Entropy-Based Applications in Economics, Finance, and Management

Entropy-Based Applications in Economics, Finance, and Management

Editor

Joanna Olbryś

MDPI • Basel • Beijing • Wuhan • Barcelona • Belgrade • Manchester • Tokyo • Cluj • Tianjin

Editor
Joanna Olbryś
Bialystok University of
Technology
Poland

Editorial Office
MDPI
St. Alban-Anlage 66
4052 Basel, Switzerland

This is a reprint of articles from the Special Issue published online in the open access journal *Entropy* (ISSN 1099-4300) (available at: https://www.mdpi.com/journal/entropy/special_issues/Finance_Management).

For citation purposes, cite each article independently as indicated on the article page online and as indicated below:

LastName, A.A.; LastName, B.B.; LastName, C.C. Article Title. *Journal Name* **Year**, *Volume Number*, Page Range.

ISBN 978-3-0365-5805-9 (Hbk)
ISBN 978-3-0365-5806-6 (PDF)

© 2022 by the authors. Articles in this book are Open Access and distributed under the Creative Commons Attribution (CC BY) license, which allows users to download, copy and build upon published articles, as long as the author and publisher are properly credited, which ensures maximum dissemination and a wider impact of our publications.

The book as a whole is distributed by MDPI under the terms and conditions of the Creative Commons license CC BY-NC-ND.

Contents

About the Editor vii

Joanna Olbryś
Entropy-Based Applications in Economics, Finance, and Management
Reprinted from: *Entropy* **2022**, 24, 1468, doi:10.3390/e24101468 1

Marc van Kralingen, Diego Garlaschelli, Karolina Scholtus and Iman van Lelyveld
Crowded Trades, Market Clustering, and Price Instability
Reprinted from: *Entropy* **2021**, 23, 336, doi:10.3390/e23030336 5

Joanna Olbryś and Krzysztof Ostrowski
An Entropy-Based Approach to Measurement of Stock Market Depth
Reprinted from: *Entropy* **2021**, 23, 568, doi:10.3390/e23050568 35

Zhewen Liao, Hongli Zhang, Kun Guo and Ning Wu
A Network Approach to the Study of the Dynamics of Risk Spillover in China's Bond Market
Reprinted from: *Entropy* **2021**, 23, 920, doi:10.3390/e23070920 57

Adina Criste, Iulia Lupu and Radu Lupu
Coherence and Entropy of Credit Cycles across the Euro Area Candidate Countries
Reprinted from: *Entropy* **2021**, 23, 1213, doi:10.3390/e23091213 77

Barbara Będowska-Sójka, Agata Kliber and Aleksandra Rutkowska
Is Bitcoin Still a King? Relationships between Prices, Volatility and Liquidity of
Cryptocurrencies during the Pandemic
Reprinted from: *Entropy* **2021**, 23, 1386, doi:10.3390/e23111386 95

Dariusz Kacprzak
A Novel Extension of the Technique for Order Preference by Similarity to Ideal Solution Method
with Objective Criteria Weights for Group Decision Making with Interval Numbers
Reprinted from: *Entropy* **2021**, 23, 1460, doi:10.3390/e23111460 113

Petre Caraiani and Alexandru Vasile Lazarec
Using Entropy to Evaluate the Impact of Monetary Policy Shocks on Financial Networks
Reprinted from: *Entropy* **2021**, 23, 1465, doi:10.3390/e23111465 133

Aleksandra Łuczak and Sławomir Kalinowski
Fuzzy Clustering Methods to Identify the Epidemiological Situation and Its Changes in
European Countries during COVID-19
Reprinted from: *Entropy* **2021**, 24, 14, doi:10.3390/e24010014 145

Renata Karkowska and Szczepan Urjasz
Linear and Nonlinear Effects in Connectedness Structure: Comparison between European Stock
Markets
Reprinted from: *Entropy* **2022**, 24, 303, doi:10.3390/e24020303 163

Loretta Mastroeni and Pierluigi Vellucci
Replication in Energy Markets: Use and Misuse of Chaos Tools
Reprinted from: *Entropy* **2022**, 24, 701, doi:10.3390/e24050701 183

Ewa Wędrowska and Joanna Muszyńska
Role of Age and Education as the Determinant of Income Inequality in Poland: Decomposition
of the Mean Logarithmic Deviation
Reprinted from: *Entropy* **2022**, 24, 773, doi:10.3390/e24060773 195

Petr Jizba, Hynek Lavička and Zlata Tabachová
Causal Inference in Time Series in Terms of Rényi Transfer Entropy
Reprinted from: *Entropy* **2022**, *24*, 855, doi:10.3390/e24070855 . . . . **213**

Joanna Olbryś and Elżbieta Majewska
Regularity in Stock Market Indices within Turbulence Periods: The Sample Entropy Approach
Reprinted from: *Entropy* **2022**, *24*, 921, doi:10.3390/e24070921 . . . . **245**

About the Editor

Joanna Olbryś

Joanna Olbryś is an Associate Professor at the Faculty of Computer Science of the Bialystok University of Technology. She obtained her Ph.D. in technical sciences from the Systems Research Institute of Polish Academy of Sciences in Warsaw. She was the head of two research projects financially supported by the Polish Ministry of Science and Higher Education (2009–2011) and the National Science Centre in Poland (2017–2020). In 2008–2012, she was the Vice-Dean for Scientific Research at the Faculty of Computer Science of the Bialystok University of Technology. She has published in various international journals. She is a member of the KES International, the Society for the Study of Emerging Markets and the Polish Mathematical Society. Since 2019, she has worked as a scientific expert and an external reviewer for the assessment of research projects submitted to the National Science Centre in Poland. Her scientific interests cover financial econometrics, computing in social science, empirical finance, time series analysis, operations research in finance, portfolio theory, asset pricing, microstructure of capital markets and information theory applications in economics and finance.

Editorial

Entropy-Based Applications in Economics, Finance, and Management

Joanna Olbryś

Faculty of Computer Science, Bialystok University of Technology, Wiejska 45a, 15-351 Białystok, Poland; j.olbrys@pb.edu.pl

Citation: Olbryś, J. Entropy-Based Applications in Economics, Finance, and Management. *Entropy* **2022**, *24*, 1468. https://doi.org/10.3390/e24101468

Received: 28 September 2022
Accepted: 8 October 2022
Published: 14 October 2022

Publisher's Note: MDPI stays neutral with regard to jurisdictional claims in published maps and institutional affiliations.

Copyright: © 2022 by the author. Licensee MDPI, Basel, Switzerland. This article is an open access article distributed under the terms and conditions of the Creative Commons Attribution (CC BY) license (https://creativecommons.org/licenses/by/4.0/).

The concept of entropy originated from physics (precisely, from thermodynamics), but it has been utilized in many research fields to characterize the complexity of a system and to investigate the information content of a probability distribution. Entropy is a general measure, and therefore, many definitions and applications of entropy have been proposed in the literature.

This Special Issue of *Entropy* was intended to be a forum for the presentation of entropy-based applications in economics, finance, and management studies. The thirteen high-quality articles included in this Special Issue propose and discuss new tools and concepts derived from information theory to investigate various aspects of entropy with assorted applications.

In the first contribution [1], the authors propose a market clustering measure using granular trading data and the maximum-entropy concept. The effect of crowded trades on stock price stability is investigated, and the evidence is that market clustering has a causal effect on the properties of the tails of the stock return distribution, particularly the positive tail, even after controlling for commonly considered risk drivers. Reduced investor pool diversity could thus negatively affect stock price stability.

The second paper [2] introduces a new methodology for the measurement of stock market depth and market liquidity. The proposed Shannon entropy-based market depth indicator is supported by an algorithm inferring the initiator of a trade. The findings of empirical experiments for real high-frequency data indicate that this new entropy-based approach can be considered as an auspicious market depth and liquidity proxy with an intuitive base for both theoretical and empirical analyses in financial markets.

The aim of the third contribution [3] is to conduct a dynamic analysis based on generalized vector autoregressive volatility spillover variance decomposition, construct a complex network, and adopt the minimum spanning tree method to clarify and analyze the risk propagation path between different bond types in China's bond market. The network's structural entropy is calculated as a useful indicator of the complexity of the network system.

The goal of the fourth paper [4] is to identify the degree of coherence of credit cycles in the countries potentially seeking to adopt the euro with the credit cycle inside the Eurozone. The indicators that define the credit cycle similarity and synchronicity in the selected countries and a set of entropy-based measures (i.e., the block entropy, the entropy rate, the Bayesian entropy) are calculated.

In the fifth paper [5], the authors try to establish the commonalities and leadership in the cryptocurrency markets by examining the mutual information and lead–lag relationships between Bitcoin and other cryptocurrencies. The transfer entropy between the volatility and liquidity of seven highly capitalized cryptocurrencies is calculated in order to determine the potential direction of information flow. Empirical results suggest the gradual increase in the role of privacy-oriented cryptocurrencies.

The sixth contribution [6] presents an extension of the Technique for Order Preference by Similarity to Ideal Solution (TOPSIS) method with objective criteria weights for Group

Decision Making (GDM) with Interval Numbers (INs). The proposed method is an alternative to popular and often used methods that aggregate the decision matrices provided by the decision makers (DMs) into a single group matrix, which is the basis for determining objective criteria weights and ranking the alternatives. The objective criteria weights are calculated using the interval entropy method. The numerical example shows the ease of use of the proposed method, which can be implemented in common data analysis software.

The seventh paper [7] analyzes the changes in the financial network built using the Dow Jones Industrial Average components following monetary policy shocks. Monetary policy shocks are measured through unexpected changes in the federal funds rate in the United States. The changes in the financial networks using singular value decomposition entropy and von Neumann entropy are investigated. The results indicate that unexpected positive shocks in monetary policy shocks lead to lower entropy.

In the eight paper [8], the main research question concerns the identification of changes in the COVID-19 epidemiological situation using fuzzy clustering methods. The identification of country types in terms of epidemiological risk is carried out using the fuzzy c-means clustering method. Moreover, the entropy index is used to measure the degree of fuzziness in the classification and evaluate the uncertainty of epidemiological states. The research concerns Europe, but the methodology is universal and can also be useful for other countries.

The purpose of the ninth contribution [9] is to compare the risk transfer structure in Central and Eastern European and Western European stock markets during the 2007–2009 financial crisis and the COVID-19 pandemic. A variety of methods, including mutual information and transfer entropy, are used. The results indicate that there are significant nonlinear correlations in the capital markets that can be practically applied for investment portfolio optimization. The study provides an insight into the risk transfer theory in developed and emerging markets as well as a cutting-edge methodology designed for analyzing the connectedness of markets.

In the tenth paper [10], the authors highlight the role of theoretical assumptions of the methods employed in the literature of energy markets. They show that the mathematical definition of chaos and the theoretical background are able to avoid possible errors from misleading results on the ostensible chaoticity of the price series. The findings indicate that both chaotic and stochastic features coexist in the energy commodity markets, although the misuse of some tests in the established practice in the literature may say otherwise.

The eleventh paper [11] focuses on the Mean Logarithmic Deviation, the measure proposed by Theil and based on the techniques of statistical information theory. The study investigates the role of age and education as the determinants of income inequality in Poland. The results confirm an association between the level of education and the average income of the groups distinguished on this basis. The study also finds that differences in the age of the household head had a smaller effect on income inequality than the level of education.

The twelfth paper [12] discusses the topic of uncovering causal interdependencies from observational data with the help of an information-theoretic concept known as the Rényi's information measure. The authors investigate the directional information flow between bivariate time series in terms of the Rényi's transfer entropy. The evidence is that the Rényi's transfer entropy not only allows us to detect a threshold of synchronization, but it also provides non-trivial insight into the structure of a transient regime that exists between the region of chaotic correlations and synchronization threshold.

Finally, in the last paper of this Special Issue [13], the authors assess and compare changes in regularity in the 36 European and the United States stock market indices within major turbulence periods. Two periods are investigated: the Global Financial Crisis in 2007–2009 and the COVID-19 pandemic outbreak in 2020–2021. To capture sequential regularity in daily financial time series, the Sample Entropy algorithm is used. The empirical findings are unambiguous and confirm that the entropy of market indices decreases during turbulence periods, which implies that the regularity and predictability of stock market returns increases in such cases.

The high-quality contributions presented in this Special Issue offer a diverse and representative portfolio of entropy-based applications in economics, finance, and management. A wide variety of tools based on entropy confirms that entropy is presumably one of the most intricate scientific concepts. However, its comprehension is a challenge to researchers. As a guest editor, I hope that the readers will enjoy the papers included in this Special Issue and will find them interesting and helpful.

Funding: The contribution was supported by the grant WZ/WI-IIT/2/22 from Bialystok University of Technology and founded by the Ministry of Education and Science.

Acknowledgments: As a guest editor, I would like to thank the authors that contributed to the Special Issue "Entropy-Based Applications in Economics, Finance, and Management" and all the anonymous peer reviewers who revised and assessed the submissions. I also would like to express special thanks to the journal *Entropy* and MDPI for their support during this work.

Conflicts of Interest: The author declares no conflict of interest.

References

1. van Kralingen, M.; Garlaschelli, D.; Scholtus, K.; van Lelyveld, I. Crowded trades, market clustering, and price instability. *Entropy* **2021**, *23*, 336. [CrossRef] [PubMed]
2. Olbryś, J.; Ostrowski, K. An entropy-based approach to measurement of stock market depth. *Entropy* **2021**, *23*, 568. [CrossRef] [PubMed]
3. Liao, Z.; Zhang, H.; Guo, K.; Wu, N. A network approach to the study of the dynamics of risk spillover in China's bond market. *Entropy* **2021**, *23*, 920. [CrossRef] [PubMed]
4. Criste, A.; Lupu, I.; Lupu, R. Coherence and entropy of credit cycles across the euro area candidate countries. *Entropy* **2021**, *23*, 1213. [CrossRef] [PubMed]
5. Będowska-Sójka, B.; Kliber, A.; Rutkowska, A. Is Bitcoin still a king? Relationships between prices, volatility and liquidity of cryptocurrencies during the pandemic. *Entropy* **2021**, *23*, 1386. [CrossRef] [PubMed]
6. Kacprzak, D. A novel extension of the technique for order preference by similarity to ideal solution method with objective criteria weights for group decision making with interval numbers. *Entropy* **2021**, *23*, 1460. [CrossRef] [PubMed]
7. Caraiani, P.; Lazarec, A. Using entropy to evaluate the impact of monetary policy shocks on financial networks. *Entropy* **2021**, *23*, 1465. [CrossRef] [PubMed]
8. Łuczak, A.; Kalinowski, S. Fuzzy clustering methods to identify the epidemiological situation and its changes in European countries during COVID-19. *Entropy* **2022**, *24*, 14. [CrossRef] [PubMed]
9. Karkowska, R.; Urjasz, S. Linear and nonlinear effects in connectedness structure: Comparison between Europen stock markets. *Entropy* **2022**, *24*, 303. [CrossRef] [PubMed]
10. Mastroeni, L.; Vellucci, P. Replication in energy markets: Use and misuse of chaos tools. *Entropy* **2022**, *24*, 701. [CrossRef] [PubMed]
11. Wędrowska, E.; Muszyńska, J. Role of age and education as the determinant of income inequality in Poland: Decomposition of the mean logarithmic deviation. *Entropy* **2022**, *24*, 773. [CrossRef] [PubMed]
12. Jizba, P.; Lavička, H.; Tabachová, Z. Causal inference in time series in terms of Rényi transfer entropy. *Entropy* **2022**, *24*, 855. [CrossRef] [PubMed]
13. Olbryś, J.; Majewska, E. Regularity in stock market indices within turbulence periods: The sample entropy approach. *Entropy* **2022**, *24*, 921. [CrossRef] [PubMed]

Article

Crowded Trades, Market Clustering, and Price Instability

Marc van Kralingen [1,†], Diego Garlaschelli [2,3,†], Karolina Scholtus [4,†] and Iman van Lelyveld [5,6,*,†]

1. Aegon N.V., Aegonplein 50, 2591 TV Den Haag, The Netherlands; marc.vankralingen@aegon.nl
2. Lorentz Institute for Theoretical Physics, Leiden University, Niels Bohrweg 2, 2333 CA Leiden, The Netherlands; garlaschelli@lorentz.leidenuniv.nl
3. IMT School of Advanced Studies, Piazza S. Francesco 19, 55100 Lucca, Italy
4. Econometric Institute, Erasmus University Rotterdam, Burg. Oudlaan 50, 3062 PA Rotterdam, The Netherlands; karolina.scholtus@gmail.com
5. Data Science Hub, De Nederlandsche Bank, Spaklerweg 4, 1096 BA Amsterdam, The Netherlands
6. Department of Finance, VU Amsterdam, De Boelelaan 1105, 1081 HV Amsterdam, The Netherlands
* Correspondence: iman.van.lelyveld@dnb.nl
† These authors contributed equally to this work.

Abstract: Crowded trades by similarly trading peers influence the dynamics of asset prices, possibly creating systemic risk. We propose a market clustering measure using granular trading data. For each stock, the clustering measure captures the degree of trading overlap among any two investors in that stock, based on a comparison with the expected crowding in a null model where trades are maximally random while still respecting the empirical heterogeneity of both stocks and investors. We investigate the effect of crowded trades on stock price stability and present evidence that market clustering has a causal effect on the properties of the tails of the stock return distribution, particularly the positive tail, even after controlling for commonly considered risk drivers. Reduced investor pool diversity could thus negatively affect stock price stability.

Keywords: crowded trading; tail-risk; financial stability; entropy

JEL Classification: G02; G14; G20

1. Introduction

This paper studies the effect of market clustering on price instability. We define market clustering as the degree to which groups of investors trade similarly. For each stock, our market clustering model measures the degree of trading overlap among any two investors that trade that particular stock. In general, stock prices are thought to adjust continuously to changes in the fundamental value of the stocks. The reactions of investors to new information determine the adjustments of prices and the resulting price dynamics. Market clustering, however, cannot be observed by individual investors and its effect on price dynamics can thus unfold unexpectedly.

Market clustering can be seen as a measure of the homogeneity of the investors' pool. Reduced diversity of the investors' pool, i.e., when the investors show similar trading behavior, means that coincidental overlap of trading strategies is more likely and overlap of trades increase the chance of crowded trades and overreactions, reflected in price fluctuations. The use of large-scale granular trading data and a novel complex network method enables us to study the effect of market clustering on price fluctuations directly. To the best of our knowledge, this is the first direct empirical investigation of the relation between market clustering and price fluctuations on individual stock level.

Studying the empirical relation between market clustering and price instability is relevant from both an academic and a supervisory point of view. First, the existing empirical literature on the topic focuses on only indirect measures of group behavior: overlapping portfolios [1,2], similarities in performance dynamics [3,4], dynamics of the number of owners per stock [5], or buyer and seller volume imbalance [6,7]. The suggestion that price fluctuations originate from uncoordinated or inefficient interaction among investors seems obvious, but due to limited data and lack of suitable methods, such effects have not yet been investigated directly.

Second, knowledge about the implications of market clustering is relevant for regulators, as market clustering can be an amplifying spillover channel for asset price fluctuations. The general implication of a causal relation between market clustering and price instability is that trading patterns through which investors react to incentives, matter for the efficiency of price discovery. Although this research focuses on the effect of market clustering on single stocks, market clustering might be a channel of volatility spillovers, because portfolio adjustments concerning other stocks in reaction to an initial price shock are more likely to overlap as well in a clustered trading environment. Therefore, market clustering might not only be a source of price instability, but also a channel of volatility spillovers, eventually resulting in correlated price jumps. In that case, market clustering would foster systemic risks. Market clustering might be an example of an existing market structure that can amplify seemingly unimportant events into widespread market volatility. In case market clusters coincide with otherwise interconnected institutions, for example, banks, common asset devaluation can be a crucial default contagion channel, as suggested in recent interdisciplinary research [8,9].

Market clustering is expected to cause price shocks, because it amplifies the effect of existing sources of price fluctuations. More specifically, market clustering is expected to increase the chance of price shocks in two different situations: Firstly, when the order deluge due to the group behavior overwhelms the supply [10,11] and, secondly, when the supply is thin due to the homogeneity of the investors' pool, i.e. a lack of liquidity at one side of the order book [12]. In both situations market clustering increases the chance that the demand exceeds the supply, either in buy or sell orders.

We start our investigation of the influence of trading patterns by studying the relation between market clustering and the price dynamics of individual stocks. Our market clustering measure is unique in the sense that it quantifies two aspects of group behavior: clustering and crowdedness. We define price instability as an increase of the number of sharp price fluctuations, such that the tails of the log return distribution are heavier. Specifically, we investigate whether there is a causal relation between market clustering and the skewness, kurtosis, tail indices, positive and negative outlier counts, changes in downside risk, and upside gains.

The analysis of trading patterns depends on the ability to distinguish to what extent the observed patterns are the result of genuinely higher-order mechanisms, like group behavior, rather than of lower-order constraints. In this research, we represent a given trade configuration as a bipartite network, i.e., a two-layer network where stocks are represented as nodes in one layer, investors as nodes in the other layer, and links can only connect nodes across the two layers. These links represent the trades during a particular time period. We use the maximum-entropy principle to generate a null model with the same lower-order properties as the empirical network, in this case the so-called "degree sequence" (i.e., the vector containing the numbers of investors per stock and the numbers of stocks per investor). Certain "apparent" network patterns can actually be explained by the lower-order properties. Observations that deviate from the random network ensemble are instead indications of higher-order trading patterns. Our approach builds on recent research on the topological structure of economic and financial networks showing that the degree sequence explains the occurrence of several higher-order structures in these networks, while still being a local property that directly reflects the intrinsic heterogeneity of market participants [13–15].

Our source data consist of granular trade-by-trade records of Dutch banks and investment funds. These data are reported under the Markets in Financial Instruments Directive (MiFID). The data available to us contain all the transactions in stocks and bonds traded by all Dutch banks and investments firms (approximately 50). These trades are either conducted as an agent or for own account. The set of investors per stock is incomplete, as trades are only reported in this data set if a Dutch bank or investment firm is involved and hence we do not observe trades between two foreign parties.

The results indicate that the prices are less (more) stable for high (low) market clustering. We find evidence for a consistent and robust positive relation between market clustering and the kurtosis of the log return distribution. Clustering thus seems to be related to large price movements. Furthermore, we find a relation between market clustering and the tail index and outlier count for the positive tail, but interestingly not for the negative tail. We hypothesize that the effect for the negative tail is conditional on volatility state in the market and test this hypothesis with the dynamic panel data approach.

We use the data limitation of not observing trading among foreign investors to mimic an experimental research design and study the causality of the relation between market clustering and price instability. Per stock we measure what percentage of its turnover is traded by investors included in the MiFID data set and compare the results for stocks that are mainly traded by included investors ("treatment group") with the results for stocks that are mainly traded by investors elsewhere ("control group"). Under assumption that Dutch and foreign investors trade in stocks with comparable properties, here we find evidence for causality as our results do not hold for stocks mostly traded by non-Dutch investors.

Finally, we examine market clustering and price instability in a dynamic panel data framework. Dynamic panel data models can account for heterogeneity bias across individual stocks and can disentangle causality effects in the presence of simultaneity driven endogeneity. These models show that clustering is a persistent process, affected by market conditions, but not by stock return momentum or fundamental variables. The only stock-related variables that matter are liquidity and market capitalization. Higher illiquidity in low volatility periods leads to higher clustering scores, indicating the investors are willing to take extra risks in low volatility periods. The model confirms the possibility that crowded trades are related to fire sales as less liquid stocks are traded more in downward markets. The relation between market capitalization and market clustering supports the presence of flight-to-safety within equities in turmoils. Thus the results are consistent with multiple equity market phenomena.

When we investigate the drivers of changes in Value-at-Risk (VaR) and Value-at-Luck (VaL; upside potential, measured as VaR but for the positive side of the return distribution), we find that our proposed clustering measure has explanatory power beyond other well-known variables. Our conditioning variables include practically all the variables suggested in the literature (i.e., market factor, book-to-market, dividend yield, size, Amihud (2002) liquidity measure, momentum, and market conditions). The findings confirm that stocks' involvement into crowded trades lead to larger price fluctuations. The effect is stronger for the positive tail (VaL) and consistent with results from group comparisons. For the negative tail, market clustering causes price instability during financial turmoil, but not during calm periods.

The setup of the remainder of the paper is as follows. First, we provide a brief overview of the relevant literature. Then, we turn to a description of the data, followed by an explanation of the method to measure market clustering we developed. To the best of our knowledge, both the data and the method are new contributions to the literature. We then describe our results and close with a discussion.

2. Literature Review

The literature studying price dynamics is rich and can be classified in many ways. Our focus here is on joint trading affecting the market in such a way that it is no longer capable to perform two key functions: efficient price discovery and providing liquidity [16]. Several related strands of the literature shed light on this important issue covering (1) similar shocks on the funding side, (2) overlapping portfolios, (3) exogenous requirements, (4) market microstructure design issues, and (5) complexity models.

First, some argue that participants in the market face very similar funding shocks or, more generally, that investment needs or beliefs are highly correlated. This affects prices because leverage cycles result in fat tails [17]. For instance, Gorban et al. [18] suggest a continuous-time model where beliefs of strategic informed traders about crowdedness of trades and strategies in the market can lead to reduced liquidity on supply side and lower market depth.

Second, given the investment needs and outlook, investors will have accumulated a portfolio of assets that might to some degree be overlapping. With homogenous agents and perfect information, all portfolios will approach the market portfolio. In practice, investors are heterogeneous and information is uncertain and not freely available, thus investors will have portfolios that overlap only partly. This does not limit itself to liquid investments but also applies to longer term and less liquid exposures such as in the syndicated loan market [19].

Common asset holdings have attracted considerable attention, especially in the context of fire-sale spillovers and cascade dynamics [20–22]. Not surprisingly, studies find that more commonality in investments increase systemic risk with an exception to Barroso et al. [23], who discover no evidence of the relation between momentum crashes and institutional crowding. Gualdi et al. [24] show that portfolio overlapping on aggregate level increased slowly before the 2008 crisis, reached a peak at the start of the crisis and then triggered fire sales. Moreover, network effects are generally important (although Glasserman and Peyton Young [25] come to the opposite conclusion). Theoretical work has evolved from analyzing the effect of fire sales on a single portfolio and a single asset [26] to continuous time models with endogenous risk and spillover from fire sales across multiple assets and multiple portfolios [27]. Empirical (stress test) exercises assess how relevant such contagion effects are in practice. The results are highly dependent on the financial system considered (see, for example, van Lelyveld and Liedorp [28] and Cont and Schaaning [29]).

A third area of the literature relevant for our analysis highlights fire sales caused by an exogenous requirement. Note that fire sales are forced sales in stressed markets under unfavorable terms and are very different compared to regular buying and selling to adjust a portfolio. External requirements are often set by regulators to safeguard sufficient buffers for various risks (credit risk—using both risk weighted and risk insensitive measures (i.e., leverage ratios), counterparty credit risk, or liquidity risk [17,29–32]).

Regulatory requirements often imply cliff effects as breaching certain thresholds come with costs. External demands leading to forced sales can sometimes also come from other market participants. For example, counterparties can call for margin. In particular, central clearing parties can require substantial margins to be delivered at very short notice [33].

Fourth, there is an established literature on mispricing because of market microstructure design and crowded trades [10,11,34]. Sometimes investors are prone to herding [35], at other times, speculators try to manipulate prices by rapidly submitting orders to drive up prices.

Finally, we develop and apply complexity models—as recently advocated by Battiston et al. [36]. Network theory in general has many applications in finance [8] and complex network theory offers reconstruction procedures and null models based on a maximization of entropy [13,14]. Such models have been applied to the world trade network [15] and banking networks [14,37–39]. A slightly different type of network emerges from order optimization as studied by Cohen-Cole et al. [40]. In studying the DOW and the S&P e-mini futures, they show that in these entirely electronic markets economically meaningful networks emerge. This happens despite the fact that the interjection of an order-matching computer makes social interaction impossible. In the method we develop here—to be elaborated on below—we incorporate the distribution of the number of links per node (degree distribution) but otherwise our expectation (or null model) is as random as possible.

To clarify our approach to crowded trading, we present a graphical representation of market clustering in Figure 1. The homogeneity of the trading behavior of the investors' pool per stock is then reflected in the market clustering measure that we will define below in Equation (1). In the most extreme case, the market breaks up into distinct submarkets, consisting of groups of investors that trade only in particular stocks which are only traded by those groups. Incorporating the effect of clustering into the measure on individual stock level is what sets our research apart from other crowdedness measures intended for individual stocks. For example, Yang and Zhou [6] differentiate between seller and buyer initiated crowded trades per stock. Their measure is based on trading volume data and thus does not reflect the (unobserved) interactions among investors. The same applies to the quarterly measure derived from mutual funds holding data in Zhong et al. [41]. The stocks that are largely held by actively managed mutual funds are classified as overcrowded but the tendency of a particular stock's owners to trade with each other is not taken into account.

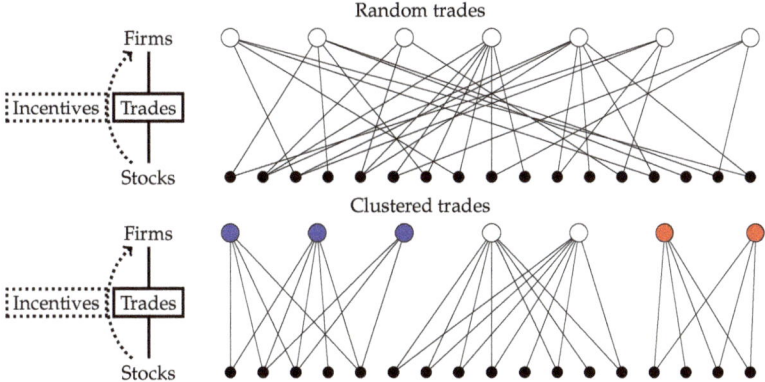

Figure 1. Market clustering in a bipartite network representation. The nodes in the top layer represent the firms and the bottom layer represents the stocks. The links between the layers represent all trades during a certain time period. Each line is a trade of the connected firm in the connected stock. In the top network, all trades are randomly distributed over the firms and stocks. The bottom trade network shows market clustering: Groups of firms trade in separated groups of stocks, while these stocks are traded only by these particular firms, which results in three distinct market clusters. The number of trades per firm and per security is the same for both random trades and the clustered trades example.

In general, peers trading similarly are likely to share common features, i.e., in case the group of investors that trade in a stock is very similar, then trading behavior might be similar, too. In our current analysis we abstract from what drives common trading. We are thus agnostic as to whether the order flows are driven by, for example, adjustments due to common asset holdings, (too) similar investment views, or shared regulatory constraints. Note that we do investigate what makes a particular stock attractive for involvement into clustered trades and how that depends on market conditions.

3. Methodology

In this section, we will first discuss our novel contribution: how to define a metric for homogeneous trading by comparing observed trade overlaps with expected overlaps under a suitable null model. We then introduce the definition of price instability and the cross-sectional comparison framework to assess the relation between clustering and price instability. Finally, we present a dynamic panel data model. We implement the latter in order to investigate the drivers of our newly defined measure as well as to show that it has additional explanatory power over and above well established covariates in models for downside risk and upside potential.

3.1. Measuring Homogeneous Trading

Our first goal here is to define a measure of similar or homogeneous trading behavior. This indicator will then be linked to the measures of price instability to investigate whether higher order patterns affect price formation. The nexus of trades between firms and stocks is complex and exhibits both lower- and higher-order network properties. Lower-order properties, such as the liquidity of a particular stock, have been researched extensively and are key determinants of price dynamics. Lower-order properties can be seen as the exogenous causes of price instability and their effects on price dynamics are direct and undelayed.

However, we focus on whether the market microstructure conceals particular grouping of trades that disturb the efficiency of the market. Particular ordering of the trades, resulting in higher-order patterns, can function as endogenous cause of price instability. Crucially, these market features are unobservable to the investors and their effects on prices can unfold unexpectedly. Such effects have not been investigated by use of granular trading data, because suitable methods had yet to developed and the data have been largely unavailable.

We develop a method that incorporates the information encoded, for each month t, in the number of unique investors per security (observed "degree" $d_{s,t}^{obs}$ of security s in month t) and the number of unique, traded securities per firm (observed "degree" $d_{f,t}^{obs}$ of firm f in month t). The observed degrees of all firms and securities during month t are combined into a vector D_t^{obs} representing the degree sequence observed in month t. We compare the observed trading network to a maximally random (i.e., maximum-entropy [13]) network ensemble based on only the observed degree sequence. The ensemble is characterized by a different connection probability $p_{sf,t}$ for each security-firm pair (s, f) and for each time t and, consequently, for combinations of links (i.e., "motifs"). Empirical deviations from the maximum-entropy ensemble are indications for higher-order patterns such as peers clustering in the same (type of) stock.

To identify market clustering, we need the observed values and the expected values based on the benchmark model. The quantity that represents the market clustering of security s during month t is

$$m_{s,t} = \frac{M_{s,t}}{\langle M_{s,t} \rangle} - 1, \tag{1}$$

where $M_{s,t}$ is the observed market clustering and $\langle M_{s,t} \rangle$ is the expected value based on the maximum-entropy model that we develop below. The observed value $M_{s,t}$ is divided by the expected value $\langle M_{s,t} \rangle$, so that deviations from the benchmark are scaled in terms of the expected value. The minimum value for the market clustering is minus one by definition and a market clustering of zero means that the market clustering has the same value as the expected value $\langle M_{s,t} \rangle$.

The observed market clustering $M_{s,t}$—visualized in Figure 2—is defined, for each security s and month t, as the number of shared securities (other than s) traded by all pairs of investors trading in s. In other words, for each pair (f, f') of firms, we first establish if they both trade in the security s during month t. If this is the case, we then count the number of securities (other than s itself) that these two firms are also trading simultaneously in the same month. The observed value of the market clustering $M_{s,t}$ for security s during month t is then given by

$$M_{s,t} = \sum_{f}^{n_{F,t}-1} \sum_{f'=f+1}^{n_{F,t}} \left(a_{sf,t} a_{sf',t} \sum_{s' \neq s} a_{s'f,t} a_{s'f',t} \right), \tag{2}$$

where the total numbers of firms and securities active in month t are denoted by $n_{F,t}$ and $n_{S,t}$, respectively. The summation $\sum_f \sum_{f'}$ runs over all possible pairs of investors and the summation $\sum_{s' \neq s}$ runs, per pair of investors, over all securities except security s. The indicator $a_{sf,t} = 1$ in case firm f trades in security s during month t and $a_{sf,t} = 0$ otherwise. $M_{s,t}$ measures all trading combinations within the pool of investors that trade in security s, forming a market clustering pattern or "motif". If investors in a security are otherwise not trading jointly, then $m_{s,t} = -1$ and we drop 3412 observations (5%) of such cases as these observations are not relevant for our analysis.

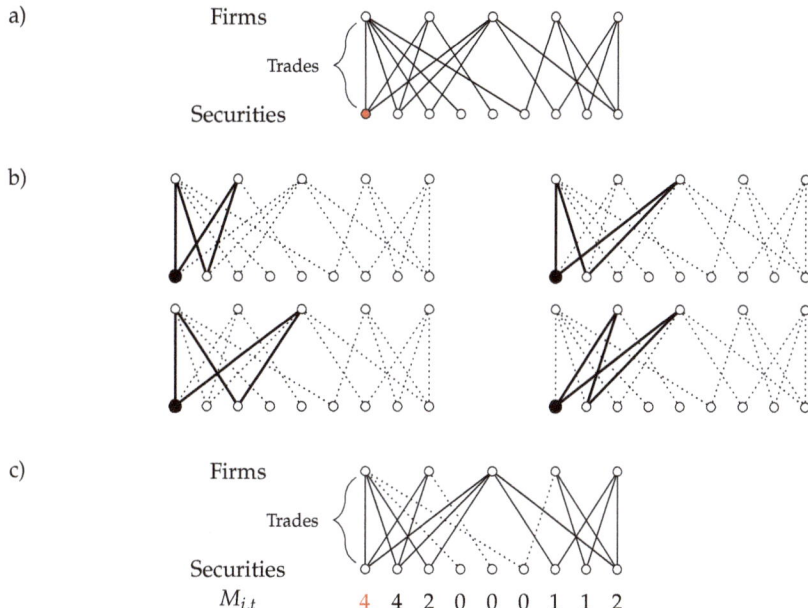

Figure 2. Example of the calculation of the observed market clustering $M_{s,t}$. (**a**) A hypothetical bipartite trading network. Each line represents a buy or sell transaction. (**b**) Counting the market clustering motifs for the first security. In these four cases shown the trading pattern exist and therefore the first security has score four. This calculation is repeated for all other securities. The summation in Equation (2) runs over all possibilities. (**c**) The same hypothetical trading situation with the observed market clustering $M_{s,t}$ for each security (lines that do not contribute to the market clustering measurements for any security are dotted).

We calculate the expected value of the market clustering based on the maximum-entropy probability distribution $P(X_t|D_t^{\text{obs}})$ derived in Appendix A based only on the observed degree sequence D_t^{obs}. As shown in Appendix A, the distribution $P(X_t|D_t^{\text{obs}})$ factorizes over pairs of edges, which are all mutually independent in the null model. The expected value of the market clustering is therefore easily calculated as the sum over all configurations weighted by the probabilities:

$$
\begin{aligned}
\langle M_{s,t} \rangle &= \sum_{X_t \in \mathcal{G}_t} P(X_t|D_t^{\text{obs}}) M_s(X_t) \\
&= \sum_{X_t \in \mathcal{G}_t} P(X_t|D_t^{\text{obs}}) \sum_{f}^{n_{F,t}-1} \sum_{f'=f+1}^{n_{F,t}} \left(a_{sf}(X_t) a_{sf'}(X_t) \sum_{s' \neq s} a_{s'f}(X_t) a_{s'f'}(X_t) \right) \\
&= \sum_{f}^{n_{F,t}-1} \sum_{f'=f+1}^{n_{F,t}} \left(p_{sf,t} p_{sf',t} \sum_{s' \neq s} p_{s'f,t} p_{s'f',t} \right),
\end{aligned}
\tag{3}
$$

where we have introduced the single security-firm pair connection probability $p_{sf,t}$, defined as

$$
p_{sf,t} = \sum_{X_t \in \mathcal{G}_t} P(X_t|D_t^{\text{obs}}) a_{sf}(X_t) \tag{4}
$$

(see in Appendix A for a detailed calculation of $p_{sf,t}$ from D_t^{obs}) and exploited the fact that, under the conditions $s \neq s'$, $f \neq f'$ guaranteed in Equation (3),

$$\sum_{X_t \in \mathcal{G}_t} P(X_t | D_t^{obs}) a_{sf}(X_t) a_{sf'}(X_t) a_{s'f}(X_t) a_{s'f'}(X_t) = p_{sf,t} p_{sf',t} p_{s'f,t} p_{s'f',t} \quad (5)$$

due to the independence of distinct edges. Figure 3 illustrates the summation process graphically.

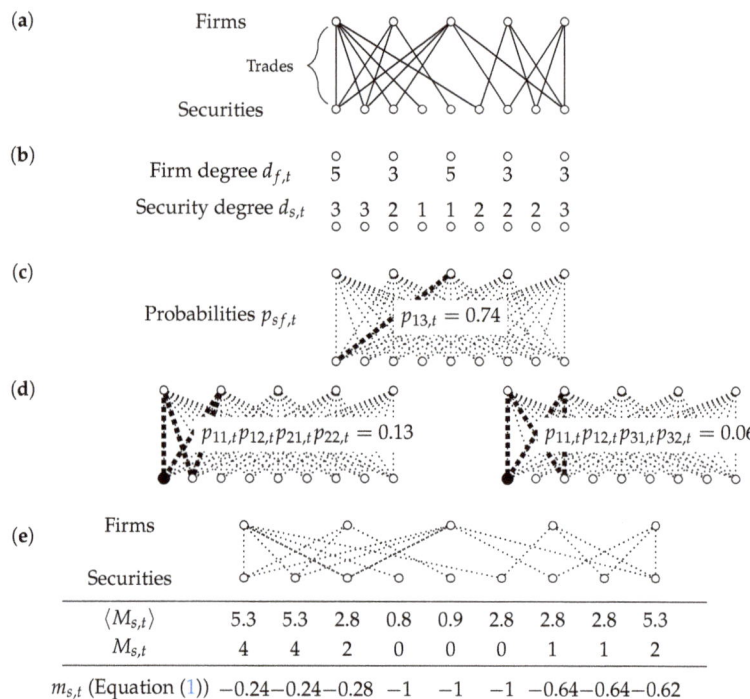

Figure 3. Calculation of the benchmark model for the market clustering $\langle M_{s,t} \rangle$. (**a**) The same hypothetical trading situation as in Figure 2. (**b**) The trading information is reduced to the degree sequence: The number of traded securities per firm and the number of trading firms per security. (**c**) The degree sequence is translated into a probability $p_{sf,t}$ for each firm–security pair (i.e., the probability of firm f trading in security s in month t). The probability and degree sequence hold the same information, as the expected value of the number of connections for each node equals the degree. (**d**) The probability of occurrence of the market clustering motifs equals the product of the four probabilities between the four involved nodes (see in Equation (3)). The expected value of the market clustering per security is the sum of all probabilities for motifs that are connected to the security. The first two motifs for the first security are shown. This calculation is repeated for each security. (**e**) The benchmark model market clustering $\langle M_{s,t} \rangle$ for each security, the observed market clustering from Figure 2, and the final market clustering measures, according to Equation (1), respectively.

The market clustering $m_{s,t}$ measures the degree of clustering for security s among its traders. Figure 4 shows examples of the performance of the method in two hypothetical situations. First, the model assigns a lower value to securities which are involved in multiple clusters. Arguably, the involvement in multiple clusters enhances the diversity of the investors group and would probably stabilize the price dynamics. Second, the work in Figure 4 shows that the model is able to indicate to what extent the security is involved in the cluster. Homogeneous trading behavior is indicated by a relatively high percentage of overlapping trades. Therefore, the number of trades that do not overlap must lower the market clustering measure. This condition is satisfied as can be seen in the second example in Figure 4.

Example 1. *Involvement in multiple clusters lowers $m_{s,t}$.*

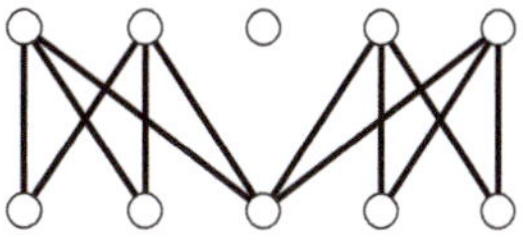

Firms
|
Trades
|
Securities

$\langle M_{s,t} \rangle$ (Figure 3)	2.6	2.6	6	2.6	2.6
$M_{s,t}$ (Figure 2)	2	2	4	2	2
$m_{s,t}$ (Equation (1))	−0.24	−0.24	−0.33	−0.24	−0.24

Example 2. *Market clustering $m_{s,t}$ indicates the degree of involvement in the cluster.*

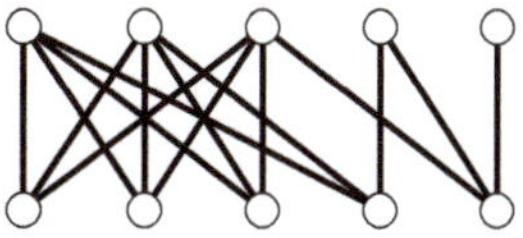

Firms
|
Trades
|
Securities

$\langle M_{s,t} \rangle$ (Figure 3)	6.5	6.5	6.5	6.5	6.5
$M_{s,t}$ (Figure 2)	7	7	7	3	0
$m_{s,t}$ (Equation (1))	0.08	0.08	0.08	−0.54	−1

Figure 4. Example of the computation of $m_{s,t}$. Example 1. The market clustering is lower when a security is involved in multiple clusters at once. In this configuration two clusters exist: one on the left and one on the right. The security in the middle is involved in both clusters. The final market clustering is lower for the security in the middle, because its four connected firms are not mutually clustered. Example 2. The market clustering $m_{s,t}$ indicates the involvement in the market cluster. All securities are traded by three firms each. The left three firms are almost fully clustered. The final market clustering $m_{s,t}$ indicates to which extent the securities are involved in the cluster.

3.2. Measuring Price Instability

We measure stock price instability with statistics that focus on tail behavior of the stock return distribution. We analyze the skewness, the kurtosis, the tail indices, the number of outliers, and the changes in the left and right 5% quantiles. The latter two can also be interpreted as changes in downside risk and upward potential and are better manageable on the time-series dimension. Ang et al. [42] show that sensitivities to downside market movements are priced in addition to the common risk factors. Thus, if market clustering leads to changes in downside risk, it implicitly shows up in the price dynamics.

Skewness and kurtosis are measures of the shape of the complete log return distribution while the outlier count and the tail index are focused on the tails of the distributions—the extreme returns. The tail index (i.e., Hill's estimator) measures the fatness of the tail according to the power law distribution. We count the number of outliers by sequentially applying the generalized Grubbs' test until no outliers are detected. The skewness, Hill indices and outlier count also allow us to distinguish the effect on price instability for up- and downward shocks separately. We measure the size of the price fluctuation relative to the yearly standard deviation of the stocks, i.e., we divide the log returns by the yearly standard deviation per stock. Complementary to the volatility normalization, we investigate the influence of market clustering on the variance and the Median Average Deviation (MAD), which is more robust to outliers than the variance.

Value-at-Risk (VaR)—often used in risk management and regulation—is an obvious choice for quantifying the downside risk. We focus on a single stock 5% VaR obtained via historical bootstrap from daily returns. Historical simulation risk measures depend on the level of volatility in the sample. However, our quantile-based variable measures change over time and, as such, it is not affected by volatility clustering. More precisely, for the monthly data set we define

$$\Delta \text{VaR}_{st} = 100 \left(\frac{\text{VaR}_s(t-11,t)}{\text{VaR}_s(t-12,t-1)} - 1 \right),$$

where $\text{VaR}_s(t_1, t_2)$ denotes a 5% VaR for stock s at the end of month t_2 obtained via historical bootstrap from daily prices over the period from month t_1 to month t_2.

Similarly, to capture tail asymmetries, we define changes in Value-at-Luck (VaL):

$$\Delta \text{VaL}_{st} = 100 \left(\frac{\text{VaL}_s(t-11,t)}{\text{VaL}_s(t-12,t-1)} - 1 \right),$$

where $\text{VaL}_s(t_1, t_2)$ denotes a 95% VaR for stock s at the end of month t_2.

3.3. Stochastic Dominance and Causality for Groups

We now compare the distributions of the price instability measures for low and high market clustering. First, the securities are ordered according to their market clustering measure. Second, the securities are divided into three groups: the lowest (L) and the highest (H) 33%. We ignore the middle group in the remainder. Finally, we collect all time series price instability measures per time window per group and assess first and second order stochastic dominance of the distributions for group L and H.

We use three tests to indicate the differences between the distributions of groups L and H. The Kolmogorov–Smirnov (KS) test and the Mann–Whitney–Wilcoxon (MWW) test are both nonparametric tests for unpaired samples. The χ^2 test is used instead of the KS test in case of binned data, because the KS test is unreliable when the number of ties is high. The KS test is sensitive to any discrepancy in the cumulative distribution function and serves as a test for the first-order stochastic dominance. The MWW is mainly sensitive to changes in the median and aids to evaluate the second-order stochastic dominance. We use visual inspection of the cumulative distributions to study the nature of the discrepancies to interpret the test results.

Using the difference-in-differences approach allows us to benefit from the partial coverage of our data set and dispel concerns over reversed causation. A concern could be that rather than market clustering causing price instability (null hypothesis), unstable and risky stocks might attract traders that prefer to trade in clusters of like-minded traders. In order to assess the effect of clustered trading in a mimicked experimental research setting, we construct a so-called control group from the stocks that are mainly traded by investors *not* included in the our data set. We look at the relation between market clustering and kurtosis in the control group. A significant relation would be speak against causality. The test is valid under an assumption that both groups of investors trade in stocks with somewhat similar properties.

3.4. Dynamic Panel Data Framework

The last part of the analysis applies a dynamic unbalanced panel data model. We aim to strengthen the high and low market clustering group results by exploring (a) the possible drivers of the clustering measure and (b) the effect that the clustering measure has on price instability. We tackle two questions in the model for the market clustering drivers. First, a group of investors may choose particular stocks because of their (latent) properties. We also include the properties that quantify a stock's riskiness and instability as an additional test on reverse causality, mentioned in the previous section. Second, crowded trading activity may depend on certain market conditions. We look at the effect of the perceived trend and volatility. In the second application, we investigate the relation between changes in left and right quantiles of log returns distribution and clustering in individual stocks. In particular, we are interested to see whether a higher clustering measure leads to larger changes in downside risk VaR and upside potential VaL after controlling for other possible individual stock risk determinants.

The general representation of the model with both lagged dependent and independent variables included, possibly of different depth, is

$$y_{st} = \sum_r \rho_r y_{s,t-r} + \sum_p \beta_p^T x_{s,t-p} + \alpha_s + \epsilon_{st}, r = 1, 2, \ldots, p = 0, 1, 2, \ldots, \quad (6)$$

where y_{st} is a dependent variable, i.e., the clustering measure or the price instability measure depending on exact specification, $x_{s,t}$ is a vector of considered covariates, α_s is an individual effect, ρ_r and β_p denote model parameters, ϵ_{st} is idiosyncratic error term, $s = 1, \ldots, N$, and $t = 1, \ldots, T$.

We opt for the fixed effects model and treat α_s as a set of N additional parameters. We do not employ time dummies for two reasons: First, time dummies would preclude including time-only varying variables of interest (like the market factor MKTF and market volatility VIX). Second, incorporation of time dummies is more suitable for panels with very small T. In fact, most of our efforts to run the dynamic model with both fixed and time effects result in singularity issues. We estimate Equation (6) with the System GMM. In particular, a two-step estimator with Windmeijer [43] correction for standard errors is used. Estimation is carried out with the R package plm [44].

Our methodology has several attractive properties. First, individual effects are allowed to be correlated with the covariates x_{st}—a likely case in our data as, e.g., firms in certain industries may have higher dividend yields or price-to-book ratios than others. Second, the fixed effects approach accounts for unobserved heterogeneity bias. All (practically) static cross-sectional stock features, like sector or exchange, are by default incorporated into α_s terms. Last but not least, we address potential endogeneity issue due to simultaneity. We hypothesize that an increase in the clustering measure leads to larger changes in downside risk. However, it is also possible that some stocks are more likely to end up in cluster trades because of their risk profile. We disentangle the causality by producing internal instruments for the right hand side variable CLUST that is not strictly exogenous.

A common approach is to use all possible lags and variables to construct GMM-style instruments. Roodman [45] warns that too many instruments result in model validity issues and, specifically, false estimation outcomes and low power of overidentification tests. Roodman suggests collapsing the instruments and using only certain lags to overcome the instrument proliferation. Wintoki et al. [46] show that both collapsing the instruments and the size of cross section increase the power of Sargan-Hansen J test. We use all available lags for selected variables and construct collapsed GMM-style instruments.

4. Data

The data have been collected as part of the Markets in Financial Instruments Directive (MiFID). MiFID is a European Union (EU) law to regulate investment services across the European Economic Area (EEA). The directive applies to all firms that perform investment services and activities. Firms that only perform ancillary services are exempted. "Post-trade transparency" is the key aspect of MiFID mandating the authorities to collect the data used here. The post-trade transparency regulation requires all firms to report all trades in all listed stocks, including the time, the price, and number of units to the supervisory authorities immediately after the trade. MiFID only contains information about the transactions and thus holdings that are not traded are not in the data.

Although MiFID collects data on a EU level, Dutch authorities only have access to the transactions of Dutch banks and investment firms. In particular, the data cover the investments in financial instruments of 86 Dutch banks and investment firms. The time span of the data covers January 2009 through April 2015. The annual cross-sectional analysis (see Section 5) is thus done for the period January 2009–December 2014. Only the face-to-market firms report their transactions. The data contain trades by the reporter as principal trader and as agents. For the market as a whole, agent trades form a limited part and are roughly at 10% of volume/trades. Furthermore, although we do not have information on the identity of the clients, it is likely that they are non-financial firms or retail clients and hence will be very heterogeneous in their trading strategies. For the moment, we thus concentrate on trades entered into as principal. In case a principal trader performs transactions via a broker, only the broker reports the transaction, but we do see it in the data.

Contrary to portfolio holdings data sets, such as the ESCB Securities Holding Statistics, which show only shifts in the portfolio holdings; the MiFID data set contains all buy and sell transactions separately. We aggregate these transaction level data to a monthly frequency, split by the total number of buy and sell transactions. Aggregation of data is necessary because trading clusters do not emerge instantaneously, but rather over time. This choice facilitates our research design, meaning that we can derive price instability metrics from less noisy daily data instead of intra-day observations.

To improve the comparability of the price dynamics, we perform the cross-sectional comparison only for equities and exclude bond trading. In general, the price dynamics and trading behavior differ markedly between equity and bond markets. In contrast to equities, most bonds are not unique as bonds issued by the same entity, but of different maturities are to a degree interchangeable (in case no arbitrage opportunities exist). In addition, we want to abstract from the dynamics at the beginning or end of the lifetime of a security (e.g., an IPO or a default). Thus we select 976 equities that are traded during each month in the period January 2009–April 2015.

The data source for the daily stock return time series is Bloomberg Professional. In case securities in our data are traded at multiple exchanges, Bloomberg chooses between the exchanges automatically. In case no transactions are registered during the day, the price of the security is kept at the price of the last transaction. After inspecting the price series for outliers, we remove two time series of penny stocks with excessive return volatility.

We apply a panel data framework for securities classified as common stocks in the Bloomberg database. The initial sample of 976 equities contains 583 common stocks. We remove 16 stocks for which the average price does not exceed 1 EUR, then 24 stocks which are thinly traded (more than 10% of days during the trading period without a single transaction), 2 stocks with non-euro currency data, and 2 stocks with suspiciously large values for some fundamentals. Next, we apply the turnover requirements for each year as in the first part of the analysis. Many of the stocks qualify for multiple years, in total we have $N = 269$ unique stocks and $T = 76$ months. The number of stocks across years fluctuates between 203 and 234.

The summary of explanatory variables and applied transformations is shown in Table 1. We consider a wide variety of potential risk and trading behavior drivers: stock market conditions, individual stock performance, liquidity, and fundamentals. MKTF and VIX are only time-varying variables, LEV3 monthly values repeat for the same fiscal quarter, and all other variables vary per stock per time period. Non-time-varying variables, like the sector of the issuer, cannot be explicitly accommodated in a panel framework with fixed effects.

The Fama and French market factor for Europe is downloaded from the Kenneth French library (See https://goo.gl/pZVmqe (accessed on 18 January 2017)). The VIX index comes from Chicago Board Options Exchange website (See https://goo.gl/zMCTa (accessed on 15 March 2017)). We obtain all stock specific information via Bloomberg terminal.

Table 1. Description of variables.

Variable	Definition
MKTF	Fama and French market factor for Europe, returns in % for a month
VIX	The CBOE Volatility index as a proxy to market conditions, level at the end of a month
MOM	12/6-month average of monthly returns in % at the end of a month
MCAP	Log of market capitalization in 10^6 EUR at the end of a month
ILLIQ	A daily ratio of absolute stock return to its euro volume, averaged over a month, also known as Amihud [47] liquidity measure, to reduce heteroskedasticity we transform as $\log(\text{ratio} + 10^{-6})$
PB3	Price-to-book ratio with a 3-month publication lag at the end of a month
DY	12-month trailing dividend yield, in % at the end of a month, we set not available values to 0
LEV3	Ratio of long-term debt to capital with a 3-month publication lag at the end of a month

Table 2 presents the descriptive statistics for variables in the panel data models. We discuss the last two columns as they offer the most valuable insights with regard to methodological choices. ΔVaR, the percentage point change in the VaR, has substantial within variation of 0.356, and thus the fixed effects model seems suitable for it. ΔVaL, the percentage point change in the upside VaR, has somewhat smaller yet acceptable within variation. We can expect effects of MKTF, VIX, and MOM to be estimated precisely because of (relatively) high within variation proportions of 1.000, 1.000, and 0.338. Perhaps we will see effects of CLUST and DY as well, but the rest of the variables are likely to have high standard errors. MCAP and ILLIQ have such high between groups variation (close to one) that their explanatory power may be subsumed by fixed effects.

Table 2. Descriptive statistics.

	N.Obs.	Mean	Median	St.dev.	Min	Max	Between	Within
ΔVaR	16216	−0.80	0.00	7.68	−39.10	82.10	0.010	0.356
ΔVaL	16216	−0.50	0.00	7.69	−59.74	98.78	0.011	0.190
CLUST	15896	0.04	0.06	0.28	−1.00	6.58	0.245	0.041
MKTF	16216	1.09	1.02	5.97	−12.33	13.86	0.003	1.000
VIX	16216	21.09	18.38	8.12	11.40	46.35	0.052	1.000
MOM	16204	0.64	0.71	3.48	−18.88	27.71	0.106	0.338
MCAP	16216	7.06	6.99	2.15	0.93	12.21	0.970	0.004
ILLIQ	16051	−3.66	−4.40	4.47	−13.82	12.48	0.957	0.007
PB3	15025	1.95	1.35	2.50	0.05	71.67	0.470	0.010
DY	16216	2.88	2.15	4.53	0.00	157.78	0.303	0.032
LEV3	15916	26.39	25.35	20.42	0.00	159.01	0.813	0.007

For each variable the table presents the number of available observations, mean, median, standard deviation, minimum, maximum, and the proportions of between and within variation. Note that the proportions of variation do not add up to one because the panel is unbalanced.

Table 3 provides information about co-movements of the variables included. The clustering measure CLUST has significant though small correlations with most variables, except for MKTF. The largest correlation of 0.102 is observed with VIX, indicating that the level of clustering could be dependent on market conditions. CLUST has marginally significant positive correlations with changes in downside risk and upside potential, i.e., ΔVaR and ΔVaL, of 0.018 and 0.020, respectively. ΔVaR and ΔVaL are also strongly correlated with VIX. In the dynamic panel data models, we aim to disentangle the causality direction and the effect of general market volatility on both clustering and risk measures. Furthermore, there is zero correlation between the changes in 5% quantiles in the left and right tail of the distribution. As within variation for these variables is non-negligible, likely, they possess very different dynamics over time supporting our choice to estimate separate models for changes in the left and the right tail.

Table 3. Correlations of pooled variables.

	ΔVaR	ΔVaL	CLUST	MKTF	VIX	MOM	MCAP	ILLIQ	PB3	DY	LEV3
ΔVaR		0.000	0.018	−0.203	0.186	−0.204	−0.039	0.047	−0.006	0.063	−0.009
ΔVaL	0.293		0.020	−0.098	0.154	−0.253	−0.053	0.047	−0.010	0.081	−0.005
CLUST	0.020	0.011		0.004	0.102	−0.036	−0.041	0.058	−0.024	0.031	−0.025
MKTF	0.000	0.000	0.613		−0.245	0.026	0.015	−0.018	−0.018	−0.021	0.015
VIX	0.000	0.000	0.000	0.000		−0.315	−0.004	0.033	−0.042	0.127	0.054
MOM	0.000	0.000	0.000	0.001	0.000		0.091	−0.088	0.152	−0.202	−0.023
MCAP	0.000	0.000	0.000	0.050	0.612	0.000		−0.620	0.046	0.096	0.227
ILLIQ	0.000	0.000	0.000	0.027	0.000	0.000	0.000		−0.069	−0.036	−0.165
PB3	0.468	0.208	0.003	0.030	0.000	0.000	0.000	0.000		−0.039	0.015
DY	0.000	0.000	0.000	0.007	0.000	0.000	0.000	0.000	0.000		0.059
LEV3	0.276	0.501	0.002	0.062	0.000	0.003	0.000	0.000	0.065	0.000	

The table presents Pearson correlations of pooled variables in the upper right triangles and the corresponding p-values to test for zero coefficient in the lower left triangles.

The autocorrelations and partial autocorrelations (Table 4) indicate the dynamic nature of all risk series and the clustering measure. Two lags seem an appropriate starting point for the dynamic models explaining CLUST, ΔVaR, and ΔVaL.

Table 4. Percentage of significant ACFs and PACFs for ΔVaR, ΔVaL, and CLUST.

Lag	ΔVaR		ΔVaL		CLUST	
	ACF	PACF	ACF	PACF	ACF	PACF
1	43.49	43.49	35.69	35.69	38.29	38.29
2	17.10	5.20	18.59	5.58	27.14	11.52
3	5.20	2.97	8.18	2.60	24.16	10.41
4	0.74	0.74	2.23	1.12	18.96	4.83
5	0.37	1.12	1.12	0.74	12.64	2.60
6	0.00	0.37	0.37	1.12	8.92	1.49
7	1.12	0.74	0.00	0.74	5.95	1.12

We obtain the autocorelations and partial autocorrelations for 269 time series per variable in the panel data set. The table contains the percentages of cases with significant coefficients for the first seven lags.

5. Results

5.1. Group Comparison

We compare distributions of price instability measures between the buckets of stocks with high and low market clustering. Our first key observation is that there seems to be a relation between the kurtosis of the log return time series and market clustering. Table 5a shows an overview of the results of the 24 test cases (MAD, variance, skewness, kurtosis where in each cell we show the results of the Kolmogorov–Smirnov (KS) test, and the Mann-Whitney-Wilcoxon (MWW) test). For all six years, both tests give significant indication for a positive relation between market clustering and the kurtosis (with significance level of 2.5%). The test results are confirmed visually by the distance between the graphs of the cumulative kurtosis distribution for low and high market clustering (see Figure A1) (Appendix B). The cumulative distribution of the kurtosis in high market clustering group stochastically dominates the cumulative distribution of the kurtosis in low market clustering group. As the sample kurtosis is a measure of tail extremity and peakedness, the stocks with a higher (lower) market clustering tend to have log return distributions which are more (less) peaked and have (less) fat tails.

Table 5. Testing for a relation between market clustering and price instability—annual window.

		2009	2010	2011	2012	2013	2014
(a)	MAD	==	==	==	==	==	++
	Variance	+=	=+	++	==	++	++
	Skewness	+=	++	++	==	++	++
	Kurtosis	++	++	++	++	++	++
(b)	Hill index neg.	−=	==	=−	==	==	==
	Hill index pos.	−−	−−	−−	==	−−	−−
(c)	Outliers neg.	≠=	==	==	==	==	≠=
	Outliers pos.	≠+	≠+	≠+	==	≠+	≠+

We compare the distributions of the four time series measures (a), the Hill indices of the negative and positive tails (b), and the number of outliers per time series (c) over six years between two groups of stocks: the lowest 33% and the highest 33% of the stocks, ranked according to their market clustering measure. The table shows for each comparison two test results. In panels a and b, the first is the Kolmogorov-Smirnov (KS) test and the second is the Mann-Whitney-Wilcoxon (MWW) test. The critical value is 0.025 for both tests. A "+"/"−"/"=" sign means that the distribution for high market clustering exceeds/undercuts/is equal to the distribution for low market clustering. In panel c the first is the χ^2-test (critical value: 0.05) and the second is the MWW test (critical value: 0.025). Contrary to the KS test, the χ^2 test results indicates only whether the hypothesis of homogeneity is accepted ("=") or rejected ("≠"). Note that we do not show 2015 because the comparison with other years would be difficult as we have significantly fewer observations.

The stochastic dominance of distributions of considered price instability measures conditional on positive and negative tail in high vs. low market clustering groups indicate that market clustering relates to a relatively heavier tail for the positive tail of the log return distribution and not for the negative tail. The results for the Hill indices (Table 5b and Figure A2) show that only the fatness of the positive tail relates to market clustering. Distribution of positive tail index in low clustering group dominates distribution of positive tail index in high clustering group. Here, a lower index implies fatter tails. The results for the outlier count (Table 5c and Figure A2) also show a clear relation between the number of positive outliers and market clustering and not for the number of negative outliers. Distribution of positive outliers in high clustering group stochastically dominates distribution of positive outlier in low clustering group. The stochastic dominance of distributions of price instability measures for the negative tail cannot be established. The tests in Table 5 provide evidence for neither first nor second order stochastic dominance.

The positive relation between the skewness and market clustering in Table 5 and Figure A1 is in accordance with the observation that the market clustering relates to a relative increase of only the upward price fluctuations. However, this does not mean that the kurtosis results in Table 5 are solely caused by the upper tail. The robustness checks in Table A1 (Appendix C) for partial data show that the relation between market clustering and the kurtosis is also significant when the tail observations of the log return distributions are left out of the analyses. Furthermore, the lack of clear unconditional relation of price instability and market clustering in the negative tail does not preclude a possibility of a conditional relation. We investigate market conditions as a possible confounding factor in the panel data framework.

The significance of the relation between market clustering and price instability varies over time, as the test results for shorter time spans indicate. Table 6 repeats the results of Table 5a for a time window of two months. Approximately half of the kurtosis test results for a time window of two months are the same as in the yearly results. For 2009, Table 6 shows a clear positive relation between the kurtosis and market clustering. During the period 2010–2011, the positive relation seems to apply to the end of 2010 and the first half of 2011. In 2012 and the first half of 2013, no consistent relation exists for any of the measures or time window. For the end of 2013 until the end of the sample, the kurtosis results are mostly positive. The significance of the results at shorter time scales is reduced because the time series measures have a higher spread at shorter time scales, while the number of observations stays the same. The significance of the relation between market clustering and price instability might vary because the samples within the time windows are too small. Nevertheless, the relation between market clustering and the kurtosis is positive in more than half the test statistics for the two month time windows.

Table 6. Testing for a relation between market clustering and price instability—2-month window.

	2009						2010					
	1	3	5	7	9	11	1	3	5	7	9	11
MAD	==	+=	==	==	==	= −	−−	= −	++	++	++	= +
Variance	==	++	++	= +	++	==	==	==	++	++	++	++
Skewness	==	==	==	++	==	==	+=	==	==	==	++	++
Kurtosis	++	==	++	++	++	+=	+=	++	==	==	++	++
	2011						2012					
	1	3	5	7	9	11	1	3	5	7	9	11
MAD	==	==	==	++	==	++	==	==	==	==	==	==
Variance	==	==	==	++	++	++	==	+=	==	==	==	+=
Skewness	++	==	++	++	++	==	==	==	==	==	==	==
Kurtosis	++	++	++	+=	==	==	==	==	==	==	==	==
	2013						2014					
	1	3	5	7	9	11	1	3	5	7	9	11
MAD	++	==	==	= +	==	++	++	++	++	++	++	==
Variance	++	++	++	++	+=	++	++	++	++	++	++	+=
Skewness	==	==	+=	==	++	==	++	++	==	++	+=	+=
Kurtosis	==	+=	++	==	++	++	++	++	= +	++	++	==

Repetition of Table 5a for time windows of two months instead of one year. Contrary to Table 5, here the critical value is 0.05. The dates in the first line indicate the first month of each time window.

The results for the skewness, kurtosis, and outlier count are normalized by the volatility. We show the relation between the variance and market clustering separately in Tables 5 and 6 and Figure A1. In addition, we analyze the results for the MAD. We find no consistent relation between market clustering and the yearly MAD. We find a weak but consistent positive relation between market clustering and the yearly variance. Figure A1 shows that the discrepancy between the distributions is smaller for the MAD and variance than for the kurtosis. The results for time spans of two months (see Table 6) show an increase in the MAD and variance during the periods where the kurtosis results are consistently positive. The relation between market clustering and the MAD and variance is not informative in itself, as the stocks are traded in different markets. The observation that more (less) market clustering relates to stronger (weaker) price fluctuations is in accordance with the observation that market clustering relates relatively more to the variance than the MAD, because the MAD is more robust to outliers than the variance. Market clustering relates also to price instability measured relative to time-varying volatility. Table A3 shows the relation between market clustering and the yearly kurtosis of log returns normalized by the conditional standard deviation estimated by various GARCH models. This indicates that the relation between market clustering and price instability is not confined to periods of high volatility.

Using the partial coverage of our data set we can dispel concerns over reversed causation. Rather than market clustering causing price instability, unstable stocks might attract traders that prefer to trade in clusters. If the latter holds, then the relation between kurtosis and market clustering would be independent of what percentage of the total turnover traded is included in the data set. Table 7 shows that the relation between market clustering and the kurtosis vanishes for stocks that are mainly traded by investors which are not included in the MiFID data set. The relation between the kurtosis and price instability is (not) significant for stocks with a high (low) percentage of the turnover traded within the data set. By difference-in-differences logic, these results indicate that market clustering leads to price instability and not the other way round.

Table 7. Relation between market clustering and price instability for stocks mainly traded by investors outside MiFID data set.

	2009	2010	2011	2012	2013	2014
Mean	= =	= −	= −	= =	− =	= =
Variance	= =	= =	= =	= =	= =	= +
Skewness	= =	= =	= =	= =	= −	= =
Kurtosis	+ =	= =	= =	= =	= =	= −

Repetition of Table 5a for the stocks for which less than 10% of the total yearly turnover is covered by the investors in the MiFID data set. This category contains on average 434 stocks, which is 44.5% of the total group of selected stocks.

5.2. Drivers of Market Clustering

An important question is whether our proposed clustering measure actually captures new, previously ignored information. To investigate which observable drive investors' pool diversity we use a dynamic panel data framework. Estimated models, shown in Table 8, suggest that clustering is quite a persistent process. Thus, if at time t clustering is high (low), it is likely to be high (low) at $t+1$, too, mainly driven by commonalities, illiquidity, and size. Other stock specific variables have little to no effect in our setting. No more than 20% of the clustering measure variation can be explained by characteristics that would proxy for investor preferences. Thus, a large part of the clustering measure variation remains unexplained and is likely due to accidental portfolio overlap.

Table 8 demonstrates that crowded trading is a persistent feature as the clustering measure exhibits significant positive dependence on the lagged values of market clustering in all models. Herding, lasting for at least multiple months in upward markets, could be one of the mechanisms related to clustering. If market clustering results from accidental portfolio overlaps, continuing clustering may be observed due to spreading the orders over time to reduce market impact. The persistence of market clustering suggests the need for further research with adjusted measures of market clustering that differentiate between buy and sell orders. Furthermore, investigation of the stability of the investors' pools involved in clustered trades would be helpful in understanding the effects of market clustering.

There is little evidence that individual downside risk affects the clustering measure. Lagged ∆VaR is marginally significant in Models 1 and 3; thus, there is not sufficient evidence to conclude that market clustering is stronger for the stocks with increasing downside risk. All of the three models in Table 8 consider downside risk as endogeneous variable in line with our hypothesis that market clustering causes price instability.

Market direction and market risk affect market clustering in multiple ways. First, all models indicate that increase (decrease) in market returns or market volatility in the previous month lead to significantly more (less) clustering per average stock. We added VIX to the GMM-style instruments to correct for potential VIX endogeneity, i.e., that clustering feeds aggregate market volatility. Second, lagged general market uncertainty (VIX_{t-2}) has a negative effect. We interpret this as a short-term corrective mechanism: when increased market volatility leads to more crowded trades, then a month afterwards the trading subsides (because the funds are used up, the interest is transferred elsewhere, investors get scared of continuing uncertainty, or some other reason) and so do the clustered activities. Third, market conditions play a role through asymmetric effects of stock size and illiquidity on clustering measure. Model 2 looks at the effect for high and low volatility states, and Model 3 shows the differences across up and down markets. The specifics of these asymmetries and implications are discussed further in the next paragraph.

Table 8. Estimation results of dynamic panel data models for the clustering measure.

	Model 1		Model 2		Model 3
GMM IV lags					
CLUST	2:75		2:75		2:75
ΔVaR	1:75		1:75		1:75
VIX	1:75		1:75		1:75
$CLUST_{t-1}$	0.122 ***		0.125 ***		0.122 ***
	(0.014)		(0.014)		(0.014)
$CLUST_{t-2}$	0.075 ***		0.078 ***		0.075 ***
	(0.014)		(0.014)		(0.014)
ΔVaR	0.025		−0.007		0.010
	(0.030)		(0.030)		(0.030)
ΔVaR_{t-1}	0.080 **		0.046		0.064 **
	(0.033)		(0.032)		(0.032)
MKTF	0.097 **		0.044		0.241***
	(0.048)		(0.049)		(0.064)
$MKTF_{t-1}$	0.172 ***		0.116 ***		0.175 ***
	(0.042)		(0.045)		(0.041)
VIX	0.082		−0.028		0.165 ***
	(0.064)		(0.080)		(0.064)
VIX_{t-1}	0.305 ***		0.333 ***		0.302 ***
	(0.093)		(0.094)		(0.092)
VIX_{t-2}	−0.282 ***		−0.245 ***		−0.276 ***
	(0.063)		(0.066)		(0.068)
MOM	−0.105	MOMhigh	−0.234	MOMup	−0.097
	(0.121)		(0.185)		(0.118)
MCAP	0.339 **	MOMlow	0.017	MOMdown	−0.055
	(0.168)		(0.122)		(0.146)
ILLIQ	0.277 **	MCAPhigh	0.734 ***	MCAPup	−0.127
	(0.108)		(0.249)		(0.156)
		MCAPlow	0.367 **	MCAPdown	0.235
			(0.175)		(0.148)
		ILLIQhigh	0.133	ILLIQup	0.159
			(0.134)		(0.113)
		ILLIQlow	0.346 ***	ILLIQdown	0.318 ***
			(0.115)		(0.104)
No. IVs	237		243		243
Sargan stat	246.290		245.255		245.197
DF	225		228		228
p-value	0.157		0.206		0.207
AR(1)	0.000		0.000		0.000
AR(2)	0.383		0.321		0.350
$corr^2(y, \hat{y})$	0.198		0.191		0.197

This table contains estimation results of Equation (6) using a two-step system GMM approach with collapsed GMM-style instruments. The dependent variable is the clustering measure. Coefficients for the price-to-book ratio (PB3), trailing dividend yield (DY), and the leverage ratio (LEV3) are insignificant in all models and are not reported to conserve space. Here, CLUST is multiplied by 100, and the number of stock-month observations is 27031. Variables with suffixes "high", "low", "up", and "down" are interacted with $\mathbb{1}_{(VIX \geq 25)}$, $\mathbb{1}_{(VIX<25)}$, $\mathbb{1}_{(MKTF \geq 0)}$, and $\mathbb{1}_{(MKTF<0)}$, respectively. Standard errors are in parentheses below the estimates. Coefficients significant at 5, and 1% level are marked with **, and ***, respectively. Obvious subscripts s and t are omitted for brevity. At the end of the table, usual dynamic panel data model diagnostics are provided: Sargan's test and p-values for Arellano–Bond test for serial correlation. $corr^2_{y,\hat{y}}$ measures squared correlation between the dependent variable and the fitted values from the model.

Illiquidity and size are the only two stock-specific variables that affect clustering, while momentum, price-to-book ratio, dividend yield, and leverage do not yield a significant coefficient in any of the models. To better understand illiquidity and size effects, we investigate asymmetries across market conditions (Models 2 and 3). We find that in quiet times market participants tend to cluster around less liquid stocks (significant coefficients for ILLIQlow and insignificant for ILLIQhigh), perhaps because they are willing to take more risks. Less liquid stocks end up in clustered trades in downward markets, too (Model 3). This resulting pattern is consistent with fire sales. When the stock owner's pool is homogeneous and the pressure to sell arises due to, for example, margin calls, selling less liquid stocks leads to higher price impact, further fueling margin calls and stock sales. Market capitalization (MCAP) has (marginally) significant coefficients in Models 1 and 2. In high volatility markets large firms attract more crowded attention than they do in low volatility markets (coefficients of 0.734 vs. 0.367). Large stocks are frequently dividend paying, are likely index constituents, and are considered less risky, thus such trading behavior may be viewed as a flight-to-safety within equities.

To summarize the insights from this section, the results support theories that market clustering could be a consequence of multiple mechanisms. For one, herding induces persistence in the clustering measure time series. Next, willingness to take up more risks in low volatility markets and fire sales in downward markets both manifest as increased clustering around less liquid stocks. Finally, more clustered trades with higher market capitalization in high volatility period can be interpreted as flight-to-safety phenomenon. Interestingly, we see no evidence that stock selection based on fundamental characteristics would lead to market clustering.

5.3. Downside Risk, Upside Potential, and Clustering

We now turn to the causal analysis of market clustering and price instability. We employ a dynamic panel data model to analyze whether our newly proposed measure actually has additional explanatory power in modeling changes in the downside risk and the upside potential in addition to all commonly used conditioning variables (as discussed in Section 4). In short, we find that market clustering indeed causes price instability, but the effect is conditional on the volatility state in the market.

Table 9 contains the results. All of the models consider the price instability measure as an endogenous variable in line with our concerns that price instability could lead to market clustering. Models 1 and 2 look at changes in the downside risk, and Models 3 and 4 look at changes in the upside potential. All models include current and lagged (conditional) values of CLUST.

Consistent with the outcome of stochastic dominance analysis, there is no causal relation between CLUST and price instability in the negative tail (Model 1). Model 2, however, reveals that in high volatility markets the relation is significant. This makes crowded trading a dangerous phenomena, likely fostering contagion. On the positive side of the return distribution (Models 3 and 4), clustering leads to price instability in both high and low volatility periods. Based on the squared correlation between the dependent variable and fitted values, the positive tail is harder to explain, nonetheless. Lagged CLUST yields insignificant coefficients in all models; thus, the direct causation for the positive tail as well as for the negative tail is contemporaneous and we find no evidence of predictive relation.

Other coefficients have the expected signs or are insignificant. Strongly significant variables come from two categories: aggregate market related (MKTF and VIX) and derived from returns (MOM, MCAP, and ILLIQ). Upward movement and trend in the market index lead to smaller individual risks (thus negative changes in VaR) and more gradual price increases (thus slightly negative changes in VaL). Current increase in volatility also increases changes in downside risk. For the positive tail of the distribution we again see the short-term corrective mechanism: higher volatility at time t implies higher average change in upside potential, but taking advantage of this will result in reducing the upside potential for the next period. Positive momentum, higher market capitalization, and higher illiquidity have negative effect on the changes in log return distribution quantiles. Fundamental characteristics (PB3, DY, and LEV3) do not consistently contribute to explaining the time variation in positive and negative quantiles of return distribution.

All in all, we show that market clustering causes contemporaneous price instability. The relation is present in the negative tail during turmoil and in the positive tail independent of the volatility level.

Table 9. Estimation results of dynamic panel models for ΔVaR and ΔVaL.

	ΔVaR		ΔVaL	
	Model 1	Model 2	Model 3	Model 4
y_{t-1}	0.136 ***	0.131 ***	0.103 ***	0.100 ***
	(0.012)	(0.013)	(0.017)	(0.017)
y_{t-2}	0.095 ***	0.090 ***	0.073 ***	0.071 ***
	(0.011)	(0.011)	(0.011)	(0.011)
CLUST	1.598		6.150 ***	
	(1.209)		(1.462)	
CLUST$_{t-1}$	0.179		−0.192	
	(0.401)		(0.387)	
CLUSTlow		1.398		3.055 **
		(1.352)		(1.44)
CLUSTlow$_{t-1}$		−0.079		−0.001
		(0.469)		(0.481)
CLUSThigh		5.315 **		7.341 ***
		(2.176)		(2.121)
CLUSThigh$_{t-1}$		1.239		−0.214
		(0.975)		(0.701)
MKTF	−0.303 ***	−0.307 ***	−0.047 ***	−0.050 ***
	(0.016)	(0.016)	(0.016)	(0.015)
MKTF$_{t-1}$	−0.144 ***	−0.146 ***	−0.107 ***	−0.105 ***
	(0.010)	(0.010)	(0.011)	(0.011)
VIX	0.117 ***	0.095 ***	0.158 ***	0.141 ***
	(0.024)	(0.027)	(0.024)	(0.026)
VIX$_{t-1}$	0.009	0.01	−0.113 ***	−0.107 ***
	(0.023)	(0.024)	(0.023)	(0.024)
MOM	−0.303 ***	−0.301 ***	−0.416 ***	−0.412 ***
	(0.030)	(0.030)	(0.036)	(0.034)
MCAP	−0.337 ***	−0.294 ***	−0.213 ***	−0.175 ***
	(0.038)	(0.043)	(0.046)	(0.049)
ILLIQ	−0.060 ***	−0.049 ***	−0.046 ***	−0.027
	(0.015)	(0.016)	(0.018)	(0.017)
PB3	0.008	0.013	0.087	0.085
	(0.053)	(0.051)	(0.056)	(0.053)
DY	0.016	0.019	0.013	0.022
	(0.023)	(0.022)	(0.033)	(0.029)
LEV3	−0.008 **	−0.007 **	−0.001	0.000
	(0.003)	(0.003)	(0.004)	(0.003)
No. IVs	241	316	241	316
Sargan stat	239.556	242.341	240.421	237.452
DF	227	300	227	300
p-value	0.271	0.994	0.258	0.997
AR(1)	0.000	0.000	0.000	0.000
AR(2)	0.265	0.146	0.355	0.504
corr$^2_{y,\hat{y}}$	0.151	0.150	0.070	0.083

This table contains the estimation results of Equation (6) using a two-step system GMM approach. All available lags for dependent variable, (conditional) CLUST, and VIX are used as collapsed GMM instruments. Here, the number of stock-month observations is 27295. Models 1 and 2 use dependent variable $y_{st} = \Delta\text{VaR}_{st}$ and Models 3 and 4 use $y_{st} = \Delta\text{VaL}_{st}$. Models 2 and 4 introduce CLUSTlow = CLUST $\times \mathbb{1}_{(\text{VIX}<25)}$ and CLUSThigh = CLUST $\times \mathbb{1}_{(\text{VIX}\geq 25)}$ to account for asymmetric effects. Standard errors are in parentheses below the estimates. Coefficients significant at 5, and 1% level are marked with **, and ***, respectively. Obvious subscripts s and t are omitted for brevity. At the end of the table, usual dynamic panel data model diagnostics are provided: Sargan's test and p-values for Arellano–Bond test for serial correlation. corr$^2_{y,\hat{y}}$ measures squared correlation between the dependent variable and the fitted values from the model.

6. Discussion

We have shown some suggestive evidence for a causal relation between market clustering and price instability on the individual stock level. There seems to be a consistent and robust positive relation between market clustering and the kurtosis, the skewness, the positive tail index, the positive outlier count, and the right 5% quantile of the log return distribution. The positive relation between market clustering and the left 5% quantile of the log return distribution is conditional on periods of high volatility. Focusing on extreme price fluctuations, that is, the tails of the normalized log return distribution, we find that market clustering generally causes an increase of large upward price shocks. Increases of large downward shocks due to market clustering turns out to be present only in financial turmoil. Findings on the positive tail are consistent with herding, while findings on the negative tail are consistent with fire sales.

We also provide some insights into investor behavior that likely lead to market clustering. The persistence of our market clustering measure could be explained by herding and order spreading over time. Market conditions obviously affect trading decisions. We find an indication that the homogeneity of the investors' pool per stock increases if there is a positive trend in the market or increase in aggregate volatility. However, the volatility effect is short-term and reverses in the month afterwards. Furthermore, we find asymmetries across market conditions. In quiet times, investors prefer less liquid stocks. Consistent with fire sales, less liquid stocks are also traded by more homogeneous groups in downward markets. We discover behavior that is consistent with flight-to-safety within equities in the sense that in high volatility markets large firms attract more crowded attention.

Our analysis contributes to the existing literature on three levels. First, we study the influence of trading behavior on price dynamics using novel granular trading data. To our knowledge, the MiFID data set has not been used for this type of market microstructure research before. Second, the idea and method to measure market clustering and its impact on price instability are new to market microstructure research. The use of complex network theory makes the method suitable for large-scale data. The methodological framework can be extended to study the effects of any feature of the market microstructure. Third, the main contribution is the indication of a causal relation between the market clustering and price instability shown in a dynamic panel data model.

The use of network theory in identifying meaningful motifs in market microstructure research is promising because the model is applicable to all types of market microstructure patterns. First, the influence of trading behavior on price dynamics can be investigated using other microstructure motifs, for example, the influence of the diversification of the investors on the price dynamics of the traded stocks. Differentiation between buy and sell orders would enhance the understanding of the difference in dependence between the positive and negative tail of the price dynamics. The persistence of the market clustering measure—evident in consistent positive dependence on past, lagged values of market clustering—is worthy of further investigation of the time dependence of the configuration of the investors' pools involved in clustered trades. Moreover, the role of news should be investigated further. It is widely accepted that negative news has a much larger impact compared to positive news. To this end, we should analyze the results on a much shorter time scale to see if common information drives clustering. Second, the method can be used for portfolio holdings data and could, for example, contribute to the literature on price comovements due to common active mutual fund owners [1]. Third, the method can be used to study trading patterns separate from price dynamics, for example, the evolution of clustering patterns over time. Furthermore, the relation between clustering and current market conditions needs further attention, for example, what is the mechanism of spillovers in each case.

Author Contributions: Conceptualization, M.v.K., D.G., and I.v.L.; methodology, M.v.K., D.G.; software, M.v.K.; validation, D.G.; formal analysis, M.v.K. and K.S.; investigation, M.v.K.; resources, I.v.L.; data curation, I.v.L.; writing—original draft preparation, M.v.K.; writing—review and editing, M.v.K., D.G., and K.S.; visualization, M.v.K.; supervision, I.v.L. and D.G.; project administration, all; funding acquisition, M.v.K., D.G., and I.v.L. All authors have read and agreed to the published version of the manuscript.

Funding: D.G. acknowledges support from the Dutch Econophysics Foundation (Stichting Econophysics, Leiden, the Netherlands), and the EU project SoBigData++ (Grant No. 871042).

Institutional Review Board Statement: Not applicable.

Informed Consent Statement: Not applicable.

Data Availability Statement: The study uses data from MIFID as explained in Section 4. This data is confidential and cannot be published.

Acknowledgments: Views expressed are those of the authors and do not necessarily reflect official positions of De Nederlandsche Bank or Aegon N.V. We would like to thank colleagues at the De Nederlandsche Bank, VU Amsterdam, Dieter Wang (World Bank), Wouter van Bronswijk (AFM), Richard Verhoef (AFM), Dick van Dijk (EUR), and participants at the Risklab/BoF/ESRB conference on Systemic Risk Analytics, Bristol Banking and Financial Intermediation Workshop, the 25th International Panel Data Conference and seminars at Banque de France and Radboud Universtiy for input received. Naturally all errors are ours.

Conflicts of Interest: The authors declare no conflict of interest.

Appendix A. Construction of the Maximum-Entropy Ensemble of Networks with Given Expected Degree Sequence

We define a bipartite network that describes the aggregate trading behavior during a particular month. For each month, t, the investment behavior comprised by the data is represented in a binary bipartite graph. The bipartite network has two (say, bottom and top) layers with edges between the two layers. No edges occur between two nodes in the same layer. The nodes of the first (say, bottom) layer represent the set S_t of securities that are traded during month t. The nodes of the second (say, top) layer represent the set F_t of firms that perform trades during month t. The individual securities are indicated by the label s each month separately, such that $s \in S_t$. The label can take the values $s = 1, ..., n_{S,t}$ with $n_{S,t} = |S_t|$ the number of elements in S_t. Similarly, the individual firms are indicated by the label f each month separately, such that $f \in F_t$. The label can take the values $f = 1, ..., n_{F,t}$ with $n_{F,t} = |F_t|$ the number of elements in F_t.

The performed transactions are represented by the edges between the firms and the securities, denoted by the rectangular binary adjacency matrix (sometimes called "bi-adjacency matrix") A_t with elements $a_{sf,t}$. The size of matrix A_t is $n_{S,t} \times n_{F,t}$. The transactions are represented as follows: $a_{sf,t} = 1$ in case firm f traded in security s during month t and $a_{sf,t} = 0$ otherwise. The observed degree of firm f during month t is given by

$$d_{f,t}^{\text{obs}} = \sum_{s=1}^{n_{S,t}} a_{sf,t} \tag{A1}$$

and the observed degree of security s is given by

$$d_{s,t}^{\text{obs}} = \sum_{f=1}^{n_{F,t}} a_{sf,t}. \tag{A2}$$

The set D_t^{obs} contains the observed degrees of all nodes in month t, such that

$$d_{s,t}^{\text{obs}}, d_{f,t}^{\text{obs}} \in D_t^{\text{obs}} \quad \forall f, s \tag{A3}$$

Note that the graph indicates only whether a trade of a firm in a security occurs. None of the following quantities are represented: the number of transactions, the number of underlying securities, or the turnover. Furthermore, the graph does not distinguish between buy and sell transactions or between agency and principal transactions.

For a given t, our goal is to find the probability distribution $P_t(X_t) = P(X_t | D_t^{\text{obs}})$ over an allowed set of alternative trading configurations, such that the ensemble of bipartite graphs generated by P_t is maximally random, apart from ensuring that the expected value $\langle D_t \rangle$ of the degree sequence under P_t equals the observed value D_t^{obs}, i.e.,

$$\langle D_t \rangle = D_t^{\text{obs}}. \tag{A4}$$

This prescription ensures that, besides the information about the observed degree sequence, all other empirical information about the actual placing of the trades is not used to determine P_t and cannot be retrieved form it. To further ensure that the inference of higher-order properties obtained using P_t is unbiased, we apply the maximum-entropy method [13] and look for the distribution $P_t(X_t)$ that maximizes Shannon's entropy functional

$$S_t[P_t] = - \sum_{X_t \in \mathcal{G}_t} P_t(X_t) \ln P_t(X_t) \tag{A5}$$

where the sum runs over the ensemble of graphs $\mathcal{G}_t$ containing all binary, bipartite networks where the number of elements in the top layer is $n_{F,t}$ and the number elements in the bottom layer is $n_{S,t}$. The resulting ensemble is a canonical one [13], which means that all the allowed graphs have the same number of nodes as the original empirical network but the number of links varies between zero and $n_{S,t} n_{F,t}$. An element $X_t \in \mathcal{G}_t$ is a $n_{S,t} \times n_{F,t}$ adjacency matrix encoding the configuration of a possible bipartite network in the ensemble. There are $2^{n_{S,t} n_{F,t}}$ possible such configurations. Each configuration X_t contains, for each security–firm pair (s, f), the information whether the firm trades the security ($a_{sf}(X_t) = 1$) or not ($a_{sf}(X_t) = 0$) during month t. X_t does not denote the observed graph configuration, but a generic allowed configuration in $\mathcal{G}_t$. Among these configurations, a particular one X_t^{obs} is the observed one, i.e., $a_{sf}(X_t^{\text{obs}}) = a_{sf,t}$ for all s, f.

Shannon's entropy can be seen as the "degree of uncertainty" encoded in the probability distribution P_t and is a weighted average of the amount of information required to identify a specific graph in the ensemble. For example, in case of no constraints, Shannon's entropy would be maximized when each configuration X_t occurs with equal probability $P_t(X_t) = 2^{-n_{S,t} n_{F,t}}$ and its value would be $S_t[P_t] = \ln 2^{n_{S,t} n_{F,t}}$. In our case, or a given month t, we instead need to maximize $S_t[P_t]$ under the constraints imposed by the degree sequence, i.e., Equation (A4), which we rewrite as

$$\langle d_{f,t} \rangle = d_{f,t}^{\text{obs}}, \quad \langle d_{s,t} \rangle = d_{s,t}^{\text{obs}} \quad \forall f, s, \tag{A6}$$

where

$$\langle d_{f,t} \rangle = \langle d_f(X_t) \rangle = \langle \sum_{s=1}^{n_{S,t}} a_{sf}(X_t) \rangle, \quad \langle d_{s,t} \rangle = \langle d_s(X_t) \rangle = \langle \sum_{f=1}^{n_{F,t}} a_{sf}(X_t) \rangle. \tag{A7}$$

Note that in total there are $n_{F,t} + n_{S,t} + 1$ constraints for each t:

$$\begin{cases} d_{f,t}^{\text{obs}} = \sum_{X_t \in \mathcal{G}_t} P_t(X_t) d_f(X_t) \quad \forall f, \\ d_{s,t}^{\text{obs}} = \sum_{X_t \in \mathcal{G}_t} P_t(X_t) d_s(X_t) \quad \forall s, \\ 1 = \sum_{X_t \in \mathcal{G}_t} P_t(X_t), \end{cases} \tag{A8}$$

where the last expression is the normalization of the probability distribution. We therefore introduce $n_{F,t} + n_{S,t} + 1$ Lagrange multipliers $\{\beta_{f,t}\}_{f=1}^{n_{F,t}}$, $\{\beta_{s,t}\}_{s=1}^{n_{S,t}}$, α_t (one for each constraint) and look for the probability distribution P_t optimizing the Lagrange function

$$\begin{aligned} L_t[P_t] &= S_t[P_t] + \alpha_t \left(1 - \sum_{X_t \in \mathcal{G}_t} P_t(X_t)\right) \\ &+ \sum_{f=1}^{n_{F,t}} \beta_{f,t} \left(d_{f,t}^{\text{obs}} - \sum_{X_t \in \mathcal{G}_t} P_t(X_t) d_f(X_t)\right) \\ &+ \sum_{s=1}^{n_{S,t}} \beta_{s,t} \left(d_{s,t}^{\text{obs}} - \sum_{X_t \in \mathcal{G}_t} P_t(X_t) d_s(X_t)\right). \end{aligned} \tag{A9}$$

Taking the functional derivative, we get

$$\frac{\delta L_t}{\delta P_t(X_t)} = \ln P_t(X_t) + 1 + \alpha_t + \sum_{f=1}^{n_{F,t}} \beta_{f,t} d_f(X_t) + \sum_{s=1}^{n_{S,t}} \beta_{s,t} d_s(X_t). \tag{A10}$$

Now the probability distribution $P_t(X_t) = P(X_t | D_t^{\text{obs}})$ is determined by the optimum:

$$\frac{\delta L_t}{\delta P_t(X_t)} = 0 \leftrightarrow P(X_t | D_t^{\text{obs}}) = \frac{e^{-H_t(X_t)}}{Z_t}, \tag{A11}$$

with $H_t(X_t)$ the so-called Hamiltonian

$$H_t(X_t) = \sum_{f=1}^{n_{F,t}} \beta_{f,t} d_f(X_t) + \sum_{s=1}^{n_{S,t}} \beta_{s,t} d_s(X_t), \tag{A12}$$

and Z_t the so-called partition function

$$Z_t = e^{1+\alpha_t} = \sum_{X_t \in \mathcal{G}_t} e^{-H_t(X_t)}. \tag{A13}$$

The partition function can be written as [13]

$$Z_t = \sum_{X_t \in \mathcal{G}_t} e^{-\sum_f \beta_{f,t} \sum_s a_{sf}(X_t) - \sum_s \beta_{s,t} \sum_f a_{sf}(X_t)} \tag{A14}$$

$$= \sum_{X_t \in \mathcal{G}_t} \prod_{s,f} e^{-\beta_{f,t} a_{sf}(X_t) - \beta_{s,t} a_{sf}(X_t)} \tag{A15}$$

$$= \prod_{s,f} \left(1 + e^{-\beta_{f,t} - \beta_{s,t}}\right). \tag{A16}$$

Now, we rewrite $P(X_t|D_t^{obs})$ in a factorized form that shows the probabilistic independence of all edges of the network (note that this independence is not an assumption or simplification, as it follows mathematically from our choice of the constraints):

$$P(X_t|D_t^{obs}) = \prod_{s,f} p_{sf,t}^{a_{sf}(X_t)} (1 - p_{sf,t})^{1-a_{sf}(X_t)}, \tag{A17}$$

where we have introduced the security-firm connection probability

$$p_{sf,t} = P(a_{sf}(X_t) = 1|D_t^{obs}) = \frac{x_{f,t} x_{s,t}}{1 + x_{f,t} x_{s,t}}, \tag{A18}$$

the complementary (no connection) probability

$$1 - p_{sf,t} = P(a_{sf}(X_t) = 0|D_t^{obs}) = \frac{1}{1 + x_{f,t} x_{s,t}}, \tag{A19}$$

and the reparametrization

$$\begin{cases} x_{f,t} = e^{-\beta_{f,t}} \\ x_{s,t} = e^{-\beta_{s,t}} \end{cases}. \tag{A20}$$

The variables $x_{f,t}$ and $x_{s,t}$ are also called "hidden variables" [13]. Their numerical value is found by solving, for each t, the $n_{F,t} + n_{S,t}$ coupled nonlinear Equation (A6) realizing the value of the imposed constraints. Noticing that

$$\langle a_{sf}(X_t) \rangle = \sum_{X_t \in \mathcal{G}_t} P_t(X_t) a_{sf}(X_t) = p_{sf,t}, \tag{A21}$$

those equations can be rewritten explicitly in terms of the hidden variables as follows:

$$\sum_{s=1}^{n_{S,t}} \frac{x_{f,t} x_{s,t}}{1 + x_{f,t} x_{s,t}} = d_{f,t}^{obs}, \quad \sum_{f=1}^{n_{F,t}} \frac{x_{f,t} x_{s,t}}{1 + x_{f,t} x_{s,t}} = d_{s,t}^{obs} \quad \forall f, s. \tag{A22}$$

It can be proven in general [13] that the values solving the above equations are unique and correspond to the values that maximize the likelihood $P_t(A_t) = P(A_t|D_t^{obs})$ of generating the observed network A_t, given the model parameters. Various efficient codes are available for solving the above type of equations [48].

Appendix B. Stochastic Dominance of Price Instability Measures

In this appendix, we report (see Figures A1 and A2) the cumulative distributions, for low and high market clustering, for all the time series measures (MAD, variance, skewness, kurtosis, number of negative outliers, number of positive outliers, Hill index for the negative tail, and Hill index for the positive tail) and all years.

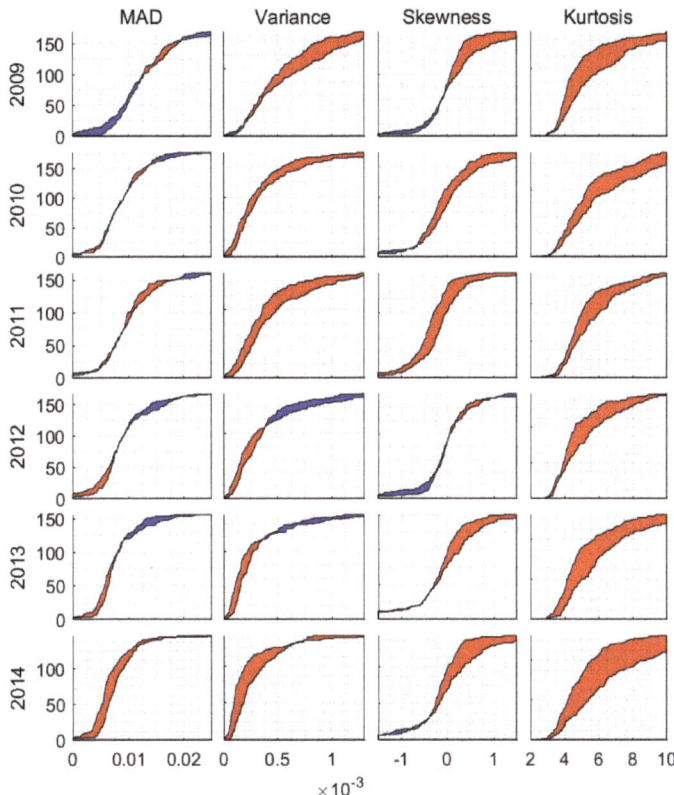

Figure A1. Cumulative distributions for low and high market clustering per time series measure (MAD, variance, skewness, and kurtosis) and per year. The space in between the distributions for low and high market clustering is colored to indicate which distribution is higher. Red means that distribution H (high market clustering) exceeds distribution L (low market clustering), and vice versa for blue.

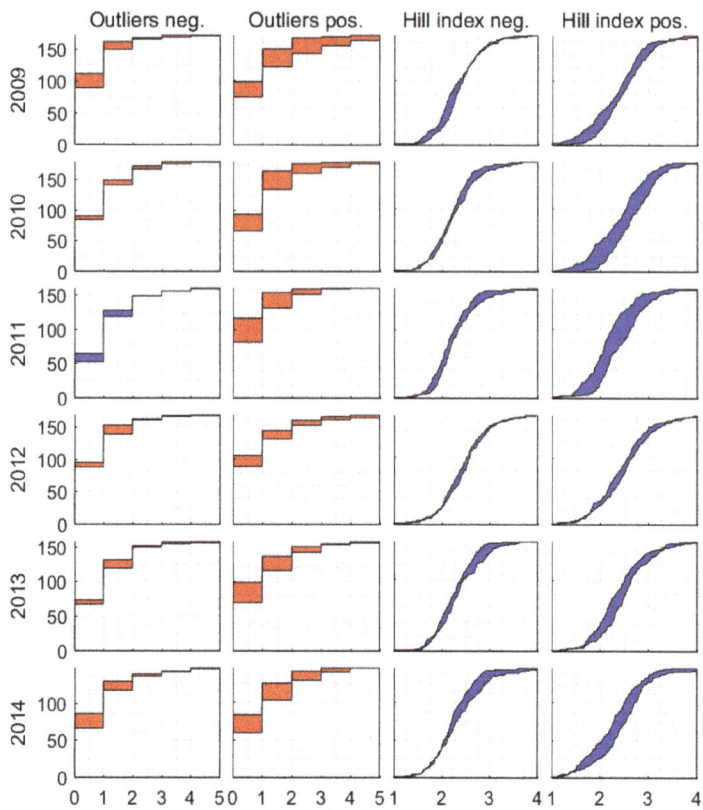

Figure A2. Cumulative distributions for low and high market clustering per time series measure (number of negative outliers, number of positive outliers, Hill index for the negative tail, and Hill index for the positive tail) and per year. See Figure A1 for explanation.

Appendix C. Robustness Checks

Table A1 shows the results for the relation between market clustering and the kurtosis for various segments of the log return distribution. The results for the kurtosis do not depend in particular on the tails of the log return distribution.

Table A1. The kurtosis results from Table 5 for partial data.

	2009	2010	2011	2012	2013	2014
10–90	++	++	++	++	++	+=
20–80	++	++	++	++	++	==
30–70	++	++	++	++	++	==
40–60	++	=+	++	=+	++	++

First, we order the log returns time series per stock and per year in ascending order. Second, we select the segments of the log return distribution as shown in the left column (in percentages). For example, the last line shows the results for the segment 40–60% (the middle part), which means that we remove the first 40% and the last 40% of the ordered log return distribution.

Table A2 shows the relation between market clustering and the kurtosis for different cross-sections of the market clustering distribution. The critical value is 0.025 in all tables. The results show no consistent variation over the different cross sections.

Table A2. The relation between market clustering and the kurtosis for different cross sections of the market clustering distribution.

	2009	2010	2011	2012	2013	2014
0–10 and 90–100	++	==	+=	++	++	++
10–30 and 70–90	++	==	++	==	=+	++
0–50 and 50–100	++	++	+=	++	++	++
20–50 and 50–80	==	=+	==	==	++	=+

For comparison, Table 5 shows the results for the highest 33% and the lowest 33% of the stocks, ranked according to their market clustering measure, i.e., the selected regions are 0–33% and 67–100%.

Table A3 shows the result for normalization by the time-varying standard deviation, estimated by various GARCH-type models. Normalization by the time-varying volatility means that the weight of the price fluctuations in periods of high volatility is effectively reduced in favor of the weight of the price fluctuations during tranquil periods. We estimate for each stock the conditional volatility time series for the complete log return time series at once instead of each year separately. The EGARCH model allows the sign and the magnitude of the log returns to have separate effects on the volatility. In the GJR-GARCH model, the effects of the positive and negative log returns are estimated separately. The EGARCH models are exponential and therefore less sensitive to outliers than the GJR-GARCH models. The addition of extra lags allows the volatility to vary on both shorter and longer time scales. For all GARCH models we we assume conditional normal distribution for the error term: $\varepsilon_{s,t} \sim \mathcal{N}(0, \sigma_{s,t}^2)$. This assumption is probably violated for some of the stocks. We assume that the consequences of this violation are limited.

The relation between market clustering and price instability remains consistently positive when we account for the time-varying volatility. We find no apparent variation of the results for the relation between market clustering and price instability for the different GARCH models for the conditional volatility. Apparently, market clustering causes downward price shocks not only during volatile periods but also when the price is more stable.

Table A3. The results for the yearly kurtosis of the log returns, normalized by the conditional standard deviation estimated by various GARCH models.

	2009	2010	2011	2012	2013	2014
GARCH(1,1)	++	++	==	++	++	++
GARCH(2,2)	++	==	==	++	++	++
EGARCH(1,1)	++	++	==	++	++	++
GJR-GARCH(1,1)	++	++	==	++	++	++

References

1. Anton, M.; Polk, C. Connected Stocks. *J. Financ.* **2014**, *69*, 1099–1127. [CrossRef]
2. Bruno, S.; Chincarini, L.B.; Ohara, F. Portfolio construction and crowding. *J. Empir. Financ.* **2018**, *47*, 190–206. [CrossRef]
3. Pojarliev, M.; Levich, R.M. Detecting Crowded Trades in Currency Funds. *Financ. Anal. J.* **2011**, *67*, 26–39. [CrossRef]
4. Kinlaw, W.B.; Kritzman, M.; Turkington, D. *Crowded Trades: Implications for Sector Rotation and Factor Timing*; SSRN Scholarly Paper ID 3182664; Social Science Research Network: Rochester, NY, USA, 2018.
5. Hong, H.G.; Jiang, W. When Some Investors Head for the Exit. In Proceedings of the AFA 2013 San Diego Meetings Paper, San Diego, CA, USA, 4–6 January 2013.
6. Yang, C.; Zhou, L. Individual stock crowded trades, individual stock investor sentiment and excess returns. *N. Am. J. Econ. Financ.* **2016**, *38*, 39–53. [CrossRef]
7. Jia, Y.; Yang, C. Disagreement and the risk-return relation. *Econ. Model.* **2017**, *64*, 97–104. [CrossRef]
8. Glasserman, P.; Young, H.P. Contagion in Financial Networks. *J. Econ. Lit.* **2016**, *54*, 779–831. [CrossRef]
9. Levy-Carciente, S.; Kenett, D.Y.; Avakian, A.; Stanley, H.E.; Havlin, S. Dynamical macroprudential stress testing using network theory. *J. Bank. Financ.* **2015**, *59*, 164–181. [CrossRef]
10. Stein, J. Presidential address: Sophisticated investors and market efficiency. *J. Financ.* **2009**, *64*, 1517–1548. [CrossRef]
11. Braun-Munzinger, K.; Liu, Z.; Turrell, A. An agent-based model of dynamics in corporate bond trading. *Quant. Financ.* **2018**, *18*, 591–608. [CrossRef]
12. Weber, P.; Rosenow, B. Large stock price changes: Volume or liquidity? *Quant. Financ.* **2006**, *6*, 7–14. [CrossRef]

13. Squartini, T.; Garlaschelli, D. *Maximum-Entropy Networks: Pattern Detection, Network Reconstruction and Graph Combinatorics*; Springer International Publishing: Berlin/Heidelberg, Germany, 2017.
14. Squartini, T.; Caldarelli, G.; Cimini, G.; Gabrielli, A.; Garlaschelli, D. Reconstruction methods for networks: The case of economic and financial systems. *Phys. Rep.* **2018**, *757*, 1–47. [CrossRef]
15. Squartini, T.; Garlaschelli, D. Triadic Motifs and Dyadic Self-Organization in the World Trade Network. *Lect. Notes Comput. Sci.* **2012**, *7166*, 24–35.
16. O'Hara, M. Liquidity and Price Discovery. *J. Financ.* **2003**, *58*, 1335–1354. [CrossRef]
17. Thurner, S.; Farmer, J.D.; Geanakoplos, J. Leverage Causes Fat Tails and Clustered Volatility. *Quant. Financ.* **2012**, *12*, 19. [CrossRef]
18. Gorban, S.; Obizhaeva, A.A.; Wang, Y. *Trading in Crowded Markets*; SSRN Scholarly Paper ID 3152743; Social Science Research Network: Rochester, NY, USA, 2018.
19. Cai, J.; Saunders, A.; Steffen, S. Syndication, Interconnectedness, and Systemic Risk. *J. Financ. Stab.* **2018**, *34*, 105–120. [CrossRef]
20. Caccioli, F.; Shrestha, M.; Moore, C.; Farmer, J.D. Stability analysis of financial contagion due to overlapping portfolios. *J. Bank. Financ.* **2014**, *46*, 233–245. [CrossRef]
21. Caccioli, F.; Farmer, J.D.; Foti, N.; Rockmore, D. Overlapping portfolios, contagion, and financial stability. *J. Econ. Dyn. Control.* **2015**, *51*, 50–63. [CrossRef]
22. Greenwood, R.; Landier, A.; Thesmar, D. Vulnerable Banks. *J. Financ. Econ.* **2015**, *115*, 471–485. [CrossRef]
23. Barroso, P.; Edelen, R.M.; Karehnke, P. *Institutional Crowding and the Moments of Momentum*; SSRN Scholarly Paper ID 3045019; Social Science Research Network: Rochester, NY, USA, 2018.
24. Gualdi, S.; Cimini, G.; Primicerio, K.; Di Clemente, R.; Challet, D. Statistically validated network of portfolio overlaps and systemic risk. *Sci. Rep.* **2016**, *6*, 39467. [CrossRef]
25. Glasserman, P.; Peyton Young, H. How Likely is Contagion in Financial Networks? *J. Bank. Financ.* **2015**, *54*, 383–399. [CrossRef]
26. Brunnermeier, M.K.; Pedersen, L.H. Predatory Trading. *J. Financ.* **2005**, *60*, 1825–1863. [CrossRef]
27. Cont, R.; Wagalath, L. Fire sales forensics: Measuring endogenous risk. *Math. Financ.* **2014**, *26*, 835–866. [CrossRef]
28. Van Lelyveld, I.P.P.; Liedorp, F. Interbank Contagion in the Dutch Banking Sector: A Sensitivity Analysis. *Int. J. Central Banking* **2006**, *31*, 99–133.
29. Cont, R.; Schaaning, E. *Systemic Stress Testing: Modelling Fire Sales in Macro Stress Tests*; Working Paper; Norges Bank: Oslo, Norway, 2017.
30. Bluhm, M.; Krahnen, J.P. Systemic risk in an interconnected banking system with endogenous asset markets. *J. Financ. Stab.* **2014**, *13*, 75–94. [CrossRef]
31. Ellul, A.; Jotikasthira, C.; Lundblad, C.T. Regulatory pressure and fire sales in the corporate bond market. *J. Financ. Econ.* **2011**, *101*, 596–620. [CrossRef]
32. Aymanns, C.; Farmer, J.D. The dynamics of the leverage cycle. *J. Econ. Dyn. Control* **2015**, *50*, 155–179. [CrossRef]
33. Glasserman, P.; Wu, Q. Persistence and Procyclicality in Margin Requirements. *Manag. Sci.* **2018**, *64*, 5705–5724. [CrossRef]
34. Madhavan, A. Market microstructure: A survey. *J. Financ. Mark.* **2000**, *3*, 205–258. [CrossRef]
35. Pedersen, L. When Everyone Runs for the Exit. *Int. J. Cent. Bank.* **2009**, *5*, 177–199.
36. Battiston, B.S.; Farmer, J.D.; Flache, A.; Garlaschelli, D.; Haldane, A.G.; Heesterbeek, H. Complexity Theory and Financial Regulation. *Science* **2016**, *351*, 818–819. [CrossRef]
37. Squartini, T.; Garlaschelli, D. Analytical maximum-likelihood method to detect patterns in real networks. *New J. Phys.* **2011**, *13*, 083001. [CrossRef]
38. Squartini, T.; van Lelyveld, I.; Garlaschelli, D. Early-Warning Signals of Topological Collapse in Interbank Networks. *Nat. Sci. Rep.* **2013**, *3*, 3357. [CrossRef] [PubMed]
39. Huang, X.; Vodenska, I.; Havlin, S.; Stanley, H.E. Cascading Failures in Bi-partite Graphs: Model for Systemic Risk Propagation. *Sci. Rep.* **2013**, *3*, 1219. [CrossRef] [PubMed]
40. Cohen-Cole, E.; Kirilenko, A.; Patacchini, E. Trading networks and liquidity provision. *J. Financ. Econ.* **2014**, *113*, 235–251. [CrossRef]
41. Zhong, L.; Ding, X.S.; Tay, N.S.P. The Impact on Stock Returns of Crowding by Mutual Funds. *J. Portf. Manag.* **2017**, *43*, 87–99. [CrossRef]
42. Ang, A.; Chen, J.; Xing, Y. Downside Risk. *Rev. Financ. Stud.* **2006**, *19*, 1191–1239. [CrossRef]
43. Windmeijer, F. A finite sample correction for the variance of linear efficient two-step GMM estimators. *J. Econom.* **2005**, *126*, 25–51. [CrossRef]
44. Croissant, Y.; Millo, G. Panel Data Econometrics in R: The plm Package. *J. Stat. Softw.* **2008**, *27*. [CrossRef]
45. Roodman, D. A Note on the Theme of Too Many Instruments. *Oxf. Bull. Econ. Stat.* **2009**, *71*, 135–158. [CrossRef]
46. Wintoki, M.B.; Linck, J.S.; Netter, J.M. Endogeneity and the dynamics of internal corporate governance. *J. Financ. Econ.* **2012**, *105*, 581–606. [CrossRef]

47. Amihud, Y. Illiquidity and stock returns: Cross-section and time-series effects. *J. Financ. Mark.* **2002**, *5*, 31–56. [CrossRef]
48. Maximum Entropy Hub. (IMT School of Advanced Studies, Lucca). Available online: http://meh.imtlucca.it (accessed on 1 February 2021).

Article

An Entropy-Based Approach to Measurement of Stock Market Depth

Joanna Olbryś * and Krzysztof Ostrowski

Faculty of Computer Science, Bialystok University of Technology, 15-351 Bialystok, Poland; k.ostrowski@pb.edu.pl
* Correspondence: j.olbrys@pb.edu.pl

Abstract: The aim of this study is to investigate market depth as a stock market liquidity dimension. A new methodology for market depth measurement exactly based on Shannon information entropy for high-frequency data is introduced and utilized. The proposed entropy-based market depth indicator is supported by an algorithm inferring the initiator of a trade. This new indicator seems to be a promising liquidity measure. Both market entropy and market liquidity can be directly measured by the new indicator. The findings of empirical experiments for real-data with a time stamp rounded to the nearest second from the Warsaw Stock Exchange (WSE) confirm that the new proxy enables us to effectively compare market depth and liquidity for different equities. Robustness tests and statistical analyses are conducted. Furthermore, an intra-day seasonality assessment is provided. Results indicate that the entropy-based approach can be considered as an auspicious market depth and liquidity proxy with an intuitive base for both theoretical and empirical analyses in financial markets.

Keywords: entropy; market microstructure; dimensions of market liquidity; market depth; high-frequency data; intra-day seasonality

Citation: Olbryś, J.; Ostrowski, K. An Entropy-Based Approach to Measurement of Stock Market Depth. *Entropy* **2021**, *23*, 568. https://doi.org/10.3390/e23050568

Academic Editors: Yong Deng and Stanisław Drożdż

Received: 8 March 2021
Accepted: 1 May 2021
Published: 3 May 2021

Publisher's Note: MDPI stays neutral with regard to jurisdictional claims in published maps and institutional affiliations.

Copyright: © 2021 by the authors. Licensee MDPI, Basel, Switzerland. This article is an open access article distributed under the terms and conditions of the Creative Commons Attribution (CC BY) license (https://creativecommons.org/licenses/by/4.0/).

1. Introduction

The original idea of entropy dates back to the fundamental Shannon's theory of communication and information [1]. Entropy was defined by Shannon as a measure of information, choice and uncertainty. The concept of entropy originates from thermodynamics, but it has been utilized in many research fields to characterize the complexity of a system and to investigate the information content of a probability distribution. Entropy is a general measure, and therefore, many definitions and applications of entropy have been proposed in the literature. Since the aim of this paper is to introduce and utilize a new entropy-based estimator of stock market depth as one of stock market liquidity dimensions, the brief literature review focuses on selected entropy-based applications in economics, finance, and management. Theoretical, empirical, and experimental aspects of entropy utilization are highlighted.

Firstly, there are quite many entropy-based applications in portfolio selection, asset pricing, and risk management, including the entropy optimization approach. Zhou et al. [2] presents a comprehensive review of applications of entropy in finance. Both primary and recent studies are included. For instance, the pioneering work of Philippatos and Wilson [3] proposed the mean-entropy concept in the efficient portfolio selection problem. The main contribution of this primary research lies in the conclusions that mean-entropy portfolios are consistent with the Markowitz and Sharpe models.

In light of the recently growing literature on the entropy-based applications, the topic concerning portfolio selection is very popular. Among others, Usta and Kantar [4] present a multi-objective method based on a mean-variance-skewness-entropy portfolio selection model to generate a well-diversified portfolio. Zhang et al. [5] deal with a multi-period portfolio selection problem with fuzzy returns. In this paper, the diversification degree of a portfolio is measured by the originally presented possibilistic entropy. Huang [6] proposes two types of credibility-based fuzzy mean-entropy models for fuzzy portfolio selection, and entropy is used as the measure of risk. Yu et al. [7] evaluate the performance of the portfolio models that are used to rebalance with short selling, considering transaction costs, minimizing portfolio risk, and utilizing entropy in modeling asset allocation. Zhou et al. [8] systematically explore the properties of six kinds of entropy-based risk measures, and develop and compare several portfolio models based on different risk measures. Yang and Qiu [9] extend the classical decision model under risk to a more general case. They propose an expected utility-entropy measure of risk and a decision-making model based on expected utility and entropy. Pele et al. [10] investigate relationship between the information entropy of the distribution of intraday returns, and intraday and daily proxies of financial market risk. They use Value-at-Risk and Expected Shortfall as risk measures for the EUR/JPY exchange rate. Gradojevic and Caric [11] concentrate on quantifying the behavioral aspects of systematic risk by utilizing a novel entropy-based approach. Their empirical results confirm the predictive usefulness of new entropy setting in stock market risk management.

In the mathematical finance literature, there are several papers dealing with entropy as an optimization criterion, especially in the context of asset and option pricing. For example, Fritelli [12] investigates the properties of the minimal entropy martingale measure, and shows that the minimization of relative entropy is equivalent to the maximization of expected exponential utility of wealth. Stutzer [13] proposes relative entropy minimization approach to derivation of a generalized Black-Scholes option pricing model. In their theoretical research concerning risk management, Geman et al. [14] use entropy maximization approach to recognize the uncertainty of asset distribution. Xu et al. [15] propose a continuous maximum entropy method to analyze the robust optimal portfolio selection problem in the case of the market with transaction costs and dividends. Brody and Hughston [16] introduce a new term structure calibration methodology based on maximization of entropy, and present some new models of interest rate. Gulko [17,18] applies the Entropy Pricing Theory to introduce new formulas for pricing European stock and bond options.

Another broad research field is information and entropy econometrics that directly or indirectly builds on the foundations of information theory and the principle of maximum entropy. Among other topics, Golan and Perloff [19] deeply investigate the generalized maximum entropy estimation method. Ullah [20] provides the uses of entropy and divergence measures for evaluating econometric approximations and inference. Kitamura and Stutzer [21] develop the relationship between entropic and linear projections in asset pricing estimation based on stochastic discount factor models. Maasoumi and Racine [22] examine the predictability of stock market returns by employing a new metric entropy measure and compare their results with a number of traditional measures. Bera and Park [23] use maximum entropy portfolio selection method in the optimal portfolio diversification problem, and their approach can be viewed as a shrinkage estimation of portfolio weights.

According to the literature, several studies propose entropy-based methods to investigate groups of stock markets in the world, especially in the context of various common features, relationships and interdependences between them. For instance, Billio et al. [24] use different entropy measures and new early warning indicator for banking crises to analyze the time evolution of systematic risk in Europe. They focus on the euro zone and analyze a total of 437 European financial institutions. Zhao et al. [25] propose copula entropy models to measure dependence in stock markets. The Authors provide an algorithm for the copula entropy approach to obtain the numerical results, and they approve the validity of the proposed method. Zunino et al. [26] introduce two quantifiers for a stock market inefficiency: the number of forbidden patterns and the normalized permutation entropy. The Authors analyze equity indexes and returns for 32 different stock exchanges. They point out that their empirical findings suggest that the proposed physical tools are helpful to discriminate the stage of stock market development.

Another promising strand of the literature concerns network entropy since Mantegna [27] first represented the financial market as a network. Financial markets are complex systems and can be represented as complex networks. Network entropy can be treated is a measure of information contained in the system [28,29].

It is worth noting that quite extensive studies consider the concepts of mutual information and transfer entropy. These tools enable us to investigate the information flow between time series and are especially useful in economic and financial applications [30–38].

The literature contains several theoretical, empirical, and experimental studies concerning entropy-based applications in market microstructure research. For instance, Liu et al. [39] use entropy-based measures to identify various types of trading behaviors. Albeit, the papers regarding dimensions of market liquidity are relatively scarce. For instance, McCauley [40] points out that interest in thermodynamic analogies in economics and finance is older than the idea of von Neumann to look for market entropy in liquidity. McCauley assumes that the definition of an asset's liquidity is analogous to this of stock market depth. However, he concludes that real financial markets cannot behave thermodynamically because they are unstable.

Order imbalance has a significant influence on stock illiquidity, considerably more important even than volume. In the recent paper, Lu et al. [41] proposed an indicator called polarity to investigate trading imbalance in Chinese stock market. This indicator is based on high-frequency transaction data. However, the definition of polarity is very similar to this of order ratio, which is well known and broadly used in the literature as an indicator of stock market depth and market illiquidity (see e.g., [42,43] and the references therein). Therefore, the aforementioned paper was our research inspiration and motivation for taking and exploring the subject of an entropy-based approach to measurement of stock market depth as one of market liquidity dimensions [44].

The aim of this study is to introduce a new entropy-based market depth proxy that is exactly based on the definition of Shannon information entropy [1]. Our proposition substantially differs from the entropy-based indicator of trading imbalance presented in [39] because we employ the Lee and Ready [45] algorithm inferring the initiator of a trade to distinguish between so-called buyer- and seller-initiated trades.

The value-added of this research derives both from the new methodology and novel empirical findings. There are some advantages of the proposed indicator. Firstly, it can be treated as a new measure of stock market liquidity. The values of the entropy-based market depth are decimal fractions that vary between zero and the exactly defined maximal value equal to one. Therefore, the entropy-based market depth values calculated for different equities can be effectively compared to each other.

Moreover, based on the Shannon entropy definition, the entropy-based market depth indicator can be used to summarize the information content of a probability distribution, and it can be treated as a measure of stock market efficiency according to the Efficient Market Hypothesis (EMH). High values of entropy are related to randomness in the evolution of stock prices [26]. Higher values of market entropy inform about higher market efficiency, and are coupled with higher values of stock liquidity. Therefore, both market entropy and market liquidity can be directly measured by the proposed new indicator.

Empirical experiments on financial markets depend on data availability. Therefore, the real-data experiments and statistical analyses are conducted for high-frequency data with a time stamp rounded to the nearest second from the Warsaw Stock Exchange (WSE). Stability and robustness tests are conducted. Moreover, an intra-day seasonality assessment is provided to recognize intra-day hourly patterns in new entropy-based market depth indicator. Results indicate that this indicator can be considered as an auspicious market depth measure with an intuitive base for both theoretical and empirical analyses in financial markets. The proposed entropy-based indictor can be successfully utilized using intra-day data from other stock markets in the world, and the results could be interesting for investors.

The remainder of the study is organized as follows: Section 2 specifies the methodological background of measurement of market depth in the context of the broad topic concerning dimensions of stock market liquidity. Section 3 contains real-data description and presents the findings of some empirical experiments, statistical analyses, and robustness tests for high-frequency data. In Section 4, we discuss and conclude the results and propose several directions for further research.

2. Methods

2.1. Depth as One of Stock Market Liquidity Dimensions

Generally speaking, stock market liquidity is not a one-dimensional variable. The literature concerning the dimensions of market liquidity has continued to grow since Kyle [44] first distinguished between three dimensions: depth, tightness, and resiliency. Depth can be defined as the ability to buy or sell a certain amount of an asset without influence on the quoted price. In other words, the depth of market captures the relation between order flow and price changes. When demand (buy) and supply (sell) sides are quantitatively the same, the quoted price will not change (there is no impulse to price changes). The definition of tightness states that this is the ability to buy and to sell an asset at about the same price at the same time. One of definitions of market resiliency specifies that this is the ability to buy or to sell a certain amount of an asset with little influence on the quoted price. Theoretical and empirical findings of research on liquidity dimensions in several stock markets in the world are reported in [46–52].

It is pertinent to notice that the studies that explore depth, tightness, and resiliency as dimensions of stock market liquidity on the WSE are rather scarce. For instance, order imbalance as a measure of market depth is assessed in the papers [42,43,53]. Market tightness as the cost of turning around a position over a short period of time on the WSE is investigated in the works [42,43]. Moreover, two new methods for measurement of intraday stock market resiliency based on the Discrete Fourier Transform and Short-Time Fourier Transform approaches are introduced and utilized for high-frequency data from the WSE in the recent papers [54,55].

2.2. Measuring Stock Market Depth

Related literature proposes various proxies of stock market depth, and a comprehensive review of them is presented e.g., in [42]. In general, the measures of order imbalance are the most frequently used.

To introduce a new entropy-based method, firstly we propose a supporting modified version of the Order Ratio (OR) indicator as a refined proxy of market depth which accurately captures market order imbalance. It is defined by the following Equation (1):

$$OR = \frac{|CTV_b - CTV_s|}{CTV_b + CTV_s}, \tag{1}$$

where $OR \in [0, 1]$ and the sums $CTV_b \sum_{i=1}^{m} Vbuy_i$, $CTV_s \sum_{j=1}^{k} Vsell_j$ denote the cumulated trading volume related to transactions classified as buyer- or seller-initiated trades, respectively. The modification lies in the denominator $\sum_{n=1}^{m+k} V_n = CTV_b + CTV_s$ which denotes the cumulated trading volume for all classified transactions within a particular period of time (in the frequently used version of the OR indicator, the denominator includes the cumulated trading volume for all transactions within an investigated period of time).

The OR indicator can be calculated within various time intervals, for example in 30-min, hourly or daily manner because the Formula (1) is the general one. The order ratio informs about imbalance in the market since it rises when the difference in the numerator rises, and therefore it measures illiquidity. High values of the order ratio indicate low market depth and low liquidity. Conversely, small values of this indicator denote high market depth and high liquidity. According to definition (1), the order ratio value is non-negative and it is equal to zero when cumulated trading volumes related to transactions classified as buyer- or seller-initiated trades are equal within a particular time interval. The order ratio value given by Equation (1) is not defined for the following two cases: (1) when all transactions within an analyzed time period are unclassified, and (2) an analyzed time period is a zero-volume period, which means the total lack of transactions. In such cases, the total trading volume in the denominator is equal to zero. The OR value is equal to one when all transactions within an analyzed time period are classified in the same manner (i.e., as only buyer- or only seller-initiated trades).

In the next step, the definitions of cumulated trading volumes related to transactions classified as buyer- or seller-initiated trades are used to define the probabilities and the entropy-based proxy of stock market depth. In light of the recently growing literature, entropy is a widely accepted measure of a generally understood diversity and disorder. In this context, an entropy-based indicator could represent the unevenness of buying and selling in trading decisions on a stock market [41]. Shannon [1] proves that quantities of the form $H = -K \cdot \sum_{i=1}^{n} p_i \cdot \log(p_i)$, where K is a positive constant that amounts to a choice of a unit of measure, play a central role in information theory as measures of information, choice, and uncertainty. Exactly based on the definition of Shannon information entropy [1] (p. 394) we propose the following new Entropy-based Market Depth (EMD) indicator given by Equation (2):

$$EMD = \frac{-1}{\log(2)} \left(P_{buy} \cdot \log\left(P_{buy}\right) + P_{sell} \cdot \log(P_{sell}) \right), \qquad (2)$$

where:

$$P_{buy} = \frac{CTV_b}{CTV_b + CTV_s} \in [0, 1], \qquad (3)$$

$$P_{sell} = 1 - P_{buy} = \frac{CTV_s}{CTV_b + CTV_s} \in [0, 1]. \qquad (4)$$

According to the Shannon definition, the EMD indicator (2) measures the entropy in the case of two possibilities with probabilities defined by Equations (3) and (4). It is scaled to obtain the EMD values that belong to the $[0; 1]$ interval (without the normalization, the maximal EMD value is equal to $\log(2) \approx 0.301$, and it is obvious based on the properties of the Shannon information entropy [1], p. 394). According to Equation (2), the EMD value is non-negative, and it is defined as equal to zero in the following two cases:

(1) If $CTV_b = 0 \Leftrightarrow P_{buy} = 0 \Leftrightarrow P_{sell} = 1 \Leftrightarrow \log(P_{sell}) = 0 \Leftrightarrow EMD = 0$;
(2) If $CTV_s = 0 \Leftrightarrow P_{sell} = 0 \Leftrightarrow P_{buy} = 1 \Leftrightarrow \log\left(P_{buy}\right) = 0 \Leftrightarrow EMD = 0$.

The EMD value given by Equation (2) is not defined for the following two cases: (1) when all transactions within an analyzed time period are unclassified, and (2) an analyzed time period is a zero-volume period, which means the total lack of transactions. In such cases, the total trading volume in the denominator in Equations (3) and (4) is equal to zero. Appendix A contains further justification for the EMD indicator in the context of the Shannon information entropy definition.

To calculate both the OR (1) and EMD (2) indicators using intraday data it is essential to recognize the side initiating a transaction. Although the WSE is a pure order-driven market with an electronic order book, information of the order book database is not publicly available. Thus, the side initiating a trade cannot be directly identified from a raw data set. Therefore, the Lee and Ready (LR) [43] algorithm inferring the initiator of a trade is used to distinguish between so-called buyer- and seller-initiated trades. Although several trade-side classification rules have been proposed in the literature, Olbryś and Mursztyn [56] confirm that the LR algorithm performs better than other procedures on the Polish stock market. For details about the LR algorithm see Table A1, in Appendix B.

As the EMD is a new both market depth and market liquidity indicator which is indirectly connected (via the probabilities defined by Equations (3) and (4)) with the supporting modified version of the OR proxy, it would be useful and informative to compare the OR and EMD values. Table 1 presents simple illustrative examples of calculations of both indicators for four selected cases within the same time period. Example 1 shows that the minimal OR value equal to zero is coupled with the maximal EMD value equal to one. In general, as the EMD values are decimal fractions that belong to the $[0;1]$ interval, the EMD values calculated for different equities can be easily compared to each other. Furthermore, Examples 2–3 illustrate that increasing values of the OR are coupled with decreasing values of the EMD indicator, and vice versa. Example 4 shows that the maximal OR value equal to one is coupled with the minimal EMD value equal to zero. It means that, on an intuitive base, the maximal value of trading imbalance indicates the lack of liquidity.

Table 1. Simple illustrative examples of the OR and EMD values for four selected cases and the same time period.

Possibilities	Probabilities	OR Indicator	EMD Indicator
Example 1—min OR and max EMD			
$CTV_b + CTV_s = 1000$ $CTV_b = 500$ $CTV_s = 500$	$P_{buy} = \frac{500}{1000} = 0.5$ $P_{sell} = \frac{500}{1000} = 0.5$	$OR = \frac{|500-500|}{1000} = 0$	$EMD = \frac{-1}{\log(2)}(2 \cdot 0.5 \cdot \log(0.5)) = 1$
Example 2			
$CTV_b + CTV_s = 1000$ $CTV_b = 600$ $CTV_s = 400$	$P_{buy} = \frac{600}{1000} = 0.6$ $P_{sell} = \frac{400}{1000} = 0.4$	$OR = \frac{|600-400|}{1000} = 0.2$	$EMD = \frac{-1}{\log(2)}(0.6 \cdot \log(0.6) + 0.4 \cdot \log(0.4)) \approx 0.971$
Example 3			
$CTV_b + CTV_s = 1000$ $CTV_b = 900$ $CTV_s = 100$	$P_{buy} = \frac{900}{1000} = 0.9$ $P_{sell} = \frac{100}{1000} = 0.1$	$OR = \frac{|900-100|}{1000} = 0.8$	$EMD = \frac{-1}{\log(2)}(0.9 \cdot \log(0.9) + 0.1 \cdot \log(0.1)) \approx 0.469$
Example 4—max OR and min EMD			
$CTV_b + CTV_s = 1000$ $CTV_b = 1000$ $CTV_s = 0$	$P_{buy} = \frac{1000}{1000} = 1$ $P_{sell} = \frac{0}{1000} = 0$	$OR = \frac{|1000-0|}{1000} = 1$	$EMD = \frac{-1}{\log(2)}(1 \cdot \log 1 + 0) = 0$

Figure 1 depicts the relationship between OR and EMD indicators. To sum up, the examples presented in Table 1 and Figure 1 show that low Order Ratio values are accompanied by high values of the Entropy-based Market Depth indicator. Otherwise, high ORs are accompanied by low values of the EMD indicator. This evidence is consistent with overall relations between these two depth estimates.

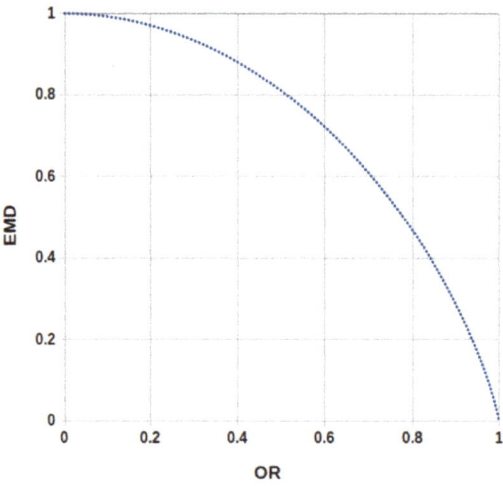

Figure 1. The relationship between the Entropy-based Market Depth (EMD) and Order Ratio (OR) indicators.

Table 2 briefly summarizes basic relationships between the indicators (1) and (2), market depth, market liquidity, and market entropy. As one can observe, the OR proxy is only a measure of depth and illiquidity, while the EMD can be treated as a measure of market depth, market liquidity and market entropy, which is the advantage of this new indicator.

Table 2. Overall relationships between two market depth indicators, market depth, market liquidity, and market entropy.

Indicator	Market Depth	Market Liquidity	Market Entropy
High order ratio (OR)	Low market depth	Low liquidity	–
Low order ratio (OR)	High market depth	High liquidity	–
High Entropy-based Market Depth (EMD)	High market depth	High liquidity	High entropy
Low Entropy-based Market Depth (EMD)	Low market depth	Low liquidity	Low entropy

3. Empirical Experiments for High-Frequency Intraday Data

As empirical experiments on financial markets depend on data availability, this section is devoted to the comparative and comprehensive investigation of the OR and EMD indicators on the Polish stock market. It presents findings of several empirical experiments and statistical analyses for high-frequency data from the Warsaw Stock Exchange. The database is large. It contains 21,010,718 records in total (see Table 3). Therefore, all computations were performed using a customized program (language C++, system: Linux, processor 3.6 GHz, RAM 4 GB).

Table 3. The averaged daily values of the Order Ratio (OR) and Entropy-based Market Depth (EMD) indicators within the whole sample period and three sub–periods for the group of 20 WSE–listed companies.

	Company	MV PLN m	No. of Records in the Database	OR indicator				EMD Indicator			
				WS	S1	S2	S3	WS	S1	S2	S3
1	PKN	36483.58	2739243	0.19 (0.13)	0.19 (0.13)	0.20 (0.14)	0.21 (0.13)	0.96 (0.05)	0.96 (0.05)	0.96 (0.05)	0.96 (0.05)
2	PKO	35175.00	3725299	0.19 (0.14)	0.24 (0.16)	0.21 (0.14)	0.20 (0.14)	0.96 (0.06)	0.94 (0.08)	0.95 (0.06)	0.96 (0.06)
3	PEO	33018.73	2210764	0.21 (0.16)	0.25 (0.19)	0.21 (0.15)	0.21 (0.15)	0.95 (0.08)	0.93 (0.11)	0.95 (0.06)	0.95 (0.06)
4	BZW	31358.11	996852	0.32 (0.25)	0.32 (0.23)	0.25 (0.18)	0.27 (0.19)	0.86 (0.21)	0.88 (0.17)	0.93 (0.10)	0.92 (0.10)
5	ING	20998.14	191091	0.48 (0.30)	0.60 (0.31)	0.55 (0.30)	0.44 (0.27)	0.73 (0.28)	0.60 (0.33)	0.67 (0.30)	0.78 (0.24)
6	KGH	18496.00	4582816	0.17 (0.13)	0.17 (0.12)	0.19 (0.14)	0.19 (0.13)	0.98 (0.05)	0.97 (0.05)	0.96 (0.05)	0.96 (0.05)
7	MBK	14174.12	930982	0.29 (0.21)	0.40 (0.27)	0.28 (0.21)	0.25 (0.17)	0.90 (0.14)	0.81 (0.22)	0.90 (0.13)	0.93 (0.08)
8	LPP	10412.23	275452	0.50 (0.33)	0.68 (0.32)	0.56 (0.31)	0.62 (0.33)	0.68 (0.35)	0.47 (0.38)	0.64 (0.33)	0.56 (0.36)
9	BHW	9981.09	498427	0.38 (0.27)	0.49 (0.30)	0.48 (0.29)	0.50 (0.29)	0.83 (0.23)	0.72 (0.29)	0.74 (0.27)	0.72 (0.27)
10	OPL	7231.09	2055914	0.22 (0.16)	0.20 (0.15)	0.20 (0.15)	0.22 (0.17)	0.95 (0.08)	0.95 (0.07)	0.95 (0.06)	0.94 (0.08)
11	MIL	6296.08	547539	0.34 (0.24)	0.40 (0.27)	0.39 (0.26)	0.30 (0.21)	0.86 (0.18)	0.81 (0.22)	0.82 (0.20)	0.90 (0.13)
12	SNS	6034.02	678481	0.32 (0.23)	0.43 (0.25)	0.39 (0.26)	0.36 (0.24)	0.88 (0.17)	0.80 (0.21)	0.82 (0.21)	0.85 (0.18)
13	BDX	5053.68	208574	0.45 (0.29)	0.58 (0.31)	0.52 (0.31)	0.46 (0.28)	0.76 (0.28)	0.62 (0.33)	0.69 (0.31)	0.76 (0.25)

41

Table 3. *Cont.*

	Company	MV PLN m	No. of Records in the Database	OR indicator				EMD Indicator			
				WS	S1	S2	S3	WS	S1	S2	S3
14	ZWC	4550.20	22181	0.65 (0.34)	0.67 (0.33)	0.63 (0.34)	0.62 (0.33)	0.50 (0.40)	0.48 (0.40)	0.53 (0.39)	0.55 (0.39)
15	CAR	3932.36	66432	0.60 (0.32)	0.62 (0.32)	0.57 (0.32)	0.59 (0.32)	0.59 (0.35)	0.56 (0.37)	0.63 (0.33)	0.60 (0.34)
16	GTC	3773.78	787020	0.32 (0.25)	0.35 (0.28)	0.25 (0.17)	0.26 (0.19)	0.86 (0.20)	0.84 (0.24)	0.93 (0.08)	0.92 (0.10)
17	KTY	3668.03	155110	0.49 (0.30)	0.45 (0.28)	0.53 (0.30)	0.52 (0.31)	0.73 (0.29)	0.76 (0.26)	0.69 (0.29)	0.69 (0.30)
18	ORB	3363.62	101850	0.55 (0.31)	0.47 (0.29)	0.52 (0.29)	0.57 (0.31)	0.65 (0.33)	0.75 (0.27)	0.70 (0.28)	0.64 (0.32)
19	STP	2929.64	74227	0.54 (0.32)	0.50 (0.31)	0.52 (0.32)	0.50 (0.31)	0.66 (0.34)	0.70 (0.31)	0.68 (0.32)	0.70 (0.32)
20	ECH	2104.99	162464	0.48 (0.31)	0.54 (0.32)	0.40 (0.27)	0.45 (0.28)	0.72 (0.30)	0.65 (0.33)	0.81 (0.22)	0.77 (0.25)
	Total	259034.50	21010718					-			

Notes: The 20 WSE–listed companies are labeled by ticker symbols and reported in decreasing order of the market value (MV) at the end of 2016. WS—the whole sample period 2 January 2005–30 December 2016; S1–the pre-crisis sub-period 6 September 2005–31 May 2007; S2—the crisis sub-period on the WSE 1 June 2007–27 February 2009; S3—the post-crisis sub-period 2 March 2009–19 November 2010. Standard deviations are given in parentheses.

3.1. Real-Data Description

The sample contains high-frequency data for 20 WSE-listed companies with the largest market capitalization (MV) at the end of 2016. Tick-by-tick transaction data is not publicly available for the WSE. Thus, in this research transaction prices and volume records with a time stamp rounded to the nearest second, for each security over one unit of time are used. The data comes from the Bank for Environmental Protection (BOS) brokerage house (available at http://bossa.pl; accessed date 5 January 2017). All stocks included in the database have been incessantly listed on the WSE through the whole sample period. This study is the continuation and extension of the research on dimensions of market liquidity on the WSE presented in the papers [54,55], and therefore the database is the same.

The sample period ranges from 2 January 2005 to 30 December 2016 (3005 trading days). To verify the robustness of the empirical findings, the calculations are provided both for the whole sample and over three consecutive sub-samples of equal length (436 trading days) [54]:

(1) The pre-crisis sub-period from 6 September 2005 to 31 May 2007 (S1);
(2) The crisis sub-period on the WSE from 1 June 2007 to 27 February 2009 (S2);
(3) The post-crisis sub-period from 2 March 2009 to 19 November 2010 (S3).

The crisis sub-period on the WSE connected to the 2007–2009 Global Financial Crisis (GFC) period was formally defined based on the paper [57], in which the statistical method for the quantitative identification of market states is used.

3.2. Estimation Results of the Order Ratio and Entropy-Based Market Depth

This subsection includes brief information on the group of 20 WSE-traded companies that are analyzed in this research (Table 3). The companies are labeled by ticker symbols and presented in decreasing order of the market value (MV) at the end of 2016. Table 3 reports the numbers of records in the database for each stock and the averaged daily values of the OR and EMD indicators. Standard deviations are given in parentheses. The evidence is that for the most liquid equities with the largest numbers of records in the database (namely PKN, PKO, PEO, KGH, OPL) the averaged daily values of the OR and EMD indicators and standard deviations of these values are stable in time. The findings confirm high market depth and high liquidity of these stocks as the averaged EMD proxy is approximately equal to one and accompanied by very low standard deviations. What is important, the experimental results reported in Table 3 show that the precise ranges of OR [0.17; 0.68] and EMD [0.47; 0.98] are equally broad (0.51 for OR and 0.51 for EMD).

Table 4 reports Pearson correlation coefficients calculated for series of daily market depth estimators given by Equations (1) and (2), for each asset separately. This table presents the results for the whole sample (WS) and three sub-samples S1, S2, S3. All correlations are significantly negative and their absolute values are very high. This evidence confirms that the information content of both market depth proxies is the same, while the main advantage of the EMD indicator is that it measures liquidity (not illiquidity, like the OR estimate). This evidence is consistent with the relationship presented in Figure 1.

Table 4. Pearson correlation coefficients between daily market depth values calculated using the alternative indicators (1) and (2).

	PKN	PKO	PEO	BZW	ING	KGH	MBK	LPP	BHW	OPL
WS	−0.927	−0.920	−0.922	−0.923	−0.946	−0.913	−0.922	−0.950	−0.938	−0.929
S1	−0.928	−0.936	−0.929	−0.934	−0.956	−0.912	−0.940	−0.955	−0.950	−0.918
S2	−0.934	−0.941	−0.944	−0.922	−0.948	−0.945	−0.925	−0.949	−0.945	−0.925
S3	−0.947	−0.931	−0.942	−0.943	−0.946	−0.944	−0.945	−0.953	−0.948	−0.929
	MIL	SNS	BDX	ZWC	CAR	GTC	KTY	ORB	STP	ECH
WS	−0.935	−0.929	−0.940	−0.953	−0.950	−0.928	−0.944	−0.948	−0.946	−0.944
S1	−0.946	−0.944	−0.949	−0.956	−0.952	−0.937	−0.939	−0.955	−0.943	−0.949
S2	−0.941	−0.941	−0.948	−0.952	−0.947	−0.944	−0.950	−0.946	−0.947	−0.940
S3	−0.938	−0.931	−0.945	−0.948	−0.952	−0.937	−0.950	−0.949	−0.946	−0.948

Notes: Notation as in Table 3.

3.3. Robustness Tests of Entropy-Based Market Depth

Various robustness analyses are standard procedures for testing stability of stock market characteristics, especially in the context of crises periods, e.g., [24,41,54,55]. The existing studies indicate that the empirical results could be diverse and economic interpretations are needed in such cases. The Entropy-based Market Depth (EMD) indicator (2) is proposed as a new estimator of a stock market depth and market liquidity. Therefore, the stability of estimation results by time periods could be assessed. To address this issue, the robustness tests over the whole sample period and three sub-periods are provided. The goal is to investigate whether the mean results of stock depth and liquidity approximated by EMD within the analyzed periods (reported in Table 3) significantly differ between each other. The following two-tailed hypothesis is tested:

$$H_0 : \mu_1 = \mu_2 \\ H_1 : \mu_1 \neq \mu_2 , \qquad (5)$$

where μ_1, μ_2 are the expected values of depth for each equity within the compared periods, and the null hypothesis assumes that two expected values are equal.

To verify the hypotheses, the Z-statistic for independent large sample means is used:

$$Z = \frac{\overline{x_1} - \overline{x_2}}{\sqrt{\frac{s_1^2}{n_1} + \frac{s_2^2}{n_2}}}, \qquad (6)$$

where $\overline{x_1}, \overline{x_2}$ are sample means, s_1^2, s_2^2 are sample variances, and n_1, n_2 denote a sample size, respectively. The numbers n_1, n_2 of trading days for each stock within each period are reported in Table A2, Appendix C. The average daily values of the EMD and standard deviations of these values are documented in Table 3. To address the multiple testing problem, the Bonferroni correction is used, and therefore the significance level is equal to $\overline{\alpha} = 0.0025$. The critical value of Z-statistic (6) at 0,25% significance level is equal to 3.03 for each test (we thank an anonymous referee for this suggestion).

Six pairs of periods are investigated, i.e., WS/S1, WS/S2, WS/S3, S2/S1, S2/S3, and S1/S3. Summarized findings for the whole group of companies are presented in Table 5 and they require some comments and economic interpretations. The hypothesis H_0 indicates that the average EMD values are stable in time within compared periods. One can observe that for the companies PKN, OPL, ZWC, CAR, STP there are no reason to reject H_0 for all six cases, for the KGH—for five cases, and for KTY—for four cases. However, for the remaining equities the results are more diverse. After deep investigation of the obtained results we can assert that there are three main reasons of this phenomenon.

Table 5. Summarized results of the significance test for the difference between two means of daily Entropy-based Market Depth (EMD) values for the group of 20 WSE–listed equities.

	PKN	PKO	PEO	BZW	ING	KGH	MBK	LPP	BHW	OPL	No. of H_0
WS/S1	H_0	H_1	H_1	H_0	H_1	H_0	H_1	H_1	H_1	H_0	4
WS/S2	H_0	H_0	H_0	H_1	H_1	H_1	H_0	H_0	H_1	H_0	6
WS/S3	H_0	H_0	H_0	H_1	H_1	H_0	H_1	H_1	H_1	H_0	5
S2/S1	H_0	H_1	H_1	H_1	H_1	H_0	H_1	H_1	H_0	H_0	4
S2/S3	H_0	H_0	H_0	H_0	H_0	H_0	H_1	H_1	H_0	H_0	7
S1/S3	H_0	H_1	H_1	H_1	H_1	H_0	H_1	H_1	H_0	H_0	4
No. of H_0	6	3	3	2	0	5	1	1	3	6	30
	MIL	SNS	BDX	ZWC	CAR	GTC	KTY	ORB	STP	ECH	No. of H_0
WS/S1	H_1	H_1	H_1	H_0	H_0	H_0	H_0	H_1	H_0	H_1	5
WS/S2	H_1	H_1	H_0	H_0	H_0	H_1	H_0	H_1	H_0	H_1	4
WS/S3	H_1	H_0	H_0	H_0	H_0	H_1	H_0	H_0	H_0	H_1	7
S2/S1	H_0	H_0	H_0	H_0	H_0	H_1	H_1	H_0	H_0	H_1	7
S2/S3	H_1	H_0	H_1	H_0	H_0	H_0	H_0	H_0	H_0	H_0	8
S1/S3	H_1	H_1	H_1	H_0	H_0	H_1	H_1	H_1	H_0	H_1	3
No. of H_0	1	3	2	6	6	2	4	3	6	1	34

Notes: Notation as in Table 3. The critical value of Z-statistic at 0.25% significance level is equal to 3.03 for each test.

Firstly, although Table 3 documents that for the most liquid equities the averaged daily values of the EMD indicator are high and approximately the same, the values of standard deviation and the significantly diverse number of trading days within the analyzed periods (reported in Table A2, Appendix C) leads to rejection of the null hypothesis (5) for some isolated cases (for instance, for PKO and PEO).

Moreover, the results depend on the pair of the sub-periods. It is important to remind that the pre-crisis (S1), crisis (S2), and post-crisis (S3) periods on the WSE are investigated, and the crisis sub-period on the WSE is connected to the 2007–2009 Global Financial Crisis (GFC). Therefore, the findings inform whether the mean results of market depth and liquidity during the GFC period on the WSE significantly differ compared to the other periods. One can observe that in the case of the pairs: S2/S1 (crisis/pre-crisis), and S2/S3 (crisis/post-crisis), the hypothesis H_0 is outweighed by the hypothesis H_1 in 9 out of 20 and 5 out of 20 cases, respectively. Moreover, for the pair WS/S2 (whole sample/crisis) the number of H_1 is equal to 10. Therefore, we can conclude that the visible influence of the GFC on market depth and liquidity was present for the following equities, including five banks: BZW, ING, MBK, LPP, BHW, MIL, SNS, BDX, GTC, ORB, ECH. In general, market depth and liquidity significantly differed during the crisis sub-period on the WSE for several analyzed companies, but not for all of them. The EMD values for the most liquid companies were much more stable. This evidence is consistent with the studies that have utilized other liquidity proxies to assess stock market liquidity dimensions on the WSE during the GFC (e.g., [42,43]).

Furthermore, the whole sample period (WS) is long (12 years), and it includes the years of substantial changes in market liquidity. The WSE was a medium-size emerging stock market during this period. Especially, the level of liquidity within the pre-crisis period (S1) was lower compared to other periods for several companies, e.g., ING, MBK, LPP, BDX, ECH (see Table 3), while the level of liquidity during the post-crisis period (S3) was higher for many stocks. As a consequence, the hypothesis H_0 is outweighed by the hypothesis H_1 in 11 out of 20 (for the pair WS/S1) and 13 out of 20 cases (for the pair S1/S3). The total number of H_1 is equal to 57 out of 120. In conclusion, the results reported in Table 5 are not homogenous but they can be explained based on the WSE liquidity behavior within the whole sample period and remaining sub-periods.

3.4. Intra-Day Seasonality in Entropy-Based Market Depth

The aim of this subsection is to assess intra-day seasonality and recognize intra-day hourly patterns in the EMD indicator of market depth. According to the literature, there are some possible shapes of intra-day patterns in various stock market characteristics such as volumes, depths, spreads, returns, transaction costs, order flows, market resiliency, etc. (see e.g., [55,58–68] and the references therein). Goodhart and O'Hara [58] emphasize that a fundamental property of high-frequency data is that observations can occur at varying time intervals. Therefore, trades are not equally spaced over the day, which may result in intra-day 'seasonal' patterns in stock market activity. Empirical investigation and visualization of these patterns may be a useful tool for decision-making process and can help an investor to state how particular characteristics vary over a session. Some shapes of intra-day patterns in stock market are possible but it is not surprising that perfectly shaped visual patterns rarely appear. There are several attributes that help to differentiate the most important shapes such as: M-similar, U-similar, W-similar, inverted-U, J-similar, and inverted-J patterns [55].

To explore intra-day patterns in the EMD indicator, the average hourly values of this indicator are calculated for each equity within the whole sample period (WS) and three sub-periods (S1, S2, S3). The WSE is an order-driven market with an electronic order book. Therefore, liquidity is provided only by limit orders submitted by investors and there are no market makers who support liquidity. Table 6 presents short market trading schedule on the WSE and the notation concerning the trading hours (H_1–H_8).

Table 6. Market trading schedule on the WSE equities–continuous trading system.

Market Phase	Time	Hours
Opening call Opening auction	8:30 am–9:00 am 9:00 am	
Continuous trading Closing call	9:00 am–4:50 pm 4:50 pm–5:00 pm	H_1: 9:00 am–10:00 am H_2: 10:00 am–11:00 am H_3: 11:00 am–12:00 am H_4: 12:00 am–1:00 pm H_5: 1:00 pm–2:00 pm H_6: 2:00 pm–3:00 pm H_7: 3:00 pm–4:00 pm H_8: 4:00 pm–5:00 pm
Closing auction Trading at last	5:00 pm 5:00 pm–5:05 pm	

ource: The WSE website (https://gpw.pl/session-details; accessed date 15 February 2021).

Figure 2 illustrates hourly patterns in the EMD values within the whole sample period. The EMD intra-day behavior during remaining periods is presented in Figures A2–A4, Appendix D. Table 7 reports summarized findings of hourly patterns in the EMD indicator for the whole group of 20 WSE–listed equities investigated in this research. The trading hours H_1–H_8 based on Table 6.

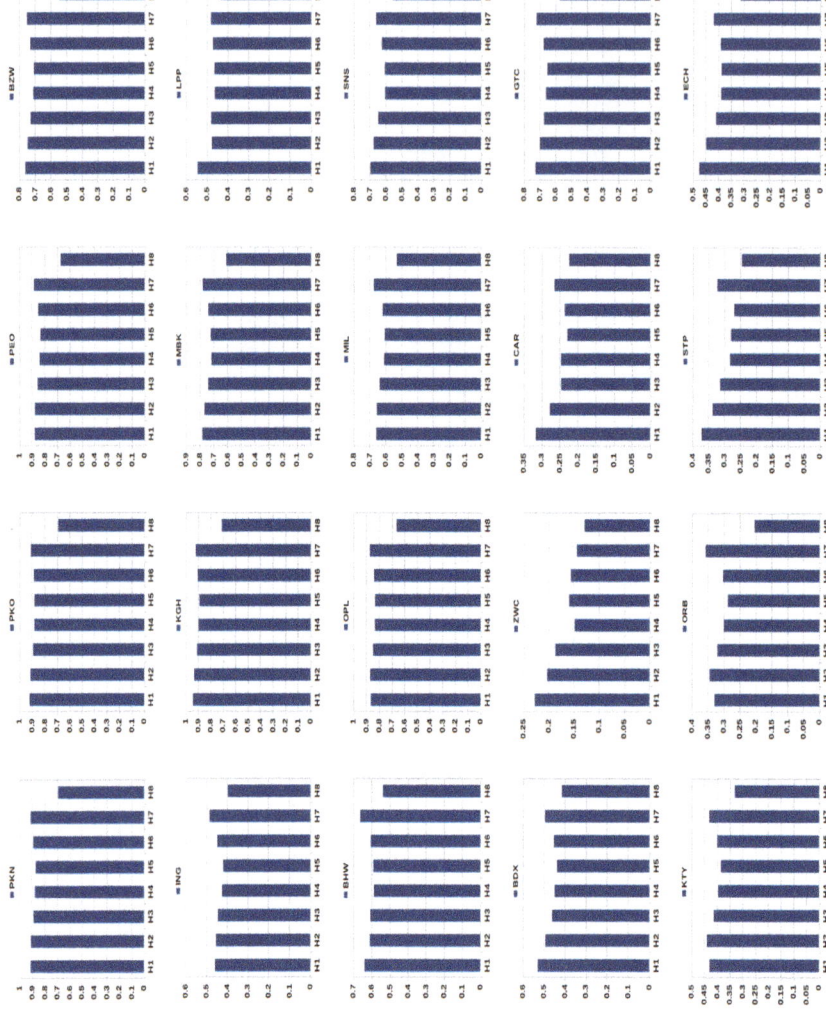

Figure 2. Intra-day hourly patterns of the EMD indicator within the whole sample period (WS) January 2005–December 2016 for the group of 20 WSE–listed equities. Notation as in Tables 3 and 6.

Table 7. Summarized findings of hourly patterns in the EMD indicator for the group of 20 WSE-listed equities.

	PKN	PKO	PEO	BZW	ING	KGH	MBK	LPP	BHW	OPL
WS	U-similar	U-similar	U-similar	U-similar	U-similar	U-similar	U-similar	U-similar	U-similar	U-similar
S1	M-similar	M-similar	M-similar	M-similar	M-similar	M-similar	M-similar	M-similar	M-similar	M-similar
S2	M-similar	M-similar	M-similar	M-similar	M-similar	M-similar	M-similar	Other	Other	M-similar
S3	U-similar	U-similar	U-similar	U-similar	U-similar	U-similar	U-similar	Other	U-similar	U-similar
	MIL	SNS	BDX	ZWC	CAR	GTC	KTY	ORB	STP	ECH
WS	U-similar	U-similar	U-similar	Other	U-similar	U-similar	M-similar	M-similar	U-similar	U-similar
S1	M-similar	M-similar	Other	Other	Other	U-similar	M-similar	M-similar	Other	M-similar
S2	M-similar	M-similar	M-similar	M-similar	U-similar	U-similar	M-similar	M-similar	M-similar	M-similar
S3	U-similar	U-similar	U-similar	Other	U-similar	U-similar	Other	U-similar	U-similar	U-similar

Notes: Notation as in Table 3. Based on Figures 2 and A2, Figures A3 and A4 (Appendix D).

It is important to notice that the results are homogenous. Except for isolated cases (e.g., LPP, ZWC), the M-similar and U-similar (with a decrease during the last hour H8) patterns dominate for the vast majority of stocks.

The M-shaped pattern depicts lower EMD values during the beginning and the ending of a session with the highest values slightly after the beginning and before the end. It is also marked by distinctively low value in the middle of a session.

The U-shaped pattern means that the value of the EMD decreases after the first hour. It then stays more or less constant, and increases during the last hour. In this context, the evidence concerning the U-similar pattern with a visible increase within the hour H7 and a pronounced decrease during the last hour H8 requires some explanations. It seems that this pattern is common for the most equities on the WSE. After deep investigation of the obtained empirical findings we can assert that the main reason of this phenomenon lies in the trade side classification results. Based on the Lee-Ready procedure presented in Appendix B (Table A1), two possible cases dominate within the last hour H8 on the WSE:

(1) The transactions are classified in the same manner (i.e., as only buyer- or only seller-initiated trades), which leads to EMD = 0 based on definition (2), and consequently decreases the average hourly value of the EMD. It's common especially for less liquid companies with a small number of transactions in H8,

(2) The transactions classified as buyer- or seller-initiated trades dominate, which leads to small EMD values approx equal to 0 (see Table 1), and as a consequence decreases the average hourly value of the EMD.

Based on the summarized findings presented in Table 7 one can observe that, in general, the M-similar pattern dominates within the sub-periods S1 (pre-crisis) and S2 (crisis), while the U-similar pattern appears for vast majority of equities during the whole sample period and the sub-period S3 (post-crisis). In our opinion, the main reason of this phenomenon can be a higher level of market liquidity on the WSE after the GFC period.

It is worthwhile to emphasize that our results concerning intra-day behavior of the EMD indictor as a measure of liquidity are consistent with the literature. For instance, Jain and Joh [60] study joint characteristics of hourly common stock trading volume and returns and they find the U-shaped pattern in volume over the trading day on the New York Stock Exchange (NYSE). They emphasize that average volume as a liquidity proxy reveals significant hour of the day effect. McInish and Wood [62] show that number of shares traded as a liquidity estimate has a U-shaped intra-day pattern for all stocks listed on the Toronto Stock Exchange. Vo [64] also assess the intra-day behavior of market activity on the Canadian stock exchange in Toronto. The results confirm that spread follows U-shaped pattern, while volume is low at the open, stable during the day, and increases at the close. Ahn and Cheung [67] investigate the Stock Exchange of Hong Kong which is a pure electronic order-driven market without market makers.

The authors find the U-shaped patterns in spread and trading volume. As for the Polish stock market, Olbryś and Oleszczak [68] conduct empirical experiments for real-data from the WSE and they document that intra-day trading volume reveals U-similar or M-similar hourly patterns in the case of all investigated equities and for all analyzed periods.

4. Discussion and Conclusions

Concept of market depth focuses on the volume which can be observed at the current price level [49]. From investors' and stock market analysts' point o view, market depth is crucial because it can be treated as quantity dimension of market liquidity [51]. Harris [69] points out that the topic concerning dimensions of liquidity is especially interesting for practitioners as they often think about liquidity quite intuitively. Thinking about liquidity, investors usually think about trading quickly, trading large size, or trading at low costs.

According to the literature related to the microstructure of markets, several proxies of market depth are proposed: (1) depth as a number of units offered at the ask price plus a number of units at the bid price (e.g., [46,51,52]), (2) dollar depth calculated in currency terms (e.g., [70]), (3) an average depth of the ask and the bid (e.g., [71]), (4) an average dollar depth measured in currency terms (e.g., [71]), (5) various versions of order ratio as a proxy of realized market depth (e.g., [43,49,51–53]). The vast majority of these depth proxies require information about ask and bid prices.

However, although the WSE is a pure order-driven market with an electronic order book, information about ask and bid prices is not publicly available. Therefore, the side initiating a transaction cannot be directly identified from a data set. This problem concerns many emerging markets in the world, and a procedure inferring the initiator of a trade is needed in such cases.

Taking the above into consideration, this research contributes to the existing literature regarding dimensions of market liquidity by introducing and utilizing a new methodology for estimation of market depth and liquidity with the EMD indicator based on the Shannon entropy and supported by an algorithm inferring the initiator of a trade. The advantage of the EMD is that it measures liquidity, and the min and max values are in accordance with an investor's intuition, i.e., EMD = 0 in the case of total illiquidity and EMD = 1 in the case of total liquidity. Hence, depth and liquidity calculated using the EMD for different stocks can be easily interpret and compared to each other. Moreover, the EMD can be treated as a measure of both market liquidity and market entropy. This is the advantage of this new indicator because higher values of entropy inform about higher market efficiency (in the sense of the EMH), and are coupled with higher values of stock liquidity.

Furthermore, intra-day behavior of the EMD indicator has been assessed and empirical findings concerning intra-day seasonal patterns in the EMD are homogenous and consistent with the existing studies on other liquidity proxies.

It is well documented in the literature that market depth varies with spread, volume, transactions, and volatility (see e.g., [49,51,70]). Therefore, one possible direction for future study could be an extensive econometric analysis of relationships between various stock market characteristics using the new EMD indicator as market depth proxy. Subject to data availability provision, the proposed entropy-based indictor could be utilized using high-frequency data from other stock markets in the world, and the results might be interesting for practitioners.

Another promising direction for further research might be to perform a theoretical analysis of the new entropy-based indictor from the perspective of the properties of extropy [72]. As the entropy and the extropy of a binary distribution are identical, the EMD indicator can be regarded also as an extropy measure (we would like to thank an anonymous referee for this valuable suggestion.).

Author Contributions: Conceptualization, J.O.; methodology, J.O.; software, K.O.; validation, J.O.; formal analysis, J.O. and K.O.; investigation, J.O. and K.O.; resources, J.O. and K.O.; data curation, J.O. and K.O.; writing—original draft preparation, J.O.; writing—review and editing, J.O.; visualization, K.O. All authors have read and agreed to the published version of the manuscript.

Funding: This research was supported by the grant WZ/WI/1/2019 from Bialystok University of Technology and founded by the Ministry of Education and Science.

Institutional Review Board Statement: Not applicable.

Informed Consent Statement: Not applicable.

Data Availability Statement: The data presented in this study are available on request from the corresponding author. The data are not publicly available at http://bossa.pl since 4 January 2021.

Conflicts of Interest: The authors declare no conflict of interest.

Appendix A

Entropy is a measure that is used to summarize the information content of a probability distribution. Specifically, the Shannon information entropy quantifies the expected value of information contained in a discrete distribution [10]. The entropy in the case of two possibilities with probabilities p and $1-p$ can be represented as a function of p [1] (p. 394). Given the probabilities defined by Equations (3) and (4), we can set $P_{buy} = p$

and $P_{sell} = 1 - p$, and then the EMD indicator (2) can be directly written as the function of probability $p = P_{buy}$:

$$\begin{aligned} EMD &= \frac{-1}{\log(2)} \left(P_{buy} \cdot \log(P_{buy}) + P_{sell} \cdot \log(P_{sell}) \right) \\ &= \frac{-1}{\log(2)} (p \log(p) + (1-p) \log(1-p)) = f(p) \end{aligned} \quad \text{(A1)}$$

By analogy with the Shannon entropy, the $f(p)$ function (A1) has several important properties which substantiate it as a reasonable measure of choice or information, and all of them are documented in [1]. In this paper, we focus on some basic properties, especially in the context of a binary distribution, and most of them are analyzed in Section 2.2. However, it is crucial to add that the $f(p)$ function (A1) is non-negative, continuous and differentiable at each point in its domain. For instance, these properties allow us to assess the sensitivity of the EMD to changes in probability p as the argument of function $f(p)$. The results could be interesting for practitioners as, from an investor's point of view, it is important to know how do changes in probability $p = P_{buy}$ (connected with cumulated trading volume) affect the EMD value (it could be a possible direction for further investigation).

Figure A1 illustrates the plot of the EMD as the function of probability $p = P_{buy}$. It is important to notice that the EMD plot is identical with the plot of entropy presented in the Shannon's seminal paper [1] (p. 394), and it confirms that the EMD measures both market liquidity and market entropy.

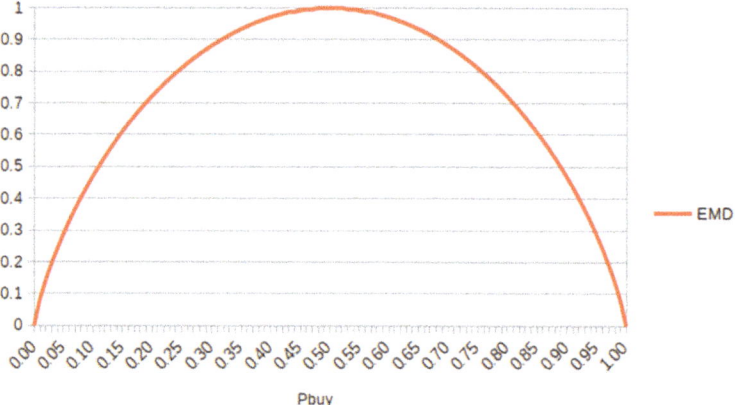

Figure A1. The Entropy-based Market Depth (EMD) as the function of probability $p = P_{buy}$.

Appendix B

Table A1 presents the Lee and Ready [45] algorithm inferring the initiator of a trade. The midpoint price P_t^{mid} at time t is calculated as the arithmetic mean of the low price P_t^L and the high price P_t^H at time t, i.e., $P_t^{mid} = \frac{P_t^L + P_t^H}{2}$. The transaction price P_t at time t is approximated by the closing price. The opening trade is treated as being unclassified according to the LR procedure.

Table A1. The Lee-Ready algorithm inferring the initiator of a trade.

Conditions	
Stage I	
$P_t > P_t^{mid}$	Trade is classified as buyer-initiated
$P_t < P_t^{mid}$	Trade is classified as seller-initiated
$P_t = P_t^{mid}$	Then:
Stage II	
$P_t^{mid} > P_{t-1}$	Trade is classified as buyer-initiated
$P_t^{mid} < P_{t-1}$	Trade is classified as seller-initiated
$P_t^{mid} = P_{t-1}$	The decision is taken using the sign of the last non-zero price change P_{t-k}.
	$P_t > P_{t-k}$ Trade is classified as buyer-initiated
	$P_t < P_{t-k}$ Trade is classified as seller-initiated

Source: [56] (p. 6).

Appendix C

Table A2 reports the number of trading days for each company and investigated period excluding the days when all of the transactions within a day are unclassified based on the Lee and Ready [45] algorithm inferring the initiator of a trade. These numbers are necessary to test the hypothesis (5) as the OR and EMD indicators are not defined when: (1) all transactions within an analyzed time period are unclassified, and (2) an analyzed time period is a zero-volume period, which means the total lack of transactions. Additionally, one can observe that for the most liquid companies (namely PKN, PKO, PEO, ING, KGH, MBK, BHW, OPL, MIL, SNS, GTC) the numbers of days reported in Table A2 are equal (or almost equal) to the particular sample size, respectively.

Table A2. The number of trading days excluding the days when: (1) all of the transactions within a day are unclassified, and (2) total daily trading volume is equal to zero.

	PKN	PKO	PEO	BZW	ING	KGH	MBK	LPP	BHW	OPL
WS	3005	3004	3005	2979	3004	3005	3005	2931	3004	3005
S1	436	436	436	436	436	436	436	411	436	436
S2	436	436	436	436	436	436	436	430	436	436
S3	436	436	436	436	436	436	436	424	436	436
	MIL	SNS	BDX	ZWC	CAR	GTC	KTY	ORB	STP	ECH
WS	3005	3005	2983	2433	2867	3003	2977	2962	2884	2967
S1	436	436	432	354	400	436	435	436	416	426
S2	436	436	435	385	433	436	436	436	432	436
S3	436	436	435	392	427	436	434	434	435	436

Notes: Notation as in Table 3. The sample size: WS (3005 trading days); S1, S2, S3 (436 trading days).

Appendix D

Figures A2–A4 illustrate intra-day seasonality results within three sub-periods S1, S2, S3 for the whole group of 20 WSE–listed companies investigated in this study. Notation as in Table 3. Information about trading hours H_1–H_8 based on Table 6.

Figure A2. Intra-day hourly patterns of the EMD indicator within the pre-crisis period (S1) for the whole group of 20 WSE–listed stocks. Notation as in Tables 3 and 6.

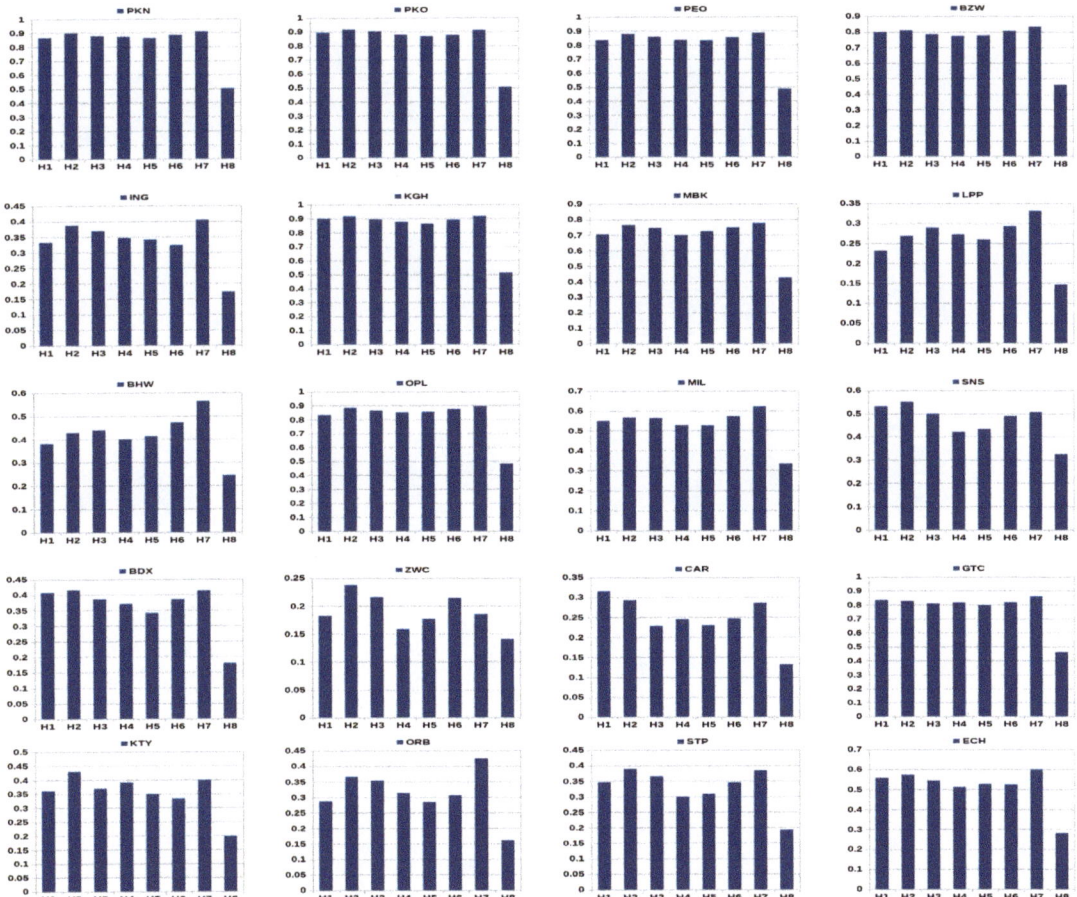

Figure A3. Intra-day hourly patterns of the EMD indicator within the crisis period (S2) for the whole group of 20 WSE–listed stocks. Notation as in Tables 3 and 6.

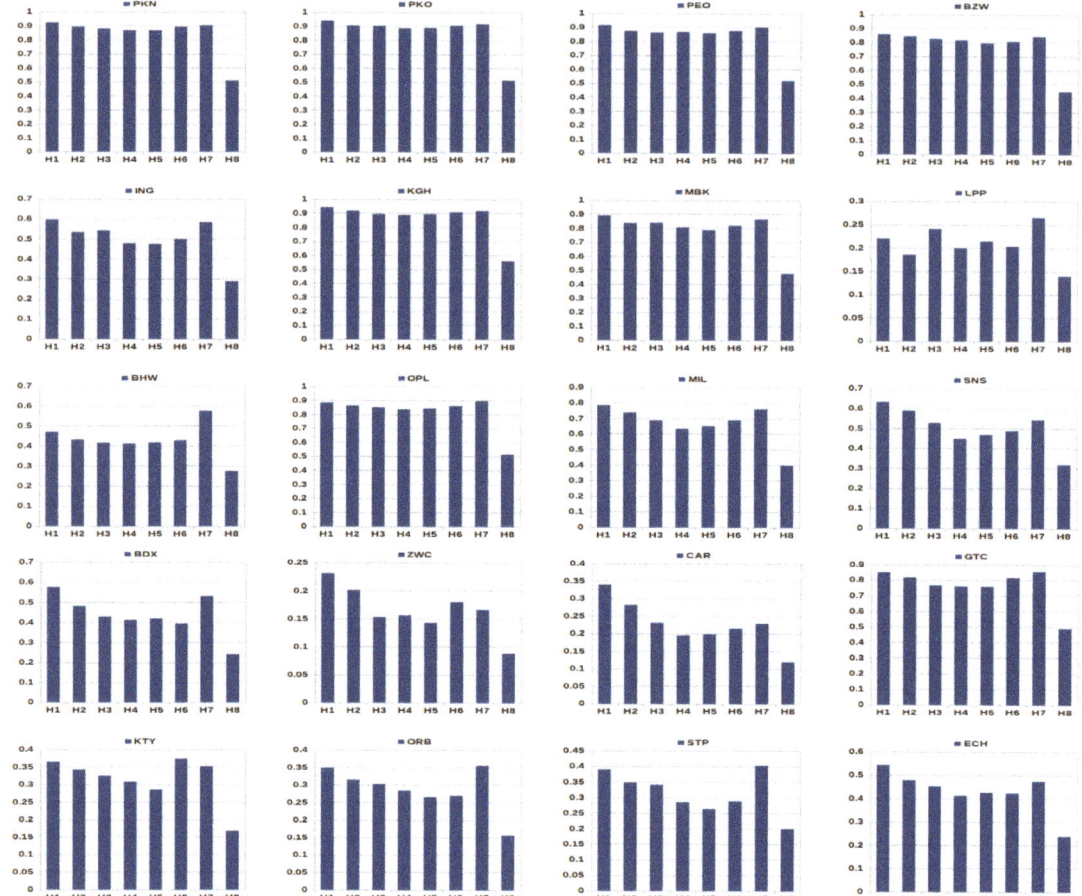

Figure A4. Intra-day hourly patterns of the EMD indicator within the post-crisis period (S3) for the whole group of 20 WSE–listed stocks. Notation as in Tables 3 and 6.

References

1. Shannon, C.E. A mathematical theory of communication. *Bell Syst. Technol. J.* **1948**, *27*, 379–423. [CrossRef]
2. Zhou, R.; Cai, R.; Tong, G. Applications of entropy in finance: A review. *Entropy* **2013**, *15*, 4909–4931. [CrossRef]
3. Philippatos, G.C.; Wilson, C.J. Entropy, market risk, and the selection of efficient portfolios. *App. Econ.* **1972**, *4*, 209–220. [CrossRef]
4. Usta, I.; Kantar, Y.M. Mean-variance-skewness-entropy measures: A multi-objective approach for portfolio selection. *Entropy* **2011**, *13*, 117–133. [CrossRef]
5. Zhang, W.-G.; Liu, Y.-J.; Xu, W.-J. A possibilistic mean-semivariance-entropy model for multi-period portfolio selection with transaction costs. *Eur. J. Oper. Res.* **2012**, *222*, 341–349. [CrossRef]
6. Huang, X. Mean-entropy models for fuzzy portfolio selection. *IEEE Trans. Fuzzy Syst.* **2008**, *16*, 1096–1101. [CrossRef]
7. Yu, J.-R.; Lee, W.-Y.; Chiou, W.-J.P. Diversified portfolios with different entropy measures. *App. Math. Comp.* **2014**, *241*, 47–63. [CrossRef]
8. Zhou, R.; Liu, X.; Yu, M.; Huang, K. Properties of risk measures of generalized entropy in portfolio selection. *Entropy* **2017**, *19*, 657. [CrossRef]
9. Yang, J.; Qiu, W. A measure of risk and decision-making model based on expected utility and entropy. *Eur. J. Oper. Res.* **2005**, *164*, 792–799. [CrossRef]
10. Pele, D.T.; Lazar, E.; Dufour, A. Information entropy and measures of market risk. *Entropy* **2017**, *19*, 226. [CrossRef]
11. Gradojevic, N.; Caric, M. Predicting systematic risk with entropic indicators. *J. Forecast.* **2017**, *36*, 16–25. [CrossRef]

12. Fritelli, M. The minimal entropy martingale measure and the valuation problem in incomplete markets. *Math. Financ.* **2000**, *10*, 39–52. [CrossRef]
13. Stutzer, M. Simple entropic derivation of a generalized Black-Scholes option pricing model. *Entropy* **2000**, *2*, 70. [CrossRef]
14. Geman, D.; Geman, H.; Taleb, N.N. Tail risk constraints and maximum entropy. *Entropy* **2015**, *17*, 3724–3737. [CrossRef]
15. Xu, Y.; Wu, Z.; Jiang, L.; Song, X. A maximum entropy method for a robust portfolio problem. *Entropy* **2014**, *16*, 3401–3415. [CrossRef]
16. Brody, D.C.; Hughston, L.P. Entropy and information in the interest rate term structure. *Quant. Financ.* **2002**, *2*, 70–80. [CrossRef]
17. Gulko, L. The entropy theory of stock option pricing. *Int. J. Theor. App. Financ.* **1999**, *2*, 331–355. [CrossRef]
18. Gulko, L. The entropy theory of bond option pricing. *Int. J. Theor. App. Financ.* **2002**, *5*, 355–383. [CrossRef]
19. Golan, A.; Perloff, J.M. Comparison of maximum entropy and higher-order entropy estimators. *J. Econ.* **2002**, *107*, 195–211. [CrossRef]
20. Ullah, A. Uses of entropy and divergence measures for evaluating econometric approximations and inference. *J. Econ.* **2002**, *107*, 313–326. [CrossRef]
21. Kitamura, Y.; Stutzer, M. Connections between entropic and linear projections in asset pricing estimation. *J. Econ.* **2002**, *107*, 159–174. [CrossRef]
22. Maasoumi, E.; Racine, J. Entropy and predictability of stock market returns. *J. Econ.* **2002**, *107*, 291–312. [CrossRef]
23. Bera, A.K.; Park, S.Y. Optimal portfolio diversification using the maximum entropy principle. *Econ. Rev.* **2008**, *27*, 484–512. [CrossRef]
24. Billio, M.; Casarin, R.; Costola, M.; Pasqualini, A. An entropy-based early warning indicator for systematic risk. *J. Int. Financ. Mark. Inst. Money* **2016**, *45*, 42–59. [CrossRef]
25. Zhao, N.; Lin, W.T. A copula entropy approach to correlation measurement at the country level. *Appl. Math. Comput.* **2011**, *218*, 628–642. [CrossRef]
26. Zunino, L.; Zanin, M.; Tabak, B.M.; Pérez, D.G.; Rosso, O.A. Forbidden patterns, permutation entropy and stock market inefficiency. *Phys. A Stat. Mech. Its Appl.* **2009**, *385*, 2854–2864. [CrossRef]
27. Mantegna, R.N. Hierarchical structure in financial markets. *Eur. Phys. J. B* **1999**, *11*, 193–197. [CrossRef]
28. Li, S.; He, J.; Song, K. Network entropies of the Chinese financial market. *Entropy* **2016**, *18*, 331. [CrossRef]
29. Lv, Q.; Han, L.; Wan, Y.; Yin, L. Stock net entropy: Evidence from the Chinese growth enterprise market. *Entropy* **2018**, *20*, 805. [CrossRef]
30. Schreiber, T. Measuring information transfer. *Phys. Rev. Lett.* **2000**, *85*, 461–464. [CrossRef]
31. Hlaváčková-Schindler, K.; Paluš, M.; Vejmelka, M.; Bhattacharya, J. Causality detection based on information-theoretic approaches in time series analysis. *Phys. Rep.* **2007**, *441*, 1–46. [CrossRef]
32. Będowska-Sójka, B.; Kliber, A. Information content of liquidity and volatility measures. *Phys. A Stat. Mech. Its Appl.* **2021**, *563*, 125436. [CrossRef]
33. Jizba, P.; Kleinert, H.; Shefaat, M. Rényi's information transfer between financial time series. *Phys. A Stat. Mech. Its Appl.* **2012**, *391*, 2971–2989. [CrossRef]
34. Syczewska, E.M.; Struzik, Z.R. Granger causality and transfer entropy for financial returns. *Acta Phys. Pol. A* **2015**, *127*, A-129. [CrossRef]
35. He, J.; Shang, P. Comparison of transfer entropy methods for financial time series. *Phys. A Stat. Mech. Its Appl.* **2017**, *482*, 772–785. [CrossRef]
36. Bossomaier, T.; Barnett, L.; Harre, M. Information and phase transitions in socio-economic systems. *Complex Adapt. Syst. Model.* **2013**, 1. [CrossRef]
37. Hmamouche, Y. NlinTS: An R package for causality detection in time series. *R J.* **2020**, *12*, 21–31. [CrossRef]
38. Allen, D.E.; McAleer, M.; Singh, A.K. An entropy-based analysis of the relationship between the DOW JONES index and the TRNA sentiment series. *App. Econ.* **2017**, *49*, 677–692. [CrossRef]
39. Liu, A.; Chen, J.; Yang, S.Y.; Hawkes, A.G. The flow of information in trading: An entropy approach to market regimes. *Entropy* **2020**, *22*, 1064. [CrossRef] [PubMed]
40. McCauley, J.L. Thermodynamic analogies in economics and finance: Instability of markets. *Phys. A Stat. Mech. Its Appl.* **2003**, *329*, 199–212. [CrossRef]
41. Lu, S.; Zhao, J.; Wang, H. Trading imbalance in Chinese stock market—A high-frequency view. *Entropy* **2020**, *22*, 897. [CrossRef] [PubMed]
42. Olbrys, J.; Mursztyn, M. Depth, tightness, and resiliency as market liquidity dimensions: Evidence from the Polish stock market. *Int. J. Comp. Econ. Econ.* **2019**, *9*, 308–326. [CrossRef]
43. Olbrys, J.; Mursztyn, M. Dimensions of Market. In *Advances in Applied Economic Research*; Tsounis, N., Vlachvei, A., Eds.; Springer: Cham, Switzerland, 2017; pp. 151–166. [CrossRef]
44. Kyle, A.S. Continuous auctions and insider trading. *Econometrica* **1985**, *53*, 1315–1336. [CrossRef]
45. Lee, C.M.C.; Ready, M.J. Inferring trade direction from intraday data. *J. Financ.* **1991**, *46*, 733–746. [CrossRef]
46. Ahn, H.-J.; Bae, K.-H.; Chan, K. Limit orders, depth, and volatility: Evidence from the Stock Exchange of Hong Kong. *J. Financ.* **2001**, *56*, 767–787. [CrossRef]

47. Chan, K.; Fong, W.-M. Trade size, order imbalance, and the volatility-volume relation. *J. Financ. Econ.* **2000**, *57*, 247–273. [CrossRef]
48. Chordia, T.; Roll, R.; Subrahmanyam, A. Order imbalance, liquidity, and market returns. *J. Financ. Econ.* **2002**, *65*, 111–130. [CrossRef]
49. Engle, R.; Lange, J. Predicting VNET: A model of the dynamics of market depth. *J. Financ. Mark.* **2001**, *4*, 113–142. [CrossRef]
50. Hmaied, D.M.; Grar, A.; Sioud, O.B. Dynamics of market liquidity of Tunisian stocks: An analysis of market resiliency. *Electron. Mark.* **2006**, *16*, 140–153. [CrossRef]
51. Lee, C.M.C.; Mucklow, B.; Ready, M.J. Spreads, depths, and the impact of earnings information: An intraday analysis. *Rev. Financ. Stud.* **1993**, *6*, 345–374. [CrossRef]
52. Ranaldo, A. Intraday market liquidity on the Swiss Stock Exchange. *Swiss Soc. Financ. Mark. Res.* **2001**, *15*, 309–327. [CrossRef]
53. Nowak, S. Order imbalance indicators in asset pricing: Evidence from the Warsaw Stock Exchange. In *Contemporary Trends and Challenges in Finance*; Jajuga, K., Orlowski, L., Staehr, K., Eds.; Springer: Cham, Switzerland, 2017; pp. 91–102. [CrossRef]
54. Olbrys, J.; Mursztyn, M. Measuring stock market resiliency with Discrete Fourier Transform for high frequency data. *Phys. A Stat. Mech. Its Appl.* **2019**, *513*, 248–256. [CrossRef]
55. Olbrys, J.; Mursztyn, M. Estimation of intraday stock market resiliency: Short-Time Fourier Transform approach. *Phys. A Stat. Mech. Its Appl.* **2019**, *535*, 122413. [CrossRef]
56. Olbryś, J.; Mursztyn, M. Evaluating trade side classification algorithms using intraday data from the Warsaw Stock Exchange. *Arch. Data Sci. A* **2018**, *4*, 1–19. [CrossRef]
57. Olbrys, J.; Majewska. E. Crisis periods and contagion effects in the CEE stock markets: The influence of the 2007 U.S. subprime crisis. *Int. J. Comput. Econ. Econ.* **2016**, *6*, 124–137. [CrossRef]
58. Goodhart, C.A.E.; O'Hara, M. High frequency data in financial markets: Issues and applications. *J. Emp. Financ.* **1997**, *4*, 73–114. [CrossRef]
59. Wood, R.; McInish, T.H.; Ord, J.K. An investigation of transactions data for NYSE stocks. *J. Financ.* **1985**, *40*, 723–739. [CrossRef]
60. Jain, C.; Joh, G.-H. The dependence between hourly prices and trading volume. *J. Financ. Quant. Anal.* **1988**, *23*, 269–283. [CrossRef]
61. Admati, A.R.; Pfleiderer, P. A theory of intraday patterns: Volume and price variability. *Rev. Financ. Stud.* **1988**, *1*, 3–40. [CrossRef]
62. McInish, T.H.; Wood, R.A. An analysis of transactions data for Toronto Stock Exchange: Return patterns and end-of-the-day effect. *J. Bank. Financ.* **1990**, *14*, 441–458. [CrossRef]
63. McInish, T.H.; Wood, R.A. Hourly returns, volume, trade size, and number of trades. *J. Financ. Res.* **1991**, *14*, 303–315. [CrossRef]
64. Vo, M.T. Limit orders and the intraday behavior of market liquidity: Evidence from the Toronto stock exchange. *Glob. Financ. J.* **2007**, *17*, 379–396. [CrossRef]
65. Hamao, Y.; Hasbrouck, J. Securities trading in the absence of dealers: Trades, and quotes on the Tokyo Stock Exchange. *Rev. Financ. Stud.* **1995**, *8*, 849–878. [CrossRef]
66. Cai, C.X.; Hudson, R.; Keasey, K. Intra day bid-ask spreads, trading volume and volatility: Recent empirical evidence from the London Stock Exchange. *J. Bus. Financ. Acc.* **2004**, *31*, 647–676. [CrossRef]
67. Ahn, H.-J.; Cheung, Y.-L. The intraday patterns of the spread and depth in a market without market makers: The Stock Exchange of Hong Kong. *Pac. Basin Financ. J.* **1999**, *7*, 539–556. [CrossRef]
68. Olbryś, J.; Oleszczak, A. Intraday Patterns in Trading Volume. Evidence from High Frequency Data on the Polish Stock Market. In *Computer Information Systems and Industrial Management. CISIM 2020. LNCS*, Saeed, K., Dvorsky, J., Eds.; Springer: Cham, Switzerland, 2020; Volume 12133, pp. 390–401. [CrossRef]
69. Harris, L. *Trading and Exchange Market: Microstructure for Practitioners*; Oxford University Press: New York, NY, USA, 2003.
70. Huberman, G.; Halka, D. Systematic liquidity. *J. Financ. Res.* **2001**, *24*, 161–178. [CrossRef]
71. Chordia, T.; Roll, R.; Subrahmanyam, A. Market liquidity and trading activity. *J. Financ.* **2001**, *56*, 501–530. [CrossRef]
72. Lad, F.; Sanfillippo, G.; Agrò, G. Extropy: Complementary dual of entropy. *Stat. Sci.* **2015**, *30*, 40–58. [CrossRef]

Article

A Network Approach to the Study of the Dynamics of Risk Spillover in China's Bond Market

Zhewen Liao [1,2,3], Hongli Zhang [1], Kun Guo [1,2,3,*] and Ning Wu [1,4]

1. School of Economics and Management, University of Chinese Academy of Sciences, Beijing 100190, China; liaozhewen16@mails.ucas.ac.cn (Z.L.); hlzhang0101@gmail.com (H.Z.); wuning20@mails.ucas.ac.cn (N.W.)
2. Key Laboratory of Big Data Mining and Knowledge Management, Chinese Academy of Sciences, Beijing 100190, China
3. Research Center on Fictitious Economy & Data Science, Chinese Academy of Sciences, Beijing 100190, China
4. National Science Library, Chinese Academy of Sciences, Beijing 100190, China
* Correspondence: guokun@ucas.ac.cn; Tel.: +86-138-1043-9286

Abstract: Since 2018, the bond market has surpassed the stock market, becoming the biggest investment area in China's security market, and the systemic risks of China's bond market are of non-negligible importance. Based on daily interest rate data of representative bond categories, this study conducted a dynamic analysis based on generalized vector autoregressive volatility spillover variance decomposition, constructed a complex network, and adopted the minimum spanning tree method to clarify and analyze the risk propagation path between different bond types. It is found that the importance of each bond type is positively correlated with liquidity, transaction volume, and credit rating, and the inter-bank market is the most important market in the entire bond market, while interest rate bonds, bank bonds and urban investment bonds are important varieties with great systemic importance. In addition, the long-term trend of the dynamic spillover index of China's bond market falls in line with the pace of the interest rate adjustments. To hold the bottom line of preventing financial systemic risks of China's bond market, standard management, strict supervision, and timely regulation of the bond markets are required, and the structural entropy, as a useful indicator, also should be used in the risk management and monitoring.

Keywords: bond market; fixed income security; risk spillovers; structural entropy; generalized variance decomposition; complex network

Citation: Liao, Z.; Zhang, H.; Guo, K.; Wu, N. A Network Approach to the Study of the Dynamics of Risk Spillover in China's Bond Market. *Entropy* 2021, 23, 920. https://doi.org/10.3390/e23070920

Academic Editor: Joanna Olbryś

Received: 9 June 2021
Accepted: 14 July 2021
Published: 20 July 2021

Publisher's Note: MDPI stays neutral with regard to jurisdictional claims in published maps and institutional affiliations.

Copyright: © 2021 by the authors. Licensee MDPI, Basel, Switzerland. This article is an open access article distributed under the terms and conditions of the Creative Commons Attribution (CC BY) license (https:// creativecommons.org/licenses/by/ 4.0/).

1. Introduction

From 2007 onwards, the Subprime Crisis brought about drastic changes in the global economic and financial system, exposing a series of loopholes in traditional financial institutions and regulatory systems, as well as showing a rising trend of cross-country risk contagion overtime [1]. Because of the down-speed shifting of economic development with a new normal medium speed after decades of high-speed and extensive growth, China's government now emphasizes quality of economic development and views financial risk management as a more important consideration than ever before.

Despite the outbreak and spread of the COVID-19 pandemic, the decoupling of the global economy, and the rise of populism having had a major impact on the global economy, China's domestic economy has endeavored to deepen supply-side structural reforms, which give full play to China's ultra-large-scale market advantages and domestic demand potential, and build new development that promotes both domestic and international cycles, as well as keeping China's economy energetic. At this stage of the pattern, China's financial system has entered a new period full of volatility and uncertainty after the long-term accumulation of systemic risks. In keeping with the findings from the research of Fang et al. [2], with the increasing openness of the Chinese economy, Chinese financial markets are becoming more integrated with those of developed markets, and Chinese financial markets are demonstrating a growing impact on global financial markets over time, especially during periods of turbulence.

Macroeconomic variables often suffer from structural changes due to changes in institutional reforms, policies, crises, and other factors [3], while systematic macroeconomic risks often tend to accumulate in the form of bubbles silently [4], only bursting with the outbreak of a crisis. When the bubble bursts, the spillover effect among institutions involved in the economic activities would become significant, expanding the range of the damage, so the systematic risks caused could not be ignored. So, understanding the risk contagion mechanism of the shocks in the financial market is significantly helpful, as well as crucial for investors for the purposes of asset allocation, asset pricing, risk management, and arbitrage trading. Generally, the investors who face asset price fluctuation, including both institute investors and individual investors, mostly use negatively correlated assets to complete their asset allocation, minimizing the portfolio risks. However, few investment institutions realize that to avoid systemic risks from being transmitted to themselves, identifying systemic risks and related systemically important institutions is a crucial step. Obviously, it is essential for regulators and governments to understand the transmission mechanism of financial shocks, since extreme volatility shock spillover causes financial unpredictability and brings about unexpected market impacts. In order to stabilize the price fluctuation in financial markets, ensuring that it is in a better condition to serve the real economy, the policymaker should develop appropriate policies to prevent large market impacts of volatility shocks from extreme events [5].

As Figure 1 shows, up until 28 October 2020, China's bond market has a tremendous scale of RMB 112 trillion, accounting for 52.41% of China's entire securities market. According to this fast-growing and tremendous volume, the bond market is almost the biggest investment area in China, only second to the real estate market. Although there are few individual investors in the bond market, the importance of the prosperity and stability of China's bond market cannot be emphasized too much, as well as the significance of controlling the volatility and risk of this market.

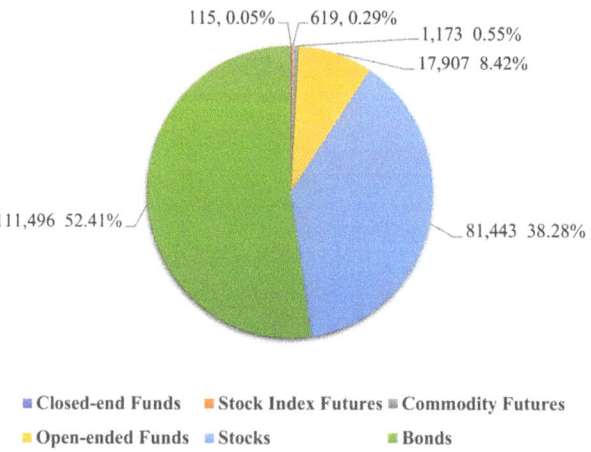

Figure 1. The scale of China's security market, as of 28 October 2020 (Unit: RMB billion).

However, few studies have focused on the inner dynamics of China's bond market. In our research, we innovatively combine the methodology of complex networks and the traditional econometric method, and instead of using the indices data of the financial market, we pioneeringly use the interest rate data of different bond types in China's bond market, which provide a better representation of the inner factors of China's bond market in a relatively micro view, instead of traditional quarterly data from the balance sheets of financial institutes.

There are 23 types of bonds included in our research. Using the traditional econometric model will face the problem of degrees of freedom caused by too many variables, so the complex network method will be more appropriate. In this paper, the bond market is regarded as a complex system that includes different types of bonds as nodes. The spillover indexes among the exchange rate fluctuations are used to construct the network. To make the relationship among bonds more intuitive and clearer, and to show the most effective path in the risk contagions process, the minimum spanning tree (MST) method is applied to analyze the influence structure. Thus, the key nodes and the key path of volatility risk contagion can be detected. This paper is organized as follows: the first section introduces the background to our research; the data are briefly introduced in Section 2; the techniques of network analysis and the results are discussed in Section 3; and finally, we end with a conclusion in Section 4.

2. Literature Review

The current economic crisis illustrates a critical need for new and fundamental understanding of the structure and dynamics of economic networks. Economic systems are increasingly built on interdependencies, implemented through trans-national credit and investment networks, trade relations, or supply chains that have proven difficult to predict and control [6]. For investigation of the risk in financial markets, various methods have been used in related research, and the simulation approach is often used, especially when a financial network is involved. Battiston and Caldarelli [7] used the simulation approach and stress tests to focus on the role of linkages within the two dimensions of contagion and liquidity, and to examine the mechanism of the contagions of systemic risk in financial networks, and they found that with respect to the issue of the determination of systemically important financial institutions, the findings indicate that both from the point of view of contagion and from the point of view of liquidity provision, there is more to systemic importance than just size. Ponta and Cincotti [8] presented and studied an information-based multi-asset artificial stock market characterized by different types of stocks and populated by heterogeneous agents to determine the influences of agents' networks on the market's structure. They concluded that the network is necessary in order to achieve the ability to reproduce the main stylized facts, but also that the market has some characteristics that are independent of the network and depend on the finiteness of traders' wealth.

The research on financial market contagion or spillover effects has been widely studied in the economic and management aspects, and is also used in our research for its robustness and interpretability. For example, Diebold and Yilmaz [9] proposed several connectedness measures built from pieces of variance decompositions, and they argued that they provide natural and insightful measure connectedness among financial asset returns and volatilities by using directed networks to make the relationship more clear. Su [10] used the MHS-EGARCH model, finding that there are negative return and volatility spillover effects between currency and stock markets, and the stock indices in emerging markets have a higher return and a higher risk. Dey and Sampath [11] analyzed spillovers in returns and volatility among five major financial assets in India, especially the shock from the USA, by using a generalized vector autoregressive model, and they find that banking, real estate and gold matter the most for India. There are a number of similar studies such as Georgiadis [12], Yang and Zhou [13], and Miranda-Agrippino and Rey [14] that show that the US monetary policy could cause a considerable spillover impact in the global financial market. Morana and Bagliano [15] analyzed business cycle spillovers and synchronization within groups of old and new European Union countries and found out that spillovers are beneficial for the common monetary policy of the European Union. Lyocsa et al. [16] studied the connectedness of a sample of 40 stock markets across five continents using daily dosing prices and return spillovers based on Granger causality by building a complex network of the global stock market. In conclusion, they found that the probability of return spillover from a given stock market to other markets increases with market volatility and market size and decreases with higher foreign exchange volatility.

In addition, closing hours are important for information propagation. The research of Tsai and I-Chun [17] is interesting, as they used the data of economic policy uncertainty (EPU) in four countries or regions, finding that EPU in China is the most influential, and its contagion risk spreads to different regional markets, except for Europe; the effect of EPU in the United States is inferior to that in China; EPU in Japan merely influences contagion risk in emerging markets; contagion risk in European markets is not influenced by the four EPU indices; and EPU in Europe is not influenced by contagion risk in the global stock market. Huo and Ahmed [18] examined the impact of the Shanghai-Hong Kong Stock Connect by using the BEKK GARCH model. They found that the new Stock Connect does contribute to the increasing importance of the Chinese mainland stock market and economic activity, and found a leading role of the Shanghai stock market in the Hong Kong stock market in terms of both mean and volatility spillover effects after the Stock Connect. Narayan et al. [19] examined the relationship between stock returns and mutual fund flows in India by applying a generalized VAR model. In addition, it was also found that the spillover index defined in their research could be used to predict stock returns and mutual fund flows. Mensi et al. [20] studied the linkages both within and between stock and foreign exchange (FX) markets via three higher moments of return distributions (volatility, skewness and kurtosis), finding that cross-asset market linkages are of a similar magnitude to intra-asset-market linkages within emerging market, but the latter are stronger in developed markets. Christiansen [21] used a GARCH volatility–spillover model to analyze the volatility spillover from the US and aggregate European bond markets into individual European bond markets, and the weekly data of multiple bond indices issued by JPMorgan were used in his research. In his conclusion, strong statistical evidence of volatility spillover from the US and aggregate European bond markets was found. Additionally, it is interesting to find that the bond markets of EMU countries became much more integrated after the Euro was first issued, and this was mainly driven by the convergence in interest rates under the unified monetary policy [22], documented asymmetry in return and volatility spillover between equity and bond markets in Australia for daily returns during the period 1992–2006 by using a bivariate GARCH modelling approach. The illuminative result from their research is that negative bond market returns spillover into lower stock market returns, whereas good news originating in the equity market leads to lower bond returns, and the spillover effects are stronger in a one-way channel from the bond market to the equity market.

There are plenty of studies using matrices and network methods to study financial markets. Junior and Franca used the eigenvalues and eigenvectors of the correlations matrices of some of the main financial market indices in the world, showing that the high volatility of markets is directly linked with strong correlations between them, and their conclusion provided a good explanation of the major financial market crises that occurred between 1987 and 2008 [23]. Matesanz's team analyzed co-movements in a wide group of commodity prices during the time period 1992–2010. Their methodological approach was based on the correlation matrix and the networks inside. Through this approach, they were able to summarize global interaction and interdependence, capturing the existing heterogeneity in the degrees of synchronization between commodity prices. Their results suggest that speculation and uncertainty are drivers of the sharp slump in commodity prices' synchronization [24]. There are also several studies on the inter-market spillover effect in China, such as the research of Zhu et al. [25], or about inter-bank spillover effect, such as the research of Bao, Wu and Li [26].

It is worth mentioning that the hybrid methods such as structural entropy have gradually become more commonly used in financial research: Murialdo and Ponta [27] presented a perspective on the intangible complexity of economic and social systems by investigating the dynamical processes producing, storing and transmitting information in financial time series by using the moving average cluster entropy approach. Shi et al. [28] used gray relational analysis and empirical mode decomposition to decompose and reconstruct the sequences to obtain the evolution trend and periodic fluctuation of systemic risk, and used structural entropy as a measurement to verify the results, showing that the systemic risk of China's stock market as a whole shows a downward trend, and the periodic fluctuation of systemic risk has a long-term equilibrium relationship with the abnormal fluctuation of the stock market. Bielik [29] used entropy combined with technical indicators of the stock market, such as MACD, to find predictable market parts and improve the automated and non-automated trading strategies in the financial market.

Except for the methods mentioned above, the rise of econophysics, a fundamentally new approach in finance, suggests that the influence between the two disciplines has become less unilateral than in the past. Jovanovic's research aimed at analyzing the unexpected influence of financial economics on physics. With this purpose, their study went one step further in the dialogue between econophysics and economics. Indeed, by investigating the reciprocal influence between the two fields, their paper identified some areas for a better cross-fertilization between the fields [30]. Kutner's research presented some of the achievements of econophysics and sociophysics which appear to us to be the most significant [31], and Schinckus' study aimed at analyzing how econophysicists implicitly promote a Duhemian way of perceiving scientific research by expanding their work into economics [32].

3. Methodology

3.1. Generalized Vector Autoregressive Forecast Error Variance Decomposition

To measure the risk spillover effect of the complex network of bond markets, we calculated the volatility spillover indices based on a generalized VAR in which the FEVD is invariant to the variable ordering initially proposed by Francis et al. [33] and Diebold and Yilmaz [34]. The details are shown as follows:

At the very first beginning, it is necessary to establish a VAR model with N variables in the lagging P period with stable covariance:

$$x_t = \sum_{i=1}^{p} \phi_i x_{t-i} + \grave{O}_t \tag{1}$$

where $x_t = (x_{1t}, x_{2t}, \cdots, x_{Nt})$ is a vector with N endogenous variables, ϕ_i, $i = 1, 2, \cdots, p$ is a N-dimensional autoregressive coefficient matrix, the mean of the error vector $\grave{O}_t$ is zero, and the covariance matrix is denoted as Σ. When the VAR model is stationary, the (1) could be convert to a moving average formula:

$$x_t = \sum_{j=0}^{\infty} A_j \grave{O}_{t-j} \tag{2}$$

A_i should meet the condition that $A_i = \phi_1 A_{i-1} + \phi_2 A_{i-2} + \cdots \phi_n A_{i-n}$, and A_0 is a N-dimensional unit matrix, and when $j < 0$, $A_i = 0$.

Secondly, in order to measure the spillover effect between variables and the total spillover effect, this study defines the spillover effect between variables: the spillover effect of variable x_j on variable x_i is defined as the variance of the H-step prediction error of x_i that is impacted by the x_j part where $i \neq j$. The H-step represents the time span of the forecast error of the VAR model—that is, the number of periods of variance decomposition, which can be represented by Formula (3):

$$\theta_{ij}^H = \frac{\sigma_{jj}^{-1} \sum_{h=0}^{H-1} \left(e_i' A_h \Sigma e_j \right)^2}{\sum_{h=0}^{H-1} \left(e_i' A_h \Sigma A_h' e_i \right)} \tag{3}$$

While σ_{jj}^{-1} is the standard deviation form of the prediction error of the jth variable, e_i is a N × 1 vector, where the ith element is 1, and the rest are zero. θ_{ij}^H represents the spillover effect of variable x_j on variable x_i, with it being noted that $\sum_{j=1}^{N} \theta_{ij}^H$, so θ_{ij}^H should be standardized:

$$\hat{\theta}_{ij}^{\tilde{H}} = \frac{\theta_{ij}^H}{\sum_{j=1}^{N} \theta_{ij}^H} \qquad (4)$$

and now $\sum_{j=1}^{N} \theta_{ij}^H = 1$, $\sum_{i,j=1}^{N} \theta_{ij}^H = N$. The matrix $\theta^H = \left[\tilde{\theta}_{ij}^H\right]$ shows the spillover effect among N variables, and the main diagonal element represents the overflow effect of the variable itself, while the non-diagonal element represents the overflow effect between different variables.

The percentage form of the total spillover effect can be obtained from Formula (4):

$$TS = \frac{\sum_{i,j=1, i \neq j}^{N} \theta_{ij}^{\tilde{H}}}{\sum_{i,j=1}^{N} \theta_{ij}^{\tilde{H}}} \times 100 = \frac{\sum_{i,j=1, i \neq j}^{N} \theta_{ij}^{\tilde{H}}}{N} \times 100 \qquad (5)$$

Regarding the total spillover index TS, add the non-diagonal elements in the resulting matrix $\theta^{\tilde{H}} = \theta_{ij}^{\tilde{H}}$ as the numerator of the total spillover index, and the denominator of the total spillover index is obtained by adding up all the elements in the matrix. In this way, the total spillover effect index measures the degree of the total spillover effect between in bond markets, so it can be used as a quantitative indicator to measure the degree of bond market correlation, as well as its risk of spreading. The bigger the spillover index is, the greater the volatility of the bond market due to the risk spillovers between different bond varieties will be, which in turn shows that the links between financial markets are very close.

3.2. The Complex Network, the MST Method and Structural Entropy

A complex network generally comprises several nodes and edges linking them. The node is the basic unit of a complex network, which is the abstract expression of an "individual" in the real world [35]. The edge is an expression of the relationship between the units and could be given weight accordingly to describe the extent of the relationships quantitatively [36]. In human social activities, the most common complex network is the small world network [37]; while talking about the Internet, scholars of complex networks usually define it as a scale-free network [38]. Different types of complex networks usually have different characteristics of their edges and nodes [39], and here in our research, w_{ij} represents the weight of the edge linking node i and node j, where $i = 1, 2, 3, \ldots, n$, $j = 1, 2, 3, \ldots, n$, where n is the amount of nodes in a certain network. For an undirected network,

$$w_{ij} = w_{ji} \qquad (6)$$

The research also uses the weighted degree to represent the importance of nodes, which is defined as:

$$dw_i = \sum_{j \in v(i)} w_{ij} \qquad (7)$$

where $v_{(i)}$ is the set of nodes linking to node i. The stronger the degree of correlation with other nodes is, the more important the node is.

In our study, the spillover index of 1st difference to the interest rate data has been used, shown as:

$$w_{ij} = (spillover\ index)_{i\ to\ j} \qquad (8)$$

It should be noted that w_{ij} here represents the weight of the edge from i to j in a directed network, and the $(spillover\ index)_{i\ to\ j}$ here could be calculated from θ_{ij}^H in Formula (3), and vice versa.

To detect a clearer structure of the complex network of bond market, we apply the minimum spanning tree (short as MST) method [40] that has been previously applied to this research aspect [41,42]. This method selects the indices with the closest interactions among all the indices and generates a visual presentation of the relationship with n − 1 edges in the tree. When using the MST method, the relatively insignificant edges are discarded and there is only one route between any two nodes, which means that the complex network constructed by the MST shows more concise and clearer risk contagion relationships in China's bond market, and that it is easier to discern the key bond types in the risk spillover complex network.

To construct the MST, the spillover index firstly needs to be converted into a "distance" coefficient as the input of the Kruskal algorithm. Following these references [28,43], we use nonlinear mapping:

$$d_{ij} = \sqrt{2\left(1 - (spillover\ index)_{ij}\right)} \qquad (9)$$

to obtain the distance d_{ij}, noting that $d_{ij} = d_{ji}$ in the undirected graph, and $(spillover\ index)_{ij}$ could be defined as:

$$(spillover\ index)_{ij} = \left((spillover\ index)_{i\ to\ j} + (spillover\ index)_{j\ to\ i}\right)/2 \qquad (10)$$

and $(spillover\ index)_{i\ to\ j}$ here represents the spillover index from node i to node j, and vice versa. It should be pointed out that the index here represents the percentage of the spillover of node i to node j to the total impact of j by the volatility spillover. The Kruskal algorithm [44] is used in this paper to construct the MST complex network.

d_{ij} represents the "distance" coefficient, which should be used as input of the Kruskal algorithm to generate an MST complex network. In an MST complex network, the relatively insignificant edges are discarded and there is only one route between any two nodes, and the weights of the edges are inversely proportional to d_{ij}.

In addition, for a better vision to observe the network's dynamics, the network's structural entropy was calculated in this study, which is often used as a quantitative measurement of the complexity of the complex network system [45]. Generally, a non-fully connected network structural entropy E_{degree} could be calculated as follows:

$$E_{degree} = -\sum_{i=1}^{N} p_i \log p_i \qquad (11)$$

where N is the total number of the nodes in the complex network, and p_i in (11) could be calculated by the degree of node i, just as follows:

$$P_i = \frac{degree(i)}{\sum_{i=1}^{N} degree(i)} \qquad (12)$$

After the complex network has been constructed, some useful indicators can be used to analyze the characteristics of the network, such as degree and centrality. For node i in the complex network, the degree of node i represents the number of its neighboring nodes. Compared with the node's degree, the centrality is a relatively complicated indicator type, which is usually used to measure the node's relationship with the other nodes in some aspect. In this research, three kinds of centrality are mentioned: closeness centrality, betweenness centrality and eigenvector centrality [46].

Closeness centrality is an indicator that the higher the closeness centrality a node has, the closer the distance from the node to other node in the complex network, and vice versa [47]. The closeness centrality C_v could be calculated as follows:

$$C_v = \frac{V-1}{\sum_{i \neq v}^{N} d_{vi}} \qquad (13)$$

where d_{vi} represents the shortest distance from node v to node i, and V is the total number of nodes.

The betweenness centrality is usually used to measure the node's central significance to a complex network; the greater the number of shortest paths passing through a node, the higher its betweenness centrality [48]. The formula of calculating betweenness centrality of node i, which is denoted as B_i, is as follows:

$$B_i = \frac{SP_i}{SP_{total}} \tag{14}$$

where SP_i represents the number of the shortest paths passing through node i, while SP_{total} stands for the total number of the shortest paths in the complex network.

The eigenvector centrality, shortened to eigen centrality, is an indicator often used to measure the number and the importance of its neighboring nodes [49]. The most famous algorithm used in search engine, called PageRank, is one kind of eigenvector centrality. The greater the number of nodes and the more important neighboring nodes the node has, the higher the eigen centrality of the node has, and the highest eigen centrality in the complex network is set as 1 by normalization. For a given graph G with v number of nodes, let $A = (a_v t)$ be the adjacency matrix, and the eigen centrality EC_i of node i can be defined as [50]:

$$EC_i = x_v = \frac{1}{\lambda} \sum_{t \in M(v)} x_t = \frac{1}{\lambda} \sum_{t \in G} a_{v,t} x_t \tag{15}$$

where $M(v)$ is a set of the neighbors of v and λ is a constant. With a small rearrangement, this can be rewritten in vector notation as the eigenvector equation:

$$Ax = \lambda x \tag{16}$$

4. Data Description

The primary goal of this study is to provide a historical narrative on the dynamics of risk spillover networks of China's bond market. For this purpose, data preprocessing of this research is shown as follows:

At the very beginning of our research, proper data type and bond maturity should be chosen. We first studied the size and liquidity of different bond type to obtain a holistic view of China's bond market today. After obtaining data from WIND, we present the data in Figure 2.

To take the multiple fundamental elements of bonds into consideration, and in order to control some factors to concentrate on the evolution of risk and volatility spillover in the network of bond markets, 23 types of bond interest rate data were chosen, including the credit spread of SOE, R007, DR007, and SHIBOR, as the benchmark interest rate data. In addition, in order to obtain a good representation of the results, and avoiding the potential price distortion of low credit rating bonds, this study mainly focuses on relatively high credit rating bonds in China, with a rating higher than AA (AA included) generally. For the same reason, this study mainly chooses the bonds which have 1 year of remaining maturity, because these bonds could reflect the features of both the monetary market and the capital market. The time interval is from 15 December 2014 to 28 October 2020, which is the time interval that guarantees that the above interest rate data could be obtained, and it is believed that the daily data, which cover almost last 6 years, ensure a good performance and representation. As Table 1 shows, all the data are stationary or stationary after the first difference, and the generalized vector autoregressive volatility spillover variance decomposition model is based on the first differenced data.

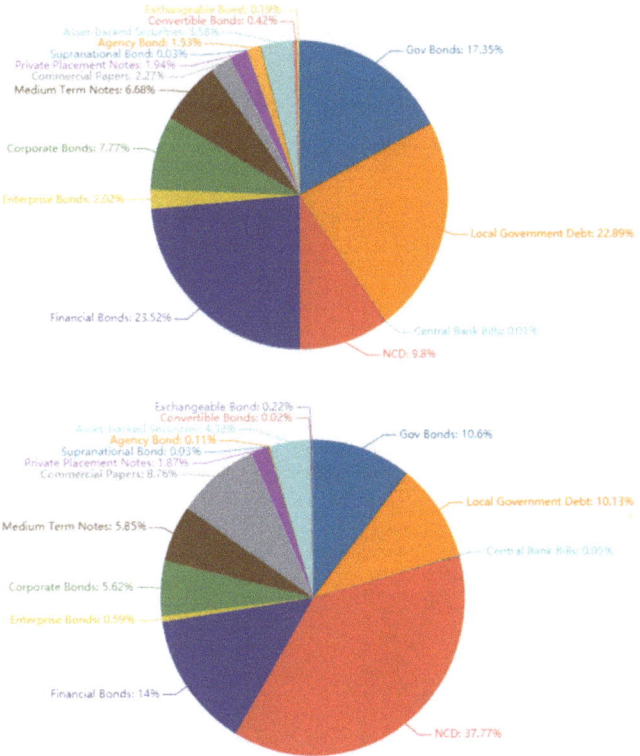

Figure 2. The percentage of the remaining size of different bond types in China's bond market (all maturities), the upper figure shows bonds with all maturity, the lower figure shows bonds with 1 year of remaining maturity; as of 28 October 2020.

Table 1. The interest data of bonds chosen by this study.

Bond Type (Remaining Maturity: 1 Year If Not Mentioned)	Details and Description	Abbreviation
Commercial Banks Bonds	Commercial Banks Bonds (Rating: AAA)	BANKAAA
Corporate Bonds	Corporate Bonds (Rating: AAA)	CORPAAA
	Corporate Bonds (Rating: AA+)	CORPAAP
	Corporate Bonds (Rating: AA)	CORPAA
Treasury	China's Treasury	TREASURY
Financial Bonds of Policy Banks	China's National Development Bond	CDB
	China's Agricultural Development Bond	ADB
	China's Export-Import Bank Bond	IEB
Short- and Medium-Term Notes	Short and Medium Term Notes (Rating: AAA)	STNAAA
	Short and Medium Term Notes (Rating: AA+)	STNAAP
NCD (Interbank negotiable certificates of deposit)	Interbank negotiable certificates of deposit (Rating: AAA)	BANKIDCAAA
	Interbank negotiable certificates of deposit (Rating: AA+)	BANKIDCAAP
Consumer Financial Asset-backed Securities	Consumer Financial Asset-backed Securities (Rating: AAA)	CFABSAAA
	Consumer Financial Asset-backed Securities (Rating: AA+)	CFABSAAP

Table 1. Cont.

Bond Type (Remaining Maturity: 1 Year If Not Mentioned)	Details and Description	Abbreviation
General Corporate Asset-backed Securities	General Corporate Asset-backed Securities (Rating: AAA)	ABSAAA
China's Railway Bond	China's Railway bond	RAILWAYB
Local Government Bond	Local Government Bond (Rating: AAA)	GOVAAA
Urban Investment Bond (Chengtou Bond)	Chengtou Bond (Rating: AAA) Chengtou Bond (Rating: AA+)	CTBAAA CTBAAP
Credit Spread of State-owned Enterprises	Credit Spread of SOE	CSPREADSOE
R007 (remaining maturity: 7 days)	Seven-day repurchase rate	R007
DR007 (remaining maturity: 7 days) SHIBOR	Seven-day repurchase rate between deposit institutions Shanghai Interbank Offered Rate	DR007 SHIBOR1Y

To take the several fundamental elements of bonds into consideration, and in order to control some factors, such as credit rating and term structure, to concentrate on the evolution of risk and volatility spillover network of bond markets as mentioned before, the descriptive statistical analysis of first differenced data are as follows in Table 2, where the t-statistics come from the Dickey–Fuller unit root test (AIC):

Table 2. The statistic feature of the bond market's interest data.

Series	T-Stats	Mean	Std Error	Minimum	Maximum	Skewness	Kurtosis	Stationary
BANKAAA	−30.887	−0.0010	0.0415	−0.4156	0.2500	−1.3653	17.5455	1st difference
CORPAAA	−24.226	−0.0011	0.0368	−0.2350	0.2292	−0.0761	6.7735	1st difference
CORPAAP	−24.188	−0.0014	0.0377	−0.2350	0.2292	−0.0117	5.5615	1st difference
CORPAA	−25.260	−0.0016	0.0391	−0.2350	0.2292	0.1380	5.0190	1st difference
TREASURY	−26.710	−0.0004	0.0335	−0.3100	0.3500	0.1439	20.1279	1st difference
CDB	−26.968	−0.0009	0.0400	−0.3529	0.2697	−0.7940	12.5871	1st difference
ADB	−23.285	−0.0009	0.0420	−0.2972	0.3673	−0.1849	13.8221	1st difference
IEB	−21.325	−0.0009	0.0403	−0.2972	0.3673	0.0009	13.2908	1st difference
STNAAA	−22.061	−0.0011	0.0368	−0.2350	0.2292	−0.0905	6.6818	1st difference
STNAAP	−22.915	−0.0014	0.0379	−0.2350	0.2292	−0.0455	5.4097	1st difference
BANKIDCAAA	−25.728	−0.0011	0.0414	−0.4130	0.2500	−1.3529	17.5522	1st difference
BANKIDCAAP	−25.493	−0.0010	0.0416	−0.4030	0.2500	−1.1148	15.1680	1st difference
CFABSAAA	−26.411	−0.0013	0.0421	−0.4088	0.2574	−0.7591	11.7487	1st difference
CFABSAAP	−26.406	−0.0015	0.0446	−0.4359	0.2744	−0.7592	12.0034	1st difference
ABSAAA	−26.326	−0.0013	0.0403	−0.3970	0.2500	−0.8645	12.9141	1st difference
RAILWAYB	−22.713	−0.0010	0.0366	−0.2325	0.2159	−0.2254	5.7954	1st difference
GOVAAA	−24.470	−0.0005	0.0323	−0.2486	0.3500	0.6673	17.5992	1st difference
CTBAAA	−24.195	−0.0012	0.0363	−0.2531	0.2889	0.0380	9.2296	1st difference
CTBAAP	−24.395	−0.0015	0.0366	−0.2531	0.2889	0.1237	8.0929	1st difference
CSPREADSOE	−60.674	−0.0002	0.1163	−0.8625	0.8883	−0.1068	33.1377	yes
R007	−30.752	−0.0004	0.2417	−2.3025	1.8934	−0.7548	20.5438	1st difference
DR007	−30.809	−0.0007	0.1125	−0.6976	1.3919	1.1032	22.9221	1st difference
SHIBOR1Y	−11.817	−0.0010	0.0153	−0.1740	0.0850	−2.8415	24.3002	1st difference

It can be clearly seen from Table 2 that all the data are stationary. In the same scale, the mean values of the data are all near zero and are all less than zero, which is mainly because the risk-free rate had a declining trend in this period, which could be indicated by the mean value of TREASURY and CDB.

5. Empirical Results

5.1. Static Spillover Effect Analysis

By using the model mentioned in Section 2, firstly, the full-sample spillover index is based on the FEV decomposition 12 days in advance. Each variable is related to the sequence of daily changes in bonds' interest rates. Therefore, the measurement of the diagonal element $i = j$ is the spillover effect within a certain type of bond, while the non-diagonal element ($i \neq j$) captures the spillover effect between different bond categories, and the last line is the acquisition of each variable Additionally, the total spillover effect passed. As is shown in Table 3, it can be concluded that:

Table 3. The static spillover effect of the full sample.

	BANK AAA	CORP AAA	CORP AAP	CORP AA	TREA-SURY	CDB	ADB	IEB	STN AAA	STN AAP	BANKIDC AAA	BANKIDC AAP	CFABS AAA	CFABS AAP	ABS AAA	RAIL WAYB	GOV AAA	CTB AAA	CTB AAP	CSPRE-ADSOE	R007	DR007	SHI-BORIY	From Others
BANKAAA	26.5	12.1	11.4	9.5	3.2	7.4	0.6	0.6	0.4	0.4	0.3	0.3	0.2	0.2	0.2	0.4	3.1	11.1	9.9	0.1	0.9	0.2	1.1	73.5
CORPAAA	8.7	19.6	17.5	14.3	2.8	6	0.5	0.5	0.4	0.4	0.3	0.3	0.1	0.1	0.2	0.3	2.5	13.1	11.4	0	0.6	0.1	0.3	80.4
CORPAAP	8.2	17.6	19.2	15.2	2.7	5.8	0.6	0.6	0.3	0.4	0.3	0.4	0.2	0.2	0.2	0.3	2.6	12.3	11.4	0	0.7	0.2	0.4	80.8
CORPAA	7.7	16.1	17	21.2	2.4	5.3	0.4	0.4	0.2	0.3	0.2	0.3	0.1	0.1	0.1	0.2	2.3	12.3	11.7	0	0.7	0.2	0.3	78.8
TREASURY	3.4	3.7	3.3	2.6	36.7	8.3	0.8	0.9	0.3	0.3	0.2	0.3	0.1	0.1	0.1	0.2	29.1	3.9	3.4	0.4	0.3	0.3	1.1	63.3
CDB	7.5	7.5	6.9	5.7	6.8	35	1.1	1	0.8	1	0.5	0.6	0.3	0.3	0.3	0.7	5.7	8	6.8	0.8	1.8	0.4	0.3	65
ADB	0.4	0.2	0.2	0.1	0.1	0.2	25	20.4	7.3	6.8	6.8	6.9	5.7	5.6	6.1	7.2	0.2	0.2	0.2	0.1	0.4	0.4	0.1	75
IEB	0.3	0.2	0.2	0.1	0.1	0.1	20.1	25.5	7.3	6.7	7	7.9	5.7	5.7	6.3	7	0.1	0.1	0	0	0.2	0.1	0.1	74.5
STNAAA	0.2	0.1	0.1	0	0	0.1	6	6.1	16.9	15.5	8.3	8.2	7.8	7.8	8.2	14.3	0	0.1	0.1	0	0.2	0	0.2	83.1
STNAAP	0.2	0.1	0.1	0.1	0	0.1	6.1	6.2	16.2	17.2	8	7.9	7.7	7.7	8.1	13.8	0	0.1	0	0	0.2	0	0.2	82.8
BANKIDCAAA	0.2	0.1	0.1	0	0	0	5.4	5.7	8	7.3	15.6	14.6	11.4	11.4	12.1	7.7	0	0.1	0.1	0	0.2	0	0.1	84.4
BANKIDCAAP	0.2	0.1	0.1	0.1	0	0	5.4	5.7	8.1	7.5	14.8	15.8	11.1	11.1	11.7	7.7	0	0.1	0.1	0	0.2	0	0.1	84.2
CFABSAAA	0.1	0	0	0	0	0	4.7	4.7	7.7	7.2	11.4	11	15.3	15.2	14.5	7.7	0	0.1	0.1	0	0.2	0	0	84.7
CFABSAAP	0.1	0	0	0	0	0	4.7	4.7	7.6	7.3	11.5	11	15.2	15.3	14.6	7.7	0	0.1	0.1	0	0.2	0	0	84.7
ABSAAA	0.1	0	0	0	0	0.1	4.8	4.9	7.8	7.3	11.9	11.3	14.2	14.2	15	7.8	0	0.1	0.1	0	0.2	0	0	85
RAILWAYB	0.2	0.1	0.1	0.1	0	0.1	6.1	6.2	14.8	13.5	8.5	8.3	8.2	8.2	8.6	17	0	0	0	0	0.2	0	0.1	83
GOVAAA	3.4	3.8	3.6	3	29.1	7.2	0.7	0.7	0.2	0.3	0.2	0.3	0.1	0.1	0.1	0.2	36.7	4.2	3.6	0.3	0.4	0.2	1.6	63.3
CTBAAA	8.3	13.6	12.6	10.9	2.9	6.6	0.5	0.6	0.4	0.5	0.5	0.6	0.3	0.3	0.3	0.4	2.7	19.7	17.2	0	0.4	0.1	0.5	80.3
CTBAAP	7.8	12.7	12.5	11	2.9	6.4	0.6	0.6	0.4	0.6	0.5	0.6	0.2	0.2	0.4	0.4	2.8	18.1	19.8	0	0.7	0.3	0.5	80.2
CSPREADSOE	0.6	0.5	0.5	2.2	0.6	1.9	0.6	0.8	0.4	0.4	0.8	1	0.7	0.7	0.7	0.6	0.5	0.4	0.4	90.3	0.7	0.2	0.4	9.7
R007	2.4	2.2	2.4	1	0.5	3.7	0.9	0.8	0.2	0.5	0.2	0.4	0.1	0.1	0.2	0.3	0.4	1.4	1.3	0.1	60	16.7	0.4	40.3
DR007	1.1	0.5	0.9	1	0.8	1.9	0.5	0.5	0.2	0.4	0.2	0.4	0.1	0.1	0.2	0.3	0.5	0.6	0.9	0.2	21	67.4	0.4	32.6
SHIBORIY	8.1	4.7	4.3	3.3	3.8	7	0.4	0.4	1.1	1	0.3	0.3	0.1	0.1	0.1	0.8	3.4	5.9	4.8	0.6	0.1	0.8	48.7	51.3
Contribution to others	69	96	93.8	79.7	58.9	68.2	71.5	72.2	90.6	85.3	92.7	91.4	89.8	89.9	93.4	85.9	56	92.3	83.8	3.1	30	20.2	8	
Contribution including own	95.4	115.6	113	100.9	95.6	103.2	96.4	97.7	107.5	102.4	108.2	107.3	105.1	105.1	108.4	102.9	92.7	111.9	103.5	93.4	89	87.6	56.7	

For bond varieties with a high liquidity and large trading volume, such as financial bonds, government bonds, short- and medium-term notes and other mainstream varieties traded in the inter-bank bond market, the volatility spillover effects of these varieties are significantly higher. The volatility of the entire bond market overflows the complex network of greater systematic importance, mainly because the price of these bonds has become the benchmark of similar bonds to some extent.

For the same types of bonds with the same maturity, the sub-categories with high credit ratings have higher spillover effects, greater system importance, and a deeper influence on the system, compared with the low-credit rating bonds. This might be attributed to the high-credit rating bonds having better liquidity and the risk aversion of investors, and, furthermore, there may be some internal regulation and guidance in investment institutions that mean that the trader could only buy bonds which have a credit rating of AAA or AA+, which might enhance these effects. This can be clearly seen from related corporate bonds, medium- and short-term notes, and urban investment bonds as to their total static spillover effect, where the high-rating bonds have a bigger contribution to others than low-rating bonds.

For the purpose of a better illustration of the result of the study regarding the mechanisms of the complex network of risk spillovers in China's bond market, we used the static spillover index to construct the relevant complex network and used Gephi to draw Figure 3a as follows, noting that the size of nodes corresponds with the importance of the bond: the bigger the node is, more important the bond is in the complex network. The thickness of the link between the nodes indicates the strength of the influence of one bond on the other bond, in the direction of the linkage.

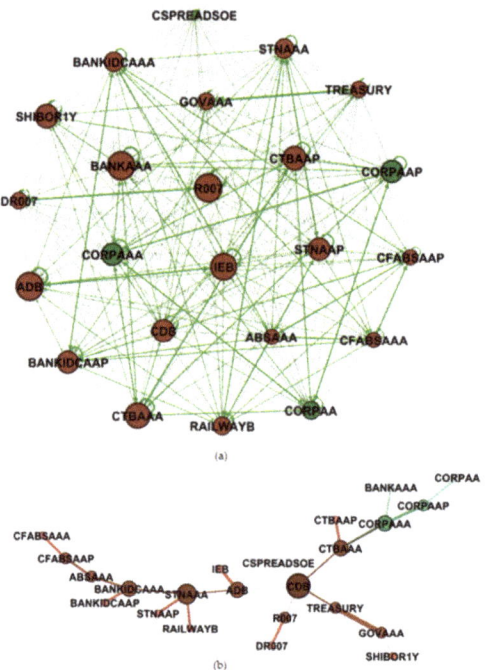

Figure 3. The complex network of bond markets constructed by the static spillover index of the full sample: (**a**) is the fully connected graph, (**b**) is the MST graph (the nodes which represent bond varieties traded in the inter-bank market are colored as red, noting that self-loops here mean the spillover effect from historical data of itself).

It can be seen from the complex network diagram in Figure 3a that as a result of their large trading volume (accounting for nearly 90% of the entire bond trading volume), good liquidity, and relatively fairer pricing, meaning they are preferred by investors, the mainstream trading bond types in the inter-bank market are more influential in the generalized volatility spillover variance decomposition network of bond markets.

It should also be noted that Figure 3b is an undirected graph. In addition, the link between the nodes means that the influence is a two-way transmission. As is shown in Figure 3b, the biggest node is CDB, which is also the most traded variety of all in China's bond market, and as the central node, it is linked with another two policy banks: ADB and IEB. CTBAAA and STNAAA are also important nodes thanks to their large trading volume.

The red nodes occupy the mainstream chain and are very closely connected, the trading volume of the inter-bank market is tremendous, and the weight of its main trading varieties is extremely significant.

After the analysis of Figure 3, the result of the MST complex network can be clearly seen in Table 4, corresponding with Figure 3.

Table 4. The statistical features of the MST complex network of China's bond market.

Bond	Degree	Closeness Centrality	Betweenness Centrality	Eigen Centrality
CDB	5	0.38	0.72	1.00
ADB	3	0.36	0.54	0.73
STNAAA	4	0.32	0.50	0.65
CTBAAA	3	0.32	0.39	0.63
TREASURY	2	0.29	0.17	0.47
R007	2	0.29	0.09	0.44
BANKIDCAAA	3	0.27	0.32	0.44
CORPAAA	3	0.26	0.26	0.41
CSPREADSOE	1	0.28	0.00	0.37
IEB	1	0.27	0.00	0.27
STNAAP	1	0.25	0.00	0.25
RAILWAYB	1	0.25	0.00	0.25
ABSAAA	2	0.22	0.17	0.25
CTBAAP	1	0.24	0.00	0.24
GOVAAA	2	0.23	0.09	0.22
CORPAAP	2	0.21	0.09	0.21
BANKIDCAAP	1	0.22	0.00	0.18
DR007	1	0.22	0.00	0.17
BANKAAA	1	0.21	0.00	0.17
CFABSAAP	2	0.19	0.09	0.15
CORPAA	1	0.18	0.00	0.09
SHIBOR1Y	1	0.19	0.00	0.09
CFABSAAA	1	0.16	0.00	0.07

It is worth mentioning these new emerging indicators, especially the centrality. In a holistic view of the results in Table 4, CDB is undeniably the most important node in the MST complex network of China's bond market, due to its dominant position in relation to all four indicator rankings, including degree, closeness centrality, betweenness centrality and eigen centrality, showing that CDB not has only the most edges, but also the most influential neighbor nodes and the minimum average distance, proving that it is actually the central node of this complex network, thus demonstrating the systemic significance of China Development Bank. ADB is second to CDB, having the second highest centrality indicator performance, with a degree of 3. From the positions of CDB and ADB, it can clearly be seen that the bonds issued by China's policy banks have great influence in the bond market, and are also frequently traded in the inter-bank market. However, the third highest ranking bond according to all the indicators is a bond issued by the left policy bank named Export-Import Bank of China (short as IEB); the main reason for this might be that the trading volume of IEB is slightly smaller than CDB and ADB. STN occupies second place in degree ranking and third place in all the centrality indicator rankings. This might also be thanks to the fact that medium- and short-term notes (short as STN) exist as a type of bond, akin to a bridge between short-term bonds and long-term bonds. The ranking of the other bonds are mainly positively related to the liquidity and trading volume, in line with common sense regarding bond trading activities, and tin varieties traded in the inter-bank market have obvious privilege.

Combined with Figure 3 and Table 4, from the perspective of the importance of bonds issued by financial institutions, the ranking is as follows: China Development Bank (bond) > Agricultural Development Bank (bond) ≈ bonds issued by banks and short- and medium-term notes with a rating of AAA (one of the most important inter-bank market trading type) >= Export-Import Bank (bond). In terms of institutional systemic importance, the regulator and policymaker must guarantee the capital adequacy ratio of these core institutions and the requirements of the Basel III, which also called «International Convergence of Capital Measurement and Capital Standards».

As the most influential type of credit bond which could also be traded in the inter-bank bond market, urban investment bonds have their own special advantages called "urban investment beliefs" and a large transaction volume. These "beliefs" stem from the implicit guarantee from the local governments, and urban investment bonds are usually invested in government-related construction projects. To prevent systemic financial risks, the default risk of urban investment bonds needs to be carefully considered in the position of systemic importance, especially there are already a few urban investment bonds which have technically defaulted recently.

5.2. Dynamic Spillover Effect Analysis

It is generally accepted that the spillover effect will change over time, and the relevance of different markets may intensify or decrease under uncertain conditions and unexpected shocks. In other words, the full-sample spillover index mentioned in the previous section is static, and might ignore the impact brought about by various political and financial events, such as the European sovereign debt crisis in 2009 and the violent fluctuations and crash of the Chinese stock market in 2015. The impact of these events during the sample period will exacerbate the spillover effect between different participants in the market and the risk crossing into different markets.

Taking the possibilities mentioned above into account, it seems that any static model with a single fixed parameter cannot reflect the evolution of the entire interval of the sample over time. Therefore, this research uses the sliding window method to study the time-varying spillover effects of different bonds, and through the total spillover index corresponding to the time series evaluates the degree and main characteristics of dynamic spillover effects. From the perspective of econometrics, the forecast step and the accuracy are negatively correlated. Perron and Qu's research [51], which identified the structural change points of the dynamic spillover index series by the unit root test, used a 200-day sliding window and a 12-day forecast step. Taking the limitation of the number of observation points in the entire sample into account, retaining more instant spillover effect information in the bond market, this study uses a 150-day sliding window and a time-varying model with a 5-day forecast step to construct a dynamic volatility spillover index.

As Figure 4 depicts, the volatility of China's bond risk spillover index from 2015 to 2020 can be divided into three stages: (1) deleveraging policy proposed by state council, (2) China–US trade disputes, and (3) outbreak of COVID-19. From the perspective of bond systemic risks represented by changes in dynamic volatility spillover variance decomposition coefficients, with the expansion of China's bond market and the continuous improvement of regulations issued by the governments, as well as with the gradual decline of real interest rates, the overall systemic risk trend falls slightly, and it is undeniable that the "Deleveraging policy" proposed by State Council played an important role in this process. However, it can also be seen that the shock caused by the rapid spread of coronavirus (COVID-19) has had dramatic impacts on financial markets all over the world [52]. It has created an unprecedented level of risk, causing investors to suffer significant loses in a very short period of time. With the tight liquidity and related expectations of the financial market, the systemic risk of China's bond market has actually increased, while the risk has slightly decreased with the government's macro-control after a short time, while finally, with the overall economic expectations moving toward pessimism and the rise of the global epidemic, the systemic risks have demonstrated a raising trend again. These pronounced and persistent impacts of the coronavirus pandemic upon Chinese financial markets correspond with recent research [53,54]. At the same time, systemic risks show a certain seasonal effect, which is related to the characteristics of liquidity changes in the bond market itself.

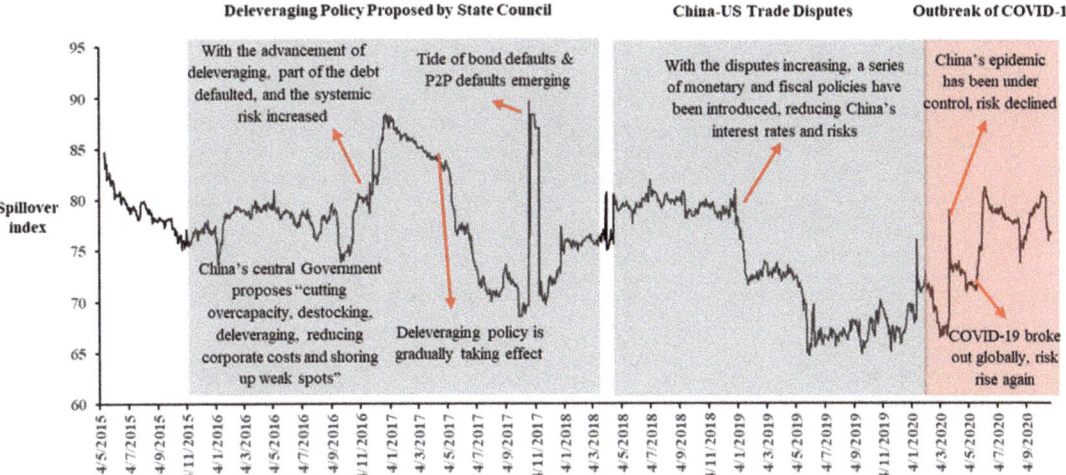

Figure 4. The dynamic evolution and trend of spillover effect of China's bond market, including description of shock events (15 December 2014–28 October 2020).

To test the robustness of the results of dynamic spillover effect analysis, several hyperparameters were applied for comparison: forecast horizons (i.e., h = 4, 5, 6 days) and rolling window width (i.e., w = 140, 150, 160 days). In Figure 5, it is shown that the spillover index of China's bond market follows a similar volatility pattern for the different values of h and w, concluding that the results of the study are robust regarding consistency.

In addition, to make the results more convincing and robust, possible future research could be expanded into several areas, such as the robustness of other methods or conducting dynamic analysis of networks [55].

To verify the analysis of the dynamic spillover effect of China's bond market and to discover the complexity of the bond market as a complex system, we calculated the structural entropy in a moving time window, which has a length of 150 days with a step size of 1 day, meaning that 1326 observations of structural entropy were generated. It is worth mentioning that from Figure 3a and Table 3, we can see that the complex network is an all-connected network, which means that the structural entropy of the network would be constant, making it worthless for the study, so the authors decided to cut some edges of weak connections, standing for the low spillover effect, to calculate the structural entropy. After observing the spillover coefficient distribution in Table 3, combining the analysis of the data correlation coefficient distribution and multiple adjustment attempts, it was found that the empirical result is relatively clear when the threshold is set to 5 percent, so the threshold was set at 5 percent, which means the edge between node i and j would exist only if w_{ij} in Formula (8) ≥ 5 percent, otherwise the edge would be cut off. After the calculation from Formula (11), the result is shown as Figure 6:

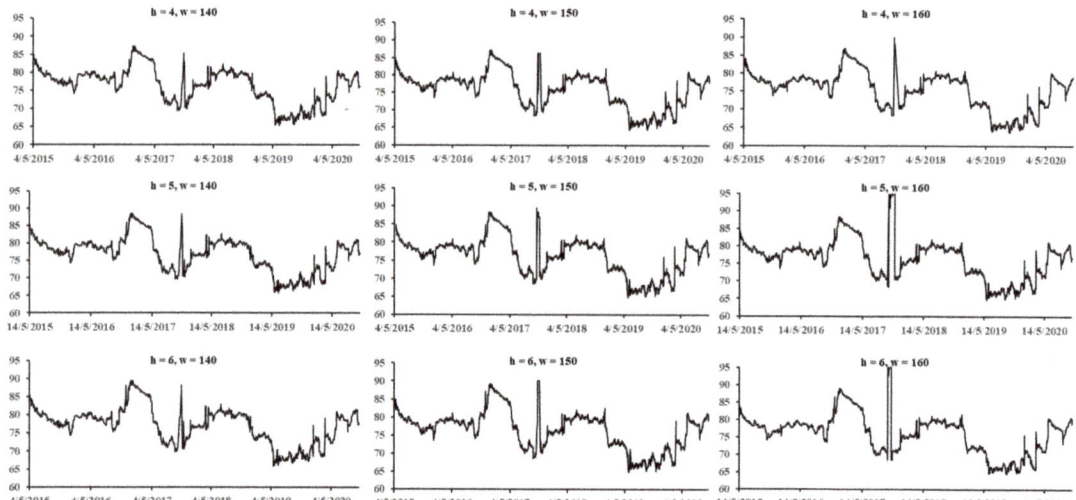

Figure 5. Robustness result of dynamic spillover effect of China's bond market, with forecast step = 4, 5, 6 days and time window = 140, 150, 160 days.

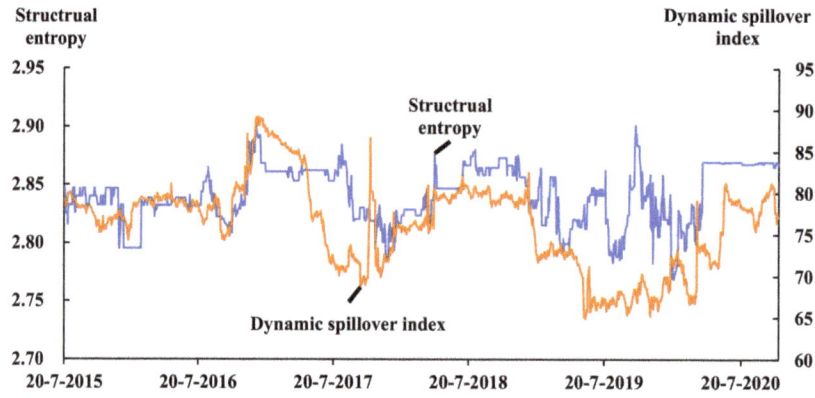

Figure 6. The complexity of the network of China's bond market and the dynamic spillover effect of China's bond market, represented by the structural entropy and the spillover index, respectively.

In this study, the node number of the complex network is always 23; that is, the increase in system complexity caused by the increase in the number of the nodes, which is a very common phenomenon as an interference, does not appear in the research [21]. From Figure 6, we can see that the structural entropy and the dynamic spillover index has the similar pattern of the fluctuation. The correlation between the structural entropy and the spillover index is 0.451, and the p-value of the correlation is 0.0000, which means that the complexity of the complex network is statistically significantly positively correlated with the spillover index, and the result is statistically reliable. From this result, it can be concluded that, with the strengthening of the node connections within the network, the structural entropy, standing for the complexity of the complex network, will rise, while the systemic risk of China's bond market also increases. The structural entropy could also be used as an effective indicator to measure the systemic risk, especially in the financial systems, which means that structural entropy could be used as a useful risk indicator to guide investment activities and show investors changes in the financial market or risk in their investment portfolio. In the meantime, structural entropy could also be an important reference for financial market regulators to assess financial risks.

6. Discussion and Conclusions

In this research, we document the evolution of the dynamics of risk spillover networks based on the complex network of China's bond market by using daily interest rate data of representative bond categories in the Chinese bond market. At the very beginning, we construct an innovative correlation complex network and an MST network of China's bond market, and these studies conduct a dynamic analysis based on a generalized vector autoregressive model, for which the volatility spillover variance decomposition method has been used to construct a complex network, and we adopt the minimum spanning tree method to analyze the clear transmission path of each bond's interest rate and its volatility. Here are the main conclusions:

Firstly, it has been concluded that the importance of each bond type in the Chinese bond market is positively correlated with the main characteristics of bond-like liquidity, transaction volume, and credit rating, etc.

Secondly, the inter-bank market is the most important market in China's entire bond market, without any doubt. In addition, interest rate bonds, commercial bank bonds and urban investment bonds are important bond types with systemic importance, which can be clearly seen in the complex networks constructed by the static spillover index.

Thirdly, from Figures 4 and 6, we can see that the long-term trend of the dynamic spillover index of China's bond market falls in line with the pace of interest rate adjustments, while several macro events such as the COVID-19 epidemic could bring instant shock which might cause systemic risk in China's bond market, and furthermore, systemic risks show a certain seasonal effect. To hold the bottom line of preventing financial systemic risks in China's bond market, standard management, strict supervision, and timely regulation of the bond markets are required, and the structural entropy, as a useful indicator for the complex network of the financial system, also should be used in risk management and monitoring.

Based on the conclusions above, corresponding policy recommendations can be put forward:

First, it is recommended to strengthen the monitoring and early warning systems of the fluctuations of China's bond market, especially for the inter-bank market. The inter-bank market has the characteristics of large transaction volumes, a variety of bond trading types, and an upstream position of the capital. Drastic fluctuations in the inter-bank market will be transmitted to the downstream financial market, and even the real economy would be affected. In order to serve the real economy better, the supervision and regulation of the inter-bank market should be one of the top priorities in the work of policymakers, implementers and regulators.

Second, for issuers of the bonds with systemic importance in the volatility spillover network, the government and regulatory agencies of China should regard them as systemically important institutions in the network of bond market participants such as bond traders and market makers, and they need to propose higher standards of capital adequacy ratio and other requirements, to ensure that it can fully comply with the requirements of the Basel Agreement.

Third, investors in China's bond market need to pay more attention to the credit rating and liquidity of bonds. Moreover, they need to pay more attention to bonds that are traded in the inter-bank market, such as commercial bank bonds and urban investment bonds.

The above conclusions have profound policy-guiding significance. On the one hand, China's policymakers could comprehensively consider financial decisions related to China's bond market from a networked perspective, thereby optimizing relevant decisions; on the other hand, from the standpoint of the China's government, identifying economic areas which are closely related to China's bonds market and financial institutes which have systemic importance in a timely manner has great forward-looking guiding significance for China's government's goal of maintaining the bottom line of preventing systemic financial risks.

Author Contributions: Data curation, Z.L.; Formal analysis, K.G. and H.Z.; Funding acquisition, K.G.; Investigation, Z.L., K.G. and H.Z.; Methodology, K.G.; Software, Z.L. and N.W.; Supervision, K.G. and H.Z.; Writing—original draft, Z.L.; Writing—review and editing, Z.L., N.W. and K.G. All authors have read and agreed to the published version of the manuscript.

Funding: The authors would like to thank the support of a financial grant from the National Natural Science Foundation of China No. 71501175 and the Fundamental Research Funds for the Central Universities.

Institutional Review Board Statement: Not applicable.

Informed Consent Statement: Not applicable.

Data Availability Statement: All the data supporting reported results could be found in WIND.

Conflicts of Interest: The authors declare no conflict of interest. The funders had no role in the design of the study; in the collection, analyses, or interpretation of data; in the writing of the manuscript; or in the decision to publish the results.

References

1. Shen, Y. International risk transmission of stock market movements. *Econ. Model.* **2018**, *69*, 220–236. [CrossRef]
2. Fang, Y.; Jing, Z.; Shi, Y.; Zhao, Y. Financial spillovers and spillbacks: New evidence from China and G7 countries. *Econ. Model.* **2021**, *94*, 184–200. [CrossRef]
3. Sun, Y.; Hong, Y.; Wang, S. Out-of-sample forecasts of China's economic growth and inflation using rolling weighted least squares. *J. Manag. Sci. Eng.* **2019**, *4*, 1–11. [CrossRef]
4. Adrian, T.; Moench, E.; Shin, H.S. Macro Risk Premium and Intermediary Balance Sheet Quantities. *IMF Econ. Rev.* **2010**, *58*, 179–207. [CrossRef]
5. Tian, S.; Hamori, S. Time-varying price shock transmission and volatility spillover in foreign exchange, bond, equity, and commodity markets: Evidence from the United States. *North Am. J. Econ. Financ.* **2016**, *38*, 163–171. [CrossRef]
6. Schweitzer, F.; Fagiolo, G.; Sornette, D.; Vega-Redondo, F.; Vespignani, A.; White, D.R. Economic networks: New Chall. *Science* **2019**, *325*, 422–425. [CrossRef] [PubMed]
7. Battiston, S.; Caldarelli, G. Systemic risk in financial networks. *J. Financ. Manag. Mark. Inst.* **2013**, *1*, 129–154.
8. Ponta, L.; Cincotti, S. Traders' networks of interactions and structural properties of financial markets: An agent-based approach. *Complexity* **2018**, *2018*. [CrossRef]
9. Diebold, F.X.; Yilmaz, K. On the network topology of variance decompositions: Measuring the connectedness of financial firms. *J. Econom.* **2014**, *182*, 119–134. [CrossRef]
10. Su, J.-B. Value-at-risk estimates of the stock indices in developed and emerging markets including the spillover effects of currency market. *Econ. Model.* **2015**, *46*, 204–224. [CrossRef]
11. Dey, S.; Sampath, A. Returns, Volatility and Spillover—A Paradigm Shift in India? *North Am. J. Econ. Financ.* **2019**, *52*, 101110. [CrossRef]
12. Georgiadis, G. Determinants of global spillovers from US monetary policy. *J. Int. Money Financ.* **2016**, *67*, 41–46. [CrossRef]
13. Yang, Z.; Zhou, Y. Quantitative Easing and Volatility Spillovers across Countries and Asset Classes. *Manag. Sci.* **2015**, *63*, 333–354. [CrossRef]
14. Miranda-Agrippino, S.; Rey, H. US monetary policy and the global financial cycle. *Rev. Econ. Stud.* **2020**, *87*, 2754–2776. [CrossRef]
15. Morana, C.; Fabio, C.B. The Great Recession: US dynamics and spillovers to the world economy. *J. Bank. Financ.* **2010**, *36*, 1–13. [CrossRef]
16. Lyocsa, S.; Vyrost, T.; Baumohl, E. Return spillovers around the globe: A network approach. *Econ. Model.* **2019**, *77*, 133–146. [CrossRef]
17. Tsai, I.-C. The source of global stock market risk: A viewpoint of economic policy uncertainty. *Econ. Model.* **2017**, *60*, 122–131. [CrossRef]
18. Huo, R.; Ahmed, A.D. Return and volatility spillovers effects: Evaluating the impact of Shanghai-Hong Kong Stock Connect. *Econ. Model.* **2016**, *61*, 260–272. [CrossRef]
19. Narayan, P.K.; Narayan, S.; Prabheesh, K.P. Stock returns, mutual fund flows and spillover shocks. *Pac. Basin Financ. J.* **2014**, *29*, 146–162. [CrossRef]

20. Mensi, W.; Al-Yahyaee, K.H.; Hoon Kang, S. Time-varying volatility spillovers between stock and precious metal markets with portfolio implications. *Resour. Policy* **2017**, *53*, 88–102. [CrossRef]
21. Christiansen, C. Volatility-Spillover Effects in European Bond Markets. *Eur. Financ. Manag.* **2007**, *13*, 923–948. [CrossRef]
22. Dean, W.G.; Faff, R.W.; Loudon, G.F. Asymmetry in return and volatility spillover between equity and bond markets in Australia. *Pac. Basin Financ. J.* **2010**, *18*, 272–289. [CrossRef]
23. Junior, L.; Franca, I. Correlation of Financial Markets in Times of Crisis. *Phys. A Stat. Mech. Its Appl.* **2012**, *391*, 187–208.
24. Matesanz, D.; Torgler, B.; Dabat, G.; Ortega, G.J. Co-movements in commodity prices: A note based on network analysis. *Agric. Econ.* **2014**, *45*, 13–21. [CrossRef]
25. Zhu, S.-Z.; Wu, J.; Li, Z.-P. Research on The Volatility Spillover Effect among Foreign Exchange Market Stock Market and Bond Market in China: Based on VS-MSV and CoVaR Models. In Proceedings of the 2nd International Conference on Information Technologies and Electrical Engineering (ICITEE-2019), New York, NY, USA, 6–7 December 2019; pp. 1–5.
26. Bao, C.; Wu, D.; Li, J. Measuring systemic importance of banks considering risk interactions: An ANOVA-like decomposition method. *J. Manag. Sci. Eng.* **2020**, *5*, 23–42. [CrossRef]
27. Murialdo, P.; Ponta, L.; Carbone, A. Long-range dependence in financial markets: A moving average cluster entropy approach. *Entropy* **2020**, *22*, 634. [CrossRef]
28. Shi, Y.; Zheng, Y.; Guo, K.; Jin, Z.; Huang, Z. The Evolution Characteristics of Systemic Risk in China's Stock Market Based on a Dynamic Complex Network. *Entropy* **2020**, *22*, 614. [CrossRef]
29. Bielik, M. Entropy and Market Prediction with Technical Indicators. *Adv. Intell. Syst. Comput.* **2014**, *289*, 347–354.
30. Jovanovic, F.; Mantegna, R.N.; Schinckus, C. When financial economics influences physics: The role of Econophysics. *Int. Rev. Financ. Anal.* **2019**, *65*, 101378. [CrossRef]
31. Kutner, R.; Ausloos, M.; Grech, D.; Di Mateo, T.; Schinckus, C.; Stanley, E. Econophysics and sociophysics: Their milestones & challenges. *Phys. A Stat. Mech. Its Appl.* **2019**, *516*, 240–253.
32. Schinckus, C. Ising model, econophysics and analogies. *Phys. A Stat. Mech. Its Appl.* **2018**, *508*, 95–103. [CrossRef]
33. Diebold, F.X.; Yilmaz, K. Measuring financial asset return and volatility spillovers, with application to global equity markets. *Econ. J.* **2009**, *119*, 158–171. [CrossRef]
34. Diebold, F.X.; Yilmaz, K. Better to Give than to Receive: Predictive Directional Measurement of Volatility Spillovers. *Int. J. Forecast.* **2012**, *28*, 57–66. [CrossRef]
35. Liao, Z.; Wang, Z.; Guo, K. The dynamic evolution of the characteristics of exchange rate risks in countries along "The Belt and Road" based on network analysis. *PLoS ONE* **2019**, *14*, e0221874. [CrossRef]
36. Mehler, A.; Lücking, A.; Wei, P. A Network Model of Interpersonal Alignment in Dialog. *Entropy* **2010**, *12*, 1440–1483. [CrossRef]
37. Watts, D.; Strogatz, S. Collective Dynamics of 'Small-World' Networks. *Nature* **1998**, *393*, 440–442. [CrossRef] [PubMed]
38. Barabási, A.; Albert, R. Emergence of Scaling in Random Networks. *Science* **1999**, *286*, 509–512. [CrossRef] [PubMed]
39. Jackson, M. *Social and Economic Networks*; Princeton University Press: Princeton, NJ, USA, 2010.
40. Bonanno, G.; Vandewalle, N.; Mantegna, R.N. Taxonomy of stock market indices. *Phys. Rev. E* **2000**, *62*, R7615. [CrossRef] [PubMed]
41. Mark, M.D.; Omer, S.; Stacy, W.; Sam, H.; Johnson, N.F. Detecting a currency's dominance or dependence using foreign exchange network trees. *Phys. Rev. E* **2005**, *72*, 046106.
42. Onnela, J.P.; Chakraborti, A.; Kaski, K.; Kertesz, J.; Kanto, A. Dynamics of market correlations: Taxonomy and portfolio analysis. *Phys. Rev. E* **2003**, *68*, 056110. [CrossRef] [PubMed]
43. Mantegna, R.N. Information and hierarchical structure in financial markets. *Comput. Phys. Commun.* **1999**, *121–122*, 153–156. [CrossRef]
44. Cormen, T.; Leiserson, C.; Rivest, R.; Stein, C. *Introduction to Algorithms*, 3rd ed.; The MIT Press: London, UK, 2009.
45. Lu, K.; Yang, Q.; Chen, G. Singular cycles and chaos in a new class of 3D three-zone piecewise affine systems. *Chaos* **2019**, *29*, 043124. [CrossRef] [PubMed]
46. Boccaletti, S.; Latora, V.; Moreno, Y.; Chavez, M.; Hwang, D.U. Complex networks: Structure and dynamics. *Phys. Rep.* **2006**, *424*, 175–308. [CrossRef]
47. Freeman, L.C. Centrality in social networks conceptual clarification. *Soc. Netw.* **1978**, *1*, 215–239. [CrossRef]
48. Freeman, L.C. A set of measures of centrality based on betweenness. *Sociometry* **1977**, *40*, 35–41. [CrossRef]
49. Solá, L.; Romance, M.; Criado, R.; Flores, J.; García del Amo, A.; Boccaletti, S. Eigenvector centrality of nodes in multiplex networks. *Chaos Interdiscip. J. Nonlinear Sci.* **2013**, *23*, 033131. [CrossRef]
50. Bonacich, P. Some unique properties of eigenvector centrality—ScienceDirect. *Soc. Netw.* **2007**, *29*, 555–564. [CrossRef]
51. Perron, P.; Qu, Z. A simple modification to improve the finite sample properties of Ng and Perron's unit root tests. *Econ. Lett.* **2007**, *94*, 12–19. [CrossRef]
52. He, Q.; Liu, J.; Wang, S.; Yu, J. The impact of COVID-19 on stock markets. *Econ. Political Stud.* **2020**, *8*, 275–288. [CrossRef]
53. Corbet, S.; Hou, Y.G.; Hu, Y.; Oxley, L.; Xu, D. Pandemic-related financial market volatility spillovers: Evidence from the Chinese COVID-19 epicentre. *Int. Rev. Econ. Financ.* **2021**, *71*, 55–81. [CrossRef]

54. Liu, X.; Liu, Y.; Yan, Y. China macroeconomic report 2020: China's macroeconomy is on the rebound under the impact of COVID-19. *Econ. Political Stud.* **2020**, *8*, 395–435. [CrossRef]
55. Ferreira, P.; Tilfani, O.; Pereira, É.; Tavares, C.; Pereira, H.; Boukfaoui, M.Y.E. Dynamic Connectivity in a Financial Network Using Time-Varying DCCA Correlation Coefficients. *Econom. Res. Financ.* **2021**, *6*, 57–75.

Article

Coherence and Entropy of Credit Cycles across the Euro Area Candidate Countries

Adina Criste [1], Iulia Lupu [1,*] and Radu Lupu [2,3]

1 "Victor Slavescu" Centre for Financial and Monetary Research, Romanian Academy, 050711 Bucharest, Romania; a.criste@icfm.ro
2 Department of International Business and Economics, Bucharest University of Economic Studies, 010404 Bucharest, Romania; radu.lupu@rei.ase.ro
3 Institute for Economic Forecasting, Romanian Academy, 050711 Bucharest, Romania
* Correspondence: iulia_lupu@icfm.ro

Abstract: The pattern of financial cycles in the European Union has direct impacts on financial stability and economic sustainability in view of adoption of the euro. The purpose of the article is to identify the degree of coherence of credit cycles in the countries potentially seeking to adopt the euro with the credit cycle inside the Eurozone. We first estimate the credit cycles in the selected countries and in the euro area (at the aggregate level) and filter the series with the Hodrick–Prescott filter for the period 1999Q1–2020Q4. Based on these values, we compute the indicators that define the credit cycle similarity and synchronicity in the selected countries and a set of entropy measures (block entropy, entropy rate, Bayesian entropy) to show the high degree of heterogeneity, noting that the manifestation of the global financial crisis has changed the credit cycle patterns in some countries. Our novel approach provides analytical tools to cope with euro adoption decisions, showing how the coherence of credit cycles can be increased among European countries and how the national macroprudential policies can be better coordinated, especially in light of changes caused by the pandemic crisis.

Keywords: credit-to-GDP gap; coherence; similarity; synchronicity; Central and Eastern European countries; entropy

Citation: Criste, A.; Lupu, I.; Lupu, R. Coherence and Entropy of Credit Cycles across the Euro Area Candidate Countries. *Entropy* **2021**, *23*, 1213. https://doi.org/10.3390/e23091213

Academic Editor: Joanna Olbryś

Received: 29 July 2021
Accepted: 11 September 2021
Published: 14 September 2021

Publisher's Note: MDPI stays neutral with regard to jurisdictional claims in published maps and institutional affiliations.

Copyright: © 2021 by the authors. Licensee MDPI, Basel, Switzerland. This article is an open access article distributed under the terms and conditions of the Creative Commons Attribution (CC BY) license (https://creativecommons.org/licenses/by/4.0/).

1. Introduction

Lending activity, which is subject to medium-term fluctuations, is one of the determining factors influencing financial stability, with excessive growth in lending activity over a period being an important signal of risk accumulation. Under the European economic integration process, financial stability and the dynamics of financial activity have increased importance. In addition to the traditional criteria of nominal economic convergence, euro area candidate countries should also take into account how their economies are prepared to join the monetary union. The synchronization of business cycles is already a much debated issue as a criterion for achieving an optimal monetary area, both theoretically and in practice, as discussed in many empirical studies; however, the synchronization of financial cycles in a monetary area is a relative recent topic. The global financial crisis has been a key factor in the increasing interest in the dynamics of lending and the financial cycle, including in European countries.

The credit cycle, which is a common way to empirically measure the financial cycle [1], is an important element that can explain the differences between countries both in terms of economic growth and stability, as well as the effects of political decisions. Moreover, Borio [1] emphasizes the importance of understanding the manifestation of the financial cycle, which is best evidenced by fluctuations in lending activity and property prices, as a premise for understanding fluctuations in economic activity and political challenges. The financial cycle was closely linked to increases in financing and intermediation in the advanced economies in the 1970s, which caused severe recessions, boom and bust cycles, and financial instability, and also to an exponential increase in cross-border lending [2].

At the level of a monetary area, the analysis of the coherence of economic and financial cycles is particularly relevant, given the conditions of the single monetary policy regime. Differences between countries in terms of business cycles increase the need for the central bank to act in accordance with the "one-size-fits-all" principle for monetary policy decisions, given that the same decision produces different effects. In this way, the divergence between economic and financial cycles can be deepened, affecting the stability of the monetary area. Moreover, the financial cycle can affect the process of convergence in a monetary area by misallocating resources to less developed countries in the union if boom–bust cycles occur, as reflected by very large amplitudes. In this regard, Oman [2] points out that the financial cycle could have played an important role in the real economic divergence between the euro area member countries since the introduction of the euro. As a result of the boom–bust lending cycles in the peripheral countries of the Eurozone, resources have been misallocated in these economies, with productivity gains being affected.

In addition to the differences between business and financial cycles, there is also the problem of differences among countries and within them, because they can create tensions and can affect the objectives of macroeconomic stabilization and financial stability.

The synchronization of financial cycles is important in the process of joining a monetary area, in implementing the macroprudential policy, and in the relationship between the macroprudential authorities at the national level and those at the level of the monetary area.

A relatively recent study by Samarina et al. [3] addressed the issue of the coherence of financial cycles within the euro area, although it would be interesting to address this issue for euro area candidate countries, given that they are in the process of joining the monetary union.

Based on the above observations and the importance of the coherence of financial cycles within a monetary area, this article aims to determine the degree of coherence of credit cycles in euro area candidate countries with the euro area credit cycle, which is taken as a reference. As described in the literature [3], the terms financial cycle and credit cycle are frequently used interchangeably, and for this reason we also adopt this approach, without excluding other empirical estimation methods; however, we often use the credit cycle wording to emphasize the chosen estimation method.

After estimating the credit cycles in the selected countries and in the euro area (at aggregate level) by using the Hodrick–Prescott filter, similarity and synchronicity indicators are calculated in the selected countries for the period 1999Q1–2020Q4. The investigation of the dynamics of these variables is further developed by using a set of entropy measures designed for certain time series. Our objectives are three-fold: first, we compute entropy measures for the filtered individual series of credit-to-GDP gap variables for the six euro area candidate countries addressed in our analysis (the block entropy and the entropy rate); second, we compute measures of entropy (transfer entropy) for the same variables in combination with the filtered credit-to-GDP indicator for the euro zone level; third, we estimate a Bayesian entropy measure for the similarity indicators of credit cycle gaps with respect to the euro zone.

The results show that a long period of low entropy before the commencement of the financial crisis matches the period in which the coherence of credit cycles of the euro area candidate countries is lower. After the crisis, the entropy is heightened, along with the degree of credit cycle coherence, particularly in terms of synchronization. We provide evidence of a high degree of heterogeneity in the dynamics of these variables and develop an analysis toolkit that is necessary to support euro adoption decisions. This data-driven set of indicators will enhance the current convergence gauges and provide new perspectives on the success of euro adoption scenarios.

In this article, we present the main landmarks from the literature in Section 2, while descriptions of the methodology and data used are given in Section 3. The obtained results are presented and interpreted in Section 4, while the main conclusions of the study are presented in Section 5.

2. Literature Review

The first studies on financial cycles were conducted by Borio et al. [4] and Borio et al. [5], although concerns have intensified since the onset of the global financial crisis. Come studies have addressed the issue of how to measure financial cycles, while others have analyzed the degree of synchronization in a group of countries [6,7], including at the level of a monetary area [3,8]. In addition, some papers have analyzed the synchronization between business and financial cycles. Among these, we mention the work of Oman [2], who focused on developed European countries, namely those that are in the euro area, as well as the work of Miteski and Georgievska [9], who analyzed emerging European countries.

A number of recent studies involving the measurement of the financial or credit cycle have differed in terms of the indicators used (credit-to-GDP or real credit in log) and the method used to obtain the credit cycle; thus, similar methods are used to measure the credit cycle to those used to measure business cycles, either by applying the turning points method [10] or frequency-based (band pass) filters [11]. Other studies have also used more complex methodologies, as mentioned by Schüler et al. [6] and Borio et al. [12].

Among the studies dedicated to the analysis of financial cycles, it is important to mention those that have analyzed European countries as benchmarks for this article. The paper by Samarina et al. [3] was particularly noteworthy, which aimed to find out whether the adoption of the euro has led to convergence of financial cycles between member states. The analysis took into account 16 Eurozone member states, including new member states (Slovakia, Slovenia, Malta, and Estonia), for a period of 25 years (1990–2015). The lending cycle was broken down into three components: total bank credit, household mortgage lending, and non-financial business loans. The authors concluded that in recent decades, both mortgage and corporate loan cycles have diverged. The study emphasized the importance of differentiating by types of credit to gain knowledge of the credit cycle, along with the importance of differentiating the transmission channels of the effects of euro adoption.

For the European Union countries, Stremmel and Zsámboki [7] noted that the amplitude of the financial cycle is largely determined by the structural characteristics of the financial sector in these states, namely the degree of concentration, share of foreign banks in the banking system, level of lending, the structure of bank loans, as well as financial integration.

Analyzing the evolution of financial and business cycles in the period 1971–2015 (on the basis of quarterly data) for the founding member countries of the Eurozone (except Luxembourg), Oman [2] showed that indigenous financial cycles (specific to each country) tend to be much broader than business cycles, noting the concordance with the results obtained by Drehmann et al. [10] and Galati et al. [13]. Additionally, during the period under review, the synchronization of financial cycles in euro area countries was weaker than that of business cycles. After the introduction of the euro, the degree of synchronization of the business cycles as an average measure of the euro area countries increased over time, while the synchronization of the financial cycles decreased on average.

Regarding the characteristics of financial cycles in euro area countries, recent results [2,6] have shown the existence of a high level of heterogeneity of financial cycles between European countries. On the other hand, Oman [2] pointed out that during the financial crisis, the synchronization of the financial cycle increased on average for their sample, reinforcing the observation made by Stremmel and Zsámboki [7], namely that the euro area countries have a lower degree of divergence, while in normal periods that financial cycles have a lower degree of synchronization.

The heterogeneous nature of financial cycles is also noticeable for other monetary areas. For example, by analyzing the issue of the coherence of financial cycles within the West African Economic and Monetary Union (WAEMU), Gammadigbe [8] showed that during the period 2005Q1–2020Q4, the national financial cycles were heterogeneous in terms of both duration and amplitude, with no convergence of financial cycles.

Some of the important benchmarks in the literature for our research are the methods used to measure the coherence of financial cycles. Aikman et al. [11] used the standard correlation coefficient of credit deviation, while Meller and Metiu [14] applied a concordance index. As mentioned by Samarina et al. [3], the disadvantage of these methods is the fact that the two dimensions of a cycle (amplitude and frequency) are not considered separately.

Regarding the issue of business cycle coherence, the studies by Harding and Pagan [15] and Mink et al. (2011) are good benchmarks for measuring the coherence of financial cycles, given that the two dimensions that define the coherence or concordance of cycles—synchronization and similarity—are assessed separately using the proposed methodologies. While cycle synchronization refers to the frequency of fluctuations, similarity is defined by the amplitude of the fluctuations. The difference between the two methodologies lies in the chosen indicator—while Harding and Pagan (2006) use the level of GDP to determine the business cycle, Mink et al. [16] use the deviation of the GDP (output gap).

The importance of financial cycles can also be seen from the perspective of the application of macroprudential instruments meant to correct possible threats to financial stability, as signaled by the evolution of the financial cycle [1]. In this sense, Samarina et al. [3] emphasized the need to capitalize on macroprudential policy instruments, given that the results of their study showed a fairly large divergence of lending cycles in the euro area. Oman [2] showed that the macroprudential instruments used for correcting the financial cycle complement those intended to correct the business cycle, especially since the two are not always synchronized.

The role played by entropy in financial research has been shown by Zhou, Cai, and Tong [17]. The authors emphasized the use of information and probability entropy as important instruments for portfolio selection issues and asset pricing, although they encouraged a wider application of different types of entropy in finance, as the results were mostly consistent with the original models, which opened up new investigation directions. With the aim of constructing a network of influences in the global financial sector, Sandoval [18] performed transfer entropy measures, showing that the 197 largest financial companies are related and obtaining stricter results than those that were obtained when the companies were analyzed through correlations. In order to compute a system credit factor, Xu and Ren [19] used the cross entropy, with their results supporting the idea of applying entropy measures to study credit cycles. In another study, the synchronization of business cycles was analyzed via the implementation of a pairwise maximum entropy model for the G7 member countries [20], showing that this is an appropriate method for small economic systems.

From the analysis of the literature, it is noted that most of the previous studies have taken into account countries with advanced economies. From this point of view, this article expands the research area in this field. Moreover, the topic of cycle coherence is relevant not only in the case of a monetary union such as the euro area, but also for countries that are about to join a monetary union, namely candidate countries for the euro area.

3. Materials and Methods

The analysis of the financial cycle in the euro area candidate countries took into account bank lending, considering the predominance of this sector in these countries, namely Bulgaria, Croatia, Czech Republic, Hungary, Poland, and Romania.

Quarterly data were extracted from the central banks' statistics for the selected countries (regarding the bank credit to the private non-financial sector) and from the Eurostat database (for GDP) for the period 1999Q1–2020Q2. Data for the euro area at the aggregate level were taken from the BIS database.

This paper had three research topics:

(1) Assessing the trajectory of credit cycles in euro area candidate countries;
(2) Assessing the coherence levels of the credit cycles in these countries with the euro area credit cycle;
(3) Performing an entropy analysis.

3.1. Estimation of the Credit Cycle

Statistical data were taken from the Eurostat and central bank databases for the period 1999–2020. In our analysis, bank credit was considered, given that in the selected countries the banking system is dominant in relation to the non-banking system [9]. Quarterly and seasonally unadjusted GDP data were taken from the Eurostat database, while the volume of bank lending to the private non-financial sector was calculated based on data provided by the central banks of the euro area candidate countries. In order to avoid the transition period, marked by major changes in the profiles of the selected economies, the time interval of 1999Q1–2020Q4 was chosen.

The credit cycle was estimated using the Hodrick–Prescott (HP) filter method. The HP filter estimates the credit cycle for euro area candidate countries by computing the credit-to-GDP gap.

The HP filter isolates the cyclical component (c_t) from the trend ($Trend_t$) of a non-stationary series

$$(y_t)_{t=0}^n \tag{1}$$

so that

$$y_t = Trend_t + c_t. \tag{2}$$

This isolation method is based on a minimization problem of the form:

$$\min_{T_1,\ldots,T_1} \left\{ \sum_{t=1}^n (y_t - Trend_t)^2 + \lambda \sum_{t=2}^{T-1} [(Trend_{t+1} - Trend_t c_t) - (Trend_t - Trend_{t-1})]^2 \right\} \tag{3}$$

The adjustment parameter or smoothing factor λ corrects the deviations from the trend and is a factor chosen by the user, depending on the frequency of the data. The following values are used for the business cycle: $\lambda = 100$ (for annual data), $\lambda = 1.600$ (for quarterly data), $\lambda = 14.400$ (for monthly data).

According to the literature, the indicator that reflects the credit cycle very well is the credit-to-GDP gap or the deviation of the Basel indicator from the long-run statistical trend, which is performed following three steps:

(1) Computing the credit-to-GDP percentage ratio in year T;
(2) Estimating the credit-to-GDP trend;
(3) Finding the "Basel gap".

Equation (4) describes the credit-to-GDP ratio at the quarterly level, q_t, as the ratio between the bank lending to the private non-financial sector (firms and households) in the q_t quarter and the cumulated GDP for four quarters prior to the quarterly credit calculation date, according to the methodology used by the Bank for International Settlements (BIS):

$$(Credit/GDP)_{q_t} = \frac{C_{bp}[q_t(T)]}{\sum_{n=t}^{t+3} GDP_n(T-1)} * 100, \tag{4}$$

where:
- q_t = quarter t, $t \in \{1; 2; 3; 4\}$;
- T = year T, $T \in \{1999; 2000; \ldots\; 2020\}$;
- C_{bp} = bank credit to the private non-financial sector
- GDP_n = quarterly and seasonally unadjusted GDP data.

For this estimation, a higher adjustment parameter was used for the credit cycle ($\lambda = 25,000$) compared to the business cycle case, in which the parameter corresponding to the quarterly period was lower (λ = 1600). This was justified by the fact that the financial cycle (with the credit cycle being a major component of the financial cycle) generally lasts about four times longer than the business cycle. On the other hand, BIS recommends a much higher parameter (λ = 400.000) for longer time series over 20 years. Moreover, recent research [21] confirmed the need to use a lower smoothing factor (λ) than that proposed by the BIS for economies with shorter financial cycles or lower levels of financial development (short financial depth), such as the emerging European countries or the transition countries. For the euro area, taken as a reference here, the smoothing factor is the one recommended by the BIS.

The credit-to-GDP gap is measured in GDP percentage units, according to the formula:

$$\left(\frac{Credit}{GDP}\right)gap_{q_t} = -\left[1 - \frac{R\left(\frac{Credit}{GDP}\right)_{q_t}}{Trend\left(\frac{Credit}{GDP}\right)_{q_t}}\right], \quad (5)$$

where:

$$R\left(\frac{Credit}{GDP}\right)_{q_t} \quad (6)$$

is the actual credit-to-GDP ratio in q_t and:

$$Trend\left(\frac{Credit}{GDP}\right)_{q_t} \quad (7)$$

is the long-term trend for credit-to-GDP ratio in q_t (estimated according to the HP filter for λ = 25.000).

3.2. The Credit Cycle Coherence

The credit cycle coherence is estimated following the methodology used by Mink et al. [16] considering the two components, i.e., the degrees of synchronization and similarity, while the benchmark used for this measurement is the euro area, as the region in which the countries from our sample are to be integrated.

We note $c_i(t)$ as the credit deviation for country i in period t (quarter) and $c_r(t)$ as the credit deviation for the euro area, taken as reference r, in the same period t.

The degree of synchronization between the credit cycle of a country i, $c_i(t)$, and the reference ($c_r(t)$) at time t is given by the formula:

$$syn_{ir}(t) = \frac{c_i(t)c_r(t)}{|c_i(t)c_r(t)|}. \quad (8)$$

The value of the coefficient, ± 1, indicates the direction of the credit cycle for i with respect to the reference. The positive value shows synchronization, while the negative value shows desynchronization (the two trajectories move in opposite directions). The degree of synchronization over 1999Q1–2020Q4 is calculated as the arithmetic mean of the values registered during this period.

The degree of similarity ($sym_{ir}(t)$) is the difference in amplitude between the credit deviation for i and the reference deviation, according to the formula:

$$sym_{ir}(t) = 1 - \frac{c_i(t) - c_r(t)}{\frac{1}{n}\sum_{i=1}^{n}|c_i(t)|}, \quad sym_{ir}(t) \in [1-n;\ 1] \quad (9)$$

A value of 1 shows that the two compared credit cycles (of country i and of reference r) have the same amplitude. The value of $1 - n$ is recorded when the values of the two indicators (country i and reference r) have opposite signs and the gap for all other countries is zero.

3.3. The Entropy Approach

As recently emphasized [22], the application of the entropy approach in economics is considered a "factor of progress", while mixing standard economic methodological approaches with natural science investigation tools is perceived as a factor for economic research development [23].

Block entropy is based on Shannon entropy [24], which is implemented on time series with *k* histories and is calculated as follows:

$$H\left(X^{(k)}\right) = -\sum_{x_i^{(k)}} p\left(x_i^{(k)}\right) log_2 p\left(x_i^{(k)}\right), \qquad (10)$$

where X is a random variable, x_i is the iteration i of the time series described by the variable X, and k denotes the histories of the time series (the block size). The probability of observing $x_i^{(k)}$ is itemized $p\left(x_i^{(k)}\right)$. According to this specification, Hlavackova-Shindler et al. [25] interpreted the Shannon entropy indicator as the "quantity of surprise one should feel upon reading the result of a measurement", which is directly proportional to uncertainty. For the application on the time series, we will interpret this indicator as the level of surprise to expect at each moment in time.

The entropy rate, also known as the source information rate, represents the entropy of the time series, in this case conditioned by the *k*-histories. In other words, it measures the quantity of needed information in order to display the $X^{(k)}$ observations. The global entropy rate is obtained from the average of the local entropy:

$$H_X(k) = h_{X,i}(k)_i = \sum_{x_i^{(k)}, x_{i+1}} p\left(x_i^{(k)}, x_{i+1}\right) log_2 \frac{p\left(x_i^{(k)}, x_{i+1}\right)}{p\left(x_i^{(k)}\right)}, \qquad (11)$$

as suggested by Cover and Thomas [26].

Two decades ago, Schreiber [27] led in the transfer entropy to measure the information that is transferred between the source and destination, taking into account the background of the system, denoted with W [28]. A local time variant is used to define the transfer entropy:

$$t_{X \to Y, W, i}(k) = log_2 \frac{p\left(y_{i+1}, x_i | y_i^{(k)}, W_{\{1,i\}}\right), \ldots, W_{\{l,i\}}}{p\left(y_{i+1} | y_i^{(k)}, W_{\{l,i\}}\right) p(x_i | y_i^{(k)}, W_{\{1,i\}}, \ldots, W_{\{l,i\}})}. \qquad (12)$$

The methodology for Bayesian entropy was previously described by Lupu et al. [29], following the study by Archer, Park, and Pillow [30]. In the estimation process of the Bayesian entropy (denoted H), we take into account that this is a deterministic function of a discrete distribution (π), which is influenced by parameter θ. Given that $p(\pi)$ is a prior distribution, $p(\pi|x)$ represents the posterior distribution over π, $p(x|\pi)$ designates the discrete likelihood, and H has a deterministic relation with π, we may consider the following expressions:

$$p(H|\pi) = \delta\left(H + \sum_i \pi_i log \pi_i\right) \qquad (13)$$

$$\hat{H}(x) = \mathbb{E}[H|x] = \int H(\pi) p(H|\pi) p(\pi|x) d\pi, \qquad (14)$$

where the last expression is the form for Bayes' least squares estimators.

The computation of these entropy indicators required the discretization of our data, for which we followed the method of Archer, Park, and Pillow [30]. The dynamic values were obtained by using a rolling window of four observations, which was equivalent to one year, given that we used quartrly data.

4. Results

The results obtained based on the HP filter method showed a rather varied picture of credit cycles in the countries considered (see Figure 1).

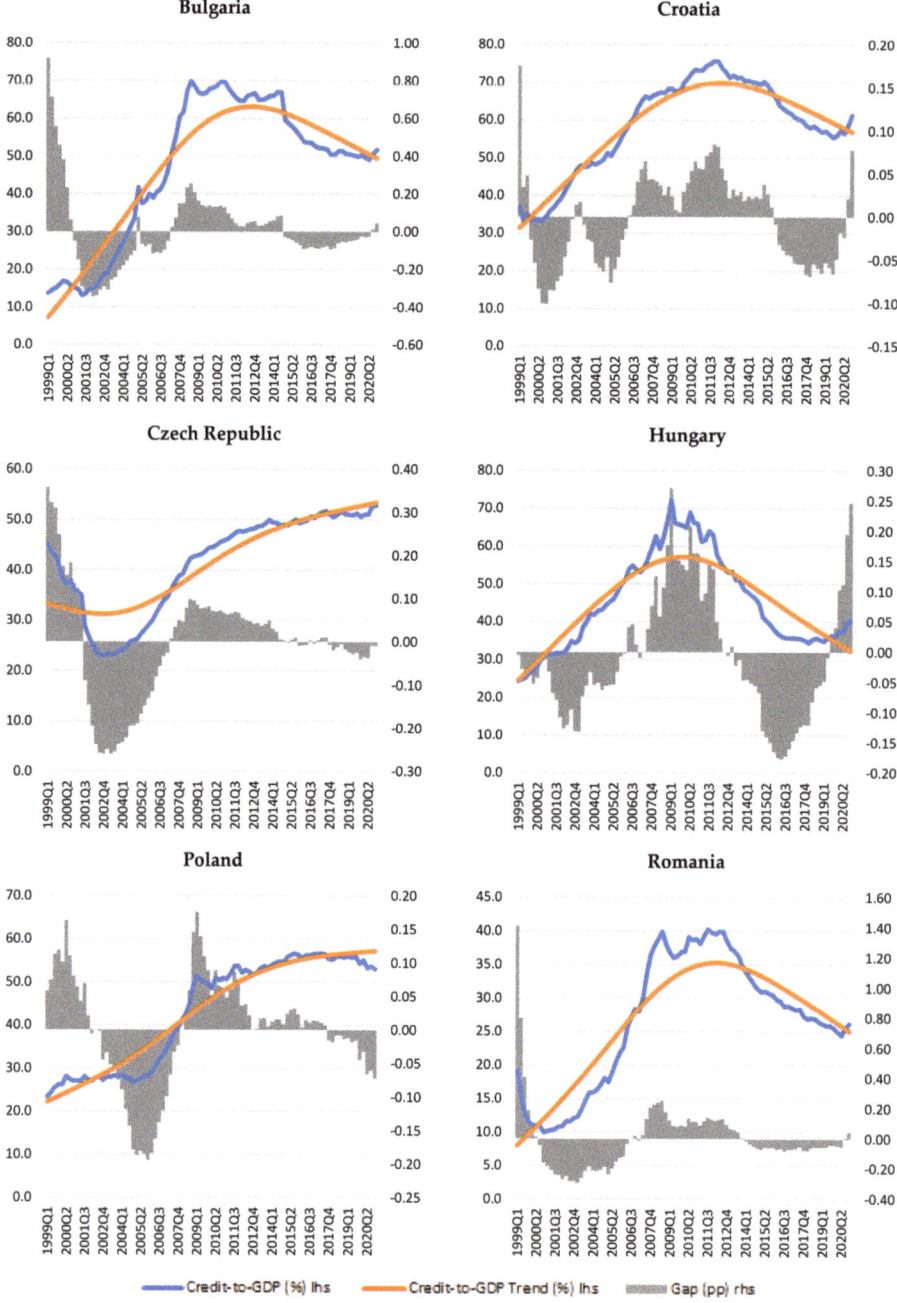

Figure 1. The bank credit cycle in the euro area candidate countries.

According to these charts (Figure 1), similar curves can be seen for Bulgaria, Croatia, Hungary, and Romania in an ascending–descending pattern, while on the other hand the Czech Republic and Poland show an ascending pattern throughout the period, especially after 2001.

Croatia, Poland, and the Czech Republic show small deviations from the trend throughout the period under review. In Hungary, there are higher levels of credit-to-GDP gaps after 2007 as compared to those recorded in the first part of the analyzed interval.

Although overall the euro area candidate countries do not have synchronized credit trajectories, it can be observed that the periods in which the credit-to-GDP gaps are positive re relatively the same for Bulgaria, Romania, and the Czech Republic (1999–2001 and 2007–2014, respectively), provided that the amplitudes are different. The highest amplitudes are shown for Bulgaria and Romania, especially in the first year (see Figure 1).

The Shannon entropies computed over the preceding year (previous four observations) for each of the six countries with filtered credit gaps provide information about the level of surprise to expect at each moment in time (Figure 2). We note that there are approximately three main regimes for Croatia and Romania, four main regimes for Bulgaria and Czech Republic, and even more for Hungary and Poland.

The most volatile series belongs to the Croatian credit-to-GDP gaps, while in Romania the stable stages are longer. We notice that these regimes do not exhibit a simultaneous structure, i.e., the credit cycles tend not to be very entropic or less entropic in the same time across these countries. For instance, the COVID-19 period tends to produce large levels of entropy in Croatia, the Czech Republic, Poland, and Hungary, but not so much in Bulgaria and Romania, which seem to continue the dynamics described by the HP filter. If we connect the concept of entropy with the idea of uncertainty, then we can say that, except for Bulgaria and Romania, the countries in our sample exhibit higher uncertainty during the pandemic period.

Further data can be revealed by observing the entropy rate, which shows the amount of information needed to describe the values of a certain variable given a sequence of observations (rolling window) from its past. The size of the rolling window is four in our case, which extends to the length of one year. Under this specification, the high levels of this indicator will correspond to situations where uncertainty existing in the data series is elevated, depicting a moment when the time series are impacted by factors that are suddenly activated or deactivated.

We note that for each of the series of gaps from credit-to-GDP variables, the values are quite volatile (Figure 3).

High levels of volatility are especially observed for Croatia, Hungary, and Poland. Romania, on the other hand, exhibits only two spikes in the dynamics of its corresponding series, revealing a rather steady entropy rate that could be caused by the fact that it has the lowest credit-to-GDP ratio among the countries in our sample.

As in the previous analysis (the Shannon entropy), no simultaneity effects can be observed for the large values of the entropy rate; however, except for Romania and Bulgaria, the pandemic period exhibits either spikes or increased volatility of this indicator.

Noting the scale of the vertical axes for these charts, we can conclude that volatility compensate for jumps. In other words, the large volatility (present for Croatia, Hungary, and Poland) also reduces the large values, as these variables do not show such large extremes as the other three countries (Figure 3).

The coherence of the credit cycles in terms of synchronicity and similarity is displayed both in Table 1, as the average values over 1999Q1–2020Q4 for these two variables, and in Table 2, with the values computed for two sub periods, i.e., before and after the global financial crisis.

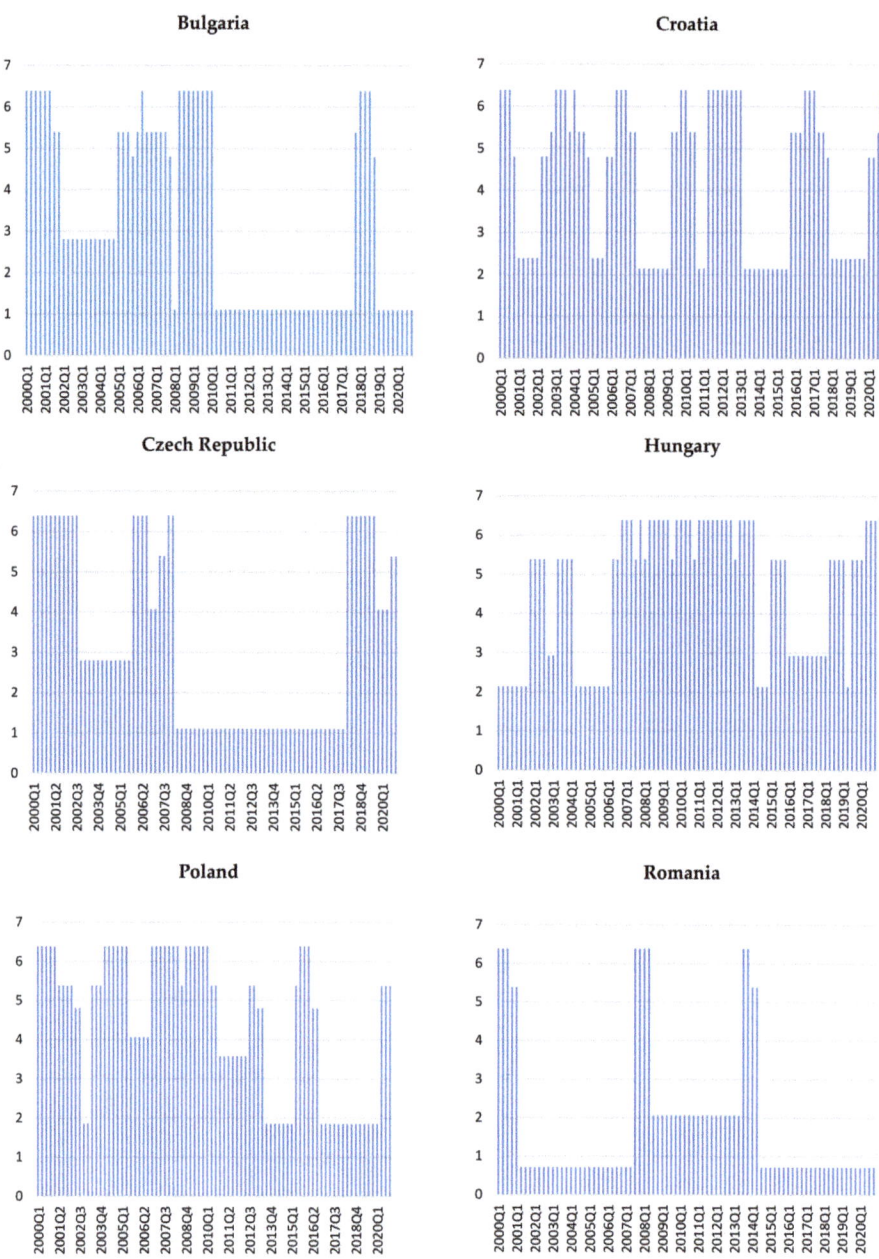

Figure 2. Shannon entropies for filtered credit gaps.

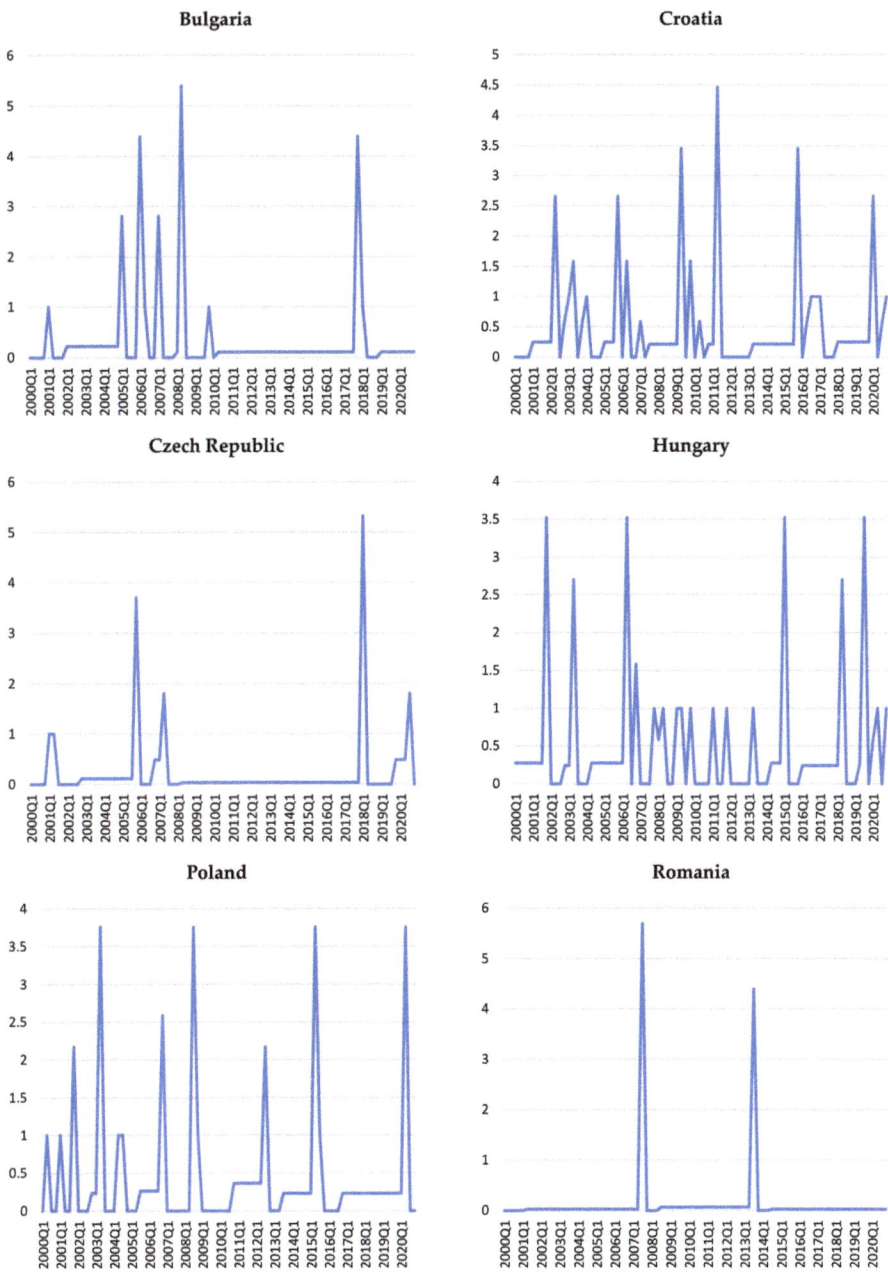

Figure 3. The entropy rates for filtered credit gaps.

Table 1. The credit cycle coherence levels for euro area candidate countries with the euro area for 1999Q1–2020Q4 [1].

	Synchronicity	Similarity
Croatia	0.773	0.638
Romania	0.545	−0.072
Bulgaria	0.523	−0.114
Hungary	0.500	−0.043
Czech Republic	0.455	0.274
Poland	0.364	0.321

[1] The means of values registered over 1999Q1–2020Q4.

Table 2. The credit cycle coherence levels of euro area candidate countries with the euro area, before and after the onset of the global financial crisis [1].

	1999–2007			2008–2020	
	Synchronicity	Similarity		Synchronicity	Similarity
Hungary	0.833	0.692	Croatia	0.875	0.650
Croatia	0.667	0.620	Bulgaria	0.708	0.162
Romania	0.500	−0.355	Poland	0.708	0.547
Bulgaria	0.278	−0.513	Czech Republic	0.667	0.630
Czech Republic	0.167	−0.241	Romania	0.583	0.123
Poland	−0.111	−0.007	Hungary	0.333	−0.552

[1] The means of values registered over the two periods.

According to the data displayed in Table 1, the highest degrees of synchronicity and similarity with the euro area credit cycle over 1999–2020 are noted for Croatia, while the lowest levels of similarity (negative levels) are recorded for Bulgaria, Romania, and Hungary.

Overall, the countries have relatively good synchronization with the euro area compared to the level of similarity, which is quite low. The large differences in amplitudes between countries in terms of lending activity can be explained by the lower levels of economic and financial development of these countries compared to the euro area.

An analysis at the level of the two-time intervals (before and after the onset of the global financial crisis) could point out the extent to which these countries are going through a process of convergence in lending activity.

As can be seen in Table 2, before the onset of the global financial crisis, Hungary shows the highest level of credit cycle coherence with the euro area, both in terms of synchronicity and similarity. It is noteworthy that after 2008, Hungary suffers a significant desynchronization from the reference and a reduction in the level of similarity.

Although in the second part of the sampled period, Croatia does not register significant increases of the two indicators, it maintains its best position among the six states. Instead, Poland, the Czech Republic, and Bulgaria show improvements in both indicators during this period. Romania shows better results in terms of synchronicity and poorer results in terms of similarity with the euro area.

The better synchronization of credit cycles in the aftermath of the global financial crisis is consistent with the observation made by Omen [2] and Stremmel and Zsámboki [7] for euro area countries, namely that the financial cycle synchronization increases in times of financial stress.

These observations are also highlighted in Figure 4, where we compare the credit cycles for each of the six countries with the euro area credit cycle. It is noted that the credit cycles in all six countries have a longer time of synchronization with the Eurozone after the global financial crisis outbreak (2007–2014). In the Czech Republic and Poland, the synchronization periods are longer at nine years (2006–2015) and ten years (2008–2017), respectively.

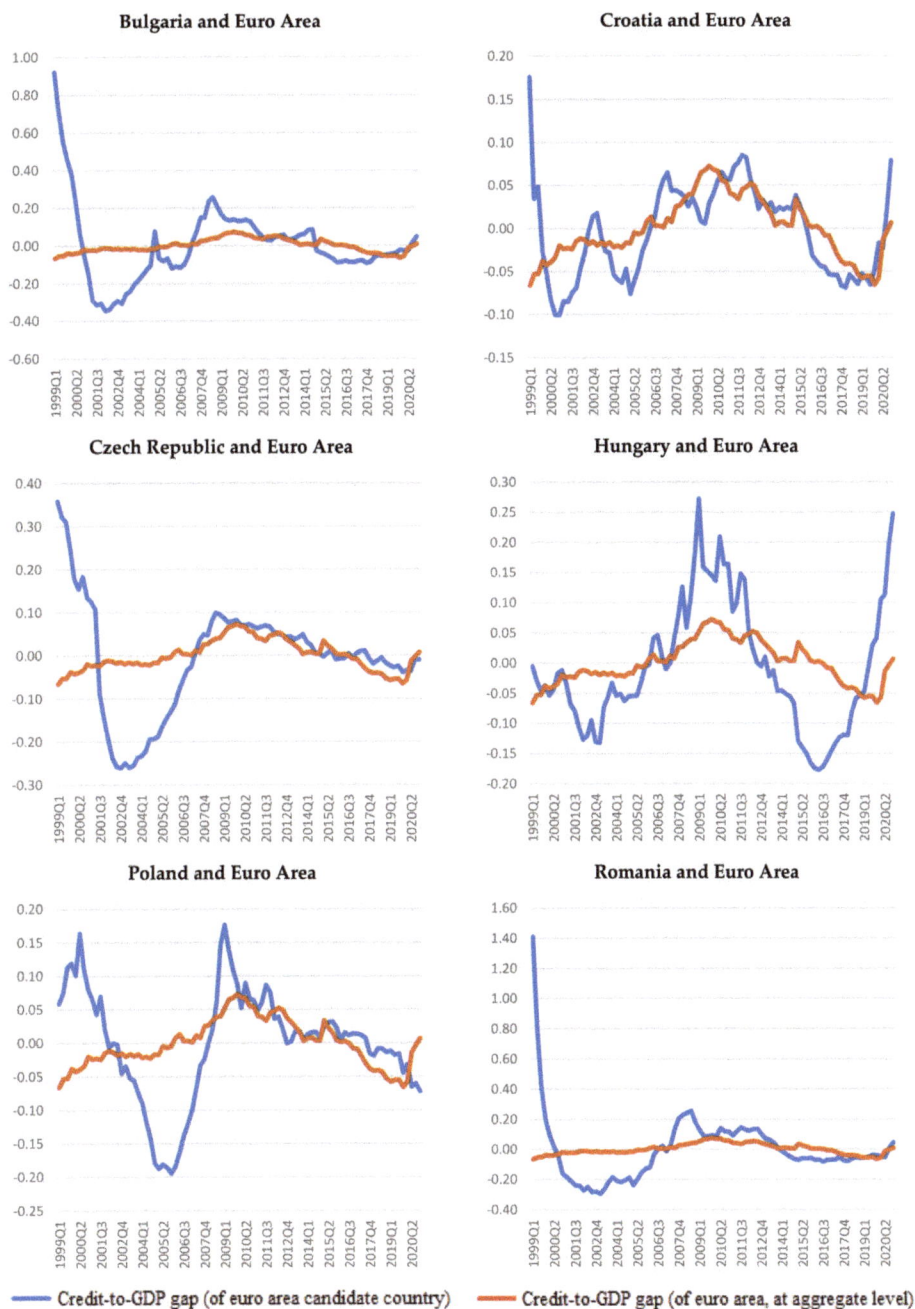

Figure 4. Credit cycles for 1999Q1–2020Q4.

Moreover, after the global financial crisis, the narrowing of the credit cycle gaps in our sample compared to the reference (euro area) is emphasized, especially for the Czech Republic and Poland and less so for Bulgaria and Romania, given the wider variation range of the credit-to-GDP gaps for these two countries (see Figure 4).

An insight into the extent to which the dynamics of the gaps in the credit-to-GDP rates for each individual series depends on the corresponding euro area values is reflected by the transfer entropy measure. As previously stated, this indicator measures the information that is transferred between the source and destination, taking into account the background of the system. Here, we consider the source to be the series of credit-to-GDP gaps for the Eurozone and the destination to be the corresponding variables for each of the countries.

In keeping with this paradigm, we interpret the transfer entropy measure as the level by which the uncertainty reduced for the credit-to-GDP gaps for each of the six countries through knowledge of the past values of the credit-to-GDP gap for the Eurozone. From this perspective, we can conjecture that the positive values reflect reductions in uncertainty, while the negative values expose increases in uncertainty.

The series with very few and lower negative values are those reflecting the credit-to-GDP gaps in Croatia, which is a country whose credit cycles seems to feature a high level of resemblance with the Eurozone (Figure 5). The negative values are also a sign of idiosyncrasy. The fact that the Eurozone induces uncertainty in the evolution of the credit-to-GDP gaps reflects the particularities of each of these countries, their cultural interpretation of credit, and their propensity to use credit for business development. We note that the negative values are not simultaneous across countries, which is another sign of these idiosyncratic effects.

The spike at the end of the series corresponds to the pandemic period. These large values reveal that the credit-to-GDP pattern in the Eurozone is informative for the evolution of the credit cycles in all countries in our sample (Figure 5).

Another perspective of the extent to which these six countries have similar credit cycles with the Eurozone is revealed by the measurement of the Bayesian entropy across all six similarity measures at each point in time. We note the existence of two regimes in the evolution of this system, with a long period of low entropy just before the large financial crisis and a long period of large entropy during 2015–2018 (Figure 6). The volatility in the last two years can first be attributed to the rather calm period in 2019 and to the start of the pandemic episode in 2020.

It should be noted that the long period of low entropy before the onset of the financial crisis corresponds to the period in which the coherence of credit cycles of the euro area candidate countries is lower, while after the crisis the entropy is increased, as well as the degree of the credit cycle coherence, especially in terms of synchronization.

The obtained results for our sample can also be seen through the lens of the differences regarding the monetary regime and the monetary policy strategy and the institutional arrangements regarding the macroprudential policy and their reporting and responsibility towards this policy. The main objective of the central banks from these countries is price stability, although the path is adapted differently to the domestic economic situation and to the history of macroeconomic imbalances. If this objective is pursued on the basis of an inflation targeting strategy for the monetary authorities of the Czech Republic, Hungary, Poland, and Romania, the emphasis is on the stability of the national currency for the central banks of Croatia and Bulgaria. With the exception of Bulgaria, which has a fixed exchange rate regime against the euro, the other countries have a more or less flexible exchange rate regime. Regarding the macroprudential policy, the profiles of the central banks are even more diverse. On the other hand, these countries are exposed to a number of common challenges they face from their current status as European Union member countries or as candidate countries for the euro area.

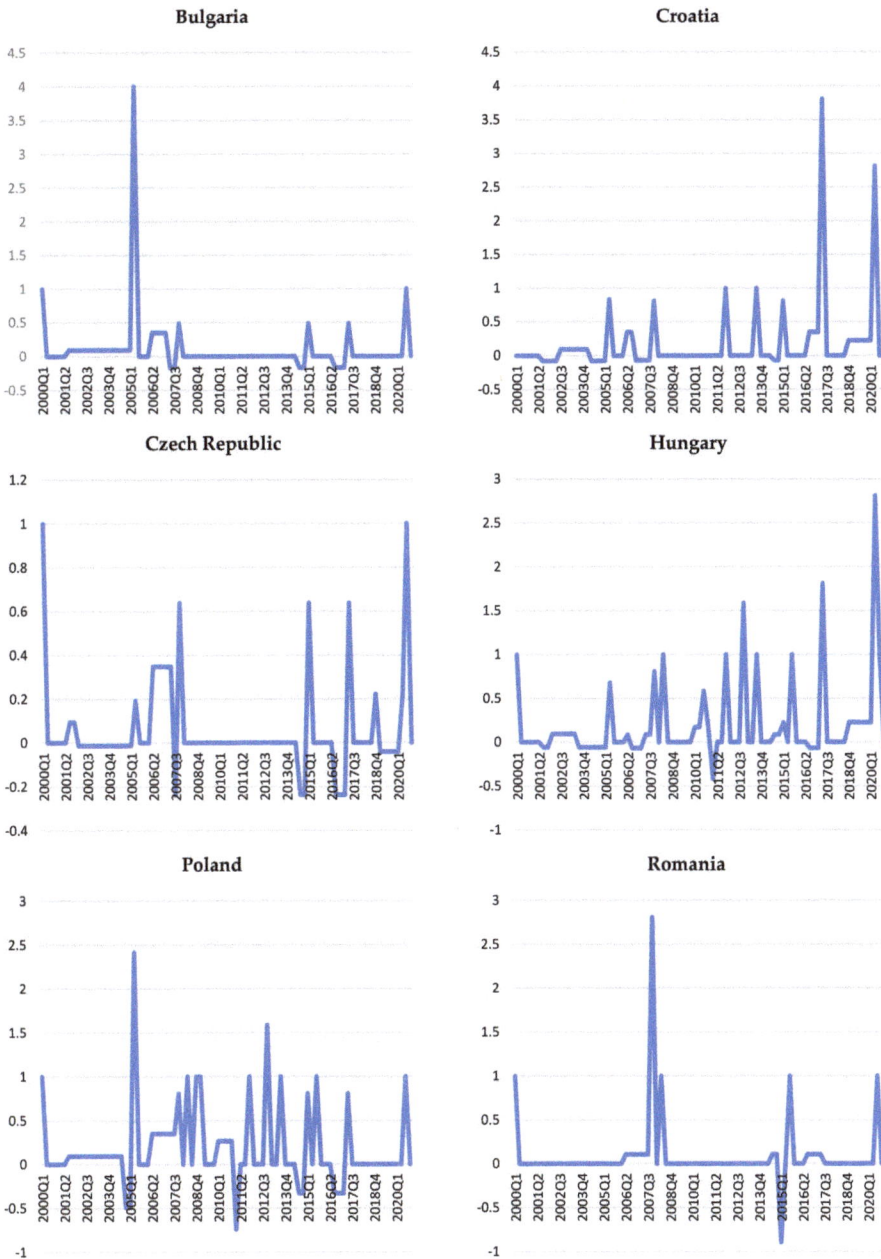

Figure 5. The transfer entropy values for filtered credit gaps in correspondence with euro area values.

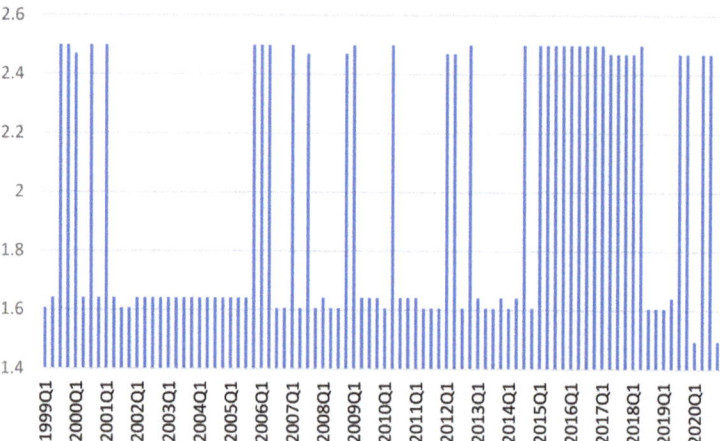

Figure 6. The Bayesian entropy values across all the six similarity measures.

5. Discussion and Conclusions

As a general conclusion that emerges from this study, the heterogeneous character of lending activity across the euro area candidate countries is highlighted, both in terms of the entropy of credit cycles and their coherence in relation to the euro area reference.

Based on the entropy measurement results, Croatia has the most volatile series (Shannon entropy) with highest level of volatility, although lower entropy rate values, as can be seen from the credit-to-GDP gap results obtained based on the HP filter method. In Poland and Hungary, the Shannon entropy also shows high levels of volatility. Unlike Poland, which has higher levels in the first half of the sampled period, Hungary shows higher entropy, especially after 2006.

Over the entire period, better coherence in terms of both synchronicity and similarity with the euro area credit cycle is shown for Croatia, while the lowest levels of similarity (negative levels) are shown for Bulgaria, Romania, and Hungary; however, separate analysis over the two-time intervals (before and after the onset of the global financial crisis) shows certain differences in the dynamics of this coherence of the countries towards the euro area. In this regard, before the onset of the global financial crisis, Hungary shows the highest level of credit cycle coherence with the euro area, both in terms of synchronicity and similarity, although after 2008 it suffers significant desynchronization from the reference area and a decrease in the level of similarity, which is more accentuated after 2014 and during the pandemic. In Hungary, the role of the central bank was neutral in adopting macroprudential policies in the lead up to the global financial crisis, while the authorities responsible for banking supervision considered "expansive" lending to be a normal reaction to the convergence process with the European Union. Although there were concerns about the expansion of foreign currency lending and mortgages, the authorities did not impose restrictions for political and social reasons. Macroprudential measures were applied more intensely during the crisis period than before the crisis in response to growing concerns about the risks to financial stability associated with foreign currency mortgages, which blocked the banks' operations.

Although in the second part of the sampled period, Croatia, a country with a high degree of euroization in the economy, does not show significant increases of the two indicators, it still holds the best position among the six states.

The data on the entropy transfer show that the credit cycle in Croatia has a high level of resemblance with the euro area, confirming its better coherence, as reflected by having the highest levels of similarity and synchronicity. It is noted that the credit cycle in Croatia has a stable path concerning the coherence with the euro area throughout the period.

It is noted that the credit cycles in all six countries have longer periods of synchronization with the Eurozone during the global financial crisis and in the first years after its onset (2007–2014). The better synchronization of the credit cycles, as perceived in the aftermath of the global financial crisis, confirms the idea mentioned in the literature, namely that financial cycle synchronization increases in times of financial stress. Overall, the countries show relatively better synchronization with the euro area than similarity. Simultaneously, during the 2007–2013 period, as compared with the period before the financial crisis, the use of macroprudential instruments is more intense, reflecting an increase in central bank activism in this regard, counteracting the effects of the crisis. This intensification is more evident for the countries that had already had similar experiences (Croatia, Bulgaria, Poland, and Romania). In addition, greater involvement is shown for Hungary as a result of the increasing role of the central bank in its macroprudential policy; however, the Czech National Bank maintained its relatively "neutral" position on the use of macroprudential measures.

This topic will remain of interest in the next future, considering not only the process of preparation for the accession to the euro area for these six countries, but also the manifestation of the COVID-19 crisis, which is supposed to change the trajectory of the financial cycles.

Credit cycle coherence with the euro area is not automatically attained by simply joining the monetary union. This observation has been mentioned in recent studies, according to which the adoption of the euro has not led to the synchronization of financial cycles in the euro area. Assuming that macroprudential policy is one of the main macroeconomic policy instruments that can influence the dynamics of the financial cycle, it is expected that better coherence of credit cycles in a monetary area will be obtained through better coordination of national macroprudential policies.

The obtained results should also be analyzed in comparison with the other components of the financial market, namely the financial assets market and the real estate market.

Author Contributions: All authors contributed equally to this paper. All authors have read and agreed to the published version of the manuscript.

Funding: This research received no external funding.

Institutional Review Board Statement: Not applicable.

Informed Consent Statement: Not applicable.

Data Availability Statement: Not applicable.

Conflicts of Interest: The authors declare no conflict of interest.

References

1. Borio, C. The financial cycle and macroeconomics: What have we learnt? *J. Bank. Financ.* **2014**, *45*, 182–198. [CrossRef]
2. Oman, W. The synchronization of business cycles and financial cycles in the euro area. *Int. J. Cent. Bank.* **2019**, *15*, 327–362.
3. Samarina, A.; Zhang, L.; Bezemer, D. Credit cycle coherence in the eurozone: Was there a euro effect? *J. Int. Money Financ.* **2017**, *77*, 77–98. [CrossRef]
4. Borio, C.; Kennedy, N.; Prowse, S.D. *Exploring Aggregate Asset Price Fluctuations across Countries: Measurement, Determinants and Monetary Policy Implications*; Bank for International Settlements, Monetary and Economic Department: Basel, Switzerland, 1994; Volume 40, pp. 1–104.
5. Borio, C.; Furfine, C.; Lowe, P. Procyclicality of the financial system and financial stability: Issues and policy options. *BIS Pap.* **2001**, *1*, 1–57.
6. Schüler, Y.S.; Hiebert, P.P.; Peltonen, T.A. Coherent financial cycles for G-7 countries: Why extending credit can be an asset. *ESRB Work. Pap. Ser.* **2017**, *43*. [CrossRef]
7. Stremmel, H.; Zsámboki, B. *The Relationship between Structural and Cyclical Features of the EU Financial Sector*; Working Paper Series 1812; European Central Bank: Frankfurt, Germany, 2015.
8. Gammadigbe, V. Financial Cycles Synchronization in WAEMU Countries: Implications for Macroprudential Policy. *Financ. Res. Lett.* **2021**, 102281. [CrossRef]
9. Miteski, M.; Georgievska, L. *Financial and Real Cycle Synchronization in Central, Eastern and Southeastern European Countries*; National Bank of North Macedonia: Skopje, North Macedonia, 2016.

10. Drehmann, M.; Borio, C.; Tsatsaronis, K. *Characterising the Financial Cycle: Don't Lose Sight of the Medium Term*; BIS Working Paper No. 380; Bank for International Settlements: Basel, Switzerland, 2012.
11. Aikman, D.; Haldane, A.G.; Nelson, B.D. Curbing the Credit Cycle. *Econ. J.* **2015**, *125*, 1072–1109. [CrossRef]
12. Borio, C.; Drehmann, M.; Xia, F.D. Forecasting recessions: The importance of the financial cycle. *J. Macroecon.* **2020**, *66*, 103258. [CrossRef]
13. Galati, G.; Hindrayanto, I.; Koopman, S.J.; Vlekke, M. Measuring financial cycles in a model-based analysis: Empirical evidence for the United States and the euro area. *Econ. Lett.* **2016**, *145*, 83–87. [CrossRef]
14. Meller, B.; Metiu, N. The synchronization of credit cycles. *J. Bank. Financ.* **2017**, *82*, 98–111. [CrossRef]
15. Harding, D.; Pagan, A. Synchronization of cycles. *J. Econom.* **2006**, *132*, 59–79. [CrossRef]
16. Mink, M.; Jacobs, J.P.A.M.; de Haan, J. *Measuring Coherence of Output Gaps with an Application to the Euro Area*; Oxford Economic Papers; Oxford University Press: Oxford, UK, 2012; Volume 64, pp. 217–236.
17. Zhou, R.; Cai, R.; Tong, G. Applications of Entropy in Finance: A Review. *Entropy* **2013**, *15*, 4909–4931. [CrossRef]
18. Sandoval, L. Structure of a Global Network of Financial Companies Based on Transfer Entropy. *Entropy* **2014**, *16*, 4443–4482. [CrossRef]
19. Xu, X.; Ren, R. Study on Credit Cycle Based on Cross Entropy. Available online: https://www-webofscience-com.am.e-nformation.ro/wos/woscc/full-record/WOS:000224824000134 (accessed on 26 July 2021).
20. Xi, N.; Muneepeerakul, R.; Azaele, S.; Wang, Y. Maximum entropy model for business cycle synchronization. *Phys. A Stat. Mech. Appl.* **2014**, *413*, 189–194. [CrossRef]
21. Wezel, T. Conceptual Issues in Calibrating the Basel III Countercyclical Capital Buffer. Available online: https://www.imf.org/en/Publications/WP/Issues/2019/05/01/Conceptual-Issues-in-Calibrating-the-Basel-III-Countercyclical-Capital-Buffer-46742 (accessed on 26 July 2021).
22. Jakimowicz, A. The Role of Entropy in the Development of Economics. *Entropy* **2020**, *22*, 452. [CrossRef]
23. Amin, T.G.; Jeppsson, F.; Haglund, J.; Strömdahl, H. Arrow of time: Metaphorical construals of entropy and the second law of thermodynamics. *Sci. Educ.* **2012**, *96*, 818–848. [CrossRef]
24. Shannon, C.E. A Mathematical Theory of Communication. *Bell Syst. Tech. J.* **1948**, *27*, 379–423. [CrossRef]
25. Hlaváčková-Schindler, K.; Paluš, M.; Vejmelka, M.; Bhattacharya, J. Causality detection based on information-theoretic approaches in time series analysis. *Phys. Rep.* **2007**, *441*, 1–46. [CrossRef]
26. Cover, T. *Elements of Information Theory*; Wiley: New York, NY, USA, 1991; ISBN 9780471062592.
27. Schreiber, T. Measuring information transfer. *Phys. Rev. Lett.* **2000**, *85*, 461–464. [CrossRef] [PubMed]
28. Lizier, J.T.; Prokopenko, M.; Zomaya, A.Y. Local information transfer as a spatiotemporal filter for complex systems. *Phys. Rev. E—Stat. Nonlinear Soft Matter Phys.* **2008**, *77*. [CrossRef]
29. Lupu, R.; Călin, A.C.; Zeldea, C.G.; Lupu, I. A Bayesian Entropy Approach to Sectoral Systemic Risk Modeling. *Entropy* **2020**, *22*, 1371. [CrossRef] [PubMed]
30. Archer, E.; Park, I.M.; Pillow, J.W. Bayesian Entropy Estimation for Countable Discrete Distributions. *J. Mach. Learn. Res.* **2014**, *15*, 2833–2868.

Article

Is Bitcoin Still a King? Relationships between Prices, Volatility and Liquidity of Cryptocurrencies during the Pandemic

Barbara Będowska-Sójka [1], Agata Kliber [2,*] and Aleksandra Rutkowska [2]

[1] Department of Econometrics, Poznan University of Economics and Business, 61-875 Poznan, Poland; barbara.bedowska-sojka@ue.poznan.pl

[2] Department of Applied Mathematics, Poznan University of Economics and Business, 61-875 Poznan, Poland; aleksandra.rutkowska@ue.poznan.pl

* Correspondence: agata.kliber@ue.poznan.pl

Abstract: We try to establish the commonalities and leadership in the cryptocurrency markets by examining the mutual information and lead-lag relationships between Bitcoin and other cryptocurrencies from January 2019 to June 2021. We examine the transfer entropy between volatility and liquidity of seven highly capitalized cryptocurrencies in order to determine the potential direction of information flow. We find that cryptocurrencies are strongly interrelated in returns and volatility but less in liquidity. We show that smaller and younger cryptocurrencies (such as Ripple's XRP or Litecoin) have started to affect the returns of Bitcoin since the beginning of the pandemic. Regarding liquidity, the results of the dynamic time warping algorithm also suggest that the position of Monero has increased. Those outcomes suggest the gradual increase in the role of privacy-oriented cryptocurrencies.

Keywords: cryptocurrencies; mutual information; transfer entropy; dynamic time warping

Citation: Będowska-Sójka, B.; Kliber, A.; Rutkowska, A. Is Bitcoin Still a King? Relationships between Prices, Volatility and Liquidity of Cryptocurrencies during the Pandemic. *Entropy* **2021**, *23*, 1386. https://doi.org/10.3390/e23111386

Academic Editor: Joanna Olbryś

Received: 7 September 2021
Accepted: 20 October 2021
Published: 22 October 2021

Publisher's Note: MDPI stays neutral with regard to jurisdictional claims in published maps and institutional affiliations.

Copyright: © 2021 by the authors. Licensee MDPI, Basel, Switzerland. This article is an open access article distributed under the terms and conditions of the Creative Commons Attribution (CC BY) license (https://creativecommons.org/licenses/by/4.0/).

1. Introduction

Bitcoin is the most noticeable cryptocurrency in the fast-growing market [1]. However, because the number of currencies has been rapidly growing and investors face different investment opportunities, its dominance is disputable. This paper aims to analyse the links between leading cryptocurrencies. These links are measured by the amount of information shared and transmitted before and during the pandemic. We also verify possible lead-lag relationships within the sample. We study seven cryptocurrencies of the highest market capitalization and a relatively long history of market quotations. The coronavirus pandemic and the resulting unprecedented crisis has affected the entire investment community, and many assets and commodities significantly dropped in value. We focus on cryptocurrencies that—on the contrary—experienced an increase in their value (at the beginning of 2020, Bitcoin price oscillated around 7200 USD). Already in April 2021, it exceeded 61,500 USD (according to coinmarketcap.com, accessed: 21 October 2021). We observe a similar enormous growth in the prices of other cryptocurrencies too. Although the prices had fallen at the end of Spring 2021, at the moment of writing this article, they still surpassed the beginning of the 2020 level.

We analysed the returns based on the closing prices, volatility approximated by Garman–Klass estimator [2] and liquidity approximated by the closing quoted spread of Chung and Zhang [3]. We calculated the amount of mutual information contained in the returns of the cryptocurrencies, their volatility and liquidity. We also examined the information transfer between them, both in the pre-COVID-19 and within the COVID-19 period. Our results are validated using the modified DTW algorithm.

Our contributions are threefold. First, we concentrate not only on the volatility but also on the liquidity of the cryptos. The former is no less important from the investors' perspective during the portfolio selection process. Secondly, we find that the amount of mutual information included in returns and volatility is much higher than the one in liquidity. The latter seems to affect the lead-lag relationships—they are indistinguishable in daily returns and volatility but relatively clear in liquidity. The amount of mutual information contained in liquidity has increased beginning from the pandemic. Moreover, there is no definite leader among cryptocurrencies when it comes to information transfer. We observe the growing role of Ripple in this process, and we link it to the fast transaction processing algorithm of this coin. According to the DTW results, Bitcoin leads all cryptocurrencies in terms of liquidity, but we observe that Monero is its close follower (probably due to the growing interest in more privacy-oriented cryptocurrencies).

Through the study, we enrich our understanding of the information transmission mechanisms in the cryptocurrency market. We also provide some practical information for market participants about the possible benefits of portfolio diversification. Thus, our results are of special importance for the investors. Investment strategies (in any cryptocurrency and not necessarily in Bitcoin) should depend on the observation of prices of a set of cryptocurrencies and not only the most popular one.

2. Literature Review

When measuring the dominance of one financial instrument (or market) over another, the most common approach is to investigate the contagion in returns or volatility. With respect to cryptocurrencies, Yi et al. (2018) [1] analysed whether Bitcoin was a dominant cryptocurrency over the period December 2016–April 2018. They found that cryptocurrencies with high market capitalization (namely Bitcoin, Litecoin and Dogecoin) propagate large volatility shocks, while small-cap cryptocurrencies are more likely to receive volatility shocks from others. Although Bitcoin plays an important role and generates strong volatility shocks to other cryptocurrencies, it does not play a role of the 'clear' leader on the market in terms of volatility connectedness.

In a similar vein, Ji et al. (2019) [4] applied the measures developed by [5] and found that the return shocks arising from Bitcoin and Litecoin had the most profound effect on the returns of other four large cryptocurrencies between 2015 and 2018. XRM and Ether mostly reacted to negative shocks, while Dash and Ether were weakly reacting to positive returns. In terms of volatility spillovers, Bitcoin was the most powerful and was followed by Litecoin. Ciaian et al. [6] reinforced the conclusion of the lack of the dominant position of Bitcoin. They show that the changes of prices of alternative coins (so-called altcoins) are driven by the development of Bitcoin in the short-run (for 15 out of 16 examined altcoins) but not in the longer term (for only four altcoins).

More closely related work to ours is [7], as that study aimed to detect the informational leadership among four cryptocurrencies, Bitcoin, Ether, Litecoin and XRM. The authors showed that the relationships between cryptocurrencies are nonlinear. Therefore, one should not apply the Granger causality or similar tools that assume linear dependencies in investigating interrelationships among such assets. The scholars utilize a method quite common in econophysics, that is, the group transfer entropy. Their findings indicate that Bitcoin is not a dominating cryptocurrency—it does not lead the information process.

In a more recent paper, Aslanidis et al. [8] documented that the cryptocurrency market experienced a strong overall increase in the connectedness both in terms of returns and volatility. In most cases over the period 2015–2020, shocks were transmitted to the other cryptocurrencies and had a short-term effect on the returns. The scholars also found evidence that the volatility transmission in the high-frequency domain becomes more important than in the low-frequency one. By analysing samples year by year, they found that the variance explained by the first principal component increased over the period both for returns and for volatility. Although over the year ending in August 2016, the percentage of variance explained by the first PC amounted 76% for Bitcoin (the values for Litecoin and Ether were 68% and 7%, respectively); in the year ending in July 2020, the first PC represented 86% of the Bitcoin variance, and the latter was exceeded by Litecoin (91%) and Ethereum (93%). Thus, Bitcoin seems to lose its superior position over time.

The goal of our analysis is to verify whether we can distinguish a leading cryptocurrency. In other words, we are interested on whether cryptocurrencies followed Bitcoin (and we observed causality) during the pandemic and before or the simultaneous increase in the prices of cryptocurrencies reflected the phenomenon of co-occurrence.

3. Data

We analyse daily closing prices of the following cryptocurrencies: Bitcoin (BTC), Ether (ETH), Ripple's XRP, Dash (DSH), Litecoin (LTC), Monero (XMR) and Iota (IOT). These cryptocurrencies vary in terms of the speed of transaction processing, privacy orientation and usage. In the investigated set, Dash and Monero are the leading privacy-oriented cryptos, while Ripple's XRP processes transactions the fastest. As literature concerning Bitcoin is already saturated [1,4,9], we focus here on the potential successors.

Ether is probably the biggest competitor of Bitcoin. At the moment of writing this article, Ether was the second-largest virtual currency by market capitalization in the world. The name Ether refers to the token (or 'coin') used through the Ethereum network, launched in 2015. Ether is a medium of exchange similarly to other cryptocurrencies. What sets them apart is that Ether tokens can be used only for one specific purpose: to facilitate the computation of decentralized applications on the Ethereum network [10]. It is possible to exchange different cryptocurrencies for Ether tokens. However, the latter cannot be substituted with other cryptocurrencies to provide computing power for Ethereum transactions.

XRP launched in 2012, and it is a cryptocurrency for products developed by Ripple Labs, and that is why these two names, XRP and Ripple, are often used interchangeably. One can use XRP coins for payment settlements, asset exchange and remittance systems. The network RippleNet is utilized by some major banks and financial institutions, e.g., Santander or American Express (see: https://www.ig.com/en/cryptocurrency-trading/cryptocurrency-comparison for details; accessed: 21 October 2021). XRP itself is pre-mined. It uses a less complicated mining method than Bitcoin, which makes the transactions much faster and of a much lower cost [11]. In July 2021, XRP was ranked sixth in terms of total market capitalization (according to coinmarketcap.com).

Dash was launched in 2014 and designed to ensure users' privacy and anonymity. Currently, Dash aims to become a medium for daily transactions, i.e., a digital currency that can be used as cash, credit card or via PayPal [12]. The main difference between Dash and Bitcoin lies in the algorithms applied to mining coins. They also have a different system of validating transactions: In the case of Bitcoin, all the nodes within a network need to validate the transaction, while Dash relies on a specific set of nodes called masternodes. The latter feature enables it to speed up the transaction process [13].

Litecoin was founded in 2011 by Christopher Lee. It is called the silver to Bitcoin gold. Its infrastructure is very similar to Bitcoin's (although the transaction processing speed is faster), so it was used as a test-net for improvements that later were applied to Bitcoin [14]. The limit of LTC coins is 84 Million (than compared to 21 Million of Bitcoin). According to coinmarketcap.com, Litecoin ranked fourteenth in terms of market capitalization in July 2021.

Monero is known as the most privacy-oriented cryptocurrency. It was launched in 2014, and its popularity stems from its anonymity orientation [15]. The capitalization of Monero in July 2021 made it 27th among the cryptocurrencies—refer to coinmarkedcap.com.

IOTA was launched in 2016. The acronym stands for Internet of Things Application. IOTA is a distributed ledger that handles transactions between connected devices in the IoT. Its cryptocurrency is known as mIOTA [16]. mIOTQ is pre-mined. The method of confirming a transaction results is based on the Tangle infrastructure, with no fees and low power consumption.

Figure 1 presents the volume of trade of the analysed cryptocurrencies, while Figure 2 shows their closing prices. Both prices and volumes are from the Bitfinex exchange. However, as [17] demonstrated, all the crypto-exchanges are very closely linked one to another, and information spills over them almost immediately. Therefore, we can assume that Bitfinex, which has the highest volume of USDBTC trade, can be representative of the market.

What we observe is the peak of volume in each cryptocurrency in March 2020. In the case of BTC, ETH and XMR, that peak is also the maximum observed in the entire analysed period. For the rest of the cryptocurrencies, the maximums of volume traded were present in 2021 (see Figure 1). However, when we compare this picture with Figure 2, we notice that this March 2020 peak was followed by a price drop. Nevertheless, the prices of all cryptocurrencies started to grow steadily, reaching their maximums in 2021.

In Table 1, we provide descriptive statistics of the returns of the analysed cryptocurrencies: mean, standard deviation and kurtosis in two subperiods. The table is accompanied by Figure 3. For mean and standard deviation, we also provide the results of the tests for the equality of the two moments in the analysed subperiods. We conclude that the means were equal in both periods, but standard deviations increased during the pandemic. That is especially visible in Figure 3—we observe an erratic behaviour of returns following the March 2020 price drop. Eventually, we note an interesting phenomenon considering kurtosis. It grew for all the coins, except for Dash. Thus, almost all cryptocurrencies experienced more cases of extreme returns during the pandemic than before it.

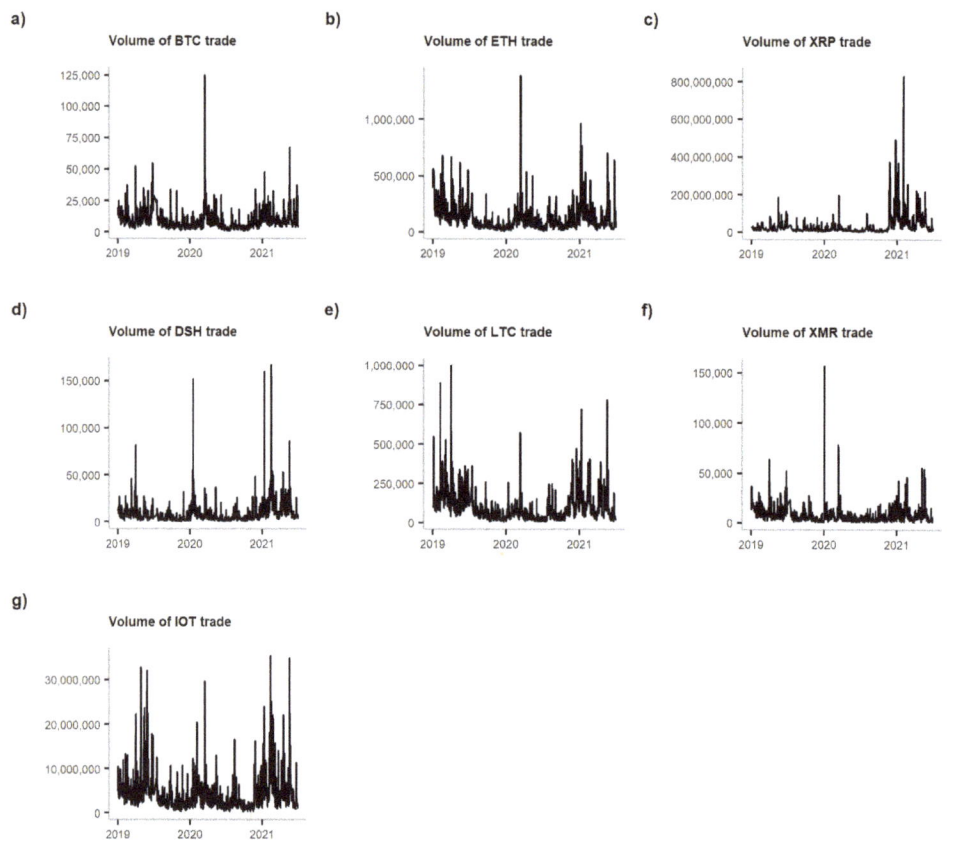

Figure 1. The volume of trade of the analysed cryptocurrencies. **Note:** The graphs are shown in the following order: (**a**) BTC, (**b**) ETH, (**c**) XRP, (**d**) DSH, (**e**) LTC, (**f**) XMR and (**g**) IOT.

Table 1. Descriptive statistics of cryptocurrencies' return series.

Moment	Period	BTC	ETH	XRP	DSH	LTC	XMR	IOT
mean μ	pre-COVID	0.002	0.001	−0.001	0.000	0.001	0.001	−0.001
	COVID	0.003	0.005	0.002	0.001	0.002	0.002	0.003
p-val for H0: $\mu_1 = \mu_2$		0.687	0.253	0.377	0.792	0.900	0.580	0.250
st.dev. σ	pre-COVID	0.033	0.043	0.040	0.050	0.051	0.041	0.045
	COVID	0.042	0.056	0.075	0.068	0.059	0.057	0.064
p-val for H0: $\sigma_1 = \sigma_2$		<0.01	<0.01	<0.01	<0.01	<0.01	<0.01	<0.01
kurtosis	pre-COVID	3.428	3.910	5.633	14.300	4.313	1.505	4.185
	COVID	8.989	8.281	11.127	8.669	7.598	12.223	6.337

Note: μ denotes mean, while σ standard deviation. The data are taken daily.

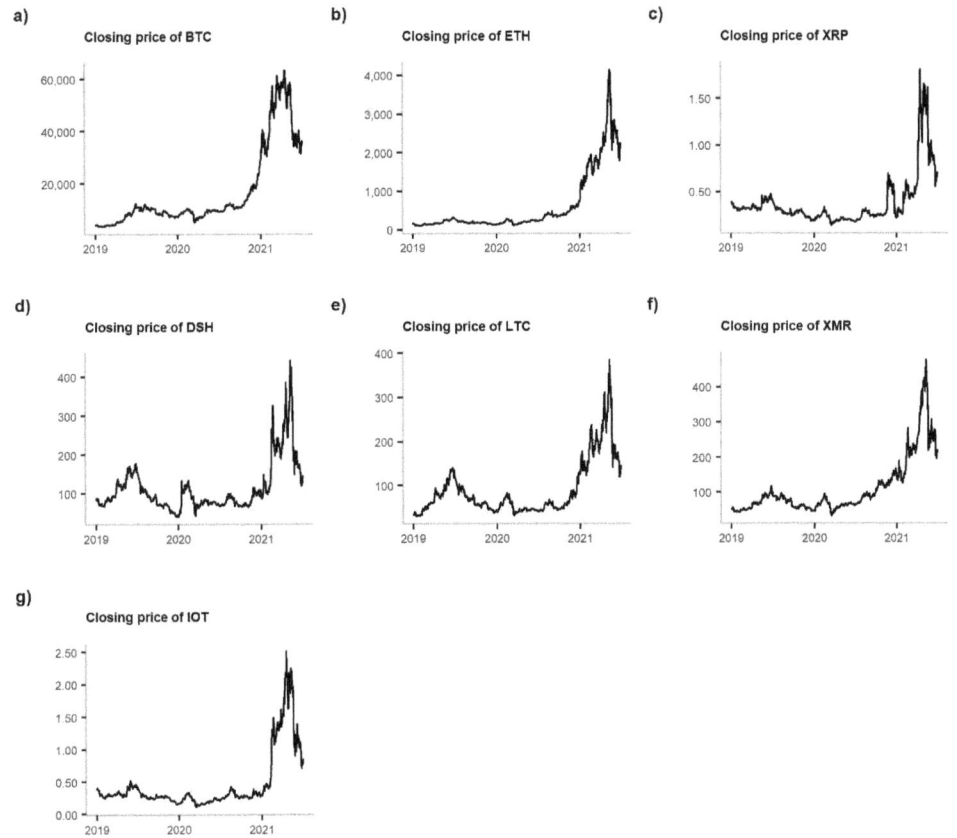

Figure 2. Closing prices (in USD) of the analysed cryptocurrencies. Note: The graphs are shown in the following order: (a) BTC, (b) ETH, (c) XRP, (d) DSH, (e) LTC, (f) XMR and (g) IOT.

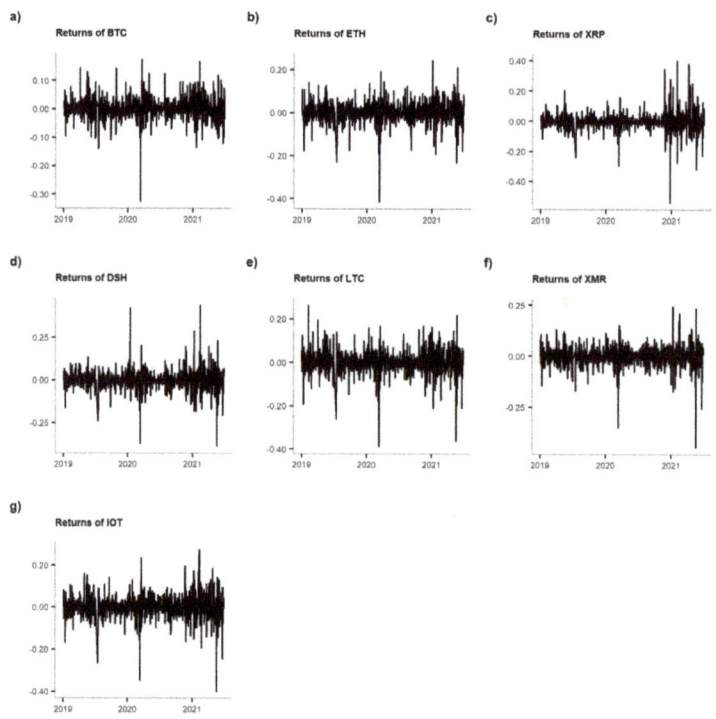

Figure 3. Log-returns of the analysed cryptocurrencies. **Note:** The graphs are shown in the following order: (**a**) BTC, (**b**) ETH, (**c**) XRP, (**d**) DSH, (**e**) LTC, (**f**) XMR and (**g**) IOT.

4. Methods

4.1. Volatility and Liquidity Measures

There are various methods to approximate liquidity and volatility. Based on the results presented in [18], we decided to use a Garman–Klass estimator to approximate volatility and the closing quoted spread of Chung and Zhang [3] to approximate liquidity of each cryptocurrency. Both measures require only daily prices; for the Garman and Klass estimator, high-low-open-close prices are employed, while in the case of the closing quoted spread, bid and ask prices are utilized.

To obtain the measures, we used the following formulas:

- The Garman–Klass ([2]) volatility estimator:

$$GK = \sqrt{0.5\left[\log\left(\frac{H_t}{L_t}\right)\right]^2 - (2\log(2) - 1) \cdot \left[\log\left(\frac{C_t}{O_t}\right)\right]^2} \quad (1)$$

where H_t, L_t, O_t and C_t are the high, low, open and close prices in day t, respectively.
- The closing quoted spread of [3]:

$$CQS_t = \frac{A_t - B_t}{0.5(A_t + B_t)}. \quad (2)$$

where B_t and A_t are the bid and the ask prices, respectively, at the end of the given day t.

We calculate both the Garman–Klass estimator and the closing quoted spread for each day and each cryptocurrency.

4.2. Mutual Information

4.2.1. The Entropy

Mutual information measures the information of a random variable contained in another random variable [19]. It is based on the concept of entropy—i.e., the measure of the uncertainty associated with a random variable (so called Shannon or information entropy [20]).

Let us denote by X and Y two random variables and assume that each of them can be described by their probability distributions (P_X and P_Y, respectively). The self-information of measuring X as outcome x is defined as follows [21]:

$$I_X(x) = -\log_2(P_X(X = x)) = \log_2 \frac{1}{P_X(X = x)}. \tag{3}$$

According to [20], for a discrete random variable X with probability distribution P_X, the average number of bits required to optimally encode independent draws can be calculated as follows:

$$H_X(X) = -\sum_x P_X(X = x) \log_2 P_X(X = x) = E[I_X(x)], \tag{4}$$

where $p_X(x)$ denotes a probability density function. The choice of the logarithm's base only impacts the unit of measurement. Base logarithm indicates bits and base digits, and the base of the natural logarithm yields nats [21]).

If we denote the joint distribution of X and Y by p_{XY}, then we can define the joint entropy by the following:

$$H(X,Y) = -\sum_x \sum_y P_{X,Y}(X = x, Y = y) \log_2(P_{X,Y}(X = x, Y = y)) \tag{5}$$

Based on the two measures, one can define conditional entropy as follows:

$$H(Y|X) = H(X,Y) - H(X). \tag{6}$$

and analogously $H(X|Y)$.

4.2.2. Mutual Information and Global Correlation

Based on the concept of entropy and self-information, one can define mutual information as the following:

$$I(X,Y) = H(X) - H(X|Y) = H(Y) - H(Y|X) = H(X) + H(Y) - H(X,Y). \tag{7}$$

Mutual information measures the reduction in uncertainty about variable X from observing variable Y. We will denote it by $I(X,Y)$. Mutual information is positive $I(X;Y) \geq 0$. It is equal to 0 if and only if X and Y are independent.

It is important that mutual information does not imply causality. To account for such a feature, one would need to use transfer entropy (see Section 4.3).

In order to normalize mutual information to take values from 0 to 1 (and be an alternative measure to linear correlation coefficient), Ref. [19] suggested to transform it to the so called global correlation coefficient λ:

$$\lambda(X,Y) = \sqrt{1 - \exp(-2I(X,Y))} \tag{8}$$

The function $\lambda(X,Y)$ captures the overall dependence: both linear and non-linear between X and Y. It can be interpreted as predictability of Y by X, where the measure of predictability is based on empirical probability distributions and is model-independent.

4.3. Transfer Entropy

Let us assume X and Y are Markov processes of order k and l, respectively. Thus, the probability to observe X at time $t+1$ in state s conditional on the k previous observations is as follows:

$$P_X(X_{t+1} = s | x_t, ..., x_{t-k+1}) = P_X(X_{t+1} = s | x_t, ..., x_{t-k}). \tag{9}$$

The average number of bits needed to encode the observation in the moment $t+1$, once the previous k values are known, is given by the following:

$$h_X(k) = -\sum_x P_X\left(X_{t+1} = s, x_t^{(k)}\right) \log_2 P_X\left(X_{t+1} = s | x_t^{(k)}\right), \tag{10}$$

where $x_t^{(k)} = x_t, ..., x_{t-k+1}$.

The information flow from process Y to process X is measured by quantifying the deviations from the generalized Markov property:

$$P_X(X_{t+1} = s | x_t^{(k)}) = P_X(X_{t+1} = s | x_t^{(k)}, y_t^{(l)}).$$

The Shannnon transfer entropy measures the information flow from Y to X and is calculated as the following:

$$T_{Y \to X}(k, l) = \sum P_X\left(X_{t+1} = s, x_t^{(k)}, y_t^{(l)}\right) \log_2 \frac{P_X\left(X_{t+1} = s | x_t^{(k)}, y_t^{(l)}\right)}{P_X\left(X_{t+1} = s | x_t^{(k)}\right)}. \tag{11}$$

To calculate the dominant direction of the information flow, one calculates the difference between $T_{Y \to X}$ and $T_{X \to Y}$.

Transfer entropy can also be based on Rényi entropy and is described as follows:

$$H_X^q(X) = \frac{1}{1-q} \log_2 \sum_x P_X^q(X = x). \tag{12}$$

It strongly depends on a weighting parameter $q : q > 0$. For $q \to 1$, Rényi entropy converges to Shannon entropy. If we take $0 < q < 1$, then events of a low probability will receive more weight. For $q > 1$, the weights favor outcomes with higher initial probabilities (for further details see: [21]). In the case of financial time series, important information comes in tails. Thus, the authors recommend using small values of q and to give more weight to extreme events.

The transfer entropy estimators are biased in small samples. To overcome this problem, one can use the effective entropy measure. It allows for correcting the bias [22]. The effective transfer entropy is defined as follows:

$$ET_{Y \to X}(k, l) = T_{Y \to X}(k, l) - T_{Y_{sh} \to X}(k, l) \tag{13}$$

where $T_{Y_{sh} \to X}(k, l)$ indicates transfer entropy and is calculated using a *shuffled* version of the time series Y. This means that the values from the observed time series Y are drawn randomly, and they are realigned to generate a new time series.

Rényi transfer entropy is calculated as [21] the following:

$$RT_{Y \to X} = \frac{1}{1-q} \log_2 \frac{\sum_x \phi_q\left(x_t^{(k)}\right) P_X\left(x_{t+1} | x_t^{(k)}\right)}{\sum_{x,y} \phi_q\left(x_t^{(k)}, y_t^{(l)}\right) P_X\left(x_{t+1} | x_t^{(k)}, y_t^{(l)}\right)}, \tag{14}$$

where the following is called *escort distribution* [21,23]:

$$\phi_q(x) = \frac{P_X^q(x)}{\sum_x P_X^q(x)} \tag{15}$$

If the values of Rényi transfer entropy are negative, then this means that the history of Y results in even greater uncertainty than only knowing the history of X alone [21].

We calculated transfer entropy and effective transfer entropy by using R package RTransferEntropy [21], and mutual information measure using Infotheo [24].

4.4. Dynamic Time Warping

Dynamic Time Warping (futher DTW) is an algorithm used for measuring similarity between two temporal sequences. The goal of the algorithm is to find an optimal alignment between two time series. By optimal alignment, we understand that it achieves the minimum global cost (distance) while ensuring time continuity. The global cost is the summation of the cost between each pair of points in the alignment. The algorithm was first used in speech recognition, where the same signals may differ in speed. It allows for a non-linear mapping of one signal to another by minimizing the distance between the two. The algorithm, unlike econometric methods, does not assume a single delay in the entire period; time series may have different delays at different times. It tries to find the smallest distance among different lags.

Let us assume that we want to compare two time series: a test/query $X = (x_1, x_2, \ldots, x_N)$ of the length N and a reference $Y = (y_1, y_2, \ldots, y_M)$ of length M. We choose a non-negative, local dissimilarity function f between any pair of elements x_i and y_j:

$$d(i,j) = f(x_i, y_j) \geq 0. \tag{16}$$

where $d(i,j)$ is small (i.e., low cost) if x_i and y_j are similar to each other, otherwise $d(i,j)$ is large (i.e., high cost). When employing one of the distance measure (most common Euclidean or Manhattan), the local cost measures for each pair of elements of the sequences X and Y are evaluated and presented in a cost matrix $C \in R^{N+M}$. A warping path ϕ is a contiguous set of matrix elements that defines a mapping between the time indices of X and Y that satisfies the boundary, monotonicy and continuity conditions. Given ϕ, the total cost d_ϕ and the average normalized accumulated cost $\bar{d}_\phi$ between the warped time series X and Y is computed as follows:

$$d_\phi(X,Y) = \sum_{k=1}^{T} d(\phi_k), \tag{17}$$

$$\bar{d}_\phi(X,Y) = \sum_{k=1}^{T} \frac{d(\phi_k) m_\phi}{M_\phi}, \tag{18}$$

where m_ϕ is a per-step weighting coefficient and M_ϕ is the corresponding normalization constant. The goal is to find an alignment between X and Y having a minimal average accumulated cost:

$$DTW(X,Y) = min_\phi \{d_\phi\} \tag{19}$$

The optimal path is computed in the reverse order of the indices, starting with (N, M).

In this study, we used extension for this algorithm that is proposed in [25] to check if one time series is forward or backward against the other. We calculated separate DTW distances with windows proposed in [25], finding an optimal path only in the upper triangular cost matrix, within different but always forward shift (called further forward distance d_f), and in the lower triangular cost matrix, within backward shift (d_b).

Let us denote two analysed time series by A and B, the distance measured between each element of A and the lagged value of B by d_f and the distance between the lagged value of A and each element of B by d_b. If the distance $d_f < d_b$, the alignment according to the forward DTW is better, and we call A the 'lead'.

5. Results

5.1. Amount of Information Shared by the Cryptocurrencies

In Table 2, we present bootstrapped values of the 95% confidence intervals of global correlation coefficients calculated for each pair of the cryptocurrencies. The coefficient measures the amount of the mutual information shared by the returns of each pair of cryptocurrencies. In general, the correlations are high. We observe that in the pre-COVID period, the highest amount of mutual information was shared between XRP and ETH (95% confidence interval of (0.81, 0.86)), BTC and ETH (0.8, 0.86) and LTC and ETH (0.78, 0.85). The pairs XMR and IOT (0.64, 0.76); BTC and IOT (0.66, 0.77); and DSH and IOT (0.66, 0.78) held the lowest amounts of mutual information. The numbers in the lower panel of Table 2 refer to the COVID-19 period. We observe a decline in the value of mutual information shared by the pairs BTC-XMR (0.65, 0.76), ETH-XRP (0.72, 0.8), EHT-XMR (0.66, 0.76) and XRP-XMR (0.63, 0.72), while an increase was observed for DSH-LTC (0.79, 0.86) and DSH-IOT (0.74, 0.82). During this period, the highest amount of information was shared by ETH and LTC (0.8, 0.87), DSH and LTC (0.79, 0.86) and BTC and LTC (0.77, 0.84), whereas the BTC-ETH pair took fourth place (0.77, 0.83).

Table 2. Global correlation coefficient for cryptocurrencies' returns: before and during pandemic.

	ETH	XRP	DSH	LTC	XMR	IOT
From 1 January 2019 to 1 March 2020						
BTC	(0.8, 0.86)	(0.71, 0.81)	(0.73, 0.81)	(0.72, 0.82)	(0.76, 0.84)	(0.66, 0.77)
ETH	–	(0.81, 0.86)	(0.74, 0.82)	(0.78, 0.85)	(0.72, 0.81)	(0.71, 0.81)
XRP	–	–	(0.71, 0.79)	(0.74, 0.83)	(0.69, 0.78)	(0.73, 0.82)
DSH	–	–	–	(0.68, 0.79)	(0.7, 0.8)	(0.66, 0.78)
LTC	–	–	–	–	(0.68, 0.78)	(0.69, 0.78)
XMR	–	–	–	–	–	(0.64, 0.76)
From 1 March 2020 to 30 June 2021						
BTC	(0.77, 0.83)	(0.68, 0.77)	(0.73, 0.82)	(0.77, 0.84)	(0.65, 0.76)	(0.68, 0.76)
ETH	–	(0.72, 0.8)	(0.75, 0.82)	(0.8, 0.87)	(0.66, 0.76)	(0.72, 0.79)
XRP	–	–	(0.73, 0.81)	(0.74, 0.81)	(0.63, 0.72)	(0.72, 0.79)
DSH	–	–	–	(0.79, 0.86)	(0.67, 0.75)	(0.74, 0.82)
LTC	–	–	–	–	(0.67, 0.77)	(0.73, 0.8)
XMR	–	–	–	–	–	(0.65, 0.74)

Note: In the table, we present the bootstrapped 95% confidence intervals of the global correlation coefficient (in nats) calculated according to Equation (8). Values closer to 1 denote a higher reduction in uncertainty when observing the returns of the cryptocurrency from the row. The global correlation coefficient is a measure of interdependence but not causality. The data have been discretized by using equal frequencies binning algorithm, and the number of bins was set to $\sqrt[3]{N}$, where N is the sample length.

In Table 3, we present 95% confidence intervals of the global correlation coefficient calculated for volatility. In the pre-COVID-19 period, we observed the highest value of λ for each pair where Ether was present: from (0.66, 0.75) for the pair ETH-XMR to (0.73, 0.81) for ETH-LTC. The values in the pandemics were slightly higher. The only decrease was for the pair ETH-XRP and ETH-IOT. However, we observed the highest increase in linkages for all pairs where LTC, DSH, XMR and IOT were included. This indicates the increase in the importance of these altcoins.

Eventually, in Table 4, we present the analogous calculations for the liquidity of the cryptocurrencies approximated by the CQS measure. In this case, we observe significant growth of relationships. The values of mutual information shared by the liquidity of the cryptocurrencies were rather low before the pandemic. The 95% confidence intervals ranged from (0.24, 0.4) for XRP-BTC to (0.43, 0.57) for IOT-DSH. In the pandemic period, the respective intervals were (0.44, 0.56) for BTC-IOT and (0.6, 0.71) for IOT-DSH. We observed that the leading pair did not change between the periods, but the amount of mutual information shared by it grew. The increase in mutual information shared by liquidity may indicate the overall growth of interest in cryptocurrency trade.

Table 3. Global correlation coefficients for cryptocurrencies volatility approximated by the Garman–Klass [2] estimator.

	ETH	XRP	DSH	LTC	XMR	IOT
From 1 January 2019 to 1 March 2020						
BTC	(0.68, 0.78)	(0.61, 0.73)	(0.58, 0.7)	(0.65, 0.75)	(0.68, 0.78)	(0.61, 0.71)
ETH	–	(0.71, 0.79)	(0.67, 0.76)	(0.73, 0.81)	(0.66, 0.75)	(0.7, 0.79)
XRP	–	–	(0.6, 0.72)	(0.65, 0.74)	(0.65, 0.73)	(0.69, 0.77)
DSH	–	–	–	(0.62, 0.73)	(0.62, 0.73)	(0.62, 0.72)
LTC	–	–	–	–	(0.63, 0.73)	(0.64, 0.74)
XMR	–	–	–	–	–	(0.6, 0.71)
From 1 March 2020 to 30 June 2021						
BTC	(0.74, 0.81)	(0.67, 0.75)	(0.71, 0.79)	(0.74, 0.8)	(0.72, 0.79)	(0.67, 0.75)
ETH	–	(0.68, 0.75)	(0.71, 0.8)	(0.75, 0.82)	(0.7, 0.78)	(0.7, 0.77)
XRP	–	–	(0.74, 0.81)	(0.79, 0.84)	(0.66, 0.75)	(0.71, 0.79)
DSH	–	–	–	(0.79, 0.85)	(0.74, 0.8)	(0.74, 0.81)
LTC	–	–	–	–	(0.71, 0.79)	(0.73, 0.8)
XMR	–	–	–	–	–	(0.7, 0.79)

Note: In the table, we present bootstrapped 95% confidence intervals of the global correlation coefficient (in nats) calculated according to Equation (8). Values closer to 1 denote a higher reduction in uncertainty when observing the volatility—Equation (1)—of the cryptocurrency from the row. The global correlation coefficient is a measure of interdependence but not causality. The data have been discretized by using equal frequencies binning algorithm, and the number of bins was set to $\sqrt[3]{N}$, where N is the sample length.

Table 4. Global correlation coefficient for cryptocurrencies liquidity approximated by the closing quoted spread of [3] (CQS).

	ETH	XRP	DSH	LTC	XMR	IOT
From 1 January 2019 to 1 March 2020						
BTC	(0.31, 0.52)	(0.24, 0.4)	(0.29, 0.47)	(0.3, 0.45)	(0.33, 0.49)	(0.29, 0.45)
ETH	–	(0.3, 0.46)	(0.3, 0.49)	(0.31, 0.5)	(0.3, 0.49)	(0.32, 0.5)
XRP	–	–	(0.33, 0.48)	(0.36, 0.51)	(0.36, 0.51)	(0.35, 0.5)
DSH	–	–	–	(0.38, 0.52)	(0.37, 0.52)	(0.43, 0.57)
LTC	–	–	–	–	(0.32, 0.49)	(0.37, 0.52)
XMR	–	–	–	–	–	(0.36, 0.5)
From 1 March 2020 to 30 June 2021						
BTC	(0.52, 0.64)	(0.5, 0.61)	(0.4, 0.54)	(0.51, 0.63)	(0.49, 0.62)	(0.44, 0.56)
ETH	–	(0.58, 0.69)	(0.53, 0.65)	(0.57, 0.69)	(0.59, 0.69)	(0.54, 0.65)
XRP	–	–	(0.55, 0.67)	(0.59, 0.69)	(0.56, 0.67)	(0.53, 0.66)
DSH	–	–	–	(0.54, 0.66)	(0.56, 0.67)	(0.6, 0.71)
LTC	–	–	–	–	(0.52, 0.63)	(0.5, 0.62)
XMR	–	–	–	–	–	(0.59, 0.7)

Note: In the table, we present bootstrapped 95% confidence intervals of the global correlation coefficient (in nats) calculated according to Equation (8). Values closer to 1 denote a higher reduction in uncertainty when observing the liquidity—Equation (2)—of the cryptocurrency from the row. The global correlation coefficient is a measure of interdependence but not causality. The data have been discretized using equal frequencies binning algorithm, and the number of bins was set to $\sqrt[3]{N}$, where N is the sample length.

5.2. Information Flow between Cryptocurrencies

The analysis of mutual information shared by the cryptocurrencies allows us to conclude that they are strongly interrelated concerning prices and volatility and less interrelated when concerning liquidity. In this section, we verify whether the relationships result in causality. We will concentrate on the causality to and from Bitcoin in the two periods.

In Figure 4, we present the point values of entropy transfer together with their 95% confidence intervals. If the interval covers 0, we conclude that the amount of information transferred is insignificantly different from 0. The calculated entropy was the Renyi one, with $q = 0.1$, i.e., stressing the information in tails. The estimates are each time ordered by the amount of the information flow from BTC.

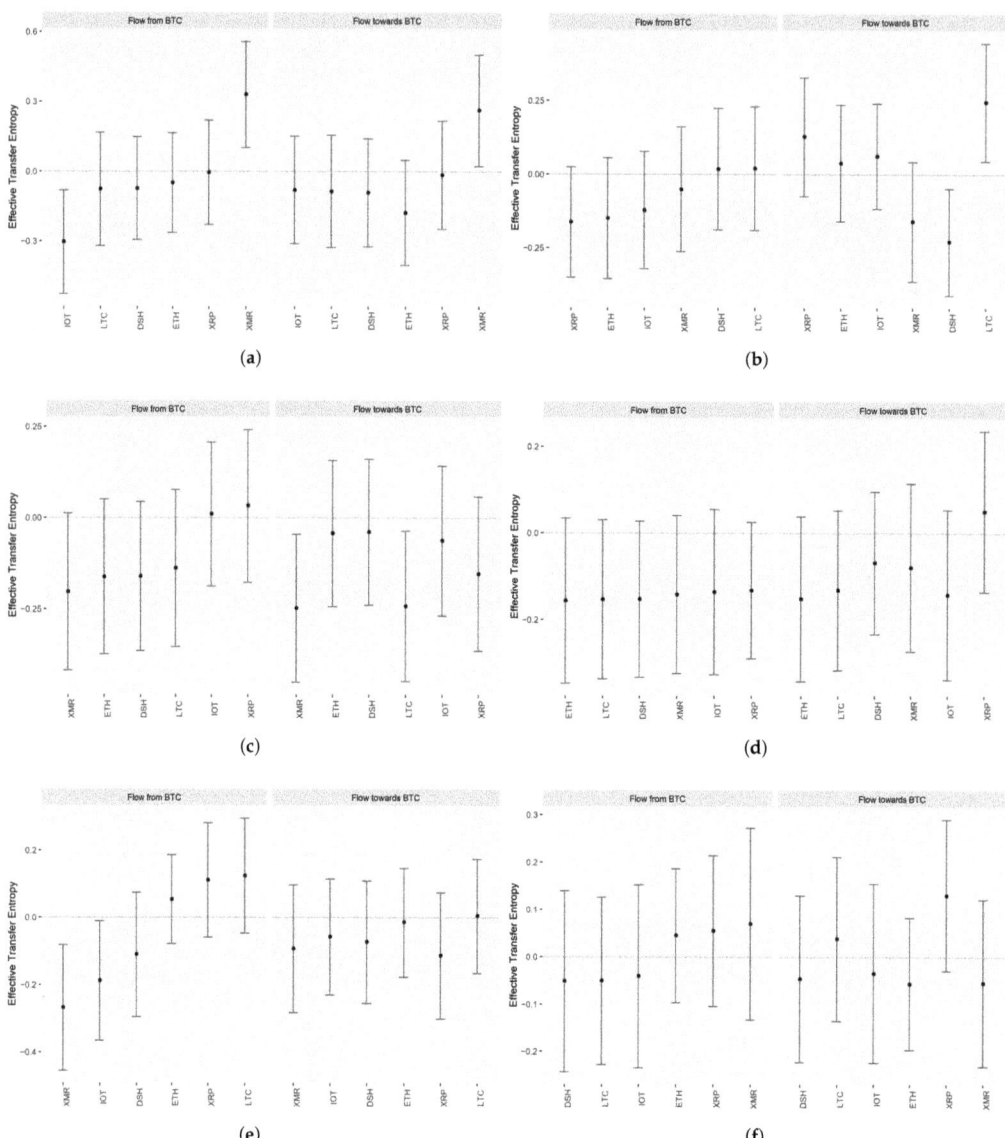

Figure 4. Effective Renyi entropy transfer from Bitcoin (BTC) to other cryptocurrencies and from those to BTC. **Note**: In the figure, we present the values of effective transfer entropy between the returns (**a,b**), volatilities (**c,d**) and liquidities (**e,f**) of cryptocurrencies calculated according to Equation (14) for $q = 0.1$, and the Markov order is set to 1 for each coin. The point values are accompanied by 95% confidence bands. Intervals covering positive values denote statistically significant causality. The negative ones indicate the increase in uncertainty when accounting for the history of other cryptocurrencies. If the intervals cover 0, we interpret it as a lack of a statistically significant relationship. The left column refers to the pre-COVID-19 period, while the right refers to the COVID-19 one. The currencies on the x-axis are ordered by the growing amount of the transfer entropy. Therefore, the order of the cryptocurrencies differs between the periods. The data have been discretized using quantiles methodology.

We observe that the causality relationships between Bitcoin and the other cryptocurrencies are in most cases insignificant, regardless of the medium of interest (returns, volatilities or liquidity). In the pre-COVID-19 period, the information from BTC flew through returns to XMR only. That changed in the COVID-period when the amount of information transmitted to XMR became insignificant. Moreover, the value of the transfer entropy became negative when we analysed the direction from BTC to XRP.

When it comes to volatility and liquidity, we observed no significantly positive information transfer from BTC in any period. On the contrary, in the pre-COVID one, the values of the transfer entropy were negative for the information transfer from BTC to XMR through volatility and liquidity and to IOT through liquidity. In the COVID period, all the values became insignificantly different from 0.

When it comes to information transfer to BTC through returns, we noted positive values in the pre-COVID-19 period for XMR and in the COVID-19 one for LTC only. The transfer entropy from DSH was significantly negative. We also emphasize that some negative values of transfer entropy observed in volatility (transfer from XMR and LTC) became insignificant in the second period. The fact that some values of transfer entropy were negative implies that any investment strategy based on inferring the returns or volatility of Bitcoin based on the historical returns or volatility dynamics of any other from our set may be ineffective.

Eventually, when we concentrate on liquidity, we observe that, during the pandemic, the values of transfer entropy were the highest in the case of XRP (the 95% interval limit still covers 0, but the part of the interval taking negative values is the shortest among all the cryptocurrencies). We explain this result by the fact that XRP is characterized by the fastest transaction processing algorithm and has the potential to lead the information process in liquidity. Moreover, interest in this cryptocurrency is steadily growing.

By summarizing the results and comparing the values of the transfer entropy to and from Bitcoin, we can say that in terms of returns, BTC is the information receiver and that returns dynamic from smaller coins influence the dynamics of the big one more than the other way round.

5.3. Lead-Lag Relationships

In order to extend the results obtained by analysing transfer entropy, we also calculated the lead-lag relationships between the cryptocurrencies using the DTW algorithm. When analysing the transfer entropy, we allowed for one lag only, while in the DTW algorithm, we took into account the 7-day history.

In Tables 5–7, we present the differences between the forward and the backward distances for returns, volatilities and liquidities, respectively. The negative values in Tables 5–7 denote that we can treat the currency in the column as the leading one relative to the one from the row. The table can be read in two directions so that the positive value shows that the currency in the row can be read as a leader. The gray colour indicates that the currency from the column switched its role from leader to follower compared to the pre-pandemic period. The orange colour signifies the change in the opposite direction.

To render the information in the tables clearer, let us concentrate on the relationship in volatility between BTC and ETH from 1 January 2019 to 1 March 2020. The forward DTW distance of the BTC to ETH takes into account the alignment of the current volatility of BTC with the future volatility of ETH, accounting for different shifts from 1 to 7 days. It amounted to 0.0080 (not included in the table). The backward DTW (the current BTC volatility match with past ETH volatility with different lags from 1 to 7 days) amounted to 0.0071. In the Table 6, we display the difference (multiplied by 100) between the two values, which are equal to 0.09. The positive sign means that BTC is the leading currency in this pair. The absolute value of these differences is not high, but we can observe that from 1 March 2020 to 30 June 2021 the value rose to 0.19. The difference has more than doubled; thus, we can conclude that the position of BTC as a volatility-leader against ETH, has strengthened.

We note two facts. First of all, the numbers presented in the tables represent differences between the distances and not the estimates of parameters. Therefore, we do not present here the significance tests. Instead, we can comment on the magnitude of the numbers. All the numbers in the tables are multiplied by 100. The differences between returns and volatilities are very small. That can suggest that daily data were not enough to capture the lead-lag relationships in returns and volatilities. It is likely that such relationships are more pronounced in intra-daily data. On the contrary, the differences between liquidities are relatively high.

The results corroborate with the one obtained by the analysis of mutual information. The highest amount of mutual information is shared by returns and volatilities. This is likely why we observed such small differences between forward and backward distances in Tables 5 and 6. Since the amount of mutual information contained in liquidities is smaller (see Table 4), clearer lead-lag relationships can be observed.

Let us concentrate on Table 5. In both periods, BTC slightly leads; however, the absolute value of the difference between the forward and backward distances is higher during the pandemic period for the relationship with ETH (0.04 versus 0), XRP(0.29 versus 0.05), DSH (0.2 versus 0.08) and XMR(0.02 versus 0) but not for IOT (0.19 versus 0.22) and LTC (0 versus 0.24). In the pandemic period, ETH is a little 'lagged' relative to XRP, BTC but also XMR. The absolute value of differences between the forward and backward distances between LTC and other cryptocurrencies decreased a little during the pandemic.

Table 5. Differences between forward and backward DTW measures of the returns.

	ETH	XRP	DSH	LTC	XMR	IOT
from 1 January 2019 to 1 March 2020						
BTC	0.00	0.05	0.08	0.24	0.00	0.22
ETH		−0.06	0.05	0.01	0.02	0.00
XRP			0.00	0.14	0.04	−0.01
DSH				0.04	0.00	0.05
LTC					−0.10	−0.05
XMR						0.00
from 1 March 2020 to 30 June 2021						
BTC	0.04	0.29	0.20	0.00	0.02	0.19
ETH		−0.01	0.02	0.00	−0.03	0.03
XRP			0.05	0.02	−0.03	0.00
DSH				0.05	0.01	0.06
LTC					0.03	0.01
XMR						−0.01

Note: In the table, we present the differences between forward and backward distances (multiplied by 100 for clarity). The negative values denote that we can treat the currency in the column as the leading one relative to the one from the row. Gray colour indicates the switch of the relationship from leaders to followers during the pandemic compared to the pre-pandemic period, while orange means changes in the opposite direction.

The results for the volatility are presented in Table 6. In the pandemic period, ETH became a slight leader relative to XRP (−0.34), DSH (−0.03), XMR (−0.01) and IOT (−0.14). LTC volatility became forward relative to ETH (−0.03), XRP (−0.22), XMR (−0.02) and IOT (−0.09), while XRP became a little backward compared to all others.

Eventually, in the case of liquidity analysis (cf. Table 7), we can draw much stronger conclusions as the numbers are much higher. BTC is forward relative to all others cryptocurrencies before as well as during the pandemic. XMR is a leader relative to all others, despite BTC in the pandemic period.

Table 6. Differences of forward and backward DTW distances of cryptocurrencies' volatility.

	ETH	XRP	DSH	LTC	XMR	IOT
		From 1 January 2019 to 1 March 2020				
BTC	0.09	0.10	0.17	0.26	0.00	0.23
ETH		−0.05	−0.03	0.14	−0.05	0.00
XRP			0.01	0.16	0.02	0.10
DSH				0.13	−0.05	0.04
LTC					−0.18	−0.09
XMR						0.09
		From 1 March 2020 to 30 June 2021				
BTC	0.19	0.66	0.18	0.18	0.13	0.30
ETH		0.34	0.03	−0.03	0.01	0.14
XRP			−0.18	−0.22	−0.34	−0.07
DSH				0.01	0.00	0.00
LTC					0.02	0.09
XMR						0.15

Note: In the table we present the differences between forward and backward distances (multiplied by 100 for clarity). The negative values denote that we can treat the currency in the column as the leading one relative to the one from the row. Gray colour indicates the switch of the relationship from leaders to followers during the pandemic compared to the pre-pandemic period, while orange means changes in the opposite direction.

Table 7. Differences of forward and backward DTW distances of the cryptocurrencies' liquidity.

	ETH	XRP	DSH	LTC	XMR	IOT
		From 1 January 2019 to 1 March 2020				
BTC	43.89	47.15	7.19	51.93	10.14	52.94
ETH		61.13	4.17	17.14	−0.17	66.92
XRP			69.65	36.22	117.58	−2.78
DSH				20.91	2.52	−64.31
LTC					−19.74	−34.53
XMR						−112.67
		From 1 March 2020 to 30 June 2021				
BTC	83.81	121.13	60.70	78.80	52.06	106.64
ETH		95.25	−10.60	6.26	−8.90	80.76
XRP			8.65	−39.52	−39.50	−6.00
DSH				13.30	−0.49	−23.75
LTC					−15.17	20.61
XMR						24.05

Note: In the table we present the differences between forward and backward distances (multiplied by 100 for clarity). The negative values denote that we can treat the currency in the column as the leading one relative to the one from the row. Gray colour indicates the switch of the relationship from leaders to followers during the pandemic compared to the pre-pandemic period, while orange means changes in the opposite direction.

6. Discussion and Conclusions

In the article, we present the results of the analysis of mutual information, information transfer and lead-lag relationships between returns, volatility and liquidity of cryptocurrencies. We found that cryptocurrencies share a relatively high amount of mutual information (especially in returns and volatility), while information transfer between them is limited. Moreover, we observed that mutual information shared in liquidity has increased since the beginning of the pandemic. The lead-lag relationships between Bitcoin and other cryptocurrencies in terms of returns and volatility are almost indistinguishable in daily data, which is probably related to the high amount of mutual information shared by these measures. Additionally, using dynamic time warping, we have found that changes in the liquidity of Monero (XMR) started to precede the changes in liquidity of all other cryptocurrencies, apart from Bitcoin.

Our results partially corroborate with the ones presented in the previous studies and obtained with different econometric methods. Similarly to [1,6,7], we show that the dominance of Bitcoin is not definite, although it has been the most recognizable cryptocurrency. Demonstrating the significant information transfer from Litecoin to Bitcoin through returns, we also corroborate the results presented in [4]. We confirm that high-capitalization cryptocurrencies (Bitcoin, Ether and Litecoin) share a large amount of mutual information with others. However, over time, the relationships become weaker. Moreover, it is most visible in returns.

We note that mutual information contained in volatility and returns is higher than the one in liquidity, and the maximal numbers are reached for returns. The latter suggests that although all cryptocurrencies may experience similar price dynamics, the market values their risk differently. We can also infer that the cryptocurrency market is divided into segments with different groups of investors. In general, the investment strategy in alternative coins based on observing Bitcoin seems to be inadequate. Investors should take into account the information flow from other currencies as well.

In future work, we plan to repeat the research for a longer time frame in order to verify the stability of the results in time. Together with extending the period of the study, we aim to include more altcoins in our research. We intend to verify the possibility of hedging the investment in the dominating cryptocurrencies with altcoins in the long run.

Author Contributions: Conceptualization, A.K., B.B.-S. and A.R.; methodology, A.K., B.B.-S. and A.R.; software, A.K. and A.R.; validation, A.K. and B.B.-S.; formal analysis, A.K., B.B.-S. and A.R.; investigation, A.K., B.B.-S. and A.R.; resources, A.K.; data curation, A.K.; writing—original draft preparation, A.K., B.B.-S. and A.R.; writing—review and editing, A.K., B.B.-S. and A.R.; visualization, A.K.; funding acquisition, A.K. All authors have read and agreed to the published version of the manuscript.

Funding: This research was funded by the Regional Initiative for Excellence programme of the Minister of Science and Higher Education of Poland, years 2019–2022, grant No. 004/RID/2018/19, financing 3,000,000 PLN. It was also supported by the National Science Centre (NCN) in Poland under the grant no. UMO-2017/25/B/HS4/01546.

Institutional Review Board Statement: Not applicable.

Informed Consent Statement: Not applicable.

Data Availability Statement: All the data comes from BitFinex exchange and were obtained through QUANDL.

Conflicts of Interest: The authors declare no conflict of interest. The funders had no role in the design of the study; in the collection, analyses or interpretation of data; in the writing of the manuscript; or in the decision to publish the results.

Abbreviations

The following abbreviations are used in this manuscript:

BTC   Bitcoin;
ETH   Ether;
XRP   Cryptocurrency for products developed by Ripple Labs;
DSH   Dash;
LTC   Litecoin;
XMR   Monero;
IOT   mIOTA, cryptocurrency used in Internet of Things Application;
GK   Garman–Klass volatility estimator;
CQS   Closing quoted spread liquidity estimator;
DTW   Dynamic time warping algorithm.

References

1. Yi, S.; Xu, Z.; Wang, G.J. Volatility connectedness in the cryptocurrency market: Is Bitcoin a dominant cryptocurrency? *Int. Rev. Financ. Anal.* **2018**, *60*, 98–114. [CrossRef]
2. Garman, M.B.; Klass, M.J. On the Estimation of Security Price Volatilities from Historical Data. *J. Bus.* **1980**, *53*, 67–78. [CrossRef]
3. Chung, K.H.; Zhang, H. A simple approximation of intraday spreads using daily data. *J. Financ. Mark.* **2014**, *17*, 94–120. [CrossRef]
4. Ji, Q.; Bouri, E.; Lau, C.K.M.; Roubaud, D. Dynamic connectedness and integration in cryptocurrency markets. *Int. Rev. Financ. Anal.* **2019**, *63*, 257–272. [CrossRef]
5. Diebold, F.; Yilmaz, K. Better to Give Than to Receive: Predictive Directional Measurement of Volatility Spillovers. *Int. J. Forecast.* **2012**, *28*, 57–66. [CrossRef]
6. Ciaian, P.; Rajcaniova, M.; Kancs, D. Virtual relationships: Short- and long-run evidence from BitCoin and altcoin markets. *J. Int. Financ. Mark. Inst. Money* **2018**, *52*, 173–195. [CrossRef]
7. Dimpfl, T.; Peter, F.J. Group transfer entropy with an application to cryptocurrencies. *Phys. A Stat. Mech. Appl.* **2019**, *516*, 543–551. [CrossRef]
8. Aslanidis, N.; Bariviera, A.F.; Perez-Laborda, A. Are cryptocurrencies becoming more interconnected? *Econ. Lett.* **2021**, *199*, 109725. [CrossRef]
9. Będowska-Sójka, B.; Kliber, A. Is there one safe-haven for various turbulences? The evidence from gold, Bitcoin and Ether. *N. Am. J. Econ. Financ.* **2021**, *56*, 101390. [CrossRef]
10. Frankenfield, J. Ether (ETH). Investopedia. 2021. Available online: https://www.investopedia.com/terms/e/ether-cryptocurrency.asp (accessed on 1 August 2021).
11. Reiff, N.; Anderson, S. Bitcoin vs. Ripple: What's the Difference? Investopedia. 2021. Available online: https://www.investopedia.com/tech/whats-difference-between-bitcoin-and-ripple/ (accessed on 1 August 2021).
12. Duffield, E.; Diaz, D. Dash: A Payments-Focused Cryptocurrency. Whitepaper. 2018. Available online: https://github.com/dashpay/dash/wiki/Whitepaper (accessed on 1 August 2021).
13. Sharma, R. What is Dash? Investopedia. 2021. Available online: https://www.investopedia.com/tech/what-dash-cryptocurrency (accessed on 1 August 2021).
14. Frankenfield, J. What Is Litecoin (LTC)? Investopedia. 2021. Available online: https://www.investopedia.com/terms/l/litecoin.asp (accessed on 1 August 2021).
15. Frankenfield, J.; Rasure, E. Monero. Investopedia. 2021. Available online: https://www.investopedia.com/terms/m/monero.asp (accessed on 1 August 2021).
16. Frankenfield, J. IOTA (MIOTA). Investopedia. 2021. Available online: https://www.investopedia.com/terms/i/iota.asp (accessed on 1 August 2021).
17. Kliber, A.; Włosik, K. Isolated Islands or Communicating Vessels?—Bitcoin Price and Volume Spillovers Across Cryptocurrency Platforms. *Financ. A Uver* **2019**, *69*, 324–341.
18. Będowska-Sójka, B.; Kliber, A. Information content of liquidity and volatility measures. *Phys. A Stat. Mech. Appl.* **2021**, *563*, 125436. [CrossRef]
19. Dionisio, A.; Menezes, R.; Mendes, D.A. Mutual information: A measure of dependency for nonlinear time series. *Phys. A Stat. Mech. Its Appl.* **2004**, *344*, 326–329. [CrossRef]
20. Shannon, C.E. A Mathematical Theory of Communication. *Bell Syst. Tech. J.* **1948**, *27*, 379–423. [CrossRef]
21. Behrendt, S.; Dimpfl, T.; Peter, F.J.; Zimmermann, D.J. RTransferEntropy—Quantifying information flow between different time series using effective transfer entropy. *SoftwareX* **2019**, *10*, 100265. [CrossRef]
22. Marschinski, R.; Kantz, H. Analysing the information flow between financial time series. *Eur. Phys. J. B Condens. Matter Complex Syst. Vol.* **2002**, *30*, 275–281. [CrossRef]
23. Beck, C.; Schögl, F. *Thermodynamics of Chaotic Systems: An Introduction*; Cambridge Nonlinear Science Series; Cambridge University Press: Cambridge, UK, 1993. [CrossRef]
24. Meyer, P.E. *Infotheo: Information-Theoretic Measures*; R Package Version 1.2.0. 2014. Available online: https://CRAN.R-project.org/package=infotheo (accessed on 1 August 2021)
25. Rutkowska, A.; Szyszko, M. New DTW Windows Type for Forward-and Backward-Lookingness Examination. Application for Inflation Expectation. *Comput. Econ.* **2021**, 1–18. [CrossRef]

Article

A Novel Extension of the Technique for Order Preference by Similarity to Ideal Solution Method with Objective Criteria Weights for Group Decision Making with Interval Numbers

Dariusz Kacprzak

Department of Mathematics, Faculty of Computer Science, Bialystok University of Technology, Wiejska 45A, 15-351 Bialystok, Poland; d.kacprzak@pb.edu.pl

Abstract: This paper presents an extension of the Technique for Order Preference by Similarity to Ideal Solution (TOPSIS) method with objective criteria weights for Group Decision Making (GDM) with Interval Numbers (INs). The proposed method is an alternative to popular and often used methods that aggregate the decision matrices provided by the decision makers (DMs) into a single group matrix, which is the basis for determining objective criteria weights and ranking the alternatives. It does not use an aggregation operator, but a transformation of the decision matrices into criteria matrices, in the case of determining objective criteria weights, and into alternative matrices, in the case of the ranking of alternatives. This ensures that all the decision makers' evaluations are taken into account instead of their certain average. The numerical example shows the ease of use of the proposed method, which can be implemented into common data analysis software such as Excel.

Keywords: interval numbers; MCGDM; TOPSIS; entropy; objective weights

Citation: Kacprzak, D. A Novel Extension of the Technique for Order Preference by Similarity to Ideal Solution Method with Objective Criteria Weights for Group Decision Making with Interval Numbers. *Entropy* **2021**, *23*, 1460. https://doi.org/10.3390/e23111460

Academic Editor: Meimei Xia

Received: 27 September 2021
Accepted: 31 October 2021
Published: 3 November 2021

Publisher's Note: MDPI stays neutral with regard to jurisdictional claims in published maps and institutional affiliations.

Copyright: © 2021 by the author. Licensee MDPI, Basel, Switzerland. This article is an open access article distributed under the terms and conditions of the Creative Commons Attribution (CC BY) license (https://creativecommons.org/licenses/by/4.0/).

1. Introduction

Recent years show that Multiple Criteria Decision Making (MCDM) methods are increasingly used to solve real decision-making problems concerning various aspects of human life [1–3]. The main application areas for these methods are supply chain management [4], logistics [5], engineering [6], technology [7], and many others. The complexity and diversity of MCDM problems have resulted in the development of a variety of methods to solve them [2]. One group of these methods are methods based on reference points. Historically, the first method which belongs to this group is the Hellwig method [8]. It uses a single reference point, called a "pattern". It is an artificial solution that maximizes benefit criteria and minimizes cost criteria. The computed synthetic indicator "proximity" of the alternatives to the "pattern" allows for their linear ordering and the identification of the best one. However, the most recognized and regularly used method in this group is TOPSIS, developed by Hwang and Yoon [9]. It uses two artificial solutions called the Positive Ideal Solution (PIS) and the Negative Ideal Solution (NIS). The PIS is equivalent to the "pattern" in Hellwig's method. In turn, the NIS minimizes the benefit criteria and maximizes the cost criteria. Taking into account the separation of the alternatives from the PIS and NIS, the Relative Closeness Coefficients (RCCs) to the PIS are calculated, which allows for the ranking of the alternatives.

The applications of the TOPSIS method are very diverse. Apart from the main applications of MCDM mentioned above, it is used in more and more new areas, such as flow control in a manufacturing system [10], the selection of sustainable acid rain control options [11], the selection of the best employees using decision support systems in internal control [12], credit risk evaluations for strategic partners [13], the investigation of aggregated social influence [14], the selection of stocks before the formation of a portfolio based on a company's financial performance [15], the identification of the best wind turbines for different locations [16], the ranking of the developmental performance of nations [17], the evaluation of the quality of institutions in the European Union countries [18], the evaluation of technologies improving the quality of life of elderly people [19], and many others.

In real-life problems, it may be difficult to measure data accurately or present the preferences of the DMs by real numbers; it may also happen that DMs use linguistic variables, in which case we can use another format of data. In such situations, MCDM methods, including TOPSIS, should be extended from real numbers to the new type of data. In the literature, we can find a number of extensions of the TOPSIS method for different types of data: fuzzy numbers [20], ordered fuzzy numbers [21], hesitant fuzzy sets [22], intuitionistic fuzzy sets [23], hesitant Pythagorean fuzzy sets [24], interval-valued fuzzy sets [25], interval neutrosophic sets [26], and others. This shows that researchers are developing new ways of presenting data to allow DMs to formulate their preferences more effectively. We can say that the choice of a data presentation method is an MCDM problem.

In this paper we use INs. An extension of the TOPSIS method to MCDM problems with INs was developed by Jahanshahloo et al. [27]. A limitation of this approach is the definitions of the PIS and NIS. These reference points are represented by real numbers selected from the lower and upper endpoints of the INs in the decision matrix, rather than by INs themselves. This can lead to incorrect results [28]. In the literature, various methods for determining the PIS and NIS for INs have been proposed. In [29,30], they are represented by real numbers instead of intervals, as in [27]. In [31,32], the PIS is defined as an interval whose endpoints are the maximum values from the lower and upper endpoints of the intervals, respectively, while for the NIS we take the minimum values of these endpoints. In [33], the PIS is the average of intervals, while for the NIS, the lower endpoints are the minimum of the lower endpoints of the intervals and the upper endpoints are the maximum of the upper endpoints of the intervals, respectively. The main limitation of these methods is that the determined elements of the PIS and NIS may not be elements of the decision matrix. Dymova et al. [28] presented a method of comparing INs to determine the minimum and maximum elements from the decision matrix. It is based on determining the distance between the midpoints of the INs being compared. In the proposed approach, we will use an analogous method of comparing INs, as proposed by Hu and Wang [34].

An important step in MCDM methods, including the TOPSIS method, is the determination of criteria weights. These describe the importance of each criterion in the decision-making process and have a key influence on the final result. We usually use subjective or objective weights in solving MCDM problems. Subjective weights are determined by the DM or an expert, using their knowledge, experience, skills, etc. In situations where we cannot obtain the appropriate weights or the cost of obtaining them is too high, we can use objective weights. These are determined by using mathematical methods based on the decision matrix. One of the popular methods for determining objective weights is the entropy method [9]. It assigns a higher weight to the given criterion, regarding which the evaluations of alternatives are more diversified. Hosseinzadeh Lotfi and Fallahnejad [35] proposed an extension of the entropy method to data in the form of INs. As a result, we can obtain objective criteria weights, also in the form of INs.

Because of the increasing complexity of decision-making problems, they are often analyzed by a group of DMs, which leads to the development of so-called Multiple Criteria Group Decision Making (MCGDM). In such situations, each member of the group defines an individual decision matrix. A common technique is to determine the aggregate (group) matrix from the individual matrices using a selected aggregation operator. This matrix is the basis for determining objective criteria weights and ranking the alternatives. One of the most popular aggregation operators is the arithmetic mean. Note, however, that this may not reflect the preferences or judgments of DMs [36]. To better explain this limitation, we present two simple numerical examples. We consider a group of two decision makers $\{DM_1, DM_2\}$ who evaluate three alternatives $\{A_1, A_2, A_3\}$ with respect to two benefit criteria $\{C_1, C_2\}$ using the following scale: $\{1, 2, 3, 4, 5\}$. Their evaluations of the alternatives with respect to the criteria are in the form of individual decision matrices X_1 and X_2; by X_{ART} we denote the aggregation results using the arithmetic mean.

Example 1. *The ratings of the alternatives with respect to the criteria provided by the DMs are:*

$$X_1 = \begin{matrix} DM_1 & C_1 & C_2 \\ A_1 \\ A_2 \\ A_3 \end{matrix} \begin{pmatrix} 1 & 1 \\ 2 & 2 \\ 4 & 3 \end{pmatrix}, \quad X_2 = \begin{matrix} DM_2 & C_1 & C_2 \\ A_1 \\ A_2 \\ A_3 \end{matrix} \begin{pmatrix} 3 & 3 \\ 2 & 2 \\ 1 & 1 \end{pmatrix}.$$

Let us note that regardless of whether the ratings of the alternatives with respect to a criterion are in the form "1 and 3", "2 and 2", or "3 and 1", the aggregation results are the same and equal to "2". The aggregation results are:

$$X_{AGG} = \begin{matrix} & C_1 & C_2 \\ A_1 \\ A_2 \\ A_3 \end{matrix} \begin{pmatrix} 2 & 2 \\ 2 & 2 \\ 2.5 & 2 \end{pmatrix}.$$

Based on matrix X_{AGG}, and using the entropy method, we can calculate the criteria weights, obtaining the following vector:

$$w_{AGG} = (1, 0).$$

This means that criterion C_2 has no influence on the ranking of the alternatives and can be omitted. On the other hand, using the proposed approach to the matrices X_1 and X_2, we obtain the following vector of criteria weights:

$$w = (0.5921, 0.4079).$$

Example 2. *The ratings of the alternatives with respect to the criteria provided by the DMs are:*

$$X_1 = \begin{matrix} DM_1 & C_1 & C_2 \\ A_1 \\ A_2 \\ A_3 \end{matrix} \begin{pmatrix} 5 & 1 \\ 3 & 2 \\ 1 & 3 \end{pmatrix}, \quad X_2 = \begin{matrix} DM_2 & C_1 & C_2 \\ A_1 \\ A_2 \\ A_3 \end{matrix} \begin{pmatrix} 1 & 3 \\ 3 & 2 \\ 5 & 1 \end{pmatrix}.$$

The aggregation results are:

$$X_{AGG} = \begin{matrix} & C_1 & C_2 \\ A_1 \\ A_2 \\ A_3 \end{matrix} \begin{pmatrix} 3 & 2 \\ 3 & 2 \\ 3 & 2 \end{pmatrix}.$$

Matrix X_{AGG} shows that all three alternatives $\{A_1, A_2, A_3\}$ are equivalent (i.e., they have the same aggregate rating) and we cannot calculate the vector of criteria weights using the entropy method. However, if we use the proposed approach, we obtain the following vector of criteria weights:

$$w = (0.6497, 0.3503).$$

From Examples 1 and 2, we can conclude that such an averaged result does not reflect the discrepancies between the individual decisions (the preferences of the DMs) and the fact that using such averaged information may lead to an incorrect final decision. The aim of this paper is to present a new approach for GDM using the TOPSIS method and objective criteria weights with INs. The first main contribution of this paper is a method for determining the objective criteria weights for GDM without aggregating individual decision matrices. The method involves transforming the individual decision matrices into criteria matrices and using the interval entropy and the interval TOPSIS methods to determine the objective criteria weights. In this method, unlike in the method proposed by Hosseinzadeh Lotfi and Fallahnejad [35], as the final result, we receive the weights in the form of real numbers. The second main contribution of this paper is the TOPSIS method for

GDM, also without the aggregation of individual decision matrices. This method involves transforming the decision matrices into matrices of alternatives and then using a new interval TOPSIS method for the ranking of alternatives.

The remainder of the paper consists of the following sections. Section 2 presents basic information about INs and a description of the classical TOPSIS method and the classical entropy method. The main section of the paper, i.e., Section 3, presents the algorithm of the proposed method in detail. Next, the proposed method is used in a numerical example and compared with other, similar approaches which are based on the aggregation of individual matrices. The paper ends with the conclusions.

2. Preliminaries

In the following, we present some basic information about INs, the classical TOPSIS method, and the entropy method of determining criteria weights.

2.1. Interval Numbers

Definition 1. *As proposed by [37]: The closed IN, denoted by $[\underline{a}, \overline{a}]$, is the set of real numbers given by:*

$$[\underline{a}, \overline{a}] = \{x \in \mathbb{R} : \underline{a} \leq x \leq \overline{a}\}. \tag{1}$$

Throughout this paper, INs will be used in the interval TOPSIS and interval entropy methods, so we assume that they are positive INs, i.e., $\underline{a} > 0$.

Definition 2. *As proposed by [37]: Let $[\underline{a}, \overline{a}]$ and $\left[\underline{b}, \overline{b}\right]$ be two positive INs, and $\lambda > 0$ be a real number. Then:*

$$[\underline{a}, \overline{a}] = \left[\underline{b}, \overline{b}\right] \text{ if } \underline{a} = \underline{b} \text{ and } \overline{a} = \overline{b},$$

$$[\underline{a}, \overline{a}] + \left[\underline{b}, \overline{b}\right] = \left[\underline{a} + \underline{b}, \overline{a} + \overline{b}\right],$$

$$[\underline{a}, \overline{a}] - \left[\underline{b}, \overline{b}\right] = \left[\underline{a} - \overline{b}, \overline{a} - \underline{b}\right],$$

$$[\underline{a}, \overline{a}] \cdot \left[\underline{b}, \overline{b}\right] = \left[\underline{a} \cdot \underline{b}, \overline{a} \cdot \overline{b}\right],$$

$$[\underline{a}, \overline{a}] / \left[\underline{b}, \overline{b}\right] = \left[\underline{a}/\overline{b}, \overline{a}/\underline{b}\right],$$

$$\lambda \cdot [\underline{a}, \overline{a}] = [\lambda \cdot \underline{a}, \lambda \cdot \overline{a}].$$

The TOPSIS method requires the determination of the minimum and maximum elements. To compare INs, we apply the method developed by Hu and Wang [34]. It is based on a different description of INs than Equation (1) used in Definition 1.

Definition 3. *As proposed by [34]: The IN $[\underline{a}, \overline{a}]$ is represented in the form:*

$$\langle m([\underline{a}, \overline{a}]); w([\underline{a}, \overline{a}]) \rangle \tag{2}$$

where $m([\underline{a}, \overline{a}])$ and $w([\underline{a}, \overline{a}])$ are its mid-point and half-width, respectively, determined as follows:

$$m([\underline{a}, \overline{a}]) = \frac{\underline{a} + \overline{a}}{2}, \tag{3}$$

and:

$$w([\underline{a}, \overline{a}]) = \frac{\overline{a} - \underline{a}}{2}. \tag{4}$$

Using the representation from Equation (2), Hu and Wang defined the order relation "$\prec_=$" for INs as follows.

Definition 4. As proposed by [34]: Let $[\underline{a}, \overline{a}]$ and $\left[\underline{b}, \overline{b}\right]$ be two INs. Then:

$$[\underline{a}, \overline{a}] \prec_= \left[\underline{b}, \overline{b}\right] iff \begin{cases} m([\underline{a}, \overline{a}]) < m\left(\left[\underline{b}, \overline{b}\right]\right), & if \quad m([\underline{a}, \overline{a}]) \neq m\left(\left[\underline{b}, \overline{b}\right]\right) \\ w([\underline{a}, \overline{a}]) \geq w\left(\left[\underline{b}, \overline{b}\right]\right), & if \quad m([\underline{a}, \overline{a}]) = m\left(\left[\underline{b}, \overline{b}\right]\right) \end{cases}. \tag{5}$$

and:

$$[\underline{a}, \overline{a}] \prec \left[\underline{b}, \overline{b}\right] iff [\underline{a}, \overline{a}] \prec_= \left[\underline{b}, \overline{b}\right] \text{ and } [\underline{a}, \overline{a}] \neq \left[\underline{b}, \overline{b}\right]. \tag{6}$$

2.2. The Classical TOPSIS Method

Suppose an MCDM problem is given. The solution of the problem involves the linear ordering of the set of possible alternatives $\{A_1, A_2, \ldots, A_m\}$ and the indication of the best one. The alternatives under consideration are evaluated with respect to a set of criteria $\{C_1, C_2, \ldots, C_n\}$ that determine the choice of a solution. An MCDM problem is represented by a decision matrix X, of the form:

$$X = \begin{pmatrix} x_{11} & x_{12} & \cdots & x_{1n} \\ x_{21} & x_{22} & \cdots & x_{2n} \\ \vdots & \vdots & \ddots & \vdots \\ x_{m1} & x_{m2} & \cdots & x_{mn} \end{pmatrix} \tag{7}$$

where x_{ij} for $i = 1, 2, \ldots, m$ and $j = 1, 2, \ldots, n$ represents the evaluation of the ith alternative with respect to the jth criterion. In addition, we determine the vector criteria weights $w = (w_1, w_2, \ldots, w_n)$. The classical TOPSIS method developed by Hwang and Yoon consists of the following steps [9]:

Step 1. The normalization of the decision matrix X and calculation of the matrix Y, of the form:

$$Y = \begin{pmatrix} y_{11} & y_{12} & \cdots & y_{1n} \\ y_{21} & y_{22} & \cdots & y_{2n} \\ \vdots & \vdots & \ddots & \vdots \\ y_{m1} & y_{m2} & \cdots & y_{mn} \end{pmatrix} \tag{8}$$

using, for $j = 1, .., n$, the following formula:

$$y_{ij} = \frac{x_{ij}}{\sqrt{\sum_{i=1}^{m} x_{ij}^2}}. \tag{9}$$

Step 2. The calculation of the weighted normalized decision matrix V, of the form:

$$V = \begin{pmatrix} v_{11} & v_{12} & \cdots & v_{1n} \\ v_{21} & v_{22} & \cdots & v_{2n} \\ \vdots & \vdots & \ddots & \vdots \\ v_{m1} & v_{m2} & \cdots & v_{mn} \end{pmatrix} \tag{10}$$

where $v_{ij} = w_j \cdot y_{ij}$ for $i = 1, 2, \ldots, m$ and $j = 1, 2, \ldots, n$.

Step 3. Determination of the PIS (A^+), of the form:

$$A^+ = (v_1^+, v_2^+, \ldots, v_n^+) = \left\{ \left(\max_i v_{ij} \mid j \in B\right), \left(\min_i v_{ij} \mid j \in C\right) \right\}, \tag{11}$$

and of the NIS (A^-), of the form:

$$A^- = (v_1^-, v_2^-, \ldots, v_n^-) = \left\{ \left(\min_i v_{ij} \mid j \in B \right), \left(\max_i v_{ij} \mid j \in C \right) \right\}, \quad (12)$$

where B and C are associated with benefit and cost criteria, respectively.

Step 4. The calculation of the distance of each A_i ($i = 1, \ldots, m$) from the PIS:

$$d_i^+ = \sqrt{\sum_{j=1}^n \left(v_{ij} - v_j^+ \right)^2}, \quad (13)$$

and from the NIS:

$$d_i^- = \sqrt{\sum_{j=1}^n \left(v_{ij} - v_j^- \right)^2}. \quad (14)$$

Step 5. The calculation of the coefficients RCC_i ($i = 1, 2, \ldots, m$) of relative closeness to the PIS for each alternative A_i ($i = 1, \ldots, m$), using the following formula:

$$RCC_i = \frac{d_i^-}{d_i^+ + d_i^-}. \quad (15)$$

Step 6. The ranking of alternatives in descending order, using RCC_i, and the determination of the best one (the one with the highest value of RCC_i).

2.3. The Entropy Method

The starting point for determining objective criteria weights by the entropy method is the decision matrix, Equation (7) (see Section 2.2). It consists of the following steps [9]:

Step 1. The normalization of the decision matrix X and the calculation of the matrix Y, of the form:

$$Y = \begin{pmatrix} y_{11} & y_{12} & \cdots & y_{1n} \\ y_{21} & y_{22} & \cdots & y_{2n} \\ \vdots & \vdots & \ddots & \vdots \\ y_{m1} & y_{m2} & \cdots & y_{mn} \end{pmatrix} \quad (16)$$

using the following formula for $j = 1, \ldots, n$:

$$y_{ij} = \frac{x_{ij}}{\sum_{i=1}^m x_{ij}}. \quad (17)$$

Step 2. The calculation of the vector of entropy $e = (e_1, e_2, \ldots, e_n)$, using the following formula for $j = 1, \ldots, n$:

$$e_j = -\frac{1}{\ln m} \sum_{i=1}^m y_{ij} \ln y_{ij}. \quad (18)$$

Moreover, when $y_{ij} = 0$ for some i, the value of $y_{ij} \ln y_{ij}$ is taken as 0, which is consistent with $\lim_{x \to 0^+} x \ln x = 0$.

Step 3. The calculation of the vector of diversification $d = (d_1, d_2, \ldots, d_n)$, using the following formula for $j = 1, \ldots, n$:

$$d_j = 1 - e_j. \quad (19)$$

Step 4. The calculation of the vector of objective criteria weights $w = (w_1, w_2, \ldots, w_n)$, where:

$$w_j = \frac{d_j}{\sum_{j=1}^n d_j}. \quad (20)$$

3. The Proposed Approach

The proposed extension of the TOPSIS method with objective criteria weights based on interval data for GDM consists of three major stages:

- The preparation of the data;
- The calculation of the objective criteria weights using the interval entropy method and the interval TOPSIS method, without the aggregation of individual decision matrices;
- The linear ordering of alternatives using the extended TOPSIS method, based on interval data, without the aggregation of individual decision matrices.

A flow chart and a graphical scheme of the proposed method are shown in Figures 1 and 2, respectively.

Stage 1: The preparation of the data. As in Section 2.2., suppose an MCDM problem for GDM is given, which consists of a set of possible alternatives $\{A_1, A_2, \ldots, A_m\}$ and a set of criteria $\{C_1, C_2, \ldots, C_n\}$. In this case, the evaluation of alternatives, with respect to the criteria, is performed by a group of DMs or experts $\{DM_1, DM_2, \ldots, DM_K\}$. In the process of GDM, each DM_k ($k = 1, 2, \ldots, K$) constructs a matrix, called the individual decision matrix, of the form:

$$X^k = \begin{array}{c} DM_k \\ A_1 \\ A_2 \\ \vdots \\ A_m \end{array} \begin{pmatrix} C_1 & C_2 & \cdots & C_n \\ x_{11}^k & x_{12}^k & \cdots & x_{1n}^k \\ x_{21}^k & x_{22}^k & \cdots & x_{2n}^k \\ \vdots & \vdots & \ddots & \vdots \\ x_{m1}^k & x_{m2}^k & \cdots & x_{mn}^k \end{pmatrix}. \quad (21)$$

In the proposed approach, each element x_{ij}^k for $i = 1, 2, \ldots, m$ and $j = 1, 2, \ldots, n$ of the matrix X^k is in the form of an IN, i.e., $x_{ij}^k = \left[\underline{x}_{ij}^k, \overline{x}_{ij}^k\right]$, and represents the evaluation of the kth DM of the ith alternative with respect to the jth criterion.

Stage 2: The calculation of the objective criteria weights for GDM, without the aggregation of individual decision matrices. The proposed method of calculation of the objective criteria weights based on interval entropy and interval TOPSIS consists of the following steps.

Step 1. The normalization, for each decision maker DM_k ($k = 1, 2, \ldots, K$), of their individual decision matrix, as given by Equation (21), and obtaining the matrix Y^k, of the form:

$$Y^k = \begin{array}{c} DM_k \\ A_1 \\ A_2 \\ \vdots \\ A_m \end{array} \begin{pmatrix} C_1 & C_2 & \cdots & C_n \\ y_{11}^k & y_{12}^k & \cdots & y_{1n}^k \\ y_{21}^k & y_{22}^k & \cdots & y_{2n}^k \\ \vdots & \vdots & \ddots & \vdots \\ y_{m1}^k & y_{m2}^k & \cdots & y_{mn}^k \end{pmatrix} \quad (22)$$

using the following formula for $j = 1, .., n$ [35]:

$$y_{ij}^k = \begin{cases} \left[\dfrac{\underline{x}_{ij}^k}{\sum_{i=1}^m \overline{x}_{ij}^k}, \dfrac{\overline{x}_{ij}^k}{\sum_{i=1}^m \underline{x}_{ij}^k}\right] & \text{if } j \in B \\ \left[\dfrac{1/\overline{x}_{ij}^k}{\sum_{i=1}^m 1/\underline{x}_{ij}^k}, \dfrac{1/\underline{x}_{ij}^k}{\sum_{i=1}^m 1/\overline{x}_{ij}^k}\right] & \text{if } j \in C \end{cases}. \quad (23)$$

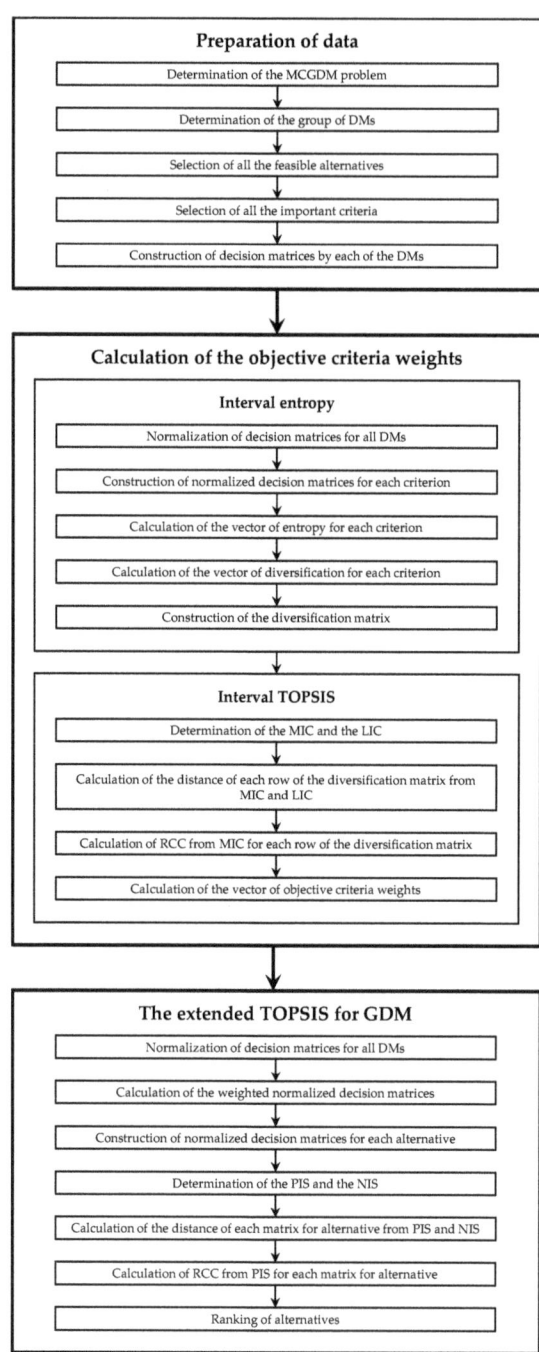

Figure 1. The conceptual framework of the proposed method.

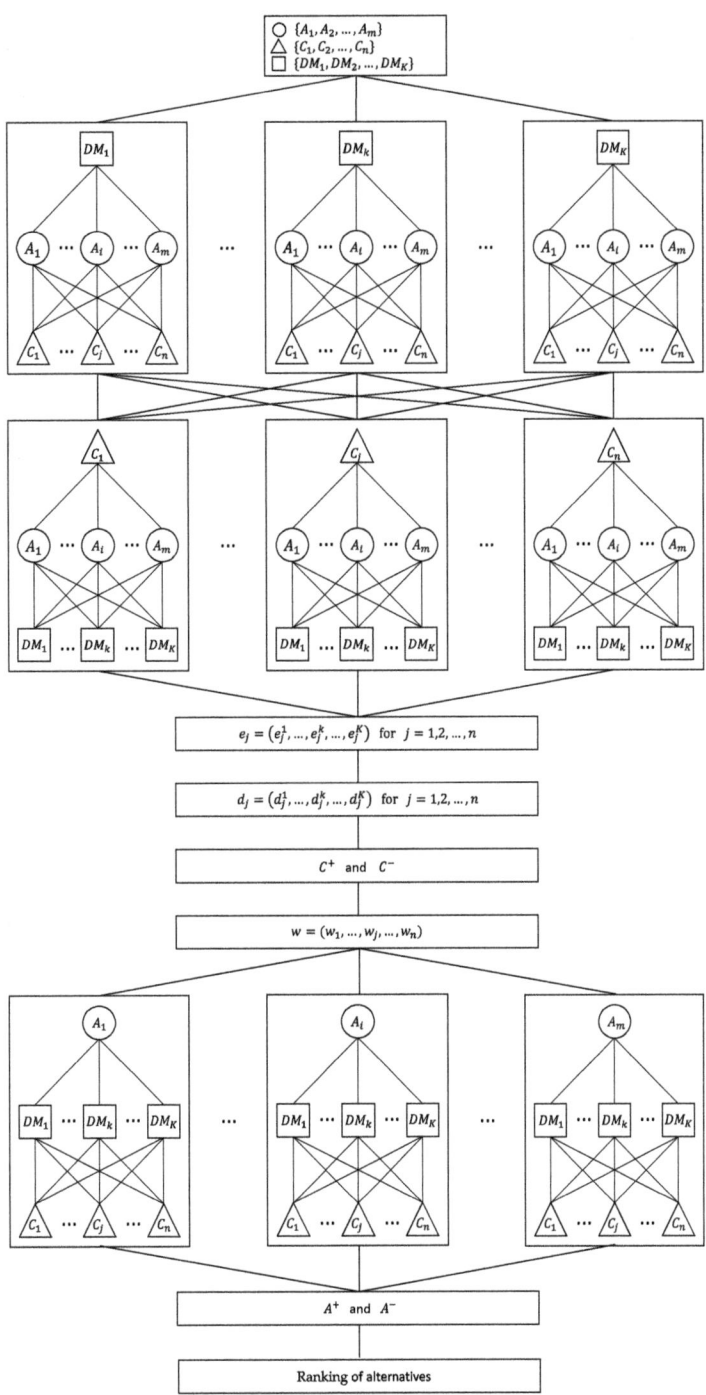

Figure 2. Hierarchical structure of the proposed method.

Step 2. The construction, for each criterion C_j $(j = 1, 2, \ldots, n)$, of the matrix V^j, of the form:

$$V^j = \begin{array}{c} C_j \\ A_1 \\ A_2 \\ \vdots \\ A_m \end{array} \begin{pmatrix} DM_1 & DM_2 & \cdots & DM_K \\ y_{1j}^1 & y_{1j}^2 & \cdots & y_{1j}^K \\ y_{2j}^1 & y_{2j}^2 & \cdots & y_{2j}^K \\ \vdots & \vdots & \ddots & \vdots \\ y_{mj}^1 & y_{mj}^2 & \cdots & y_{mj}^K \end{pmatrix}. \qquad (24)$$

Step 3. The calculation, for each criterion C_j $(j = 1, 2, \ldots, n)$, of the entropy vector e_j, of the form:

$$e_j = \left(e_j^1, e_j^2, \ldots, e_j^K \right) \qquad (25)$$

based on the matrix V^j, where $e_j^k = \left[\underline{e}_j^k, \overline{e}_j^k \right]$ for $k = 1, 2, \ldots, K$ and:

$$\underline{e}_j^k = \min\left\{ -\frac{1}{\ln m} \sum_{i=1}^m \underline{y}_{ij}^k \ln \underline{y}_{ij}^k, -\frac{1}{\ln m} \sum_{i=1}^m \overline{y}_{ij}^k \ln \overline{y}_{ij}^k \right\}, \qquad (26)$$

and:

$$\overline{e}_j^k = \max\left\{ -\frac{1}{\ln m} \sum_{i=1}^m \underline{y}_{ij}^k \ln \underline{y}_{ij}^k, -\frac{1}{\ln m} \sum_{i=1}^m \overline{y}_{ij}^k \ln \overline{y}_{ij}^k \right\}, \qquad (27)$$

and $\underline{y}_{ij}^k \ln \underline{y}_{ij}^k$ or $\overline{y}_{ij}^k \ln \overline{y}_{ij}^k$ is defined to be 0 if $\underline{y}_{ij}^k = 0$ or $\overline{y}_{ij}^k = 0$ [35], respectively.

Step 4. The calculation, for each criterion C_j $(j = 1, 2, \ldots, n)$, of the diversification vector d_j, of the form:

$$d_j = \left(d_j^1, d_j^2, \ldots, d_j^K \right) \qquad (28)$$

where $d_j^k = 1 - e_j^k = \left[1 - \overline{e}_j^k, 1 - \underline{e}_j^k \right]$ for $k = 1, 2, \ldots, K$, and the construction of diversification matrix D, of the form:

$$D = \begin{array}{c} C_1 \\ C_2 \\ \vdots \\ C_n \end{array} \begin{pmatrix} DM_1 & DM_2 & \cdots & DM_K \\ d_1^1 & d_1^2 & \cdots & d_1^K \\ d_2^1 & d_2^2 & \cdots & d_2^K \\ \vdots & \vdots & \ddots & \vdots \\ d_n^1 & d_n^2 & \cdots & d_n^K \end{pmatrix}. \qquad (29)$$

Step 5. The determination of the Most Important Criterion (MIC):

$$C^+ = \left(c_1^+, c_2^+, \ldots, c_K^+ \right) \qquad (30)$$

where $c_k^+ = \max_j d_j^k$ for $k = 1, 2, \ldots, K$, and of the Least Important Criterion (LIC):

$$C^- = \left(c_1^-, c_2^-, \ldots, c_K^- \right) \qquad (31)$$

where $c_k^- = [0, 0]$ for $k = 1, 2, \ldots, K$, based on the matrix D.

Step 6. The calculation of the distance of each diversification vector d_j, representing the weight of criterion C_j $(j = 1, 2, \ldots, n)$, from the MIC:

$$d_j^{C+} = \sqrt{ \sum_{k=1}^K \left[\left(\underline{d}_j^k - \underline{c}_k^+ \right)^2 + \left(\overline{d}_j^k - \overline{c}_k^+ \right)^2 \right] }, \qquad (32)$$

and from the LIC:

$$d_j^{C-} = \sqrt{\sum_{k=1}^{K}\left[\left(\underline{d}_j^k - \underline{c}_k^-\right)^2 + \left(\overline{d}_j^k - \overline{c}_k^-\right)^2\right]}. \tag{33}$$

Step 7. The calculation of the coefficients RCC_j^C ($j = 1, 2, \ldots, n$) of relative closeness to the MIC for each diversification vector d_j, using the following formula:

$$RCC_j^C = \frac{d_j^{C-}}{d_j^{C+} + d_j^{C-}}. \tag{34}$$

Step 8. The calculation of the vector of objective criteria weights:

$$w = (w_1, w_2, \ldots, w_n) \tag{35}$$

where:

$$w_j = \frac{RCC_j^C}{\sum_{j=1}^{n} RCC_j^C} \tag{36}$$

for $j = 1, 2, \ldots, n$.

Stage 3: The extended TOPSIS method for GDM without the aggregation of individual decision matrices.

The developed extended TOPSIS for GDM without the aggregation of individual decision matrices consists of the following steps.

Step 1. The normalization, for each decision maker DM_k ($k = 1, 2, \ldots, K$), of their individual decision matrix, as given by Equation (21), and obtaining the matrix Y^k, of the form

$$Y^k = \begin{array}{c} DM_k \\ A_1 \\ A_2 \\ \vdots \\ A_m \end{array} \begin{pmatrix} C_1 & C_2 & \cdots & C_n \\ y_{11}^k & y_{12}^k & \cdots & y_{1n}^k \\ y_{21}^k & y_{22}^k & \cdots & y_{2n}^k \\ \vdots & \vdots & \ddots & \vdots \\ y_{m1}^k & y_{m2}^k & \cdots & y_{mn}^k \end{pmatrix} \tag{37}$$

using the following formula for $j = 1, \ldots, n$ [38]:

$$y_{ij}^k = \begin{cases} \left[\dfrac{\underline{x}_{ij}^k}{\sum_{i=1}^{m} \overline{x}_{ij}^k}, \dfrac{\overline{x}_{ij}^k}{\sum_{i=1}^{m} \underline{x}_{ij}^k}\right] & \text{if } j \in B \\ \left[\dfrac{1/\overline{x}_{ij}^k}{\sum_{i=1}^{m} 1/\underline{x}_{ij}^k}, \dfrac{1/\underline{x}_{ij}^k}{\sum_{i=1}^{m} 1/\overline{x}_{ij}^k}\right] & \text{if } j \in C \end{cases}. \tag{38}$$

Remark 1. *Note that the normalization method, Equation (38), used above does not provide the property that the normalized elements y_{ij}^k belong to the interval $[0, 1]$. If we require this property to be satisfied, the elements of the matrix Y^k can be recalculated using the following formula [38]:*

$$z_{ij}^k = \left[\frac{\underline{y}_{ij}^k}{\sqrt{\sum_{i=1}^{m}\left[\left(\underline{y}_{ij}^k\right)^2 + \left(\overline{y}_{ij}^k\right)^2\right]}}, \frac{\overline{y}_{ij}^k}{\sqrt{\sum_{i=1}^{m}\left[\left(\underline{y}_{ij}^k\right)^2 + \left(\overline{y}_{ij}^k\right)^2\right]}}\right]. \tag{39}$$

As the final result, we obtain normalized decision matrices Z^k ($k = 1, 2, \ldots, K$):

$$Z^k = \begin{array}{c} DM_k \\ A_1 \\ A_2 \\ \vdots \\ A_m \end{array} \begin{pmatrix} C_1 & C_2 & \cdots & C_n \\ z^k_{11} & z^k_{12} & \cdots & z^k_{1n} \\ z^k_{21} & z^k_{22} & \cdots & z^k_{2n} \\ \vdots & \vdots & \ddots & \vdots \\ z^k_{m1} & z^k_{m2} & \cdots & z^k_{mn} \end{pmatrix} \qquad (40)$$

Step 2. The calculation of the weighted normalized individual matrices V^k ($k = 1, 2, \ldots, K$):

$$V^k = \begin{array}{c} DM_k \\ A_1 \\ A_2 \\ \vdots \\ A_m \end{array} \begin{pmatrix} C_1 & C_2 & \cdots & C_n \\ v^k_{11} & v^k_{12} & \cdots & v^k_{1n} \\ v^k_{21} & v^k_{22} & \cdots & v^k_{2n} \\ \vdots & \vdots & \ddots & \vdots \\ v^k_{m1} & v^k_{m2} & \cdots & v^k_{mn} \end{pmatrix} \qquad (41)$$

where:

$$v^k_{ij} = w_j z^k_{ij} = \left[w_j \underline{z}^k_{ij}, w_j \overline{z}^k_{ij} \right] \qquad (42)$$

and w_j ($j = 1, 2, \ldots, n$) are the objective criteria weights obtained in Stage 2.

Step 3. The construction, for each alternative A_i ($i = 1, 2, \ldots, m$), of the matrix A^i:

$$A^i = \begin{array}{c} A_i \\ DM_1 \\ DM_2 \\ \vdots \\ DM_K \end{array} \begin{pmatrix} C_1 & C_2 & \cdots & C_n \\ v^1_{i1} & v^1_{i2} & \cdots & v^1_{in} \\ v^2_{i1} & v^2_{i2} & \cdots & v^2_{in} \\ \vdots & \vdots & \ddots & \vdots \\ v^K_{i1} & v^K_{i2} & \cdots & v^K_{in} \end{pmatrix}. \qquad (43)$$

Step 4. The determination of the PIS (A^+):

$$A^+ = \begin{array}{c} DM_1 \\ DM_2 \\ \vdots \\ DM_K \end{array} \begin{pmatrix} C_1 & C_2 & \cdots & C_n \\ v^{1+}_1 & v^{1+}_2 & \cdots & v^{1+}_k \\ v^{2+}_1 & v^{2+}_2 & \cdots & v^{2+}_n \\ \vdots & \vdots & \ddots & \vdots \\ v^{K+}_1 & v^{K+}_2 & \cdots & v^{K+}_n \end{pmatrix} \qquad (44)$$

where $v^{k+}_j = \max\limits_i v^k_{ij}$ for $j = 1, 2, \ldots, n$ and $k = 1, 2, \ldots, K$ and of NIS (A^-):

$$A^- = \begin{array}{c} DM_1 \\ DM_2 \\ \vdots \\ DM_K \end{array} \begin{pmatrix} C_1 & C_2 & \cdots & C_n \\ v^{1-}_1 & v^{1-}_2 & \cdots & v^{1-}_k \\ v^{2-}_1 & v^{2-}_2 & \cdots & v^{2-}_n \\ \vdots & \vdots & \ddots & \vdots \\ v^{K-}_1 & v^{K-}_2 & \cdots & v^{K-}_n \end{pmatrix} \qquad (45)$$

where $v^{k-}_j = \min\limits_i v^k_{ij}$ for $j = 1, 2, \ldots, n$ and $k = 1, 2, \ldots, K$.

Step 5. The calculation of the distance of each matrix A^i, representing the alternative A_i ($i = 1, \ldots, m$), from the PIS:

$$d_i^{A+} = \sqrt{\sum_{k=1}^{K} \sum_{j=1}^{n} \left[\left(\underline{v}_{ij}^k - \underline{v}_j^{k+} \right)^2 + \left(\overline{v}_{ij}^k - \overline{v}_j^{k+} \right)^2 \right]}, \qquad (46)$$

and from the NIS:

$$d_i^{A-} = \sqrt{\sum_{k=1}^{K} \sum_{j=1}^{n} \left[\left(\underline{v}_{ij}^k - \underline{v}_j^{k-} \right)^2 + \left(\overline{v}_{ij}^k - \overline{v}_j^{k-} \right)^2 \right]}. \qquad (47)$$

Step 6. The calculation of the coefficients RCC_i^A ($i = 1, 2, \ldots, m$) of relative closeness to the PIS for each alternative A_i ($i = 1, \ldots, m$), using the following formula:

$$RCC_i^A = \frac{d_i^{A-}}{d_i^{A-} + d_i^{A+}}. \qquad (48)$$

Step 7. The ranking of alternatives in descending order, using RCC_i^A, and the determination of the best one.

4. A Numerical Example and Results

The approach proposed in Section 3 will now be illustrated with a numerical example, taken from [38], related to the evaluation of the authorities of a university in China. The set of alternatives $\{A_1, A_2, A_3\}$ consists of the president and two vice presidents, who are evaluated by teams of teachers, DM_1, researchers, DM_2, and undergraduates, DM_3. The DMs evaluate the presidents with respect to leadership, C_1, performance, C_2, and style of work, C_3, using a point scale from 0 to 100. The team ratings are represented by INs, where the lower end is the minimum and the upper end is the maximum ratings among the group members. The individual decision matrices are presented in Table 1.

Table 1. Individual decision matrices.

		C_1	C_2	C_3
	A_1	[60, 90]	[72, 86]	[85, 92]
DM_1	A_2	[77, 81]	[69, 93]	[83, 88]
	A_3	[80, 96]	[59, 87]	[68, 85]
	A_1	[77, 83]	[68, 86]	[82, 90]
DM_2	A_2	[93, 98]	[76, 86]	[65, 87]
	A_3	[79, 85]	[72, 92]	[81, 97]
	A_1	[85, 86]	[76, 86]	[80, 97]
DM_3	A_2	[79, 87]	[75, 89]	[81, 93]
	A_3	[62, 82]	[84, 89]	[78, 82]

The first main step of the proposed approach is to determine the objective criteria weights, as described in Stage 2 of Section 3. The individual decision matrices are normalized (see Table 2) and then transformed into matrices of criteria (see Table 3). Next, for each criterion matrix, the entropy and diversification vectors are determined (see Tables 4 and 5). Using the diversification vectors, we construct a diversification matrix, which is the basis for calculating the objective criteria weights using the interval TOPSIS method. Table 6 presents reference points—in this case, the MIC and LIC. After calculating the distance of each row of the diversification matrix from the MIC and LIC, the RCCs are calculated (see Table 7). These coefficients, after normalization, are the objective criteria weights (see Table 7 and Figure 3). In our example, we obtain the following vector:

$$w = (0.3049, 0.4372, 0.2579).$$

Table 2. Normalized individual decision matrices for the calculation of criteria weights.

		C_1	C_2	C_3
DM_1	A_1	[0.2247, 0.3371]	[0.2707, 0.3233]	[0.3208, 0.3472]
	A_2	[0.2884, 0.3034]	[0.2594, 0.3496]	[0.3132, 0.3321]
	A_3	[0.2996, 0.3596]	[0.2218, 0.3271]	[0.2566, 0.3208]
DM_2	A_1	[0.2895, 0.3120]	[0.2576, 0.3258]	[0.2993, 0.3285]
	A_2	[0.3496, 0.3684]	[0.2879, 0.3258]	[0.2372, 0.3175]
	A_3	[0.2970, 0.3195]	[0.2727, 0.3485]	[0.2956, 0.3540]
DM_3	A_1	[0.3333, 0.3373]	[0.2879, 0.3258]	[0.2941, 0.3566]
	A_2	[0.3098, 0.3412]	[0.2841, 0.3371]	[0.2978, 0.3419]
	A_3	[0.2431, 0.3216]	[0.3182, 0.3371]	[0.2868, 0.3015]

Table 3. Matrices for each criterion.

		DM_1	DM_2	DM_3
C_1	A_1	[0.2247, 0.3371]	[0.2895, 0.3120]	[0.3333, 0.3373]
	A_2	[0.2884, 0.3034]	[0.3496, 0.3684]	[0.3098, 0.3412]
	A_3	[0.2996, 0.3596]	[0.2970, 0.3195]	[0.2431, 0.3216]
C_2	A_1	[0.2707, 0.3233]	[0.2576, 0.3258]	[0.2879, 0.3258]
	A_2	[0.2594, 0.3496]	[0.2879, 0.3258]	[0.2841, 0.3371]
	A_3	[0.2218, 0.3271]	[0.2727, 0.3485]	[0.3182, 0.3371]
C_3	A_1	[0.3208, 0.3472]	[0.2993, 0.3285]	[0.2941, 0.3566]
	A_2	[0.3132, 0.3321]	[0.2372, 0.3175]	[0.2978, 0.3419]
	A_3	[0.2566, 0.3208]	[0.2956, 0.3540]	[0.2868, 0.3015]

Table 4. Vectors of entropy.

e_1	([0.9605, 0.9978], [0.9893, 0.9975], [0.9767, 0.9997])
e_2	([0.9446, 0.9995], [0.9669, 0.9995], [0.9834, 0.9999])
e_3	([0.9807, 0.9995], [0.9672, 0.9990], [0.9820, 0.9977])

Table 5. Vectors of diversification.

d_1	([0.0022, 0.0395], [0.0025, 0.0107], [0.0003, 0.0233])
d_2	([0.0005, 0.0554], [0.0005, 0.0331], [0.0001, 0.0166])
d_3	([0.0005, 0.0193], [0.0010, 0.0328], [0.0023, 0.0180])

Table 6. MIC and LIC.

C^+	([0.0005, 0.0554], [0.0010, 0.0328], [0.0003, 0.0233])
C^-	([0, 0], [0, 0], [0, 0])

Table 7. Objective criteria weights.

	d_j^{C+}	d_j^{C-}	RRC_j^C	w_j
C_1	0.0272	0.0472	0.6340	0.3049
C_2	0.0067	0.0666	0.9091	0.4372
C_3	0.0365	0.0422	0.5362	0.2579

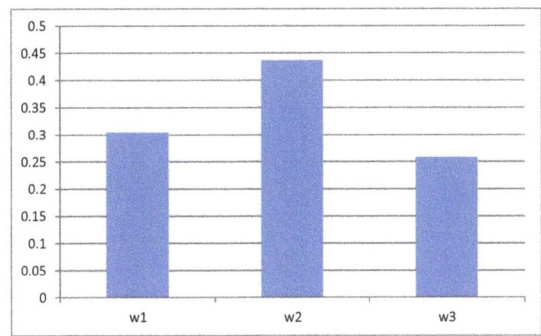

Figure 3. Objective criteria weights.

The second main step of the proposed approach is to use an extension of the TOPSIS method for GDM without the aggregation of individual matrices, as described in Stage 3 of Section 3. The individual decision matrices (see Table 1) are normalized (see Table 8) using Equation (38) and then Equation (39). Using objective criteria weights (see Table 7), we calculate the weighted normalized decision matrices (see Table 9). These matrices are the basis for constructing the matrix for each alternative (see Table 10) of the form (43). Now, we apply the extended TOPSIS method for the matrices of alternatives for ranking the alternatives. Table 11 presents reference points—in this case, the PIS and NIS. Finally, the distances of the alternatives from the PIS and NIS and the RCCs are calculated (see Table 12). Based on these coefficients, the ranking of the alternatives is as follows:

$$A_3 \prec A_1 \prec A_2$$

where " $\prec$ " means "inferior to" (see Table 12 and Figure 4). It means that the highest rating is given to the vice president, A_2. The symbol J in Table 12 represents the normalized RCCs.

Table 8. Normalized individual decision matrices for the TOPSIS method.

		C_1	C_2	C_3
	A_1	[0.1572, 0.2902]	[0.1876, 0.2980]	[0.2260, 0.2747]
DM_1	A_2	[0.2018, 0.2611]	[0.1798, 0.3223]	[0.2207, 0.2628]
	A_3	[0.2096, 0.3095]	[0.1537, 0.3015]	[0.1808, 0.2538]
	A_1	[0.2045, 0.2354]	[0.1803, 0.2787]	[0.2098, 0.2768]
DM_2	A_2	[0.2470, 0.2780]	[0.2015, 0.2787]	[0.1663, 0.2676]
	A_3	[0.2098, 0.2411]	[0.1909, 0.2982]	[0.2073, 0.2983]
	A_1	[0.2348, 0.2681]	[0.2029, 0.2579]	[0.2071, 0.2858]
DM_3	A_2	[0.2183, 0.2712]	[0.2002, 0.2669]	[0.2097, 0.2740]
	A_3	[0.1713, 0.2556]	[0.2242, 0.2669]	[0.2019, 0.2416]

Table 9. Weighted normalized individual decision matrices for the TOPSIS method.

		C_1	C_2	C_3
DM_1	A_1	[0.0479, 0.0885]	[0.0820, 0.1303]	[0.0583, 0.0708]
	A_2	[0.0615, 0.0796]	[0.0786, 0.1409]	[0.0569, 0.0678]
	A_3	[0.0639, 0.0944]	[0.0672, 0.1318]	[0.0466, 0.0655]
DM_2	A_1	[0.0623, 0.0718]	[0.0788, 0.1219]	[0.0541, 0.0714]
	A_2	[0.0753, 0.0848]	[0.0881, 0.1219]	[0.0429, 0.0690]
	A_3	[0.0640, 0.0735]	[0.0835, 0.1304]	[0.0535, 0.0769]
DM_3	A_1	[0.0716, 0.0817]	[0.0887, 0.1128]	[0.0534, 0.0737]
	A_2	[0.0666, 0.0827]	[0.0875, 0.1167]	[0.0541, 0.0707]
	A_3	[0.0522, 0.0779]	[0.0980, 0.1167]	[0.0521, 0.0623]

Table 10. Matrices of alternatives.

		C_1	C_2	C_3
A_1	DM_1	[0.0479, 0.0885]	[0.0820, 0.1303]	[0.0583, 0.0708]
	DM_2	[0.0623, 0.0718]	[0.0788, 0.1219]	[0.0541, 0.0714]
	DM_3	[0.0716, 0.0817]	[0.0887, 0.1128]	[0.0534, 0.0737]
A_2	DM_1	[0.0615, 0.0796]	[0.0786, 0.1409]	[0.0569, 0.0678]
	DM_2	[0.0753, 0.0848]	[0.0881, 0.1219]	[0.0429, 0.0690]
	DM_3	[0.0666, 0.0827]	[0.0875, 0.1167]	[0.0541, 0.0707]
A_3	DM_1	[0.0639, 0.0944]	[0.0672, 0.1318]	[0.0466, 0.0655]
	DM_2	[0.0640, 0.0735]	[0.0835, 0.1304]	[0.0535, 0.0769]
	DM_3	[0.0522, 0.0779]	[0.0980, 0.1167]	[0.0521, 0.0623]

Table 11. PIS and NIS.

		C_1	C_2	C_3
A^+	DM_1	[0.0639, 0.0944]	[0.0786, 0.1409]	[0.0583, 0.0708]
	DM_2	[0.0753, 0.0848]	[0.0835, 0.1304]	[0.0535, 0.0769]
	DM_3	[0.0716, 0.0817]	[0.0980, 0.1167]	[0.0534, 0.0737]
A^-	DM_1	[0.0479, 0.0885]	[0.0672, 0.1318]	[0.0466, 0.0655]
	DM_2	[0.0623, 0.0718]	[0.0788, 0.1219]	[0.0429, 0.0690]
	DM_3	[0.0522, 0.0779]	[0.0887, 0.1128]	[0.0521, 0.0623]

Table 12. The ranking of the alternatives—R.

	d_j^{A+}	d_j^{A-}	RCC_j^A	R	J
A_1	0.0313	0.0322	0.5076	2	0.3322
A_2	0.0255	0.0364	0.5884	1	0.3851
A_3	0.0340	0.0258	0.4318	3	0.2826

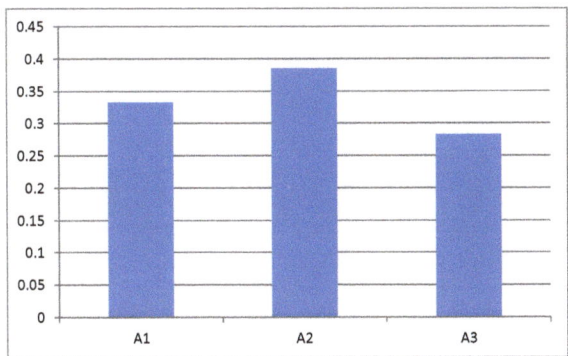

Figure 4. The ranking of the alternatives.

5. Comparison of the Proposed Method with Other, Similar Approaches

In the following, the approach proposed in Section 3 will be compared with other, similar approaches. In practice, the most common methods for GDM use a certain operator to aggregate the individual decision matrices, given by Equation (21), into a group matrix X of the form Equation (7), which is the starting point for the ranking of alternatives. To compare the results obtained by the proposed method (PM), we use the following operators:

- AM—arithmetic mean, defined by:

$$x_{ij} = \frac{1}{K}\sum_{k=1}^{K} x_{ij}^k = \left[\frac{1}{K}\sum_{k=1}^{K} \underline{x}_{ij}^k, \frac{1}{K}\sum_{k=1}^{K} \overline{x}_{ij}^k\right];$$

- GM—geometric mean, defined by:

$$x_{ij} = \left(\prod_{k=1}^{K} x_{ij}^k\right)^{\frac{1}{K}} = \left(\left(\prod_{k=1}^{K} \underline{x}_{ij}^k\right)^{\frac{1}{K}}, \left(\prod_{k=1}^{K} \overline{x}_{ij}^k\right)^{\frac{1}{K}}\right);$$

- WM—weighted mean, defined by:

$$x_{ij} = \sum_{k=1}^{K} \lambda_k x_{ij}^k = \left(\sum_{k=1}^{K} \lambda_k \underline{x}_{ij}^k, \sum_{k=1}^{K} \lambda_k \overline{x}_{ij}^k\right)$$

where λ_k are weights that determine the importance of the DMs, such that $\lambda_k \in [0,1]$ and $\sum_{k=1}^{K} \lambda_k = 1$.

In the WM method, the vector of DM weights $\lambda = (0.2661, 0.3573, 0.3766)$ is determined by the method proposed by [38]. Next, based on the matrix X, we determine the objective criteria weights using the method proposed by Lotfi and Fallahnejad [35]. In this case, the criteria weights are in the form of INs, so we do not compare them with the criteria weights obtained by the proposed method described in Stage 2 of Section 3 and presented in Table 7. To obtain the ranking of the alternatives, we use the normalization method proposed by Jahanshahloo et al. [27]; the PIS and NIS are determined using Equations (5) and (6), whereas the distances of the alternatives from the PIS and NIS are calculated using Equations (46) and (47), where $K = 1$. Because the analyzed methods are significantly different, to compare the final results we use the indicator J instead of the RRCs. Table 13 and Figure 5 present the results obtained. We can notice that all the analyzed methods indicated alternative A_2 as the best one, and the obtained values of the indicator J are similar. On the other hand, methods that use an aggregation operator give a different ranking than the proposed method, of the form:

$$A_1 \prec A_3 \prec A_2$$

where alternatives A_1 and A_3 are swapped.

Table 13. Comparison of results.

	PM	AM	GM	WM
A_1	0.332244	0.291138	0.297903	0.297472
A_2	0.385121	0.385427	0.384682	0.385048
A_3	0.282635	0.323435	0.317416	0.317480

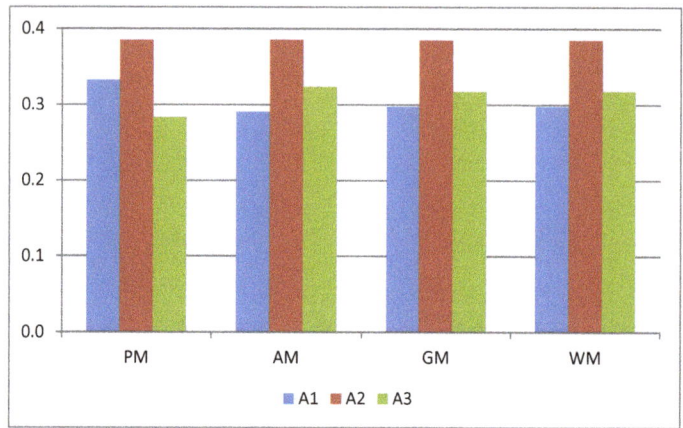

Figure 5. Comparison of results.

6. Conclusions

This paper presents a new extension of the TOPSIS method for GDM, using INs. It is an alternative to methods based on the aggregation of individual matrices. It uses the transformation of decision matrices into criteria matrices to determine objective criteria weights, while it uses alternatives matrices to create rankings of alternatives. The numerical example shows that the results obtained by the proposed method differ from the results obtained by the methods based on the aggregation of individual matrices using the arithmetic mean, geometric mean, and weighted mean (with weights reflecting the importance assigned to the DMs).

However, it is worth noting that the proposed method has some limitations, as it uses data in the form of INs. This implies the necessity of extending the proposed method to other types of imprecise data, which will be the subject of further research. Furthermore, the proposed method should be extended by taking into account the subjective criteria weights and the subjective and objective weights of the DMs, to ensure that all key elements in the decision-making process are taken into account.

Funding: The work was performed in the framework of project WZ/WI-IIT/1/2020 at the Bialystok University of Technology and financed by the Ministry of Science and Higher Education.

Data Availability Statement: Not applicable.

Acknowledgments: The author would like to thank the editor of the *Entropy* journal and the two anonymous reviewers for their valuable comments and suggestions.

Conflicts of Interest: The author declare no conflict of interest.

Abbreviations

TOPSIS	Technique for Order Preference by Similarity to Ideal Solution
GDM	Group Decision Making
IN	Interval Number
DM	Decision Maker
MCDM	Multiple Criteria Decision Making
PIS	Positive Ideal Solution
NIS	Negative Ideal Solution
RCC	Relative Closeness Coefficient
MCGDM	Multiple Criteria Group Decision Making
MIC	Most Important Criterion
LIC	Least Important Criterion
PM	Proposed Method
AM	Arithmetic Mean
GM	Geometric Mean
WM	Weighted Mean

References

1. Behzadian, M.; Otaghsara, S.K.; Yazdani, M.; Ignatius, J. A state-of the art survey of TOPSIS applications. *Expert Syst. Appl.* **2012**, *39*, 13051–13069. [CrossRef]
2. Mardani, A.; Jusoh, A.; Zavadskas, E.K. Fuzzy multiple criteria decision-making techniques and applications—Two decades review from 1994 to 2014. *Expert Syst. Appl.* **2015**, *42*, 4126–4148. [CrossRef]
3. Palczewski, K.; Sałabun, W. The fuzzy TOPSIS applications in the last decade. *Procedia Comput. Sci.* **2019**, *159*, 2294–2303. [CrossRef]
4. Koganti, V.K.; Menikonda, N.; Anbuudayasankar, S.P.; Krishnaraj, T.; Athhukuri, R.K.; Vastav, M.S. GRAHP TOP model for supplier selection in Supply Chain: A hybrid MCDM approach. *Decis. Sci. Lett.* **2019**, *8*, 65–80. [CrossRef]
5. Zhang, X.; Lu, J.; Peng, Y. Hybrid MCDM model for location of logistics hub: A case in China under the belt and road initiative. *IEEE Access* **2021**, *9*, 41227–41245. [CrossRef]
6. Stojčić, M.; Zavadskas, E.K.; Pamučar, D.; Stević, Ž.; Mardani, A. Application of MCDM Methods in Sustainability Engineering: A Literature Review 2008–2018. *Symmetry* **2019**, *11*, 350. [CrossRef]
7. Ghasempour, R.; Nazari, M.A.; Ebrahimi, M.; Ahmadi, M.H.; Hadiyanto, H. Multi-Criteria Decision Making (MCDM) Approach for Selecting Solar Plants Site and Technology: A Review. *Int. J. Renew. Energy Dev.* **2019**, *8*, 15–25. [CrossRef]
8. Hellwig, Z. *Procedure of Evaluating High-Level Manpower Data and Typology of Countries by Means of the Taxonomic Method*; COM/WS/91, UNESCO Working Paper; UNESCO: Warsaw, Poland, 1967.
9. Hwang, C.L.; Yoon, K. *Multiple Attribute Decision Making: Methods and Applications*; Springer: Berlin, Germany, 1981.
10. Rudnik, K.; Kacprzak, D. Fuzzy TOPSIS method with ordered fuzzy numbers for flow control in a manufacturing system. *Appl. Soft Comput.* **2017**, *52*, 1020–1041. [CrossRef]
11. Onu, P.U.; Quan, X.; Xu, L.; Orji, J.; Onu, E. Evaluation of sustainable acid rain control options utilizing a fuzzy TOPSIS multi-criteria decision analysis model frame work. *J. Clean. Prod.* **2017**, *141*, 612–625. [CrossRef]
12. Rahim, R.; Supiyandi, S.; Siahaan, A.P.U.; Listyorini, T.; Utomo, A.P.; Triyanto, W.A.; Khairunnisa, K. TOPSIS Method Application for Decision Support System in Internal Control for Selecting Best Employees. *J. Phys. Conf. Ser.* **2018**, *1028*, 012052. [CrossRef]
13. Shen, F.; Ma, X.; Li, Z.; Xu, Z.; Cai, D. An extended intuitionistic fuzzy TOPSIS method based on a new distance measure with an application to credit risk evaluation. *Inf. Sci.* **2018**, *428*, 105–119. [CrossRef]
14. Kong, Y.S.; Dankyi, A.B.; Ankomah-Asare, E.T.; Addo, A.A. An Application of TOPSIS Approach in Determination of Spread Influencers in a Competitive Industrial Space: Evidence from the Banking Network of Ghana. *J. Hum. Resour. Sustain. Stud.* **2019**, *7*, 312–327. [CrossRef]
15. Fauzi, N.A.M.; Ismail, M.; Jaaman, S.H.; Kamaruddin, S.N.D.M. Applicability of TOPSIS Model and Markowitz Model. *J. Phys. Conf. Ser.* **2019**, *1212*, 012032. [CrossRef]
16. Rehman, S.; Khan, S.A.; Alhems, L.M. Application of TOPSIS Approach to Multi-Criteria Selection of Wind Turbines for On-Shore Sites. *Appl. Sci.* **2020**, *10*, 7595. [CrossRef]
17. Narayan, N.; Singh, K.K.; Srivastava, U. Developmental Performance Ranking of SAARC Nations: An Application of TOPSIS Method of Multi-Criteria Decision Making. *Inter. Multidiscip. J. Soc. Sci.* **2020**, *9*, 26–50. [CrossRef]
18. Balcerzak, A.P. Quality of institutions in the European Union countries. Application of TOPSIS based on entropy measure for objective weighting. *Acta Polytech. Hung.* **2020**, *17*, 101–122. [CrossRef]
19. Halicka, K.; Kacprzak, D. Linear ordering of selected gerontechnologies using selected MCGDM methods. *Technol. Econ. Dev. Econ.* **2021**, *27*, 921–947. [CrossRef]
20. Chen, C.T. Extensions of the TOPSIS for group decision-making under fuzzy environment. *Fuzzy Sets Syst.* **2000**, *114*, 1–9. [CrossRef]

21. Roszkowska, E.; Kacprzak, D. The fuzzy SAW and fuzzy TOPSIS procedures based on ordered fuzzy numbers. *Inf. Sci.* **2016**, *369*, 564–584. [CrossRef]
22. Senvar, O.; Otay, I.; Boltürk, E. Hospital site selection via hesitant fuzzy TOPSIS. *IFAC-PapersOnLine* **2016**, *49*, 1140–1145. [CrossRef]
23. Boran, F.E.; Genc, S.; Kurt, M.; Akay, D. A multi-criteria intuitionistic fuzzy group decision making for supplier selection with TOPSIS method. *Expert Syst. Appl.* **2009**, *36*, 11363–11368. [CrossRef]
24. Garg, H. Hesitant Pythagorean fuzzy sets and their aggregation operators in multiple attribute decision making. *Int. J. Uncertain. Quantif.* **2018**, *8*, 267–289. [CrossRef]
25. Ashtiani, B.; Haghighirad, F.; Makui, A.; Montazer, G. Extension of fuzzy TOPSIS method based on interval-valued fuzzy sets. *Appl. Soft Comput.* **2009**, *9*, 457–461. [CrossRef]
26. Chi, P.; Liu, P. An Extended TOPSIS Method for the Multiple Attribute Decision Making Problems Based on Interval Neutrosophic Set. *Neutrosophic Sets Sys.* **2013**, *1*, 63–70.
27. Jahanshahloo, G.R.; Hosseinzadeh Lotfi, F.; Izadikhah, M. An Algorithmic Method to Extend TOPSIS for Decision Making Problems with Interval Data. *Appl. Math. Comput.* **2006**, *175*, 1375–1384. [CrossRef]
28. Dymova, L.; Sevastjanov, P.; Tikhonenko, A. A direct interval extension of TOPSIS method. *Expert Syst. Appl.* **2013**, *40*, 4841–4847. [CrossRef]
29. Jahanshahloo, G.R.; Hosseinzadeh Lotfi, F.; Davoodi, A.R. Extension of TOPSIS for decision-making problems with interval data: Interval efficiency. *Math. Comput. Model.* **2009**, *49*, 1137–1142. [CrossRef]
30. Jahanshahloo, G.R.; Khodabakhshi, M.; Hosseinzadeh Lotfi, F.; Moazami Goudarzi, M.R. Across-efficiency model based on super-efficiency for ranking units through the TOPSIS approach and its extension to the interval case. *Math. Comput. Model.* **2011**, *53*, 1946–1955. [CrossRef]
31. Ye, F.; Li, Y.N. Group multi-attribute decision model to partner selection in the formation of virtual enterprise under incomplete information. *Expert Syst. Appl.* **2009**, *36*, 9350–9357. [CrossRef]
32. Tsaur, R.C. Decision risk analysis for an interval TOPSIS method. *Appl. Math. Comput.* **2011**, *218*, 4295–4304. [CrossRef]
33. Yue, Z. An extended TOPSIS for determining weights of decision makers with interval numbers. *Knowl. Based Syst.* **2011**, *24*, 146–153. [CrossRef]
34. Hu, B.Q.; Wang, S. A Novel Approach in Uncertain Programming Part I: New Arithmetic and Order Relation for Interval Numbers. *J. Ind. Manag. Optim.* **2006**, *2*, 351–371.
35. Hosseinzadeh Lotfi, F.; Fallahnejad, R. Imprecise Shannon's Entropy and Multi Attribute Decision Making. *Entropy* **2010**, *12*, 53–62. [CrossRef]
36. Kacprzak, D. An extended TOPSIS method based on ordered fuzzy numbers for group decision making. *Artif. Intell. Rev.* **2020**, *53*, 2099–2129. [CrossRef]
37. Moore, R.E.; Kearfott, R.B.; Cloud, M.J. *Introduction to Interval Analysis*; SIAM: Philadelphia, PA, USA, 2009.
38. Yue, Z. Developing a straightforward approach for group decision making based on determining weights of decision makers. *Appl. Math. Model.* **2012**, *36*, 4106–4117. [CrossRef]

Article

Using Entropy to Evaluate the Impact of Monetary Policy Shocks on Financial Networks

Petre Caraiani [1,2] and Alexandru Vasile Lazarec [3,*]

[1] Institute for Economic Forecasting, Romanian Academy, 050711 Bucharest, Romania; petre.caraiani@fabiz.ase.ro
[2] Faculty of Business Administration in Foreign Languages, Bucharest University of Economic Studies, 010374 Bucharest, Romania
[3] Department of Economics, Sociology and Law, The School of Advanced Studies of the Romanian Academy, 010071 Bucharest, Romania
* Correspondence: alexandrulazarec@gmail.com; Tel.: +40-07-5622-2061

Abstract: We analyze the changes in the financial network built using the Dow Jones Industrial Average components following monetary policy shocks. Monetary policy shocks are measured through unexpected changes in the federal funds rate in the United States. We determine the changes in the financial networks using singular value decomposition entropy and von Neumann entropy. The results indicate that unexpected positive shocks in monetary policy shocks lead to lower entropy. The results are robust to varying the window size used to construct financial networks, though they also depend on the type of entropy used.

Keywords: entropy; financial markets; monetary policy; networks

Citation: Caraiani, P.; Lazarec, A.V. Using Entropy to Evaluate the Impact of Monetary Policy Shocks on Financial Networks. *Entropy* **2021**, *23*, 1465. https://doi.org/10.3390/e23111465

Academic Editor: Joanna Olbryś

Received: 27 September 2021
Accepted: 3 November 2021
Published: 6 November 2021

Publisher's Note: MDPI stays neutral with regard to jurisdictional claims in published maps and institutional affiliations.

Copyright: © 2021 by the authors. Licensee MDPI, Basel, Switzerland. This article is an open access article distributed under the terms and conditions of the Creative Commons Attribution (CC BY) license (https://creativecommons.org/licenses/by/4.0/).

1. Introduction

With the rapid increase of the use of network based approaches in economics, more and more key questions are approached from this perspective. The applications are diverse, and many times, they bring new insights. Without trying to exhaust an already large literature, we can mention the applications to business cycles [1], systemic risk [2–6], and contagion and spillovers [7–9].

In this paper, we aim at studying a less discussed topic from a network perspective. We aim at analyzing the transmission of monetary policy shocks to the financial markets. In this sense, we look at the way financial networks modify following monetary policy shocks. To measure the change, we use an entropy measure of networks based on singular value decomposition and on von Neumann entropy. The main question of this paper is as follows: do monetary policy shocks impact the financial networks?

There are several directions in which we contribute to the literature. Our first contribution is related to the analysis of monetary policy shocks in the context of networks. There is a rapidly growing literature, with contributions mainly focusing on the role of production networks. A reference paper in this direction is one published by Weber and Ozdagli [10], who used the spatial structure of production in the United States (based on the input–output structure) to measure how this affects the transmission of monetary policy shocks. We can also mention Caraiani et al. [11], who studied the propagation of monetary policy shocks using specific measures of production networks such as upstreamness and downstreamness, finding that they matter for the transmission of monetary policy shocks. In a related paper [12], Caraiani studied in an international context the transmission of oil shocks using network measures such as density and skewness of links, finding again that the network structure matters significantly for the transmission of (oil) shocks.

A second contribution is to the field of financial networks. We have already cited some reference papers applying networks approaches to the financial markets. Here, we contribute to the understanding of the relationship between monetary policy shocks and the stock market, but we also quantify the structural changes in the financial markets networks using an entropy measure.

Finally, our last contribution is related to the use of entropy in measuring the changes in the financial markets networks following a particular shock—here, a monetary policy shock. There are various ways to measure the entropy of financial markets. A discussion of the various ways to measure entropy in financial networks is conducted in [13]. Below, we also review a few contributions on this topic and outline our contribution in this direction.

A significant contribution was made by [14], who applied transfer entropy to study the relationships between 187 companies in the world. This approach allowed him to identify a central role for insurance companies from large economies such as the United States and the Euro Area.

A different contribution looked at the ability of singular-value-based entropy of financial markets to signal the state of the market. In [15], entropy is measured using a singular value decomposition of the matrix of correlations of financial stock. Caraiani also showed that this entropy measure has predictive ability for the dynamics of the stock market. More recently, Caraiani [16] extended the work to the case of international financial markets, showing that there are spillovers of entropy between the big financial markets, with entropy measured again based on the singular value based decomposition of the financial stock.

Another contribution on the use of entropy was given by Bekiros et al. [17], who used entropy measures of the financial markets to show that there is a decoupling between commodity and equity markets. Another approach consisted of showing that we can use permutation entropy to analyze how the degree of information changes during a market crash [18]. The main result of this latter paper was that during financial market crashes, the permutation entropy decreases.

In this paper, we extend previous research from several literature strands (i.e., networks and monetary policy, financial networks, and entropy of financial networks) by making several contributions. First, we show that we can approach the topic of the changes in the financial networks following monetary policy shocks using networks measures. As far as we know, this has not been studied extensively before. There are, however, a few studies that are close to ours. For example, Beltran et al. [19] found that Fed Funds networks (along with abundant reserves) tend to dampen the impact of monetary policy transmission. In a different framework, using agent-based modeling, Riccetti et al. [20] found a significant role for a financial accelerator that was founded on three dimensions: a leverage one, a stock market one, and a network one. We can also mention the study by Silva et al. [21], who consider a granular approach that takes into consideration the network relationships between agents, along with the balance sheets compositions. The inclusion of network data allowed them to study contagion effects as well. They applied their model to Brazilian data. However, our focus is rather on detecting the changes in financial networks following monetary policy shocks.

Second, we quantify the changes in the financial markets networks based on different measures of entropy. Different from previous studies, we focus on event studies with monetary policy shocks precisely identified following FED communications. Thus, we can to isolate the impact of such announcements by considering the changes in entropy. Since we consider windows of data before and after these announcements, we can isolate the impact solely of these announcements.

The paper is structured as follows. We first discuss the methodology used throughout the paper in the following section. In the third section, we present the data used in the empirical analysis. In the fourth section, we perform the empirical analysis by looking at the impact of monetary policy shocks on financial networks. Finally, in section five, we discuss the results and suggests possible extensions of the present result.

2. Methodology

We detail here the main tools used in the empirical analysis. While most of the methods applied here have been extensively used in the literature, they might still be unknown to some readers.

Our research builds on the recent work on financial networks and measuring the key properties of networks by applying network-based measures of entropy. We use these well-studied and understood methods to approach the impact of monetary policy shocks on financial networks in a novel manner.

2.1. Correlation Networks of Stocks

In the first stage, we construct correlation-based networks. Since our sample of financial series comprises the components of the Dow Jones Industrial Average index (while considering also the historical changes in its composition; see Appendix A for the composition of the DJIA index), we construct time-varying correlation matrices of the returns. Returns for a stock i, r_i, are measured through the log-difference in prices at time t, i.e., $P_i(t)$, namely:

$$r_i(t) = log[P_i(t)] - log[P_i(t-1)] \tag{1}$$

We further compute the standard correlation between two stocks using:

$$\rho_{i,j} = \frac{cov(r_i, r_j)}{\sigma_{r_i} \sigma_{r_j}} \tag{2}$$

Here, r_i represents again the return of the stock i. σ_{r_i} is the standard deviation for the return of the stock i.

Our approach to constructing networks relies on correlations. While we admit that there are other approaches, this approach remains one of the standard ones. Further discussions on this can be found in [22], in which the authors discuss various approaches based on correlations, and also in [23], in which the authors use VAR models and compute the financial networks based on the variance decomposition.

Once correlation matrices are obtained, we can derive the corresponding adjacency matrix and build the financial networks. Our focus is on measuring the structural change in financial networks (and their corresponding adjacency matrices) following changes in monetary policy, as revealed by the series in monetary policy announcements (see below).

2.2. Singular-Value-Decomposition-Based Entropy

Many measures can be used to characterize a (financial) network quantitatively. Here, we focus on a simple measure that measures the degree of entropy in a (financial network). This measure has been used in the past, and it was shown to have significant predictive and/or informational content for a financial network (see [15,16]).

We start from a standard singular value decomposition (SVD, hereafter) applied to the adjacency matrix that we have obtained:

$$A = USV^T \tag{3}$$

The SVD decomposition is applied to the adjacency matrix of returns as computed in Section 2.1, denoted by A, characterized by n rows and n columns (the matrix is square). Furthermore, the resulting matrix U has n rows and n columns, and the matrix V has n rows and n columns. We can further write the matrix S as follows:

$$S = \text{diag}(\lambda_1, \lambda_2, \ldots, \lambda_n) \tag{4}$$

The literature shows that the resulting matrix consists only of positive elements, which are also ordered decreasingly.

We further employ the SVD decomposition to measure the entropy of the adjacency matrix and, implicitly, of the financial networks that we built. There are many ways to measure the entropy of a financial network and market; for examples, see the recent contributions by Nie and Song [13] and Anand and Bianconi [24]. The approach employed here is based on the key contribution by [25] as well as the more recent application by [26].

To measure the entropy, we use the approach employed in [15,26,27] in the context of financial networks. Based on the singular value derived above, λ_n, we first compute the normalized values using:

$$\bar{\lambda}_k = \frac{\lambda_k}{\sum \lambda_k} \quad (5)$$

In the next step, we measure the entropy employing the normalized singular values as follows:

$$En = -\sum \bar{\lambda}_k ln(\bar{\lambda}_k) \quad (6)$$

Our key measure of interest is En, which stands for the singular-value-decomposition-based entropy. We can measure the entropy for each financial network that we construct. As explained in the empirical part, we will aim to measure the changes in the financial networks following monetary policy shocks. Details about constructing the change in the entropy are given in Section 4.1.

2.3. Von Neumann Entropy

To obtain the von Neumann entropy, denoted by En_{vne}, we use the Laplacian matrix of the graph, denoted by L. If Λ is the spectrum (or the set of eigenvalues) of the Laplacian matrix, we can compute the von Neumann entropy via a similar formula:

$$En_{vne} = -\sum_{\lambda \in \Lambda} \lambda_k ln(\lambda_k) \quad (7)$$

We also consider the normalized Laplacian, $\bar{L}$ for which we compute the set of eigenvalues $\bar{\Lambda}$, and derive a normalized measure of entropy (denoted by En_{vnen}):

$$En_{vnen} = -\sum_{\lambda \in \bar{\Lambda}} \bar{\lambda}_k ln(\bar{\lambda}_k) \quad (8)$$

3. Data

We selected data for the stock components of the Dow Jones Industrial Average Index, DOW30 (see Appendix A). We selected daily data to ensure larger samples and thus to construct financial networks before and after monetary policy announcements. Contrary to previous studies (see, for example, [15]), we also account for the time changes in the Dow Jones structure since the index is updated constantly. Given the components' historical changes, we update the series used following the official date when changes occurred. To simplify the analysis, we focus only on data starting with 2000.

A second series we use is that of monetary policy announcements. This is based on the study by [28]. We then use the updated data set of announcements as in [29]. The data set spans from 1990 to 2016, but we focus only on 2000 to 2016. Appendix B, Figure A1 displays the monetary policy shocks series. The time x-axis indicates the observations that we have on the dates shocks produce. Shocks are produced at irregular dates. The y-axis stands for the magnitude of the shock that is observed.

4. Results

4.1. Measuring the Entropy

In this section, we derive the measure of entropy that we are interested in. In contrast to previous contributions that have also used singular-value-based entropy to characterize financial networks (see [15] or [16]), we focus here on measuring the change in the singular-value-based or von Neumann entropy in pre- versus post- dates when the monetary policy shocks occur.

An informational issue is also critical to ensure that the change in the financial network(s) comes only from the current monetary policy shock. To counter this effect, we isolate the impact of each monetary policy shock by considering the state of the financial network (as characterized by the entropy) before and after each event (or monetary policy shock). The informational issue that we discuss is represented below, see Figure 1:

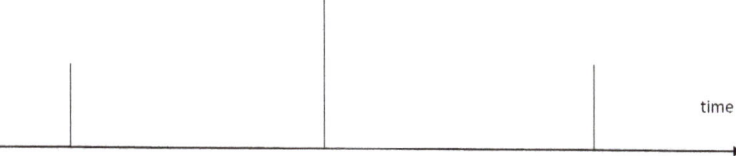

Financial network before event: T_{-30}-T_0 MP shock: T_0 Financial network after event: T_0-T_{+30}

Figure 1. The informational timing. Note: T_0 is the moment the monetary policy is produced, $T_{-30} - T_0$ is the window of 30 days before the event, and $T_0 - T_{+30}$ is the window after the monetary policy shock. The size of the window is varied for robustness reasons.

While previous studies (see [15,16]) relied on a sliding window, here, we compute for each monetary policy shock that entropy for the financial networks before the event and after the event. We consider a window for which the financial network is derived. This is used only before and after the event. Thus, the resulting series is the series of changes in the singular-value-based entropy ex post compared to ex ante.

To control for the robustness of the results to the size of the window used, we vary the window's dimension and consider windows of 20, 30, and 45 days (these correspond to calendar days, while the trading days are just at most five each week). Our main interest relies on financial networks that are affected only by the events we consider, i.e., monetary policy shocks. In this sense, considering that only windows of 20, 30, or 45 days fulfills this essential criterion while ensuring enough observations to construct the financial networks. We also consider a larger window of 60 days (with the results available at request) for robustness. However, it might sometimes overlap with previous or subsequent monetary policy shocks, but this should be taken only as additional evidence.

In Appendixes B and C, we show the log-difference of the Shannon entropy measure for the different window sizes used, namely for 20, 30, and 45 days (the figures for von Neumann entropy are similar, and they are available at request). Our data start from 2000, ensuring that there are enough observations to carry the statistical analysis. The dot-com crisis from 2001 is marked through a decreasing value of entropy. A similar pattern is noticed after about eight years, corresponding to the timing of the great financial crisis. The x-axis is interpreted as showing the observations on entropy changes, while the y-axis shows the magnitude of the change.

4.2. The Impact of Monetary Policy Shocks on Financial Networks

This section aims to answer the paper's central research question: do monetary policy shocks impact the financial networks? We use the singular-value-based entropy and von Neumann entropy measures derived in the last section to answer this question. We test the hypothesis of whether monetary policy shocks have a significant impact on financial networks as measured through the change in the entropy of the financial networks.

We consider the following basic regression models. The model aims at capturing the relations between the shocks (the change in the monetary policy stance) and the entropy of the financial markets.

$$dEn_t = c + MP_t + u_t \qquad (9)$$

Here, dEn_t is the change in the entropy, while MP_t are the monetary policy shocks. c is a constant, while u_t are the residuals of the regression. For robustness, we use the Shannon entropy and the von Neumann entropy, including one based on a normalized version of the Laplacian.

Before performing the regression, we also test for the unit root in both monetary policy shocks and the change in entropy for various window sizes. The results are shown in Appendix D. The unit root hypothesis is strongly rejected in each case, for either of the monetary policy shocks, for the different measures of entropy based on different approaches and window sizes.

Table 1 shows the regression results described in Equation (1) for the Shannon entropy for the various window sizes considered: 20, 30, and 45 days. Although the R^2 is low, the F-test indicates that the model is significant from a statistical point of view (For those not familiar with the regression analysis, the F-test is an overall test of significance for the estimated regression. The null hypothesis is that the model does not have significant explanatory power).

However, the key result is the statistically significant and negative coefficient associated with the MP shock in each case considered. In other words, monetary policy shocks lead to a reduction in the financial network's entropy, as measured by the change in the singular-value-based entropy. The results are robust to the window size used, and they tend to become stronger for larger windows.

Additionally, we consider in Tables 2 and 3 the von Neumann entropy, varying the window size as well. However, the results are not statistically significant.

Table 1. Monetary policy shocks and the change in Shannon entropy for different window sizes.

Variable	Entropy +/− 20 Days	Entropy +/− 30 Days	Entropy +/− 45 Days
Intercept	−0.06351 **	−0.05160	−0.01865
MP shock	−1.28732 **	−1.58216 **	−1.55791 **
R^2	0.04149	0.04576	0.04374
F-test	6.06 **	6.714 **	6.403 **

Note: * denotes statistical significance of the F-test at the 0.10 level, ** statistical significance at the 0.05 level, and *** at the 0.01 level.

Table 2. Monetary policy shocks and the change in von Neumman entropy for different window sizes: normalized.

Variable	Entropy +/− 20 Days	Entropy +/− 30 Days	Entropy +/− 45 Days
Intercept	0.006243	0.001215	−0.0005439
MP shock	0.106932	0.070585	0.0608659
R^2	0.01106	0.007153	0.008522
F-test	1.566	1.009	1.203

Note: * denotes statistical significance of the F-test at the 0.10 level, ** statistical significance at the 0.05 level, and *** at the 0.01 level.

Table 3. Monetary policy shocks and the change in von Neumman entropy for different window sizes: not normalized.

Variable	Entropy +/− 20 Days	Entropy +/− 30 Days	Entropy +/− 45 Days
Intercept	0.006880	0.001546	0.000870
MP shock	0.135886	0.089820	0.089003
R^2	0.01425	0.01599	0.01261
F-test	2.024	2.016	1.788

Note: * denotes statistical significance of the F-test at the 0.10 level; ** statistical significance at the 0.05 level, and *** at the 0.01 level.

In Appendix E, we further test whether controlling for the correlation threshold changes the results for the Shannon entropy (we set the correlation weaker than 0.30 to 0). We were able to derive the results only for two types of windows of 20 and 30 observations. The results remain negative and statistically significant, and the magnitude is even larger than for the baseline case. We tried the same exercise for the von Neumann entropy; however, the results remained the same.

5. Discussion

In this paper, we aimed at approaching the issue of monetary policy effects on the financial markets from a network perspective. We analyzed whether monetary policy shocks statistically impact the financial networks (as constructed from the Dow Jones Industrial Average components). To measure the change in the financial networks, we used the change in the entropy (either singular-value-based or von Neumann).

The main contribution of this paper was to show that monetary policy shocks have indeed a statistically significant impact on financial networks: a positive monetary policy shock (corresponding to a tightening of the monetary policy and a higher interest rate) had a negative impact on the singular-value-based entropy of the financial networks. Our results are robust to varying the size of the window used to construct the financial networks. They are also robust to controlling for the significance of correlation. However, the results using the von Neumann entropy are not statistically significant.

The interpretation of the result is that the release of the new information through the Fed communications on the interest decreases the entropy of the financial market networks. This is a somewhat expected result since it reduces the degree of uncertainty in the financial markets.

There are a few novel results that can be outlined. First, we highlight the fact that monetary policy shocks do affect the financial networks. Previous studies (see [10,12,16]) considered (production) networks that are invariant to changes in aggregate shocks, including monetary policy shocks. Our focus was on financial networks and how they respond to monetary policy shocks. Second, we also show that entropy measures of networks can be used to detect the changes in financial networks. This has been used before in a few studies; however, in this paper, we show that event studies can be combined with entropy to evaluate the impact of financial networks.

The results here can be further extended in various ways. For example, one can consider different ways to construct entropy from financial networks. Furthermore, financial networks can also be characterized in many ways, including based on measures that are more intuitively linked to financial and economic concepts (such as risk, for example), which can be further used to analyze the impact of monetary policy shocks in a network context.

Author Contributions: P.C. and A.V.L. wrote the paper. P.C. gathered the data and performed the technical work. All authors have read and agreed to the published version of the manuscript.

Funding: This work was supported by a grant of the Romanian Ministry of Education and Research, CNCS-UEFISCDI, project number PN-III-P4-ID-PCE-2020-0557, within PNCDI III, contract number 112/2021.

Conflicts of Interest: The authors declare no conflict of interest.

Abbreviations

The following abbreviations are used in this manuscript:

DJIA   Dow Jones Industrial Average
SvdEn Singular Value Decomposition Entropy
MP   Monetary Policy
ADF   Augmented Dickey–Fuller
PP   Phillips–Perron

Appendix A. DJIA Index Components

Table A1. DOW Jones Industrial Average Components as of end of 2015.

Company	Abbreviation
3M Company	MMM
American Express Company	AXP
Apple Inc.	AAPL
Boeing Company	BA
Caterpillar, Inc.	CAT
Cisco Systems, Inc.	CSCO
Chevron Corporation	CVX
Dow Chemical Company	DD
Exxon Mobil Corporation	XOM
General Electric Company	GE
The Goldman Sachs Group, Inc.	GS
Home Depot, Inc. (The)	HD
Intel Corporation	INTC
International Business Machines	IBM
Johnson & Johnson	JNJ
JP Morgan Chase & Co.	JPM
Coca-Cola Company (The)	KO
McDonald's Corporation	MCD
Merck & Company, Inc.	MRK
Microsoft Corporation	MSFT
Nike, Inc.	NKE
Pfizer, Inc.	PFE
Procter & Gamble Company (The)	PG
Raytheon Technologies	RTX
The Travelers Companies, Inc.	TRV
United Health Group Inc.	UNH
Verizon Communications Inc.	VZ
Visa Inc.	V
WalMart Stores, Inc.	WMT
Walt Disney Company (The)	DIS

Appendix B. Monetary Policy Shocks and Entropy

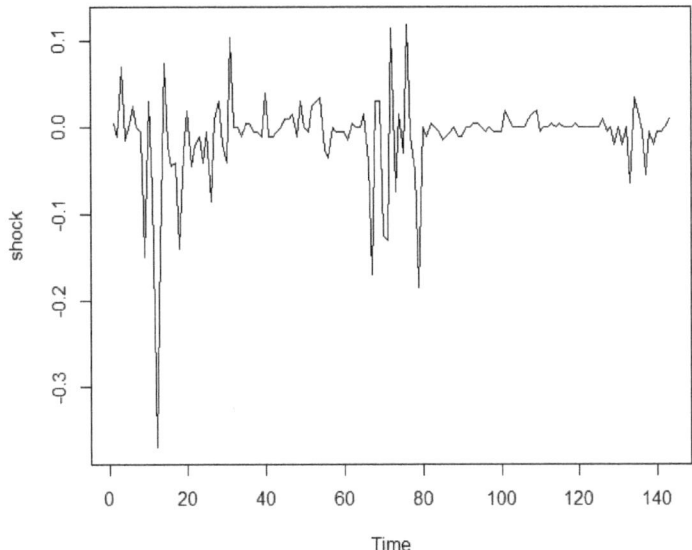

Figure A1. Monetary policy shocks.

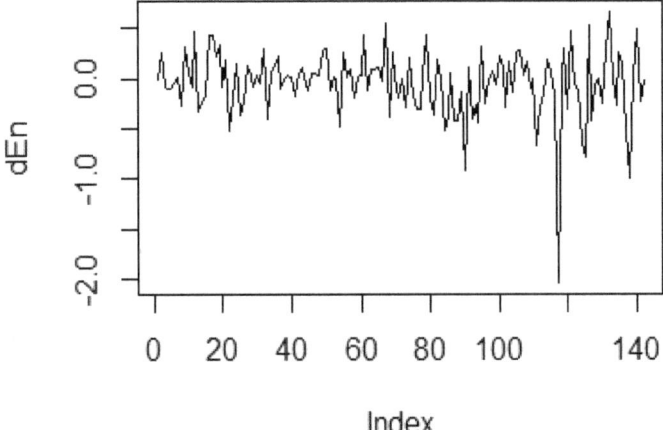

Figure A2. The change in singular-value-based entropy-20 days window.

Appendix C. Entropy at 30 and 45 Days Windows

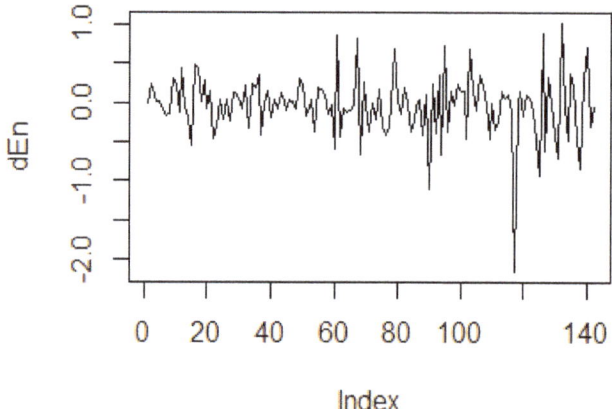

Figure A3. The change in singular-value-based entropy-30 days window.

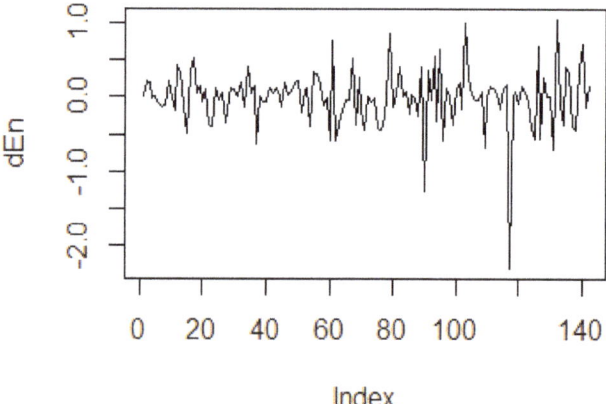

Figure A4. The change in singular-value-based entropy-45 days window.

Appendix D. Unit Root Tests

Table A2. Unit Root Tests: Shannon Entropy.

Country	ADF Test	PP Test
Monetary Policy Shock	−5.7318 **	−124.91 **
Entropy—20 days window	−4.8608 **	−136.29 **
Entropy—30 days window	−5.4853 **	−159.48 **
Entropy—45 days window	−5.7318 **	−162.22 **

Note: * denotes statistical significance of the unit root test at 0.10 level; ** at 0.05 level; *** at 0.01 level.

Table A3. Unit Root Tests: Von Neumann Entropy—normalized.

Country	ADF Test	PP Test
Entropy—20 days window	−4.7529 **	−121.16 **
Entropy—30 days window	−4.555 **	−186.99 **
Entropy—45 days window	−5.0434 **	−172.26 **

Note: * denotes statistical significance of the unit root test at the 0.10 level, ** at the 0.05 level, and *** at the 0.01 level.

Table A4. Unit Root Tests: Von Neumann Entropy—not normalized.

Country	ADF Test	PP Test
Entropy—20 days window	−4.8207 **	−116.98 **
Entropy—30 days window	−4.4355 **	−185.88 **
Entropy—45 days window	−5.0565 **	−170.02 **

Note: * denotes statistical significance of the unit root test at the 0.10 level, ** at the 0.05 level, and *** at the 0.01 level.

Appendix E. Robustness Exercise: Taking into Account a Correlation Threshold

Table A5. Monetary policy shocks and the change in Shannon entropy for different window sizes. Controlling for correlation threshold.

Variable	Entropy +/− 20 Days	Entropy +/− 30 Days
Intercept	0.11335 ***	0.15085 ***
MP shock	−1.72342 **	−1.88651 ***
R^2	0.04601	0.0483
F-test	6.75 **	7.125 ***

Note: * denotes statistical significance of the F-test at the 0.10 level, ** statistical significance at the 0.05 level, and *** at the 0.01 level.

References

1. Acemoglu, D.; Carvalho, V.M.; Ozdaglar, A.; Tahbaz-Salehi, A. The Network Origins of Aggregate Fluctuations. *Econometrica* **2012**, *80*, 1977–2016. [CrossRef]
2. Acemoglu, D.; Ozdaglar, A.; Tahbaz-Salehi, A. Systemic Risk and Stability in Financial Networks. *Am. Econ. Rev.* **2015**, *105*, 564–608. [CrossRef]
3. Bisias, D.; Flood, M.; Lo, A.W.; Valavanis, S. A Survey of Systemic Risk Analytics. *Annu. Rev. Financ. Econ.* **2014**, *4*, 255–296. [CrossRef]
4. Markose, S.; Giansante, S.; Shaghaghi, A.R. 'Too interconnected to fail' financial network of US CDS market: Topological fragility and systemic risk. *J. Econ. Behav. Organ.* **2012**, *83*, 627–646. [CrossRef]
5. Bilio, M.; Getmansky, M.; Lo, A.W.; Pelizzon, L. Econometric measures of connectedness and systemic risk in the finance and insurance sectors. *J. Financ. Econ.* **2012**, *104*, 535–559. [CrossRef]
6. Cimini, G.; Squartini, T.; Garlaschelli, D.; Gabrielli, A. Systemic Risk Analysis on Reconstructed Economic and Financial Networks. *Sci. Rep.* **2015**, *5*, 15758, [CrossRef] [PubMed]
7. Glasserman, P.; Young, H.P. How likely is contagion in financial networks? *J. Bank. Financ.* **2015**, *50*, 383–399. doi: 10.1016/j.jbankfin.2014.02.006. [CrossRef]
8. Wang, G.J.; Xie, C.; He, K.; Stanley, E.H. Extreme risk spillover network: Application to financial institutions. *Quant. Financ.* **2017**, *17*, 1417–1433. [CrossRef]
9. Wang, G.J.; Xie, C.; Stanley, E.H. Correlation Structure and Evolution of World Stock Markets: Evidence from Pearson and Partial Correlation-Based Networks. *Comput. Econ.* **2018**, *51*, 607–635. [CrossRef]
10. Weber, C.; Ozdagli, A. Monetary Policy through Production Networks: Evidence from the Stock Market. Available online: https://www.nber.org/papers/w23424 (accessed on 15 September 2021).
11. Caraiani, P.; Dutescu, A.; Hoinaru, R.; Stănilă, G.O. Production network structure and the impact of the monetary policy shocks: Evidence from the OECD. *Econ. Lett.* **2020**, *193*, 109271. [CrossRef]
12. Caraiani, P. Oil shocks and production network structure: Evidence from the OECD. *Energy Econ.* **2019**, *84*, 109271. [CrossRef]
13. Nie, C.X.; Song, F.T. Entropy of Graphs in Financial Markets. *Comput. Econ.* **2020**. [CrossRef]
14. Sandoval, S., Jr. Structure of a Global Network of Financial Companies Based on Transfer Entropy. *Entropy* **2014**, *16*, 4443–4482. [CrossRef]

15. Caraiani, P. The predictive power of singular value decomposition entropy for stock market dynamics. *Phys. A* **2014**, *393*, 571–578. [CrossRef]
16. Caraiani, P. Modeling the Comovement of Entropy between Financial Markets. *Entropy* **2018**, *20*, 417. [CrossRef] [PubMed]
17. Bekiros, S.; Nguyen, D.K.; Sandoval, S., Jr.; Uddin, G.S. Information diffusion, cluster formation and entropy-based network dynamics in equity and commodity markets. *Eur. J. Oper. Res.* **2017**, *256*, 945–961. [CrossRef]
18. Hou, Y.; Young, H.P. Characterizing Complexity Changes in Chinese Stock Markets by Permutation Entropy. *Entropy* **2017**, *19*, 514. [CrossRef]
19. Beltran, D.O.; Bolotnyy, V.; Klee, E. The federal funds network and monetary policy transmission: Evidence from the 2007–2009 financial crisis. *J. Mon. Econ.* **2021**, *117*, 187. [CrossRef]
20. Riccetti, L.; Russo, A.; Gallegati, M. Stock market dynamics, leveraged network-based financial accelerator and monetary policy. *Int. Rev. Econ. Financ.* **2016**, *43*, 509. [CrossRef]
21. Silva, T.C.; Guerra, S.M.; Alexandre, M.; Tabak, B.M. Micro-level transmission of monetary policy shocks: The trading book channel. *JEBO* **2020**, *179*, 279. [CrossRef]
22. Kennett, D.Y.; Shapira, Y.; Madi, A.; Bransburg-Zabary, S.; Gur-Gershgoren, G.; Ben-Jacob, E. Index Cohesive Force Analysis Reveals That the US Market Became Prone to Systemic Collapses Since 2002. *PLoS ONE* **2011**, *6*, e19378. [CrossRef]
23. Diebold, F.; Yilmaz, K. On the network topology of variance decompositions: Measuring the connectedness of financial firms. *J. Econom.* **2014**, *182*, 119–134. [CrossRef]
24. Anand, K.; Bianconi, G. Entropy measures for networks: Toward an information theory of complex topologies. *Phys. Rev. E* **2009**, *80*, 045102. [CrossRef] [PubMed]
25. Shannon, C.E. A Mathematical Theory of Communication. *Bell* **1948**, *27*, 379–423. [CrossRef]
26. Sabatini, A.M. Analysis of postural sway using entropy measures of signal complexity. *Med. Biol. Eng. Comput.* **2000**, *38*, 617. [CrossRef] [PubMed]
27. Anagnoste, S.; Caraiani, P. The Impact of Financial and Macroeconomic Shocks on the Entropy of Markets. *Entropy* **2019**, *21*, 316. [CrossRef] [PubMed]
28. Gurkaynak, R.S.; Sack, B.; Swanson, E. Do Actions Speak Louder Than Words? The Response of Asset Prices to Monetary Policy Actions and Statements. *IJCB* **2005**, *1*, 1. Available online: https://www.ijcb.org/journal/ijcb05q2a2.htm (accessed on 15 September 2021).
29. Jarociński, M.; Karadi, P. Deconstructing Monetary Policy Surprises—The Role of Information Shocks. *Am. Econ. J. Macroecon.* **2020**, *2*, 12. [CrossRef]

Article

Fuzzy Clustering Methods to Identify the Epidemiological Situation and Its Changes in European Countries during COVID-19

Aleksandra Łuczak [1,*] and Sławomir Kalinowski [2,*]

1. Department of Finance and Accounting, Faculty of Economics, Poznań University of Life Sciences, ul. Wojska Polskiego 28, 60-637 Poznan, Poland
2. Institute of Rural and Agricultural Development, Polish Academy of Sciences, ul. Nowy Świat 72, 00-330 Warsaw, Poland
* Correspondence: aleksandra.luczak@up.poznan.pl (A.Ł.); skalinowski@irwirpan.waw.pl (S.K.)

Abstract: The main research question concerned the identification of changes in the COVID-19 epidemiological situation using fuzzy clustering methods. This research used cross-sectional time series data obtained from the European Centre for Disease Prevention and Control. The identification of country types in terms of epidemiological risk was carried out using the fuzzy c-means clustering method. We also used the entropy index to measure the degree of fuzziness in the classification and evaluate the uncertainty of epidemiological states. The proposed approach allowed us to identify countries' epidemic states. Moreover, it also made it possible to determine the time of transition from one state to another, as well as to observe fluctuations during changes of state. Three COVID-19 epidemic states were identified in Europe, i.e., stabilisation, destabilisation, and expansion. The methodology is universal and can also be useful for other countries, as well as the research results being important for governments, politicians and other policy-makers working to mitigate the effects of the COVID-19 pandemic.

Keywords: fuzzy c-means classification method; entropy; COVID-19; epidemic states; Europe

1. Introduction

In the recent past, the coronavirus has become an anomalous part of everyday life worldwide. Moreover, it deepens a sense of insecurity in society and brings confusion due to the lack of standards and rules to fit the new reality. The spread rate of the severe acute respiratory syndrome coronavirus 2 (SARS-CoV-2) that causes COVID-19 and its scale has clearly made everyone aware of how powerful the phenomenon we are dealing with is. In the macro-social dimension, it was associated with disturbances in the economy, i.e., an increase in unemployment, inflation, the budget deficit or a decrease in GDP cf. [1]. On the one hand, people were looking for solutions that would rationalise their everyday life, consisting in a change in everyday functioning, reorganisation of professional life, or changes in the education system. On the other hand, the authorities, started actions aimed at counteracting the unfavourable phenomena in the economy and society. There are many studies and articles on COVID-19 that point to different human behaviour, adaptation to COVID reality, and people's fear of changes, as well as the process of entering the "new normality" but also negating this phenomenon [2–25]. These papers contribute to the literature on the potential healthcare, financial, social, and economic impacts of the COVID-19 pandemic. The importance of this research is highlighted by the European Commission's "Sustainable Europe 2030", in which more than half of the ten essential changes needed in the fight the pandemic are economic. These include support for restoring the economy; job protection; financial aid for EU member states; broadening European solidarity, and assisting the economic sectors hit hardest. This goes to show just how vital it is to research the pandemic's effects.

There are analyses of the situation in countries such as Italy [26], the United States [27,28], United Kingdom [4], Poland [10], Russia [29], Germany [30], China [21,31], Lebanon [23], Kenya [22], Uganda [22,32], Brazil [33], and India [6]. Analyses in these countries reveal various problems, such as rural areas with fewer opportunities for medical services, poorer health and sanitation infrastructure, insufficient social care and numerous problems in managing rural areas, and sometimes endemic poverty. In many countries, such as Canada, the United States, Australia, and Norway, people escaping to the countryside from cities is also a problem, because rural areas have been recognised as places of relative safety [34].

Some studies address issues of studying COVID-19 and its consequences using various mathematical models. Many possible approaches for this modelling can be considered, i.e., non-linear regression, Markov models, differential equation systems (continuous time), and difference equations (discrete time). There are many infectious disease-spread models, such as SIR, SIS, SIRS, SEIR, SEIRD, and SEIHR see e.g., [35,36]. Ivorra et al. [31] developed a mathematical model for the spread of the coronavirus. They proposed the θ-SEIHRD model based on the Be-CoDiS model. Rajaei et al. [37] proposed a different type of nonlinear model for COVID-19. They used a state-estimation-based nonlinear robust control method for state estimation, tracking control, and robustness against uncertainties. Earlier, Sharifi and Moradi [38] proposed a nonlinear epidemiological model of influenza. Shadabfar et al. [28] proposed a probabilistic method to predict the spreading profile of the coronavirus. Their research applied an extended susceptible-exposed-infected-vaccinated-recovered (SEIVR) epidemic model. Moreover, Monte Carlo sampling was used to calculate the exceedance probabilities for three parameters, i.e., the final number of deaths and recovered cases, as well as the maximum number of the infected cases. Moreover, artificial intelligence was applied "in battling against the difficulties the outbreak has caused" [39].

However, there is little research on multiple country analyses together. An interesting example is research by Mahmoudi et al. [40], who studied the situation in the United States, Spain, Italy, Germany, the United Kingdom, France, and Iran. They used a fuzzy clustering technique to compare and cluster the distributions of the spread of COVID-19. It should be noted that, recently, approaches based on soft clustering algorithms have become more popular, having fewer limitations and disadvantages than traditional hard clustering algorithms. Just and Łuczak [41] stated that the "application of classical clustering methods is burdened with some restrictions, which often result in an oversimplification of the actual course of investigated phenomena". They also added that "the clustering methods based on fuzzy sets provide a much greater amount of information on clustering of objects than classical methods, which only allow the unambiguous assignment each element to one of the clusters".

Mirkin [42] pointed out that it is possible to "distinguish two overlapping mainstreams potentially leading to bridging the gaps within the clustering discipline. One is related to modeling cluster structures in terms of observed data, and the other is connected with analyzing particular kinds of phenomena". It is worth adding an observation by Sato-Ilic and Jain [43] that "fuzzy clustering is one method which can capture the uncertainty situation of real data and it is well known that fuzzy clustering can obtain a robust result as compared with conventional hard clustering".

The statement of these facts leads to reflection on the current situation countries and its changes during the COVID-19 pandemic. Research gaps were identified based on a broad review of the source literature on the classification of objects and studies related to the COVID-19 pandemic. Our goal was to fill a significant research gap in the assessment of the epidemiological situation and its changes in European countries during the coronavirus pandemic on the basis of empirical studies and on this basis to formulate answers to the following research questions:

Q1. What were the typical epidemiological states in Poland and other European countries, from 4 March to 24 June 2020?

Q2. What was the variability of the epidemiological states in the countries analysed from the beginning of the epidemic in Poland until the end of the second stage of the survey?

Q3. Were epidemiological states clearly recognizable in the countries analysed during the given time period?

The main objective of this paper is to identify the epidemic states in the countries investigated from 4 March 2020 (the beginning of the epidemic in Poland) to 24 June 2020 (the first phase—the abolition of most restrictions related to COVID-19 in Poland). Furthermore, the following research hypothesis was formulated: the epidemiological situation in Poland in the period from 4 March to 24 June 2020 was stable compared to other European countries.

To fill the existing research gap, our study identified epidemic states in European countries using the fuzzy c-means classification method. The proposed approach not only makes the identification of epidemic states possible, but also provides information on the time of transition from one state to another. Thus, this paper is an important complement to and extension of existing studies on changes in the situation of countries affected by the COVID-19 epidemic. Other authors' contribution concerned the ability of the entropy of the classification to signal the uncertainty of epidemiological states.

Apart from the introduction, the paper is composed as follows: part 2 presents the methods and data used in the empirical study; part 3 presents the results of the research on the epidemiological situation and its changes in European countries. The final parts (5–7) of the paper present a discussion of the research together with conclusions and recommendations.

2. Materials and Methods

The study includes the identification of epidemic states, as well as their changes in European countries from the beginning of the epidemic in Poland (4 March 2020) until the abolition of most restrictions related to COVID-19 in Poland (24 June 2020). The country types were distinguished regarding their epidemiological risk. The cross-sectional time series data from the European Centre for Disease Prevention and Control [44] constitute the empirical basis of the study. Changes in the countries' epidemic states were identified using the fuzzy c-means clustering (FCM) method. FCM "is one of the most classical prototype-based clustering methods" [45]. Yang and Sinaga [46] noted that this method has been "widely extended and applied in various real-world problems, such as pattern recognition, image segmentation, medical diagnostic, economics, cell formation, gene expression, and data mining".

A methodological approach based on clustering methods was proposed (Figure 1). The clustering process consists in the grouping of similar objects [47]. "Clustering mainly aims to partition data into clusters with a maximum similarity in a cluster (homogeneous), as well as a maximum dissimilarity between clusters (heterogeneous)" [48] (p. 297). In other words, Liao [49] (p. 1857) states that "the within-group-object similarity is minimized and the between-group-object dissimilarity is maximized". It aims to identify relatively homogeneous groups of objects in terms of similar characterising variables. The most frequent clustering methods are the disjoint methods, where each object is assigned only to one class. This indicates that each object is assigned properties of only one type. Such an identification of types is a great simplification of the state of the objects examined, as they frequently possess variables of many types. Methods based on the fuzzy-sets theory help to resolve this issue [50]. This theory was developed to describe highly complex phenomena or poorly defined concepts which cannot be precisely described by the classical mathematical apparatus. In fuzzy-clustering methods, objects may belong to different classes. These methods make it possible to assign objects to all classes with a certain degree of membership.

Prior to the clustering process, it is necessary to establish the main criterion regarding the process (e.g., identification of pandemic states), as well as the objects (e.g., countries) intended for clustering (stage 1). An important stage in the clustering process comprises an appropriate selection of variables (stage 2), which is based on substantive and statistical analyses. The established values of the K variables for n countries and T

moments in time are compiled in $T \cdot N \times K$ dimensional data matrix $\mathbf{X}^* = [x^*_{tik}]$, where x^*_{tik} ($t = 1, 2, \ldots, T; n = 1, 2, \ldots, N; k = 1, 2, \ldots, K$) is the value of the k-th variable for the i-th country at time t.

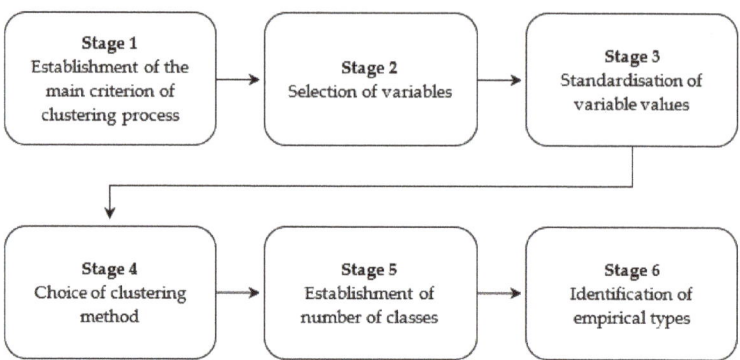

Figure 1. Stages of the clustering process. Source: Own elaboration based on Wysocki [51].

Variables describing the objects examined may assume a different nature and their range of maximum and minimum values also varies. The values of variables should be standardised to ensure comparability of data (stage 3). The standardisation, recorded in the form of a matrix $\mathbf{X}^*$, is conducted according to the formula:

$$x_{tik} = \frac{x^*_{tik} - \overline{x}^*_k}{s^*_k} \qquad (t = 1, 2, \ldots, T; i = 1, \ldots, N; k = 1, \ldots, K), \qquad (1)$$

where x_{tik}—the standardised value of the k-th variable for the i-th object at time t, x^*_{tik}—an initial value of the k-th variable for the i-th object at time t, $\overline{x}^*_k$—arithmetical mean of the k-th variable, and s^*_k—a standard deviation of the k-th variable.

The clustering process is based on the distances between pairs of the multi-variable objects [51–53]. The most frequently applied distance measure is the Minkowski distance [52]:

$$d_{ts} = \left\{ \sum_{k=1}^{K} |x_{tik} - x_{sik}|^p \right\}^{1/p} \qquad (t, s = 1, \ldots, T; i = 1, \ldots, N) \qquad (2)$$

The formula (2) for $p = 1$ comprises a city block (taxicab, Manhattan) distance, which for $p = 2$ is referred to as a Euclidean distance, while for $p \rightarrow \infty$ as a Chebyshev distance. The application of the city block distance results in cubic clustering, while spherical clustering is identified for Euclidean distances. It should be emphasised that the Minkowski distance is employed to study the similarity of objects with regard to the level of the variable values.

Moreover, it is necessary to add that it is not possible to indicate a universal clustering method. All methods involve a limitation related to the interpretation of the results obtained, which decreases with the number of objects classified. The most common clustering methods include the k-means method and its rarely used fuzzy c-means version, both of which were used in this study (stage 4). Knowledge regarding the number of classes, as well as the initial clustering of objects, is required in case of the application of these methods. In the subsequent stages of the clustering process, objects are transferred from one class to another in a way that enables them to minimise the difference from certain class variables (prototypes) within the specific class. The iterative process is repeated until the clustering approaches the assumed level of stability [43,51,54,55].

The clustering of objects requires the number of classes to be determined (stage 5), which may be established by different methods [56,57]. In this paper, the number of classes was determined in two steps. In the initial step, separable clustering was generated using the k-means method, then assessed with the Krzanowski–Lai [58] clustering quality index calculated according to the formula

$$KL(G) = \left| \frac{DIFF(G)}{DIFF(G+1)} \right|, \quad KL(G) \in R \quad (3)$$

where $DIFF(G) = (G-1)^{2/K} tr\mathbf{W}(G-1) - G^{2/K} tr\mathbf{W}(G)$. When $KL(G)$ reaches the first local maximum for the number of clusters G *, the best partition of the population is into G * clusters.

In the fifth stage of the clustering, the number of classes adopted was determined by the chosen disjoint clustering method for the identical data matrix. Next, the clustering was conducted using the fuzzy c-means method [59–61]. The problem of fuzzy clustering was presented as a non-linear issue of mathematical programming [59–61]:

$$\text{Minimise} \quad J_m(\mathbf{U}, \mathbf{C}, \mathbf{X}) = \sum_{t=1}^{T} \sum_{i=1}^{N} \sum_{g=1}^{G} u_{tig}^m \sum_{k=1}^{K} (x_{tik} - c_{gk})^2 \quad (4)$$

Subject to:

$$\sum_{g=1}^{G} u_{tig} = 1 \quad (t = 1, \ldots, T; i = 1, \ldots, N) \quad (5)$$

$$\sum_{t=1}^{T} \sum_{i=1}^{N} u_{tig} > 0 \quad (g = 1, \ldots, G), \quad (6)$$

$$u_{tig} \geq 0 \quad (t = 1, \ldots, T; i = 1, \ldots, N; g = 1, \ldots, G), \quad (7)$$

where T—the number of moments in time (e.g., days), N—the number of objects (e.g., countries), G—the number of fuzzy classes, K—the number of variables, m—the parameter which regulates the degree of fuzziness of the clustering process, $\mathbf{U} = [u_{tig}] - (T \cdot N \times G)$, a dimensional matrix of the degrees of membership of objects belonging to fuzzy classes, $\mathbf{C} = [c_{gk}] - (G \times K)$, a dimensional matrix of the centroids (centres of gravity) of classes, and $\mathbf{X} = [x_{tik}] - (T \cdot N \times K)$, a dimensional data matrix, where x_{tik} represents the standardised value of the k-th variable in the i-th object at time t.

As a result of the fuzzy clustering process, each object (e.g., a country at a given moment of time) is classified into each class (epidemic states) with a certain degree of membership, that is, a number between 0 and 1. Additionally, the sum of degrees of membership for each object equals one. The degree of membership determines the strength with which a given object belongs to a particular class (epidemic states). The higher the degree of membership, the more strongly the object is characterised by the variables of a given state. Fuzzy clustering methods provide more information on the clustering of objects than classical methods, which only make it possible to unambiguously assign each object to one of the classes (states) created. The proposed approach not only allows for the identification of epidemic states but also provides information on the time of transition from one state to another, as well as presenting the opportunity to illustrate the fluctuations occurring when states change.

The next stage of the procedure is to identify epidemic states (stage 6). The identification of states may be divided into the formal and the substantive. Formal identification consists of determining the name, while substantive identification involves descriptive statistics of indicators. It is likewise worth paying attention to the fuzziness degree of the classification—we used the entropy index to measure this and at the same time to assess the uncertainty of epidemiological states. Entropy is a measure of the indeterminacy, chaos, and degree of disorder in a structure. It is greater when the states are more equal, and smaller when one state is more pronounced. The entropy of a fuzzy set [62] is a measure of the total amount of information in the missing fuzzy structure, given by a fuzzy set, to such a state that there is no uncertainty in the classification of the elements. The research used the normalized entropy index see [53,60,63,64]:

$$H_i = \frac{1}{T} \sum_{t=1}^{T} \sum_{g=1}^{G} h(u_{tig}) (i = 1, \ldots, N) \quad (8)$$

where:

$$h(u_{tig}) = \begin{cases} -u_{tig} \log_a u_{tig} & \text{for } u_{tig} > 0 \\ 0 & \text{for } u_{tig} = 0 \end{cases} \qquad (9)$$

u_{tig} is the degree of membership of the i-th object (country) at time t belonging to g-th fuzzy class, and $a \in (1, \infty)$, but usually $a = G$. Then, this index ranges from 0 to 1. The lower the entropy value, the lower the hesitancy of the states in the period analyzed. In other words, the lower the entropy, the more pronounced is one state, while the higher the entropy, the higher the uncertainty states.

We also determine the changes in the epidemiological states using the daily entropy index:

$$H_{ti} = \sum_{g=1}^{G} h(u_{tig}) \qquad (10)$$

Equation (10) "represents Shannon's measure of statistical uncertainty" [65]. The daily entropy is computed similarly to the normalized entropy index, but aggregating per day. The greater H_{ti}, the greater the uncertainty of fuzzy classification; the greater the fuzziness, and the greater the uncertainty in the identification of epidemiological states. It is worth noting that in two extreme cases, if $H_{ti} = 0$ then there is no uncertainty in the identification of states, and if $H_{ti} = 1$ then we identify the most uncertain situation.

3. Results

The examination of the epidemiological situation, as well as its changes, initiates the adoption of the main objective of the clustering process, comprising the identification of epidemic states. The study covered the European countries and was based on daily data from 4 March to 24 June 2020. A set of four variables (indicators) was selected to identify the epidemic states in the countries studied, as follows:

- COVID-19 cases per 100,000 population (x_1),
- COVID-19 deaths per 100,000 population (x_2),
- share of COVID-19 deaths in COVID-19 cases (%) (x_3),
- active cases—cumulative number for 14 days of COVID-19 cases per 100,000 (x_4).

A statistical description of the variables was presented in Table 1. On this basis, it may be concluded that the variables selected significantly differentiate the countries analysed. Such a conclusion is indicated by a significant range between the maximum and minimum values, as well as by the analysis of the variation coefficient. The largest diversity of values characterised the x_2 COVID-19 deaths per 100,000 population, in which the average diversity of values of this variable in European countries was 339.94%. In European countries, the coefficient of variation of the x_1 COVID-19 cases per 100,000 population was also high (329.17%). The analysis of the variable values based on positional statistics reveals a slightly lower differentiation in their values.

Selected diagnostic variables constitute important information on the epidemiological situation of the countries studied. Initially, sequences of disjoint classifications from 2 to 10 classes were generated using the *k*-means method. The calculations were performed in the R program [66] with the *clusterSim* package [67]. As part of this package, we used a function of the same name, cluster. Sim, for a *k*-means method with the classical standardisation formula for data. The divisions were assessed using the Krzanowski–Lai index, which achieved the first local extremum for three classes. It was therefore assumed that three epidemiological states would be identified in the countries analysed. Subsequently, applying information from the previous research stage, the fuzzy clustering of objects was conducted based on the fuzzy *c*-means method. The calculations were performed in the R program with the *fclust* package [68]. We used the FKM procedure including the fuzzy *c*-means clustering algorithm. The results of the state identification in the countries analysed are presented in Figure 2.

Table 1. Values of the selected descriptive statistics of variables characterising the epidemiological situation in the countries examined from 4 March to 24 June 2020.

Variables	Classical Measures					Positional Measures				
	min	mean	max	SD	CV	Q_1	Q_2	Q_3	IQR	QCOD
x_1	0.00	3.04	490.80	10.00	329.17	0.16	0.82	2.65	2.48	88.41
x_2	0.00	0.16	17.42	0.53	339.94	0.00	0.01	0.09	0.09	100.00
x_3	0.00	6.07	400.00	16.27	268.05	0.00	0.72	6.39	6.39	100.00
x_4	0.00	39.80	858.90	74.90	188.20	3.77	12.74	40.78	37.02	83.09

Note: SD—standard deviation, CV—coefficient of variation (%), Q_1—1st quartile, Q_2—median, Q_3—3rd quartile, IQR—interquartile range, QCOD—quartile coefficient of dispersion (%). Source: own calculation based on statistical data from [44].

Figure 2 presents the degrees of membership of countries to the three epidemic states in the period examined. The closer the line is to 1, the more identifiable is the state. The change in the membership degrees of countries to specific states indicates a change in the epidemiological state. The method applied makes it possible not only to identify the epidemic states but also provides information on the time of transition from one state to another.

We observed that for Germany, from 20 March 2020 the values of the degrees of membership of the stabilisation state began to decline. This situation lasted until 30 March 2020, with slight fluctuations in the degrees of membership to the stable state. The transition time from stable to destabilisation in Germany was 11 days. On 31 March the degrees of membership to the state of stabilisation and destabilisation were identical at 0.48. From 1 April 2020 Germany entered the state of destabilisation, which finished on 16 April 2020. For the next 19 days, the situation was unstable, and on 5 May (as on March 31), there was no single dominant state and the degrees of membership to the stabilisation and destabilisation states were 0.48. It was only on 6 May that Germany entered the state of stabilisation of the epidemiological situation.

In France, too, the situation began to destabilise around 20 March 2020. The state of destabilisation began after a week. Although this state prevailed until 9 May 2020, sometimes it was only partial (a degree of membership less than 0.5). The situation was ambiguous for the 19 days following 10 May 2020. Only on 29 May 2020 did France enter a state of relative stabilisation of the epidemiological situation. Until the end of the period studied, one can observe a quite regular—about a week apart—sharp decrease in the degree of membership of the state of stabilisation.

In Italy, from 9 March a decrease in the degree of membership of the stabilisation state was observed, lasting about a week. From 16 to 23 May 2020, a state of destabilisation was observed. However, for 23 days from the beginning of May, declining degrees of membership of this state was mostly identified, indicating a potential change in state. For three weeks from 24 May 2020, the situation was unclear. The state of epidemiological stabilisation was mostly identified, but to a large extent it was partial. For three more weeks the situation was not clear. It was only from 14 June that the situation began to stabilise. It should be noted that in Germany, France and Italy the transition from stabilised to destabilised was faster than the other way around.

In Spain, the situation was more complicated. On 16 March 2020 there was a sharp decline in the degree of membership. However, from 12 March a slight decrease in the values of membership degrees was already observed. After about a week, Spain went into a destabilised state. After another week, the expansion of the epidemiological situation already dominated and was identified until 13 April 2020. From 14 April a partial state of destabilisation began to manifest itself, which after a week was already quite intense (membership degrees above 0.7). After another week (27 April 2020), there was a one-day breakdown, followed by a state of destabilisation for the next 19 days. From 17 May 2020 the situation began to stabilise for nine days. This was clear until the end of the period analysed, excluding 16 June 2020, where the degrees of membership to the states were similar (approximately 0.3).

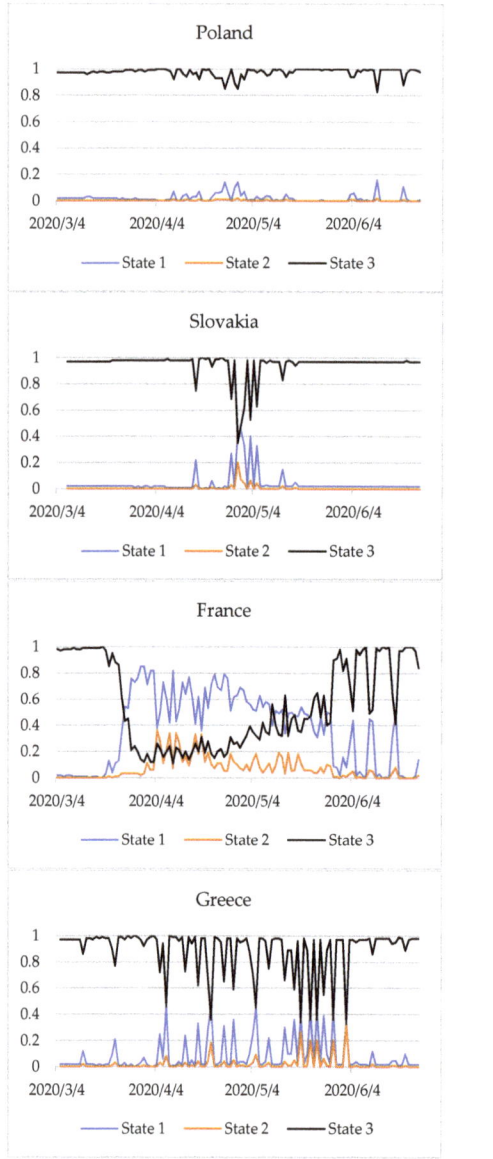
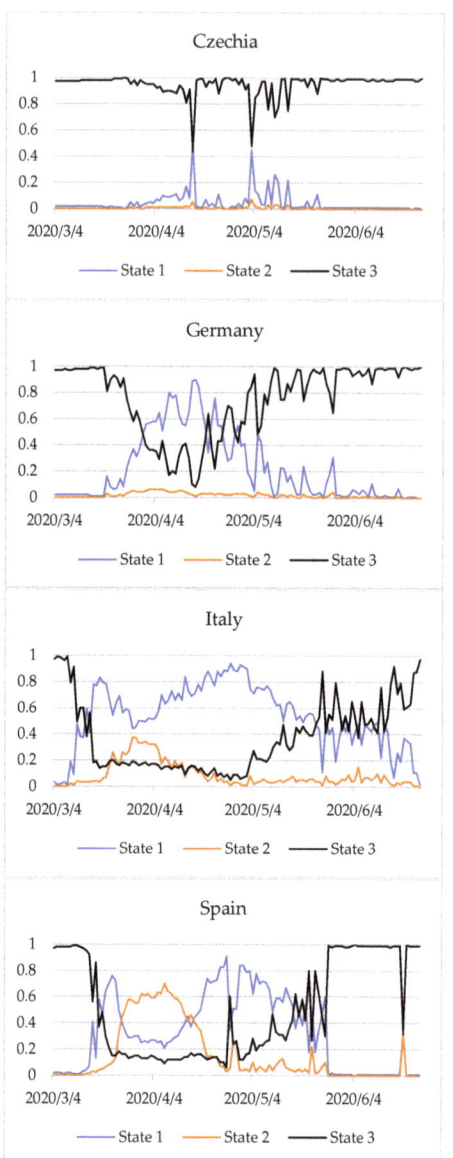

Figure 2. Epidemic states in selected European countries from 4 March to 24 June 2020. Note: The ordinate axis shows the membership degrees of a country for states of the epidemic. Source: own elaboration based on statistical data from [44].

Some countries displayed a stable state throughout the study period. These include Poland, the Czech Republic, and Slovakia. However, Greece was dominated by one epidemiological state—stabilization, but sometimes it was only partial (degrees of membership less than 0.5). This was especially visible in two-week intervals, from 7 to 21 April, from 5 to 19 May and from 22 May to 2 June at intervals of two to four days.

However, in the latter two countries, a less stable dominant state, as well as small periodic fluctuations were observed. Additionally, Figures 3 and 4 show the values of the COVID-19 cases and present deaths per 100,000 population.

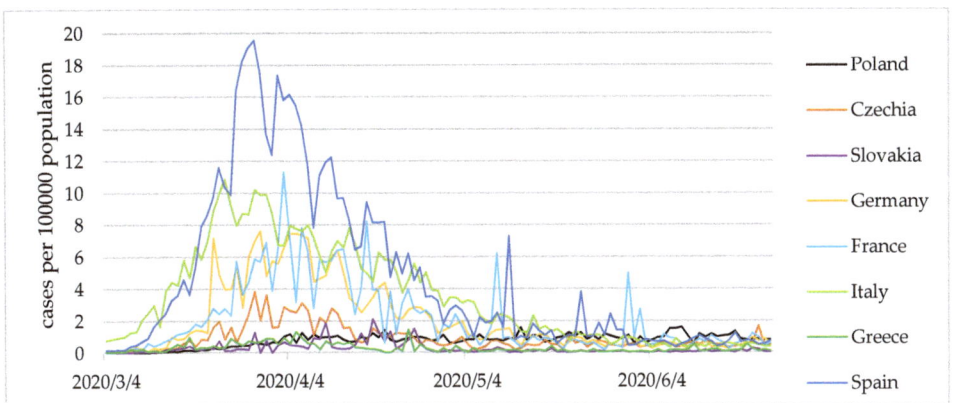

Figure 3. COVID-19 cases per 100,000 population in selected European countries from 4 March to 24 June 2020. Source: own elaboration based on statistical data from [44].

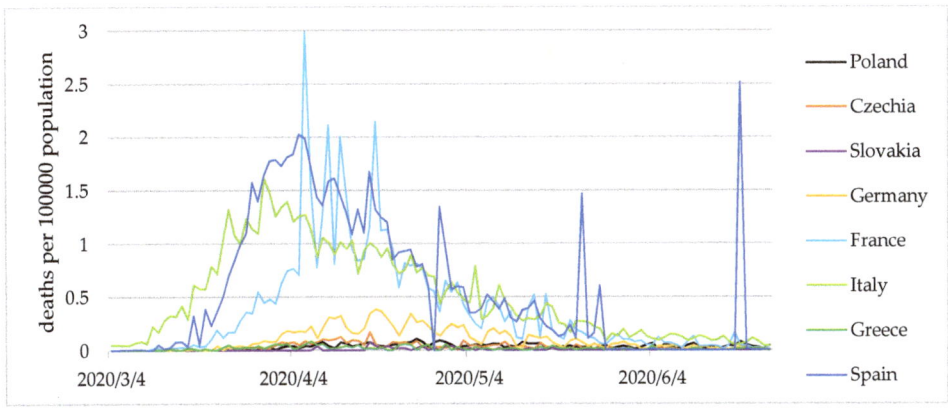

Figure 4. COVID-19 deaths per 100,000 population in selected European countries from 4 March to 24 June 2020. Source: own elaboration based on statistical data from [44].

Table 2 presents the affiliation of countries to specific states in three crucial periods: 4 March 2020 (the start of the epidemic in Poland), 15 April 2020, and 24 June 2020. The study identified three main epidemic states in the European countries defined as follows: stabilization, destabilization, and expansion of COVID-19. A state was defined as partial, provided that the highest membership degree of the country was less than 0.5. The degree of membership determines the strength with which a country belongs to a particular epidemic state. The higher the degree of membership, the more strongly the country is characterised by the variables of a given state. The typology of states was conducted using the average values of variables for epidemic states identified in European countries (Table 3).

Table 2. Pandemic states in European countries in crucial study periods.

Date	States	Types of State [1]	Countries [2]
4 March 2020	1	destabilisation	not identified
	2	expansion	not identified
	3	stabilisation	France (0.98) [3], Austria (0.97), Belarus (0.97), Belgium (0.97), Croatia (0.97), Czechia (0.97), Denmark (0.97), Estonia (0.97), Finland (0.97), Germany (0.97), Iceland (0.97), Ireland (0.97), Italy (0.97), Netherlands (0.97), Norway (0.97), Poland (0.97), Portugal (0.97), Romania (0.97), Russia (0.97), Spain (0.97), Sweden (0.97), Switzerland (0.97), Ukraine (0.97), United Kingdom (0.97), San Marino (0.84)
15 April 2020	1	destabilisation	Germany (0.89), Netherlands (0.89), Switzerland (0.87), Portugal (0.8), Sweden (0.76), Italy (0.69), France (0.63), Denmark (0.62), Norway (0.59), Czechia (0.51)
		partial destabilisation	United Kingdom (0.48), Iceland (0.46), Luxembourg (0.43)
	2	expansion	Ireland (0.70), San Marino (0.57),
		partial expansion	Belgium (0.49), Spain (0.46)
	3	stabilisation	Armenia (1.00), Kosovo (0.99), Russia (0.99), Slovakia (0.99), Ukraine (0.99), Bosnia and Herzegovina (0.99), Georgia (0.98), Lithuania (0.98), Latvia (0.98), Poland (0.96), Greece (0.94), Liechtenstein (0.94), Finland (0.92), Belarus (0.9), Malta (0.88), Bulgaria (0.87), Albania (0.82), Cyprus (0.81), Romania (0.79), Slovenia (0.79), Croatia (0.77), Moldova (0.77), Montenegro (0.72), Monaco (0.63), Serbia (0.63), Austria (0.62), Hungary (0.61), Estonia (0.54), North Macedonia (0.53),
24 June 2020	1	destabilisation	Moldova (0.65), North Macedonia (0.65), Sweden (0.51), Belarus (0.51)
		partial destabilisation	Ireland (0.48), Russia (0.48), Lithuania (0.47)
	2	expansion	Armenia (0.85)
	3	stabilisation	Belgium (1.00), Czechia (1.00), Denmark (1.00), Germany (1.00), Bulgaria (0.99), Serbia (0.99), Spain (0.99), Albania (0.98), Bosnia and Herzegovina (0.98), Croatia (0.98), Cyprus (0.98), Estonia (0.98), Finland (0.98), Georgia (0.98), Greece (0.98), Iceland (0.98), Luxembourg (0.98), Malta (0.98), Monaco (0.98), Montenegro (0.98), Norway (0.98), Poland (0.98), Switzerland (0.98), Ukraine (0.98), Hungary (0.97), Latvia (0.97), Liechtenstein (0.97), Slovakia (0.97), San Marino (0.96), Netherlands (0.94), Romania (0.93), Austria (0.90), Portugal (0.85), France (0.84), United Kingdom (0.80), Kosovo (0.76), Italy (0.72), Slovenia (0.72)

Note: [1] A type of state was defined as partial, provided that the highest membership degree of the country to a specific state amounted to less than 0.5. The research also included: Armenia, Kosovo, Georgia and Cyprus. [2] Countries reporting COVID-19 in a particular period. [3] The highest membership degree of a country to the specific state. The calculations were performed with the *fclust* package [68] in R. Source: own elaboration based on statistical data from [44].

Table 3. The average values of variables for epidemic states identified in European countries (average values for fuzzy classes).

Specification	Variables			
	x_1	x_2	x_3	x_4
State 1	5.66	0.39	13.55	76.73
State 2	13.70	0.67	14.23	183.62
State 3	1.57	0.06	3.65	19.64
Mean	3.04	0.16	6.07	39.80

Source: own elaboration based on statistical data from [44].

The analysis of the variable values in the period examined made it possible to identify three epidemic states in Europe. The first state was defined as a total or partial destabilisation. Such a nomenclature was influenced by high values of the indicators. Each of these exceeded the average for Europe as a whole. The number of COVID-19 cases amounted to 5.66 per 100,000 population, with the average for European countries close to 3. It should be noted that there were almost 4 COVID-19 deaths per 1 million population, which represented more than 13.5% of the total COVID-19 cases (%). Simultaneously, the active number of cases within the destabilisation state amounted to nearly 77 COVID-19 cases per 100,000 population. This state constitutes a threat to countries' economies; however, the level of variables associated with infections and deaths allows for a certain limited functioning of economies.

We called the second state expansion, which constitutes an escalation of the phenomena, noticeable in various intensities. The indicators for state 2 assume significantly worse values than for state 1. The state of expansion was characterised by more than twice as many COVID-19 cases than the state of destabilisation. In the state of coronavirus expansion, the number of active cases increased rapidly, amounting to over 183 COVID-19 cases per 100,000 population. The values of indicators enabled the formulation of a thesis assuming that the situation threatens the country's stability. They also comprise the basis for social and economic restrictions, resulting in a loss of economic security in the micro- and macro-economic dimensions. Such a state should constitute a premise for a complete or significant closure of the economy to prevent a further uncontrolled expansion of the disease.

In state 3—stabilisation—the values of the indicators were below the European average. The number of COVID-19 cases amounted to 1.57 per 100,000 population, while deaths were at 1 person in over a million. The number of active cases was therefore low (19.64 per 100,000 population), with the European average at 39.8. State 3 does not pose a significant threat to national economies. It appears to constitute a premise for complying with certain hygiene and safety standards, such as the use of masks, hand-washing, and refraining from shaking hands; however, it should not result in a freeze of the national economies. Unfortunately, the absence of recognition of the disease's effects caused many countries to introduce lockdowns at this level, which resulted in their economic destabilisation.

Figure 5 shows values of the normalised entropy index in selected European countries. A high value of the entropy index was revealed for Italy (0.653). This proves the high uncertainty of the epidemiological situation in the period analysed. A slightly lower value of the entropy index was identified for France (0.537) and Spain (0.510). A very low entropy index value and, at the same time, the most stable epidemiological situation was observed in Poland (0.084). In even greater detail, the uncertainty in the epidemiological situation of countries is shown in the daily entropy index (Figure 6). The results showed that a period of low entropy in countries primarily matches the epidemiological state of stabilisation. This situation was observed especially in Poland (during almost the entire period analysed), Czechia, and Slovakia (from March to until around mid-April and from the end of May to June).

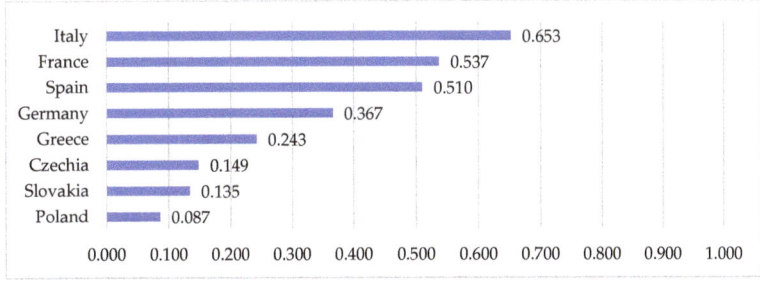

Figure 5. Values of normalised entropy index in selected European countries. Source: own elaboration based on statistical data from [44].

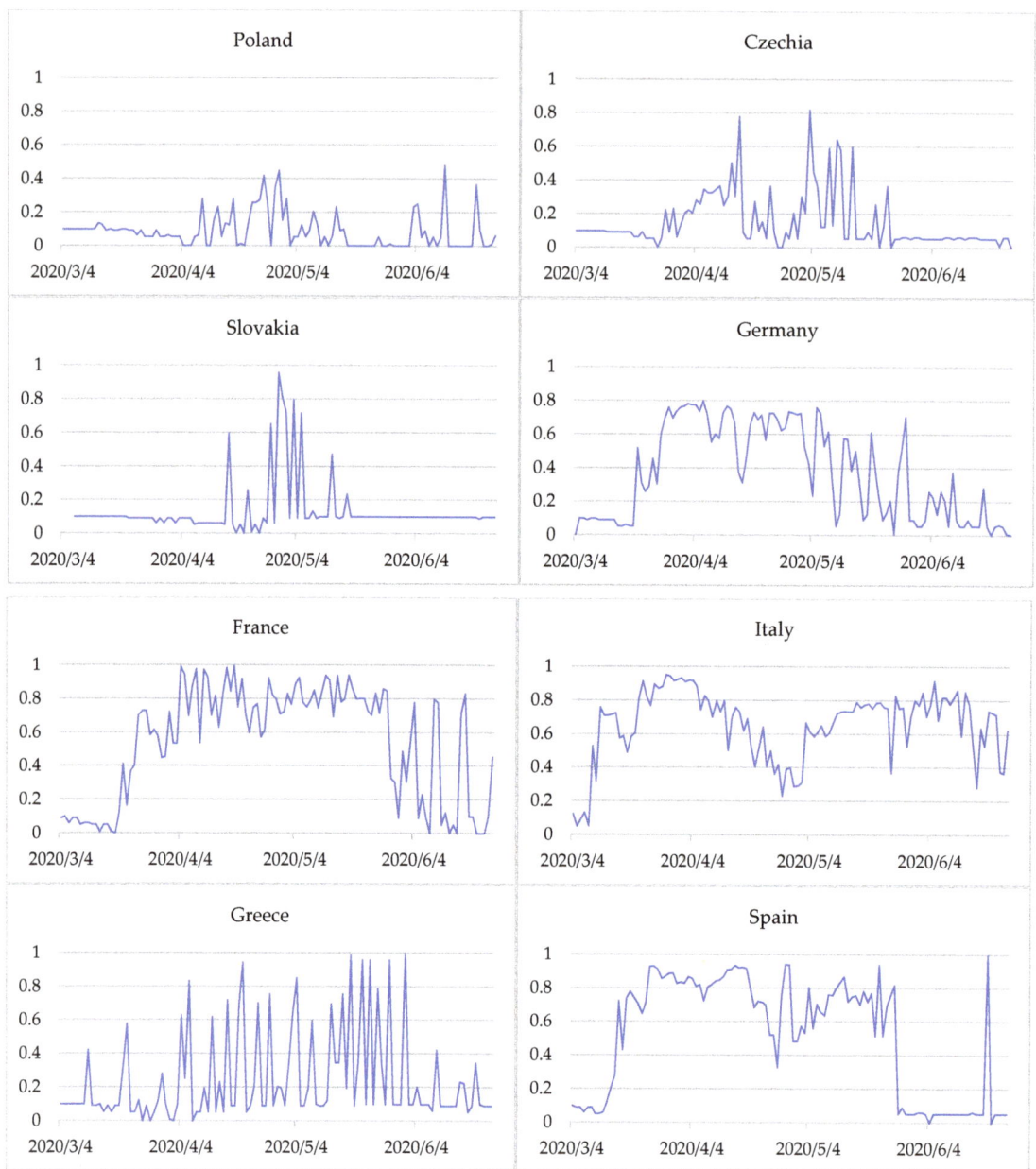

Figure 6. Changes in daily entropy index in selected European countries from 4 March to 24 June 2020. Source: own elaboration based on statistical data from [44].

After COVID-19 cases and deaths increased, the entropy was heightened. This shows a destabilisation of the epidemiological situation in Germany, France, Italy, and Spain during almost the entire period considered. In Germany, France, and Italy, during the period studied, there was a transition from a stabilization state (with fewer COVID-19 cases and deaths) to destablilization (with a sharp increase in COVID-19 cases and deaths) and back to a stabilization state (Figure 2). In Spain, the situation was similar, but the state of expansion was also partially identified. Moreover, since the end of May, when the number of COVID-19 cases and deaths was lower, the stabilization state was identified (Figure 2), and the daily entropy index was predominantly at a very low level (Figure 6).

In Greece, the situation was quite different. In this case entropy measure describes the high degree of chaoticity. Although the epidemiological state in the country was mainly identified as stabilization (Figure 2), and the entropy index is quite low—0.243 (Figure 5), the daily entropy shows great variability. This demonstrates the instability of the epidemiological state, despite the country keeping closer to the state of stabilization.

4. Discussion

Some studies use models (e.g., the recursive bifurcation model) to describe the infection processes as first- and second-order phase transitions. Such approaches make it possible to show two states, i.e., "the possibility of the population returning to a state with a low level of cases or the epidemic returning" [35]. The advantage of our approach is that more than two states of the epidemic can be revealed. In addition, the proposed fuzzy technique also makes it possible to observe the fluctuations and transition times from one state to another. Variability of states shows the intensity of the process and the hidden diversity in phases of the pandemic.

Moreover, the idea of the proposed fuzzy clustering approach proposed is based on more complex mathematical modelling then in the case of traditional clustering. Important in this approach is the concept of partial membership of a country in more than one class (state). Each country can belong to more than one epidemic state at the same time, but one state a day tends to predominate. The transition from membership to non-membership is gradual. An abrupt transition from one state to another is less common. This relates to the fuzziness of the degree of membership, because "the essence of fuzzy clustering is to consider not only the belonging status to the clusters, but also to consider to what degree do the objects belong to the clusters" [43].

Mahmoudi et al. [40] compared and clustered selected countries using the fuzzy clustering approach. This work describes the distributions of the spread of COVID-19. They also state that "to determine the policies and plans, the study of the relations between the distributions of the spread of this virus in other countries is critical". Although our research differs, we agree with this statement. It should be emphasised that our research brings a new quality by proposing a fuzzy classification approach to the study of epidemic states in European countries. This approach makes it possible to identify states of pandemic and define the time of transition from one state to another. Our manuscript presents research on the situation of selected European countries, but the research has been conducted for all other countries for which data were available. Our research complements other studies around the world. It outlines the most important background aspects on the epidemiological situation and changes in European countries.

D'Urso et al. [69] used spatial robust fuzzy clustering to identify a clustering structure for the 20 Italian regions according to the main variables related to the COVID-19 pandemic. The exponential distance-based fuzzy c-medoids clustering algorithm based on B-splines with a spatial penalty term was applied to the clustering of time series. Although a different fuzzy approach was used and objects at the regional level were studied, three clusters were identified, similar to our study at the European country level. D'Urso et al. [69] obtained "on the entire period almost the same partition". Our research showed that the variability of epidemic states differed depending on the country. According to our research, in Italy, epidemic states fluctuated even in the initial months of the epidemic.

We should also mention interesting research carried out by Afzal et al. [70]. They used c-means and fuzzy c-means algorithms for partitioning COVID-19 data. Their results focused mainly on the comparison of the optimum cluster size obtained using both methods. They stated that "the clustering of COVID-19 data from the available data revealed that there were five optimal clusters based on the location and the cases observed so far", but that "the three main COVID-19 clusters have been identified". The main number of clusters is therefore in line with our research, although the characteristics of the classes are different and, in our case, more detailed and specific. In our opinion our research allows for a more complex analysis.

Moreover, Ghanbari et al. [71] mentioned that "entropy is related to the missing information on the concrete state of a system and it shows a measure of the disorder of a system". In that sense we point out that entropy of fuzzy classification can be an effective measure for assessment of an epidemiological situation in a country because it can express a grade of uncertainty (or sometimes stability) of the situation as a single number per day or in a given time period.

It should be emphasised that our research can be extended to include other elements. The research is ongoing and in our opinion, it is interesting to find a connection between studies from the initial pandemic period, which we present in this manuscript, and further studies covering the later phases of the pandemic (e.g., from an annual perspective) and other types of research during the COVID-19 pandemic.

5. Conclusions

The study attempted to identify of the COVID-19 epidemic states in European countries. During the period studied, epidemic states and their changes in Poland and other European countries were therefore identified. The fuzzy c-means clustering method allowed us to identify countries' epidemic states. This approach also made it possible to determine the time of transition from one state to another, as well as to observe fluctuations during changes of state. The innovation is the application of fuzzy clusters, which are more appropriate for the characteristics of the variability epidemic states because they avoid a binary split between membership and non-membership.

With this work, we have demonstrated that the entropy analysis of fuzzy classification can contain relevant information concerning the epidemiological states of COVID-19. We demonstrated that the entropy measure of classification can be used to detect the grade of uncertainty in countries' epidemiological situations. The greater value of the entropy index for a country, the more equal the degrees of membership and, consequently, epidemiological states are less unrecognized (i.e., no one state predominates); the smaller the entropy, the more pronounced is one state. It proved possible to positively verify the paper's research hypothesis, which stated that the epidemiological situation in Poland from 4 March to 24 June 2020 was stable compared to the other European countries. Three COVID-19 epidemic states were identified in Europe, i.e., stabilisation, destabilisation, and expansion. Our research revealed that one state, defined as stability, dominated the period studied in Poland. The Czech Republic and Slovakia displayed a similar state; however, they had greater fluctuations in the values of the indicators analysed during the same period. Additionally, we also propose a simple way of visualising the countries' epidemic trajectories in order to enable trend observation and easy comparison. The graphic representation allows for day-by-day monitoring of the epidemic state and its changes.

The message of this research is also that the new public policies currently being introduced have positive but insufficient effects on preventing the spread of COVID-19, and increasing their effectiveness is a must. Hence, the search for new solutions through various types of analysis and research paths concerning the assessment of the epidemiological situation of countries, including changes in their states and dynamics, is very important. Quickly recognising not only states but also the timing of changes from one state to another is extremely important in regard to the authorities' possible reactions. Producers and consumers alike react to these changes, trying to adapt to them to a certain extent. The accurate identification of any dependencies will, in the future, allow faster responses to threats at an earlier stage.

We believe that research into the epidemiological situation in countries is important in order to understand the trajectory of the COVID-19 pandemic. We believe that scientific analysis and understanding of the various changes in the COVID-19 pandemic can help society better prepare for future outbreaks and support informed decision making in light of societal values. In addition, it should be added that the research results are important for governments, politicians, and other decision-makers who are involved in the process of preventing and reducing the effects of the COVID-19 pandemic.

6. Recommendations

The research results can be useful in deepening the understanding of the phenomenon of the COVID-19 pandemic. Above all, the research is significant in illustrating the links between theory and practice in terms of the study of the epidemiological situation in countries. Understanding states of COVID-19 as well as their evolution is of paramount importance for controlling and preventing this disease, and also mitigating the devastating effects of the pandemic. They can therefore be useful in diagnosing and solving real problems, and thus will be useful for decision-makers and politicians involved in the process of developing and implementing COVID-19 prevention policies. Undoubtedly, our research may be useful because it allows us to classify certain groups of countries, to which aid as well as tools for counteracting unfavourable circumstances within the economy and society can, to a greater extent, be standardised. The research makes it possible to get to know the essence of the phenomenon and, as a result, create strategies to prevent threats from occurring or, at the very least, mitigate their effects in the future.

The research concerned European countries, but the results may also be useful for other countries. It is emphasised that the results of this research are based on the state of the COVID-19 pandemic in European countries during its first months, but we are also convinced that the results of this study can be useful for further research during its future phases.

Author Contributions: Conceptualization, A.Ł. and S.K.; methodology, A.Ł. and S.K.; validation, A.Ł. and S.K.; formal analysis, A.Ł.; investigation, A.Ł. and S.K.; resources, A.Ł. and S.K.; data curation, A.Ł. and S.K.; writing—original draft preparation, A.Ł. and S.K.; writing—review and editing, A.Ł. and S.K.; visualization, A.Ł. and S.K. supervision, A.Ł. and S.K.; project administration, A.Ł. and S.K.; funding acquisition, A.Ł. and S.K. All authors have read and agreed to the published version of the manuscript.

Funding: The research was financed from resources of the Faculty of Economics, Poznań University of Life Sciences.

Institutional Review Board Statement: Not applicable.

Informed Consent Statement: Not applicable.

Data Availability Statement: All the data supporting reported results comes from: https://data.europa.eu/euodp/en/data/dataset/covid-19-coronavirus-data (accessed on 11 October 2020).

Conflicts of Interest: The authors declare no conflict of interest.

References

1. Djankov, S.; Panizza, U. (Eds.) *COVID in Developing Economies*; Centre for Economic Policy Research (CEPR): London, UK, 2020. Available online: https://voxeu.org/content/covid-19-developing-economies (accessed on 6 July 2021).
2. Asmundson, G.J.; Taylor, S. Coronaphobia: Fear and the 2019-nCoV outbreak. *J. Anxiety Disord.* **2020**, *70*, 102196. [CrossRef]
3. Baldwin, R.; di Mauro, B.W. *Economics in the Time of COVID-19*; Centre for Economic Policy Research (CEPR): London, UK, 2020. Available online: https://voxeu.org/article/economics-time-covid-19-new-ebook (accessed on 23 August 2021).
4. Bu, F.; Steptoe, A.; Fancourt, D. Loneliness during a strict lockdown: Trajectories and predictors during the COVID-19 pandemic in 38,217 United Kingdom adults. *Soc. Sci. Med.* **2020**, *265*, 113521. [CrossRef]
5. Cassandro, D. Siamo in Guerra! Il Coronavirus e le Sue Metafore [We Are at War: The Coronavirus and Its Metaphors]. *L'Internazionale*. 22 March 2020. Available online: https://www.internazionale.it/opinione/daniele-cassandro/2020/03/22/coronavirus-metafore-guerra?fbclid=IwAR0kZCnNmLZLENFTAPUIFtkq8bqrabqMe-vEoZpQZ6Wig55XdPEWlzdzRkE (accessed on 19 October 2020).
6. Dutta, A.; Fischer, H.W. The local governance of COVID-19: Disease prevention and social security in rural India. *World Dev.* **2021**, *138*, 105234. [CrossRef] [PubMed]

7. Hall, M.C.; Prayag, G.; Fieger, P.; Dyason, D. Beyond panic buying: Consumption displacement and COVID-19. *J. Serv. Manag.* **2020**, *32*, 113–128. [CrossRef]
8. International Labour Organization. ILO Monitor: COVID-19 and the World of Work (2nd ed.). 2020. Available online: https://www.ilo.org/wcmsp5/groups/public/---dgreports/---dcomm/documents/briefingnote/wcms_740877.pdf (accessed on 19 October 2020).
9. Jribi, S.; Ben Ismail, H.; Doggui, D.; Debbabi, H. COVID-19 virus outbreak lockdown: What impacts on household food wastage? *Environ. Dev. Sustain.* **2020**, *22*, 3939–3955. [CrossRef] [PubMed]
10. Kalinowski, S. Od paniki do negacji: Zmiana postaw wobec COVID-19 [From panic to negation: A change in attitudes towards COVID-19]. *Wieś Rol.* **2020**, *3*, 45–65. [CrossRef]
11. McCarthy, J.U.S. Coronavirus Concerns Surge, Government Trust Slides. *Politics*. 16 March 2020. Available online: https://news.gallup.com/poll/295505/coronavirus-worries-surge.aspx (accessed on 11 October 2020).
12. Mertens, G.; Gerritsen, L.; Duijndam, S.; Salemink, E.; Engelhard, I.M. Fear of the coronavirus (COVID-19): Predictors in an online study conducted in March 2020. *J. Anxiety Disord.* **2020**, *74*, 102258. [CrossRef]
13. Taylor, S.; Landry, C.A.; Paluszek, M.M.; Fergus, T.A.; McKay, D.; Asmundson, G.J.G. Development and initial validation of the COVID Stress Scales. *J. Anxiety Disord.* **2020**, *72*, 102232. [CrossRef]
14. Venuleo, C.; Gelo, C.G.O.; Salvatore, S. Fear, affective semiosis, and management of the pandemic crisis: COVID-19 as semiotic vaccine? *Clin. Neuropsychiatry* **2020**, *17*, 117–130. [CrossRef]
15. Patel, J.A.; Nielsen, F.; Badiani, A.A.; Assi, S.; Unadkat, V.A.; Patel, B.; Ravindrane, R.; Wardle, H. Poverty, inequality and COVID-19: The forgotten vulnerable. *Public Health* **2020**, *183*, 110–111. [CrossRef] [PubMed]
16. Tran, P.B.; Hensing, G.; Wingfield, T.; Atkins, S.; Annerstedt, K.S.; Kazibwe, J.; Tomeny, E.; Biermann, O.; Thorpe, J.; Forse, R.; et al. Income security during public health emergencies: The COVID-19 poverty trap in Vietnam. *BMJ Glob. Health* **2020**, *5*, e002504. [CrossRef]
17. Wang, C.; Pan, R.; Wan, X.; Tan, Y.; Xu, L.; Ho, C.S.; Ho, R.C. Immediate Psychological Responses and Associated Factors during the Initial Stage of the 2019 Coronavirus Disease (COVID-19) Epidemic among the General Population in China. *Int. J. Environ. Res. Public Health* **2020**, *17*, 1729. [CrossRef] [PubMed]
18. Akhtar, R. *Coronavirus (COVID-19) Outbreaks, Environment and Human Behaviour*; Springer: Cham, Switzerland, 2021. [CrossRef]
19. Henao-Cespedes, V.; Garcés-Gómez, Y.A.; Ruggeri, S.; Henao-Cespedes, T.M. Relationship analysis between the spread of COVID-19 and the multidimensional poverty index in the city of Manizales, Colombia. *Egypt. J. Remote. Sens. Space Sci.* **2021**. [CrossRef]
20. Bobba, G.; Hubé, N. *Populism and the Politicization of the COVID-19 Crisis in Europe*; Palgrave Macmillan: Cham, Switzerland, 2021. [CrossRef]
21. Jia, Z.; Xu, S.; Zhang, Z.; Cheng, Z.; Han, H.; Xu, H.; Wang, M.; Zhang, H.; Zhou, Y.; Zhou, Z. Association between mental health and community support in lockdown communities during the COVID-19 pandemic: Evidence from rural China. *J. Rural. Stud.* **2021**, *82*, 87–97. [CrossRef]
22. Kansiime, M.K.; Tambo, J.A.; Mugambi, I.; Bundi, M.; Kara, A.; Owuor, C. COVID-19 implications on household income and food security in Kenya and Uganda: Findings from a rapid assessment. *World Dev.* **2021**, *137*, 105199. [CrossRef] [PubMed]
23. Kerbage, A.; Matta, M.; Haddad, S.; Daniel, P.; Tawk, L.; Gemayel, S.; Amine, A.; Warrak, R.; Germanos, M.; Haddad, F.; et al. Challenges facing COVID-19 in rural areas: An experience from Lebanon. *Int. J. Disaster Risk Reduct.* **2020**, *53*, 102013. [CrossRef]
24. Naeem, M. Do social media platforms develop consumer panic buying during the fear of Covid-19 pandemic. *J. Retail. Consum. Serv.* **2020**, *58*, 102226. [CrossRef]
25. Zaremba, A.; Kizys, R.; Tzouvanas, P.; Aharon, D.Y.; Demir, E. The quest for multidimensional financial immunity to the COVID-19 pandemic: Evidence from international stock markets. *J. Int. Financial Mark. I* **2021**, *71*, 101284. [CrossRef]
26. Agnoletti, M.; Manganelli, S.; Piras, F. Covid-19 and rural landscape: The case of Italy. *Landsc. Urban Plan.* **2020**, *204*, 103955. [CrossRef]
27. Cuadros, D.F.; Branscum, A.J.; Mukandavire, Z.; Miller, F.D.; MacKinnon, N. Dynamics of the COVID-19 epidemic in urban and rural areas in the United States. *Ann. Epidemiol.* **2021**, *59*, 16–20. [CrossRef]
28. Shadabfar, M.; Mahsuli, M.; Khoojine, A.S.; Hosseini, V.R. Time-variant reliability-based prediction of COVID-19 spread using extended SEIVR model and Monte Carlo sampling. *Results Phys.* **2021**, *26*, 104364. [CrossRef] [PubMed]
29. Starostin, V.; Samokhodkin, E.; Elzon, A. Changing Consumer and Brand Behavior in the Early Stages of the COVID-19 Pandemic in Russia. *Eur. Res. Stud. J.* **2020**, *XXIII*, 531–543. [CrossRef]
30. Nolting, T. COVID-19 (SARS-CoV-2) in Germany: A Holistic Approach. Duesseldorf. 2020. Available online: https://www.researchgate.net/publication/345136477_COVID-19_SARS-CoV-2_in_Germany_A_holistic_approach (accessed on 1 December 2020).
31. Ivorra, B.; Ferrández, M.; Vela-Pérez, M.; Ramos, A. Mathematical modeling of the spread of the coronavirus disease 2019 (COVID-19) taking into account the undetected infections. The case of China. *Commun. Nonlinear Sci.* **2020**, *88*, 105303. [CrossRef]
32. Mahmud, M.; Riley, E. Household response to an extreme shock: Evidence on the immediate impact of the Covid-19 lockdown on economic outcomes and well-being in rural Uganda. *World Dev.* **2021**, *140*, 105318. [CrossRef]
33. Tavares, F.F.; Betti, G. The pandemic of poverty, vulnerability, and COVID-19: Evidence from a fuzzy multidimensional analysis of deprivations in Brazil. *World Dev.* **2021**, *139*, 105307. [CrossRef]

34. Malatzky, C.; Gillespie, J.; Couch, D.L.; Cosgrave, C. Why place matters: A rurally-orientated analysis of COVID-19's differential impacts. *Soc. Sci. Humanit. Open* **2020**, *2*, 100063. [CrossRef]
35. Soukhovolsky, V.; Kovalev, A.; Pitt, A.; Kessel, B. A new modelling of the COVID 19 pandemic. *Chaos Solitons Fractals* **2020**, *139*, 110039. [CrossRef] [PubMed]
36. Niu, R.; Chan, Y.-C.; Wong, E.W.M.; van Wyk, M.A.; Chen, G. A stochastic SEIHR model for COVID-19 data fluctuations. *Nonlinear Dyn.* **2021**, *106*, 1311–1323. [CrossRef] [PubMed]
37. Rajaei, A.; Raeiszadeh, M.; Azimi, V.; Sharifi, M. State estimation-based control of COVID-19 epidemic before and after vaccine development. *J. Process. Control* **2021**, *102*, 1–14. [CrossRef]
38. Sharifi, M.; Moradi, H. Nonlinear robust adaptive sliding mode control of influenza epidemic in the presence of uncertainty. *J. Process Contr.* **2017**, *56*, 48–57. [CrossRef]
39. Tayarani, M.-H.N. Applications of artificial intelligence in battling against covid-19: A literature review. *Chaos Solitons Fractals* **2020**, *142*, 110338. [CrossRef]
40. Mahmoudi, M.R.; Baleanu, D.; Mansor, Z.; Tuan, B.A.; Pho, K.-H. Fuzzy clustering method to compare the spread rate of Covid-19 in the high risks countries. *Chaos Solitons Fractals* **2020**, *140*, 110230. [CrossRef]
41. Just, M.; Łuczak, A. Assessment of Conditional Dependence Structures in Commodity Futures Markets Using Copula-GARCH Models and Fuzzy Clustering Methods. *Sustainability* **2020**, *12*, 2571. [CrossRef]
42. Mirkin, B. Mathematical Classification and Clustering. In *Nonconvex Optimization and Its Applications*; Springer: Boston, MA, USA, 1996; Volume 11. [CrossRef]
43. Sato-Ilic, M.; Jain, L.C. *Innovations in Fuzzy Clustering. Theory and Applications*; Studies in Fuzziness and Soft Computing; Springer: Berlin, Germany, 2006; Volume 205. [CrossRef]
44. European Centre for Disease Prevention and Control. COVID-19 Coronavirus Data [Data Set]. European Union Open Data Portal. 2020. Available online: https://data.europa.eu/euodp/en/data/dataset/covid-19-coronavirus-data (accessed on 11 October 2020).
45. Wang, Y.; Li, T.; Chen, L.; Xu, G.; Zhou, J.; Chen, C.L.P. Random Fourier feature-based fuzzy clustering with p-Laplacian regularization. *Appl. Soft Comput.* **2021**, *111*, 107724. [CrossRef]
46. Yang, M.S.; Sinaga, K.P. Collaborative feature-weighted multi-view fuzzy c-means clustering. *Pattern Recognit.* **2021**, *119*, 108064. [CrossRef]
47. Hartigan, J.A. *Clustering Algorithms*; John Wiley & Sons: New York, NY, USA, 1975.
48. Salehi, F.; Keyvanpour, M.R.; Sharifi, A. GT2-CFC: General type-2 collaborative fuzzy clustering method. *Inf. Sci.* **2021**, *578*, 297–322. [CrossRef]
49. Liao, T.W. Clustering of time series data—A survey. *Pattern Recognit.* **2005**, *38*, 1857–1874. [CrossRef]
50. Zadeh, L.A. Fuzzy sets. *Inf. Control* **1965**, *8*, 338–353. [CrossRef]
51. Wysocki, F. *Metody Taksonomiczne w Rozpoznawaniu Typów Ekonomicznych Rolnictwa i Obszarów Wiejskich [Taxonomic Methods in Recognizing Economic Types of Agriculture and Rural Areas]*; Wydawnictwo Uniwersytetu Przyrodniczego: Poznań, Poland, 2010.
52. Grabiński, T. *Metody Taksonometrii [Taxonometric Methods]*; Akademia Ekonomiczna: Kraków, Poland, 1992.
53. Wysocki, F. Metody statystycznej analizy wielowymiarowej w rozpoznawaniu typów struktury przestrzennej rolnictwa [Methods of multidimensional statistical analysis in recognizing types of spatial structure of agriculture]. *Rocz. Akad. Rol. Pozn. Rozpr. Nauk.* **1996**, *266*, 1–176.
54. Kim, T.; Bezdek, J.C.; Hathaway, R.J. Optimality tests for fixed points of the fuzzy c-means algorithm. *Pattern Recognit.* **1988**, *21*, 651–663. [CrossRef]
55. Wu, J. *Advances in K-Means Clustering: A Data Mining Thinking*; Springer Theses; Springer: Berlin, Germany, 2012. [CrossRef]
56. Milligan, G.W.; Cooper, M.C. An examination of procedures for determining the number of clusters in a data set. *Psychometrika* **1985**, *50*, 159–179. [CrossRef]
57. Fischer, A. On the number of groups in clustering. *Stat. Probab. Lett.* **2011**, *81*, 1771–1781. [CrossRef]
58. Krzanowski, W.J.; Lai, Y.T. A Criterion for Determining the Number of Groups in a Data Set Using Sum-of-Squares Clustering. *Biometrics* **1988**, *44*, 23–34. [CrossRef]
59. Bezdek, J.C. Fuzzy Mathematics in Pattern Classification. Doctoral Dissertation, Cornell University, Ithaca, NY, USA, 1973.
60. Bezdek, J.C. *Pattern Recognition with Fuzzy Objective Function Algorithms*; Plenum Press: New York, NY, USA, 1981.
61. Pal, N.R.; Bezdek, J.C. On cluster validity for the fuzzy c-means model. *IEEE Trans. Fuzzy Syst.* **1997**, *3*, 370–379, Correction in *IEEE Trans. Fuzzy Syst.* **1997**, *5*, 152–153. [CrossRef]
62. Kacprzyk, J. *Zbiory Rozmyte w Analizie Systemowej [Fuzzy Sets in System Analisis]*; PWN: Warsaw, Poland, 1986.
63. Bodjanova, S. Využitie niektórych poznatkov z teorje fuzzy mnozin pri typologii a klasyfikacii vjacrozmernych pozorovani. *Ekon.-Mat. Obzor.* **1988**, *4*, 439–449.
64. Wysocki, F.; Wagner, W. Some remarks on the determination of the initial matrix of membership degree in fuzzy classification of objects. *Ekon. Mat. Obzor.* **1990**, *4*, 414–419.
65. Bodjanova, B. Exploratory analysis of empirical frequency distributions based on partition entropy. *Inf. Sci.* **1999**, *121*, 135–147. [CrossRef]
66. R Core Team. *R. A Language and Environment for Statistical Computing*; R Foundation for Statistical Computing: Vienna, Austria, 2020. Available online: https://www.R-project.org/ (accessed on 19 October 2020).

67. Walesiak, M.; Dudek, A. Package 'ClusterSim': Searching for Optimal Clustering Procedure for a Data Set. R Package Version 0.49-1. CRAN. 2020. Available online: https://cran.r-project.org/web/packages/clusterSim/clusterSim.pdf (accessed on 19 October 2020).
68. Giordani, P.; Ferraro, M.B.; Serafini, A. Package 'Fclust': Fuzzy Clustering. R Package Version 2.1.1. CRAN. 2019. Available online: https://cran.r-project.org/web/packages/fclust/fclust.pdf (accessed on 19 October 2020).
69. D'Urso, P.; De Giovanni, L.; Vitale, V. Spatial robust fuzzy clustering of COVID 19 time series based on B-splines. *Spat. Stat.* **2021**, 100518. [CrossRef]
70. Afzal, A.; Ansari, Z.; Alshahrani, S.; Raj, A.K.; Kuruniyan, M.S.; Saleel, C.A.; Nisar, K.S. Clustering of COVID-19 data for knowledge discovery using c-means and fuzzy c-means. *Results Phys.* **2021**, *29*, 104639. [CrossRef]
71. Ghanbari, A.; Khordad, R.; Ghaderi-Zefrehei, M. Non-extensive thermodynamic entropy to predict the dynamics behavior of COVID-19. *Phys. B Condens. Matter* **2021**, *624*, 413448. [CrossRef]

Article

Linear and Nonlinear Effects in Connectedness Structure: Comparison between European Stock Markets

Renata Karkowska * and Szczepan Urjasz *

Faculty of Management, University of Warsaw, Szturmowa Street 1/3, 02-678 Warsaw, Poland
* Correspondence: rkarkowska@wz.uw.edu.pl (R.K.); surjasz@wz.uw.edu.pl (S.U.)

Abstract: The purpose of this research is to compare the risk transfer structure in Central and Eastern European and Western European stock markets during the 2007–2009 financial crisis and the COVID-19 pandemic. Similar to the global financial crisis (GFC), the spread of coronavirus (COVID-19) created a significant level of risk, causing investors to suffer losses in a very short period of time. We use a variety of methods, including nonstandard like mutual information and transfer entropy. The results that we obtained indicate that there are significant nonlinear correlations in the capital markets that can be practically applied for investment portfolio optimization. From an investor perspective, our findings suggest that in the wake of global crisis and pandemic outbreak, the benefits of diversification will be limited by the transfer of funds between developed and developing country markets. Our study provides an insight into the risk transfer theory in developed and emerging markets as well as a cutting-edge methodology designed for analyzing the connectedness of markets. We contribute to the studies which have examined the different stock markets' response to different turbulences. The study confirms that specific market effects can still play a significant role because of the interconnection of different sectors of the global economy.

Keywords: stock market; market connectedness; mutual information; transfer entropy; COVID-19; crisis

1. Introduction

Correlation estimates are crucial not only for asset allocation decisions but also for risk management and hedge. Following the global financial crisis (GFC), we have another critical period in the financial market—global outbreak of the coronavirus (COVID-19) [1]. The pandemic is influencing a number of channels, including commercial activities, consumption, labor markets, and international supply chains. Among these channels, one of the most important components is the stock markets [2,3].

As a result, investors are more active and efficient in transferring their investments from one market to another in the event of a financial crisis, particularly at the first signs of economic or political instability. However, at a time when financial crises and pandemic turbulences are systemic in nature, the process of international diversification of assets may not fulfill its basic role—risk reduction. Additionally, empirical studies confirm that correlations between markets change over time, which makes the benefits of the theory of diversification of investment portfolio selection questionable [4]. The main goal of this paper is to verify the risk transfer between US stock market indices and six European stock market indices under the 2007–2009 global financial crisis and COVID-19 outbreak.

In our study, we compare the Central and Eastern European (CEE) and Western European markets, even though these countries are forming a common area of the European Union together. The motivation to perform this division is to compare markets from countries with different levels of economic development, including the financial market. Keeping this in mind, the risk transfer structure may be different for these two regions. Our previous research confirms this relationship [5]. Our interest in that group of countries stems from several insights. Firstly, CEE countries have made major structural changes and reforms to integrate into European structures. Therefore, verification of how the financial markets of transition countries interact with other markets is an interest for both policy makers and investors. Secondly, CEE countries offer high returns on capital market investments with relatively low risk. Additionally, as the financial systems of CEE countries are strongly bank-based, an analysis of stock market development may still provide useful information.

The main contributions of this paper could be capitulated as follows. Firstly, we contribute to the studies which have examined the different stock markets' response to different turbulences (financial crisis and pandemic outbreak). Thus, we answer the question whether they can be equally responsible for the intensification of the impact of the US stock market on the stock exchanges of Central and Eastern Europe. Secondly, we employ a variety of methods to separately analyze the linear and nonlinear effect of connectedness structures for international equity markets. The area of transfer entropy has not been explored in depth. Therefore, using linear and nonlinear methodology, we can compare the complexity of the behavior of stock markets. Interesting results were obtained by Olbryś and Majewska [6], who examined the benefits of diversifying their international portfolio to the largest European stock markets (i.e., the UK, France, and Germany) during the period 2003–2013. To the best of our knowledge, no current study has analyzed connectedness structures by verifying the linear and nonlinear effect in CEE stock markets compared to Western European markets during the COVID-19 pandemic.

Thirdly, we can observe that the correlations between US and other European markets are unstable. Additionally, we confirm that Western European markets displayed higher results of the correlations with the US stock market in comparison to CEE [7].

Fourthly, the study emphasizes that while globalization has contributed to a more integrated financial system, specific market effects can still play a significant role because of the interconnection in different countries of the global economy. From an investor perspective, our findings suggest that in the wake of the global crisis and pandemic outbreak, the benefits of diversification will be limited by the transfer of funds between developed and developing country markets.

The analysis by Gao and Mei [8] examined the structure of the correlation between the US and Asian stock indices during the global financial crisis of 2007–2009 with the use of a sliding window. As part of our article, we carried out verification of the method used by Gao and Mei [8] in relation to European indices, extending the research sample to the period of the COVID-19 pandemic. The sliding window is a technique used by [8–10] to obtain dynamically changing results in observation windows. Using various parameters of sliding windows allowed for receiving distinctive outputs that presented slightly different trends in the time series. Using the methods of linear correlations, mutual information, and transfer entropy, which take into account the sliding window, it was possible to build a network of risk transfer structure relationships for the daily rates of return of selected Western European markets and Central and Eastern European equity markets. We show that these networks detect significant differences in the behavior of individual stock indices, especially in turbulent market periods, thus highlighting the strongly changing relationships between stock markets in different countries.

The rest of the paper is organized as follows. Section 2 presents the literature review, while Section 3 provides the description of the data. Section 4 presents methodology. Section 5 analyzes the results of the linear and nonlinear effect in connectedness structures. Finally, Section 6 concludes with some discussion regarding the implications of the findings and possible extensions to future work.

2. Literature Review

Although there is no consensus in studies on the reasons for increasing inter-market correlations in times of market turbulences, most researchers accept that correlations change fundamentally during market crises. The empirical results of Boubaker and Raza [4] provide strong evidence of cross-market movement between US and CEE stock markets and show that joint movement exhibits large time differences and asymmetry in the tails of return distributions. The analysis demonstrated that changes in volatility in the US and the euro area are relevant factors causing risk shocks in European markets.

Studies on the impact of COVID-19 on the financial market spread rapidly; however, they still do not cover all economic aspects of the pandemic. The overall economic impacts are not yet straight, and there is no consensus in the research. For example, Ashraf [11], Zhang et al. [12], Akhtaruzzaman et al. [13], and Zaremba et al. [14] confirm that the last pandemic has led to a growth in global financial market risk. On the other hand, Sharif et al. [15] indicate that the COVID-19 pandemic affects the US economic risk much less than the geopolitical risk. Given a slower economic growth and relatively not liquid capital markets, it is possible that emerging markets have limited resources to cope with the pandemic. According to Topcu and Gulal [16], the negative impact of COVID-19 on emerging stock markets has gradually fallen and began to taper off by mid-April 2020. The recent result of the TGARCH model estimated in Visegrad group countries' markets reveals that there is a negative link between the stock market indices and COVID-19 spread [17].

Even though the correlation coefficient and regression models are measures of linear relation between the markets, there are also nonlinear effects that may not be captured with the linear methods. The vast majority of research in transfer entropy estimation concerns developed markets. For example, Qiu and Yang [18] verify the estimation of transfer entropy for short time sequences, using 38 important stock market indices from four continents to create further financial networks, omitting nevertheless Central and Eastern European markets. Similarly, Kuang [19] aims to construct the information flow networks on multi-time-scales among 31 international stock markets between 2007 and 2018, finding that developed markets are more dominant but vulnerable to short-term risk contagion. An interesting study was conducted by Karaca, Zhang, and Muhammad [20] to optimize the stock indices' forecasting model in the stock indices dataset; however, in their study, they used only the French and German indices. Nevertheless, developing stock market connectedness based on nonlinear methods such as mutual information and transfer entropy is still at a very early stage [21–27].

Mutual information and entropy transfer are frequently used methods to study the effect of long-memory volatility. Long-memory volatility can be seen as evidence of market participants' inability to use the information available on the market and can, therefore, be linked to the issue of (not) market efficiency. For example, Dima and Dima [28] analyze the case of the Bucharest stock exchange, where they suspect endogenous and exogenous causes of nonlinear volatility effects. They suggest that mutual information can be an alternative method of checking persistence, which can be understood as evidence of long memory in the financial market. Caginalp and Desantis [29] emphasize that the role of long-term volatility is not the explicit opposite of a risk/return relationship but rather that there is an ambiguous and complex relationship between volatility and return. Khoojine and Han [30] used the mutual information method to build a structure describing the return and trading volume network of the Chinese stock. You, Fiedor, and Hołda [24] use mutual information to analyze the correlation structure of the stock market in Shanghai and find that the Chinese stock market is not structurally riskier than US and Western Europe markets. Barbi and Prataviera [21] study nonlinear dependencies on the Brazilian equity network and underline the particular benefit of mutual information network analysis to identify the characteristics of financial markets due to nonlinear relationships. Ferreira, Dionísio, Almeida, Quintino, and Aslam [31] review the influential dynamics of CEE stock indices as well as US, German, UK, and Chinese indices and find strongly influential correlations between some CEE indices and the impactful character of the US index. They argue that the COVID-19 pandemic could intensify the influence of Chinese and US indices.

Thus, we believe that there is a need for development of a study that provides an insight into the cutting-edge methodology for analyzing the connectedness of stock markets, together with a structural and time analysis of the stock exchange in CEE and Western Europe comparing the 2007–2009 financial crisis and the COVID-19 pandemic outbreak.

3. Data Characteristics

The data used in this study were taken from the Stooq website and consist of daily logarithmic returns of one US stock market index: SPX (S&P500 Index–New York) and six European market indices, of which three are from developed countries: UKX (FTSE 100 Index–London), CAC (CAC40 Index–Paris), DAX (DAX Index–Frankfurt), and three are from developing countries: WIG20 (WIG20 Index–Warsaw), PX (PX Index–Praha), BUX (BUX Index–Budapest). The allocation was made in accordance with the classification used by MSCI Inc. [32].

There are 4773 observations for each time series in the period between January 2000 and August 2020. Table 1 presents preliminary statistics of the daily logarithmic returns for all indices. The measure of skewness demonstrates that all-time series are skewed. On the basis of excess kurtosis, we can see that almost all series are highly leptokurtic with respect to the normal distribution. The Doornik–Hansen tests show a rejection (at the 5% level) of the null hypothesis of normality for each of the return series.

Table 1. Summarized statistics for daily returns.

Index	Mean	Standard Deviation	Skewness	Excess Kurtosis	Doornik–Hansen Test
SPX	0.0001839	0.0131	−0.482 [0.000]	10.584 [0.000]	4805.214 [0.000]
UKX	−0.0000148	0.0124	−0.289 [0.000]	7.956 [0.000]	1515.870 [0.000]
CAC	−0.0000208	0.0152	−0.297 [0.000]	6.630 [0.000]	1892.501 [0.000]
DAX	0.0001436	0.0156	−0.251 [0.000]	5.931 [0.000]	2270.681 [0.000]
WIG20	0.0000092	0.0157	−0.288 [0.000]	5.111 [0.000]	819.241 [0.000]
PX	0.0001328	0.0143	−1.041 [0.000]	19.041 [0.000]	7536.307 [0.000]
BUX	0.0003067	0.0156	0.123 [0.000]	13.298 [0.000]	3660.866 [0.000]

4. Methods

4.1. Cross-Market Correlations

As a first step, we use the Pearson correlation coefficient to measure the linear relationship. Next, we proposed an adjusted correlation coefficient following studies by Forbes and Rigobon [33], Olbryś and Majewska [6], and Rigobon [34]:

$$\rho_{\hat{VA}} = \frac{\hat{\rho_C}}{\sqrt{1 + \delta\left[1 - (\hat{\rho_C})^2\right]}} \tag{1}$$

where:
$\rho_{\hat{VA}}$—the adjusted correlation coefficient;
$\hat{\rho_C}$—the conditional (unadjusted) correlation coefficient;
δ—the change in turbulent period (crisis) volatility compared to the tranquil period (pre-crisis):

$$\delta = \frac{\hat{\sigma}_C^2}{\hat{\sigma}_{PC}^2} - 1 \tag{2}$$

where $\hat{\sigma}_C^2, \hat{\sigma}_{PC}^2$ are the variances in the turbulent and tranquil periods.

Following that, the formula to transform Pearson correlations to a Fisher Z transformation is [35]:

$$\rho_{VA}* = \frac{1}{2}[\ln(\hat{\rho_C} + 1) - \ln(\hat{\rho_C} - 1)] \tag{3}$$

To obtain approximately standard normal distributed z-statistic values, the difference is formed as follows:

$$Z = \frac{(\rho_C - \rho_{PC})}{\sqrt{\frac{1}{n_C - 3} + \frac{1}{n_{PC} - 3}}} \quad (4)$$

where ρ_C, ρ_{PC} are the cross-correlation coefficient in the turbulent and tranquil periods and n_C and n_{PC} are the sample sizes of the turbulent periods and tranquil period.

To verify the existence of significant change in cross-market correlations, we can test the hypotheses as follows:

$$H_0: \rho_{VA} = \rho_{PC} \quad H_1: \rho_{VA} \neq \rho_{PC} \quad (5)$$

where H_0 states that there are no significant changes in adjusted correlation.

4.2. Larntz–Perlman Procedure

We used the Larntz–Perlman procedure [36] for testing the equality of correlation matrices computed over non-overlapping subsamples: the pre-crisis and crisis periods in the group of markets investigated. Longin and Solnik [37] affirmed that the knowledge about international covariance and correlation matrices of asset returns and their behaviors is essential for the calculation of portfolios.

To examine the equality of correlation matrices, we can test the pair of hypotheses:

$$H_0: P_C = P_{PC} \quad H_1: P_C \neq P_{PC} \quad (6)$$

where P_C and P_{PC} are population correlation matrices in the turbulent and tranquil periods. Rejection of the H_0 indicates lack of equality of correlation matrices in a turbulent episode.

In this article, we used the test statistic proposed by Larntz and Perlman [36]:

$$T_{LP} = \sqrt{\frac{n-3}{2}} * \max_{1 \leq i < j \leq p} \left| z_{ij}^C - z_{ij}^{PC} \right| \quad (7)$$

where z_{ij}^C and z_{ij}^{PC} are the Fisher z-transformed correlation between $\hat{\rho}_{ij}^C$ and $\hat{\rho}_{ij}^{PC}$.

4.3. Mutual Information

Mutual information (MI) is a measure of statistical independence between two random variables, and it has its usage in evaluating both linear and nonlinear relationships [9]. Moreover, MI is defined as the amount of information transferred between studied systems [27].

There is no single commonly used MI estimator, but there are studies that compare them [38–44]. Determined by the sample size and underlying distribution or process, the MI rises with partition of an interval for time series. There are three main groups of estimators: histogram-based estimators, k-nearest neighbors, and kernel estimators [39,40]. Among histogram-based estimators we can distinguish three main subgroups: equidistant partitioning—bins of equal length [44]; equiprobable partitioning—each bin has the same occupancy, i.e., marginal equiquantization [45]; and adaptive partitioning as an extension of the previous two proposed by Darbellay and Vajda [41]. The k-nearest neighbors method takes into account the probability distributions for the distance between the point at which the density is to be estimated and its k-th nearest neighbor [40]. Another approach is to apply the kernel mutual information estimator constructed by Moon et al. [39] to centering kernel function at the data samples. According to the approach proposed by Darbellay [45], the marginal equiquantization estimation process allows one to maximize mutual information. Furthermore Dionísio et al. [46] emphasize that the comparison of MI is difficult in some contexts; therefore, it should apply a normalized measure of MI. Nevertheless, in order to ensure the comparability of our results with the study conducted by Gao and Mei [8], we will use the equidistant partitioning estimation process for our calculations.

In the study of MI, the selected method to discretize the time series is the binning method [9]. We fragmentize the range of the time series into n disjoint intervals $x_n(n = 1,2,3,\ldots,N;\ x_n = 0, 1, 2, 3)$ with fraction of all measurements equal to $p(x_n) = 1/n$. By grouping the time series into bins $I : x_n(n = 1,2,3,\ldots,N;\ x_n = 0, 1, 2, 3)$ and $J : y_n(n = 1,2,3,\ldots,N;\ y_n = 0, 1, 2, 3)$ that share identical length N, we create two discrete processes. The MI is given as:

$$M(X;Y) = \sum_{x_n,y_n} p(x_n, y_n) \log \frac{p(x_n, y_n)}{p(x_n)p(y_n)} \tag{8}$$

4.4. Transfer Entropy

Transfer entropy (TE) was introduced by Schreiber [47] as an approach to measuring the direct exchange of the flow of information between two systems evolving in time. Considering two stationary and discrete processes $I : x_n(n = 1,2,3,\ldots,N;\ x_n = 0, 1, 2, 3)$ and $J : y_n(n = 1,2,3,\ldots,N;\ y_n = 0, 1, 2, 3)$ that share identical length N, we measure the TE with $J \to I$ as the deviation of information collected from the previous state of I that comes purely from the latest state of I, which in turn was received from the last joint state of I and J [8,48]. The information propagation about the subsequent state of x_{n+1} of I was received from the last joint state of I and J:

$$h_1 = - \sum_{x_{n+1}} p(x_{n+1}, x_n, y_n) * \log p(x_{n+1}|x_n, y_n) \tag{9}$$

The state of the subsequent observation x_{n+1} of I is not based on the state of J; therefore, the information was received only from the state of I:

$$h_2 = - \sum_{x_{n+1}} p(x_{n+1}, x_n) * \log p(x_{n+1}|x_n) \tag{10}$$

The transfer entropy with processes $J \to I$:

$$T_{J \to I} = h_2 - h_1 = \sum_{x_{n+1}, x_n, y_n} p(x_{n+1}, x_n, y_n) * \log \frac{p(x_{n+1}|x_n, y_n)}{p(x_{n+1}|x_n)} \tag{11}$$

4.5. Summary of Methods

We would like to use a variety of methods, such as the cross-correlation, volatility-adjusted cross-correlation, Larntz–Perlman procedure [36], and the mutual information and transfer entropy approaches, to separately analyze the correlation structures for testing the linear and nonlinear relationships in returns between selected markets. Each method has advantages and disadvantages.

There is a sizeable empirical literature that presents nonlinear effects in financial time series [9]. It is not possible to model such behavior in a sufficient manner using Pearson correlation, due to the fact that it explores only linear relationships, ignoring a meaningful amount of information [49]. For this reason, it would be favorable to model both linear and nonlinear information using different methods.

Mutual information has solid foundations in the mathematical concept of information theory and can be used to model both linear and nonlinear connections but is easily influenced by dependencies that are not found in the covariance [40]. On the other hand, MI does not provide directional or dynamical information because of its static, symmetric property [47]. Furthermore, the amount of received information relies on discretization algorithms and bin size [9]. In comparison to MI, transfer entropy is more adequate for detecting the direct exchange of information between two systems, but, as Kaiser and Schreiber [50] pointed out, no similar monotonic convergence seems to hold. In contrast to MI, transfer entropy is created to avoid static correlations due to the common input signals [47]. This tool is widely used due to its close relationship to the concept of Granger causality [51], which is the cause for combining two approaches (information-theoretic and predictive) to analyze directional relations between processes [52].

5. Results
5.1. Cross-Market Correlations

In the first step, using linear correlations, we examine whether the degree of stock market connectedness between the US stock market and CEE differs from that in developed markets. Figure 1 shows the mean linear correlations between each index and the rest of the indices received by using overlapping windows. We split the time series into sequence based on the fixed-size sliding window of 220 days (up) and 1000 days (down), with 1 trading day window step length. After exploring different values, we identified the optimal parameters that ensure smoothly but dynamically changing results. Using various parameters of sliding windows allowed for receiving distinctive outputs that presented slightly different trends in the time series. The selected values are similar to Onnela, Chakraborti, Kaski, Kertész, and Kanto [10]. The mean linear correlations of the Western European markets are higher than in CEE indices. We can observe that UKX, CAC, and DAX indices move together throughout the complete sample, and the mean linear correlation of the CAC index is the highest. On the other hand, the mean linear correlation of the UKX index from 2016 (Brexit) to March 2020 (COVID-19 pandemic) has a weaker relationship with other Western European indices. The relationship between the mean linear correlations of CEE markets fluctuates during the whole period. In the time of the crisis, the mean linear correlation of the BUX index rose until 2013 and then dropped dramatically. Between 2009 and 2015, the mean correlation of the WIG20 is higher than other CEE indices. From 2016, the mean correlation of the PX index is higher than the WIG20 and BUX. Out of the CEE markets, the mean correlation of the BUX index increased the most during the COVID-19 pandemic. This evidence is consistent with the study on CEE indices during the COVID-19 period [17]. When the fixed-size sliding window is 220 days, the mean linear correlations of European markets bounce after falling in 2005, 2015, 2018, and in early 2020. The mean linear correlation of stock exchanges in the US (presented as a black line) declined from 2007 to 2009 and then began to rise again. Even with the 1000-day fixed size sliding window, it is still clear that the trend is going up, especially starting from March 2020.

For further observation, the data were split into five short, distinctive periods: pre-crisis (1 September 2006 to 30 November 2007), crisis (1 December 2007 to 28 February 2009), post-crisis (1 March 2009 to 25 May 2010), pre-COVID-19 (30 September 2019 to 11 March 2020), and COVID-19 (12 March 2020 to 14 August 2020) in order to provide information on the strength and direction of the linear relationship. The results of the preliminary analysis are presented in Figure 2. We can see there that in all analyzed periods, linear correlations between the SPX and Western European indices achieve higher values than with CEE indices in all periods. The results show that COVID-19 has a considerable impact on all analyzed indices. The mean linear correlations of European and US markets prove to be higher during the COVID-19 period than in the crisis period. Furthermore, Western European indices are more affected by COVID-19 compared to CEE indices. During the COVID-19 period, the highest value of the correlation coefficient was observed in three cases: between the SPX and UKX, the SPX and CAC, and the SPX and DAX. In the group of CEE indices in the pre-crisis period, the linear correlation coefficients between the US and the WIG20 were at the highest level. During the crisis, this role is taken over by the BUX index; after the crisis, the PX index; and after that, during pre-COVID-19 and COVID-19 periods, again by the BUX index. Excluding the BUX index, all linear correlation coefficients between the US equity markets and selected European stock exchanges were higher in the post-crisis period than during and before the crisis. It is worth noting that only the linear correlation coefficient between the US equity markets and UKX index was lower in the COVID-19 period than in the pre-COVID-19 period.

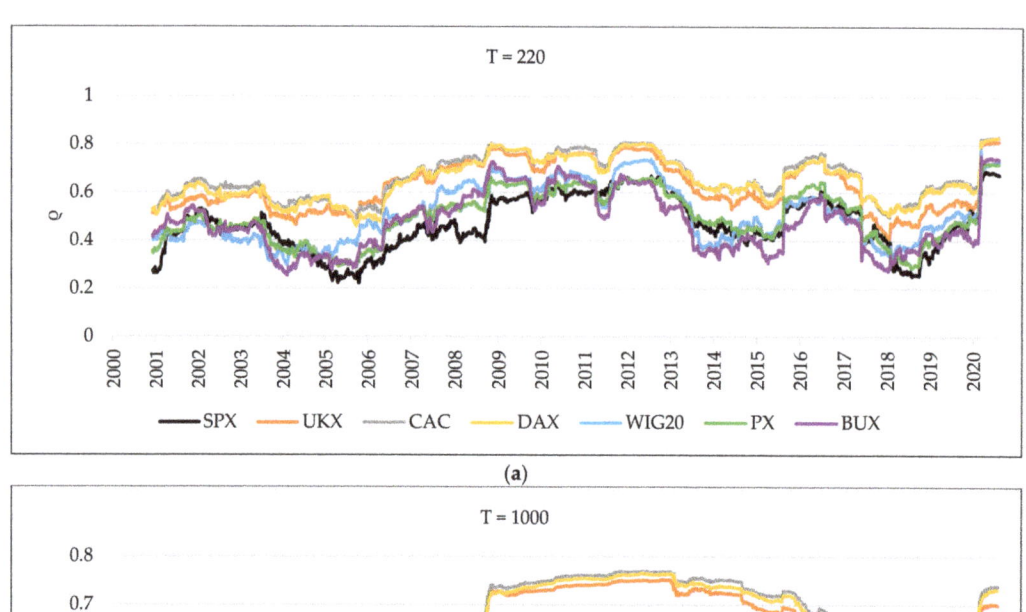

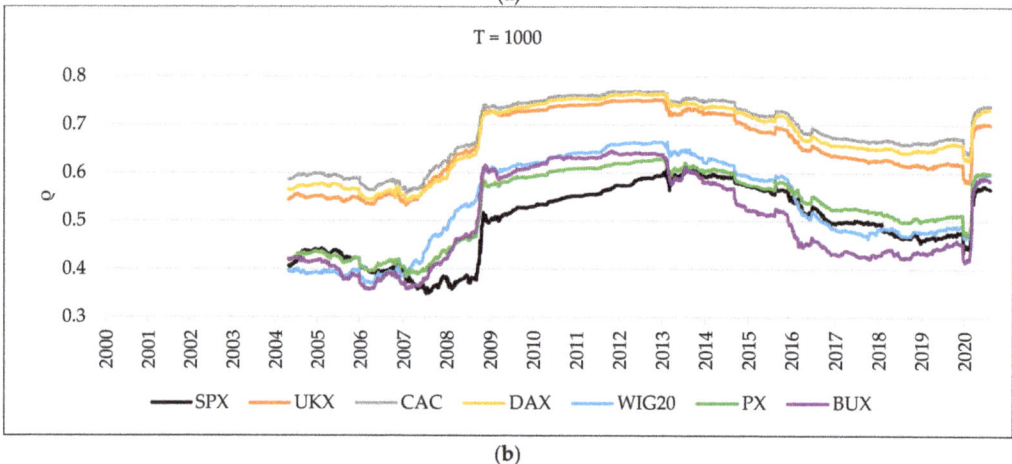

Figure 1. The mean linear correlations between each index and the rest of the indices using overlapping windows. The upper part is a 220-day fixed-size sliding window (**a**), and the one below is a 1000-day fixed-size sliding window (**b**).

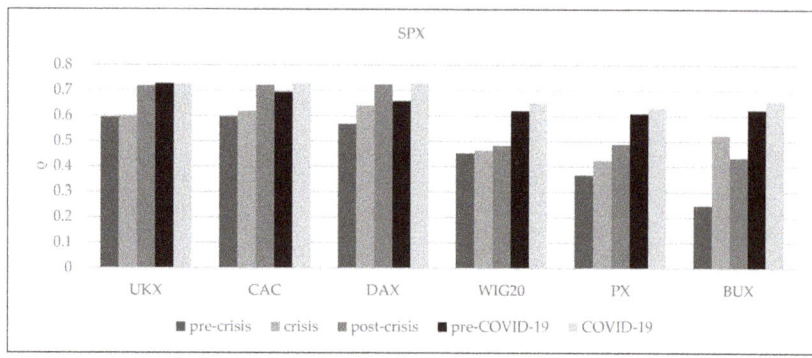

Figure 2. The linear correlations between the US and European stock market indices in the selected periods.

Table 2 shows the standard contemporaneous cross-market correlations and adjusted correlation coefficients, as seen in (1), of daily logarithmic returns on pairs of indices—the SPX/stock market index. We take into consideration the dependencies in the complete sample (January 2000–mid-August 2020) as well as in two equally sized subsamples: the pre-crisis period, September 2006–November 2007 (290 days), and the crisis period, December 2007–February 2009 (290 days). We analyze the changes in cross-market linkages after the economic shock to the US financial market. The supporting values are equal to: $\hat{\sigma}_C^2 = 0.0006661542$ (the variance in the turbulent period in the US stock market) and $\hat{\sigma}_{PC}^2 = 0.0000864396$ (the variance in the tranquil period in the US stock market), while the relative increase in the variance of the SPX returns, given by (2), is equal to $\delta = 6.706584$.

Table 2. Contemporaneous cross-correlations and adjusted correlations of daily logarithmic returns in pairs—the SPX/stock market index—subsamples: the pre-crisis and crisis.

	Contemporaneous Cross-Correlations						Adjusted Correlations ([33])			
	Complete Sample (1)	Pre-Crisis (2)	Crisis (3)				Crisis (3)			
Index	$\hat{\rho}$	$\hat{\rho}_{PC}$	$\hat{\rho}_C$	Change Compared to the Period (2)	Z-Statistic	Hypothesis	$\hat{\rho}_{VA}$	Change Compared to the Period (2)	Z-Statistic	Hypothesis
UKX	0.598 [0.000]	0.595 [0.000]	0.600 [0.000]	0.008	0.089	H0	0.261	−0.562	−5.011	H0
CAC	0.615 [0.000]	0.598 [0.000]	0.618 [0.000]	0.034	0.382	H0	0.273	−0.544	−4.917	H0
DAX	0.634 [0.000]	0.568 [0.000]	0.640 [0.000]	0.127	1.366	H0	0.287	−0.494	−4.175	H0
WIG20	0.407 [0.000]	0.452 [0.000]	0.464 [0.000]	0.027	0.182	H0	0.185	−0.590	−3.586	H0
PX	0.382 [0.000]	0.366 [0.000]	0.424 [0.000]	0.157	0.816	H0	0.166	−0.546	−2.592	H0
BUX	0.395 [0.000]	0.246 [0.000]	0.524 [0.000]	1.130	3.960	H1	0.216	−0.121	−0.376	H0

Notes: The table presents the data received through the analysis of the complete sample period of January 2000–December 2019 (4623 days); the pre-crisis period of September 2006–November 2007 (290 days); and the crisis period of December 2007–February 2009 (290 days). The numbers in brackets are p-values. Fisher Z-statistic tests were null for no changes in correlation. Critical value of Student's t distribution is 1.711 (at the 10% significance level).

The results received in Table 2 for the crisis period indicate that the contemporaneous correlations between the US and other stock exchanges were higher than during the pre-crisis period, but the differences were low. In both periods, the values of contemporaneous correlations were higher in Western Europe than in CEE. The results of the Forbes and Rigobon methodology [33] show the absence of significant changes in cross-market linkages. The value of adjusted correlation between US and European stock markets decreased during crisis. There is no reason to reject the null hypothesis that states that there are no significant changes in the adjusted correlation for all analyzed markets. For this method as well, the values of adjusted correlations were higher in Western Europe than in CEE.

Moreover, we take into consideration the dependencies in the complete sample (January 2000–mid-August 2020) as well as in two equally sized subsamples: the pre-COVID-19 period of 30 September 2019–11 March 2020 (103 days) and the COVID-19 period of 12 March 2020–14 August 2020 (103 days). As shown in Table 3, we analyze the changes in cross-market linkages after the COVID-19 shock to the US financial market. The supporting values are equal to: $\hat{\sigma}_C^2 = 0.0008037915$ (the variance in the COVID-19 period in the US stock market) and $\hat{\sigma}_{PC}^2 = 0.0002521314$ (the variance in the tranquil period in the US stock market), while the relative increase in the variance of the SPX returns, given by (3), is equal to $\delta = 2.187987$.

Table 3. Contemporaneous cross-correlations and adjusted correlations of daily logarithmic returns in pairs—the SPX/stock market index—subsamples: pre-COVID-19 and COVID-19.

	Contemporaneous Cross-Correlations						Adjusted Correlations ([33])			
	Complete Sample (1)	Pre-COVID-19 (2)	COVID-19 (3)				COVID-19 (3)			
Index	$\hat{\rho}$	$\hat{\rho}_{PC}$	$\hat{\rho}_C$	Change Compared to the Period (2)	Z-Statistic	Hypothesis	$\hat{\rho}_{VA}$	Change Compared to the Period (2)	Z-Statistic	Hypothesis
UKX	0.598 [0.000]	0.726 [0.000]	0.725 [0.000]	−0.001	1.651	H_0	0.508	−0.300	−0.882	H_0
CAC	0.615 [0.000]	0.693 [0.000]	0.729 [0.000]	0.051	1.674	H_0	0.512	−0.261	−0.878	H_0
DAX	0.634 [0.000]	0.657 [0.000]	0.729 [0.000]	0.110	1.990	H_1	0.512	−0.221	−0.559	H_0
WIG20	0.407 [0.000]	0.619 [0.000]	0.650 [0.000]	0.050	2.046	H_1	0.432	−0.302	−0.169	H_0
PX	0.382 [0.000]	0.608 [0.000]	0.630 [0.000]	0.036	2.529	H_1	0.414	−0.319	0.397	H_0
BUX	0.395 [0.000]	0.622 [0.000]	0.658 [0.000]	0.058	3.805	H_1	0.440	−0.293	1.560	H_0

Notes: The table presents the data received through the analysis of the complete sample period of January 2000–mid-August 2020 (4773 days); the pre-COVID-19 period of 30 September 2019–11 March 2020 (103 days); and the COVID-19 period of 12 March 2020–14 August 2020 (103 days). The numbers in brackets are p-values. Fisher Z-statistic tests were null for no changes in correlation. Critical value of Student's t distribution is 1.711 (at the 10% significance level).

The results received in Table 3 for the COVID-19 period indicate that the contemporaneous correlations between the US and other stock exchanges (except UKX) were higher than during the pre-COVID-19 period; however, the differences were low. These results provide support for the theory of Ferreira, Dionísio, Almeida, Quintino, and Aslam [31] that the pandemic crisis may be a factor for the intensification of US indices. Similar results were obtained in the study by Czech, Wielechowski, Kotyza, Benešová, and Laputková [17] and Aslam et al. [53], who emphasize that the COVID-19 pandemic caused great impacts on CEE stock markets. In both periods, the values of contemporaneous correlations were higher in Western Europe than in CEE. For DAX, WIG20, PX, and BUX, we reject the null hypothesis, which suggests the existence of changes in correlation. On the other hand, the results of the Forbes and Rigobon methodology [33] show the absence of significant changes in cross-market linkages. The value of adjusted correlation between US and European stock markets decreased during the pandemic. There is no reason to reject the null hypothesis that states that there are no significant changes in the adjusted correlation for all analyzed markets. For this method as well, the values of adjusted correlations were higher in Western Europe than in CEE.

We observed that, compared to the 2007–2009 crisis, contemporaneous correlations between the US and other stock exchanges increased significantly during the pre-COVID-19 and COVID-19 periods (Tables 2 and 3). In the case of the 2007–2009 crisis, we find one market (BUX) which indicates the lack of equality of correlation matrices, while during the COVID-19 period we find as many as four markets (DAX, WIG20, PX, BUX).

5.2. Larntz–Perlman Procedure

Table 4 summarizes the Larntz–Perlman test [36] performed on the SPX and the six European stock indices. We have reason to reject the null hypothesis (6), which suggests the stability of the correlation matrix via three adjacent sub-periods:

- the pre-crisis period, September 2006–November 2007 (290 days), and the crisis period, December 2007–February 2009 (290 days);
- the crisis period, December 2007–February 2009 (290 days), and the post-crisis period, March 2009–May 2010 (290 days); and
- the pre-COVID-19 period, 30 September 2019–11 March 2020 (103 days), and the COVID-19 period, 12 March 2020–14 August 2020 (103 days).

Table 4. Results of the Larntz–Perlman test.

Test Periods	Larntz–Perlman Test				
	Test Statistic T_{LP}	b_α Critical Value (5%)		b_α Critical Value (10%)	
September 2006–November 2007 and December 2007–February 2009	5.257	2.63	H_0	2.38	H_0
December 2007–February 2009 and March 2009–May 2010	3.076	2.63	H_0	2.38	H_0
30 September 2019–11 March 2020 and 12 March 2020–14 August 2020	3.006	2.63	H_0	2.38	H_0

5.3. Mutual Information

Figure 3 shows the outcome of average mutual information evolving in time. When the fixed-size sliding window equals 220 days, the average mutual information of European markets bounced after the fall that happened at the end of 2005, which is consistent with the mean linear correlation. Starting from March 2020, we can observe another soaring growth in the average mutual information of European markets. For the 1000-day fixed-size sliding window, the average mutual information showed an upward trend until 2013, when it peaked. It is worth noting that, starting from March 2020, we can see the growing tendency again; however, the UKX index is no longer so closely associated with other Western countries. Our main interest is in analyzing the connection between the US equity markets and European stock exchanges in the financial crisis of 2007–2009 and during the COVID-19 pandemic. The results received by comparing the MI in pre-crisis, crisis, and post-crisis periods are shown in Figure 4. Except for Hungary's stock exchange, the MI between the US equity markets and other European stock indices is lower during the crisis in comparison to the pre-crisis period. We observe similar results for COVID-19 in comparison to the pre-COVID-19 period, except for Hungary's and Czech Republic's stock exchanges.

5.4. Transfer Entropy

Figure 5 presents quickly changing outcomes of the average transfer entropy. We can observe that the average transfer entropy of the US stock market index reaches higher levels in comparison to the other markets. When the fixed-size sliding window is 220 days, the average transfer entropy of the US stock market index before January 2009 soars, but the peaks that it exhibits are sharp and narrow. A similar situation can be observed in March 2020. When the fixed-size sliding window is 1000 days, the average transfer entropy of the US stock market index grows continuously, then starts to decline after 2009, and rises again in March 2020. Figure 6 shows the outcomes of the TE values of the US equity markets of six European stock exchanges during the pre-crisis, crisis, post-crisis, pre-COVID-19, and COVID-19 periods. The TE from the US equity markets to Western Europe stock indices present higher values than CEE ones in the pre-crisis period. We observe the opposite situation in the pre-COVID-19 period. On the other hand, the TE from the US equity markets to CEE stock indices in the crisis period is higher than to Western Europe indices. In the COVID-19 period, the TE from the US equity markets to DAX and BUX stock indices was the highest. In the pre-crisis period, the TE from the US equity market to Poland is the weakest in comparison to other countries, but, during the crisis, it increased the most, reaching a level similar to Western Europe. On the other hand, in the pre-COVID-19 period, the TE from the US equity market to Germany is the weakest in comparison to other countries, but during the pandemic it increased the most. The TE from the US equity markets to selected European stock indices in the crisis period reaches a higher level in comparison to the pre-crisis period, with France being the exception. Contrary to that, the TE from the US equity markets to selected European stock indices in the COVID-19 period reaches lower levels in comparison to the pre-COVID-19 period, with Germany being the exception. During the crisis, the TE from the US equity markets to the BUX index is the highest in the group of CEE countries and the UKX index in the group of Western Europe. In the post-crisis period, the TE from the US equity markets to other indices decreased dramatically, especially the BUX and UKX indices. During COVID-19, the TE from the US equity markets to the BUX index is the highest in the group of CEE countries and the DAX index in the group of Western Europe. Based on the presented outcomes, we deduce that when the fixed-size sliding window equals 1000 days, the growth of mean linear correlations slows down considerably after 2009. At the same time, the average mutual information continues to rise until it peaks around 2013. Thus, we conclude that the stronger dependencies between all indices that can be observed after 2009 are due to the nonlinear effect. Similar results have been obtained by Gao and Mei [8] and Haluszczynski et al. [9].

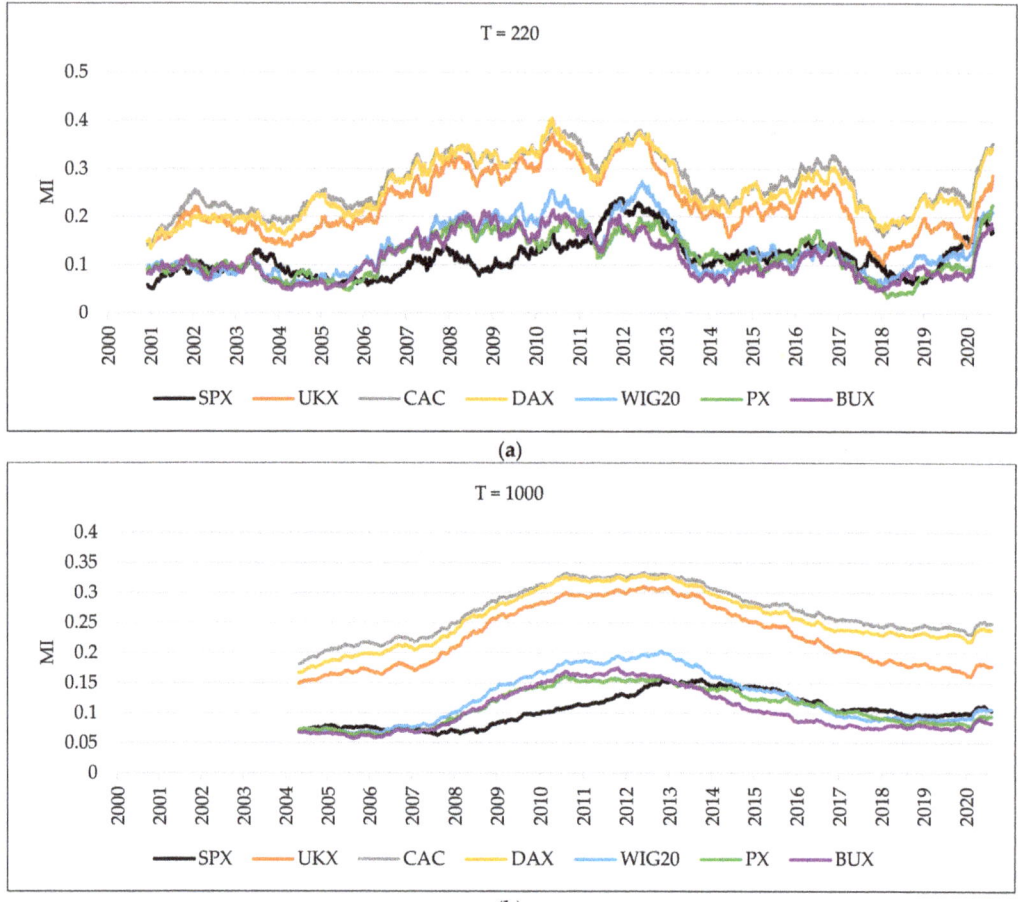

Figure 3. The average mutual information between each index and the rest of the indices using overlapping windows. The upper part is a 220-day fixed-size sliding window (**a**), and the one below is a 1000-day fixed-size sliding window (**b**).

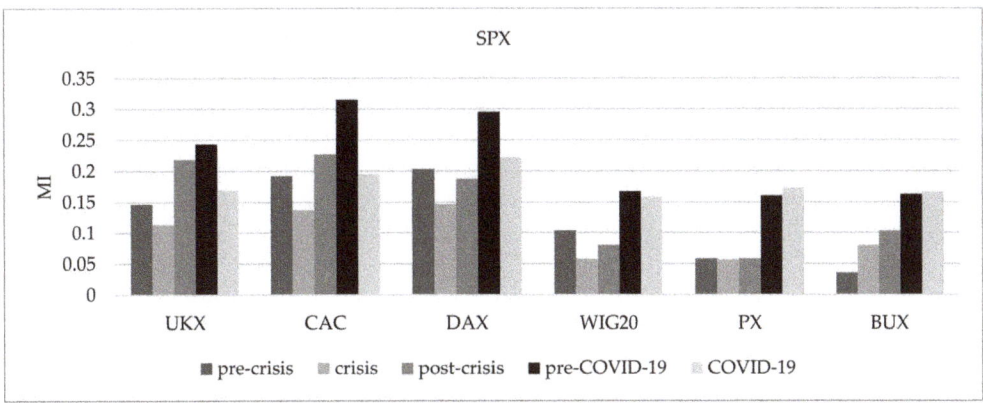

Figure 4. The mutual information between the US stock index and six European stock indices during the selected periods.

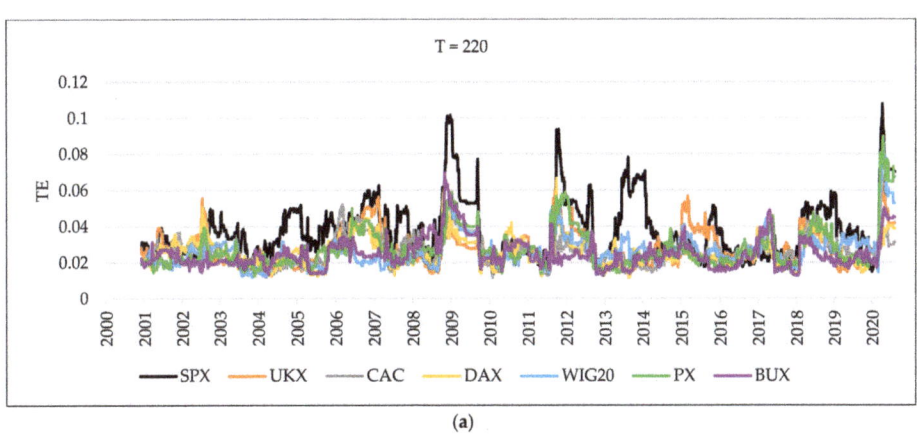

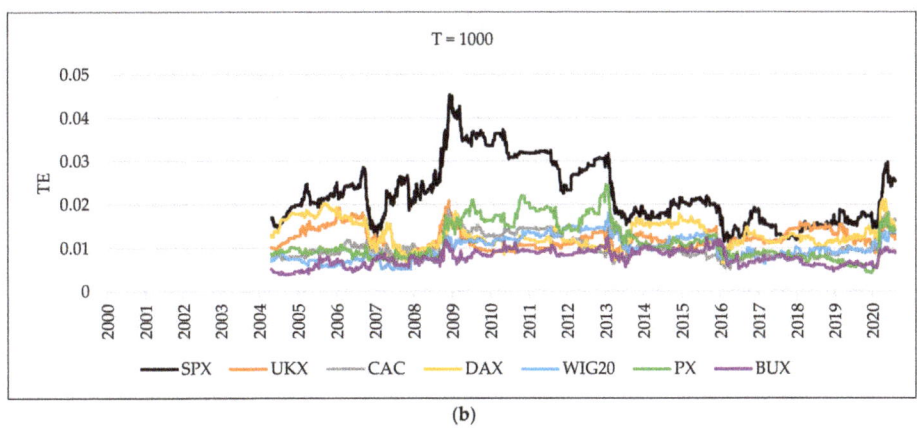

Figure 5. The average transfer entropy between each index and the rest of the indices using overlapping windows. The upper part is a 220-day fixed-size sliding window (**a**), and the one below is a 1000-day fixed-size sliding window (**b**).

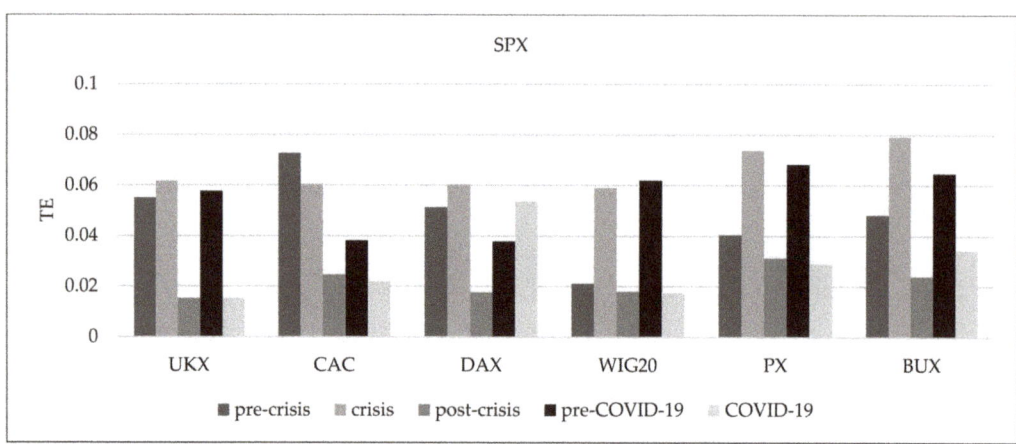

Figure 6. The transfer entropy from the US equity markets to six European equity markets during selected periods.

5.5. Comparison of Results

We would like to model linear and nonlinear behavior in financial time series through the evaluation of information on dynamic correlations. Due to that, we used not only linear Pearson correlation but also mutual information, which can be used both for linear and nonlinear connections, as well as transfer entropy, which allows one to examine nonlinear connections.

Table 5 shows the comparison of different methods used to measure the dependence between the US stock index and selected European stock indices. For each of the three methods, we compute the values for pre-crisis, crisis, post-crisis, pre-COVID-19, and COVID-19 periods. The correlation coefficient values range from 0.246 to 0.729. In the case of examined countries, there is a clear separation between two strongly connected groups: Western European indices and CEE indices. We recognize that Western Europe has higher linear correlation coefficient values (from 0.568 to 0.729) than CEE (from 0.246 to 0.658). The levels of correlation increased significantly in the pre-COVID-19 and COVID-19 periods in all markets (the highest for CAX and DAX indices from Western Europe and for PX and BUX from CEE in the COVID-19 period). The results confirm that the COVID-19 pandemic has led to a growth in European financial market risk, which is in line with Zhang et al. [12], Akhtaruzzaman et al. [13], Shehzad et al. [54], and Zaremba et al. [14]. It should be stressed that the amplitude of growth was much higher in CEE markets, which is similar to the findings of Topcu and Gulal [16] and Tilfani, Ferreira, and Boukfaoui [55]. The most stable level of correlation in all analyzed periods is presented by the UKX index (from 0.595 to 0.726) and the CAC index (from 0.598 to 0.729). On the other hand, BUX increased the most between pre-crisis and crisis periods (from 0.246 to 0.524). After the crisis, BUX began to behave like other CEE countries. Overall, relationships between local centers are greater within these groups than between them. These results are in line with those obtained by Stoica and Diaconașu [56] and Gradojević and Dobardžić [57]. The results demonstrated that regional market integration is strengthened in times of crisis or pandemic.

Table 5. Comparison of different methods used to measure the dependence between the US stock index and European indices during pre-crisis, crisis, post-crisis, pre-COVID-19, and COVID-19 periods.

Period	Group of Countries	Index	Linear Correlations	Mutual Information	Transfer Entropy
Pre-crisis	West Europe	UKX	0.595	0.146	0.055
		CAC	0.598	0.192	0.073
		DAX	0.568	0.203	0.051
	CEE	WIG20	0.452	0.103	0.021
		PX	0.366	0.058	0.041
		BUX	0.246	0.035	0.048
Crisis	West Europe	UKX	0.600	0.113	0.062
		CAC	0.618	0.137	0.060
		DAX	0.64	0.146	0.060
	CEE	WIG20	0.464	0.058	0.059
		PX	0.424	0.057	0.074
		BUX	0.524	0.080	0.079
Post-crisis	West Europe	UKX	0.717	0.219	0.015
		CAC	0.721	0.227	0.025
		DAX	0.723	0.187	0.018
	CEE	WIG20	0.483	0.080	0.018
		PX	0.489	0.058	0.031
		BUX	0.434	0.103	0.024
Pre-COVID-19	West Europe	UKX	0.726	0.243	0.058
		CAC	0.693	0.315	0.038
		DAX	0.657	0.295	0.038
	CEE	WIG20	0.619	0.167	0.062
		PX	0.608	0.160	0.068
		BUX	0.622	0.163	0.065
COVID-19	West Europe	UKX	0.725	0.169	0.015
		CAC	0.729	0.195	0.022
		DAX	0.729	0.222	0.054
	CEE	WIG20	0.650	0.159	0.017
		PX	0.630	0.173	0.029
		BUX	0.658	0.167	0.034

Notes: The rows of a heat map represent stock indices in specific periods, and the columns represent the methods used to measure the dependence between the US stock index and six European stock indices during pre-crisis, crisis, post-crisis, pre-COVID-19, and COVID-19 periods. Each cell in the particular methods is colorized based on the values (from green for the lowest values to red for the highest ones).

As can be observed in Table 5, similar conclusions to those received by using linear correlation can be obtained with mutual information. For both methods, Western Europe is the region that attains the largest values. Furthermore, the highest values of mutual information are achieved in the pre-COVID-19 period for Western Europe and in the COVID-19 period for CEE regions. It is interesting to note that the transfer entropy presents slightly different results. The values of transfer entropy in CEE are higher (from 0.017 to 0.079) than in Western Europe (from 0.015 to 0.025), which can be especially observed in the crisis and pre-COVID-19 periods. As per our results, notable information cannot be expressed well by linear measure, hence the usage of different methods that intercept linear and nonlinear correlations. In conclusion, our analysis suggests that stock indices quickly responded to the GFC as well as the COVID-19 pandemic, and these responses changed over time depending on the information flowing through markets.

6. Discussion and Conclusions

This study provides an analysis of the effect of the GFC and the COVID-19 pandemic on European stock markets. The main goal of this paper is to compare the risk transfer between US stock market indices and six European stock market indices before, during, and after the GFC, as well as before and during the COVID-19 outbreak. In our study, we also emphasize the differences in the correlation structure between CEE and Western European markets. We used a variety of methods to separately analyze the correlation structures for testing the linear and nonlinear structure of relationships in returns between the US stock index and selected European stock indices.

Testing the connectedness during the crisis period, the correlation between SPX and CEE indices changed more in terms of growth than in Western European indices. This is only a partial confirmation of earlier research [7], stating that the CEE stock exchanges are not more vulnerable to contagion, even if they are less liquid than Western European markets. Additionally, our findings stress that the amplitude of growth in the pre-COVID-19 period is much higher in CEE markets. Given a slower economic growth and relatively not liquid capital markets, emerging markets have probably limited resources to cope with the pandemic.

Nevertheless, the relationship between the mean linear correlations of CEE markets fluctuates during the whole period. In the years 2009–2015, the mean linear correlation for WIG20 is higher than for other CEE indices, but, starting from 2016, the correlation index for the PX is higher than for the WIG20 and the BUX. In the analyzed period, the stock markets in CEE were not stable or resistant to crisis shocks. This result may be explained by the smaller integration of CEE stock markets with global capital markets. For investors, this means another source of risk diversification in CEE markets.

Comparing to the GFC, our findings emphasize that the linear correlations between the S&P 500 and all European indices increased significantly in the pre-COVID-19 period. The negative impact of COVID-19 on stock markets continued or slightly increased by mid-August 2020. The results show that the COVID-19 pandemic has led to a growth in European financial market risk. These findings confirm those of earlier studies, such as Ferreira [58] and Grabowski [59]. An analysis of the volatility spillovers indicates that CEE markets are the recipients of volatility. As opposed to the previous research of Topcu and Gulal [16], our findings do not confirm that the influence of COVID-19 on emerging stock markets has gradually fallen and began to taper off by mid-April 2020.

The results that we obtained indicate that there are relatively significant differences between linear and nonlinear estimation. The transfer entropy from the US equity markets to CEE stock indices during the crisis is higher than to Western Europe indices. Before the crisis, the transfer entropy from the US equity market to Poland is the weakest compared to other countries, but, during the crisis, it increased the most. During the crisis, the transfer entropy from the US equity market to Poland is similar to Western Europe. Additionally, we infer that nonlinear effects lead to stronger dependencies between all indices after 2009. Starting from the COVID-19 pandemic period, we can observe soaring growth in the average mutual information and transfer entropy of all European markets.

Our study of European stock markets shows that cases of intensified and broken links between markets are particularly visible in CEE countries. This evidence may suggest that emerging equity markets are increasingly integrated into mature markets, thus becoming dependent on certain crises and pandemic outbreaks. This may be explained by short-term capital flows from less stable markets, changing political circumstances. Undoubtedly, research should provide an interesting insight for potential investors diversifying their stock portfolio. Our research has implications for risk management and asset pricing. Although CEE countries are considered a homogeneous group by international investors, the financial markets of these countries show varying degrees of integration. Therefore, from a portfolio diversification perspective, less developed markets may offer risk diversification opportunities that investors can capitalize on. For the purpose of portfolio risk management, information about the linkages between markets can be important for investors in making decisions. In addition, information on the increasing connectedness between markets may be relevant when portfolios are reallocated.

We believe that this study may be a benchmark for financial market network structure for further research in this area. Therefore, future researchers should test whether the results remain insignificant over a longer time horizon. Additionally, similar to the vast majority of research on contagion in emerging economies, our research focuses on the analysis of daily and weekly data. However, it would be worthwhile to investigate the connectedness of European stock markets with high-frequency information.

Author Contributions: Conceptualization, R.K.; methodology, R.K.; software, S.U.; validation, S.U.; formal analysis, S.U.; investigation, S.U.; resources, S.U.; data curation, S.U.; writing—original draft preparation, R.K. and S.U.; writing—review and editing, R.K. and S.U.; visualization, S.U.; supervision, R.K.; project administration, R.K.; funding acquisition, R.K. All authors have read and agreed to the published version of the manuscript.

Funding: This research received no external funding.

Data Availability Statement: All the data supporting reported results come from: https://stooq.pl (accessed on 9 February 2022).

Conflicts of Interest: The authors declare no conflict of interest.

References

1. WHO. Director-General's Opening Remarks at the Media Briefing on COVID-19. 11 March 2020. Available online: https://www.who.int/dg/speeches/detail/who-director-general-s-opening-remarks-at-the-media-briefing-on-covid-19---11-march-2020 (accessed on 1 September 2020).
2. Ahmar, A.S.; del Val, E.B. SutteARIMA: Short-Term Forecasting Method, a Case: Covid-19 and Stock Market in Spain. *Sci. Total Environ.* **2020**, *729*, 138883. [CrossRef] [PubMed]
3. Al-Awadhi, A.M.; Alsaifi, K.; Al-Awadhi, A.; Alhammadi, S. Death and Contagious Infectious Diseases: Impact of the COVID-19 Virus on Stock Market Returns. *J. Behav. Exp. Financ.* **2020**, *27*, 100326. [CrossRef] [PubMed]
4. Boubaker, H.; Raza, S.A. On the Dynamic Dependence and Asymmetric Co-Movement between the US and Central and Eastern European Transition Markets. *Phys. A Stat. Mech. Its Appl.* **2016**, *459*, 9–23. [CrossRef]
5. Karkowska, R.; Urjasz, S. Connectedness Structures of Sovereign Bond Markets in Central and Eastern Europe. *Int. Rev. Financ. Anal.* **2021**, *74*, 101644. [CrossRef]
6. Olbryś, J.; Majewska, E. Increasing Cross-Market Correlations during the 2007–2009 Global Financial Crisis: Contagion or Integration Effects? *Argum. Oeconomica* **2017**, *39*, 263–278. [CrossRef]
7. Gao, H.L.; Mei, D.C. The Correlation Structure in the International Stock Markets during Global Financial Crisis. *Phys. A Stat. Mech. Its Appl.* **2019**, *534*, 122056. [CrossRef]
8. Haluszczynski, A.; Laut, I.; Modest, H.; Räth, C. Linear and Nonlinear Market Correlations: Characterizing Financial Crises and Portfolio Optimization. *Phys. Rev. E* **2017**, *96*, 062315. [CrossRef]
9. Onnela, J.P.; Chakraborti, A.; Kaski, K.; Kertész, J.; Kanto, A. Dynamics of Market Correlations: Taxonomy and Portfolio Analysis. *Phys. Rev. E* **2003**, *68*, 056110. [CrossRef]
10. Serwa, D.; Bohl, M.T. Financial Contagion Vulnerability and Resistance: A Comparison of European Stock Markets. *Econ. Syst.* **2005**, *29*, 344–362. [CrossRef]
11. Ashraf, B.N. Stock Markets' Reaction to COVID-19: Cases or Fatalities? *Res. Int. Bus. Financ.* **2020**, *54*, 101249. [CrossRef]
12. Zhang, D.; Hu, M.; Ji, Q. Financial Markets under the Global Pandemic of COVID-19. *Financ. Res. Lett.* **2020**, *36*, 101528. [CrossRef] [PubMed]
13. Akhtaruzzaman, M.; Boubaker, S.; Sensoy, A. Financial Contagion during COVID–19 Crisis. *Financ. Res. Lett.* **2020**, *38*, 101604. [CrossRef] [PubMed]
14. Zaremba, A.; Kizys, R.; Aharon, D.Y.; Demir, E. Infected Markets: Novel Coronavirus, Government Interventions, and Stock Return Volatility around the Globe. *Financ. Res. Lett.* **2020**, *35*, 101597. [CrossRef]
15. Sharif, A.; Aloui, C.; Yarovaya, L. COVID-19 Pandemic, Oil Prices, Stock Market, Geopolitical Risk and Policy Uncertainty Nexus in the US Economy: Fresh Evidence from the Wavelet-Based Approach. *Int. Rev. Financ. Anal.* **2020**, *70*, 101496. [CrossRef]
16. Topcu, M.; Gulal, O.S. The Impact of COVID-19 on Emerging Stock Markets. *Financ. Res. Lett.* **2020**, *36*, 101691. [CrossRef]
17. Czech, K.; Wielechowski, M.; Kotyza, P.; Benešová, I.; Laputková, A. Shaking Stability: COVID-19 Impact on the Visegrad Group Countries' Financial Markets. *Sustainability* **2020**, *12*, 6282. [CrossRef]
18. Qiu, L.; Yang, H. Transfer Entropy Calculation for Short Time Sequences with Application to Stock Markets. *Phys. A Stat. Mech. Its Appl.* **2020**, *559*, 125121. [CrossRef]
19. Kuang, P.C. Measuring Information Flow among International Stock Markets: An Approach of Entropy-Based Networks on Multi Time-Scales. *Phys. A Stat. Mech. Its Appl.* **2021**, *577*, 126068. [CrossRef]
20. Karaca, Y.; Zhang, Y.D.; Muhammad, K. Characterizing Complexity and Self-Similarity Based on Fractal and Entropy Analyses for Stock Market Forecast Modelling. *Expert Syst. Appl.* **2020**, *144*, 113098. [CrossRef]
21. Barbi, A.Q.; Prataviera, G.A. Nonlinear Dependencies on Brazilian Equity Network from Mutual Information Minimum Spanning Trees. *Phys. A Stat. Mech. Its Appl.* **2019**, *523*, 876–885. [CrossRef]

22. Ponta, L.; Carbone, A. Information Measure for Financial Time Series: Quantifying Short-Term Market Heterogeneity. *Phys. A Stat. Mech. Its Appl.* **2018**, *510*, 132–144. [CrossRef]
23. Guo, X.; Zhang, H.; Tian, T. Development of Stock Correlation Networks Using Mutual Information and Financial Big Data. *PLoS ONE* **2018**, *13*, e0195941. [CrossRef] [PubMed]
24. You, T.; Fiedor, P.; Hołda, A. Network Analysis of the Shanghai Stock Exchange Based on Partial Mutual Information. *J. Risk Financ. Manag.* **2015**, *8*, 266–284. [CrossRef]
25. Sharma, C.; Habib, A. Mutual Information Based Stock Networks and Portfolio Selection for Intraday Traders Using High Frequency Data: An Indian Market Case Study. *PLoS ONE* **2019**, *14*, e0221910. [CrossRef] [PubMed]
26. Villaverde, A.F.; Ross, J.; Morán, F.; Banga, J.R. MIDER: Network Inference with Mutual Information Distance and Entropy Reduction. *PLoS ONE* **2014**, *9*, e96732. [CrossRef] [PubMed]
27. Fiedor, P. Networks in Financial Markets Based on the Mutual Information Rate. *Phys. Rev. E* **2014**, *89*, 052801. [CrossRef]
28. Dima, B.; Dima, Ş.M. Mutual Information and Persistence in the Stochastic Volatility of Market Returns: An Emergent Market Example. *Int. Rev. Econ. Financ.* **2017**, *51*, 36–59. [CrossRef]
29. Caginalp, G.; Desantis, M. Nonlinearity in the Dynamics of Financial Markets. *Nonlinear Anal. Real World Appl.* **2011**, *12*, 1140–1151. [CrossRef]
30. Khoojine, A.S.; Han, D. Network Analysis of the Chinese Stock Market during the Turbulence of 2015–2016 Using Log-Returns, Volumes and Mutual Information. *Phys. A Stat. Mech. Its Appl.* **2019**, *523*, 1091–1109. [CrossRef]
31. Ferreira, P.; Dionísio, A.; Almeida, D.; Quintino, D.; Aslam, F. A New Vision about the Influence of Major Stock Markets in CEEC Indices: A Bidirectional Dynamic Analysis Using Transfer Entropy. *Post-Communist Econ.* **2021**, 1–16. [CrossRef]
32. MSCI Global Market Accessibility Review. 2020. Available online: https://www.msci.com/documents/1296102/1330218/MSCI_2021_Global_Market_Accessibility_Review_Report.pdf/d88d8bc0-a882-58c7-35f0-bef191e0ebe2 (accessed on 9 February 2022).
33. Forbes, K.J.; Rigobon, R. No Contagion, Only Interdependence: Measuring Stock Market Comovements. *J. Financ.* **2002**, *57*, 2223–2261. [CrossRef]
34. Rigobon, R. Contagion: How to Measure It? In *Preventing Currency Crises in Emerging Markets*; University of Chicago Press: Chicago, IL, USA, 2002; pp. 269–334.
35. Hon, M.T.; Strauss, J.; Yong, S.K. Contagion in Financial Markets after September 11: Myth or Reality? *J. Financ. Res.* **2004**, *27*, 95–114. [CrossRef]
36. Larntz, K.; Perlman, M.D. A Simple Test for the Equality of Correlation Matrices. 1985. Available online: https://citeseerx.ist.psu.edu/viewdoc/download?doi=10.1.1.142.7301&rep=rep1&type=pdf (accessed on 9 February 2022).
37. Longin, F.; Solnik, B. Is the Correlation in International Equity Returns Constant: 1960-1990? *J. Int. Money Financ.* **1995**, *14*, 3–26. [CrossRef]
38. Papana, A.; Kugiumtzis, D. Evaluation of Mutual Information Estimators on Nonlinear Dynamic Systems. *arXiv* **2008**, arXiv:0809.2149.
39. Moon, Y.-I.; Rajagopalan, B.; Lall, U. Estimation of Mutual Information Using Kernel Density Estimators. *Phys. Rev. E* **1995**, *52*, 2318. [CrossRef]
40. Kraskov, A.; Stögbauer, H.; Grassberger, P. Estimating Mutual Information. *Phys. Rev. E* **2004**, *69*, 16. [CrossRef]
41. Darbellay, G.A.; Vajda, I. Estimation of the Information by an Adaptive Partitioning of the Observation Space. *IEEE Trans. Inf. Theory* **1999**, *45*, 1315–1321. [CrossRef]
42. Steuer, R.; Kurths, J.; Daub, C.O.; Weise, J.; Selbig, J. The Mutual Information: Detecting and Evaluating Dependencies between Variables. *Bioinformatics* **2002**, *18*, S231–S240. [CrossRef]
43. Daub, C.O.; Steuer, R.; Selbig, J.; Kloska, S. Estimating Mutual Information Using B-Spline Functions–an Improved Similarity Measure for Analysing Gene Expression Data. *BMC Bioinform.* **2004**, *5*, 1–12. [CrossRef]
44. Cellucci, C.J.; Albano, A.M.; Rapp, P.E. Statistical Validation of Mutual Information Calculations: Comparison of Alternative Numerical Algorithms. *Phys. Rev. E* **2005**, *71*, 066208. [CrossRef]
45. Darbellay, G.A. An Estimator of the Mutual Information Based on a Criterion for Independence. *Comput. Stat.* **1999**, *32*, 1–17. [CrossRef]
46. Dionisio, A.; Menezes, R.; Mendes, D.A. An Econophysics Approach to Analyse Uncertainty in Financial Markets: An Application to the Portuguese Stock Market. *Eur. Phys. J. B* **2006**, *50*, 161–164. [CrossRef]
47. Schreiber, T. Measuring Information Transfer. *Phys. Rev. Lett.* **2000**, *85*, 461–464. [CrossRef] [PubMed]
48. Kwon, O.; Yang, J.S. Information Flow between Composite Stock Index and Individual Stocks. *Phys. A Stat. Mech. Its Appl.* **2008**, *387*, 2851–2856. [CrossRef]
49. Onnela, J.P.; Kaski, K.; Kertész, J. Clustering and Information in Correlation Based Financial Networks. *Eur. Phys. J. B* **2004**, *38*, 353–362. [CrossRef]
50. Kaiser, A.; Schreiber, T. Information Transfer in Continuous Processes. *Phys. D Nonlinear Phenom.* **2002**, *166*, 43–62. [CrossRef]
51. Barnett, L.; Barrett, A.B.; Seth, A.K. Granger Causality and Transfer Entropy Are Equivalent for Gaussian Variables. *Phys. Rev. Lett.* **2009**, *103*, 2–5. [CrossRef]
52. Montalto, A.; Faes, L.; Marinazzo, D. MuTE: A MATLAB Toolbox to Compare Established and Novel Estimators of the Multivariate Transfer Entropy. *PLoS ONE* **2014**, *9*, e109462. [CrossRef]

53. Aslam, F.; Nogueiro, F.; Brasil, M.; Ferreira, P.; Mughal, K.S.; Bashir, B.; Latif, S. The Footprints of COVID-19 on Central Eastern European Stock Markets: An Intraday Analysis. *Post-Communist Econ.* **2021**, *33*, 751–769. [CrossRef]
54. Shehzad, K.; Xiaoxing, L.; Kazouz, H. COVID-19's Disasters Are Perilous than Global Financial Crisis: A Rumor or Fact? *Financ. Res. Lett.* **2020**, *36*, 101669. [CrossRef]
55. Tilfani, O.; Ferreira, P.; El Boukfaoui, M.Y. Revisiting Stock Market Integration in Central and Eastern European Stock Markets with a Dynamic Analysis. *Post-Communist Econ.* **2020**, *32*, 643–674. [CrossRef]
56. Stoica, O.; Diaconașu, D.-E. Analysis of Interdependencies between Austrian and CEE Stock Markets. 2011. Available online: https://scholar.google.com/scholar?hl=en&as_sdt=0%2C5&q=56.%09Stoica%2C+O.%3B+Diacona%C8%99u%2C+D.-E.+Analysis+of+Interdependencies+between+Austrian+and+CEE+Stock+Markets.+Sch.+Bus.+Administration&btnG= (accessed on 9 February 2022).
57. Gradojević, N.; Dobardžić, E. Causality between Regional Stock Markets: A Frequency Domain Approach. *Panoeconomicus* **2013**, *60*, 633–647. [CrossRef]
58. Ferreira, P. What Guides Central and Eastern European Stock Markets? A View from Detrended Methodologies. *Post-Communist Econ.* **2018**, *30*, 805–819. [CrossRef]
59. Grabowski, W. Givers or Recipients? Co-Movements between Stock Markets of CEE-3 and Developed Countries. *Sustainability* **2019**, *11*, 6495. [CrossRef]

Article

Replication in Energy Markets: Use and Misuse of Chaos Tools

Loretta Mastroeni *,† and Pierluigi Vellucci †

Department of Economics, University of Roma Tre, 00145 Roma, Italy; pierluigi.vellucci@uniroma3.it
* Correspondence: loretta.mastroeni@uniroma3.it
† These authors contributed equally to this work.

Abstract: As pointed out by many researchers, replication plays a key role in the credibility of applied sciences and the confidence in all research findings. With regard, in particular, to energy finance and economics, replication papers are rare, probably because they are hampered by inaccessible data, but their aim is crucial. We consider two ways to avoid misleading results on the ostensible chaoticity of price series. The first one is represented by the proper mathematical definition of chaos and the related theoretical background, while the latter is represented by the hybrid approach that we propose here—i.e., consisting of considering the dynamical system underlying the price time series as a deterministic system with noise. We find that both chaotic and stochastic features coexist in the energy commodity markets, although the misuse of some tests in the established practice in the literature may say otherwise.

Keywords: nonlinear dynamics; chaos; butterfly effect; energy futures

JEL Classification: C650; G140; Q470

Citation: Mastroeni, L.; Vellucci, P. Replication in Energy Markets: Use and Misuse of Chaos Tools. *Entropy* **2022**, *24*, 701. https://doi.org/10.3390/e24050701

Academic Editor: Joanna Olbryś

Received: 16 April 2022
Accepted: 14 May 2022
Published: 16 May 2022

Publisher's Note: MDPI stays neutral with regard to jurisdictional claims in published maps and institutional affiliations.

Copyright: © 2022 by the authors. Licensee MDPI, Basel, Switzerland. This article is an open access article distributed under the terms and conditions of the Creative Commons Attribution (CC BY) license (https://creativecommons.org/licenses/by/4.0/).

1. Introduction

As pointed out by many researchers (see, for example, [1]), replication is the key to credibility in applied sciences and confidence in all research findings. With regard in particular to energy finance and economics, replication papers are rare, probably because they are hampered by inaccessible data [1], but their aim is crucial and twofold. First, they wonder if the old results resist if more recent data are added and if the methods are updated, and if not, why this is so. Second, they take into account a large number of recent (or older) articles to check whether the results are still valid when compared with other contributions. For instance, the same data may be examined by different authors with different methodological approaches. Can the difference in results be explained? Is it possible to distinguish credible results from others that are less so?

Recently, we started to focus on this question by considering, in particular, the findings of the so-called "chaos theory" on the energy commodity markets [2–4]. An important reason to be interested in chaotic behavior is that it resembles random behavior (even if they cannot be treated as the same).

In particular, it is interesting to know whether the fluctuations in many time series are really random or they are instead the product of a (complex) deterministic system [3–6]. The behavior of a completely random system is not predictable anyway. Otherwise, if it were completely deterministic, even if chaotic, its behavior could be predicted in the short term.

It is straightforward that evidence on deterministic chaos would have important implications for regulators and short-term trading strategies, in all financial markets and in particular in energy markets.

Energy commodity prices have been examined over the last 20 years to detect the presence of chaos as an alternative to stochastic models, but they revealed contrasting results: some papers highlighted the presence of chaos, while some others did not, and this has led to a gradual loss of interest in the chaos theory applied to energy commodity markets. For example, the papers we have examined in this field—we have selected only those relating to crude oil, diesel, natural gas and copper—are refs. [7–17], but eight of them fall before 2009 and only three after. (For the discussion of the previous literature, see [2–4]).

The conflicting results of identifying chaos in the energy commodity markets can be seen as a replication problem.

Hence, in this paper, we highlight the role of theoretical assumptions of the methods employed in the literature of energy markets. In particular, we show that the mathematical definition of chaos and the theoretical background recalled and discussed here are able to avoid possible errors from misleading results on ostensible chaoticity of the price series.

After showing the importance of the theoretical background in the light of the problem of replication, we also discuss the hybrid approach introduced in [3,4]—i.e., consisting in considering the dynamical system underlying the price time series as a deterministic system with noise—in order to re-evaluate the presence of a chaotic feature in the energy commodity markets. This hybrid approach is based on the introduction of tools that take into account the co-existence of stochastic and chaotic behavior in the same time series, such as modified correlation entropy, noise level estimation and recurrence analysis.

The result is that chaotic characteristics coexist with stochastic ones in the time series of energy commodity prices.

The remainder of this article is structured as follows. Section 2 introduces the chaos definition. Section 3 presents the tools we employ in our analysis, while Section 4 discusses the results. In addition, Section 5 provides the conclusions of our paper.

2. The "Core" of Chaos: Its Definition

Who remembers Ian Malcolm, the mathematician of Jurassic Park? In a scene where he tries to explain the chaos theory to Ellie Sattler, he says: "It simply deals with unpredictability in complex systems. The shorthand is the Butterfly Effect. A butterfly can flap its wings in Peking and in Central Park you get rain instead of sunshine." That is very effective, simple and straightforward.

The chaos definition, however, goes deeper. According to one of the most widely accepted definitions of chaos, introduced by Robert L. Devaney [18] (hence known as *Devaney's chaos definition*), sensitive dependence on initial conditions, topological transitivity and density of periodic points are the "ingredients" of chaos (for the self-consistency of Devaney's definition, see the references in [2]). The intuitive meaning of sensitive dependence on initial conditions is straightforward: tiny differences become amplified. It is the most popular property of a chaotic system. Also called "butterfly effect", it is immediate enough to be cited in a popular film, as we said. This is probably why the "butterfly effect" becomes so predominant that in many contexts, it constitutes, itself, a definition of chaos. There is a lot of numerical evidence for this experimental definition of chaos, but it is not satisfactory, both theoretically and experimentally.

From a theoretical point of view, see, for example, the counterexample 3.3 introduced by Martelli et al. in [19]. Their counterexample shows that, although the "experimental" definition of chaos is easy to check, it defines as chaotic systems those which are not.

As far as the experimental point of view is concerned, however, it has been noted that the time series generated by stochastic systems can also show a sensitive dependence on the initial conditions [20–22] and, since chaos theory is an alternative paradigm to the stochastic approach, a problem arises with the definitions—what is chaotic and what is not.

In addition, while some tests for sensitive dependence on initial conditions have been introduced, for the other two properties that build the Devaney chaos definition, we have far fewer tests, and further, no tests for transitivity conditions of the chaos definition have been found [23].

For this reason, it is inappropriate to talk about chaos tests. We should instead refer to the specific property we are going to test. For example, all the papers considered in this article [7–17] resort to the experimental definition of chaos, testing sensitive dependence on initial conditions. However, the implications that the butterfly effect may have in the energy markets make this property interesting to study, as remarked in [2], but... how?

Is there a dichotomy between the butterfly effect and stochastic features? Or is it possible to think of a paradigm that can include both? The answer to this question is, yes, this dichotomy does not need to be a strict rule, as proved in [3,4]. Hence, in the following, we propose a systematic approach to detect the correct tests to work in this "hybrid" framework.

3. Methodologies

In this paper, entropy and recurrence analysis tools represent the key methodologies to assess the presence of the butterfly effect. Moreover, we extend some of them in order to deal with the coexistence of chaotic and stochastic behaviors.

In the following, p_t and $\kappa_t = \ln \frac{p_t}{p_{t-1}}$ are, respectively, the price and log returns at time t. The time series we will work on is defined as follows: $\{\kappa_t, t = 1, 2, \ldots, n\}, n \in \mathbb{N}$.

3.1. Phase Space Reconstruction

Embedding the time series in a phase space is an important research topic on chaotic time series analysis [24]. In this case, the time evolution of returns is represented by the dynamical system that comes out of the phase space independent variables. The asymptotic behavior of the dynamical system is described by an *attractor*, whose dimension provides a measure of the minimum number of independent variables able to describe the dynamical system.

The scalar time series is topologically equivalent to the attractor, which can be reconstructed from a time series by using the method of the time delay coordinate [25,26]. The reconstructed attractor of the original system is given by the vector sequence

$$\zeta(i) = \left(\kappa_i, \kappa_{i+\tau}, \kappa_{i+2\tau}, \ldots, \kappa_{i+(m-1)\tau}\right) \qquad (1)$$

where m is the embedding dimension, and τ is an appropriate time delay.

The choice of the time delay τ could be a potential issue. For example, the authors in [27] showed that the chaos measures estimation for stock price data is affected by the wrong choice of τ.

The authors in [8] estimated the optimal time delay as the one where average mutual information reaches its first minimum, obtaining a time lag greater than 1.

In [3,4], we employed the average mutual information (AMI) technique to select a proper value of τ. A proper value of τ can be determined using the first minimum of average mutual information (AMI) function, as done in [8]. The method of false nearest neighbors (FNN), introduced by [28], is an algorithm to estimate the minimal embedding dimension m. Let r be the threshold on the distance between two neighboring points, $k(i)$ be the index of the time series element for which we have the minimum $|\zeta(k(i)) - \zeta(i)|$, $\zeta(k(i))^{(m)}$ be the closest neighbor to $\zeta(i)$ in m dimensions, σ be the standard deviation of the data, and $\Theta(\cdot)$ the Heaviside step function, i.e.,

$$\Theta(x) = \begin{cases} 0, & x < 0, \\ 1, & x \geq 0. \end{cases}$$

Hence, the *false nearest neighbor* (FNN) metric is defined as

$$\mathrm{FNN}(r) = \frac{\sum_{i=1}^{n-m-1} \Theta\left(\frac{|\zeta(i)^{(m+1)} - \zeta(k(i))^{(m+1)}|}{|\zeta(i)^{(m)} - \zeta(k(i))^{(m)}|} - r\right) \Theta\left(\frac{\sigma}{r} - |\zeta(i)^{(m)} - \zeta(k(i))^{(m)}|\right)}{\sum_{i=1}^{n-m-1} \Theta\left(\frac{\sigma}{r} - |\zeta(i)^{(m)} - \zeta(k(i))^{(m)}|\right)}, \qquad (2)$$

A proper value of m can be selected by imposing a threshold FNN* (in our case FNN* = 0.5%, as done in [3,4]) so that, if FNN is larger than FNN*, the neighbor is false. Since the FNN decreases with the threshold r, this is the equivalent of selecting as the embedding dimension the minimum value of m such that FNN < FNN*.

3.2. Modified Correlation Entropy

Let $\{\kappa_i\}$ be the result of phase space reconstruction described by Equation (1). Hence, the authors in [29] showed that the Kolmogorov–Sinai (KS) entropy can be approximated by the correlation sum

$$C_m(r) = \frac{1}{n(n-1)} \sum_{\substack{i,j=1 \\ i \neq j}}^{n} \Theta(r - \|\zeta(i) - \zeta(j)\|), \tag{3}$$

where the distance metric is given by the Euclidean norm. From Equation (3), it is possible to achieve an early estimate of the KS entropy

$$K \simeq \frac{1}{\tau} \ln \frac{C_m(r)}{C_{m+1}(r)}. \tag{4}$$

and its adjusted estimation

$$K \simeq \frac{1}{\tau} \ln \frac{C_m(r)}{C_{m+1}(r)} - \frac{D}{2\tau} \ln \frac{m+1}{m}. \tag{5}$$

given by [30], where D is the correlation dimension.

Nevertheless, the computation of the correlation sum is affected by noise, which produces errors in these formulas, used instead in the literature so far.

The authors in [31] introduced the *modified correlation entropy* (MCE), which estimates the KS entropy for noisy time series. It is based on the correlation integral derived in [32] and assumes the presence of Gaussian additive noise.

3.3. Noise Level

Let $0.1 = r_1 < r_2 < \cdots < r_i < \cdots < r_L = 0.3$ with a uniform step $\Delta r = r_{i+1} - r_i$. The noise level is estimated by means of a linear least-squares method

$$\bar{\sigma}^2 = \frac{\sum_{i=2}^{L-2}(v_{i+1} - v_i)(u_{i+1} - u_i)}{2\sum_{i=2}^{L-2}(u_{i+1} - u_i)^2}. \tag{6}$$

as obtained in [33]. It is based on an auxiliary time series (u_i, v_i), $i = 1, \ldots, L$

$$u_i = \frac{(m-1)\Delta r(c_i - c_{i-1}) - r_i(c_{i-1} - 2c_i + c_{i+1}) - r_i(c_i - c_{i-1})^2}{r_i(\Delta r)^2}$$

$$v_i = r_i \frac{c_i - c_{i-1}}{\Delta r},$$

$$\tag{7}$$

where $c_i = \ln C_0(r_i)$.

3.4. Recurrence Analysis

Recurrence quantification analysis (RQA) can be considered as another important tool in chaotic time series analysis [34,35]. The *recurrence plot* (RP), introduced by [36], is defined by the matrix

$$M_{ij} = \Theta(\epsilon - \|\zeta(i) - \zeta(j)\|), \tag{8}$$

where ϵ is a tolerance parameter to be chosen and $\zeta(i)$ is derived by Equation (1). Since the distance is symmetric, we have that the matrix M is in turn symmetric and, then, the recurrence plot is symmetric with respect to the diagonal, by definition.

The parameter ϵ, which determines the density of RP, can be selected according to the criterion introduced in [37]:

$$\epsilon = k \cdot \max_{i,j}\|\zeta(i) - \zeta(j)\|. \tag{9}$$

provided that $k < 10\%$ [34,38,39].

Related to the RP is the *recurrence rate* [34], which can be defined as follows:

$$RR(\tau) = \frac{1}{N-\tau} \sum_{i=1}^{N-\tau} M_{ij}. \tag{10}$$

The *recurrence quantification analysis* contains several measures of complexity. Its aim is to go beyond the visual impression yielded by RPs [34].

Some of them resort to the histogram $P(l)$ of diagonal lines of length l, i.e.,

$$P(l) = \sum_{i,j=1}^{N} \left(1 - M_{i-1,j-1}\right)\left(1 - M_{i+l,j+l}\right) \prod_{k=0}^{l-1} M_{i+k,j+k}.$$

As recalled in [34], "processes with uncorrelated or weakly correlated, stochastic or chaotic behaviour cause none or very short diagonals, whereas deterministic processes cause longer diagonals and less single, isolated recurrence points". From this, it is natural to take

$$DET = \frac{\sum_{l=l_{min}}^{N} lP(l)}{\sum_{l=1}^{N} lP(l)} \tag{11}$$

as a measure for *determinism* of the system—percentage of recurrence points which form diagonal structures (of at least length l_{min}) over the total number of recurrence points.

Moreover, given the histogram $P(v)$ of vertical lines of length v, i.e.,

$$P(v) = \sum_{i,j=1}^{N} \left(1 - M_{i,j}\right)\left(1 - M_{i,j+v}\right) \prod_{k=0}^{v-1} M_{i,j+k}.$$

it is possible to define the percentage of recurrence points which form vertical structures in the RP, the so-called *laminarity*:

$$LAM = \frac{\sum_{v=v_{min}}^{N} vP(v)}{\sum_{v=1}^{N} vP(v)}$$

whereas the average length of vertical structures is given by

$$TT = \frac{\sum_{v=v_{min}}^{N} vP(v)}{\sum_{v=v_{min}}^{N} P(v)}$$

and is called the *trapping time*.

4. Implications of the New Approach

We now turn to recall the main findings enclosed in [3,4], discussing them in the framework of our approach, i.e., the coexistence of the stochastic and chaotic paradigms.

Before embracing this hybrid paradigm for energy markets, it is very important to determine the two embedding parameters for the reconstruction of the phase space, namely, the time delay τ and the embedding dimension m. In Table 1, we recall the embedding parameters of some of the future contracts analyzed in [4], as collected by the U.S. Energy

Information Administration (EIA). As we can see, the optimal time lags are not always equal to 1.

Table 1. τ and m for futures prices (FNN* = 0.5%).

Futures Contract	Time Delay	Embedding Dimension
Crude oil Contract 1	4	11
Crude oil Contract 3	4	10
Heating oil Contract 1	1	13
Heating oil Contract 3	1	11
Natural gas	1	14

According to our framework, the impact of the stochastic component can be initially estimated through the modified correlation entropy. An example of MCE estimation is depicted in Figure 1, where MCE and CE are compared depending on the threshold r [4].

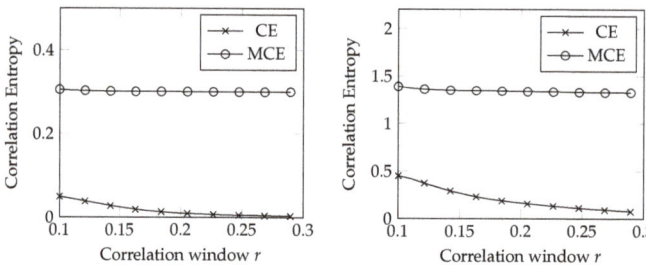

Figure 1. MCE vs. CE; Cushing Crude Oil Contract 1 (on the **left**) and Natural Gas (on the **right**).

In Figure 1, we see the following:
- The KS entropy estimated with a noise-oblivious approach is much smaller than the MCE;
- The CE decays as the size of the correlation window increases, whereas the MCE is rather steady.

Since MCE ≡ CE for noise-free data, these two points show the relevance of the stochastic component in our dataset of prices. The steadiness of MCE is typical of deterministic systems with noise (see Figure 11.3 of [40]).

Connected to this point is the noise level estimation. Few examples of noise level estimation are represented in Table 2 and, as discussed in [4], it shows that the level of noise cannot be ignored.

Table 2. Noise level estimation.

Commodity Contract	$\tilde{\sigma}$	Noise Level %
Crude oil C1	0.02363634	57.9%
Crude oil C3	0.02432642	57.1%
Heating oil C1	0.02032667	51.7%
Heating oil C3	0.02334584	53.5%
Natural gas	0.02591293	40.1%

We now turn to prove these insights through the use of recurrence analysis. We show an example of the recurrence plot for copper dataset, examined in [3], in Figure 2, for $\epsilon = 6\%$.

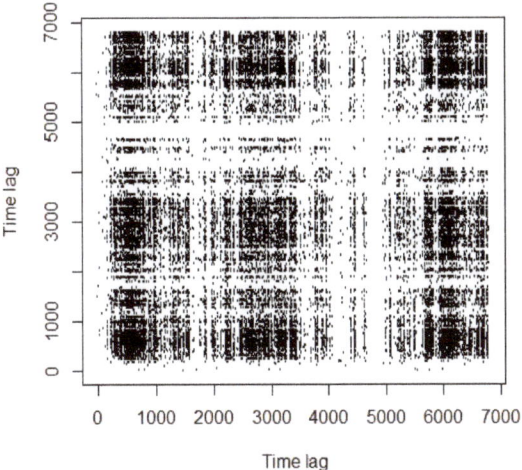

Figure 2. Recurrence plot, copper (6%).

In Figure 2, black rectangles and single dots alternate along the entire picture. In the recurrence analysis, single points denote noisy behavior [34] because they indicate strongly uncorrelated, fluctuating data, whereas black rectangles characterize *laminar* behaviors. The latter are indicative of states that do not change or change slowly for some time [34,41]. Therein, periods are related to *intermittency*, a behavior of dynamical systems which has been extensively studied in the literature [42–45].

In economics and finance, intermittency results in the irregular alternation of phases of boom and of depression [46,47].

The authors in [48] showed "how economic intermittency is induced by an attractor merging crisis and how to recognize different recurrent patterns in the intermittent time series of economic cycles by separating them into laminar (weakly chaotic) and bursty (strongly chaotic) phases". Moreover, intermittency is related to the emergence of bubbles [3,35,49,50].

Intermittency is one of the common routes to chaos [51]. In such a state, the dynamical system switches between two different kinds of behavior called phases. Complex systems which exhibit intermittency can be described by a control parameter p. It is characterized by a critical threshold p_T, which marks the switch from different dynamic regimes [51]. For example, the dynamical system underlying the copper time series is such that $p > p_T$, because the laminar phases in Figure 2 are still pretty recognizable ([3]).

White areas or bands in the RPs are caused by abrupt changes and extreme events in the dynamics (*disrupted* typology [36]). They are indicative of transient activities and may reflect an underlying state change [34]. White bands with no recurrent points appear in Figure 2.

Pomeau and Manneville introduced three types of intermittency [42], whose structure were examined in [52] afterwards. According to [52], it is possible to distinguish the kind of intermittency showed by the system by looking at the patterns of RPs. Hence, following [52], the pattern in Figure 2 suggests the presence of a type I intermittency (Figure 3).

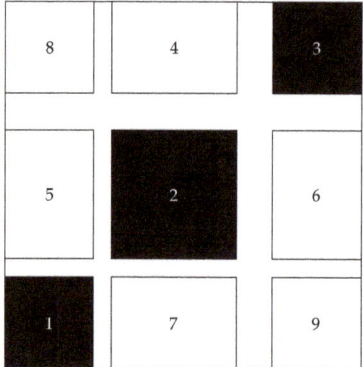

Figure 3. Type I intermittency, positioning of the rectangles in the RP (see Figure 8 in [52]).

Quite different is the RP depicted in Figure 4, for natural gas. We can spot the presence of a larger number of black rectangles, even if they are smaller.

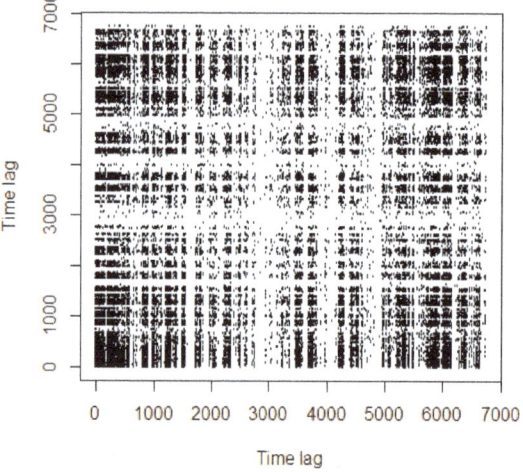

Figure 4. Recurrence plot, natural gas (6%).

Then it is clear that, in this context, we cannot talk about purely chaotic (or stochastic) time series and that the energy commodity markets follow instead a hybrid paradigm—both chaotic and stochastic. However, do you remember Ian Malcolm's words? Rearranging them, *the shorthand of chaos is the butterfly effect*. In Section 2, we explained why this cannot be true, and the energy commodity markets give us a *counterexample*. Actually, we estimated the maximal Lyapunov exponent (MLE) for some of the datasets previously examined in [3,4] obtaining: MLE (copper) = −0.78; MLE (oil contract 1) = −0.68; MLE (natural gas) = 0.14. From these findings, according to the experimental definition of chaos, we may infer that the natural gas time series is chaotic [2].

MCE, noise level estimation and RP tell us a different story: the stochastic component is too large to be neglected. This result is also confirmed by the measure for determinism enclosed in Equation (11). For natural gas, DET= 0.22, which denotes a very high level of stochastic component. The choice of $l_{min} = 10$ satisfies the suggestions contained in [34,40]; the choice of ϵ ($k = 6\%$) follows the criterion fixed by (9).

5. Conclusions

As pointed out by many researchers, replication is the key to credibility in applied sciences and confidence in all research findings. With regard, in particular, to energy finance and economics, replication papers are rare, probably because they are hampered by inaccessible data, but their aim is crucial and twofold. First, they wonder if the old results resist the addition of more recent data and the updating of new methods and, if not, why this is so. Second, they take into account a large number of recent (or older) articles to check whether the results are still valid when compared with other contributions.

While in [3,4] we proved that the contrasting results in chaos theory applied to energy economics are due to replication issues, in this paper, we consider two ways to avoid misleading results on the ostensible chaoticity of price series. The first one is represented by the proper mathematical definition of chaos and the related theoretical background, while the latter is represented by the hybrid approach that we propose here—which consists in considering the dynamical system underlying the price time series as a superposition of deterministic and stochastic systems. This hybrid approach is based on the introduction of tools that take into account the co-existence of stochastic and chaotic behaviors in the same time series, such as modified correlation entropy, noise level estimation and recurrence analysis.

We find that the chaotic and stochastic features coexist in the energy commodity markets, although the misuse of some tests in the established practice in literature—like CE or MLE—may say otherwise.

Our results are in line with the seminal paper by Barnett and Serletis who, more than 20 years ago, conjectured that controversies concerning the application of chaos theory in economics "might stem from the high noise level that exists in most aggregated economic time series and the relatively low sample sizes that are available with economic data" [53]. However, we should observe that the long debate produced by this paper did not answer the question, and, instead, papers dealing with the existence of chaos in economic and financial data continued to be published in the subsequent years [3,4]. Moreover, we do not completely agree with the conclusions enclosed in [53]: "However, it also appears that the controversies are produced by the nature of the tests themselves, rather than by the nature of the hypothesis, since linearity is a very strong null hypothesis, and hence should be easy to reject with any test and any economic or financial time series on which an adequate sample size is available". We do not believe that "the controversies are produced by the nature of the tests themselves", and instead we showed here that it would be more correct to speak of the superposition of chaotic and stochastic systems.

The consequences of such findings, though not investigated here, deserve further investigations and suggest, for future works, the adoption of different approaches to predict the behavior of energy commodity prices.

As for future works, artificial intelligence (AI) methods, such as machine learning, offer new possibilities to forecast energy consumption prices. Unlike conventional algorithms, which tend to follow explicit instructions to perform a specific task, machine learning (ML) takes into account various context variables and their mutual relationship while training. For example, in price prediction, supervised learning algorithms can already produce good results, which in turn are applied to time series data. There are already several studies on the predictability of time series data for various applications, including in the energy sector [54–57].

For the future, it would be therefore good to address these AI/ML-driven techniques for a robust evaluation and estimation of energy consumption prices in the outlook.

Author Contributions: Conceptualization, L.M. and P.V.; Data curation, L.M. and P.V.; Formal analysis, L.M. and P.V.; Validation, L.M. and P.V.; Writing—original draft, L.M. and P.V.; Writing—review & editing, L.M. and P.V. All authors have read and agreed to the published version of the manuscript.

Funding: This research received no external funding.

Institutional Review Board Statement: Not applicable.

Informed Consent Statement: Not applicable.

Data Availability Statement: The data presented in this study are available on request from the corresponding author.

Conflicts of Interest: The authors declare no conflict of interest.

References

1. Tol, R.S. Special issue on replication. *Energy Econ.* **2018**, *82*, 1–3. [CrossRef]
2. Mastroeni, L.; Vellucci, P. Chaos versus stochastic paradigm in energy markets. In *Handbook of Energy Finance: Theories, Practices and Simulations*; World Scientific: Singapore, 2019; pp. 765–786.
3. Mastroeni, L.; Vellucci, P.; Naldi, M. Co-existence of stochastic and chaotic behaviour in the copper price time series. *Resour. Policy* **2018**, *58*, 295–302. [CrossRef]
4. Mastroeni, L.; Vellucci, P.; Naldi, M. A reappraisal of the chaotic paradigm for energy commodity prices. *Energy Econ.* **2019**, *82*, 167–178. [CrossRef]
5. Orlando, G.; Bufalo, M.; Stoop, R. Financial markets' deterministic aspects modeled by a low-dimensional equation. *Sci. Rep.* **2022**, *12*, 1693. [CrossRef] [PubMed]
6. Hirata, Y. Recurrence plots for characterizing random dynamical systems. *Commun. Nonlinear Sci. Numer. Simul.* **2021**, *94*, 105552. [CrossRef]
7. Adrangi, B.; Chatrath, A.; Dhanda, K.K.; Raffiee, K. Chaos in oil prices? Evidence from futures markets. *Energ. Econ.* **2001**, *23*, 405–425. [CrossRef]
8. Barkoulas, J.T.; Chakraborty, A.; Ouandlous, A. A metric and topological analysis of determinism in the crude oil spot market. *Energ. Econ.* **2012**, *34*, 584–591. [CrossRef]
9. Carrasco, R.; Vargas, M.; Alfaro, M.; Soto, I.; Fuertes, G. Copper Metal Price Using Chaotic Time Series Forecasting. *IEEE Lat. Am. Trans.* **2015**, *13*, 1961–1965. [CrossRef]
10. Chwee, V. Chaos in Natural Gas Futures? *Energy J.* **1998**, *19*, 149–164. [CrossRef]
11. Cortez, C.A.T.; Hitch, M.; Sammut, C.; Coulton, J.; Shishko, R.; Saydam, S. Determining the embedding parameters governing long-term dynamics of copper prices. *Chaos Solitons Fractals* **2018**, *111*, 186–197. [CrossRef]
12. Kyrtsou, C.; Malliaris, A.G.; Serletis, A. Energy sector pricing: On the role of neglected nonlinearity. *Energ. Econ.* **2009**, *31*, 492–502. [CrossRef]
13. Matilla-García, M. Nonlinear Dynamics in Energy Futures. *Energy J.* **2007**, *28*, 7–29. [CrossRef]
14. Moshiri, S.; Foroutan, F. Forecasting nonlinear crude oil futures prices. *Energy J.* **2006**, *27*, 81–95. [CrossRef]
15. Panas, E. Long memory and chaotic models of prices on the London Metal Exchange. *Resour. Policy* **2001**, *27*, 235–246. [CrossRef]
16. Panas, E.; Ninni, V. Are oil markets chaotic? A non-linear dynamic analysis. *Energ. Econ.* **2000**, *22*, 549–568. [CrossRef]
17. Serletis, A.; Gogas, P. The North American Natural Gas Liquids Markets are Chaotic. *Energy J.* **1999**, *20*, 83–103. [CrossRef]
18. Devaney, R.L. *An Introduction to Chaotic Dynamical Systems*; Addison-Wesley Reading: Reading, MA, USA, 1989; Volume 13046.
19. Martelli, M.; Dang, M.; Seph, T. Defining chaos. *Math. Mag.* **1998**, *71*, 112–122. [CrossRef]
20. Ikeguchi, T.; Aihara, K. Lyapunov spectral analysis on random data. *Int. J. Bifurcat. Chaos* **1997**, *7*, 1267–1282. [CrossRef]
21. Tanaka, T.; Aihara, K.; Taki, M. Lyapunov exponents of random time series. *Phys. Rev. E* **1996**, *54*, 2122. [CrossRef]
22. Tanaka, T.; Aihara, K.; Taki, M. Analysis of positive Lyapunov exponents from random time series. *Phys. D* **1998**, *111*, 42–50. [CrossRef]
23. Yousefpoor, P.; Esfahani, M.; Nojumi, H. Looking for systematic approach to select chaos tests. *Appl. Math. Comput.* **2008**, *198*, 73–91. [CrossRef]
24. Packard, N.H.; Crutchfield, J.P.; Farmer, J.D.; Shaw, R.S. Geometry from a time series. *Phys. Rev. Lett.* **1980**, *45*, 712. [CrossRef]
25. Takens, F. Detecting strange attractors in turbulence. In *Dynamical Systems and Turbulence, Warwick 1980*; Springer: Berlin/Heidelberg, Germany, 1981; pp. 366–381.
26. Ruelle, D. *Chaotic Evolution and Strange Attractors*; Cambridge University Press: Cambridge, UK, 1989; Volume 1.
27. Mayfield, E.S.; Mizrach, B. On Determining the Dimension of Real-Time Stock-Price Data. *J. Bus. Econ. Stat.* **1992**, *10*, 367–374. [CrossRef]
28. Kennel, M.B.; Brown, R.; Abarbanel, H.D.I. Determining embedding dimension for phase-space reconstruction using a geometrical construction. *Phys. Rev. A* **1992**, *45*, 3403–3411. [CrossRef] [PubMed]
29. Grassberger, P.; Procaccia, I. Estimation of the Kolmogorov entropy from a chaotic signal. *Phys. Rev. A* **1983**, *28*, 2591. [CrossRef]
30. Frank, M.; Blank, H.R.; Heindl, J.; Kaltenhäuser, M.; Köchner, H.; Kreische, W.; Müller, N.; Poscher, S.; Sporer, R.; Wagner, T. Improvement of K2-entropy calculations by means of dimension scaled distances. *Phys. D Nonlinear Phenom.* **1993**, *65*, 359–364. [CrossRef]
31. Jayawardena, A.W.; Xu, P.; Li, W.K. Modified correlation entropy estimation for a noisy chaotic time series. *Chaos Interdiscip. J. Nonlinear Sci.* **2010**, *20*, 023104. [CrossRef]
32. Diks, C. *Nonlinear Time Series Analysis: Methods and Applications*; World Scientific: Singapore, 1999.

33. Jayawardena, A.W.; Xu, P.; Li, W.K. A method of estimating the noise level in a chaotic time series. *Chaos Interdiscip. J. Nonlinear Sci.* **2008**, *18*, 023115. [CrossRef]
34. Marwan, N.; Romano, M.C.; Thiel, M.; Kurths, J. Recurrence plots for the analysis of complex systems. *Phys. Rep.* **2007**, *438*, 237–329. [CrossRef]
35. Orlando, G.; Zimatore, G. Recurrence quantification analysis of business cycles. *Chaos Solitons Fractals* **2018**, *110*, 82–94. [CrossRef]
36. Eckmann, J.P.; Kamphorst, S.O.; Ruelle, D. Recurrence Plots of Dynamical Systems. *EPL Europhys. Lett.* **1987**, *4*, 973. [CrossRef]
37. Mindlin, G.M.; Gilmore, R. Topological analysis and synthesis of chaotic time series. *Phys. D Nonlinear Phenom.* **1992**, *58*, 229–242. [CrossRef]
38. Koebbe, M.; Mayer-Kress, G. Use of recurrence plots in the analysis of time-series data. In *Santa Fe Institute Studies in Sciences of Complexity*; Addison-Wesley Publishing Co.: Boston, MA, USA, 1992; Volume 12, pp. 361–361.
39. Zbilut, J.P.; Webber, C.L. Embeddings and delays as derived from quantification of recurrence plots. *Phys. Lett. A* **1992**, *171*, 199–203. [CrossRef]
40. Kantz, H.; Schreiber, T. *Nonlinear Time Series Analysis*; Cambridge University Press: Cambridge, UK, 2004; Volume 7.
41. Bianchi, F.M.; Livi, L.; Alippi, C. Investigating Echo-State Networks Dynamics by Means of Recurrence Analysis. *IEEE Trans. Neural Netw. Learn. Syst.* **2016**, *29*, 427–439. [CrossRef] [PubMed]
42. Pomeau, Y.; Manneville, P. Intermittent transition to turbulence in dissipative dynamical systems. *Commun. Math. Phys.* **1980**, *74*, 189–197. [CrossRef]
43. Bergé, P.; Dubois, M.; Mannevillel, P.; Pomeau, Y. Intermittency in Rayleigh-Bénard convection. *J. Phys. Lett.* **1980**, *41*, 341–345. [CrossRef]
44. Bersini, H.; Sener, P. The connections between the frustrated chaos and the intermittency chaos in small Hopfield networks. *Neural Netw.* **2002**, *15*, 1197–1204. [CrossRef]
45. Peterka, F.; Kotera, T.; Čipera, S. Explanation of appearance and characteristics of intermittency chaos of the impact oscillator. *Chaos Solitons Fractals* **2004**, *19*, 1251–1259. [CrossRef]
46. Reinhart, C.M.; Rogoff, K.S. *This Time Is Different: Eight Centuries of Financial Folly*; Princeton University Press: Princeton, NJ, USA, 2009.
47. Chen, P. *Economic Complexity and Equilibrium Illusion: Essays on Market Instability and Macro Vitality*; Routledge: London, UK, 2010.
48. Chian, A.C.L.; Rempel, E.L.; Rogers, C. Crisis-induced intermittency in non-linear economic cycles. *Appl. Econ. Lett.* **2007**, *14*, 211–218. [CrossRef]
49. Bornholdt, S. Expectation bubbles in a spin model of markets: Intermittency from frustration across scales. *Int. J. Mod. Phys. C* **2001**, *12*, 667–674. [CrossRef]
50. Orlando, G.; Zimatore, G. Business cycle modeling between financial crises and black swans: Ornstein–Uhlenbeck stochastic process vs Kaldor deterministic chaotic model. *Chaos Interdiscip. J. Nonlinear Sci.* **2020**, *30*, 083129. [CrossRef] [PubMed]
51. Ott, E. *Chaos in Dynamical Systems*; Cambridge University Press: Cambridge, UK, 2002.
52. Klimaszewska, K.; Żebrowski, J.J. Detection of the type of intermittency using characteristic patterns in recurrence plots. *Phys. Rev. E* **2009**, *80*, 026214. [CrossRef] [PubMed]
53. Barnett, W.A.; Serletis, A. Martingales, nonlinearity, and chaos. *J. Econ. Dyn. Control* **2000**, *24*, 703–724. [CrossRef]
54. Antonopoulos, I.; Robu, V.; Couraud, B.; Kirli, D.; Norbu, S.; Kiprakis, A.; Flynn, D.; Elizondo-Gonzalez, S.; Wattam, S. Artificial intelligence and machine learning approaches to energy demand-side response: A systematic review. *Renew. Sustain. Energy Rev.* **2020**, *130*, 109899. [CrossRef]
55. Crespo-Vazquez, J.L.; Carrillo, C.; Diaz-Dorado, E.; Martinez-Lorenzo, J.A.; Noor-E-Alam, M. A machine learning based stochastic optimization framework for a wind and storage power plant participating in energy pool market. *Appl. Energy* **2018**, *232*, 341–357. [CrossRef]
56. Ghoddusi, H.; Creamer, G.G.; Rafizadeh, N. Machine learning in energy economics and finance: A review. *Energy Econ.* **2019**, *81*, 709–727. [CrossRef]
57. Herrera, G.P.; Constantino, M.; Tabak, B.M.; Pistori, H.; Su, J.J.; Naranpanawa, A. Long-term forecast of energy commodities price using machine learning. *Energy* **2019**, *179*, 214–221. [CrossRef]

Article

Role of Age and Education as the Determinant of Income Inequality in Poland: Decomposition of the Mean Logarithmic Deviation

Ewa Wędrowska [1,*] and Joanna Muszyńska [2]

[1] Department of Economic Applications of Informatics and Mathematics, Faculty of Economic Sciences and Management, Nicolaus Copernicus University in Toruń, ul. Gagarina 13a, 87-100 Toruń, Poland
[2] Econometrics and Statistics Department, Faculty of Economic Sciences and Management, Nicolaus Copernicus University in Toruń, ul. Gagarina 13a, 87-100 Toruń, Poland; jmus@umk.pl
* Correspondence: ewaw@umk.pl

Citation: Wędrowska, E.; Muszyńska, J. Role of Age and Education as the Determinant of Income Inequality in Poland: Decomposition of the Mean Logarithmic Deviation. *Entropy* **2022**, *24*, 773. https://doi.org/10.3390/e24060773

Academic Editor: Joanna Olbryś

Received: 15 May 2022
Accepted: 29 May 2022
Published: 30 May 2022

Publisher's Note: MDPI stays neutral with regard to jurisdictional claims in published maps and institutional affiliations.

Copyright: © 2022 by the authors. Licensee MDPI, Basel, Switzerland. This article is an open access article distributed under the terms and conditions of the Creative Commons Attribution (CC BY) license (https://creativecommons.org/licenses/by/4.0/).

Abstract: Measures of inequality can be used to illustrate inequality between and within groups, but the choice of the appropriate measure can have different implications. This study focused on the Mean Logarithmic Deviation, the measure proposed by Theil and based on the techniques of statistical information theory. The MLD was selected because of its attractive properties: fulfillment of the principle of monotonicity and the possibility of additive decomposition. The following study objectives were formulated: (1) to assess the degree of inequality in the population and in the distinguished subgroups, (2) to determine the extent to which education and age influence the level of inequality, and (3) to ascertain what factors contribute to changes in the level of inequality in Poland. The study confirmed an association between the level of education and the average income of the groups distinguished on this basis. The education level of the household head remains an important determinant of household income inequality in Poland, despite the decline in the "educational bonus". The study also found that differences in the age of the household head had a smaller effect on income inequality than the level of education. However, it can be concluded that the higher share of older people may contribute to an increase in income inequality between groups, as the income from pension in Poland is more homogeneous than the income from work in younger groups. Moreover, the current paper seeks to situate Theil's approach in the context of scholarly writings since 1967.

Keywords: Mean Logarithmic Deviation; Shannon entropy; income inequality; household income; decomposition of income inequality; EU-SILC

1. Introduction

It is well-known that entropy can be considered a measure of uncertainty in probability distribution [1]. Historically, numerous definitions of entropy have been advanced [2–8] that subsequently are encountered in numerous contexts (thermodynamics, statistical mechanics, information theory, topological dynamics, economy, etc.). The most broadly recognized is Shannon's information entropy [5]. Statistical entropy introduced by Shannon is an essential concept in information theory, quantifies the unevenness of the probability distribution [9], and may be interpreted as an index of concentration [10]. Furthermore, it needs the straightforward condition of being additive, which was adopted as one of the functional requirements of entropy. According to Theil [11], these properties made it legitimate for entropy to be employed to devise measures that served to quantify income inequality, while the indexes the latter introduced, i.e., the Theil index (TI) and the Mean Logarithmic Deviation (MLD), entered widespread application as instruments for computing concentration and inequality of income distribution. Then, by subtracting Shannon's entropy of the actual distribution of income shares from the maximum possible value of this entropy, one arrives at the Theil index. Both the TI and the MLD are instances of application of relative entropy or Kullback–Leibler divergence between two income distributions, i.e., actual distribution and equal distribution. Simultaneously, relative entropy introduces alternative variants of the comparative distribution for each Theil measure [12].

Having advanced income inequality measures based on the techniques of statistical information theory, Theil put forward another intellectual concept to define and measure inequality. Not only did he pioneer using entropy to determine inequality, but he also contributed an important set of functional forms by which inequality could be modeled and analyzed. Thanks to Theil, the concepts of information theory became the cornerstone of a new understanding of inequality in income distribution, where it was construed as a discrepancy between the actual income distribution and an implicitly egalitarian reference distribution or some other distribution of economic relevance. In a sense, Theil focused on inequality as a "by-product" of the information content in the income distribution structure. Cowell [13] goes as far as stating that this landmark in comprehending inequality may not have been fully appreciated for some time, and Theil's contribution may have been more far-reaching than usually assumed. Indeed, there is an extensive amount of works in the literature offering cogent arguments favoring the information theory techniques Theil innovatively employed in studying income inequality. Theil's proposal engendered a discussion on various theoretical aspects resulting from using information theory methods in the study of inequality. First, one could cite a more flexible general class of measures introduced by Cowell [12] and Cowell and Kuga [14] known as the Generalized Entropy (GE) measures, in which the two Theil indices are special instances. The GE measures constitute the single-parameter entropy family, and their concept is based on comparing observed income distribution with a reference distribution using Csiszár's divergence (f-divergence) [15]. Talih [16] observes that the GE class is a special case of alpha divergence. The idea of applying dissimilarity measures deriving from the information theory in the study of income inequality was elaborated by References [17–23]. Second, numerous papers have been devoted to the axiomatization of Theil indices [14,24,25] and, in particular, to the capacity of GE measures (including the TI and the MLD) to additively decompose into within-group and between-group inequalities [17,26–28]. Third, the innovative methods introduced by Theil led to a debate on measures of inequality derived from information theory from "ethical" (or prescriptive), as well as "statistical" (or descriptive) standpoints [13,29].

One common application of Theil indices involves the relation between inequality of total income and the values obtained for population subgroups. Theil indices can be easily resolved into terms interpreted as measures of within-group and between-group inequality for population subgroups. This property of additive decomposition is an attractive feature of both Theil indices, promoting numerous applications of the TI and the MLD in the study of the degree of inequality and when examining the factors behind it [27,30–34].

The total income inequality of a population is generated within groups (sub-populations) and between groups. Following this premise, measures based on entropy—which can be easily aggregated (and disaggregated)—are extremely useful for analyzing income inequality in a population divided according to identifiable sociodemographic characteristics such as place of residence, race, gender, age, education, labor market status, etc. The decomposition of an inequality measure enables one to determine how much of the total income inequality can be attributed to variation within groups or, alternatively, to differences between groups. The emergence of comprehensive and detailed micro-data sets made it possible to examine the extent of inequality between people or households. In this study, attention was focused on the equivalized income among Poles in 2005 and 2019. Using EU-SILC data, the age and education of the household head were considered as potential factors of income inequality. Taking these circumstances into account, the following study objectives were formulated: (1) to assess the degree of inequality in the population and in the distinguished subgroups, (2) to determine the extent to which education and age influence the level of inequality, and (3) to ascertain what factors (changes in population structure and changes in income distribution and/or income inequality within subgroups) contribute to changes in the level of inequality in Poland. Therefore, the following hypotheses were formulated:

1. Changes in the age structure of the population in Poland (population aging) increase the importance of age as a determinant of income inequality.
2. Due to the increase of well-educated persons in the share of population, the effect of differences in the level of education on the level of income inequality decreases.

Moreover, the current paper seeks to situate Theil's approach in the context of scholarly writings since 1967. Specifically, the Mean Logarithmic Deviation is considerably highlighted, given that the Theil index treats differences in all parts of the distribution equally, while the MLD is more responsive to changes at the bottom tail [35]. The Mean Logarithmic Deviation was selected from among all additively decomposable inequality measures because it is the sole measure that allows unequivocal partitioning of the total inequality due to differences between subgroups [27]. The decomposition methodology relies on an a priori approach which derives from theoretical axioms and employs a decomposition technique by population subgroups consistent with Shorrocks [17,27] and Mookherjee and Shorrocks [36].

The structure of this paper is as follows: Section 2 outlines the conceptual background, particularly the intellectual basis for defining the MLD, along with its properties and decomposition techniques based on the axiomatic approach. Section 3 describes the dataset used in the study. The subsequent section provides the results of the empirical analysis, while the conclusions are stated in the final section.

2. Conceptual Background

2.1. Notation and Concepts

To clarify the notation used throughout the paper, let $y_i \in R_+$ represent the (positive) individual income of a person i ($i = 1, 2, \ldots, n$), and $y := (y_1, y_2, \ldots, y_n) \in R_+^n$ is the income distribution vector for a population of n individuals. The set of all possible income distributions, D, was also defined with specific income distribution, $y \in R_+^n$, and mean income level, $\mu = \mu(y) = \frac{Y}{n}$, where $Y = \sum_{i=1}^{n} y_i$ denotes the total number of income units. A parameter vector $\theta(y) = (\mu(y), n(y))$ of the distribution y is introduced following Shorrocks [17], where $n(y) = n$ denotes the dimension of any vector y (i.e., the population size).

Mean income is most often adopted as a natural point of reference in the study of income inequality [37]. For this reason, vector $\bar{y} := (\mu, \mu, \ldots, \mu) \in R_+^n$ will be employed to signify the equalized version of y. Vector $\bar{y}$ represents a perfectly equal distribution in a situation in which the income of all persons is equal. The mean vector, $\bar{y}$, shall be referred to as the reference distribution for perfect equality.

The connection between information theory and the economic interpretation of income distributions is established by exploiting the close relationship between entropy measures (based on probability distributions) and measures of inequality (based on distributions of income shares) (Reference [22], p. 422). Therefore, based on individual income for each i person, it is possible to determine their share in total income, Y: $q_i = \frac{y_i}{Y}$. The actual vector of income shares is structured as $q := \left(\frac{y_1}{Y}, \frac{y_2}{Y}, \ldots, \frac{y_n}{Y}\right) = \left(\frac{y_1}{n\mu}, \frac{y_2}{n\mu}, \ldots, \frac{y_n}{n\mu}\right)$, whereas the vector of equal income shares is as follows: $p := \left(\frac{1}{n}, \frac{1}{n}, \ldots, \frac{1}{n}\right)$.

Finally, the designated notation will be used to describe the division of n income-receiving units into $G \geq 2$ mutually exclusive and exhaustive subgroups (e.g., by education, age, gender, race, occupation, or region). The overall distribution, y, is partitioned into G subgroup distributions: $y = (y^1, y^2, \ldots, y^G)$. The mean income of the g subgroup is denoted as $\mu^g = \mu(y^g)$, while $n^g = n(y^g)$ describes its numerical strength ($\sum_{g=1}^{G} n^g = n$). Let $\bar{\mu} = (\mu^1, \mu^2, \ldots, \mu^G)$, and $\bar{n} = (n^1, n^2, \ldots, n^G)$ represents the vectors of subgroup means and population sizes, respectively. For each distribution y^g ($g = 1, \ldots, G$), the parameter vector is as follows: $\theta^g(y^g) = (\mu(y^g), n(y^g)) = (\mu^g, n^g)$. Furthermore, $v^g = \frac{n^g}{n}$ denotes subgroup population shares, $\lambda^g = \frac{\mu^g}{\mu}$ stands for relative mean income, and $\theta^g = v^g \lambda^g$ signifies g group income share in the income of the entire population.

An inequality measure is normally a real-valued function, $I(y) : D \to R$, which is given meaning by axioms that integrate criteria derived from ethics, intuition, or mathematical convenience [13]. In the pertinent literature, the Mean Logarithmic Deviation index is most often presented by using the formula below:

$$MLD = \frac{1}{n}\sum_{i=1}^{n} \ln \frac{\mu}{y_i} = -\frac{1}{n}\sum_{i=1}^{n} \ln \frac{y_i}{\mu}. \tag{1}$$

However, for a comprehensive picture of inequality in income distribution as a concept of disparity between the actual income distribution, y, and the equal distribution, $\bar{y}$, based on information theory techniques, Formula (1) is expressed as follows:

$$MLD = \frac{1}{n}\sum_{i=1}^{n} [\ln \mu - \ln y_i] \tag{2}$$

or

$$MLD = \frac{1}{n}\sum_{i=1}^{n} \ln \frac{\mu}{y_i} = \frac{1}{n}\sum_{i=1}^{n} \ln \frac{\frac{y_i}{nq_i}}{y_i} = \frac{1}{n}\sum_{i=1}^{n} \ln \frac{1}{nq_i} = \frac{1}{n}\sum_{i=1}^{n}\left[\ln \frac{1}{n} - \ln q_i\right]. \tag{3}$$

Formula (2) represents the average deviation between average income logarithm, μ, and income logarithm, y_i. In turn, Formula (3) analogously allows for the combined concept of distance between vectors q and p. It may thus be said that it represents the average deviation between the income share logarithm and the logarithm of shares which would constitute perfect equality.

Straightforward conversions of the Formula (2) make it possible to demonstrate that the MLD index is the difference between the logarithm of the arithmetic mean of income (μ) and the logarithm of the geometrical mean (μ_g):

$$\begin{aligned} MLD &= \frac{1}{n}\sum_{i=1}^{n}[\ln \mu - \ln y_i] = \frac{1}{n}\sum_{i=1}^{n} \ln \mu - \frac{1}{n}\sum_{i=1}^{n} \ln y_i \\ &= \ln \mu - \frac{1}{n}\ln(\prod_{i=1}^{n} y_i) = \ln \mu - \ln \mu_g. \end{aligned} \tag{4}$$

Ultimately, it may be shown that the Mean Logarithmic Deviation is simply tantamount to the Kullback–Leilber divergence (KL divergence), in which prior distribution constitutes the actual vector of income shares, $q = \left(\frac{y_1}{n\mu}, \frac{y_2}{n\mu}, \ldots, \frac{y_n}{n\mu}\right)$, whereas posterior distribution is the vector of equal income shares, $p := \left(\frac{1}{n}, \frac{1}{n}, \ldots, \frac{1}{n}\right)$:

$$D(p\|q) = \sum_{i=1}^{n} p_i \ln\left(\frac{p_i}{q_i}\right) = \sum_{i=1}^{n} \frac{1}{n} \ln\left(\frac{\frac{1}{n}}{\frac{y_i}{n\mu}}\right) = \sum_{i=1}^{n} \frac{1}{n} \ln \frac{\mu}{y_i} = MLD. \tag{5}$$

$D(p\|q)$ measures the divergence between actual income distribution, q, and the perfectly equal distribution, p. Taking advantage of the interpretation known in information theory, it may be said that $D(p\|q)$ quantifies the amount of information obtained following a transformation of the prior distribution (q) into posterior distribution (p). $D(p\|q)$ is a measure of the information lost when q is used to approximate p. The Kullback–Leilber divergence may also be construed as a measure of surprise [38]. Therefore, the MLD is the surprise in transitioning from the income distribution one actually has to a hypothetical equal distribution. As is commonly known, the KL divergence is non-symmetric: ($D(p\|q) \neq D(q\|p)$) and $D(p\|q) \geq 0$, whereby its value is equal to 0 when the compared distributions are identical. When quantifying the level of income inequality, if it is assumed that the reference distribution is even, it is evident that $D(p\|q) = 0$ when the examined distribution is $q = \left(\frac{1}{n}, \frac{1}{n}, \ldots, \frac{1}{n}\right)$. Consequently, the MLD index assumes 0 value if (and only if) income distribution, y, is completely equal, meaning that the MLD index meets the property known as normalization.

The Kullback–Leibler divergence does not have an upper-bound. The maximum value of the *MLD* depends on how small an income is determined for y_i. This may be a certain shortcoming of the *MLD* index in the assessment of income inequality, in particular when contrasted with the Gini coefficient, for example, which also easily yields to interpretation. Nonetheless, the many attractive properties of the *MLD* that come to light in the next section have made it one of the commonly used measures of inequality.

The Mean Logarithmic Deviation belongs to a more flexible general family of inequality measures. Cowell extended the class of inequality measures based on information theory techniques to the Generalized Entropy measures [12,14]:

$$GE_\alpha(y) = \begin{cases} \sum_{i=1}^n \left((y_i/\mu)^\alpha\right)/n(\alpha^2 - \alpha) & \alpha \neq 0,1 \\ -\sum_{i=1}^n \ln(y_i/\mu)/n & \alpha = 0 \\ \sum_{i=1}^n (y_i/\mu)\ln(y_i/\mu)/n & \alpha = 1 \end{cases}, \quad (6)$$

where $\alpha \epsilon(-\infty, +\infty)$ is a parameter capturing the sensitivity of a particular GE measure to different parts of the distribution. This class includes, as is widely acknowledged, the Theil index (for $\alpha = 1$), the Mean Logarithmic Deviation (for $\alpha = 0$), and monotonic transformations of the coefficient of variation of the entire Atkinson family of indices. The GE measures constitute a class of relative indices which are normalized by the mean.

The Generalized Entropy measures offer the ability to examine the effects of inequalities in different areas of the income spectrum, enabling more meaningful quantitative assessments of qualitatively different inequalities. As α decreases, the measure's sensitivity to the lower tail, i.e., the poor, increases. Cowell [13] observes that GE is more sensitive to income variation in the upper tail of distribution for high and positive α, whereas, with negative α, the index becomes sensitive to income variation in the lower tail of distribution. In particular, the MLD displays greater sensitivity to changes at the bottom tail.

2.2. Axiomatic Approach

Comparative reference, which provides the basis for inequality measurement using techniques of the statistical information theory, is usually a permanent component of investigations into inequality. Often enough, it is not transparent without verifying mathematical properties which lie at the foundation of the structure of a given inequality measure. Roberto [39] argues that there are many measures which operationalize any given dimension of inequality and divides inequality measures with respect to two dimensions: evenness and diversity. Coulter [40], on the other hand, split inequality measures into four categories in accordance with their basic mathematical model: combinatorics, entropy, deviations, and social-welfare function. However, the most widely adopted classification criterion is the link between measures of inequality and the concept of social welfare. According to Sen [41], measures of inequality can be divided into two broad classes: normative and positive. The former measure the level of inequality in terms of the normative notion of social welfare and the loss incurred as a result of unequal income distribution. They rely on the "ethical" link to social-welfare functions developed by Kolm [42], Atkinson [43], and Sen [41] and are thus informed by value judgements. Conversely, positive measures do not make explicit use of the concept of social welfare and serve only a descriptive function, suitably conveying the degree of inequality in an appropriate way and help one to assess the significance of the impact of various factors. However, Sen [41] notes that this division is not precise since any positive measure of inequality is always entangled with a social welfare function. He cites the Theil index, which, in terms of form, almost fully corresponds with the utilitarian social-welfare function, as a result of which individual welfare components are equal to $y_i \ln\left(\frac{1}{y_i}\right)$ (see Reference [41], p. 43). Shorrocks [29] adds that the descriptive and ethical aspects of inequality measures are complementary.

In describing the properties of the *MLD* index, an axiomatic approach will be used which seeks to characterize measures that satisfy relevant properties in the context of income inequality analysis. Magdalou [44] underlines that such an approach usually yields a unique class of indices which the Generalized Entropy measures represent.

The *MLD* index satisfies five key axioms: symmetry, the principle of population replication, scale invariance, the Pigou–Dalton transfer principle, and an additive decomposition property. It may be interesting to note that any inequality measure that satisfies these axioms must belong to the Generalized Entropy class or its ordinal transformations [27].

1. *Symmetry.* Let $y' = (y'_1, y'_2, \ldots, y'_n) \in D$, which is obtained from $y = (y_1, y_2, \ldots, y_n) \in D$ by a permutation of incomes y_i. $MLD(y') = MLD(y)$ whenever y' is obtained from y by a permutation.
2. *Principle of Population Replication (Replication Invariance).* Let $x = (y, y, \ldots, y) \in D$, which is obtained from $y = (y_1, y_2, \ldots, y_n) \in D$ by a replication. The incomes in x are simply the incomes in y repeated a finite number of times. If x is obtained from y by a replication: $MLD(x) = MLD(y)$ whenever x is obtained from y by a replication.
3. *Scale Invariance (Scale Independence).* Let $x = (\alpha y) = (\alpha y_1, \alpha y_2, \ldots, \alpha y_n) \in D$, which is obtained from $y = (y_1, y_2, \ldots, y_n) \in D$ by a scalar multiple for some positive real α. $MLD(x) = MLD(y)$ whenever x is obtained from y by a scalar multiple.
4. *The Pigou–Dalton Transfer Principle.* Let $x = (x_1, x_2, \ldots, y_i - t, \ldots, y_j + t, \ldots, x_n) \in D$, which is obtained from $y = (y_1, y_2, \ldots, y_i, \ldots, y_j, \ldots, y_n) \in D$ by regressive transfer $t > 0$. This means that, for any given income value, y_i and y_j, which satisfy $y_i < y_j$, transfer $t > 0$ proceeds as follows: $y_i - t = x_i$ and $y_j + t = x_j$, $x_i \leq x_j$, whereas, for any given $k \neq i, j$, we obtain $x_k = y_k$ ($y_i - x_i = x_j - y_j > 0$). $MLD(x) = MLD(y)$ whenever x is obtained from y by a regressive transfer.
5. *Additively decomposable.* Suppose that the overall distribution y is partitioned into G subgroup distributions: $y = (y^1, y^2, \ldots, y^G)$. Additive decomposition property is defined according to References [20,27,45]. The decomposition formula will make use of a parameter vector $\bar{\theta} = (\bar{\mu}, \bar{n}) \in R_+^G \times N^G$ for both the weights employed in the within-group term and the distribution used to define the between-group term. For each vector $\bar{\theta} = (\bar{\mu}, \bar{n}) \in R_+^G \times N^G$, let us define a weighting function, $w(\bar{\mu}, \bar{n}) := (w^1(\bar{\mu}, \bar{n}), w^2(\bar{\mu}, \bar{n}), \ldots, w^G(\bar{\mu}, \bar{n}))$, for which $w^g(\bar{\mu}, \bar{n}) \geq 0$ is the weight attached to the g subgroup inequality, assuming that it depends on $\bar{\mu}$ and $\bar{n}$. The between-group term is based on the smoothed distribution, $\chi(\bar{\mu}, \bar{n}) := \left(\mu^1 1^{n^1}, \mu^2 1^{n^2}, \ldots, \mu^G 1^{n^G} \right)$, which replaces the income of each person in the g subgroup with a correspondingly mean subgroup income, μ^g (1^{n^g} is n^g-coordinated vector of ones).

The *MLD* is additively decomposable, as shown below:

$$MLD\left(y^1, y^2, \ldots, y^G\right) = \sum_{g=1}^{G} w^g(\bar{\mu}, \bar{n}) MLD(y^g) + MLD(\chi(\bar{\mu}, \bar{n})). \tag{7}$$

Belonging to the family of Generalized Entropy measures, the *MLD* satisfies the above measure properties for that class. Still, the *MLD* is a particular instance of median-normalized inequality measures suggested by Reference [37]. These measures were devised by using the median (m) as the equality reference point; in contrast, mean income is adopted as a reference point for the mean-normalized GE.

A median-based class of Generalized Entropy inequality measures is defined as follows:

$$I_\alpha(y/m; \mu) := \frac{1}{\alpha(\alpha-1)} \frac{1}{n} \sum_{i=1}^{n} \left[\left(\frac{y_i}{m}\right)^\alpha - \left(\frac{\mu}{m}\right)^\alpha \right], \quad \alpha \neq 0, 1. \tag{8}$$

By applying de l'Hôpital's rule for $\alpha = 0$ and $\alpha = 1$, we obtain the following, respectively:

$$I_0(y/m; \mu) := -\frac{1}{n} \sum_{i=1}^{n} \ln \frac{y_i}{\mu}, \tag{9}$$

$$I_1(y/m; \mu) := \frac{1}{n} \sum_{i=1}^{n} \frac{y_i}{m} \ln \frac{y_i}{\mu}. \qquad (10)$$

Let us note that the particular case of the median-normalized inequality measures for $\alpha = 0$ is independent of the median, and Formula (9) describes the Mean Logarithmic Deviation index.

Cowell and Flachaire [37] demonstrated that the median-normalized inequality measures satisfy the property known as monotonicity in distance for $\alpha \geq 0$. The principle of monotonicity in distance was advanced by Cowell [18] as a certain generalization of the transfer principle. Magdalou and Nock [21] draw attention to the fact that the property is "quite demanding". The principle of monotonicity in distance means that a departure of any income, y_i, from the reference point, e, should be interpreted as an increase of inequality.

2.3. The MLD Decomposition by Subgroups

The decomposition criterion is to be met by inequality measures when the assessment of the level of income inequality in a population involves the premise that inequality is not an inherent characteristic of the community but a certain function of its component elements. It is assumed that the level of inequality in the entire society is contingent on the degree of inequality in the subgroups isolated on the basis of certain traits, and precisely those traits. This study sought to establish how the overall level of inequality may be decomposed into contributions resulting from (1) income inequality within each subgroup and (2) inequality between groups that arise from differences between the mean level of income in those subgroups.

Shorrocks [27] identified a class of relative inequality measures which are additively decomposable by subgroups. The Generalized Entropy measures—inclusive of the MLD—constitute a family of those measures. Subgroup decomposable indices are also known in the literature as additively decomposable or, more concisely, additive indices [45].

Let us assume yet again that the studied population into G of mutually exclusive and exhaustive subgroups. The Mean Logarithmic Deviation is additively decomposable in accordance with Formula (7), in which weights $w^g(\overline{\mu}, \overline{n})$ linked to the g subgroup income level equal $v^g = \frac{n^g}{n}$. In other words, the within-group term MLD_W is a weighted sum of inequalities in subgroups, and it is expressed in the following formula:

$$MLD_W = \sum_{g=1}^{G} w^g(\overline{\mu}, \overline{n}) MLD(y^g) = \sum_{g=1}^{G} \frac{n_g}{n} MLD(y^g). \qquad (11)$$

The within-group component describes a part of the overall inequality which is due to the inequalities in the subgroups.

Between-group term MLD_B quantifies income inequalities in the smoothed distribution $\left(\mu^1 1^{n^1}, \mu^2 1^{n^2}, \ldots, \mu^G 1^{n^G}\right)$, which would result from replacing each income, y_i, with the g subgroup mean income, in which the i person is classified. Therefore, the between-group component $MLD(\chi(\overline{\mu}, \overline{n}))$ found in Formula (7) may be expressed as follows:

$$MLD_B = \sum_{g=1}^{G} \frac{n_g}{n} \ln\left(\frac{\mu}{\mu_g}\right). \qquad (12)$$

In other words, the between-group component describes the scale of inequality resulting exclusively from the differences in mean income of the subgroups. The ratio of inequality between subgroups to overall inequality reflects the extent to which the feature on the basis of which the subgroups are distinguished contributes to household income inequality [46].

Theil [11] formulated a vital requirement that subgroup decomposable inequality measures should satisfy. Specifically, the within-group and their associated weights should be independent of the between-group component. This is because a major problem arises when mutually independent within-group and between-group terms cannot be defined. Shorrocks [27] and Anand [47] also highlight the problem, stressing that changes in inequality between groups can induce modifications not only in the between-group component but also in the within-group component, even if within-group income inequality has registered no change. With the issue in mind, Foster and Shneyerov [48] examine an additive decomposition property which they refer to as "path independent decomposability". This property requires that the between-group and within-group components be independent. Foster and Shneyerov [48] introduced a class of inequality measures which satisfy this property, designated as path-independent indices. Path-independent inequality measures have within-group terms that can be expressed as population-share weighted sums of the subgroup inequalities. Path-independent inequality measures have within-group terms that can be expressed as population-share weighted sums of the subgroup inequalities. The researchers demonstrate that the Mean Logarithmic Deviation and the variance of logarithms $V_L = \sum_{i=1}^{n} (\ln y_i - \ln \mu_g)^2 / n$ belong to this class and, thus, satisfy the path-independent decomposability property. The *MLD* index has a path-independent decomposition that uses the arithmetic mean as the representative income, while the variance of logarithms is path-independent relative to the geometric mean.

Another relevant issue involved in the interpretation of the results obtained from the decomposition of inequality measures was identified by Shorrocks [27]. This problem concerns the interpretation of statements such as "X per cent of inequality is due to Y". To understand this issue better, let us consider a possible answer to the question "What proportion of total inequality is due to income differences due to attribute (characteristic) Y?" This may be interpreted as follows: (1) What decrease in inequality will be observed if differences in the studied attribute Y are the only source of income differences? (2) How far will inequality decrease if income differences due to attribute Y disappear? Since these interpretations are equivalent modes of answering the same question, the inequality measure is expected to yield the same answer for both cases (1) and (2). Only inequality measures for which the weights of the within-group expressions do not depend on the subgroup means will generate the same answer for (1) and (2). Given that GEs are additively decomposable with weights $w^g(\overline{\mu}, \overline{n}) = \left(\frac{n^g}{n}\right)\left(\frac{\mu^g}{\mu}\right)^\alpha$ [20,27], there is only one member of the Generalized Entropy family to satisfy this property, namely the *MLD*. Therefore, Shorrocks (Reference [27], p. 625) underlines that the *MLD* "is the most satisfactory of the decomposable measures, allowing total inequality to be unambiguously split into the contribution due to differences between subgroups".

The decomposition of inequality indices by population subgroups has often been used to explain trends in income distribution. With the population divided into subgroups, the decomposed inequality (into within- and between-group components) in a given year may be expressed as a function of three components: subgroup population shares, subgroup mean incomes, and subgroup inequalities. The change in inequality between the two examined periods can therefore be linked to changes in these three components. Therefore, three main components are identified in the decomposition of the inequality trend, corresponding respectively to the following: changes in population structure (Δv^g), relative fluctuations in subgroup mean incomes ($\Delta \ln \mu_g$), and changes in subgroup inequality values ($\Delta MLD(y^g)$) [36]. Since the *MLD* is an index for which indices expressing subgroup inequality are weighted by subgroup shares in a population, Mookherjee and Shorrocks [36] show that changes in inequality between two periods (t_0 and t_1) can be noted as follows:

$$\Delta MLD = MLD(t_1) - MLD(t_0)$$
$$= \sum_{g=1}^{G} \overline{v}^g \Delta MLD(y^g) + \sum_{g=1}^{G} \overline{MLD}(y^g) \Delta v^g - \sum_{g=1}^{G} \overline{\ln \lambda^g} \Delta v^g - \sum_{g=1}^{G} \overline{v}^g \Delta \ln \lambda^g, \quad (13)$$

where Δ is the difference operator, and a bar over variables indicates an average of base and current period value ($\overline{v^g} = (v^g(t_0) + v^g(t_1))/2$, etc.).

The MLD can be approximately decomposed into the contributions of changes in inequality within groups, changes in inequality between groups, changes in the population share of each group, and changes in the subgroup means:

$$\approx \sum_{g=1}^{G} \overline{v}^g \Delta MLD(y^g) \underbrace{+ \sum_{g=1}^{G} \overline{MLD}(y^g) \Delta v^g}_{[\text{termB}]} \underbrace{+ \sum_{g=1}^{G} \left(\overline{\lambda^g} - \overline{\ln \lambda^g} \right) \Delta v^g}_{[\text{termC}]} \underbrace{+ \sum_{g=1}^{G} \left(\overline{\theta^g} - \overline{v}^g \right) \Delta \ln \mu_g}_{[\text{termD}]} , \quad (14)$$

The term A of the expression (14) represents the impact of changes in within-subgroup inequality ("pure" inequality changes); terms B and C indicate the effect of changes in the population shares on the within-group and between-group components (allocation effect); and term D (income effect) is the contribution to overall inequality change attributable to relative changes in the subgroup means [34,36].

Formula (14) is employed to assess changes in inequality, because, as Jenkins [34] argues, "the approximation is more useful than the exact decomposition because it relates inequality changes to changes in subgroup inequalities, shares and means (rather than relative means)".

3. Data

The current study employed data from the EU-SILC survey conducted by Eurostat. The EU-SILC is an annual EU-wide household survey which provides information on the income and living conditions of a sample of households. The micro-data were obtained under the project entitled *Income and inequality of income of European households* (RPP 162/2018-EU-SILC). The current study used data extracted from the cross-sectional database of the EU-SILC 2019 (version as of March 2021). As the EU-SILC adopts the preceding year as the income reference period for the vast majority of countries, including Poland, the data taken from 2005 and 2019 surveys cover information about incomes achieved by individual members of Polish households in 2004 and 2018, respectively.

Considering data availability, in 2005 and 2019, the samples of raw micro-data obtained from the cross-sectional EU-SILC data set spanned 16,263 households, i.e., 49,044 individuals and 19,874 households with 50,788 persons, respectively. Due to the lack of information on the education and age of the household head, the number of observations was limited to 48,916 individuals in 2005 and 43,935 persons in 2019. In the analysis, the authors also omitted 117 observations with zero and negative incomes in 2005 and disregarded 103 such observations in 2019. All the inequality measures reported in the study were calculated by using personal cross-sectional weights.

Throughout the empirical analysis, the authors employed the annual equivalized household disposable income per household member. The total household disposable income was calculated as a sum of gross personal income components for all household members and gross income components at the household level reduced by taxes, social insurance contributions, and inter-household cash transfers paid. To compensate for different household structures and possible economies of scale within households, household income was size-adjusted by dividing total income by the equivalized household size and assigning this value to each household member. To size-adjust household disposable income, the study used the OECD-modified equivalence scale, which assigns a weight of 1.0 to the head of household, 0.5 to every household member aged 14 or more, and 0.3 to each child aged under 14. Summing up the individual weights gives the equivalized household size.

For years, income inequality (as well as its sources) has been the subject of numerous studies. The micro-determinants of household income inequality, referred to in the relevant literature, can be assembled into two groups: sources of household income and sociodemographic attributes associated with the household and its members. In the current study, we focused on the personal characteristics of household members, specifically the head of household, and considered two possible drivers of inequality: the level of education and the age of the household head.

Various approaches to selecting the head of the household can be found in empirical research. Very often, the household head was considered to be the member of the household who had made the largest contribution to the household income [33,49]. Kranziger [50] designated the oldest member of the household as its head, while, in Papatheodorou's analysis [51] of inequality in Greece, the male was presumed to be the head of the household. In the current study, Medgyesi's approach [52] was employed; it defined the household head on a demographic basis. The oldest male of working age (16–64 years old) in the household was considered to be the head of the household. In case there was no such individual, the oldest working-age female was taken as the household head. If no working-age persons resided in the household, the oldest male member was considered the household head, or, alternatively, the oldest female was. We decided to follow Medgyesi because, due to the economic situation in Poland, housing shortages, as well as Polish culture, many young, well-educated people with high incomes share dwellings with their relatives. Even if their income exceeds that of their parents, the oldest working male (usually the father) is still considered the head of the household.

For the age of the head of household, the following household subgroups were distinguished: 18–35, 36–49, 50–64, and above 65 years of age. Figure 1a,b presents the estimation of the Kernel density of equivalized disposable income for the subgroups, which were distinguished based on the age of the household head in 2005 (Figure 1a) and 2019 (Figure 1b), respectively.

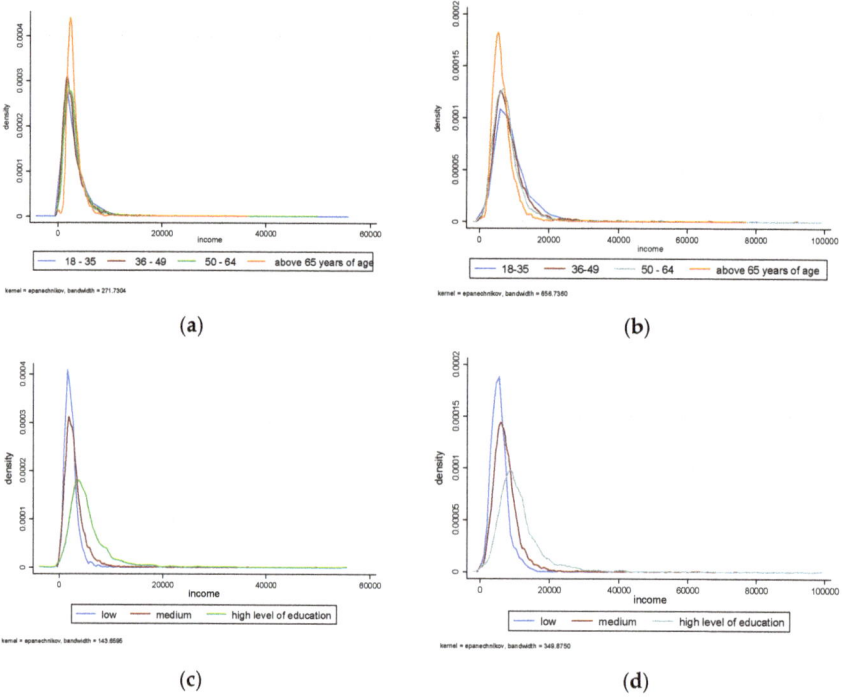

Figure 1. The Kernel density estimates of equivalized disposable income for the subgroups were distinguished based on the age of the household head in 2005 (**a**) and 2019 (**b**), and for the subgroups distinguished by the education of the household head in 2005 (**c**) and 2019 (**d**), respectively. Source: Own elaboration based on the EU-SILC data.

The estimation of the Kernel density of equivalized disposable income for the subgroups distinguished by the education of the household head in 2005 (Figure 1c) and 2019 (Figure 1d), respectively, is presented in Figure 1c,d.

In the SILC, the level of education is assigned according to the International Standard Classification of Education (ISCED 2011), which comprises nine categories of educational attainment. In the current analysis, it was decided to merge certain education levels and create three subgroups of households with low, medium, and high education levels of the household head. The first subgroup (low level) included early childhood education, primary, and lower secondary education. The subgroup of medium educational level would have completed upper-secondary and post-secondary education. The last subgroup (high level) included short-cycle tertiary, bachelor's, master's, doctoral, or equivalent education.

4. Empirical Analysis

The first step in the analysis was to estimate the level of household income inequality in Poland in both examined years. The level of income inequality measured by the value of the MLD of equivalized household disposable income amounted to 0.2319 in 2005 and to 0.1465 in 2019. Although the level of income inequality in both years can be considered moderate, there has been a significant decline in inequality between the years in question.

In analyzing income inequality in the current study, the authors focused on the personal attributes of the household head (age and education) as the possible determinant of income disparities between households. An attempt was made to assess the extent to which the selected factors affect household income inequality, as well as whether their impact is stable over time.

Table 1 presents the summary statistics on equivalized disposable income and population of the subgroups of households distinguished relative to the age of the household head.

Table 1. Summary statistics for the subgroups were distinguished based on the age of the household head.

Age	Population Share		Income Share		Relative Mean		MLD	
	2005	2019	2005	2019	2005	2019	2005	2019
18–35	0.170	0.121	0.177	0.138	1.038	1.142	0.276	0.158
36–49	0.378	0.345	0.361	0.364	0.957	1.054	0.257	0.156
50–64	0.369	0.424	0.378	0.407	1.025	0.960	0.215	0.138
above 65	0.083	0.109	0.084	0.090	1.004	0.825	0.097	0.103

Source: Own computations based on the EU-SILC data.

After dividing the households into four subgroups by the age of the household head, it was found that, in 2005, households headed by a person aged 36–49 were as common as households run by a person aged 50–64. Their share in the population was 37.8% and 36.9%, respectively. In 2005, the smallest share of the population (8.3%) lived in households run by a person aged above 65. While in the first year under study, two subgroups of household accounted for the dominant share of the population, in the second year, there were greater disparities in the proportion of the population. In 2019, the most numerous group of households was headed by a person aged 50–64, comprising over 42% of the population. The share of households run by the oldest persons (above 65) also increased. On the other hand, the shares of households headed by persons aged 36–49 and 18–35 decreased to 34.5% and 12.1%, respectively. The changes observed in the structure of households confirm the aging of Polish society.

An examination of the level and structure of income indicated that, in 2005 the average income of the defined subgroups was very close to the Polish average. The youngest households achieved the highest average income, but it was only 3.8% higher than the national average. The lowest average income was achieved by households run by a person aged 36–49. Their average income was 4.3% lower than the national one. A different situation was observed in 2019, when there was a negative correlation between the age of the household head and the average income in the subgroups. The youngest households achieved the highest average income, exceeding the national by 14.2%. The average income of households headed by a person aged 36–49 was also higher than the national average, but only by 5.4%. The remaining subgroups, run by people aged 50–64 and above 65, achieved lower average income than the national average by 4% and 17.5%, respectively.

The unfavorable changes observed in the case of households headed by the oldest persons indicate a deterioration of their relative income situation.

It was also found that, in 2005, the structure of income corresponded to the structure of the population. The largest proportion of income was distributed among the most numerous subgroups, where household heads were aged 36–49 and 50–64, with a slight advantage of the latter. Their shares in the structure of income amounted to 36.1% and 37.8%, respectively. In 2019, households headed by a person aged 50–64 increased their share in the income structure to over 40%, while the share of the youngest households decreased by approximately 4 percentage points. The shares of households run by people aged 36–49 and aged above 65 remained almost unchanged.

The overall income inequality consists of both the differences between average income in the distinguished subgroups and the differentiation of income within these subgroups. Despite the differences in average incomes of the subgroups distinguished by the age of the household head, more inequality was observed within the subgroups than between them. In both examined years, the only subgroup with significantly lower inequality than overall inequality was that of the oldest households. It was also the only subgroup in which there was a slight increase in inequality between the studied years.

With respect to the level of income inequality within the distinguished subgroups, a negative correlation was found between the age of the household head and the level of inequality; that is, the older the head of the household, the lower the level of income inequality within the subgroup. It was also observed that in 2019 a higher average income of the subgroup was accompanied by a higher level of inequality.

To assess whether the age of the household head contributes to household income inequality, we employed the ratio of inequality between subgroups to overall inequality. The results of the *MLD* decomposition are presented in Table 2.

Table 2. Results of the *MLD* static decomposition.

	2005			2019		
	MLD_W	MLD_B	Ratio	MLD_W	MLD_B	Ratio
Age	0.2313	0.0006	0.3%	0.1427	0.0039	2.6%
Education	0.1953	0.0365	15.8%	0.1231	0.0234	16.0%

Source: Own computations based on the EU-SILC data.

It was determined that the age of the household head was of negligible importance in 2005, and it accounted for 0.3% of overall inequality. However, the importance of this determinant increased significantly in 2019, and the ratio of the between-group component to overall inequality was almost tenfold higher. It may be expected that the observed process of the aging of society will entail a further increase in the importance of the age of the household head as a factor in household income inequality.

The level of education of the household head was the second factor to be analyzed. The summary statistics reflecting equivalized disposable income and population of the subgroups of households distinguished by education of the household head are presented in Table 3. As a result of dividing households on this basis, three subgroups of households were obtained with a "low", "medium", or "high" education level of the household head. As regards the structure of the household population, it was found that the subgroup of households run by a person with a medium level of education was the most numerous in both examined years. While the dominant share of households with medium education of the household head was expected, substantial changes were noted in the proportions of the population in the remaining subgroups between the studied years. In 2005, households run by a person with a low level of education accounted for 21.5%, whereas households headed by a person with a high education level constituted 12.7%. In 2019, the opposite was observed. The share of households with a low-educated household head decreased to 11%, while the proportion of households headed by a highly educated person rose to 23%.

The observed changes may have been due to "the fashion for having higher education" (even inconsistent with one's adopted profession) prevailing in Poland in the first decade of the 21st century.

Table 3. Summary statistics for the subgroups distinguished by the education of the household head.

Education	Population Share		Income Share		Relative Mean		MLD	
	2005	2019	2005	2019	2005	2019	2005	2019
Low	0.215	0.110	0.156	0.077	0.725	0.701	0.162	0.104
Medium	0.659	0.660	0.620	0.601	0.941	0.911	0.204	0.116
High	0.127	0.230	0.224	0.322	1.773	1.398	0.206	0.153

Source: Own computations based on the EU-SILC data.

As for the distribution of income among the distinguished subgroups, the share of income of the "medium" group corresponded to its share in the population. Households in this subgroup accounted for 66% of the population and accumulated over 60% of income. The smallest part of income belonged to households headed by a person with a low level of education. In 2005, the share of this subgroup in income accounted for 15.6% and decreased twofold between the studied years, as did its share in the population. A reverse tendency was observed in the subgroup of households run by a person with a high level of education. As in the population, the income share of the "high" subgroup rose by ten percentage points.

The average income of a household run by persons with a low or medium level of education was lower than the average income in Poland and amounted to 70% and 90% of the national average, respectively. The highest average income was observed in the "high" subgroup, although the advantage in relation to the national average decreased by almost half in the examined years, from 77% to 40%. When comparing the average income in the defined subgroups, we found a positive correlation between income and education, and a higher education level of the household head coincided with a higher level of income inequality within the subgroup. In the examined years, the level of within-group inequality decreased significantly. The most substantial drop (over 43%) was recorded in the subgroup of households run by a person with a medium level of education. In the subgroups of households with "low" and "high" education level of the household head, the declines were also considerable, but not that high, and amounted to 36% and 26%, respectively.

The ratio of inequality between subgroups to overall inequality was 16% in both analyzed years (Table 2). This means that, if the average incomes of the subgroups distinguished on the basis of the education of the household head were equal, and within-group inequality remained unchanged, the level of overall income inequality would decrease by 16%. The high ratio confirmed the role of education as a determinant of income inequality. In 2005, the impact of education of the household head on household income inequality was significant, and its importance did not change over time.

In order to identify the factors associated with changes in income inequality in 2005–2019, a dynamic decomposition of the *MLD* was used. The results are presented in Table 4.

Table 4. Results of the *MLD* dynamic decomposition.

	Within-Group Component		Between-Group Component	
	Inequality Effect	Allocation Effect		Income Effect
Age	−98.1%	−5.8%	0.0%	3.9%
Education	−92.4%	5.8%	9.9%	−23.2%

Source: Own computations based on the EU-SILC data.

The overall change in income inequality was partitioned into four components. The first component, showing the effect of inequality, described the impact of changes on within-group inequality. The allocation effect, broken down into two components, showed how changes in population shares affected the within-group and between-group component, respectively. The latter component represented the income effect. It showed the impact of relative changes in the average incomes of the distinguished subgroups.

In the study, the level of household income inequality was analyzed in two distributions: by age and by the level of education of the household head. As shown in Table 4, the decline in household income inequality in Poland in both distributions resulted chiefly from the decline in within-group inequality. Changes in the population structure by age, i.e., an increase in the share of households run by persons aged 50+, contributed to a decline in the level of income inequality, reducing the within-group component. On the other hand, relative changes in the average income of the age subgroups fostered an increase in the level of inequality. The changes observed in the structure of the household population with respect to the education of the household head adversely affected the level of income inequality, contributing to its increase and adding to the within-group and between-group component alike. However, relative changes in the average income of the subgroups distinguished by education supported a decrease in the level of inequality.

5. Discussion and Conclusions

The empirical aim of the study was to assess the extent to which education and age affect household income inequality, as well as whether their impact is stable over time. Therefore, in order to attain the aim, our analysis was based on micro-data obtained from the EU-SILC database and employed MLD as a research tool.

The literature on the subject indicates education as one of the most crucial factors influencing income inequality. However, the impact of education on income inequality is yet to be fully understood and may differ from economy to economy. The association of education and income inequality is also frequently examined in empirical studies, and their results—sometimes contradictory—reflect the complexity of the discussed issue. Chevan and Stokes [53] even refer to education as "the Pandora's box of income inequality", claiming that both low and high levels of education can foster income inequality. Checchi [54] claims that facilitated access to tertiary education can increase earning opportunities of the poorest groups of the population and can lead to a reduction of income inequality. Moreover, Rodríguez-Pose and Tselios [55] confirm that education is considered one of the most powerful known instruments for reducing income inequality. However, they emphasize that an increase in the share of the population with tertiary education leads to a reduction of the value of education and, in the longer term, to a decrease in the wages of some workers with tertiary education.

The current study confirmed an association between the level of education and the average income of the groups distinguished on this basis. Based on the obtained results, it can be concluded that the education level of the household head remains an important determinant of household income inequality in Poland, despite the decline in the "educational bonus". Although the predominance of average income of households with "high" education of the household head, over the national average, has almost halved (from 77% to 40%), the differences in the level of education still account for 16% of income inequality. The current results are in line with the results of other empirical studies on the causes of income inequality [32,52,56]. All of these studies confirmed that, in the post-transition countries, the level of education remains one of the important sources of income inequality.

The current study also found that differences in the age of the household head had a smaller effect on income inequality than the level of education. Since the results have shown that only 2.6% of income inequality can be explained by the age of the household head, the contribution of this characteristic to total income inequality may seem to be negligible. However, the results prove that the aging of the population can foster income inequality in Poland and may increase the impact of age on income inequality. The results achieved are in line with the report of the RAND Corporation [57], which points out that income inequality in Europe is sensitive to an aging of population.

Brandolini and D'Alessio [58] indicate that the age structure of population can affect income inequality because the amount and composition of personal incomes (from work, property, and transfer) vary over life, and also because individual experiences mirror the different historical periods. Typically, an individual's income over the entire life is hump-shaped: it usually increases from the moment of entering the labor market to approximately the age of 65 and then decreases when the income from work is replaced by the income from pension. However, a precise form of the hump-shaped curve is not fixed and responds to redistribution between generations due to changes in labor market relations and the trends in economic and social policies. The current study does not reveal the inverted U-shape (hump-shaped) pattern in household incomes in Poland, but it does confirm the deterioration of the relative income situation in the case of households headed by the oldest persons.

Household income may not confirm the hump-shaped pattern due to the fact that the household, by accumulating and redistributing the income of its members, acts as a redistributor of resources [59]. Households combine the incomes of all their members, thereby equalizing their level and eliminating the income disparities within the household, and this, in turn, reduces the income inequality between households.

However, the aging of the population may substantially reduce the redistributive role of the household. Therefore, it can be concluded that the higher share of older people may contribute to an increase in income inequality between groups, as the income from pension in Poland is more homogeneous than the income from work in younger groups.

In addition to empirical research, the current paper sought to situate Theil's approach in the context of scholarly writings since 1967, and the Mean Logarithmic Deviation was selected because of its attractive properties. Firstly, the choice of the MLD resulted from an emphasis on the sensitivity of this measure to the lower tail of the income distribution. Secondly, as discussed at length in this paper, the MLD shares many of the well-established properties of the Generalized Entropy measures, the median-normalized inequality measures, and path-independent inequality measures. The MLD also respects the principle of monotonicity in distance and is decomposable for arbitrary partitions with the path-independence property. As Cowell and Flachaire [37] showed, the lack of the principle of monotonicity in distance may have strong implications in empirical studies. Moreover, the properties of additive decomposition fulfilled by MLD cannot be overestimated, namely the between-group and within-group components are independent, and the weights of the within-group expressions do not depend on the subgroup means.

The empirical study was based on the income data derived directly from the household survey. When using such data, it should be remembered that low- and high-income households can be underrepresented in the survey data due to the fact that people often refuse to provide any information about their income or understate it. As a result, the measures of income inequality can be underestimated. Furthermore, different approaches to selecting the head of the household can affect the results of empirical studies.

Author Contributions: Conceptualization, E.W. and J.M.; methodology, E.W.; software, J.M.; validation, E.W. and J.M.; formal analysis E.W.; investigation, J.M.; resources, E.W. and J.M.; data curation, E.W. and J.M.; writing—original draft preparation E.W. and J.M.; writing—E.W. and J.M.; visualization, E.W. and J.M.; supervision, E.W. and J.M.; project administration, E.W. and J.M.; funding acquisition, E.W. and J.M. All authors have read and agreed to the published version of the manuscript.

Funding: The research was financed from resources of the Faculty of Economic Sciences and Management, Nicolaus Copernicus University in Toruń, Poland.

Institutional Review Board Statement: Not applicable.

Informed Consent Statement: Not applicable.

Data Availability Statement: Restrictions apply to the availability of these data. Data were obtained from Eurostat and are only available from Eurostat.

Acknowledgments: This paper was developed as part of the research project *Income and Inequality of Income of European Households* (Eurostat, No. 162/2018-EU-SILC) and is based on data from Eurostat, EU Statistics on Income and Living Conditions—EU-SILC CROSS-SECTIONAL UDB 2019–version 2021-03. The responsibility for all conclusions drawn from the data lies entirely with the authors.

Conflicts of Interest: The authors declare no conflict of interest.

References

1. Wang, Q.A. Probability distribution and entropy as a measure of uncertainty. *J. Phys. A Math. Theor.* **2008**, *41*, 065004. [CrossRef]
2. Clausius, R. *The Mechanical Theory of Heat*; McMillan and Co.: London, UK, 1865; pp. 1–376.
3. Boltzmann, L. Weitere Studien über das Wärmegleichgewicht unter Gasmolekülen. *Kinet. Theor. II WTB Wiss. Taschenb.* **1970**, *67*, 111–225. [CrossRef]
4. Gibbs, J.W. *Elementary Principles in Statistical Mechanics—Developed with Especial References to the Rational*; C. Scribner's Sons: New York, NY, USA, 1902; pp. 1–207.
5. Shannon, C.A. A Mathematical Theory of Communication. *Bell Syst. Tech. J.* **1948**, *27*, 379–423. [CrossRef]
6. Kolmogorov, A.N. A new metric invariant of transitive dynamical systems and Lebesgue space. *Dokl. Russ. Acad. Sci.* **1958**, *119*, 851–864.
7. Rényi, A. On measures of entropy and information. In *Berkeley Symposium on Mathematical Statistics and Probability*; Neyman, J., Ed.; University of California Press: Berkeley, CA, USA, 1961; pp. 547–561.
8. Tsallis, C. Possible generalization of Boltzmann–Gibbs statistics. *J. Stat. Phys.* **1988**, *52*, 479–487. [CrossRef]
9. Lesne, A. Shannon entropy: A rigorous notion at the crossroads between probability, information theory, dynamical systems and statistical physics. *Math. Struct. Comput. Sci.* **2014**, *24*, e240311. [CrossRef]
10. Chakravarty, S.R.; Weymark, J.A. Axiomatizations of the entropy numbers equivalent index of industrial concentration. In *Measurement in Economics. Theory and Applications of Economic Indices*; Eichhorn, W., Ed.; Springer: Berlin/Heidelberg, Germany, 1988; pp. 383–398.
11. Theil, H. *Economics and Information Theory*; North-Holland Publishing Company: Amsterdam, The Netherlands, 1967; pp. 1–488.
12. Cowell, F.A. Generalized entropy and the measurement of distributional. *Eur. Econ. Rev.* **1980**, *13*, 147–159. [CrossRef]
13. Cowell, F.A. Theil, Inequality and the Structure of Income Distribution. DARP Discussion Paper 2003. Available online: http://eprints.lse.ac.uk/2288/1/Theil%2C_Inequality_and_the_Structure_of_Income_Distribution.pdf (accessed on 20 February 2022).
14. Cowell, F.A.; Kuga, K. Additivity and the entropy concept: An axiomatic approach to inequality measurement. *J. Econ. Theory* **1981**, *25*, 131–143. [CrossRef]
15. Csiszár, I. Information-Type Measures of Difference of Probability Distributions and Indirect Observations. *Studia Sci. Math. Hung.* **1967**, *2*, 299–318.
16. Talih, M. A reference-invariant health disparity index based on R'enyi divergence. *Ann. Appl. Stat.* **2013**, *7*, 1217–1243. [CrossRef]
17. Shorrocks, A.F. Inequality Decomposition by Population Subgroups. *Econometrica* **1984**, *52*, 1369–1385. [CrossRef]
18. Cowell, F.A. Measures of distributional change: An axiomatic approach. *Rev. Econ. Stud.* **1985**, *52*, 135–151. [CrossRef]
19. Jenkins, S.P.; O'Higgins, M. Inequality measurement using 'norm incomes': Were Garvy and Paglin onto something after all? *Rev. Income Wealth* **1989**, *35*, 265–282. [CrossRef]
20. Foster, J.E.; Shneyerov, A.A. A general class of additively decomposable inequality measures. *Econ. Theory* **1999**, *14*, 89–111. [CrossRef]
21. Magdalou, B.; Nock, R. Income Distributions and Decomposable Divergence Measures. *J. Econ. Theory* **2011**, *146*, 2440–2454. [CrossRef]
22. Cowell, F.A.; Flachaire, E.; Bandyopadhyay, S. Reference distributions and inequality measurement. *J. Econ. Inequal.* **2013**, *11*, 241–437. [CrossRef]
23. Rodhe, N. J-divergence measurements of economic inequality. *J. R. Stat. Soc. Ser. A* **2016**, *179*, 847–870. [CrossRef]
24. Foster, J.E. An axiomatic characterization of the Theil measure of income inequality. *J. Econ. Theory* **1983**, *31*, 105–121. [CrossRef]
25. Lasso de la Vega, C.; Volij, O. A simple proof of Foster's (1983) characterization of the Theil measure of inequality. *Econ. Model.* **2013**, *35*, 940–943. [CrossRef]
26. Bourguignon, F. Decomposable Income Inequality Measures. *Econometrica* **1979**, *47*, 901–920. [CrossRef]
27. Shorrocks, A.F. The Class of Additively Decomposable Inequality Measures. *Econometrica* **1980**, *48*, 613–625. [CrossRef]
28. Elbers, C.; Lanjouw, P.; Mistiaen, J.A.; Özler, B. Reinterpreting between-group inequality. *J. Econ. Inequal.* **2008**, *6*, 231–245. [CrossRef]
29. Shorrocks, A.F. Aggregation Issues in Inequality Measurement. In *Measurement in Economics. Theory and Applications of Economic Indices*; Eichhorn, W., Ed.; Springer: Berlin/Heidelberg, Germany, 1988; pp. 429–451.
30. Shorrocks, A.F. Inequality Decomposition by Factor Components. *Econometrica* **1982**, *50*, 193–211. [CrossRef]
31. Paulus, A. Income inequality and its decomposition: The case of Estonia. In *Modelling the Economies of the Baltic Sea Region*; Pass, T., Tafenau, E., Eds.; Tartu University Press: Tartu, Estonia, 2004; pp. 206–235.
32. Militaru, E.; Stanila, L. Income variability in Romania: Decomposing income inequality by household characteristics. *Procedia Econ. Financ.* **2015**, *26*, 227–233. [CrossRef]

33. Muszyńska, J.; Wędrowska, E. Income Inequality of Households in Poland: A Subgroup Decomposition of Generalized Entropy Measures. *Econom. Ekonom. Adv. Appl. Data Anal.* **2018**, *22*, 43–64. [CrossRef]
34. Jenkins, S.P. Accounting for Inequality Trends: Decomposition Analyses for the UK, 1971–86. *Economica* **1995**, *62*, 29–63. [CrossRef]
35. Sarabia, J.M.; Jorda, V.; Remuzgo, L. The Theil indices in parametric families of income distributions—A short review. *Rev. Income Wealth* **2017**, *63*, 867–880. [CrossRef]
36. Mookherjee, D.; Shorrocks, A.F. A Decomposition Analysis of the Trend in UK Income Inequality. *Econ. J.* **1982**, *92*, 886–902. [CrossRef]
37. Cowell, F.A.; Flachaire, E. Inequality Measurement and the Rich: Why Inequality Increased More than We Thought. STICERD—Public Economics Programme Discussion Papers 2018. Available online: https://sticerd.lse.ac.uk/dps/pep/pep36.pdf (accessed on 2 August 2021).
38. Itti, L.; Baldi, P. A principled approach to detecting surprising events in video. In Proceedings of the 2005 IEEE Computer Society Conference on Computer Vision and Pattern Recognition (CVPR'05), San Diego, CA, USA, 20–25 June 2005. [CrossRef]
39. Roberto, E. The Divergence Index: A Decomposable Measure of Segregation and Inequality. 2016. Available online: https://arxiv.org/abs/1508.01167 (accessed on 24 July 2021).
40. Coulter, P.B. *Measuring Inequality: A Methodological Handbook*; Westview Press: Boulder, CO, USA, 1989; pp. 1–216.
41. Sen, A. *On Economic Inequality*; Clarendon Press: Oxford, UK, 1973; pp. 1–276. [CrossRef]
42. Kolm, S.C. The Optimal Production of Social Justice. In *Public Economics*; Margolis, J., Guitton, H., Eds.; Macmillan: London, UK, 1969; pp. 145–200.
43. Atkinson, A.B. On the measurement of inequality. *J. Econ. Theory* **1970**, *2*, 244–263. [CrossRef]
44. Magdalou, B. Income inequality measurement: A fresh look at two old issues. *Soc. Choice Welf.* **2018**, *51*, 415–435. [CrossRef]
45. Charkavarty, S.R. The Variance as a Subgroup Decomposable Measure of Inequality. *Soc. Indic. Res.* **2001**, *53*, 79–95. [CrossRef]
46. Muszyńska, J.; Wędrowska, E. The effect of household type on income inequality: Evidence from the EU-15 countries. In Proceedings of the 36th International Business Information Management Association Conference (IBIMA): Sustainable Economic Development and Advancing Education Excellence in the Era of Global Pandemic, Granada, Spain, 4–5 November 2020.
47. Anand, S. *Inequality and Poverty in Malaysia: Measurement and Decomposition*; Oxford University Press: New York, NY, USA, 1983; pp. 1–371. [CrossRef]
48. Foster, J.E.; Shneyerov, A.A. Path Independent Inequality Measures. *J. Econ. Theory* **2000**, *91*, 199–222. [CrossRef]
49. Turcinkova, J.; Stavkova, J. Does the Attained Level of Education Affect the Income Situation of Households? *Procedia-Soc. Behav. Sci.* **2012**, *55*, 1036–1042. [CrossRef]
50. Kranzinger, S. The decomposition of income inequality in the EU-28. *Empirica* **2020**, *47*, 643–668. [CrossRef]
51. Papatheodorou, C. Decomposing Inequality by Population Subgroups in Greece: Results and Policy Implications. DARP Discission Paper 2000. Available online: http://eprints.lse.ac.uk/6568/1/Decomposing_Inequality_in_Greece_Results_and_Policy_Implications.pdf (accessed on 23 February 2022).
52. Medgyesi, M. Components of income inequality and its change in EU countries, 2004–2010. ImPRovE Discussion Paper 2014, 14/01. Available online: https://www.researchgate.net/publication/312552806_Components_of_income_inequality_and_its_change_in_EU_countries_2004-2010 (accessed on 23 February 2022).
53. Chevan, A.; Stokes, R. Growth in family income inequality, 1970–1990: Industrial restructuring and demographic change. *Demography* **2000**, *37*, 365–380. [CrossRef] [PubMed]
54. Checchi, D. Does Educational Achievement Help to Explain Income Inequality? Working Papers of Department of Economics, University of Milan 2000. Available online: http://wp.demm.unimi.it/files/wp/2000/DEMM-2000_011wp.pdf (accessed on 23 February 2022).
55. Rodríguez-Pose, A.; Tselios, V. Education and income inequality in the regions of the European Union. *J. Reg. Sci.* **2009**, *49*, 411–437. [CrossRef]
56. Muszyńska, J.; Wędrowska, E. Income inequality in the Visegrad Group countries. Decomposition of Generalized Entropy measures. In Proceedings of the 12th International Days of Statistics and Economics, Prague, Czech Republic, 6–8 September 2018.
57. Guerin, B. Demography and Inequality: How Europe's Changing Population will Impact on Income Inequality. RAND Corporation Report 2013. Available online: https://www.rand.org/pubs/research_reports/RR183.html (accessed on 23 February 2022).
58. Brandolini, A.; D'Alessio, G. Household Structure and Income Inequality, LIS Working Paper Series 2001. Available online: http://hdl.handle.net/10419/160926 (accessed on 23 February 2022).
59. Blossfeld, H.P.; Buchholz, S. Increasing resource inequality among families in modern societies: The mechanisms of growing educational homogamy, changes in the division of work in the family and the decline of the male breadwinner model. *J. Comp. Fam. Stud.* **2009**, *40*, 603–616. [CrossRef]

Article

Causal Inference in Time Series in Terms of Rényi Transfer Entropy

Petr Jizba [1,*,†], Hynek Lavička [1,†,‡] and Zlata Tabachová [2,†]

1. Faculty of Nuclear Sciences and Physical Engineering, Czech Technical University in Prague, Břehová 7, 115 19 Prague, Czech Republic; hynek.lavicka@fjfi.cvut.cz
2. Complexity Science Hub Vienna, Josefstädter Straße 39, 1080 Vienna, Austria; zlata.tabachova@fjfi.cvut.cz
* Correspondence: p.jizba@fjfi.cvut.cz; Tel.: +420-775-317-309
† These authors contributed equally to this work.
‡ Current address: Blocksize Capital GmbH, Taunusanlage 8, D-60329 Frankfurt am Main, Germany.

Abstract: Uncovering causal interdependencies from observational data is one of the great challenges of a nonlinear time series analysis. In this paper, we discuss this topic with the help of an information-theoretic concept known as Rényi's information measure. In particular, we tackle the directional information flow between bivariate time series in terms of Rényi's transfer entropy. We show that by choosing Rényi's parameter α, we can appropriately control information that is transferred only between selected parts of the underlying distributions. This, in turn, is a particularly potent tool for quantifying causal interdependencies in time series, where the knowledge of "black swan" events, such as spikes or sudden jumps, are of key importance. In this connection, we first prove that for Gaussian variables, Granger causality and Rényi transfer entropy are entirely equivalent. Moreover, we also partially extend these results to heavy-tailed α-Gaussian variables. These results allow establishing a connection between autoregressive and Rényi entropy-based information-theoretic approaches to data-driven causal inference. To aid our intuition, we employed the Leonenko et al. entropy estimator and analyzed Rényi's information flow between bivariate time series generated from two unidirectionally coupled Rössler systems. Notably, we find that Rényi's transfer entropy not only allows us to detect a threshold of synchronization but it also provides non-trivial insight into the structure of a transient regime that exists between the region of chaotic correlations and synchronization threshold. In addition, from Rényi's transfer entropy, we could reliably infer the direction of coupling and, hence, causality, only for coupling strengths smaller than the onset value of the transient regime, i.e., when two Rössler systems are coupled but have not yet entered synchronization.

Keywords: Rényi entropy; Rényi transfer entropy; Rössler system; multivariate time series

1. Introduction

The time evolution of a complex system is usually recorded in the form of a time series. Time series analysis is a traditional field of mathematical statistics; however, the development of nonlinear dynamical systems and the theory of deterministic chaos have opened up new vistas in the analysis of nonlinear time series [1,2]. The discovery of the synchronization of chaotic systems [3] has changed the study of interactions and cooperative behavior of complex systems and brought new approaches to studying the relations between nonlinear time series [4]. During the process of synchronization, two systems can either mutually interact or only one can influence the other. In order to distinguish these two ways, and to find which system is the driver ("master") and which is the response ("slave") system, a number of approaches from the dynamical system theory have been proposed [5–8]. The aforementioned problem of synchronization can be seen as part of a broader framework known as *causality* or *causal relations between systems*, processes, or phenomena. The mathematical formulation of causality, in terms of predictability, was first proposed by Wiener [9] and formulated for the time series by

Granger [10]. In particular, Granger introduced what is now known as *Granger causality*, which is a statistical concept of causality that is based on the evaluation of predictability in bivariate autoregressive models.

Extracting causal interdependencies from observational data is one of the key tasks in a nonlinear time series analysis. Apart from the linear Granger causality and various nonlinear extensions thereof [11–13], existing methods for this purpose include state-space-based approaches, such as conditional probabilities of recurrence [14–16], or information-theoretic quantities, such as conditional mutual information [17,18] and *transfer entropies* [2,19–21]. In particular, the latter information-theoretic quantities represent powerful instruments in quantifying causality between time-evolving systems. This is because ensuing information-theoretic functionals (typically based on Shannon entropy) quantify—in a non-parametric and explicitly non-symmetric way—the flow of information between two (or more) time series. In particular, transfer entropies (TEs) have recently received considerable attention. The catalyst was the infusion of new (numerical and conceptional) ideas. For instance, the performances of the Shannon entropy-based conditional entropies and conditional mutual entropies have been, in recent years, extensively tested using numerically-generated time series [17,22]. Sophisticated algorithms have been developed to uncover direct causal relations in multivariate time series [23–25]. In parallel, increasing attention has been devoted to the development of reliable estimators of entropic functionals to detect causality from nonlinear time series [26]. At the same time, it has been recognized that information-theoretic approaches play important roles in dealing with complex dynamical systems that are multiscale and/or non-Gaussian [21,27–29]. The latter class includes complex systems with heavy-tailed probability distributions epitomized, e.g., in financial and climatological time series [30,31].

In this paper, we extend the popular Shannon entropy-based TE (STE), which represents a prominent tool for assessing directed information flow between joint processes, and quantifies information transfer in terms of *Rényi's TE* (RTE). RTE was introduced by one of us (PJ) in reference [21] in the context of a bivariate financial time series. The original idea was to use the RTE in order to exploit the theoretical formulation that could identify and quantify peculiar features in multiscale bivariate processes (e.g., multiscale patterns, generalized fractal dimensions, or multifractal cross-correlations) that are often seen in finance. In contrast to [21], where the focus was mostly on qualitative aspects of Rényian information flow between selected stock-market time series, in the present work, we wish to be more quantitative by analyzing coupled time series that are numerically generated from known dynamics. Specifically, we demonstrate how *the RTE method performs in the detection of the coupling direction and onset of synchronization between two Rössler oscillators* [32] *that are unidirectionally coupled in the first variable x*. The Rössler system (RS) is a paradigmatic and well-studied low-dimensional chaotic dynamical system. When coupled, RSs allow for *synchronization* as well as a subtle phenomenon known as "phase synchronization", i.e., when the amplitudes of both systems are not correlated while the phases are approximately equal. In this respect, the synthetic bivariate time series (generated from coupled RSs) serves as an excellent test-bed, allowing to numerically analyze, e.g., drive–response relationships or identify the ensuing onset (or threshold) of synchronization. In doing so, we identify factors and influences that can lead to either decreases in the RTE sensitivity or false detections and propose some ways to cope with them. The aforementioned issues have not been explicitly studied in the framework of the RTE; this work presents the first attempt in this direction.

To set the stage, we shall first, in Section 2, provide the information-theoretic background on Rényi entropy (RE), which will be needed in the main body of the text. For self-consistency of our exposition, we briefly review Shannon's transfer entropy of Schreiber and motivate and derive the core quantity of this work—the Rényi transfer entropy. The issue of causality (and its connection to RTE) is examined in Section 3. In particular, we prove that the Granger causality is entirely equivalent to the RTE for Gaussian processes and show how the Granger causality and the RTE are related in the case of heavy-tailed (namely α-Gaussian) processes. Section 4 is dedicated to derived information-theoretic concepts, such as the balance of transfer entropy and effective transfer entropy that will be employed in our analysis. The proposed framework is then illustrated on two unidirectionally coupled Rössler systems as a paradigmatic example. To cultivate our intuition about the latter RSs, we discuss in Section 5 the inner workings of such RSs in terms of simple numerical experiments. The ensuing numerical analysis is presented in Section 6, where we discuss how the RTE can be used to detect causality and the onset of synchronization in the two coupled RSs. We also demonstrate how the RTE provides non-trivial insight into the structure of a transient regime that exists between the regions of chaotic correlations and the onset of synchronization. Finally, Section 7 summarizes our theoretical and numerical findings and discusses possible extensions of the present work. For the reader's convenience, we relegate some technical issues concerning the RE estimator employed and the statistical significance of results presented to Appendices A and B.

2. Rényi Entropy

Information theory approaches based on Shannon entropy currently belong in the portfolio of techniques and tools that are indispensable in addressing causality issues in complex dynamical systems. At the same time, Shannon's information theory is limited in its scope. In fact, since Shannon's seminal papers [33], it has been known that Shannon's information measure (or entropy) represents mere idealized information, appearing only in situations when the buffer memory (or storage capacity) of a transmitting channel is infinite. In particular, Shannon's source coding theorem (or noiseless coding theorem), which establishes the limits to possible data compression and, thus, provides operational meaning to the Shannon entropy, assumes that the *cost* of a codeword is a linear function of its length (so the optimal code has a minimal cost out of all codes). However, the linear costs of codewords are not always desirable. For instance, when the storage capacity is finite one would aim to penalize excessively lengthy codewords with a price that is, e.g., exponential rather than the linear function of the length.

For these reasons, information theorists have devised various remedies to deal with such cases. This usually consists of substituting Shannon's information measure with information measures of other types. Consequently, numerous generalizations of Shannon's entropy have started to proliferate in the information-theory literature, ranging from additive entropies [34,35] to a rich class of non-additive entropies [36–40], to more exotic types of entropies [41]. The one-parametric class of information measures, known as *Rényi entropies*, introduced by Hungarian mathematician and information theorist Alfred Rényi in the early 1960s [42,43], is particularly prominent among such generalizations. Applications of RE in information theory, namely its generalization to coding theorems, were carried over by Campbel [44], Csiszár [45,46], Aczél [47], and others. In a physical setting, RE was popularized in the context of chaotic dynamical systems by Kadanoff et al. [48] and in connection with multifractals by Mandelbrot [49]. RE is also indispensable in the quantum information theory where it quantifies multipartite entanglement [50].

In its essence, REs constitute a one-parametric family of information measures labeled by parameter α, fulfilling the additivity with respect to the composition of statistically independent systems. The special case with $\alpha = 1$ corresponds to ordinary Shannon's entropy. REs belong to a broader class of so-called Uffink entropic functionals [51,52], i.e., the most general class of solutions that satisfy Shorem–Johnson axioms for the maximum entropy principle in the statistical estimation theory. Moreover, it might be shown that Rényi entropies belong to the class of the so-called mixing homomorphic functions [53] and that they are analytic for $\alpha \in \mathbb{C}_{I \cup IV}$, cf. [34].

2.1. Definition

RE is defined as an exponentially weighted mean of the *Hartley information measure* $-\log p$ (i.e., elementary measure of information) [54]. In fact, it was shown by Rényi that, except for a linearly-weighted average (which leads to Shannon entropy), exponential weighting is the only possible averaging that is both compatible with the Kolmogorov–Nagumo average prescription and leads to entropies that are additive, with respect to independent systems [42,43]. RE, associated with a system described with a probability distribution $\mathcal{P}$, reads

$$H_\alpha[\mathcal{P}] = \frac{1}{1-\alpha} \log_2 \sum_{i=1}^n p_i^\alpha. \tag{1}$$

RE has the following properties [34,43]:

- RE is symmetric, i.e., $H_\alpha[\{p_1,\ldots,p_n\}] = H_\alpha[\{p_{\pi(1)},\ldots,p_{\pi(n)}\}]$;
- RE is non-negative, i.e., $H_\alpha \geq 0$;
- $\lim_{\alpha \to 1} H_\alpha = H_1$, where $H_1 = H$ is the Shannon entropy;
- $H_0 = \log_2 n$ is the *Hartley* entropy and $H_2 = -\log_2 \sum_{i=1}^n p_i^2$ is the *Collision entropy*;
- $0 \leq H_\alpha[\mathcal{P}] \leq \log_2 n$;
- H_α is a positive, decreasing the function of $\alpha \geq 0$.

Let us mention that $H_\alpha[\mathcal{P}]$ with different αs complement each other. This is because for each specific α, the ensuing $H_\alpha[\mathcal{P}]$ carries extra information that is not present in any other $H_\beta[\mathcal{P}]$ with $\beta \neq \alpha$. In information theory, this fact is known as the *reconstruction theorem*, namely, the underlying distribution $\mathcal{P}$ can be uniquely reconstructed only if all $H_\alpha[\mathcal{P}]$ are known, [21,34,55]. In chaotic dynamical systems, the reconstruction theorem goes under the name *complementary generalized dimensions* [56] (cf. also next subsection).

2.2. Multifractals, Chaotic Systems, and Rényi Entropy

Another appealing property of the Rényi entropy is its close connection to *multifractals*, i.e., the mathematical paradigm that is often encountered in complex dynamical systems with examples ranging from turbulence and strange attractors to meteorology and finance, see, e.g., [57]. The aforementioned connection is established through the so-called *generalized dimensions*, which are defined as [2,48]

$$D_\alpha = -\lim_{\delta \to 0} \frac{H_\alpha(\delta)}{\log \delta} \tag{2}$$

where δ is a size of a $\delta-$mesh covering of a configuration space of a system. Generalized dimensions D_α are conjugate to the *multifractal spectrum* $f(\beta)$ through the Legendre transform [48]

$$(\alpha - 1)D_\alpha = \alpha\beta - f(\beta). \tag{3}$$

The function $f(\beta)$ is called the multifractal spectrum because β plays the role of the scaling exponent in the local probability distribution, e.g., distribution with support on the i-th hypercube of a mesh size δ scale, as $p_i(\delta) \sim \delta^{\beta_i}$. The key assumption in the multifractal analysis is that in the small $\delta-$ limit, the local probability distribution depends smoothly on β. It can be argued that $f(\beta)$ corresponds to the (box-counting) fractal dimension of the portion of the configuration space where local probability distributions have the scaling exponent β, cf., e.g., reference [34]. In this way, the multifractal can be viewed as an ensemble of intertwined (uni)fractals, each with its own fractal dimension $f(\beta)$.

The multifractal paradigm is particularly pertinent in the *theory of chaotic systems*. For instance, chaotic dynamics and strange attractors, in particular, are uniquely characterized by the infinite sequences of generalized dimensions D_α, cf. reference [56]. In particular, the generalized dimensions can help to recognize (in a quantitative way) the main geometric features of chaotic systems. For instance, they may help to distinguish chaotic behavior from noisy behavior, determine the number of variables that are needed to model the dynamics of the system or classify systems into universality classes. On the other hand, dynamical features of chaotic systems are often analyzed through such quantifiers as *Lyapunov exponent*, which is a measure of the divergence of nearby trajectories, or ensuing *Kolmogorov-Sinai entropy rate* (KSE), which quantifies the change of entropy as the system evolves and is given by the sum of all positive Lyapunov exponents. The connection between KSE and the time evolution of the information-theoretic or statistical entropy is quite delicate, see, e.g., the discussion in reference [58], though the upshot is clear, in order to describe the dynamics of a (complex) system, the temporal change or the difference in entropy is more relevant than the entropy itself. Consequently, while RE (alongside with D_α) is a suitable quantifier of geometric properties of chaotic systems, its temporal differences or temporal rates are useful for the description of the dynamics of such systems. Rényi's transfer entropy follows the latter route.

2.3. Shannon Transfer Entropy

In order to understand the concept of Rényi transfer entropy, we recall first its Shannon's counterpart.

Let $X = \{x_i\}_{i=1}^{N}$ be a discrete random variable with ensuing probability distribution $\mathcal{P}_X$, then the Shannon entropy of this process is

$$H(X) \equiv H(\mathcal{P}_X) = -\sum_{x \in \mathcal{X}} p(x) \log_2 p(x). \tag{4}$$

Let $Y = \{y_i\}_{i=1}^{N}$ be another random variable, then *mutual information* between X and Y is

$$\begin{aligned} I(X:Y) &= \sum_{x \in X, y \in Y} p(x,y) \log_2 \frac{p(x,y)}{p(x)p(y)} \\ &= H(X) - H(X|Y) = H(Y) - H(Y|X), \end{aligned} \tag{5}$$

where quantity $H(X|Y)$ is the *conditional entropy*, defined as

$$H(X|Y) = -\sum_{x \in X, y \in Y} p(x,y) \log_2 p(x|y). \tag{6}$$

Mutual information quantifies an average reduction in uncertainty (i.e., gain in information) about X resulting from the observation of Y, or vice versa. Since $I(X:Y) = I(Y:X)$, it cannot be used as a measure of directional information flow. Note also that the amount of information contained in X about itself is just the Shannon entropy, i.e., $I(X:X) = H(X)$.

The mutual information between two processes X and Y conditioned on the third process Z is called *conditional mutual information* and is defined as

$$I(X:Y|Z) = H(X|Z) - H(X|Y,Z) = I(X:(Y,Z)) - I(X:Y). \tag{7}$$

Let us now consider two time sequences (e.g., two stock market time series) described by stochastic (possibly vector-type) random variables X_t and Y_t. Let us assume further that the time steps (e.g., data ticks) are discrete with the time step τ and with $t_n = t_0 + n\tau$ where t_0 is some reference time. For practical purposes, it is also useful to assume that X_t and Y_t represent discrete-time stochastic Markov processes of order k and l, respectively.

We wish to know what information will be gained on $X_{t_{n+1}}$ by observing Y_t up to time t_n. To this end, we introduce the joint process $X_{t_n}, X_{t_{n-1}}, \ldots, X_{t_{n-k+1}}$, which we denote as $X_n^{(k)}$, and similarly, we define the joint process $Y_n^{(l)} \equiv Y_{t_n}, Y_{t_{n-1}}, \ldots, Y_{t_{n-l+1}}$. By replacing X in (7) by $X_{t_{n+1}}$, Y by $Y_n^{(l)}$, and Z by $X_n^{(k)}$, we obtain the desired conditional mutual information

$$\begin{aligned} I(X_{t_{n+1}} : Y_n^{(l)} | X_n^{(k)}) &= H(X_{t_{n+1}} | X_n^{(k)}) - H(X_{t_{n+1}} | Y_n^{(l)}, X_n^{(k)}) \\ &= \sum_{x_n^{(k)} \in X_{n+1}^{(k)}, y_n^{(l)} \in Y_n^{(l)}} p(x_{n+1}, x_n^{(k)}, y_n^{(l)}) \log_2 \left(\frac{p(x_{n+1} | x_n^{(k)}, y_n^{(l)})}{p(x_{n+1} | x_n^{(k)})} \right). \end{aligned} \tag{8}$$

The conditional mutual information (8) is also known as *Shannon transfer entropy* from Y_t to X_t (or simply from Y to X) and as a measure of the directed (time asymmetric) information transfer between joint processes, it was introduced by Schreiber in reference [19]. The latter is typically denoted as

$$T_{Y \to X}(k, l) \equiv I(X_{t_{n+1}} : Y_n^{(l)} | X_n^{(k)}). \tag{9}$$

As already mentioned, for independent processes, TE is equal to zero. For a non-zero case transfer, entropy measures the deviation from the independence of the two processes. An important property of the transfer entropy is that it is directional, i.e., in general, $T_{Y \to X} \neq T_{X \to Y}$.

2.4. Rényi Transfer Entropy

In the same manner as in (7), we can introduce the *Rényi transfer entropy of order* α from Y to X (see also reference [21]) as

$$\begin{aligned} T_{\alpha, Y \to X}^R(k, l) &= H_\alpha(X_{t_{n+1}} | X_n^{(k)}) - H_\alpha(X_{t_{n+1}} | X_n^{(k)}, Y_n^{(l)}) \\ &= I_\alpha(X_{t_{n+1}} : Y_n^{(l)} | X_n^{(k)}), \end{aligned} \tag{10}$$

where $H_\alpha(X|Y)$ is the *conditional entropy of order* α and $I_\alpha(X : Y)$ is the *mutual information of order* α. These can be explicitly written as [21,43]

$$\begin{aligned} H_\alpha(X|Y) &= \frac{1}{1-\alpha} \log_2 \frac{\sum_{x \in X, y \in Y} p^\alpha(x, y)}{\sum_{y \in Y} p^\alpha(y)}, \\ I_\alpha(X : Y) &= \frac{1}{1-\alpha} \log_2 \frac{\sum_{x \in X, y \in Y} p^\alpha(x) p^\alpha(y)}{\sum_{x \in X, y \in Y} p^\alpha(x, y)}. \end{aligned} \tag{11}$$

It can be checked (via L'Hospital's rule) that Rényi's transfer α-entropy reduces to Shannon TE in the $\alpha \to 1$ limit, i.e.,

$$\lim_{\alpha \to 1} T_{\alpha, Y \to X}^R = T_{Y \to X}. \tag{12}$$

From (10), we see that $T_{\alpha, Y \to X}^R(k, l)$ may be intuitively interpreted as the degree of ignorance (or uncertainty) about $X_{t_{n+1}}$ resolved by the past states $Y_n^{(l)}$ and $X_n^{(k)}$, over and above the degree of ignorance about $X_{t_{n+1}}$ already resolved by its own past state alone. Here, the ignorance is quantified by the Rényi information measure (i.e., RE) of order α.

Rényi TE can also be negative (unlike the Shannon TE). This means that the uncertainty of the process X_t becomes bigger knowing the past of Y_t, i.e., $H_\alpha(X_{t_{n+1}} | X_n^{(k)}) \leq H_\alpha(X_{t_{n+1}} | X_n^{(k)}, Y_n^{(l)})$. If X_t and Y_t are independent, then $T_{\alpha, Y \to X}^R = T_{\alpha, X \to Y}^R = 0$. However, in contrast to Shannon's case, the fact that $T_{\alpha, Y \to X}^R = 0$ does necessarily imply the independence of the two underlying stochastic processes. Nonetheless, in Section 3, we prove that in case of Gaussian (Wiener) processes, 0-valued RTE is a clear signature of independence.

Due to the *reconstruction theorem* mentioned in Section 2.1, RTE $T_{\alpha, Y \to X}^R$ conveys for each α a different type of directional information from Y to X. The essence of this statement can be understood qualitatively by introducing the so-called *escort distribution*.

2.5. Escort Distribution

Because of the nonlinear way in which probability distributions enter in the definition of RE, cf. Equation (1), the RTE represents a useful measure of transmitted information that quantifies the dominant information flow between certain parts of underlying distributions. In fact, for $0 < \alpha < 1$, the corresponding information flow accentuates marginal events, while for $\alpha > 1$, more probable (close-to-average) events are emphasized [21]. In this respect, one can zoom or amplify different parts of probability density functions involved by merely choosing appropriate values of α. This is particularly useful in studies of time sequences, where marginal events are of crucial importance, for instance, in financial time series.

In order to better understand the aforementioned "zooming" property of RTE, we rewrite (10) in the form

$$T^R_{\alpha, Y \to X}(k,l) = \frac{1}{1-\alpha} \log_2 \left(\frac{\sum \frac{p^\alpha(x_n^{(k)})}{\sum p^\alpha(x_n^{(k)})} p^\alpha(x_{n+1}|x_n^{(k)})}{\sum \frac{p^\alpha(x_n^{(k)}, y_n^{(l)})}{\sum p^\alpha(x_n^{(k)}, y_n^{(l)})} p^\alpha(x_{n+1}|x_n^{(k)}, y_n^{(l)})} \right). \tag{13}$$

This particular representation shows how the underlying distribution changes (or deforms) with the change of parameter α. The numerator and denominator inside the log-function contain the so-called *escort* (or *zooming*) *distributions* ρ_α

$$\rho_\alpha(x) \equiv \frac{p^\alpha(x)}{\sum_{x \in X} p^\alpha(x)}, \tag{14}$$

which emphasize less probable events for $0 < \alpha < 1$ and more probable events when $\alpha > 1$, see Figure 1.

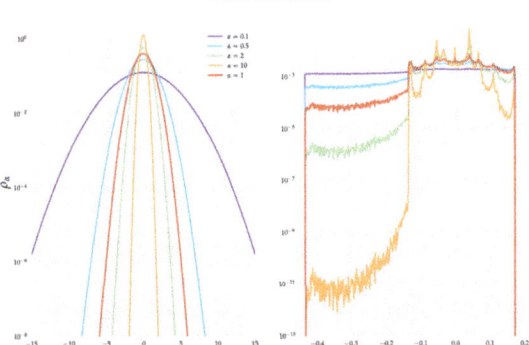

Figure 1. Illustration of the concept of escort distribution ρ_α on histograms. The left figure depicts log-scaled normal distribution $\mathcal{N}(0,1)$, while in the right figure, we show the log-scaled histogram for x_1–projection increments from the Rössler system (51). Both figures demonstrate that the escort distribution deforms the original distribution ($\alpha = 1$) so that $0 < \alpha < 1$ less probable events are emphasized (the smaller, α the greater emphasis) while high probable events are accordingly suppressed. For $\alpha > 1$, the situation is reversed.

Note also that $\rho_\alpha(x_n^{(k)}, y_n^{(l)})$ is not the joint probability distribution of $X_n^{(k)}$ and $Y_n^{(l)}$ as it does not satisfy the Kolmogorov–de Finetti relation for conditional probabilities [59].

In connection with (13), we may note that for $0 < \alpha < 1$ the multiplicative factor is positive, and so the RTE is negative if, by learning $Y_n^{(l)}$, the rare events are (on average) more emphasized than in the case when only $X_n^{(k)}$ alone is known. Analogically, for $\alpha > 1$ the RTE can be negative when—by learning $Y_n^{(l)}$—the more probable events are (on average) more accentuated in comparison with the situation when $Y_n^{(l)}$ is not known. It should be stressed that the analogous situation does not hold for Shannon's TE. This is because in the limit $\alpha \to 1$ we regain expression (8), which is nothing but relative entropy, and as such, it is always non-negative due to Gibbs inequality. At the same time, Shannon's TE is, by its very definition, also mutual information. While RTE is also defined to be a mutual information, it is not relative entropy (in the RE case, those two concepts do not coincide). It can be shown (basically via Jensen's inequality) [34] that the relative entropy based on

RE is also non-negative but this is not true for ensuing mutual information, which serves as a conceptual basis for the definition of RTE.

3. Rényi Transfer Entropy and Causality

As already seen, Rényi TE (analogously to Shannon TE) is a directional measure of information transfer. Let us now comment on the connection of the RTE with the causality concept.

3.1. Granger Causality—Gaussian Variables

The first general definition of causality, which could be quantified and measured computationally was given by Wiener in 1956, namely "... *For two simultaneously measured signals, if we can predict the first signal better by using the past information from the second one than by using the information without it, then we call the second signal causal to the first one...*" [9].

The introduction of the concept of causality into the experimental practice, namely into analyses of data observed in consecutive time instants (i.e., time series), is due to the Nobel prize winner (economy, 2003) C.W.J. Granger. The so-called *Granger causality* is defined so that the process Y_t *Granger causes* another process X_t if, in an appropriate statistical sense, Y_t assists in predicting the future of X_t beyond the degree to which X_t already predicts its own future.

The standard test of the Granger causality was developed by Granger himself [10] and it is based on a linear regression model, namely

$$X_t = a_{0t} + \sum_{\ell=1}^{k} a_{1\ell} X_{t-\ell} + \sum_{\ell=1}^{l} a_{2\ell} Y_{t-\ell} + e_t, \quad (15)$$

where $a_0, a_{1\ell}, a_{2\ell}$ are (constant) regression coefficients, l and k represent the maximum number of lagged observations included in the model (i.e., memory indices), t is a discrete time with the time step τ (ℓ is also quantified in units of τ) and e_t is the uncorrelated random variable (residual) with zero mean and variance σ^2. The *null hypothesis* that Y_t does not cause X_t (in the sense of Granger) is not rejected if and only if $a_{2\ell} = 0$ for $\ell = 1, \ldots, l$. In the latter case, we will call the ensuing regression model the *reduced regression model*.

It is not difficult to show that for Gaussian variables, the RTE and Granger causality are entirely equivalent. To see this, we use the *standard measure* of the Granger causality, which is defined as [60]

$$\mathcal{F}_{Y \to X}^{(k,l)} = \log_2 \frac{|\Sigma(e_t')|}{|\Sigma(e_t)|}, \quad (16)$$

where $\Sigma(\ldots)$ is the covariance matrix, $|\ldots|$ denotes the matrix determinant, and e_t, e_t' are residuals in the full and reduced regression model, respectively. We chose the logarithm to the base 2, rather than e for technical convenience. We now prove the following theorem:

Theorem 1. *If the joint process X_t, Y_t is Gaussian, then there is an exact equivalence between the Granger causality and RTE, namely*

$$\mathcal{F}_{Y \to X}^{(k,l)} = 2 T_{\alpha, Y \to X}^{R}(k,l). \quad (17)$$

This can be proved in the following way (for an analogous proof for Shannon's TE, see [61]). We first define the *partial covariance* as

$$\Sigma(\mathbf{X}|\mathbf{Y}) = \Sigma(\mathbf{X}) - \Sigma(\mathbf{X}, \mathbf{Y})\Sigma(\mathbf{Y})^{-1}\Sigma(\mathbf{X}, \mathbf{Y})^\top, \quad (18)$$

where $\Sigma(\mathbf{X})_{ij} = \text{cov}(X_i, X_j)$ and $\Sigma(\mathbf{X}, \mathbf{Y})_{ij} = \text{cov}(X_i, Y_j)$ with $\mathbf{X}$ and $\mathbf{Y}$ being random vector (or multivariate) variables. Let $\mathbf{X}$ and $\mathbf{Y}$ be jointly distributed random vectors in the linear regression model

$$\mathbf{X} = \mathbf{a} + \mathbf{Y}\mathbb{A} + \mathbf{e}. \tag{19}$$

Here, $\mathbf{a}$ is a constant vector, $\mathbb{A}$ contains regression coefficients, and $\mathbf{e}$ is a residual random vector with zero mean. In the subsequent, we will identify both $\mathbf{X}$ and $\mathbf{Y}$ with stochastic vectors (see text after Equation (28)). In such a case, one can always choose a specified number of time lags, so that system (19) (or better (23) and, consequently, (22)) is uniquely solvable, as neither vector $\mathbf{a}$ nor matrix $\mathbb{A}$ are time-dependent.

We now apply the least square method to the mean square error

$$\mathcal{E}^2 \equiv \sum_i \mathbb{E}(e_i^2) = \sum_i \mathbb{E}\left[(\mathbf{X} - \mathbf{Y}\mathbb{A} - \mathbf{a})_i^2\right], \tag{20}$$

Here, $\mathbb{E}(\ldots)$ denotes the average value. The ensuing least square equations

$$\frac{\partial \mathcal{E}^2}{\partial \mathbb{A}_{ij}} = 0 \quad \text{and} \quad \frac{\partial \mathcal{E}^2}{\partial a_k} = 0, \tag{21}$$

yield

$$a_l = \mathbb{E}(X_l) - \sum_k \mathbb{E}(Y_k)\mathbb{A}_{kl}, \tag{22}$$

$$\mathbb{A}_{li} = \sum_j [\Sigma(\mathbf{X})]_{lj}^{-1} \Sigma(\mathbf{Y}, \mathbf{X})_{ji}. \tag{23}$$

From (19) follows that

$$\mathbb{E}(X_i X_j) = \mathbb{E}\left[(\mathbf{a} + \mathbf{Y}\mathbb{A} + \mathbf{e})_i (\mathbf{a} + \mathbf{Y}\mathbb{A} + \mathbf{e})_j\right], \tag{24}$$

which after employing (22) can be equivalently rewritten as

$$\mathrm{cov}(X_i, X_j) = \sum_{l,k} \mathrm{cov}(Y_l, Y_k) \mathbb{A}_{li} \mathbb{A}_{kj} + \mathrm{cov}(e_i, e_j), \tag{25}$$

or equivalently

$$\Sigma(\mathbf{X}) = \mathbb{A}^\top \Sigma(\mathbf{Y}) \mathbb{A} + \Sigma(\mathbf{e}). \tag{26}$$

If we now insert (23)–(26), we obtain

$$\mathrm{cov}(e_i, e_j) = \mathrm{cov}(X_i, X_j) - \mathrm{cov}(X_i, Y_k) [\mathrm{cov}(Y_k, Y_l)]^{-1} [\mathrm{cov}(X_i, Y_j)]^\top, \tag{27}$$

which might be equivalently written as

$$\Sigma(\mathbf{e}) = \Sigma(\mathbf{X}|\mathbf{Y}). \tag{28}$$

If we now take $\mathbf{X} = (X_{t_{n+1}})$, $\mathbf{a} = (a_0)$, $\mathbf{Y} = (X^{(k)}, Y^{(l)})$, $\mathbb{A} = \mathrm{diag}(a_{1n}^{(k)}, a_{2n}^{(l)})$ for the full regression model and $\mathbf{Y} = (X_n^{(k)})$, $\mathbb{A} = \mathrm{diag}(a_1^{(k)})$ for the reduced regression model, we might write that

$$\mathcal{F}_{Y \to X}^{(k,l)} = \log_2 \frac{|\Sigma(e_t')|}{|\Sigma(e_t)|} = \log_2 \left(\frac{|\Sigma(X_{t_{n+1}}|X_n^{(k)})|}{|\Sigma(X_{t_{n+1}}|X_n^{(k)}, Y_n^{(l)})|} \right). \tag{29}$$

At this stage, we can use the fact that RE of the multivariate Gaussian variable $\mathbf{X}$ is [62]

$$H_\alpha(\mathbf{X}) = \frac{1}{2} \log_2 |\Sigma(\mathbf{X})| + \frac{D_\mathbf{X}}{2} \log_2 \left(2\pi \alpha^{\alpha'/\alpha}\right). \tag{30}$$

Here, D_X is the dimension of X and α' is a Hölder dual variable to α (i.e., $1/\alpha + 1/\alpha' = 1$). In particular, for jointly multivariate Gaussian variables X and Y, we can use (11) to write

$$\begin{aligned} H_\alpha(X|Y) &= \left[\frac{1}{2}\log_2|\Sigma(X \oplus Y)| + \frac{D_X + D_Y}{2}\log_2\left(2\pi\alpha^{\alpha'/\alpha}\right)\right] \\ &\quad - \left[\frac{1}{2}\log_2|\Sigma(Y)| + \frac{D_Y}{2}\log_2\left(2\pi\alpha^{\alpha'/\alpha}\right)\right] \\ &= \frac{1}{2}\log_2|\Sigma(X|Y)| + \frac{D_X}{2}\log_2\left(2\pi\alpha^{\alpha'/\alpha}\right). \end{aligned} \qquad (31)$$

Here, $\oplus$ denotes the direct sum. Employing finally the defining relation (10), we obtain

$$\begin{aligned} T^R_{\alpha,Y\to X}(k,l) &= H_\alpha(X_{t_{n+1}}|X_n^{(k)}) - H_\alpha(X_{t_{n+1}}|X_n^{(k)}, Y_n^{(l)}) \\ &= \frac{1}{2}\log_2\left(\frac{|\Sigma(X_{t_{n+1}}|X_n^{(k)})|}{|\Sigma(X_{t_{n+1}}|X_n^{(k)}, Y_n^{(l)})|}\right). \end{aligned} \qquad (32)$$

This confirms the statement of Theorem 1. In addition, since the standard measure of Granger causality (16) is typically defined only for the univariate target and source variables X_t and Y_t, we can omit $|\ldots|$ in (29) and (32).

Theorem 1 deserves two comments. First, the theorem is clearly true for any α. In fact, it is α independent, which means that for Gaussian processes we can employ any RTE to test the Granger causality. This naturally generalizes the classical result of Barnett et al. [61] (see also [1]) that is valid for Shannon's TE. When TE is phrased in terms of the Shannon entropy, it is typically easier to use various multivariate autoregressive model fitting techniques (e.g., the Lewinson–Wiggins–Robinson algorithm or the least-squares linear regression approach [63]) to derive $\mathcal{F}^{(k,l)}_{Y\to X}$ more efficiently than by employing direct entropy/mutual information-based estimators. On the other hand, since the efficiency and robustness of RTE estimators crucially hinge on the parameter α employed [64] (see also our discussion in Section 4), it might be, in many cases, easier to follow the information-theoretic route to the Granger causality (provided the Gaussian framework is justified). One can even test the Gaussian assumption in the actual time series by determining the RTE for various α parameters and checking if the results are α independent.

Second, the exact equivalence between the Granger causality and RTE can be (in the Gaussian case) retraced to the fact that in Equation (30) the second additive term on the RHS is proportional to D_X. It is not difficult to see (by a direct inspection) that this proportionality will be preserved in many other exponential distributions that satisfy the Markov factorization property. In these cases, the equivalence between the Granger causality and RTE statistics will also be preserved. However, for generic distributions, the additive term in (30) will no longer be a linear function of D_X and, hence, it will not be canceled. This, in turn, spoils the desired equivalence. In the following section, we will discuss one possible generalization of Theorem 1 in the context of heavy-tailed distributions.

3.2. Granger Causality—Heavy-Tailed Variables

It is not difficult to find relations analogous to (32) in a more general setting. Here, we will illustrate this point with heavy-tailed (namely α-Gaussian) random variables, where computations can be conducted analytically.

It is well known that if variance and mean are the only statistical observables, then the conventional maximum entropy principle (MaxEnt) based on Shannon entropy yields Gaussian distribution. Similarly, if the very same MaxEnt is applied to Rényi entropy H_α, one obtains the so-called α-Gaussian distribution [34] (cf. also Figure 2)

$$p_i = \frac{1}{\mathcal{Z}_\alpha}\left[1 - \beta(\alpha-1)x_i^2\right]_+^{1/(\alpha-1)}, \qquad (33)$$

that decays asymptotically following power law. Here, $\beta \in \mathbb{R}^+$ and $[z]_+ = z$ if $z \geq 0$ and 0, otherwise, $\mathcal{Z}_\alpha$ is the normalization factor. It is more conventional to write (33) as

$$p_i = \mathcal{Z}_\alpha^{-1} \exp_{\{2-\alpha\}}(-\beta x_i^2), \qquad (34)$$

where

$$e_{\{\alpha\}}^x = [1 + (1-\alpha)x]_+^{1/(1-\alpha)}, \qquad (35)$$

is the Box–Cox α-exponential [30].

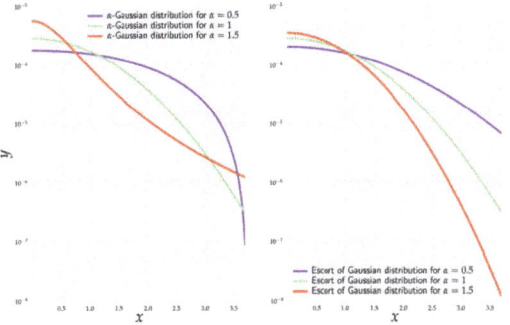

Figure 2. Comparison of the escort distributions ρ_α of the Gaussian (normal) distribution $\mathcal{N}(0,1)$ and α-Gaussian distributions (in log-linear plots) with a choice of β in (33), such that variances are the same for equal αs. For $\alpha = 1$, the two distributions correspond to the Gaussian distribution $\mathcal{N}(0,1)$. Even though ρ_α and α-Gaussian distributions deform the same underlying Gaussian distribution $\mathcal{N}(0,1)$, α-Gaussian is (save for $\alpha = 1$) heavy-tailed, while ρ_α remains Gaussian.

α-Gaussian distribution (33) has finite variance (and, more generally, the covariance matrix) for $\frac{D}{2+D} < \alpha \leq 1$. Let us now assume that Granger's linear (full/reduced) regression model is described by joint processes X_t and Y_t that are α-Gaussian. We now prove the following theorem:

Theorem 2. *If the joint process X_t, Y_t is α-Gaussian with $\alpha \in \left(\frac{1+k+l}{3+k+l}, 1\right]$ (i.e., a finite covariance matrix region) then $\mathcal{F}_{Y \to X}^{(k,l)} - 2T_{\alpha, Y \to X}^R(k,l)$ is a monotonically decreasing function of α (at fixed k and l) with zero reached at a stationary point $\alpha = 1$. The leading-order correction to the Granger causality is "k"-independent and has the form*

$$\mathcal{F}_{Y \to X}^{(k,l)} = 2T_{\alpha, Y \to X}^R(k,l) + \frac{l(\alpha-1)^2}{4} + \mathcal{O}((\alpha-1)^3). \qquad (36)$$

This result explicitly illustrates how certain "soft" heavy-tailed processes can be related to the concept of the Granger causality via universal types of corrections that are principally discernible in data analysis.

Theorem 2 can be proved in close analogy with our proof of Theorem 1. In fact, all steps in the proof are identical up to Equation (29). For the D-dimensional α-Gaussian process, the scaling property (30) reads

$$H_\alpha(\mathbf{X}) = \frac{1}{2} \log_2 |\Sigma(\mathbf{X})| + H_\alpha(\mathbf{Z}_\alpha^{1,D}). \qquad (37)$$

Here, $\mathbf{Z}_\alpha^{1,D}$ represents an α-Gaussian random vector with zero mean and unit ($D \times D$) covariance matrix. Relation (37) results from the following chain of identities

$$\begin{aligned}
H_\alpha(\mathbf{X}) &= H_\alpha(\sqrt{\Sigma(\mathbf{X})}\,\mathbf{Z}_\alpha^{1,D}) \\
&= \frac{1}{1-\alpha}\log_2 \int_{\mathbb{R}^D} d^D\mathbf{y}\left(\int_{\mathbb{R}^D} d^D\mathbf{z}\,\delta\left(\mathbf{y} - \sqrt{\Sigma(\mathbf{X})}\,\mathbf{z}\right)\mathcal{F}(\mathbf{z})\right)^\alpha \\
&= \frac{1}{1-\alpha}\log_2\left[|\Sigma(\mathbf{X})|^{(1-\alpha)/2}\int_{\mathbb{R}^D} d^D\mathbf{y}\,\mathcal{F}^\alpha(\mathbf{y})\right] \qquad (38)\\
&= \frac{1}{2}\log_2|\Sigma(\mathbf{X})| + H_\alpha(\mathbf{Z}_\alpha^{1,D}),
\end{aligned}$$

which is clearly valid for any non-singular covariance matrix. The derivation $\mathcal{F}(\dots)$ denoted the α-Gaussian probability density function with the unit covariance matrix and zero mean. We can now use the simple fact that

$$\begin{aligned}
H_\alpha(\mathbf{Z}_\alpha^{1,D}) &= \log_2\left[\left(\frac{\pi}{\mathfrak{b}(1-\alpha)}\right)^{D/2}\frac{\Gamma\left(\frac{1}{1-\alpha}-\frac{D}{2}\right)}{\Gamma\left(\frac{1}{1-\alpha}\right)}\left(1-\frac{D}{2\alpha}(1-\alpha)\right)^{1/(\alpha-1)}\right] \\
&= \frac{D}{2}\log_2[2\pi\alpha] + \log_2\left[\frac{\Gamma\left(\frac{1}{1-\alpha}-\frac{D}{2}\right)}{(1-\alpha)^{D/2}\Gamma\left(\frac{1}{1-\alpha}\right)}\right] + \log_2\left[\left(1-\frac{D}{2\alpha}(1-\alpha)\right)^{\frac{D}{2}-\frac{1}{1-\alpha}}\right], \qquad (39)
\end{aligned}$$

(where $\mathfrak{b} = [2\alpha - D(1-\alpha)]^{-1}$), to write

$$H_\alpha(\mathbf{X}|\mathbf{Y}) = \frac{1}{2}\log_2|\Sigma(\mathbf{X}|\mathbf{Y})| + H_\alpha(\mathbf{Z}_\alpha^{1,D_X+D_Y}) - H_\alpha(\mathbf{Z}_\alpha^{1,D_Y}). \qquad (40)$$

At this stage, we note that

$$\begin{aligned}
H_\alpha(\mathbf{Z}_\alpha^{1,D_X+D_Y}) &- H_\alpha(\mathbf{Z}_\alpha^{1,D_Y}) - H_\alpha(\mathbf{Z}_\alpha^{1,D_X}) \\
&= H_\alpha(\mathbf{Z}_\alpha^{1,D_X}|\mathbf{Z}_\alpha^{1,D_Y}) - H_\alpha(\mathbf{Z}_\alpha^{1,D_X}), \qquad (41)
\end{aligned}$$

which is not zero as it was in the case of the Gaussian distribution. In fact, from the foregoing discussion, it is clear that for the α-Gaussian random variables, we can write the RTE in the form

$$\begin{aligned}
T_{\alpha,Y\to X}^R(k,l) &= H_\alpha(X_{t_{n+1}}|X_n^{(k)}) - H_\alpha(X_{t_{n+1}}|X_n^{(k)}, Y_n^{(l)}) \\
&= \frac{1}{2}\log_2\left(\frac{\Sigma(X_{t_{n+1}}|X_n^{(k)})}{\Sigma(X_{t_{n+1}}|X_n^{(k)}, Y_n^{(l)})}\right) + H_\alpha(\mathbf{Z}_\alpha^{1,1}|\mathbf{Z}_\alpha^{1,k}) - H_\alpha(\mathbf{Z}_\alpha^{1,1}|\mathbf{Z}_\alpha^{1,k+l}) \qquad (42)\\
&= \frac{1}{2}\mathcal{F}_{Y\to X}^{(k,l)} + I_\alpha(\mathbf{Z}_\alpha^{1,1}:\mathbf{Z}_\alpha^{1,l}|\mathbf{Z}_\alpha^{1,k}).
\end{aligned}$$

Here, we have set $\mathbf{Z}_\alpha^{1,1}$ to correspond to the random variable $X_{t_{n+1}}$ with unit variance. Similarly, $\mathbf{Z}_\alpha^{1,k}$ and $\mathbf{Z}_\alpha^{1,l}$ correspond to unit covariance random variables $X_n^{(k)}$ and $Y_n^{(l)}$, respectively.

Clearly, when Y_t and X_t processes are independent (and, hence, *not causal* in the Granger sense), their joint distribution factorizes and, thus, $H_\alpha(\mathbf{Z}_\alpha^{1,D_X+D_Y}) \mapsto H_\alpha(\mathbf{Z}_\alpha^{1,D_X} \times \mathbf{Z}_\alpha^{1,D_Y})$. Additivity of the RE then ensures that $H_\alpha(\mathbf{Z}_\alpha^{1,1}|\mathbf{Z}_\alpha^{1,k}) = H_\alpha(\mathbf{Z}_\alpha^{1,1}|\mathbf{Z}_\alpha^{1,k+l})$ and, hence, $I_\alpha(\mathbf{Z}_\alpha^{1,1}:\mathbf{Z}_\alpha^{1,l}|\mathbf{Z}_\alpha^{1,k})$ is zero. In other words, when two processes are not Granger causal, their RTEs are zero. Actually, it is not difficult to see that this is true irrespective of a specific form of the distribution involved. However, the opposite is not true since $I_\alpha(\mathbf{Z}_\alpha^{1,1}:\mathbf{Z}_\alpha^{1,l}|\mathbf{Z}_\alpha^{1,k})$ might be (unlike in Shannon's case) negative; consequently, $T_{\alpha,Y\to X}^R(k,l)$ can be zero even if

$\mathcal{F}_{Y \to X}^{(k,l)}$ is not. To understand this point better, we explicitly evaluate $I_\alpha(\mathbf{Z}_\alpha^{1,1} : \mathbf{Z}_\alpha^{1,l} | \mathbf{Z}_\alpha^{1,k})$ for our α-Gaussian random variables. Using (39), we can write

$$I_\alpha(\mathbf{Z}_\alpha^{1,1} : \mathbf{Z}_\alpha^{1,l} | \mathbf{Z}_\alpha^{1,k}) = \log_2 \left[\frac{\Gamma\left(\frac{1}{1-\alpha} - \frac{1+k}{2}\right) \Gamma\left(\frac{1}{1-\alpha} - \frac{k+l}{2}\right)}{\Gamma\left(\frac{1}{1-\alpha} - \frac{k}{2}\right) \Gamma\left(\frac{1}{1-\alpha} - \frac{1+k+l}{2}\right)} \right]$$

$$+ \log_2 \left[\frac{\left(\frac{\alpha}{1-\alpha} - \frac{1+k}{2}\right)^{\frac{1+k}{2} - \frac{1}{1-\alpha}} \left(\frac{\alpha}{1-\alpha} - \frac{k+l}{2}\right)^{\frac{k+l}{2} - \frac{1}{1-\alpha}}}{\left(\frac{\alpha}{1-\alpha} - \frac{k}{2}\right)^{\frac{k}{2} - \frac{1}{1-\alpha}} \left(\frac{\alpha}{1-\alpha} - \frac{1+k+l}{2}\right)^{\frac{1+k+l}{2} - \frac{1}{1-\alpha}}} \right]. \quad (43)$$

By setting $\zeta = \frac{1}{1-\alpha} - \frac{k}{2}$ and $\tilde{\zeta} = \frac{1}{1-\alpha} - \frac{k+l}{2}$, we can rewrite (43) as

$$I_\alpha(\mathbf{Z}_\alpha^{1,1} : \mathbf{Z}_\alpha^{1,l} | \mathbf{Z}_\alpha^{1,k}) = \log_2 \left[\frac{\Gamma\left(\zeta - \frac{1}{2}\right)}{\Gamma(\zeta)} \frac{(\zeta-1)^\zeta}{\left(\zeta - \frac{3}{2}\right)^{\zeta - \frac{1}{2}}} \frac{\Gamma(\tilde{\zeta})}{\Gamma\left(\tilde{\zeta} - \frac{1}{2}\right)} \frac{\left(\tilde{\zeta} - \frac{3}{2}\right)^{\tilde{\zeta} - \frac{1}{2}}}{(\tilde{\zeta}-1)^{\tilde{\zeta}}} \right]$$

$$= \log_2 \left[\frac{\Gamma\left(\zeta - \frac{3}{2}\right)}{\Gamma(\zeta - 1)} \frac{(\zeta-1)^{\zeta-1}}{\left(\zeta - \frac{3}{2}\right)^{\zeta - \frac{3}{2}}} \frac{\Gamma(\tilde{\zeta} - 1)}{\Gamma\left(\tilde{\zeta} - \frac{3}{2}\right)} \frac{\left(\tilde{\zeta} - \frac{3}{2}\right)^{\tilde{\zeta} - \frac{3}{2}}}{(\tilde{\zeta}-1)^{\tilde{\zeta}-1}} \right] \quad (44)$$

$$\leq -\frac{1}{2} \log_2 \left[\frac{(\zeta - 1)}{\left(\zeta - \frac{3}{2}\right)} \right] \leq 0,$$

where on the last line we use the Kečkić–Vasić inequality [65]

$$\frac{(x+1)^{x+1}}{(x+s)^{x+s}} e^{s-1} \leq \frac{\Gamma(x+1)}{\Gamma(x+s)} \leq \frac{(x+1)^{x+\frac{1}{2}}}{(x+s)^{x+s-\frac{1}{2}}} e^{s-1}, \quad (45)$$

valid for $s \in (0,1)$. In addition, it can be numerically checked that $\frac{dI_\alpha(\mathbf{Z}_\alpha^{1,1}:\mathbf{Z}_\alpha^{1,l}|\mathbf{Z}_\alpha^{1,k})}{d\alpha} > 0$, for all l, k from the definition, so the maximum of $I_\alpha(\mathbf{Z}_\alpha^{1,1} : \mathbf{Z}_\alpha^{1,l} | \mathbf{Z}_\alpha^{1,k})$ is attained at $\alpha = 1$, see Figure 3. When α is close to 1, then one can employ the asymptotic relation $\Gamma[x + \gamma] \sim \Gamma[x]x^\gamma$ valid for $x \gg 1$, $\gamma \in \mathbb{C}$, and rewrite (39) in the form $(D/2) \log_2[2\pi\alpha e^\alpha]$. In this case, (43) tends to zero and we obtain equivalence between TE and the Granger causality. This result should not be so surprising because in the limit $\alpha \to 1$, RE tends to Shannon's entropy and the α-Gaussian distribution tends to the Gaussian distribution.

The leading order behavior near $\alpha = 1$ can be obtained directly from (43). The ensuing Taylor expansion gives

$$I_\alpha(\mathbf{Z}_\alpha^{1,1} : \mathbf{Z}_\alpha^{1,l} | \mathbf{Z}_\alpha^{1,k}) = -\frac{l(\alpha - 1)^2}{8} + \mathcal{O}((\alpha - 1)^3), \quad (46)$$

so, the point $\alpha = 1$ is a *stationary point* of $I_\alpha(\mathbf{Z}_\alpha^{1,1} : \mathbf{Z}_\alpha^{1,l} | \mathbf{Z}_\alpha^{1,k})$. This closes the proof.

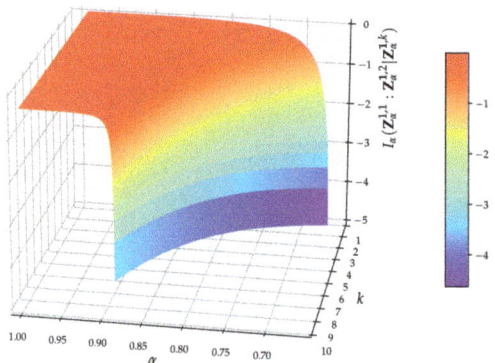

Figure 3. Example of $I_\alpha(\mathbf{Z}_\alpha^{1,1} : \mathbf{Z}_\alpha^{1,l} | \mathbf{Z}_\alpha^{1,k})$ for $l = 2$ and $k = 1, 2, \ldots, 10$. Range validity of α is thus between $\frac{3+k}{5+k}$ and 1.

4. Estimation of Rényi Entropy

4.1. RTE and Derived Concepts

From a data analysis point of view, it is not very practical to use the full joint processes $X_n^{(k)}$ and $Y_n^{(l)}$ (cf. the defining relation (10)) because (possibly) high values of k and l negatively influence the accuracy of estimation of RTE. In the following sections, we will thus switch to a more expedient definition of RTE given by

$$\begin{aligned}T^R_{\alpha,Y\to X}(\{k\},\{m\},\{l\}) &= H_\alpha(X_n^{\{m\},+}|X_n^{\{k\},-}) - H_\alpha(X_n^{\{m\},+}|X_n^{\{k\},-}, Y_n^{\{l\},-}) \\ &= I_\alpha(X_n^{\{m\},+} : Y_n^{\{l\},-}|X_n^{\{k\},-}),\end{aligned} \quad (47)$$

where $X_n^{\{k\},\Omega}$ is a subset of past ($\Omega = -$) or future ($\Omega = +$) values of X_{t_n} with the number of elements equal to k, such that $\{k\} = \{\kappa_1, \ldots, \kappa_k\}$ is a set of indices and $X_n^{\{k\},\Omega} \equiv X_{t_n \Omega \kappa_1}, X_{t_n \Omega \kappa_2}, \ldots, X_{t_n \Omega \kappa_k}$ is a selected subsequence of X_{t_n}, i.e., n_X-dimensional vectors. The same notational convention applies to $Y_n^{\{l\},\Omega}$ as a subsequence of Y_{t_n}, i.e., n_Y-dimensional vectors. In definition (47), we added a third parameter, m—the so-called *future step*. Though such a parametrization is often used in the literature on Shannon's TE, cf., e.g., reference [17], we will (in the following) only employ $m = \{1\}$ so as to conform with the definition (10). In such a case, we will often omit the middle index in $T^R_{\alpha,Y\to X}(\{k\},\{1\},\{l\})$.

4.1.1. Balance of Transfer Entropy

In order to compare RTE that flows in the direction from $Y \to X$ with the RTE that flows in the opposite direction $X \to Y$, we define the *balance of transfer entropy*

$$T^{R,\text{balance}}_{\alpha,Y\to X}(\{k\},\{l\}) = T^R_{\alpha,Y\to X}(\{k\},\{l\}) - T^R_{\alpha,X\to Y}(\{k\},\{l\}). \quad (48)$$

4.1.2. Effective Transfer Entropy

To mitigate the finite size effects, we employ the idea of a surrogate time series. To this end, we define the *effective transfer entropy*

$$T^{R,\text{effective}}_{\alpha,Y\to X}(\{k\},\{l\}) = T^R_{\alpha,Y\to X}(\{k\},\{l\}) - T^R_{\alpha,Y^{(\text{sur})}\to X}(\{k\},\{l\}), \quad (49)$$

where $Y^{(\text{sur})}$ stands for the randomized (reordered) time series—the surrogate data sequence. Such a series has the same mean, the same variance, the same autocorrelation function and, therefore, the same power spectrum as the original sequence, but (nonlinear) phase relations are destroyed. In effect, all the potential correlations between $X_n^{\{k\}}$ and $Y_n^{\{l\}}$

are removed, which means that $T^R_{\alpha,Y^{(\text{sur})} \to X}(\{k\},\{l\})$ should be zero. In practice, this is not the case, despite the fact that there are no obvious structures in the data. The non-zero value of $T^R_{\alpha,Y^{(\text{sur})} \to X}(\{k\},\{l\})$ must then be a byproduct of the finite data set. Definition (49) then ensures that spurious effects caused by finite k and l are removed. In our computations, we used the Fisher–Yates algorithm [66] together with Mersenne twister random generation algorithm [67] for the randomized surrogates. For a more technical exposition, see, e.g., refs. [68–70].

4.1.3. Balance of Effective Transfer Entropy

Finally, we combined both previous definitions to form the *balance effective transfer entropy*

$$
\begin{aligned}
T^{R,\text{balance, effective}}_{\alpha,Y \to X}(\{k\},\{l\}) &= T^{R,\text{effective}}_{\alpha,Y \to X}(\{k\},\{l\}) - T^{R,\text{effective}}_{\alpha,X \to Y}(\{k\},\{l\}) \\
&= T^R_{\alpha,Y \to X}(\{k\},\{l\}) - T^R_{\alpha,Y^{(\text{sur})} \to X}(\{k\},\{l\}) \\
&\quad - T^R_{\alpha,X \to Y}(\{k\},\{l\}) + T^R_{\alpha,X^{(\text{sur})} \to Y}(\{k\},\{l\}),
\end{aligned}
\tag{50}
$$

to quantify the direction of flow of transfer entropy without finite size effects.

4.1.4. Choice of Parameters k and l

The choice of the parameters k and l is essential to reliably analyze the information transfer between variables in a system. So, a natural question arises as to how one should choose such parameters.

The order of k and l, both in the RTE and Shannon's TE, but also in approximating autoregression in the Granger case, is often (in practice) set rather arbitrarily at some moderately high number. In the literature, there are theoretical criteria for optimal choices of k and l—with no unique answer. In our numerical simulations, we employed two pragmatic criteria: (a) results should be stable under the increase of k and l and, additionally, (b) k, and l should be equal to—or higher than—those used in the literature for the analysis of Shannon's TE in Rössler systems, e.g., references [18,22], so that we could make a comparison with the existence results. The chosen values $(\{k\},\{l\}) \equiv (\{k\},\{1\},\{l\}) = (\{0,1\},\{1\},\{0\})$ often well-satisfied both aforementioned conditions. In Section 6.3, it was sufficient to set $\{k\} = \{0\}$ and $\{l\} = \{0\}$, in agreement with [18]. When a need has arisen to emphasize some finer details in the behavior of the RTE (cf. Figures 6 and 10), $\{k\}$ was chosen to be $\{0,1,2,3,4\}$ or even $\{0,1,2,3,4,5,6\}$.

5. Rössler System

5.1. Equations for Master System

In order to illustrate the use of RTE, we considered two unidirectionally coupled Rössler systems (oscillators). These often serve as testbeds for various measures of synchronization, including Shannon's TE [71–73]. Rössler's system is described by three non-linearly coupled partial differential equations

$$
\begin{aligned}
\dot{x}_1 &= -\omega_1 x_2 - x_3, \\
\dot{x}_2 &= \omega_1 x_1 + a x_2, \\
\dot{x}_3 &= b + x_3(x_1 - c),
\end{aligned}
\tag{51}
$$

with four coefficients ω_1, a, b, and c. Strictly speaking, only three coefficients are independent, as ω_1 can be set to one by appropriately rescaling x_2. RS was invented in 1976 by O.E. Rössler [32] and it likely represents the most elementary geometric construction of chaos in the continuous systems. In fact, since the Poincaré–Bendixson theorem precludes the existence of (other than) steady, periodic, or quasi-periodic attractors in autonomous systems, defined in one- or two-dimensional manifolds, the minimal dimension for chaos is three [74]. The simplicity of the RS is bolstered by the fact that it only has one nonlinear (quadratic) coupling.

RS classifies as the *continuous (deterministic) chaotic system*, and more specifically as the *chaotic attractor*. The word "attractor" refers to the fact that whatever is the initial condition for the solution of the differential Equation (52), the trajectory $\mathbf{x}(t)$ ends up (after a short transient period) at the same geometrical structure (see Figure 5), which is neither a fixed point nor a limit cycle. This attractive geometrical structure is known as the Rössler attractor.

For future convenience, we will call the RS (51) as *driving* or *master system* and denote it as $\{X\}$.

5.2. Equations for the Slave System

In the following, we investigate RTE between two Rössler systems that are unidirectionally coupled in the variable x_1 via a small adjustable parameter ε. The corresponding second RS—*driven* or *slave system*, is defined as

$$
\begin{aligned}
\dot{y}_1 &= -\omega_2 y_2 - y_3 + \varepsilon(x_1 - y_2), \\
\dot{y}_2 &= \omega_2 y_1 + a y_2, \\
\dot{y}_3 &= b + y_3(y_1 - c).
\end{aligned}
\quad (52)
$$

Here, we fix the coefficients so that $a = 0.15, b = 0.2, c = 10.0$, and frequencies $\omega_1 = 1.015$ and $\omega_2 = 0.985$, and initial conditions $(x_1(0), x_2(0), x_3(0)) = (0, 0, 0)$ and $(y_1(0), y_2(0), y_3(0)) = (0, 0, 1)$. This parametrization is adopted from reference [18] where Shannon's TE between systems (51) and (52) was studied. In the following, we will denote the slave system also as $\{Y\}$.

5.3. Numerical Experiments with Coupled RSs

Before we embark on the RTE analysis, let us first take a look at the phenomenology of the coupled RSs (51) and (52) by means of simple numerical experiments. In our numerical treatment, we simulate coupled RSs by using the integration method, which is implemented in a package SciPy named `solve_ivp` with the LSODA option that exploits the Addams/BDF method, see, e.g., reference [75]. Projections of the ε-dependent RSs dynamics to various planes are presented in Figure 5. For visualization purposes, we used the toolkit Matplotlib [76] that exploits toolkit NumPy [77]. The sources are part of the Pyclits project [78]. In the future, the work can be rebased. The resulting data set analyzed consisted of 100,000 data points. To gain insight into the transient region, we chose shorter time lags in the data set generated from RS with $0.1 \leq \varepsilon \leq 0.15$, namely, we reduced the time steps from 0.01 to 0.001. In parallel, we display in Figure 4 the behaviors of the corresponding Lyapunov exponents, as adapted from [22], which help to elucidate our discussion.

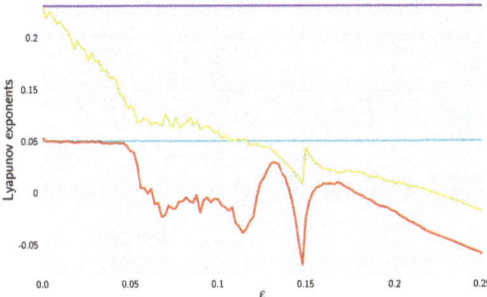

Figure 4. The two largest Lyapunov exponents of the master system (constant—violet and green) and the slave system (decreasing—red and yellow). So, for small ε, the signature of LE is $++00--$, while after synchronization, we end up with the signature $+0----$. After synchronization, there is a "collaps" of the dimension, in the sense that the slave system is completely dependent on the master system, so that there is only one dimension (direction) in which there is an expansion. Accordingly, there is only one LE with a positive sign. The LEs are measured in nats per time unit.

Projections

Instead of a conventional stereoscopic plotting, we found it more convenient (and illuminating) to focus on various plane projections of the coupled RSs. First, we noticed that, in Figure 5, the projections of RSs on the x_2-x_1, x_3-x_2, and x_1-x_3 planes do not depend on the coupling between systems (i.e., they are ε-independent), as expected, because the slave system (52) does not influence dynamics of the master system (51), which is autonomous (irrespective of ε). However, it is clear that signatures of the interaction between non-symmetrically coupled RSs (51) and (52) will show up in projections on the x_i-y_j and y_i-y_j planes.

Secondly, when the RSs are not coupled (i.e., when $\varepsilon = 0$), we have two autonomous RSs—in fact, two strange attractors that differ only by values of their frequency coefficients and initial values. The autonomies of the respective RSs are clearly seen in projections on the x_i-x_j and y_i-y_j planes (cf. Figure 5). A different density of trajectories (in a given time window $t = 100{,}000$) can be ascribed to the frequency mismatch. Projections on the x_1-y_1 and x_2-y_2 planes show how the ensuing chaotic and (component-wise) uncorrelated trajectories fill their support regions. In particular, we can observe that on the background of densely packed chaotic trajectories, clear vertical stripes of dominantly-visited regions appear in the slave system. Vertical stripes are clearly visible because limit cycles in the autonomous slave system are far more localized than in the master system. The projection on the x_3-y_3 plane indicates that (most of the time) the master system orbits venture to the x_3 direction, the slave system orbits are in the vicinity of the y_1-y_2 plane, and vice versa.

By continuously increasing the coupling strength ε from the zero value, we can observe that, already, a small interaction significantly changes the evolution of the slave system. For instance, in Figure 5, we see that when $\varepsilon = 0.01$, then the diffusive term $\varepsilon(x_1 - y_2)$ significantly disperses the limit cycles in the slave system. This is reflected not only in all projections on the y_i-y_j planes but also in projections on the x_1-y_1 and x_2-y_2 planes. In the latter two cases, the diffusion causes that horizontal stripes to completely disappear. Finally, the projection on the x_3-y_3 plane does not change significantly from the $\varepsilon = 0$ case.

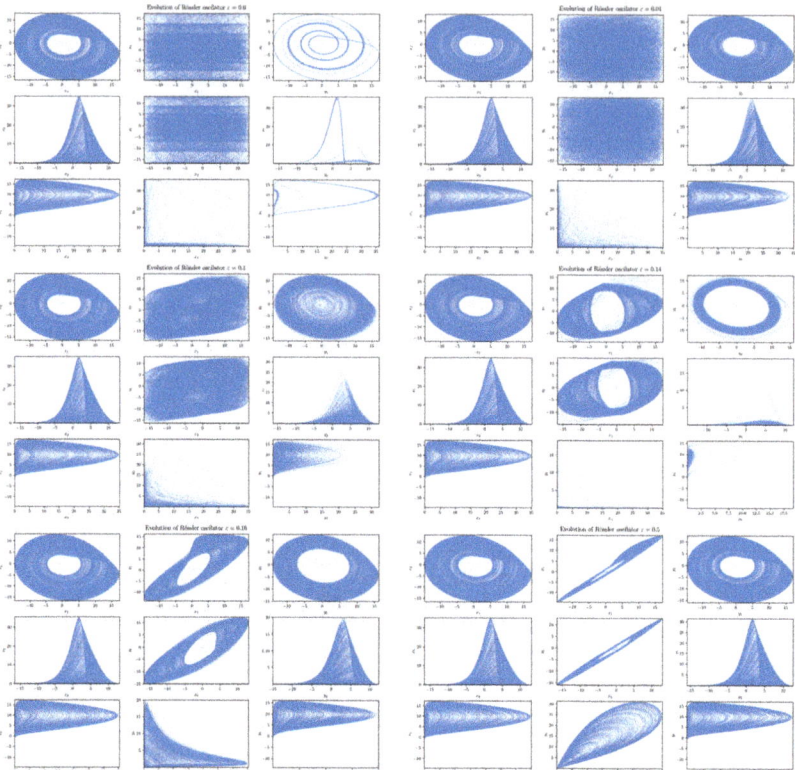

Figure 5. Projections of the RSs (51) and (52) on various planes. For each fixed ε, we depict nine figures that correspond (from top to bottom and left to right) to projections on the x_2-x_1, x_3-x_2, x_1-x_3, x_1-y_1, x_2-y_2, x_3-y_3, y_2-y_1, y_3-y_2, and y_1-y_3 planes. In the figure, we display, altogether, nine values of ε corresponding (from left to right and top to bottom) to $\varepsilon = 0, 0.01, 0.1, 0.14, 0.16$ and 0.5. The initial values are chosen as $x_1(0), x_2(0), x_3(0) = 0, y_1(0), y_2(0) = 0$, and $y_3(0) = 1$. Further projections for the transient region $0.12 \lesssim \varepsilon \lesssim 0.15$ are shown in Figure 8. All RSs are depicted in the time window $t = 10,000$.

When we further increase ε, we see that the behavior of the slave system starts to qualitatively depart from that of the master system. For ε, around 0.1, the slave system orbit diffuses to the region around the origin that is basically not visited (apart from an initial transient orbit) by the master system orbit (cf. projections on the y_i-y_j planes). In addition, projections on the x_1-y_1 and x_2-y_2 planes disclose that the ensuing support areas are not filled anymore. In fact, we can see a development of a slant stripe structure. On the other hand, the projection on the y_3-x_3 plane reveals that the slave system orbits stop visiting regions further from $y_3 = 0$. A yet higher ε (around 0.14) orbit of the system $\{Y\}$ first converges to a single limit cycle before it makes (again) a transition into a chaotic regime. Finally, we can observe that at $\varepsilon \sim 0.14$, the slave system rarely deviates far from $y_3 = 0$ and spends most of its time in the close vicinity of the y_1-y_2 plane—its evolution is "flattened".

Moreover, at $\varepsilon \sim 0.14$, we can also notice that projections on the y_1-x_1 and y_2-x_2 planes underwent a change in topology (in fact, this happened already at around $\varepsilon \sim 0.12$). The onset of this "topological phase transition" is closely correlated with the behavior of the largest Lyapunov exponent (LE) of the slave system. In fact, coupled RSs altogether have six Lyapunov exponents. The $\varepsilon = 0$ one has two autonomous RSs each with three LEs—one positive, one zero, and one negative (signature $+0-$ is a typical hallmark of a strange attractor in three dimensions). While at $\varepsilon = 0$, the signature of LEs is $++00--$, increasing ε all three LEs associated with $\{Y\}$ decreasing (initially) monotonically, cf. Figure 4. After a transient negativity and a return to zero (red curve in Figure 4), the originally positive LE of the slave system monotonically decreases and the negative for $\varepsilon \gtrsim 0.15$. In particular, we see that the critical value $\varepsilon \sim 0.12$ at which the "topological phase transition" occurs coincides with the value at which the largest LE of the system $\{Y\}$ crosses zero.

What is particularly noteworthy is an abrupt (non-analytic) change in the behavior of LEs at the value $\varepsilon \sim 0.145$. At this value, the LE changes direction and starts to increase with increasing ε. The increase stops at $\varepsilon \sim 0.15$ when the yellow-colored LE in Figure 4 reaches (approximately) value zero, after which it monotonically decreases. Such a decrease also starts for the second red-colored LE, but at a slightly different value of ε.

For stronger interactions with $0.15 \lesssim \varepsilon \lesssim 0.2$, we see (cf. Figure 5 with $\varepsilon = 0.16$) that the slave system starts to approach the structure of the master system strange attractor (cf. x_i-x_j and y_i-y_j projections). From the tilt and thinning of projections on the x_1-y_1 and x_2-y_2 planes, one may deduce that the amplitude synchronizations in the x_1 and y_1 (as well as x_2 and y_2) directions increase. Projection on the x_3-y_3 plane shows that amplitudes in the x_3 and y_3 directions are also synchronized (being roughly a half-cycle behind each other).

Finally, for very strong interactions, e.g., for $\varepsilon \sim 0.5$, the synchronization is almost complete: the system $\{Y\}$ basically fully emulates the master system's behavior with both systems now being structurally identical (cf. x_i-x_j and y_i-y_j projections). Full synchronization is nicely seen in projections on the x_1-y_1 and x_2-y_2 planes. Note that the amplitudes in the x_3 and y_3 directions start to synchronize.

6. Numerical Analysis of RTE for Coupled RSs

In the previous section, we learned some essentials about the coupled RS (51) and (52). In order to demonstrate the inner workings of the RTE and to gain further insight into how the two RSs approach synchronization, we compute here the RTE for various salient situations, such as the RTE between the x_1- and y_1-component, between the x_1- and y_3-component, or RTE between the full master and slave system. In our numerical analysis, we employed the RE estimator introduced by Leonenko et al. [26]. Some fundamentals associated with this estimator are relegated to Appendix A.

6.1. Effective RTE between x_1 and y_1 Directions

In order to understand the dynamics of the two coupled nonlinear dynamical systems (51) and (52) on their routes to synchronization, we first analyzed the effective RTE between the x_1 and y_1 components. Corresponding plots for different coupling strengths ε and different orders α are depicted in Figure 6. We can observe first that the effective RTE from x_1 to y_1 gradually increases with the increasing coupling strength until $\varepsilon \sim 0.12$. The regime between $\varepsilon \sim 0.12$ and $\varepsilon \sim 0.15$, as seen from Figure 5, corresponds to a transient synchronization behavior, which stabilizes only after $\varepsilon \sim 0.15$. This can also be seen from the behavior of the LEs at Figure 4. It should also be noted that the behavior of effective RTEs in the transient regime is apparently almost identical for all α in both $T^{R, \text{effective}}_{\alpha, x_1 \to y_1}(\{0,1\},\{1\},\{0\})$ and $T^{R, \text{effective}}_{\alpha, y_1 \to x_1}(\{0,1\},\{1\},\{0\})$. This would, in turn, indicate that the information transfer is the same across all sectors of the underlying probability distributions. Upon closer inspection though, such a highly correlated behavior will disappear when more historic data on $\{X\}$ and $\{Y\}$ are included (cf. $T^{R, \text{effective}}_{\alpha, x_1 \to y_1}(\{0,1,2,3,4,5,6\},\{1\},\{0\})$ and $T^{R, \text{effective}}_{\alpha, y_1 \to x_1}(\{0,1,2,3,4,5,6\},\{1\},\{0\})$ in Figure 6).

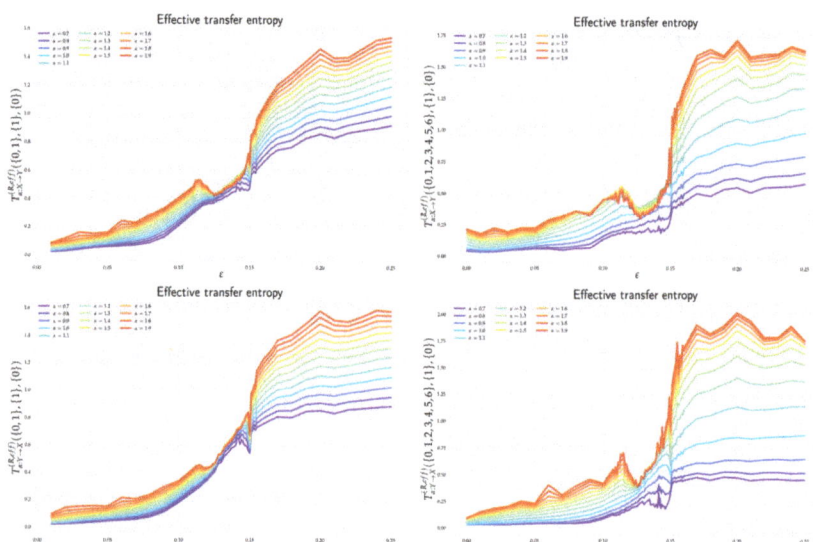

Figure 6. Effective RTE between x_1 and y_1 for two different histories of x_1, i.e., $T_{\alpha,x_1\to y_1}^{R,\text{effective}}(\{0,1\},\{1\},\{0\})$, $T_{\alpha,x_1\to y_1}^{R,\text{effective}}(\{0,1,2,3,4,5,6\},\{1\},\{0\})$, $T_{\alpha,y_1\to x_1}^{R,\text{effective}}(\{0,1\},\{1\},\{0\})$, $T_{\alpha,y_1\to x_1}^{R,\text{effective}}(\{0,1,2,3,4,5,6\},\{1\},\{0\})$, respectively, from left to right and top to bottom. RTE is measured in nats.

The same conclusion can be reached when the effective RTEs for the full six-dimensional systems are considered, cf. Figure 7.

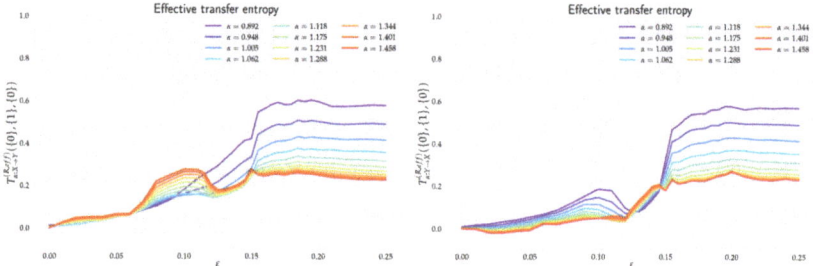

Figure 7. Effective transfer entropy for the full system ($n_X = 3$ and $n_Y = 3$) and for different values of α as functions of the coupling ε. We depict $T_{\alpha,X\to Y}^{R,\text{effective}}(\{0\},\{1\},\{0\})$ (**left**) and $T_{\alpha,Y\to X}^{R,\text{effective}}(\{0\},\{1\},\{0\})$ (**right**). RTE is measured in nats.

Nevertheless, from Figure 6, it can clearly be inferred that—in the transient region—strong correlations do exist, albeit not for all αs. In particular, one starts with the correlated flow for $\alpha \gtrsim 1.2$, which becomes stronger as ε increases. On the other hand, as ε approaches 0.15, the information flow decreases for $\alpha \lesssim 1$. This can be seen clearly in both Figures 6 and 7. At $\varepsilon = 0.15$, the information flow abruptly increases for all αs. This is similar to a first order phase transition in statistical physics. In this respect, our "topological phase transition" would be more similar to a second order phase transition due to a smooth change in the entropic flow across the critical point $\varepsilon = 0.12$. This scenario is also supported by Figure 8, where the actual behavior of the RS between the two critical points for four selected values of ε's is depicted. Note, in particular, how the increase in the RTE for $\alpha \gtrsim 1.2$ (as well as the decrease of RTE for $\alpha \lesssim 1$) are reflected in the contractions (measure concentrations) of the regions with denser orbit populations in the slave system. This, in turn, reinforces the picture that RTEs with higher αs describe the transfer of information between more central parts of underlying distributions, which, in this case, relate to higher occupation densities of the $\{Y\}$ system orbit. From Figure 8, we can also note that, at the critical point $\varepsilon = 0.15$, the contracted orbit regions abruptly expand and the slave system starts its way toward full synchronization with the master system. This is again compatible with the fact that the RTE abruptly increases for all αs at this point—i.e., all parts of underlying distributions participate in this transition and, consequently, the occupation density of the $\{Y\}$ system orbit spreads. In this respect, point $\varepsilon = 0.15$ represents the *threshold to full synchronization* while point $\varepsilon = 0.12$ denotes the *threshold to transient behavior prior to full synchronization*. The latter can be identified with a phase synchronization threshold, which should be at (or very close to) this point [22].

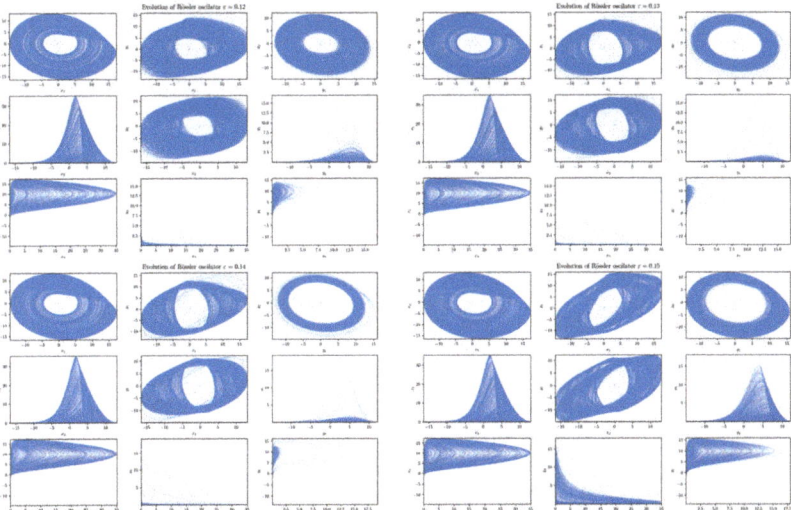

Figure 8. Four projections of the RSs (51) and (52) in the transient region $0.12 \lesssim \varepsilon \lesssim 0.15$. Depicted are projections (from left to right, from top to bottom) with $\varepsilon = 0.12, 0.13, 0.14,$ and 0.15. With increasing ε, one can observe the contractions (measure concentrations) of the regions with denser orbit populations in the slave system. At the critical point $\varepsilon = 0.15$, the contracted orbit regions abruptly expand and the slave system starts its way toward full synchronization with the master system (cf. also Figure 5). All RSs are depicted in the time window $t = 10,000$.

After the critical point $\varepsilon \sim 0.15$, both RSs enter full synchronization. In fact, the full synchronization starts when the information flow from all sectors of underlying distributions (i.e., for all αs) starts to be (almost) ε-independent and when $T_{\alpha,X \to Y}^{R, \text{balance, effective}}$ approach zero—so there is a one-to-one relation between the states of the systems, and the time series of the $\{X\}$ system can be predicted from the time series $\{Y\}$ system, and vice versa. Indeed, from Figure 6 (cf. also Figures 7 and 9), we see that all $T_{\alpha,Y \to X}^{R, \text{effective}}$ proceed in a slow increase toward their asymptotic values in the fully-synchronized state.

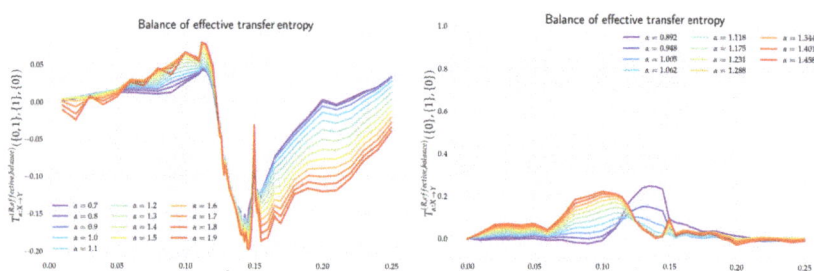

Figure 9. Balance of effective RTEs from x_1 to y_1 $T^{R,\text{balance, effective}}_{\alpha, x_1 \to y_1}(\{0,1\},\{1\},\{0\})$ (**left**, $n_{x_1}=1$ and $n_{y_1}=1$) and the balance of effective RTEs for the full system $T^{R,\text{balance, effective}}_{\alpha, X \to Y}(\{0\},\{1\},\{0\})$ (**right**, $n_X=3$ and $n_Y=1$) with Y being y_1.

6.2. Effective RTE between x_3 and y_3 Directions

As already seen from Figures 5 and 8, projections in the x_3-y_3 plane are particularly distinct. In Figure 10, we see the ensuing effective RTE between x_3 and y_3 directions.

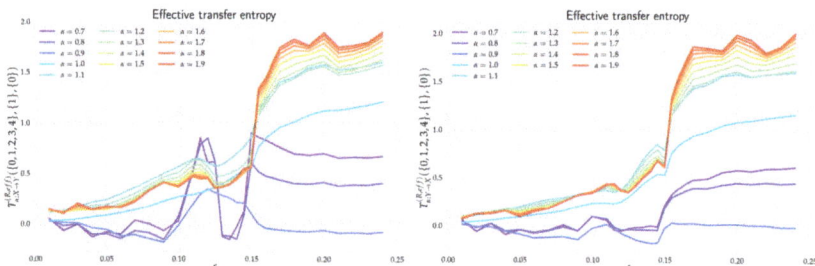

Figure 10. Effective RTE between x_3 and y_3 directions. From left to right: $T^{R,\text{effective}}_{\alpha, x_3 \to y_3}(\{0,1,2,3,4\},\{1\},\{0\})$ and $T^{R,\text{effective}}_{\alpha, y_3 \to x_3}(\{0,1,2,3,4\},\{1\},\{0\})$. Note a sudden increase in entropy transfer from the master to slave system at $\varepsilon = 0.12$ (i.e., threshold to transient behavior) for $\alpha < 1$. RTE is measured in nats.

What is particularly noticeable is a sudden increase in entropy transfer from the master to slave system at $\varepsilon = 0.12$ (i.e., at the threshold to transient behavior) for $\alpha < 1$. No comparable increase is observed from slave to master. This, might be explained as an influx of information needed to organize the chaotically correlated regime that exists prior the (correlated) transient regime (cf. x_i-y_i projections in Figures 5 and 8). It should also be noticed that ordinary Shannonian TE ($\alpha = 1$) is completely blind to such an information transfer.

As for the transient region, we can observe that the effective RTE has qualitatively very similar behavior to the effective RTE between x_1 and y_1, namely a distinct decrease in the information transfer for $\alpha < 1$ and an increase for $\alpha > 1$. This again reveals a measure concentration. In this case, the orbit occupation density concentrates around the y_1-y_2 plane of the slave systems, cf. projections depicted in Figure 8. The situation abruptly changes at the synchronization threshold $\varepsilon = 0.15$ after which the effective RTE approaches for each α a fixed asymptotic value that turns out to be the same for both $T^{R,\text{effective}}_{\alpha, x_3 \to y_3}$ and $T^{R,\text{effective}}_{\alpha, y_3 \to x_3}$.

6.3. Effective RTE for the Full System

In general, for a reliable inference, it is desirable that the conditioning variable in the definition or RTE (10) contains all relevant information about future values of the system or processes generating this variable in the uncoupled case. So, it should be a full three-dimensional vector X or Y in the case of RS. To this end, we display in Figure 7 the effective RTE for the full six-dimensional RS with information transfers in both $X \to Y$

and $Y \to X$ directions. Corresponding plots are depicted for different coupling strengths ε, different order αs, and different memories.

In particular, we can see that the information flow in the transient region starts after a brief decrease at around $\varepsilon \sim 0.12$ and sharply increases (in both directions) for $\alpha \gtrsim 1.2$. This implies that there is an increase in the correlating activity in between regions with higher occupation densities in both REs. The behavior depicted in Figure 8 can help us to better understand this situation. In particular, we see that in the transient region the $\{Y\}$ system reshapes its orbit occupation density so that the ensuing measure concentrates more around its peak while its tail parts are thinner. In fact, Figure 8 also shows that this measure concentration increases until almost $\varepsilon \sim 0.15$. The measure concentration behavior is reflected by the decrease of the RTE for $\alpha \lesssim 1$, i.e., decreasing information transfers between tail parts. This situation is even more pronounced when more memory is included in the effective RTEs, cf. both right pictures in Figure 7.

At the synchronization threshold $\varepsilon = 0.15$, the information flow abruptly changes for all αs, with a particularly strong increase for $\alpha \lesssim 1$. This indicates that the orbit occupation density of the $\{Y\}$ system abruptly reshapes by lowering the measure concentrated around its peak and broadening it in tails, so that the tail parts may also enter the full synchronization regime.

Let us finally comment on the issue of bidirectional information flown for single-component RTEs. By envisioning the discretized versions of RSs, (51) and (52), one can see that RTE from the slave to the master system (e.g., between the x_3 and y_3 direction) cannot easily be zero. This is because $H_\alpha(X_{3,t_{n+1}}|X_{3,n}^{(k)}, Y_{3,n}^{(l)})$ in the relation (10) is not simply $H_\alpha(X_{3,t_{n+1}}|X_{3,n}^{(k)})$. Note that due to the nonlinear nature of the coupled RSs, $y_3(t_n)$ depends both on $y_1(t_n)$ and $y_1(t_{n-1})$ (via the third equation in (52)), while $y_1(t_n)$ depends on $x_1(t_n)$ and $x_1(t_{n-1})$ (via the first equation in (52)); finally, $x_1(t_n)$ depends on $x_3(t_n)$ and $x_3(t_{n-1})$ and also $x_2(t_n)$ and $x_2(t_{n-1})$ (via the first equation in (51)); hence, $y_3(t_n)$ depends not only on $x_3(t_n)$, $x_3(t_{n-1})$, $x_3(t_{n-2})$ and $x_3(t_{n-3})$ but also on historical values of x_2. In this way, $H_\alpha(X_{3,t_{n+1}}|X_{3,n}^{(k)}, Y_{3,n}^{(l)}(\mathbf{X}))$ is not simply $H_\alpha(X_{3,t_{n+1}}|X_{3,n}^{(k)})$, as other components beyond $X_{3,n}$ are also needed. Consequently, when single-component RTEs for RS are computed, we inevitably find a non-zero information transfer from the slave to the master system. The latter is not so much a problem of k and l but rather the fact that we did not account for all relevant components (we simply missed some information).

It is true that for a reliable inference, in general, it would be desirable to obtain a zero value in the uncoupled direction $Y \to X$. This should be attained by proper conditioning—the conditioning variable should contain full information about future values of the system or processes generating this variable in the uncoupled case. So, it should be a three-dimensional vector $\mathbf{X}$ or $\mathbf{Y}$ for RS. Here, we computed effective RTE for the full six-dimensional system (vectors $\mathbf{X}$ and $\mathbf{Y}$). From Figure 7, we can see that $T_{\alpha,Y \to X}^{R, \text{effective}}$ in the uncoupled direction stays at the zero value (particularly for larger values of α) up to close to the synchronization threshold ($\varepsilon = 0.12$), while $T_{\alpha,X \to Y}^{R, \text{effective}}$ is distinctly positive there. So, RTE is a good *causal measure* only if the conditioning has a sufficient dimension (in our case, 3); otherwise, it can be viewed only as a measure of dependence.

6.4. Balance of Effective RTE

In order to quantify the difference between coupled ($X \to Y$) and uncoupled ($Y \to X$) information flow directions, we depict in Figure 9 the balance of effective RTEs between $T_{\alpha,X \to Y}^{R, \text{effective}}$ and $T_{\alpha,Y \to X}^{R, \text{effective}}$ for two different situations. Let us first concentrate on the balance of effective RTE $T_{\alpha,x_1 \to y_1}^{R, \text{balance, effective}}(\{0,1\},\{1\},\{0\})$. There, we can clearly see that before the synchronization threshold ("topological phase transition"), i.e., for $\varepsilon \lesssim 0.12$, we have $T_{\alpha,x_1 \to y_1}^{R, \text{effective}} > T_{\alpha,y_1 \to x_1}^{R, \text{effective}}$, which indicates the correct direction of coupling. The fact that for $\alpha > 1.6$ and $\varepsilon \lesssim 0.04$ one has $T_{\alpha,x_1 \to y_1}^{R, \text{balance, effective}}(\{0,1\},\{1\},\{0\}) < 0$ can be attributed to smaller reliability of the estimator in this region, cf. Figure 11 for estimation of ensuing the standard deviations. We can also observe that the synchronization threshold

$T_{\alpha,x_1 \to y_1}^{R, \text{balance, effective}}(\{0,1\},\{1\},\{0\})$ changes sign and slowly return back to positive values in the fully synchronized regime. Similar behavior was reported in [22] for Shannon's TE. Moreover, in this transient region, the effective RTEs have the same values irrespective of α, or, in other words, information transfer is the same across all sectors of the underlying probability distributions. This is akin to the behavior, which, in statistical physics, is typically associated with phase transitions—except for the fact that now we have a critical line rather than a critical point. However, as we already mentioned in the previous two paragraphs, this degeneracy is only spurious and will be removed by considering either the effective RTE for the full (six-dimensional) RS or longer memory.

After $\varepsilon \sim 0.15$, the approach to full synchronization proceeds at slightly different rates for different αs. This can equivalently be restated as saying that different parts of the underlying distributions enter synchronization differently. The dependence of the balance of effective RTE for the full (six-dimensional) system is shown on the right in Figure 9. Here, the behavior is less reliable for larger values of α ($\alpha \gtrsim 1.2$) and for smaller αs ($\alpha \lesssim 0.8$), cf. Figure 11. In the region of reliable αs, the behavior is qualitatively similar to that of $T_{\alpha,x_1 \to y_1}^{R, \text{balance, effective}}(\{0,1\},\{1\},\{0\})$. On the other hand, apart from the region of a transient synchronization, we clearly have $T_{\alpha,X \to Y}^{R, \text{effective}} > T_{\alpha,Y \to X}^{R, \text{effective}}$, which implies the correct direction of coupling. The approach to full synchronization is also easily recognized—the RTEs saturate to constant values (i.e., information transfer is ε-independent) and both $T_{\alpha,X \to Y}^{R, \text{effective}}$ and $T_{\alpha,Y \to X}^{R, \text{effective}}$ start to approach each other. In this respect, RTEs with lower αs enter the synchronization regime slower than RTEs with larger αs. In other words, events described by the tail parts of the distributions $p(x_{n+1}|x_n^{(k)})$ and $p(x_{n+1}|x_n^{(k)}, y_n^{(l)})$ (corresponding to $\alpha < 1$) will fully synchronize at higher values of ε than corresponding events described by central parts ($\alpha > 1$).

In passing, we might notice that since both $T_{\alpha,X \to Y}^{R, \text{effective}}$ and $T_{\alpha,Y \to X}^{R, \text{effective}}$ approach each other in the fully synchronized state, both the $\{X\}$ and $\{Y\}$ systems have to have the same underlying distributions (due to the reconstruction theorem for REs [21,34]) and, hence, they are indistinguishable, as one would expect.

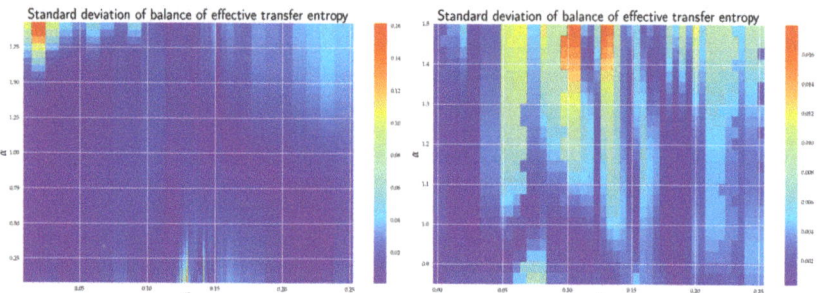

Figure 11. Dependence of standard deviation of the balance of effective RTEs $T_{\alpha,x_1 \to y_1}^{R, \text{balance, effective}}(\{0,1\},\{1\},\{0\})$ (**left**) and $T_{\alpha,X \to Y}^{R, \text{balance, effective}}(\{0\},\{1\},\{0\})$ (**right**).

7. Discussion and Conclusions

7.1. Theoretical Results

How one discerns 'cause' from 'effect' is the main question in many scientific areas. The seminal contribution of Wiener and Granger led to the so-called Granger causality principle and time series analysis method for inference of causality from experimental data. The traditional Granger causality method is based on linear autoregressive processes. However, nonlinear complex systems cannot be well-described by linear autoregressive models and require appropriate generalizations of the Granger causality method. One successful generalization stems from information theory, using a form of conditional mutual information, also known as transfer entropy. Shannon entropy-based TE has become a standard tool used for inferring causality from time series in all areas of science (including finance, climatology, neuroscience, etc.).

In this paper, instead of the Shannon entropy, we employed yet another information quantity, namely Rényi entropy. The ensuing RTE has the principal advantage that it is based on *a bona fide* information measure. In this way, one has a clear quantifier of the conveyed directional information (measured in bits or nats). Consequently, statements, such as: "the conveyed directional information from a tail part of the distribution is comparable with information from central part of distribution" or "information transfer is small/large (or good/bad)" are meaningful. RE is a measurable quantity; in principle, it can be measured directly (similar to Clausius entropy or Shannon entropy) without invoking the concept of the underlying distribution. This is because RE has an operational meaning given by various coding theorems. In practice, this is how RE is measured, e.g., in quantum optics (or more generally quantum information theory) [50,55]. In a conventional time series, one does not proceed this way because coding theorems (such as the Campbell coding theorem [44]) are difficult to implement for a large number of data.

As a proof of principle, we tested the concept of RTE on two unidirectionally coupled Rössler systems. The idea was to illustrate how the RTE can deal with such issues as synchronization and, more generally, causality in systems that are complex enough and yet amenable to a numerical analysis. Coupled RS is one of a handful of (simple) coupled chaotic systems that have been studied in the literature by means of Shannon's TE. This point is particularly important because we needed a gauge to which we could compare our results (and to which our results should reduce for $\alpha = 1$). Despite the earlier applications of the RTE in bivariate (mostly financial) time series, many questions remained unanswered about how to properly qualify and quantify the results obtained. Here, we went 'some way' toward this goal.

First, we showed that the concept of the Granger causality is exactly equivalent to the RTE for Gaussian processes, which may, in turn, be used as a test of Gaussianity. This is because RTEs are in the Gaussian framework all the same, and, hence, the results should be α-independent. On the other hand, since the efficiency and robustness of RTE estimators crucially hinge on the parameter α employed, it might be (in many cases) easier to follow the information-theoretic route to Granger causality (provided the Gaussian framework is justified).

Second, we demonstrated that the equivalence between the Granger causality and RTE can also be established for certain heavy-tailed processes—for instance, for soft α-Gaussian processes. In particular, in this latter case, one could clearly see the connection between Granger causality, Rényi's parameter α, and the heavy-tail power.

7.2. Numerical Analysis of RTE for Rössler Systems

In order to estimate the RTE, we employed the ℓ-nearest-neighbor entropy estimator of Leonenko et al. [26]. The latter is not only suitable for RE evaluation but it can also be easily numerically implemented to RTEs so that these can be computed almost in real time, which is relevant, e.g., in finance, regarding various risk-aversion decisions. Spurious effects caused by the finite size of the data set were taken into account by working with effective RTEs.

In order to gain further insight into the practical applicability and efficiency of the RTE, we tested it on two unidirectionally coupled Rössler systems—the master and slave system. To have a clear idea about what to expect, we first looked at the phenomenology of the coupled RSs by means of simple numerical simulations (presented in Figure 5). This was also accompanied by comparisons with Lyapunov exponents computed in references [18,22] and reproduced in Figure 4. In particular, we could clearly observe how the RSs synchronized with the increasing value of coupling strength. In this connection, we also identified critical values of coupling strengths at which *thresholds to transient behavior* (or the "topological phase transition") and the *threshold to full synchronization* occurred.

More specifically, we were particularly interested in the transient region between chaotic correlation regimes and full synchronization, which had not as yet been discussed in the literature. To gain a better understanding of this region, we employed in the range $\varepsilon \in [0.1, 0.15]$ a higher frequency sampling, namely 0.001, in contrast to the standard 0.01 one used for other εs. The threshold to transient behavior was identified at the scale $\varepsilon = 0.12$ where the positive LE crossed to negative values and where the projection on the x_1-y_1 and x_2-y_2 planes underwent topology changes (cf. Figure 5). From the point of view of RTEs, this threshold behavior was reflected in peaking the information flow in various directions. The increase in the effective RTE between x_1 and y_1 (in both directions) for $\alpha > 1$ was pronounced, in particular, which reflected the increase in orbit occupation density around the peak in the y_1-y_2 plane in the slave system. Even more marked was the high peak in information flow from x_3 to y_3 for $\alpha < 1$ (see Figure 10), which described an influx of information needed to "organize" chaotic correlations that existed between the x_3 and y_3 directions prior to $\varepsilon \lesssim 0.12$. Furthermore, the RTE was especially instrumental in understanding the measure concentration phenomenon in the transient regime. Finally, after a sharp "first-order-type" transition at the threshold of synchronization, the effective RTEs slowly approached their asymptotic values (distinct for each α) in the synchronized state. In addition, in the synchronized state, both $T_{\alpha, X \to Y}^{R, \text{effective}}$ and $T_{\alpha, Y \to X}^{R, \text{effective}}$ approached each other, which reveals that both $\{X\}$ and $\{Y\}$ systems have the same underlying distributions and, hence, they are indistinguishable.

As for the causality issue, we observed that the RTE is a good *causal measure* only if the conditioning has a sufficient dimension (in our case 3); otherwise, it is merely a *measure of dependence*. By employing effective RTE for the full system, we could reliably infer the coupling direction but only until $\varepsilon \lesssim 0.12$, i.e., until the threshold to transient behavior. After this value, the RSs started to synchronize, first partially (in the transient regime) and then fully $\varepsilon = 0.15$. In fact, the full synchronization started when the information flows from all sectors of underlying distributions (i.e., for all αs) began to be (almost) ε independent and when $T_{\alpha, X \to Y}^{R, \text{balance, effective}}$ approached zero— so there was a one-to-one relation between the states of the systems and the time series of the $\{X\}$ system could be predicted from the time series $\{Y\}$ system, and vice versa; hence, one could not make any statement about the coupling direction.

We should also reemphasize that the standard deviation of the RTE importantly depends on α, cf. Equation (11). For instance, the balance effective RTE for the full system is around the transient region quite reliably described by $0.8 \lesssim \alpha \lesssim 1.25$, though the minimal noise value is not attained at $\alpha = 1$ (Shannon transfer entropy) but at $\alpha = 1.16$. Clearly, the α-dependence of fluctuations is generally dynamics-dependent, and in many interesting real-world processes, it is simply more reliable to utilize non-Shannonian TEs.

7.3. Conclusions

In this paper, we discussed the Rényi transfer entropy and its role in the inference of causal relations between two systems, i.e., in the identification of the driving and driven systems from the experimental time series. On the theoretical side, our focus was on understanding the connection between RTE and Granger causality. In particular, we proved that the Granger causality is entirely equivalent to the RTE for Gaussian processes. This generalizes the classic result of Barnett et al. [61] that is valid for Shannon's TE. Furthermore, we have also shown how the Granger causality and the RTE are related in the case of heavy-tailed (namely α-Gaussian) processes. These results allow one to bridge the gap between autoregressive and Rényi entropy-based information-theoretic approaches.

On the experimental side, we illustrated the inner workings of the RTE by analyzing RTE between the synthetic time series generated from two unidirectionally coupled Rössler systems that are known to undergo synchronization. The route to synchronization was scrutinized by considering the effective RTE (and other derived concepts) between various master–slave components as well as between the full master and slave systems. We observed that with the effective RTE one could clearly identify a transient synchronization region (in the coupling strength), i.e., the regime between chaotic (master–slave) correlations and the synchronization threshold. In the transient region, the effective RTE allowed inferring the measure concentration for the orbit occupation density. It is noteworthy to mention that the latter cannot be deduced from Shannon's TE alone.

We also saw that the direction of coupling and, hence, causality, could be reliably inferred only for coupling strengths $\varepsilon < 0.12$ (the onset of the transient regime), i.e., when two RSs were coupled, but not yet fully. This is in agreement with earlier observations, cf., e.g., reference [22]. As soon as the RSs were synchronized, they produced identical time series; hence, there is no way to infer the correct causality relation solely from the measured data.

We conclude with a general observation—a clear conceptual advantage of information-theoretic measures in general, and RTE in particular, as compared to the standard Granger causality, are sensitive to nonlinear signal properties, as they do not rely on linear regression models. On the other hand, a clear limitation of RTEs, in comparison to the Granger causality, is that they are—by their very formulation—restricted to bivariate situations (though multivariate generalization is possible, it substantially increases dimensionality in the estimation problem, which might be hard to solve with a limited amount of available data). In addition, the RTEs often require substantially more data than regression methods.

Author Contributions: Conceptualization, P.J.; formal analysis, H.L. and Z.T.; methodology, P.J., H.L. and Z.T.; validation, H.L. and Z.T.; software design, data structures, computer calculation, and visualization, H.L.; writing—original draft, P.J.; writing—review and editing, P.J., H.L. and Z.T. All authors have read and agreed to the published version of the manuscript.

Funding: P.J. and H.L. were supported by the Czech Science Foundation, grant no. 19-16066S and Z.T. by the Jubiläumsfonds der Österreichischen Nationalbank Project 18696. This work was also in part supported by the U.S. Army RDECOM—Atlantic Grant No. W911NF-17-1-0108.

Institutional Review Board Statement: Not applicable.

Informed Consent Statement: Not applicable.

Data Availability Statement: Not applicable.

Acknowledgments: We thank Milan Paluš for the helpful comments and discussions and for providing us with source code for Figure 4.

Conflicts of Interest: The authors declare no conflict of interest.

Abbreviations

The following abbreviations are used in this manuscript:

RE	Rényi entropy
TE	transfer entropy
RTE	Rényi transfer entropy
PDF	probability density function
ITE	information-theoretic entropy
RS	Rössler system
KSE	Kolmogorov–Sinai entropy rate
LE	Lyapunov exponent

Appendix A

Here, we provide a brief technical exposition of the RE estimator employed.

Finding good estimators for the RE is an open research area. The estimators for the Shannon entropy based on ℓ-nearest-neighbor in one-dimensional spaces were studied in statistics almost 60 years ago by Dobrushin [79] and Vašíček [80]. One disadvantage of these estimators is that they cannot easily be generalized to higher-dimensional spaces, so they are inapplicable to the TE calculations. Nowadays, there are many usable frameworks—

most of them, of course, in the Shannonian setting (see reference [2] for a recent review). However, it is important to stress that the naive estimation of TE by partitioning of the state space is problematic [19] and that such estimators frequently fail to converge to the correct result [81]. In practice, more sophisticated techniques, such as kernel [82] or ℓ–nearest-neighbor estimators [83,84], need to be utilized. However, the latter techniques may bring about their own assumptions about the empirical distributions of the data (see [81] for a discussion about the issues involved).

In our work, we used the ℓ-nearest-neighbor entropy estimator for higher-dimensional spaces introduced by Leonenko et al. [26]. This estimator is suitable for RE and it can be effectively adapted and implemented by using formulas from the above-mentioned papers. In particular, the approach is based on an estimator of the RE from a finite sequence of N points that is defined as

$$\widehat{H}_{N,\ell,\alpha} = \begin{cases} \alpha \neq 1 & \log_B((N-1) \cdot V_m) + \frac{1}{1-\alpha}\left[\log_B \frac{\Gamma(\ell)}{\Gamma(\ell+1-\alpha)} \right. \\ & \left. + \log_B \left(\frac{1}{N}\sum_{i=1}^N \left(\rho_\ell^{(i)}\right)^{m(1-\alpha)}\right)\right] \\ \alpha = 1 & \log_B((N-1) \cdot \exp(-\psi(\ell)) \cdot V_m) \\ & + \frac{m}{N}\sum_{i=1}^N \log_B\left(\rho_\ell^{(i)}\right) \end{cases} \quad (A1)$$

Here, $\Gamma(x)$ is Euler's gamma function, $\psi(x) = -\Gamma'(x)/\Gamma(x)$ is the (negative) digamma function, $m = \dim X_t$ is the dimension of the data set space X_t, and $\rho_\ell^{(i)}$ is the distance from the data i to the ℓ-th nearest data counterpart using a metric in the space X_t. Moreover, V_m is the size of the ball in space X_t defined via the same metric. Finally, $\log_B$ is the logarithm with base B (we typically use $B = e$). In our computations, we employed the Euclidean metric, which has $V_m = \pi^{\frac{m}{2}}/\Gamma(\frac{m}{2}+1)$. Note that the estimator basically depends on N, i.e., the number of data in a data set and on ℓ, i.e., the rank of the nearest-neighbor used.

The advantages of the estimator (A1) in contrast to the standard histogram method are:

- It has relative accuracy for a small data set;
- It has applicability for high-dimensional data;
- The set estimators provide statistics for the estimation.

We should also note that, in contrast to other RE estimators, such as *fixed-ball* estimator [2], the estimator (A1) is not confined to any specific ranges of α values, though the efficiency of the estimator is, of course, α-dependent. We comment more on this point in Section 6. On the other hand, the disadvantage of this method involves the computational complexity of the algorithm and the complicated data container.

To calculate RTE and the related quantities (48)–(50), we apply the estimator Equation (A1). Ensuing estimators to (47)–(50)—let us call them generically $\mathcal{X}$—become dependent on ℓ (i.e., the nearest-neighbor rank). We exploit this feature and define the mean value $\overline{\mathcal{X}}$ and standard deviation $\sigma_\mathcal{X}$ with the Bessel correction, respectively, as

$$\overline{\mathcal{X}} = \frac{\sum_{\ell=n_{min}}^{n_{max}} \mathcal{X}_\ell}{n_{max} - n_{min} + 1}, \quad (A2)$$

$$\sigma_\mathcal{X} = \sqrt{\frac{\sum_{\ell=1}^n (\mathcal{X}_\ell - \overline{\mathcal{X}})^2}{n_{max} - n_{min}}}. \quad (A3)$$

Here, n_{max} and n_{min} are the highest and the lowest orders of the nearest data counterparts, respectively. Theoretically, we should use $n_{max} = M$, where M stands for the number of samples, but such a setup would require an enormous amount of computer memory to hold the distances.

In our calculations, we used $n_{max} = 50$, which turned out to be a good compromise between accuracy and computer time. On the other hand, for n_{min}, we were a little bit restricted by the fact that n_{min} influenced the interval of convergence of the estimator for various α (cf. discussion and proof in [26]). For instance, for $\ell = 1$, the estimator converged in the interval $\alpha \in [0, 1 + \frac{1}{2\dim(X_t)}]$, while for $\ell > 1$, one had $\alpha \in [0, \frac{\ell+1}{2}]$. For our particular purpose, it will suffice to set $n_{min} = 5$, so that the interval of convergence will be $\alpha \in [0, 3]$. This will fully suit our needs.

Appendix B

Here, we provide the heat maps for the relevant figures from the main text. These depict standard deviations (A2) and their dependencies on both α and ε.

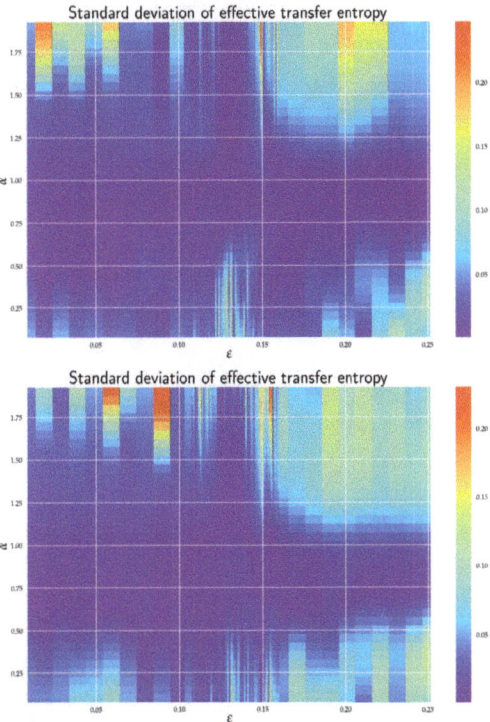

Figure A1. Standard deviation of the effective RTE between x_1 and y_1 $T^{R,\text{ effective}}_{\alpha, x_1 \to y_1}(\{0,1,2,3,4,5,6\}, \{1\}, \{0\})$, and $T^{R,\text{ effective}}_{\alpha, y_1 \to x_1}(\{0,1,2,3,4,5,6\}, \{1\}, \{0\})$.

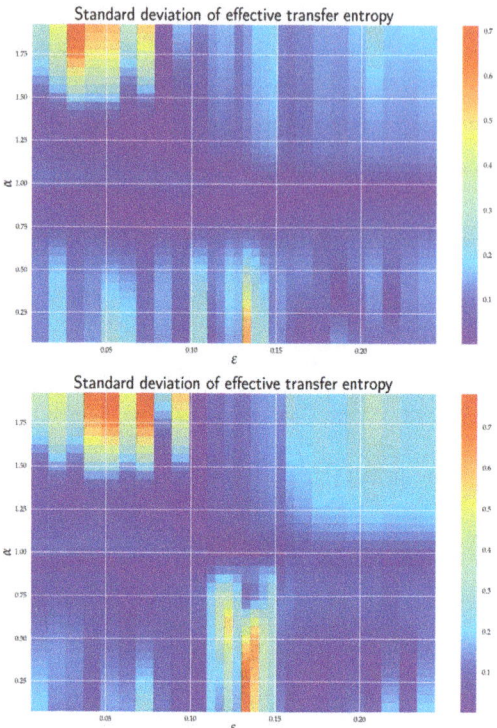

Figure A2. Standard deviation of the effective RTE between x_3 and y_3 for $T_{\alpha,x_3 \to y_3}^{R,\text{effective}}(\{0,1,2,3,4\},\{1\},\{0\})$, and $T_{\alpha,y_3 \to x_3}^{R,\text{effective}}(\{0,1,2,3,4\},\{1\},\{0\})$.

References

1. Schreiber, T. Interdisciplinary application of nonlinear time series methods. *Phys. Rep.* **1999**, *308*, 1–64. [CrossRef]
2. Kantz, H.; Schreiber, T. *Nonlinear Time Series Analysis*; Cambridge University Press: Cambridge, UK, 2010.
3. Pecora, L.M.; Carroll, T.L. Synchronization in chaotic systems. *Phys. Rev. Lett.* **1990**, *64*, 821–824. [CrossRef] [PubMed]
4. Boccaletti, S.; Kurths, J.; Osipov, G.; Valladares, D.L.; Zhou, C.S. The synchronization of chaotic systems. *Phys. Rep.* **2002**, *366*, 1–101. [CrossRef]
5. Quiroga, R.Q.; Arnhold, J.; Grassberger, P. Learning driver-response relationships from synchronization patterns. *Phys. Rev.* **2000**, *E61*, 5142–5148. [CrossRef]
6. Nawrath, J.; Romano, M.C.; Thiel, M.; Kiss, I.Z.; Wickramasinghe, M.; Timmer, J.; Kurths, J.; Schelter, B. Distinguishing Direct from Indirect Interactions in Oscillatory Networks with Multiple Time Scales. *Phys. Rev. Lett.* **2010**, *104*, 038701. [CrossRef]
7. Sugihara, G.; May, R.; Ye, H.; Hsieh, C.; Deyle, E.; Fogarty, M.; Munch, S. Detecting causality in complex ecosystems. *Science* **2012**, *338*, 496–500. [CrossRef]
8. Feldhoff, J.H.; Donner, R.V.; Donges, J.F.; Marwan, N.; Kurths, J. Geometric detection of coupling directions by means of inter-system recurrence networks. *Phys. Lett.* **2012**, *A376*, 3504–3513. [CrossRef]
9. Wiener, N. *Modern Mathematics for Engineers*; Beckenbach, E.F., Ed.; McGraw-Hill: New York, NY, USA, 1956.
10. Granger, C.W.J. Investigating Causal Relations by Econometric Models and Cross-spectral Methods. *Econometrica* **1969**, *37*, 424–438. [CrossRef]
11. Ancona, N.; Marinazzo, D.; Stramaglia, S. Radial basis function approach to nonlinear Granger causality of time series. *Phys. Rev.* **2004**, *R70*, 056221. [CrossRef]
12. Chen, Y.; Rangarajan, G.; Feng, J.; Ding, M. Analyzing multiple nonlinear time series with extended Granger causality. *Phys. Lett.* **2004**, *A324*, 26–35. [CrossRef]
13. Wismüller, A.; Souza, A.M.D.; Vosoughi, M.A.; Abidin, A.Z. Large-scale nonlinear Granger causality for inferring directed dependence from short multivariate time-series data. *Sci. Rep.* **2021**, *11*, 7817. [CrossRef]
14. Zou, Y.; Romano, M.; Thiel, M.; Marwan, N.; Kurths, J. Inferring indirect coupling by means of recurrences. *Int. J. Bifurc. Chaos* **2011**, *21*, 1099–1111. [CrossRef]

15. Donner, R.V.; Small, M.; Donges, J.F.; Marwan, N.; Zou, Y.; Xiang, R.; Kurths, J. Recurrence-based time series analysis by means of complex network methods. *Int. J. Bifurc. Chaos* **2011**, *21*, 1019–1046. [CrossRef]
16. Romano, M.; Thiel, M.; Kurths, J.; Grebogi, C. Estimation of the direction of the coupling by conditional probabilities of recurrence. *Phys. Rev.* **2007**, *E76*, 036211. [CrossRef]
17. Vejmelka, M.; Paluš, M. Inferring the directionality of coupling with conditional mutual information. *Phys. Rev.* **2008**, *77*, 026214. [CrossRef] [PubMed]
18. Paluš, M.; Krakovská, A.; Jakubík, J.; Chvostekova, M. Causality, dynamical systems and the arrow of time. *Chaos* **2018**, *28*, 075307. [CrossRef] [PubMed]
19. Schreiber, T. Measuring Information Transfer. *Phys. Rev. Lett.* **2000**, *85*, 461–464. [CrossRef]
20. Marschinski, R.; Kantz, H. Analysing the Information Flow Between Financial Time Series. *Eur. Phys. J. B* **2002**, *30*, 275–281. [CrossRef]
21. Jizba, P.; Kleinert, H.; Shefaat, M. Rényi's information transfer between financial time series. *Physica A* **2012**, *391*, 2971–2989. [CrossRef]
22. Paluš, M.; Vejmelka, M. Directionality of coupling from bivariate time series: How to avoid false causalities and missed connections. *Phys. Rev.* **2007**, *75*, 056211. [CrossRef]
23. Runge, J.; Heitzig, J.; Petoukhov, V.; Kurths, J. Escaping the Curse of Dimensionality in Estimating Multivariate Transfer Entropy. *Phys. Rev. Lett.* **2012**, *108*, 258701. [CrossRef] [PubMed]
24. Faes, L.; Kugiumtzis, D.; Nollo, G.; Jurysta, F.; Marinazzo, D. Estimating the decomposition of predictive information in multivariate systems. *Phys. Rev.* **2015**, *91*, 032904. [CrossRef] [PubMed]
25. Sun, J.; Taylor, D.; Bollt, E.M. Causal Network Inference by Optimal Causation Entropy. *SIAM J. Appl. Dyn. Syst.* **2015**, *14*, 73–106. [CrossRef]
26. Leonenko, N.; Pronzato, L.; Savani, V. A class of Rényi information estimators for multidimensional densities. *Ann. Stat.* **2008**, *36*, 2153–2182; Correction in *Ann. Stat.* **2010**, *38*, 3837–3838. [CrossRef]
27. Lungarella, M.; Pitti, A.; Kuniyoshi, Y. Information transfer at multiple scales. *Phys. Rev.* **2007**, *76*, 056117. [CrossRef]
28. Faes, L.; Nollo, G.; Stramaglia, S.; Marinazzo, D. Multiscale Granger causality. *Phys. Rev.* **2017**, *76*, 042150. [CrossRef]
29. Paluš, M. Multiscale Atmospheric Dynamics: Cross-Frequency Phase-Amplitude Coupling in the Air Temperature. *Phys. Rev. Lett.* **2014**, *112*, 078702. [CrossRef]
30. Tsallis, C. *Introduction to Nonextensive Statistical Mechanics: Approaching a Complex World*; Springer: New York, NY, USA, 2009.
31. Thurner, S.; Hanel, R.; Klimek, P. *Introduction to the Theory of Complex Systems*; Oxford University Press: London, UK, 2018.
32. Rössler, O.E. An equation for continuous chaos. *Phys. Lett.* **1976**, *57*, 397–398. [CrossRef]
33. Shannon, C.E. A Mathematical Theory of Communication. *Bell Syst. Tech. J.* **1948**, *5*, 379–423, 623–656. [CrossRef]
34. Jizba, P.; Arimitsu, T. The world according to Rényi: Thermodynamics of multifractal systems. *Ann. Phys.* **2004**, *312*, 17–59. [CrossRef]
35. Burg, J.P. The Relationship Between Maximum Entropy Spectra In addition, Maximum Likelihood Spectra. *Geophysics* **1972**, *37*, 375–376. [CrossRef]
36. Tsallis, C. Possible generalization of Boltzmann-Gibbs statistics. *J. Stat. Phys.* **1988**, *52*, 479–487. [CrossRef]
37. Havrda, J.; Charvát, F. Quantification Method of Classification Processes: Concept of Structural α-Entropy. *Kybernetika* **1967**, *3*, 30–35.
38. Frank, T.; Daffertshofer, A. Exact time-dependent solutions of the Rényi Fokker–Planck equation and the Fokker–Planck equations related to the entropies proposed by Sharma and Mittal. *Physica A* **2000**, *285*, 352–366. [CrossRef]
39. Sharma, B.D.; Mitter, J.; Mohan, M. On measures of "useful" information. *Inf. Control* **1978**, *39*, 323–336. [CrossRef]
40. Jizba, P.; Korbel, J. On q-non-extensive statistics with non-Tsallisian entropy. *Physica A* **2016**, *444*, 808–827. [CrossRef]
41. Vos, G. Generalized additivity in unitary conformal field theories. *Nucl. Phys. B* **2015**, *899*, 91–111. [CrossRef]
42. Rényi, A. *Probability Theory*; North-Holland: Amsterdam, The Netherlands, 1970.
43. Rényi, A. *Selected Papers of Alfréd Rényi*, 2nd ed.; Akademia Kiado: Budapest, Hungary, 1976.
44. Campbell, L.L. A coding theorem and Rényi's entropy. *Inf. Control* **1965**, *8*, 423–429. [CrossRef]
45. Csiszár, I. Generalized cutoff rates and Rényi's information measures. *IEEE Trans. Inform. Theory* **1995**, *26*, 26–34. [CrossRef]
46. Csiszár, I.; Shields, P.C. *Information and Statistics: A Tutorial*; Publishers Inc.: Boston, MA, USA, 2004.
47. Aczél, J.; Darótzy, Z. *Measure of Information and Their Characterizations*; Academic Press: New York, NY, USA, 1975.
48. Halsey, T.C.; Jensen, M.H.; Kadanoff, L.P.; Procaccia, I.; Schraiman, B.I. Fractal measures and their singularities: The characterization of strange sets. *Phys. Rev.* **1986**, *A33*, 1141–1151. [CrossRef]
49. Mandelbrot, B.B. *Fractals: Form, Chance and Dimension*; W. H. Freeman: San Francisco, CA, USA, 1977.
50. Bengtsson, I.; Życzkowski, K. *Geometry of Quantum States. An Introduction to Quantum Entanglement*; Cambridge University Press: Cambridge, UK, 2006.
51. Jizba, P.; Korbel, J. Maximum Entropy Principle in Statistical Inference: Case for Non-Shannonian Entropies. *Phys. Rev. Lett.* **2019**, *122*, 120601. [CrossRef] [PubMed]
52. Jizba, P.; Korbel, J. When Shannon and Khinchin meet Shore and Johnson: Equivalence of information theory and statistical inference axiomatics. *Phys. Rev.* **2020**, *E101*, 042126. [CrossRef] [PubMed]
53. Lesche, B. Instabilities of Rényi entropies. *J. Stat. Phys.* **1982**, *27*, 419–422. [CrossRef]

54. Rényi, A. On measures of entropy and information. In Proceedings of the Fourth Berkeley Symposium on Mathematical Statistics and Probability, Berkeley, CA, USA, 20–30 June 1961; pp. 547–561.
55. Jizba, P.; Ma, Y.; Hayes, A.; Dunningham, J.A. One-parameter class of uncertainty relations based on entropy power. *Phys. Rev. E* **2016**, *93*, 060104(R). [CrossRef]
56. Hentschel, H.G.E.; Procaccia, I. The infinite number of generalized dimensions of fractals and strange attractors. *Physica D* **1983**, *8*, 435–444. [CrossRef]
57. Harte, D. *Multifractals Theory and Applications*; Chapman and Hall: New York, NY, USA, 2019.
58. Latora, V.; Baranger, M. Kolmogorov–Sinai Entropy Rate versus Physical Entropy. *Phys. Rev. Lett.* **1999**, *82*, 520–523. [CrossRef]
59. Jizba, P.; Korbel, J. On the Uniqueness Theorem for Pseudo-Additive Entropies. *Entropy* **2017**, *19*, 605. [CrossRef]
60. Geweke, J. Measurement of Linear Dependence and Feedback between Multiple Time Series. *J. Am. Stat. Assoc.* **1982**, *77*, 304–313. [CrossRef]
61. Barnett, L.; Barrett, A.B.; Seth, A.K. Granger Causality and Transfer Entropy are Equivalent for Gaussian Variables. *Phys. Rev. Lett.* **2009**, *103*, 238701. [CrossRef]
62. Jizba, P.; Dunningham, J.A.; Joo, J. Role of information theoretic uncertainty relations in quantum theory. *Ann. Phys.* **2015**, *355*, 87–114. [CrossRef]
63. Seth, A.K. A MATLAB toolbox for Granger causal connectivity analysis. *J. Neurosci. Methods* **2010**, *186*, 262–273. [CrossRef] [PubMed]
64. Jizba, P.; Korbel, J. Multifractal Diffusion Entropy Analysis: Optimal Bin Width of Probability Histograms. *Physica A* **2014**, *413*, 438–458. [CrossRef]
65. Kečkić, J.D.; Vasić, P.M. Some inequalities for the gamma function. *Publ. De L'Institut Mathématique* **1971**, *11*, 107–114.
66. Fisher, R.A.; Yates, F. *Statistical Tables for Biological, Agricultural and Medical Research*, 3rd ed.; Oliver & Boyd: Edinburgh, UK, 1963.
67. Matsumoto, M.; Nishimura, T. Mersenne Twister: A 623-Dimensionally Equidistributed Uniform Pseudo-Random Number Generator. *ACM Trans. Model. Comput. Simul.* **1998**, *8*, 3–30. [CrossRef]
68. Theiler, J.; Eubank, S.; Longtin, A.; Galdrikian, B.; Farmer, J.D. Testing for nonlinearity in time series: The method of surrogate data. *Physica D* **1992**, *58*, 77–94. [CrossRef]
69. Schreiber, T.; Schmitz, A. Improved Surrogate Data for Nonlinearity Tests. *Phys. Rev. Lett.* **1996**, *77*, 635–638. [CrossRef]
70. Schreiber, T.; Schmitz, A. Surrogate time series. *Physica D* **2000**, *142*, 346–382. [CrossRef]
71. Paluš, M., Linked by Dynamics: Wavelet-Based Mutual Information Rate as a Connectivity Measure and Scale-Specific Networks. In *Advances in Nonlinear Geosciences*; Springer International Publishing: Cham, Switzerland, 2018; pp. 427–463.
72. Rosenblum, M.G.; Pikovsky, A.; Kurths, J. Phase Synchronization of Chaotic Oscillators. *Phys. Rev. Lett.* **1996**, *76*, 1804–1807. [CrossRef]
73. Cheng, A.L.; Chen, Y.Y. Analyzing the synchronization of Rössler systems—When trigger-and-reinject is equally important as the spiral motion. *Phys. Lett.* **2017**, *381*, 3641–3651. [CrossRef]
74. Rössler, O.E. Different Types of Chaos in Two Simple Differential Equations. *Z. Naturforsch.* **1976**, *31*, 1664–1670. [CrossRef]
75. Virtanen, P.; Gommers, R.; Oliphant, T.; Travis, E.; Haberland, M.; Reddy, T.; Cournapeau, D.; Burovski, E.; Peterson, P.; Weckesser, W.; et al. SciPy 1.0: Fundamental Algorithms for Scientific Computing in Python. *Nat. Methods* **2020**, *17*, 261–272. [CrossRef] [PubMed]
76. Hunter, J.D. Matplotlib: A 2D Graphics Environment. *Comput. Sci. Eng.* **2007**, *9*, 90–95. [CrossRef]
77. Harris, C.R.; Millman, K.J.; van der Walt, S.J.; Gommers, R.; Virtanen, P.; Cournapeau, D.; Wieser, E.; Taylor, J.; Berg, S.; Smith, N.J.; et al. Array programming with NumPy. *Nature* **2020**, *585*, 357–362. [CrossRef]
78. Use Branch `tranfer_entropy`. Available online: https://github.com/jajcayn/pyclits (accessed on 16 March 2022).
79. Dobrushin, R.L. A simplified method of experimentally evaluating the entropy of a stationary sequence. *Teor. Veroyatnostei I Ee Primen.* **1958**, *3*, 462–464. [CrossRef]
80. Vašíček, O. A test for normality based on sample entropy. *J. Roy. Stat. Soc. Ser. B Methodol.* **1976**, *38*, 54–59.
81. Kaiser, A.; Schreiber, T. Information transfer in continuous processes. *Physica D* **2002**, *166*, 43–62. [CrossRef]
82. Silverman, B.W. *Density Estimation for Statistics and Data Analysis*; Chapman & Hall: London, UK, 1986.
83. Kraskov, A.; Stögbauer, H.; Grassberger, P. Estimating mutual information. *Phys. Rev.* **2004**, *69*, 066138. [CrossRef]
84. Frenzel, S.; Pompe, B. Partial Mutual Information for Coupling Analysis of Multivariate Time Series. *Phys. Rev. Lett.* **2007**, *99*, 204101. [CrossRef]

Article

Regularity in Stock Market Indices within Turbulence Periods: The Sample Entropy Approach

Joanna Olbryś [1,*] and Elżbieta Majewska [2]

[1] Faculty of Computer Science, Bialystok University of Technology, Wiejska 45a, 15-351 Białystok, Poland
[2] Faculty of Economics and Finance, University of Bialystok, Warszawska 63, 15-062 Białystok, Poland; e.majewska@uwb.edu.pl
* Correspondence: j.olbrys@pb.edu.pl

Abstract: The aim of this study is to assess and compare changes in regularity in the 36 European and the U.S. stock market indices within major turbulence periods. Two periods are investigated: the Global Financial Crisis in 2007–2009 and the COVID-19 pandemic outbreak in 2020–2021. The proposed research hypothesis states that entropy of an equity market index decreases during turbulence periods, which implies that regularity and predictability of a stock market index returns increase in such cases. To capture sequential regularity in daily time series of stock market indices, the Sample Entropy algorithm (SampEn) is used. Changes in the SampEn values before and during the particular turbulence period are estimated. The empirical findings are unambiguous and confirm no reason to reject the research hypothesis. Moreover, additional formal statistical analyses indicate that the SampEn results are similar both for developed and emerging European economies. Furthermore, the rolling-window procedure is utilized to assess the evolution of SampEn over time.

Keywords: Sample Entropy (SampEn); stock market index; regularity; predictability; Global Financial Crisis; COVID-19; rolling-window

---

Citation: Olbryś, J.; Majewska, E. Regularity in Stock Market Indices within Turbulence Periods: The Sample Entropy Approach. *Entropy* **2022**, *24*, 921. https://doi.org/10.3390/e24070921

Academic Editor: Damián H. Zanette

Received: 12 May 2022
Accepted: 28 June 2022
Published: 1 July 2022

Publisher's Note: MDPI stays neutral with regard to jurisdictional claims in published maps and institutional affiliations.

Copyright: © 2022 by the authors. Licensee MDPI, Basel, Switzerland. This article is an open access article distributed under the terms and conditions of the Creative Commons Attribution (CC BY) license (https://creativecommons.org/licenses/by/4.0/).

1. Introduction

The vast majority of the literature in finance relies on the informational market efficiency assumption, which implies unpredictability of financial markets. The concept of informational efficiency is central in finance and it is strictly connected with the Efficient Market Hypothesis (EMH) [1]. An efficient market is defined as one in which new information is quickly and correctly reflected in current security prices [2]. The classic taxonomy of information sets distinguishes between: (1) weak-form efficiency (the information set includes only the history of prices or returns), (2) semi-strong-form efficiency (the information set includes all public available information), and (3) strong-form efficiency (the information set includes all information known to any market participant) [3]. Although the EMH is simple in principle, it remains an elusive concept [4]. Therefore, testing for efficiency and predictability of markets is difficult, which implies that empirical results are ambiguous [2].

There is an important strand of the existing literature, known as Algorithmic Information Theory (AIT), that explores predictability in terms of sequential regularity of time series based on the existence of patterns. The AIT could be employed to investigate the regularity/irregularity in data series by analyzing its entropy [5].

Entropy was defined by Shannon as a measure of information, choice and uncertainty [6]. The concept of entropy has originated from physics (precisely, from thermodynamics), but it has been employed in various research fields to assess the information content of a probability distribution, and to describe the complexity of a system. Entropy properly characterizes the uncertainty, particularly the unpredictability, of a random variable [7]. The highest uncertainty of the system corresponds to the highest entropy.

Specifically, high values of entropy are related to randomness in the evolution of stock prices [8]. In contrast, when no uncertainty exists in the system, entropy is minimized.

Entropy is an universal measure, and therefore many applications of entropy have been proposed in the literature, including economic, finance, and management studies (for a brief literature review see for instance [9–16] and the references therein).

It is important to emphasize that the fundamental mathematical entropy definitions, for instance the Kolmogorov-Sinai entropy ([17,18]), were not formulated for statistical applications. For this reason, Pincus [19] introduced the Approximate Entropy (ApEn) as a new statistic for experimental and empirical data series. The ApEn statistic was constructed along similar line to the Kolmogorov-Sinai entropy. Unfortunately, the ApEn procedure has some disadvantages which make that the results suggest more regularity than there is in reality (e.g., [5,20]).

The alternative statistic, the so-called Sample Entropy (SampEn), was proposed by Richman and Moorman [20] to avoid the ApEn bias. The SampEn algorithm solves the self-matching problem and eliminates the ApEn bias. The SampEn was initially used in physiological time series analyses, but it is also a suitable indicator for economic and financial data sets (e.g., [21,22]). Both ApEn and SampEn statistics are model-independent measures of sequential regularity in experimental or empirical data series. They are based on the existence of patterns. Moreover, they can quantify the regularity in time series with a relatively small number of data. However, due to the ApEn bias reporting in the literature, the SampEn algorithm is used in this study since it works better than the ApEn procedure (e.g., [5,20,23]).

The terms *regularity/irregularity* and *sequential regularity/irregularity* are connected with the terms *complexity* and *randomness* of data series [19]. The AIT procedure (ApEn or SampEn) assigns a nonnegative number to a sequence or time series, with larger values corresponding to greater apparent serial randomness or irregularity, and smaller values corresponding to more instances of recognizable features in the data [24]. Pincus [25] emphasizes that the need to assess potentially exploitable changes in serial structure is paramount in analyses of financial and econometric data.

The goal of this research is to assess and compare changes in sequential regularity in the 36 European and the U.S. stock market indices within major turbulence periods with the use of the SampEn statistic. Two periods are investigated: the Global Financial Crisis (GFC) in 2007–2009 and the COVID-19 pandemic outbreak in 2020–2021.

According to the literature, there is no unanimity in determining the phases of the GFC among the researchers (see, e.g., [26–30] and the references therein). Therefore, in our research, the GFC period was formally detected with the use of the Pagan and Sossounov [31] statistical method of dividing market states into bullish and bearish markets. The results reported in the papers [29,32,33] revealed the period from October 2007 to February 2009 as the GFC period for the U.S. and the majority of the European financial markets. The results are consistent with the literature (see, e.g., [26,27]).

The COVID-19 pandemic period comprised two years (2020–2021), since on 30 January 2020, the COVID-19 outbreak was declared as a Public Health Emergency of International Concern by the World Health Organization (WHO), while on 11 March 2020, the WHO officially declared the COVID-19 outbreak to be a global pandemic [34].

The proposed main research hypothesis states that entropy of an equity market index decreases during turbulence periods. It means that regularity and predictability of a stock market index increases within such periods. To examine the hypothesis, changes in the SampEn values for the pre-turbulence and turbulence periods are estimated.

The contribution of our study is twofold. First, the empirical findings are unambiguous and confirm no reason to reject the research hypothesis. The comparative results are especially homogenous for the pre-COVID-19 and COVID-19 sub-periods, and they support the evidence that regularity and predictability of the U.S. and almost all European stock markets indices increased during the COVID-19 outbreak. Moreover, the rolling-window approach is used to assess the evolution of entropy over time. The empirical findings are illustrated with the corresponding graphs which indicate that entropy (measured by SampEn) substantially decreased during the COVID-19 pandemic, especially in March–April 2020.

Second, the results are similar both for developed and emerging economies, and document that entropy of European developed markets does not differ significantly compared to the European emerging markets. Therefore, the findings do not support the hypothesis that developed markets are generally more efficient than emerging ones (see, e.g., [35]).

The value-added of this research derives from novel empirical findings that have not been reported in the literature thus far. These findings are important for academics and practitioners as they support the thesis that a sequential regularity in financial time series exists and even rises during extreme event periods, which implies a possibility of returns prediction. To the best of the authors' knowledge, this is the first comparative study that investigates the group of 36 European stock markets in the context of their sequential regularity measured by SampEn.

The rest of this study is organized as follows. Section 2 presents a brief literature review. Section 3 describes the methodological background concerning the SampEn algorithm and contains data description. Section 4 presents and compares empirical results on the European stock markets and the U.S. market. The last section summarizes and discusses the main findings and indicates some further research directions. The paper is supplemented with three appendixes.

2. Literature Review

In light of the recently growing literature, a fairly broad research field regards assessing informational efficiency and predictability of financial markets with various entropy-based methods (e.g., [8,21,35–46]).

For instance, Zunino et al. [8] introduce and utilize two quantifiers for stock market (in)efficiency, namely the number of forbidden patterns and the normalized permutation entropy. Maasoumi and Racine [36] use a metric entropy measure of dependence to examine predictability of stock market returns. Oh et al. [37] assess efficiency of 17 foreign exchange markets using the approximate entropy approach. Risso ([35,38]) investigates informational efficiency of various stock market indices utilizing the Shannon entropy and the symbolic time series analysis. Eom et al. [39] evaluate the relationship between efficiency and predictability in 27 stock markets. They use the Hurst exponent and the approximate entropy procedure to analyse a long period of time. Gu [40] aims to predict the DJIA Index values in both short-term and long-term employing the multi-scale Shannon entropy. Ortiz-Cruz et al. [41] investigate informational complexity and efficiency of several crude oil markets with the multi-scale approximate entropy approach. Liu et al. [42] develop the conditional entropy and the transfer entropy to accommodate various trading activities in the context of market efficiency. Alvarez-Ramirez et al. [46] use entropy methods for measuring a time-varying structure of the U.S. stock market informational efficiency. Bekiros and Marcellino [43] propose a new wavelet-based approach with minimum-entropy decomposition to explore predictability of currency markets at different timescales. Gencay and Gradojevic [44] use parametric and non-parametric entropy-based methods in order to obtain an early indication of financial crisis and to predict market behavior. Wang and Wang [45] employ a multi-scale entropy-based method to analyse efficiency of various financial time series during the COVID-19 pandemic. Kim and Lee [21] use the approximate entropy, the sample entropy, and the Lempel-Ziv measure for the complexity of a time sequence to investigate predictability in cryptocurrency markets during the pandemic period. However, studies that deeply explore wide groups of stock markets in the context of their regularity and predictability are scarce.

3. Methodological Background and Data Description

This section presents the methodological background concerning the Sample Entropy algorithm (SampEn) and contains the real-data description.

3.1. The Sample Entropy Algorithm

In this research, the SampEn algorithm code in R has been implemented based on the paper [5], and therefore the similar notation has been used.

Let us consider a time sequence $u = \{u(1), u(2), \ldots, u(N)\}$ of length N, an integer $0 \leq m \leq N$, which is the length of sequences to be compared, and a real number $r > 0$, which denotes the tolerance for accepting matches. The parameters N, m, and r must be fixed for each computation.

The vectors $x_m(i) = \{u(i), u(i+1), \ldots, u(i+m-1)\}$ and $x_m(j) = \{u(j), u(j+1), \ldots, u(j+m-1)\}$ are defined and then the Chebyshev distance between them is calculated based on Equation (1):

$$d[x_m(i), x_m(j)] = max_{k=1,2,\ldots,m}(|u(i+k-1) - u(j+k-1)|). \tag{1}$$

The number of vectors $x_m(j)$ within r of $x_m(i)$ without allowing self-counting is defined by Equation (2):

$$B_i^m(r) = \frac{1}{N-m-1} \sum_{j=1, j \neq i}^{N-m} (\text{number of times that } d[x_m(i), x_m(j)] \leq r). \tag{2}$$

In the next step, the total number of possible vectors $B^m(r)$ is calculated based on Equation (3), and it denotes the empirical probability that two sequences match for m points:

$$B^m(r) = \frac{1}{N-m} \sum_{i=1}^{N-m} B_i^m(r). \tag{3}$$

Analogically, the number of vectors $x_{m+1}(j)$ at a distance r of $x_{m+1}(i)$ without allowing self-matching is defined by Equation (4):

$$A_i^m(r) = \frac{1}{N-m-1} \sum_{j=1, j \neq i}^{N-m} (\text{number of times that } d[x_{m+1}(i), x_{m+1}(j)] \leq r). \tag{4}$$

Next, the total number of matches $A^m(r)$ is computed based on Equation (5), and it denotes the empirical probability that two sequences are similar for $m+1$ points (matches).

$$A^m(r) = \frac{1}{N-m} \sum_{i=1}^{N-m} A_i^m(r). \tag{5}$$

Since the number of matches $(A^m(r))$ is always less than or equal to the number of possible vectors $(B^m(r))$, the ratio $\frac{A^m(r)}{B^m(r)} < 1$ is a conditional probability [5].

In the last step, the SampEn value of the time sequence u is computed as follows:

$$SampEn(m, r, N)(u) = -log\left(\frac{A^m(r)}{B^m(r)}\right). \tag{6}$$

The $SampEn(m, r, N)$ given by Equation (6) is the statistical estimator of the parameter $SampEn(m, r)$:

$$SampEn(m, r) = \lim_{N \to \infty} \left[-log\left(\frac{A^m(r)}{B^m(r)}\right) \right]. \tag{7}$$

For regular, repeating data, the term $\frac{A^m(r)}{B^m(r)}$ in Equation (7) nears one, and therefore Sample Entropy nears zero [47].

3.2. Real-Data Description

The data set includes daily observations for the 36 European stock market indices and the S&P500 index. The sample covers the period from January, 2006 to December, 2021. The returns of stock market indices are calculated as daily logarithmic rates of return given by Equation (8):

$$r_t = \ln P_t - \ln P_{t-1}, \qquad (8)$$

where P_t is the daily value of the particular market index on day t.

Table 1 presents brief information about all analyzed indices, in order of decreasing value of stock market capitalisation in 31 December 2020, as well as the basic statistics for daily logarithmic rates of return within the whole sample period. Several results in Table 1 need comments. The sample means are not statistically different from zero. The test statistic for skewness and excess kurtosis is the conventional t-statistic. The measure for skewness indicate that almost all series are skewed at the 0.05 level of significance, except for Cyprus (p-value 0.287) and Bosnia and Herzegovina (p-value 0.894). The values of excess kurtosis show that all series are highly leptokurtic with respect to the normal distribution. Furthermore, the Jarque-Bera (J-B) test [48] rejects normality for each return series as all of the J-B statistic values are greater than 3505 with the p-value approximately equal to zero (these values are not reported in Table 1 but are available upon a request). It is worth noting that the obtained empirical findings are typical for return time series and are consistent with the literature (e.g., [49]). The similar Tables A1 and A2 that report the basic statistics for daily logarithmic rates of return within the turbulence sub-periods are presented in Appendix A.

Table 1. The information about the analyzed stock market indices and the basic statistics for daily logarithmic rates of return within the whole sample period.

	Country	Index	Market Cap. EUR Billion Dec 2020	Mean (in %)	Std. Dev. (in %)	Skewness	Excess Kurtosis
	United States	S&P500	18,435.290	0.0329	1.26	−0.567	13.739
1	France	CAC40	2480.404	0.0100	1.39	−0.290	8.324
2	United Kingdom	FTSE100	2411.490	0.0065	1.18	−0.390	9.829
3	Germany	DAX	1870.687	0.0264	1.37	−0.239	8.257
4	Switzerland	SMI	1639.314	0.0130	1.11	−0.418	9.700
5	Netherlands	AEX	1149.619	0.0145	1.29	−0.396	9.549
6	Sweden	OMXS30	873.404	0.0229	1.37	−0.200	5.724
7	Spain	IBEX35	621.765	−0.0052	1.48	−0.378	9.717
8	Italy	FTSEMIB	600.652	−0.0067	1.59	−0.679	9.848
9	Russia	RTSI	568.992	0.0073	2.09	−0.574	11.988
10	Denmark	OMXC20	506.525	0.0385	1.28	−0.352	5.983
11	Belgium	BEL20	306.132	0.0046	1.27	−0.666	10.853
12	Finland	OMXH25	289.000	0.0105	1.34	−0.272	5.332
13	Norway	OSEAX	273.141	0.0309	1.42	−0.705	7.149
14	Turkey	XU100	194.491	0.0383	1.63	−0.467	4.479
15	Poland	WIG	145.379	0.0163	1.25	−0.746	7.141
16	Ireland	ISEQ	138.719	0.0033	1.47	−0.713	8.157
17	Austria	ATX	108.176	0.0012	1.59	−0.515	8.205
18	Portugal	PSI20	73.361	−0.0106	1.25	−0.387	7.323
19	Greece	ATHEX	41.758	−0.0356	2.00	−0.478	7.140
20	Hungary	BUX	22.908	0.0221	1.50	−0.274	8.436
21	Czechia	PX	21.797	−0.0010	1.34	−0.628	17.455
22	Romania	BET	20.895	0.0162	1.42	−0.749	12.300
23	Croatia	CROBEX	18.206	0.0010	1.10	−0.502	23.966
24	Bulgaria	SOFIX	14.505	−0.0065	1.11	−1.253	15.194
25	Lithuania	OMXV	12.114	0.0192	0.99	−0.749	26.775

Table 1. Cont.

	Country	Index	Market Cap. EUR Billion Dec 2020	Mean (in %)	Std. Dev. (in %)	Skewness	Excess Kurtosis
26	Iceland	OMXI	9.752	−0.0171	2.06	−36.153	1806.18
27	Slovenia	SBITOP	6.919	0.0073	1.04	−0.716	10.209
28	Serbia	BELEXLINE	4.437	−0.0032	0.81	0.156	16.365
29	Malta	MSE	4.161	−0.0058	0.67	0.141	8.658
30	Cyprus	GENERAL	3.844	−0.0820	2.28	0.042	7.862
31	Ukraine	UX	3.615	0.0186	1.88	−0.283	9.630
32	Montenegro	MONEX	3.178	0.0001	1.25	0.733	13.045
33	Estonia	OMXT	3.014	0.0275	1.04	−0.412	14.786
34	Latvia	OMXR	2.971	0.0152	1.24	0.080	18.658
35	Bosnia and Herzegovina	BIFX	2.698	−0.0369	0.86	0.005	9.535
36	Slovakia	SAX	2.648	−0.0006	1.11	−0.959	21.294

4. Results

This section presents empirical findings concerning sequential regularity and predictability of the 36 European stock markets and the U.S. market within the turbulence periods.

4.1. Empirical Experiments

In this subsection, the research hypothesis proposed in Introduction is examined. Changes in the SampEn values for the pre-turbulence and turbulence periods are estimated to assess whether entropy of equity market indices decreased during extreme event periods. To calculate the changes in entropy before and during the particular turbulence period, the following pairs of sub-periods of equal length are investigated:

1. For the Global Financial Crisis (GFC):
   - The pre-GFC period from May 2006 to September 2007 (17 months);
   - The GFC period from October 2007 to February 2009 (17 months).
2. For the COVID-19 pandemic outbreak:
   - The pre-COVID-19 pandemic period from January 2018 to December 2019 (24 months);
   - The COVID-19 pandemic period from January 2020 to December 2021 (24 months).

As was emphasized in Introduction, the aforementioned turbulence periods are based on the references [26,27,32–34].

An important expected feature of the SampEn algorithm is the relative consistency (e.g., [20,50]). This property follows from the Kolmogorov-Sinai definition of entropy [17]. The notion of relative consistency was introduced by Pincus [19]. In terms of the SampEn procedure, this can be written as the following property:

For dynamical processes A, B, if $SampEn(m_1, r_1)(A) < SampEn(m_1, r_1)(B)$, then $SampEn(m_2, r_2)(A) < SampEn(m_2, r_2)(B)$.

This property means that if series A exhibits more sequential regularity than series B for one set of the parameters (m_1, r_1), then this holds true for any other set (m_2, r_2) [20]. This expected property enables us to compare two processes for a single set (m_1, r_1) and draw conclusions for all sets of input parameters.

As mentioned in Section 3.1, the SampEn statistic depends on three parameters: N, m, and r, where N is a time series length, m is the length of sequences to be compared, and a real number $r > 0$ denotes the tolerance for accepting matches. Based on the literature, the suggestion is that m should be 1 or 2, since there are more template matches for $m = 1$, but $m = 2$ (or greater) reveals more of the dynamics of the data. Moreover, the authors of the SampEn procedure suggest that r should be 0.2 times the standard deviation σ of the empirical data set [47]. Therefore, in this research, the $m = 2$ and $r = 0.2\sigma$ parameters are used.

Table 2 includes the SampEn empirical findings within the Global Financial Crisis and COVID-19 pandemic outbreak. The columns entitled 'Change' report changes in entropy before and during particular turbulence period. The down arrows show entropy decrease, while the (rare) up arrows visualize entropy increase.

Table 2. The SampEn empirical findings within the Global Financial Crisis and COVID-19 pandemic outbreak.

	Stock Market	Pre-GFC	SampEn GFC	Change	Pre-COVID-19	SampEn COVID-19	Change
	United States	1.798	1.734	−0.064 ↓	1.801	1.305	−0.496 ↓
1	France	1.962	1.772	−0.189 ↓	1.972	1.489	−0.482 ↓
2	United Kingdom	1.897	1.878	−0.019 ↓	2.107	1.481	−0.626 ↓
3	Germany	1.900	1.786	−0.115 ↓	1.970	1.405	−0.565 ↓
4	Switzerland	1.967	1.993	0.025 ↑	2.010	1.577	−0.432 ↓
5	Netherlands	1.950	1.773	−0.177 ↓	1.945	1.561	−0.384 ↓
6	Sweden	1.778	1.787	0.010 ↑	2.126	1.624	−0.502 ↓
7	Spain	1.884	1.796	−0.088 ↓	1.901	1.673	−0.228 ↓
8	Italy	1.850	1.695	−0.155 ↓	2.037	1.543	−0.494 ↓
9	Russia	1.803	1.278	−0.525 ↓	2.103	1.762	−0.341 ↓
10	Denmark	1.871	1.766	−0.104 ↓	2.010	2.001	−0.009 ↓
11	Belgium	1.980	1.812	−0.168 ↓	2.073	1.547	−0.526 ↓
12	Finland	1.825	1.994	0.169 ↑	2.253	1.680	−0.573 ↓
13	Norway	1.964	1.744	−0.221 ↓	2.078	1.660	−0.419 ↓
14	Turkey	2.074	1.945	−0.129 ↓	2.172	1.789	−0.383 ↓
15	Poland	2.054	1.991	−0.063 ↓	2.121	1.680	−0.442 ↓
16	Ireland	1.735	1.811	0.075 ↑	2.089	1.699	−0.390 ↓
17	Austria	1.817	1.728	−0.090 ↓	1.950	1.584	−0.366 ↓
18	Portugal	1.787	1.700	−0.086 ↓	2.069	1.728	−0.341 ↓
19	Greece	1.904	1.607	−0.297 ↓	2.084	1.559	−0.524 ↓
20	Hungary	2.118	1.525	−0.593 ↓	2.124	1.823	−0.301 ↓
21	Czechia	1.855	1.511	−0.344 ↓	2.037	1.515	−0.522 ↓
22	Romania	2.034	1.827	−0.207 ↓	1.672	1.498	−0.173 ↓
23	Croatia	2.053	1.505	−0.547 ↓	2.079	1.310	−0.769 ↓
24	Bulgaria	1.730	1.499	−0.231 ↓	1.961	1.647	−0.314 ↓
25	Lithuania	1.764	1.530	−0.234 ↓	1.520	1.408	−0.112 ↓
26	Iceland	1.743	0.554	−1.189 ↓	2.044	1.825	−0.219 ↓
27	Slovenia	1.693	1.386	−0.307 ↓	2.105	1.740	−0.364 ↓
28	Serbia	1.508	1.570	0.061 ↑	1.949	1.585	−0.364 ↓
29	Malta	1.478	1.531	0.053 ↑	1.936	1.701	−0.236 ↓
30	Cyprus	1.739	2.078	0.339 ↑	1.979	1.898	−0.081 ↓
31	Ukraine	1.486	1.466	−0.020 ↓	1.201	1.858	0.658 ↑
32	Montenegro	1.740	1.480	−0.260 ↓	1.832	1.437	−0.395 ↓
33	Estonia	1.600	1.627	0.027 ↑	1.811	1.403	−0.408 ↓
34	Latvia	1.974	1.467	−0.507 ↓	1.584	1.496	−0.089 ↓
35	Bosnia and Herzegovina	1.701	1.800	0.099 ↑	0.730	0.566	−0.164 ↓
36	Slovakia	1.641	1.106	−0.534 ↓	1.247	0.934	−0.313 ↓
	Max	2.118	2.078	−0.040 ↓	2.253	2.001	−0.253 ↓
	Min	1.478	0.554	−0.924 ↓	0.730	0.566	−0.164 ↓
	Median	1.838	1.714	−0.124 ↓	2.010	1.584	−0.426 ↓
	Mean	1.829	1.648	−0.182 ↓	1.913	1.575	−0.339 ↓
	Std. Dev.	0.164	0.284	0.120 ↑	0.310	0.258	−0.052 ↓

The results presented in Table 2 require some explanations and interpretations. In general, the empirical findings are unambiguous and confirm no reason to reject the research hypothesis. The evidence is that entropy decreased within the GFC period for the U.S. and the vast majority of the European markets, except for nine countries (i.e., Switzerland, Sweden, Finland, Ireland, Serbia, Malta, Cyprus, Estonia, Bosnia and Herzegovina). Both developed and emerging markets are among them. The probable reason of the differences in the obtained results is that the GFC periods for some countries were slightly different (for details see, e.g., [33]).

However, the comparative results for the pre-COVID-19 and COVID-19 sub-periods are homogenous and they decidedly support the evidence that regularity and predictability of the U.S. and almost all European stock markets (apart from Ukraine) increased during the COVID-19 outbreak. Due to the investigated period (2020-2021), the isolated case of Ukraine is rather coincidental and is not connected with the Russian aggression in Ukraine on 24 February 2022.

The ranges of the SampEn values for the European market indices are: $[1.478; 2.118]$ (Pre-GFC), $[0.554; 2.078]$ (GFC), $[0.730; 2.253]$ (Pre-COVID), and $[0.566; 2.001]$ (COVID). The minimum, maximum, median, and mean values decreased substantially during both extreme event periods.

To formally test whether the mean results of SampEn for the whole group of markets during the turbulence period differ significantly compared to the corresponding pre-turbulence period, the t statistic for sample means given by Equation (9) is utilized:

$$t = \frac{(\overline{x_1} - \overline{x_2})\sqrt{n}}{\sqrt{s_1^2 + s_2^2}}, \qquad (9)$$

where $\overline{x_1}$ and $\overline{x_2}$ are sample means, s_1^2 and s_2^2 are sample variances, while $n = 36$ denotes the stock markets sample size.

The following two-tailed hypothesis is tested:

$$H_0 : \mu_1 = \mu_2 \\ H_1 : \mu_1 \neq \mu_2, \qquad (10)$$

where μ_1 and μ_2 are the expected values of SampEn for the whole group of stock market indices during the compared periods, and the null hypothesis states that two expected values are equal. Calculations of the t statistic values (Equation (9)) are based on the results presented in Table 2. The null hypothesis is rejected when $|t| > t^*$, where the critical value of t-statistic at the α significance level is equal to $t^* = t_{\alpha;2n-2}$. In our research, the critical values are equal to: $t^* = 1.667$ ($\alpha = 0.10$), $t^* = 1.994$ ($\alpha = 0.05$), and $t^* = 2.648$ ($\alpha = 0.01$), respectively.

The obtained empirical t-statistics are equal to: (1) $t = 3.325 > t^*$ for the pair of periods (pre-GFC, GFC), and (2) $t = 5.036 > t^*$ for the pair of periods (pre-COVID, COVID). This indicates that the H_0 hypothesis was rejected in both cases and the SampEn mean values substantially differed (specifically, decreased) during both extreme event periods.

What is important, the SampEn findings are consistent with the literature as they confirm that entropy of stock market indices usually decreases during the economic downturns (see, e.g., [41,45]). The equity market crash initiates a declining trend, which reduces entropy but increases time series regularity. As a consequence, predictability of a market increases within turbulence periods since a number of repeated patterns increases. It is worth noting that this evidence is in accordance with investors' intuition.

4.2. Sample Entropy of Developed versus Emerging European Stock Markets

An interesting and important question is whether developed stock markets differ substantially from emerging markets in their predictability, in the sense of their sequential regularity. Therefore, in this subsection, the comparative assessment of regularity/irregularity in the European developed and emerging markets is presented.

Based on the recent MSCI reports, and especially on the report "MSCI Global Market Accessibility Review. Country comparison" [51], the following 15 European countries are classified as developed markets (in the order of decreasing value of stock market capitalisation in 31 December 2020 reported in Table 1): France, United Kingdom, Germany, Switzerland, Netherlands, Sweden, Spain, Italy, Denmark, Belgium, Finland, Norway, Ireland, Austria, and Portugal. The remaining 21 European countries are recognized as emerging, including also frontier and stand-alone equity markets (see Table A3 in Appendix B).

Figure 1 presents the boxplots of the SampEn results within the pre-turbulence and turbulence periods, for two groups of the European developed (the yellow boxplots) and emerging (the green boxplots) stock markets. The boxplots that visualize the SampEn results are based on Tables A4 and A5 (Appendix B). The boxplot width depends on the number of the stock market indices, and these numbers are: 15 (the European developed markets) and 21 (the European emerging markets).

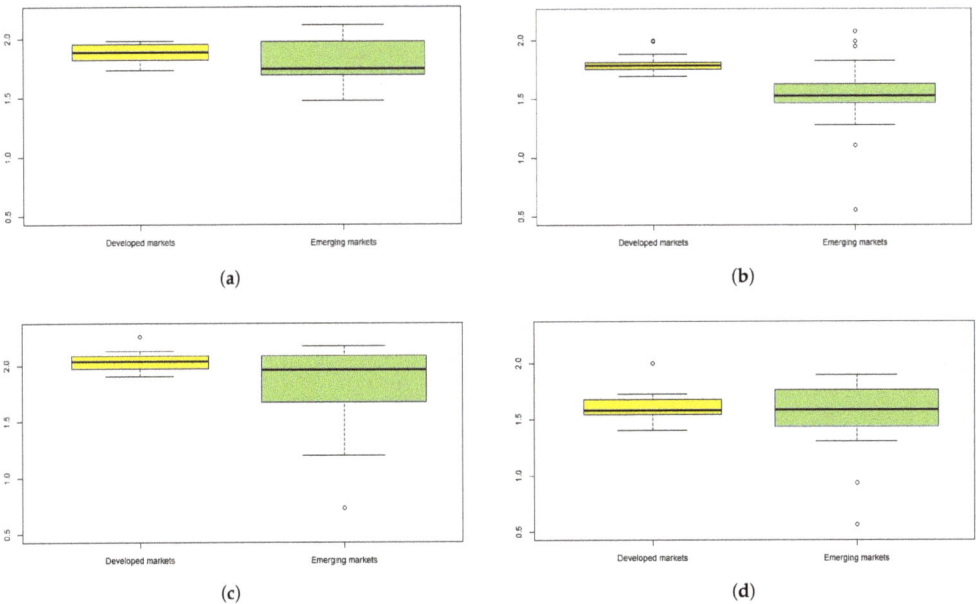

Figure 1. The boxplots of the SampEn results for the European developed (the yellow boxplots) and emerging (the green boxplots) countries: (**a**) the SampEn within the pre-GFC period, (**b**) the SampEn within the GFC period, (**c**) the SampEn within the pre-COVID-19 pandemic period, (**d**) the SampEn within the COVID-19 pandemic period.

One can observe that entropy measured by the SampEn statistic substantially fell during the turbulence periods compared to the pre-turbulence periods, respectively. The down arrows in Tables A4 and A5 illustrate the substantial falls of median and percentile values.

The SampEn median for the European developed markets was equal to 1.88 (within the pre-GFC period) versus 1.79 (within the GFC period). Similarly, the corresponding SampEn median values for the European emerging markets were equal to: 1.74 (within the pre-GFC period) and 1.53 (within the GFC period), respectively (see Table A4).

As for the pre-COVID-19 and COVID-19 sub-periods, the changes in entropy were even more significant. For the European developed markets the SampEn median values were equal to 2.04 versus 1.58, while for the European emerging markets, 1.96 versus 1.59 (see Table A5).

To formally test the hypothesis concerning the median values within pre-turbulence and turbulence periods, the following conditions are proposed:

$$H_0 : Me_1 = Me_2$$
$$H_1 : Me_1 > Me_2, \quad (11)$$

where Me_1 is a SampEn median value before particular turbulence period, while Me_2 denotes a SampEn median value during a turbulence period, respectively. The null hypothesis states that two median values are equal. To examine the hypothesis, the Wilcoxon-Mann-Whitney test [52] is used and the calculations are reported in Table 3. The numbers in brackets are p-values. The test results indicate that the null hypothesis H_0 should be rejected in all cases, both for developed and emerging markets. Hence, the evidence is that the median values during the turbulence periods were significantly lower compared to the corresponding pre-turbulence periods.

Table 3. The comparison of SampEn median values between pre-turbulence and turbulence periods—the Wilcoxon-Mann-Whitney test summary.

	Pre-GFC vs. GFC	Pre-COVID vs. COVID
European developed markets	170 (0.0082)	220 (0.0000)
European emerging markets	337 (0.0014)	345 (0.0007)

The numbers in brackets are p-values.

The boxplot height means the interquartile range, which is a measure of statistical dispersion as it is equal to the difference between Q3 (75th) and Q1 (25th) percentiles. The evidence is that the level of entropy dispersion for the European developed market indices was similar and low, regardless of the time period choice. The results for the European emerging markets are mixed, but the main probable reason is that these markets are much more diverse. However, one can observe that the interquartile range for the emerging markets has substantially decreased during the turbulence periods (see Tables A4 and A5).

The singular points denote outliers. The SampEn outliers were: (1) within the GFC period: Switzerland, Finland, Turkey, Poland, Cyprus (significantly higher values of the SampEn) and Slovakia (significantly lower value of the SampEn), (2) within the pre-pandemic period: Finland (significantly higher value of the SampEn) and Bosnia and Herzegovina (significantly lower value of the SampEn), and (3) within the pandemic period: Denmark (significantly higher value of the SampEn) and Slovakia and Bosnia and Herzegovina (significantly lower values of the SampEn). Within the pre-GFC period outliers did not appear.

To formally test the hypothesis concerning the comparison between the SampEn median values of the European developed and emerging stock markets within various sub-periods, the following H_0 and H_1 conditions (Equation (12)) are proposed:

$$H_0 : Me_1 = Me_2$$
$$H_1 : Me_1 \neq Me_2, \quad (12)$$

where Me_1 is a SampEn median value of the group of the European developed markets, while Me_2 denotes a SampEn median value of the group of the European emerging markets, respectively. The null hypothesis states that two median values are equal. To examine the hypothesis, the Wilcoxon-Mann-Whitney test [52] for two independent groups is used, and the calculations are reported in Table 4. The numbers in brackets are p-values. The test results indicate that the null hypothesis H_0 should be rejected only during the GFC period (p-value 0.0019), while there is no reason to reject the null hypothesis for other periods. Therefore, the evidence is that the SampEn median values did not differ significantly between developed and emerging markets during the remaining three sub-periods.

Table 4. The comparison of SampEn median values between the European developed and emerging stock markets. The Wilcoxon-Mann-Whitney test results.

	European Developed vs. Emerging Stock Markets
Pre-GFC period	203 (0.1504)
GFC period	252 (0.0019)
Pre-COVID period	202.5 (0.1533)
COVID period	160 (0.9495)

The numbers in brackets are p-values.

To summarize, the findings for both the European developed and emerging equity markets are homogenous. The analyzed groups of market indices do not differ substantially in their sequential regularity. The aforementioned SampEn results indicate that entropy visibly fell during each extreme event period compared to the corresponding pre-event period. It implies that predictability of market indices rose, which confirmed no reason to reject the main research hypothesis.

4.3. The Evolution of Sample Entropy over Time

In this subsection, the evolution of SampEn over time is analyzed. A rolling-window dynamic approach is employed to capture the changes in market index regularity (measured by SampEn) through time, for daily logarithmic index returns.

In line of the existing literature, the sample size N should be within the range of $[10^m, 30^m]$ (see, e.g., [5,45]). As pointed out in Section 4.1, in this research $m = 2$, hence the minimal time window length should be equal to 100. Therefore, a window $N = 100$ business days is utilized in this study.

The broad group of 36 stock markets is explored. The use of the rolling-window method requires the corresponding figures that show the changes in SampEn over time. Hence, it should be 36 × 2 = 72 figures reported in the paper as the graphic representation of the rolling-window procedure. Therefore, only selected dynamic SampEn results for developed and emerging markets are illustrated, i.e., the results for stock markets with the highest absolute value of the change in SampEn (based on Table 2). Due to the space restriction, the remaining figures are available upon a request.

Subsequent Figures 2–4 show the evolution of SampEn over time within the period from January 2018 to December 2021 (two combined pre-COVID-19 and COVID-19 sub-periods). Figures 2 and 3 present graphs for the European developed and emerging markets, respectively. Finally, Figure 4 plots the dynamics of SampEn for S&P500 index. The SampEn procedure implemented on the rolling-window scheme indicates and confirms that entropy visibly decreased during the COVID-19 pandemic, especially in March-April 2020, both for developed and emerging markets. It is rather clear that the main reason of such homogenous results is that all investigated stock markets have been affected by the COVID-19 pandemic in the same time and to the similar extent.

By analogy, the rolling-window procedure is utilized to investigate the evolution of the SampEn during the period from May 2006 to February 2009 (two combined pre-GFC and GFC sub-periods). The findings are reported and discussed in Appendix C.

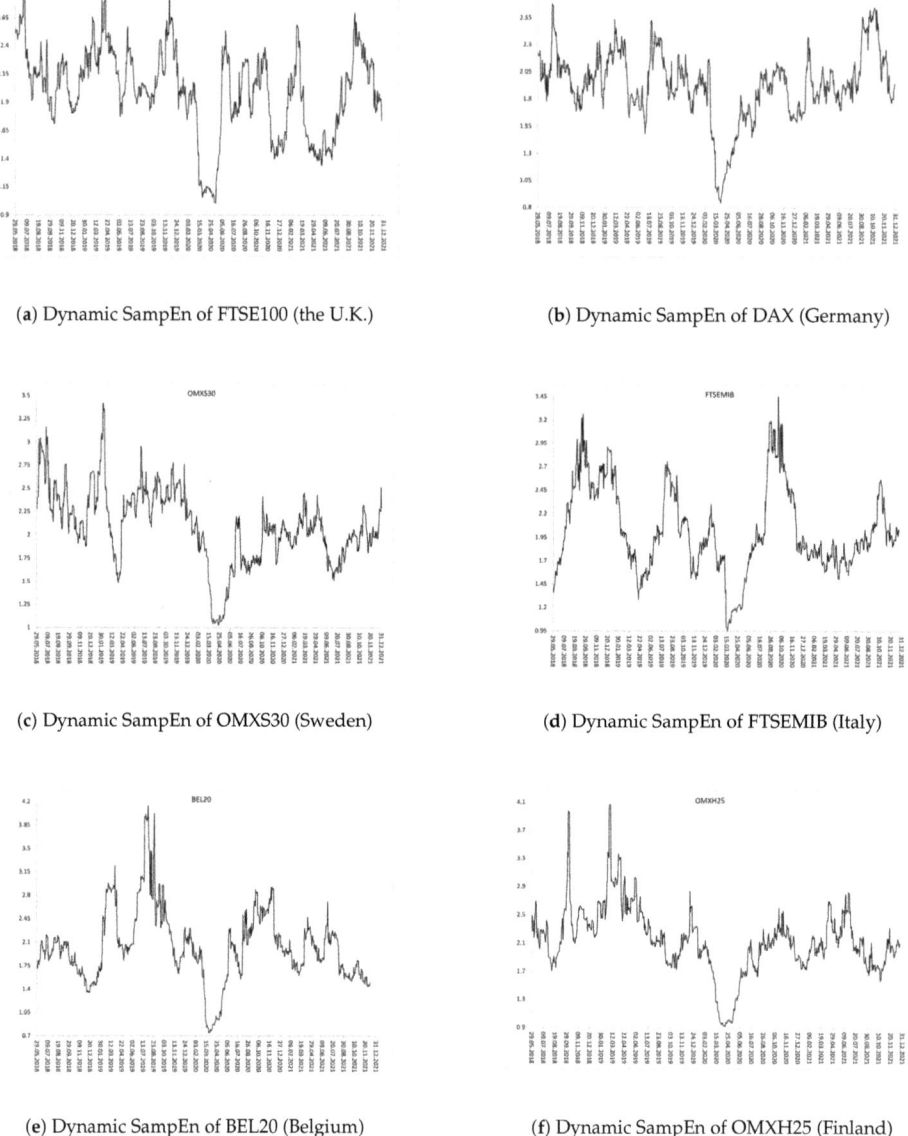

Figure 2. Dynamic SampEn of the selected European developed market indices within the period from January 2018 to December 2021 (two combined pre-COVID-19 and COVID-19 sub-periods): (**a**) FTSE100 (the U.K.), (**b**) DAX (Germany), (**c**) OMXS30 (Sweden), (**d**) FTSEMIB (Italy), (**e**) BEL20 (Belgium), (**f**) OMXH25 (Finland). The rolling-window $N = 100$ business days.

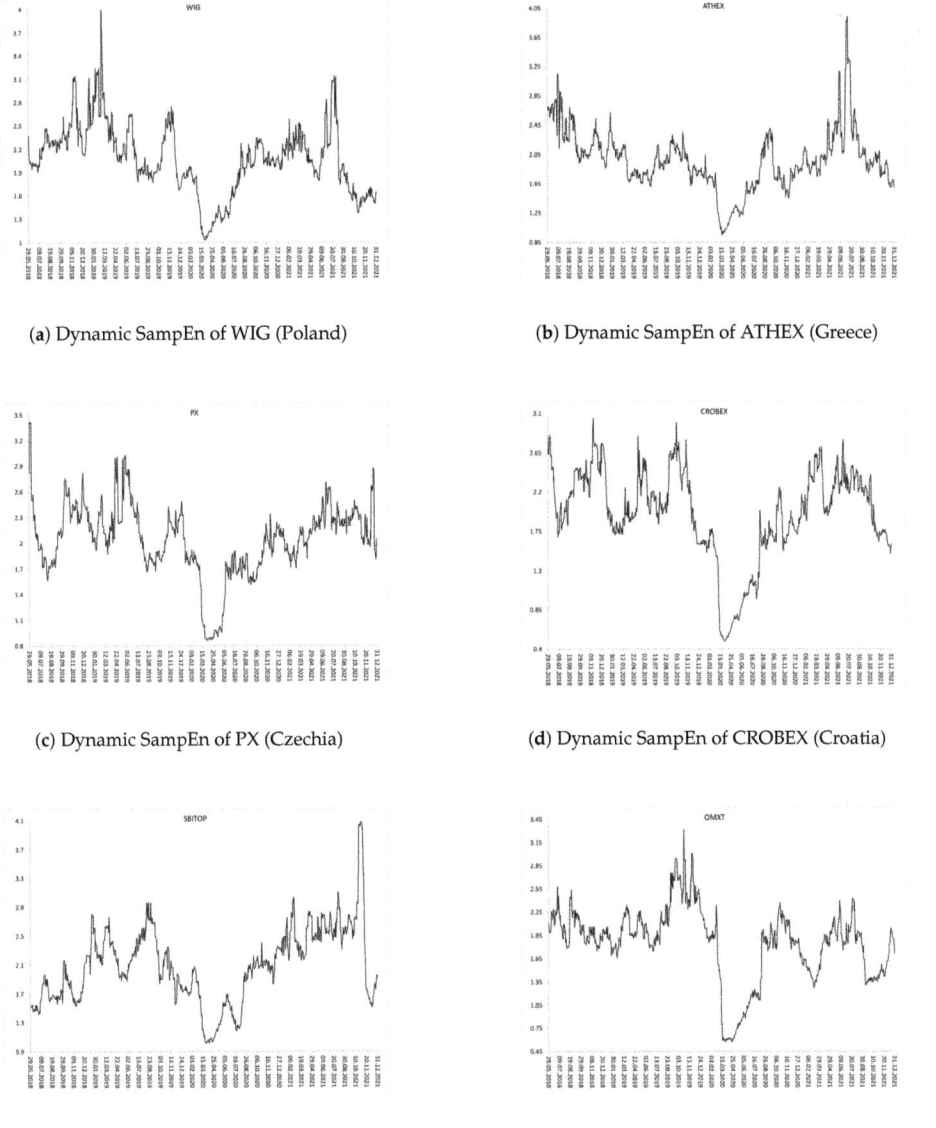

(a) Dynamic SampEn of WIG (Poland) (b) Dynamic SampEn of ATHEX (Greece)

(c) Dynamic SampEn of PX (Czechia) (d) Dynamic SampEn of CROBEX (Croatia)

(e) Dynamic SampEn of SBITOP (Slovenia) (f) Dynamic SampEn of OMXT (Estonia)

Figure 3. Dynamic SampEn of the selected European emerging market indices within the period from January 2018 to December 2021 (two combined pre-COVID-19 and COVID-19 sub-periods): (**a**) WIG (Poland), (**b**) ATHEX (Greece), (**c**) PX (Czechia), (**d**) CROBEX (Croatia), (**e**) SBITOP (Slovenia), (**f**) OMXT (Estonia). The rolling-window $N = 100$ business days.

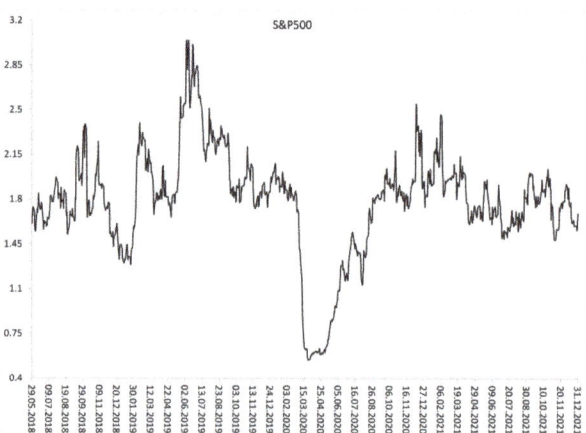

Figure 4. Dynamic SampEn of the S&P500 index (the U.S.) within the period from January 2018 to December 2021 (two combined pre-COVID-19 and COVID-19 periods). The rolling-window $N = 100$ business days.

5. Discussion and Conclusions

The goal of this empirical study was to investigate changes in sequential regularity in the 36 European and the U.S. stock market indices within major turbulence periods. Two periods were analyzed: the Global Financial Crisis in 2007–2009 and the COVID-19 pandemic outbreak in 2020–2021. To capture regularity in the daily time series of stock market indices, the SampEn algorithm was utilized. Changes in the SampEn values before and during the particular turbulence period were calculated and compared. The research hypothesis that entropy of an equity market index decreases during turbulence periods was examined. The main contribution of this research lies in important empirical findings which indicate no reason to reject the research hypothesis. Our research belongs to the strand of the literature known as Algorithmic Information Theory (AIT). The AIT explores predictability in terms of sequential regularity in various time series based on the existence of patterns.

The obtained results are homogenous and statistically significant for both investigated turbulence periods, and for both independent groups of stock markets (developed and emerging). The findings imply that regularity in stock market index returns increases during extreme event periods.

Our results contribute to the discussion concerning predictability of financial markets. It seems that the conclusions could be generalized as the SampEn empirical findings are in line with the relatively scarce previous literature which documents that entropy of various financial time series usually decreases during market crashes, financial crisis and other turbulence periods. For instance, Ortiz-Cruz et al. [41] utilized the multi-scale approximate entropy procedure and they indicated that returns from crude oil markets were less uncertain during economic downturns. Wang and Wang [45] assessed informational efficiency of S&P500 Index, gold, Bitcoin, and US Dollar Index during the COVID-19 pandemic with a multi-scale entropy-based method. They confirmed that a decline of entropy was particularly large for S&P500 Index. Moreover, their results of dynamic informational efficiency of the S&P500 Index are similar to ours. Risso [38] investigated several market indices during financial crashes. He showed that short-time market trends (both 'up' and 'down') usually reduce entropy of an index daily time series due to more frequent patterns.

Moreover, it is worth noting that, during the turbulence periods, all public information is especially important for investors and determines investment decisions. However, the used information set includes only the history of index returns. Therefore, our research relates to the literature concerning the weak form of market informational efficiency. The obtained results indicate that informational efficiency of stock market indices decreases during turbulence periods. This evidence is especially useful for investors as it provides information about a possibility of financial forecasting.

The findings of our research might be interesting for academics and practitioners since the entropy-based indicators can generate predictive signals and can be useful in predictive modelling (see, e.g., [44,53]). Moreover, there are some innovative applications of entropy for financial time series forecasting (see, e.g., [43,54]). Gradojevic and Caric [54] emphasize that although volatility and entropy are related measures of market risk and uncertainty, entropy can be more useful in predictive modelling. Taking the above into consideration, we hope that the results of our research could be generally of special importance for investors as the entropy-based procedures might be used as helpful tools in various systems that support investment decisions.

Since the analyzed GFC and COVID-19 periods have affected all financial markets in the world, the promising direction for further research could be an extensive comparative assessment of predictability in the context of sequential regularity in time series of stock market indices within the world, for instance in continent-based regions. Moreover, the influence of the recent extreme event, i.e., the Russian invasion in Ukraine, could be investigated.

Author Contributions: Conceptualization, J.O.; methodology, J.O. and E.M.; software, E.M.; validation, J.O. and E.M.; formal analysis, J.O. and E.M.; investigation, J.O. and E.M.; resources, J.O. and E.M.; data curation, E.M.; writing—original draft preparation, J.O.; writing—review and editing, J.O.; visualization, E.M.; supervision, J.O.; funding acquisition, J.O. All authors have read and agreed to the published version of the manuscript.

Funding: The contribution of the first named author was supported by the grant WZ/WI-IIT/2/22 from Bialystok University of Technology and founded by the Ministry of Education and Science.

Institutional Review Board Statement: Not applicable.

Informed Consent Statement: Not applicable.

Data Availability Statement: The data comes from the following web pages: Stooq (https://stooq.pl, 15 January 2022); Yahoo (https://finance.yahoo.com, 15 January 2022); Malta Stock Exchange (https://www.borzamalta.com.mt, 15 January 2022); Cyprus Stock Exchange (http://www.cse.com.cy, 15 January 2022); Nasdaq (http://www.nasdaqomxnordic.com, 15 January 2022); Zagreb Stock Exchange (http://zse.hr, 15 January 2022); Ljubljana Stock Exchange (http://www.ljse.si, 15 January 2022); Montenegro Stock Exchange (http://mnse.me, 15 January 2022); Belgrade Stock Exchange (http://www.belex.rs, 15 January 2022); The Sarajevo Stock Exchange (http://www.sase.ba, 15 January 2022).

Conflicts of Interest: The authors declare no conflict of interest.

Abbreviations

The following abbreviations are used in this manuscript:

AIT	Algorithmic Information Theory
ApEn	Approximate Entropy
SampEn	Sample Entropy
GFC	Global Financial Crisis
COVID-19	COVID-19 pandemic

Appendix A. Basic Statistics for Sub-Periods

Tables A1 and A2 report the basic statistics for daily logarithmic rates of return within the turbulence sub-periods. N denotes the number of observations. The stock markets are presented in the same order as in Table 1.

Table A1. The basic statistics for daily logarithmic rates of return within the pre-GFC and GFC periods.

	Country	Pre-GFC			GFC		
		N	Mean (in %)	Std. Dev. (in %)	N	Mean (in %)	Std. Dev. (in %)
	United States	356	0.044	0.80	355	−0.210	2.37
1	France	362	0.024	1.05	360	−0.211	2.29
2	United Kingdom	358	0.017	0.97	358	−0.148	2.13
3	Germany	361	0.072	1.02	356	−0.203	2.17
4	Switzerland	355	0.028	0.93	351	−0.186	1.98
5	Netherlands	362	0.039	0.97	360	−0.253	2.39
6	Sweden	356	0.044	1.33	353	−0.185	2.36
7	Spain	362	0.055	1.02	356	−0.183	2.24
8	Italy	360	0.012	0.91	355	−0.274	2.17
9	Russia	354	0.053	1.79	346	−0.383	3.78
10	Denmark	356	0.063	1.07	351	−0.212	2.24
11	Belgium	362	0.026	0.97	361	−0.275	2.12
12	Finland	357	0.071	1.17	353	−0.290	2.20
13	Norway	356	0.053	1.45	354	−0.226	2.69
14	Turkey	359	0.057	1.87	353	−0.230	2.53
15	Poland	355	0.089	1.37	351	−0.291	1.91
16	Ireland	360	−0.001	1.20	358	−0.376	2.78
17	Austria	350	0.020	1.36	348	−0.323	2.81
18	Portugal	362	0.049	0.74	360	−0.196	1.84
19	Greece	357	0.055	1.14	350	−0.345	2.25
20	Hungary	355	0.041	1.38	348	−0.296	2.51
21	Czechia	354	0.058	1.25	354	−0.296	2.71
22	Romania	353	0.071	1.38	349	−0.469	2.64
23	Croatia	354	0.197	0.93	347	−0.374	2.39
24	Bulgaria	353	0.209	0.87	345	−0.565	2.25
25	Lithuania	346	0.093	0.93	340	−0.373	1.85
26	Iceland	353	0.105	0.94	350	−0.789	6.18
27	Slovenia	350	0.239	1.00	349	−0.319	1.99
28	Serbia	357	0.214	0.83	357	−0.432	1.47
29	Malta	350	−0.060	0.77	346	−0.159	0.68
30	Cyprus	354	0.165	1.52	344	−0.555	3.03
31	Ukraine	343	0.250	1.67	347	−0.475	2.82
32	Montenegro	348	0.377	1.66	345	−0.425	2.66
33	Estonia	358	0.085	1.02	352	−0.341	1.60
34	Latvia	354	0.051	0.80	348	−0.357	1.90
35	Bosnia and Herzegovina	357	0.186	1.42	349	−0.428	1.42
36	Slovakia	344	0.012	0.72	343	−0.077	0.95

Table A2. The basic statistics for daily logarithmic rates of return within the pre-COVID and COVID periods.

	Country	Pre-COVID-19			COVID-19		
		N	Mean (in %)	Std. Dev. (in %)	N	Mean (in %)	Std. Dev. (in %)
	United States	502	0.036	0.94	504	0.075	1.65
1	France	509	0.024	0.86	514	0.033	1.58
2	United Kingdom	504	−0.003	0.77	506	−0.006	1.43
3	Germany	501	0.006	0.94	508	0.034	1.61
4	Switzerland	497	0.023	0.80	505	0.037	1.17
5	Netherlands	509	0.020	0.80	514	0.051	1.42
6	Sweden	499	0.023	0.92	504	0.058	1.44
7	Spain	509	−0.011	0.82	512	−0.021	1.69
8	Italy	503	0.015	1.05	510	0.027	1.74
9	Russia	504	0.053	1.28	504	0.004	2.05
10	Denmark	495	0.021	0.94	500	0.099	1.27
11	Belgium	509	−0.001	0.85	514	0.014	1.61
12	Finland	499	0.007	0.86	497	0.045	1.38
13	Norway	497	0.026	0.90	503	0.045	1.41
14	Turkey	499	−0.005	1.35	500	0.094	1.66
15	Poland	494	−0.020	0.89	502	0.032	1.51
16	Ireland	505	0.004	0.93	509	0.029	1.59
17	Austria	497	−0.016	0.95	505	0.0356	1.82
18	Portugal	509	−0.009	0.78	514	0.011	1.38
19	Greece	495	0.023	1.23	497	−0.008	2.01
20	Hungary	489	0.032	0.98	502	0.018	1.52
21	Czechia	498	0.006	0.62	500	0.048	1.24
22	Romania	497	0.047	1.04	500	0.055	1.23
23	Croatia	493	0.019	0.46	499	0.005	1.08
24	Bulgaria	491	−0.038	0.58	492	0.023	1.01
25	Lithuania	495	0.016	0.57	498	0.060	0.86
26	Iceland	494	0.033	0.80	498	0.108	1.16
27	Slovenia	490	0.031	0.55	503	0.060	1.05
28	Serbia	502	0.009	0.46	502	−0.001	0.56
29	Malta	493	0.009	0.47	493	−0.034	0.82
30	Cyprus	489	−0.012	0.83	492	0.010	1.05
31	Ukraine	488	0.024	0.95	493	0.027	1.38
32	Montenegro	493	0.024	0.63	498	−0.029	0.72
33	Estonia	500	0.004	0.45	500	0.090	1.18
34	Latvia	494	0.007	1.07	496	0.041	1.27
35	Bosnia and Herzegovina	496	0.034	0.78	502	0.004	0.37
36	Slovakia	482	0.016	0.95	490	0.026	1.07

Appendix B. Developed and Emerging Markets

Table A3 presents two groups of the investigated stock markets: (1) the European developed markets and (2) the European emerging markets. This division is the recent one since it is based on the report "MSCI Global Market Accessibility Review. Country comparison" [51].

Tables A4 and A5 report the SampEn basic statistics within the pre-turbulence and turbulence periods, respectively. Two groups of the European countries (presented in Table A3) are explored.

Table A3. The European developed and emerging stock markets.

European Developed Markets	European Emerging Markets
France, U.K., Germany, Switzerland, Netherlands, Sweden, Spain, Italy, Denmark, Belgium, Finland, Norway, Ireland, Austria, Portugal	Russia, Turkey, Poland, Greece, Hungary, Czechia, Romania, Croatia, Bulgaria, Lithuania, Iceland, Slovenia, Serbia, Malta, Cyprus, Ukraine, Montenegro, Estonia, Latvia, Bosnia and Herzegovina, Slovakia

Based on the MSCI report [51], in the market order as in Table 1.

Table A4. The SampEn basic statistics within the pre-GFC and GFC periods for developed and emerging European stock markets.

	Pre-GFC					GFC				
	Min	Max	Median	Q1	Q3	Min	Max	Median	Q1	Q3
Developed markets	1.74	1.98	1.88	1.82	1.96	1.69	1.99	1.79 ↓	1.76 ↓	1.81 ↓
Emerging markets	1.48	2.12	1.74	1.69	1.97	0.55	2.08	1.53 ↓	1.47 ↓	1.63 ↓

Table A5. The SampEn basic statistics within the pre-COVID-19 and COVID-19 periods for developed and emerging European stock markets.

	Pre-COVID-19					COVID-19				
	Min	Max	Median	Q1	Q3	Min	Max	Median	Q1	Q3
Developed markets	1.90	2.25	2.04	1.97	2.08	1.41	2.00	1.58 ↓	1.54 ↓	1.68 ↓
Emerging markets	0.73	2.17	1.96	1.67	2.08	0.57	1.90	1.59 ↓	1.44 ↓	1.76 ↓

Appendix C. Dynamic SampEn Results during the period from May 2006 to February 2009

According to the literature, the financial crisis timeline, from the U.S. perspective, was marked by the following events: (1) the increase in subprime delinquency rates in the spring of 2007, (2) the ensuing liquidity crunch in late 2007, (3) the liquidation of Bear Stearns in March 2008, and (4) the failure of Lehman Brothers in September 2008. The U.S. economy officially slipped into a recession following the peak in December 2007. It is important to note that the crisis began in the U.S., but initially it did not fully and strongly affect all financial markets. For instance, Claessens et al. [30] identify five groups of countries based on the date they were affected by the crisis. Hence, the investigated stock markets were not affected by the GFC in the same time and to the same extent. This is the probable reason why empirical findings of the SampEn dynamics for various countries are ambiguous.

Figure A1 shows the dynamics of SampEn of the S&P500 index. Moreover, Figures A2 and A3 illustrate the rolling-window dynamic results of the SampEn algorithm within the period from May 2006 to February 2009 (two combined pre-GFC and GFC sub-periods), for selected European developed and emerging markets, respectively. The highest absolute value of the change in SampEn (reported in Table 2) was the main criterion for the choice.

As reported in Section 4.1 (Table 2), formal statistical analyses confirm that the basic statistics of entropy (measured by SampEn) decreased significantly during the GFC period but, in general, the results are not such homogenous as in the case of the COVID-19 pandemic period. This evidence can be observed in Figures A1–A3.

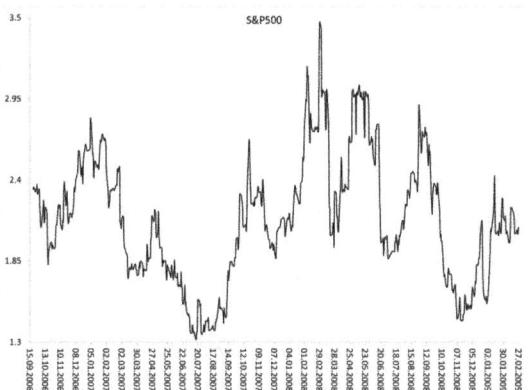

Figure A1. Dynamic SampEn of the S&P500 index (the U.S.) within the period from May 2006 to February 2009 (two combined pre-GFC and GFC sub-periods). The rolling-window $N = 100$ business days.

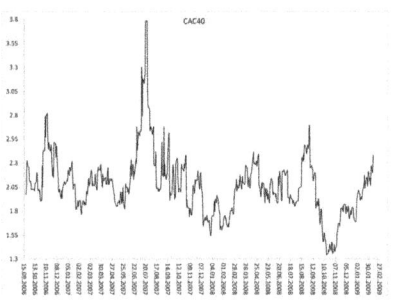

(**a**) Dynamic SampEn of CAC40 (France)

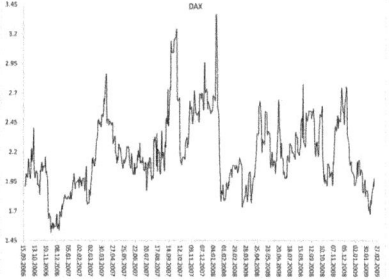

(**b**) Dynamic SampEn of DAX (Germany)

(**c**) Dynamic SampEn of BEL20 (Belgium)

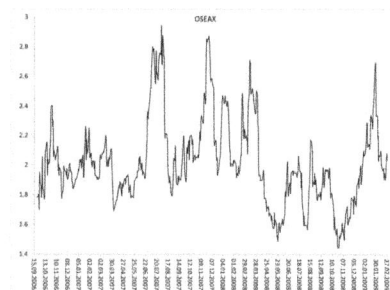

(**d**) Dynamic SampEn of OSEAX (Norway)

Figure A2. Dynamic SampEn of the selected European developed market indices within the period from May 2006 to February 2009 (two combined pre-GFC and GFC sub-periods): (**a**) CAC40 (France), (**b**) DAX (Germany), (**c**) BEL20 (Belgium), (**d**) OSEAX (Norway). The rolling-window $N = 100$ business days.

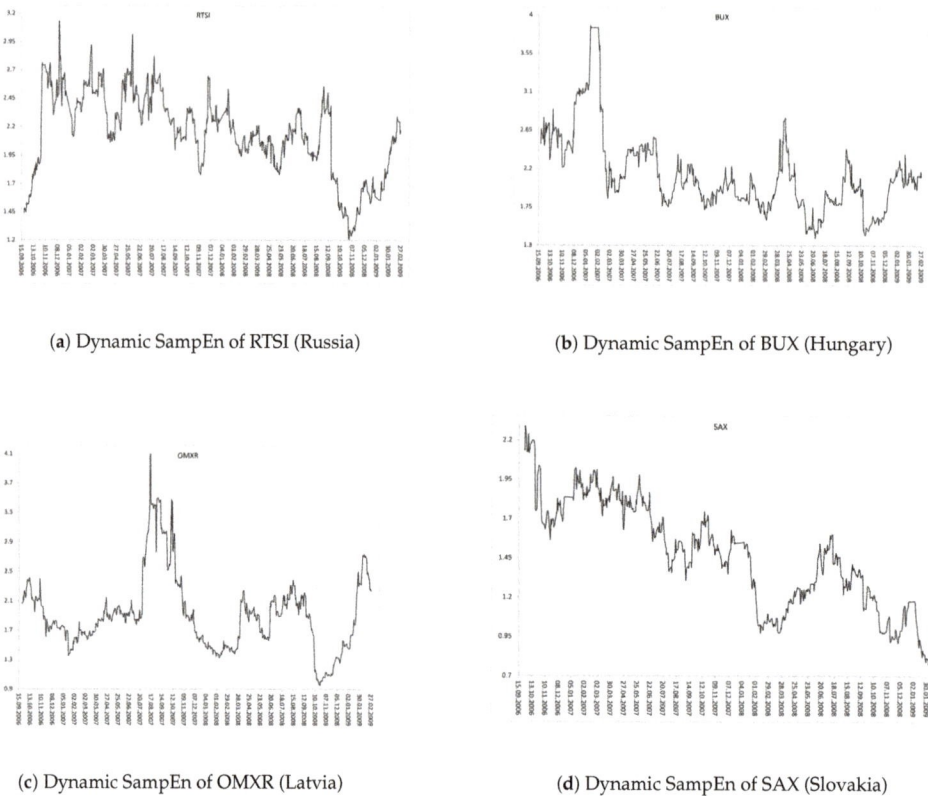

Figure A3. Dynamic SampEn of the selected European emerging market indices within the period from May 2006 to February 2009 (two combined pre-GFC and GFC sub-periods): (**a**) RTSI (Russia), (**b**) BUX (Hungary), (**c**) OMXR (Latvia)), (**d**) SAX (Slovakia). The rolling-window $N = 100$ business days.

References

1. Fama, E. Efficient capital markets: A review of theory and empirical work. *J. Financ.* **1970**, *25*, 383–417. [CrossRef]
2. Lim, K.P.; Brooks, R. The evolution of stock market efficiency over time: A survey of the empirical literature. *J. Econ. Surv.* **2011**, *25*, 69–108. [CrossRef]
3. Campbell, J.; Lo, A.; MacKinlay, A. *The Econometrics of Financial Markets*; Princeton University Press: Princeton, NJ, USA, 1997.
4. Dimson, E.; Mussavian, M. A brief history of market efficiency. *Eur. Financ. Manag.* **1998**, *4*, 91–103. [CrossRef]
5. Delgado-Bonal, A.; Marshak, A. Approximate Entropy and Sample Entropy: A comprehensive tutorial. *Entropy* **2019**, *21*, 541. [CrossRef] [PubMed]
6. Shannon, C. A mathematical theory of communication. *Bell Syst. Tech. J.* **1948**, *27*, 379–423. [CrossRef]
7. Ahn, K.; Lee, D.; Sohn, S.; Yang, B. Stock market uncertainty and economic fundamentals: An entropy-based approach. *Quant. Financ.* **2019**, *19*, 1151–1163. [CrossRef]
8. Zunino, L.; Zanin, M.; Tabak, B.; Pérez, D.G.; Rosso, O. Forbidden patterns, permutation entropy and stock market inefficiency. *Phys. A* **2009**, *385*, 2854–2864. [CrossRef]
9. Zhou, R.; Cai, R.; Tong, G. Applications of entropy in finance: A review. *Entropy* **2013**, *15*, 4909–4931. [CrossRef]
10. Olbryś, J.; Ostrowski, K. An entropy-based approach to measurement of stock market depth. *Entropy* **2021**, *23*, 568. [CrossRef]
11. Jakimowicz, A. The role of entropy in the development of economics. *Entropy* **2020**, *22*, 452. [CrossRef] [PubMed]
12. Kitamura, Y.; Stutzer, M. Connections between entropic and linear projections in asset pricing estimation. *J. Econom.* **2002**, *107*, 159–174. [CrossRef]
13. Stutzer, M. The role of entropy in estimating financial network default impact. *Entropy* **2018**, *20*, 369. [CrossRef]

14. Bowden, R. Directional entropy and tail uncertainty, with applications to financial hazard. *Quant. Financ.* **2011**, *11*, 437–446. [CrossRef]
15. Bekiros, S. Timescale analysis with an entropy-based shift-invariant discrete wavelet transform. *Comput. Econ.* **2014**, *44*, 231–251. [CrossRef]
16. Gencay, R.; Gradojevic, N. Crash of '87—Was it expected? Aggregate market fears and long-range dependence. *J. Emp. Finance* **2010**, *17*, 270–282. [CrossRef]
17. Kolmogorov, A. A new metric invariant of transient dynamical systems and automorphisms in Lebesgue spaces. *Dokl. Russ. Acad. Sci.* **1958**, *119*, 861–864.
18. Sinai, Y. On the notion of entropy of a dynamical system. *Dokl. Russ. Acad. Sci.* **1959**, *124*, 768–771.
19. Pincus, S. Approximate entropy as a measure of system complexity. *Proc. Natl. Acad. Sci. USA* **1991**, *88*, 2297–2301. [CrossRef]
20. Richman, J.; Moorman, J. Physiological time-series analysis using approximate entropy and sample entropy. *Am. J. Physiol. Heart Circ. Physiol.* **2000**, *278*, H2039–H2049. [CrossRef]
21. Kim, K.; Lee, M. The impact of the COVID-19 pandemic on the unpredictable dynamics of the cryptocurrency market. *Entropy* **2021**, *23*, 1234. [CrossRef]
22. Xu, M.; Shang, P.; Zhang, S. Multiscale analysis of financial time series by Renyi distribution entropy. *Phys. A* **2019**, *536*, 120916. [CrossRef]
23. Olbrys, J.; Majewska, E. Approximate entropy and sample entropy algorithms in financial time series analyses. In Proceedings of the 26th International Conference on Kowlegde-Based and Intelligent Information & Engineering Systems (KES 2022), Verona, Italy, 7–9 September 2022.
24. Pincus, S.; Kalman, R. Irregularity, volatility, and financial market time series. *Proc. Natl. Acad. Sci. USA* **2004**, *101*, 13709–13714. [CrossRef]
25. Pincus, S. Approximate entropy as an irregularity measure for financial data. *Econom. Rev.* **2008**, *27*, 329–362. [CrossRef]
26. Bartram, S.; Bodnar, G. No place to hide: The global crisis in equity markets in 2008/2009. *J. Int. Money Financ.* **2009**, *28*, 1246–1292. [CrossRef]
27. Dooley, M.; Hutchison, M. Transmission of the U.S. subprime crisis to emerging markets: Evidence on the decoupling–recoupling hypothesis. *J. Int. Money Financ.* **2009**, *28*, 1331–1349. [CrossRef]
28. Boyarchenko, N. Ambiguity shifts and the 2007-2008 financial crisis. *J. Mon. Econ.* **2012**, *59*, 493–507. [CrossRef]
29. Olbrys, J.; Majewska, E. Bear market periods during the 2007-2009 financial crisis: Direct evidence from the Visegrad countries. *Acta Oecon.* **2015**, *65*, 547–565. [CrossRef]
30. Claessens, S.; Dell'Ariccia, G.; Igan, D.; Laeven, L. Cross-country experience and policy implications from the Global Financial Crisis. *Econ. Policy* **2010**, *62*, 267–293. [CrossRef]
31. Pagan, A.; Sossounov, K. A simple framework for analysing bull and bear markets. *J. App. Econom.* **2003**, *18*, 23–46. [CrossRef]
32. Majewska, E.; Olbrys, J. Formal identification of crises on the euro area stock markets, 2004–2015. In *Advances in Applied Economic Research*; Tsounis, N., Vlachvei, A., Eds.; Springer Proceedings in Business and Economics; Springer: Berlin/Heidelberg, Germany, 2017; pp. 167–180. [CrossRef]
33. Olbrys, J. The Global Financial Crisis: A Survey. Available online: https://ssrn.com/abstract=3872477 (accessed on 10 May 2022). [CrossRef]
34. WHO. Timeline of WHO's Response to COVID-19. Available online: https://www.who.int/emergencies/diseases/novel-coronavirus-2019/interactive-timeline (accessed on 31 March 2022).
35. Risso, W. The informational efficiency: The emerging versus the developed markets. *Appl. Econ. Lett.* **2009**, *16*, 485–487. [CrossRef]
36. Maasoumi, E.; Racine, J. Entropy and predictability of stock market returns. *J. Econom.* **2002**, *107*, 291–312. [CrossRef]
37. Oh, G.; Kim, S.; Eom, C. Market efficiency in foreign exchange markets. *Phys. A* **2007**, *382*, 209–212. [CrossRef]
38. Risso, W. The informational efficiency and the financial crashes. *Res. Int. Bus. Financ.* **2008**, *22*, 396–408. [CrossRef]
39. Eom, C.; Oh, G.; Jung, W.S. Relationship between efficiency and predictability in stock price change. *Phys. A* **2008**, *387*, 5511–5517. [CrossRef]
40. Gu, R. Multiscale Shannon entropy and its application in the stock market. *Phys. A* **2012**, *484*, 215–224. [CrossRef]
41. Ortiz-Cruz, A.; Rodriguez, E.; Ibarra-Valdez, C.; Alvarez-Ramirez, J. Efficiency of crude oil markets: Evidences from informational entropy analysis. *Energ. Policy* **2012**, *41*, 365–373. [CrossRef]
42. Liu, A.; Chen, J.; Yang, S.; Hawkes, A. The flow of information in trading: An entropy approach to market regimes. *Entropy* **2020**, *22*, 1064. [CrossRef]
43. Bekiros, S.; Marcellino, M. The multiscale causal dynamics of foreign exchange markets. *J. Int. Money Financ.* **2013**, *33*, 282–305. [CrossRef]
44. Gencay, R.; Gradojevic, N. The tale of two crises: An entropic perspective. *Entropy* **2017**, *19*, 244. [CrossRef]
45. Wang, J.; Wang, X. COVID-19 and financial market efficiency: Evidence from an entropy-based analysis. *Financ. Res. Lett.* **2021**, *42*, 101888. [CrossRef]
46. Alvarez-Ramirez, J.; Rodriguez, E.; Alvarez, J. A multiscale entropy approach for market efficiency. *Int. Rev. Financ. Anal.* **2012**, *21*, 64–69. [CrossRef]
47. Richman, J.; Lake, D.; Moorman, J. Sample Entropy. *Method. Enzymol.* **2004**, *384*, 172–184.

48. Jarque, C.; Bera, A. A test for normality of observations and regression residuals. *Int. Stat. Rev.* **1987**, *55*, 163–172. [CrossRef]
49. Tsay, R. *Analysis of Financial Time Series*; John Wiley: New York, NY, USA, 2010.
50. Xie, H.B.; He, W.X.; Liu, H. Measuring time series regularity using nonlinear similarity-based sample entropy. *Phys. Lett. A* **2008**, *372*, 7140–7146. [CrossRef]
51. MSCI. MSCI Global Market Accessibility Review. Country Comparison (June 2021). Available online: https://www.msci.com/our-solutions/indexes/market-classification (accessed on 31 March 2022).
52. Fay, M.; Proschan, M. Wilcoxon-Mann-Whitney or t-test? On assumptions for hypothesis tests and multiple interpretations of decision rules. *Stat. Surv.* **2010**, *4*, 1–39. [CrossRef]
53. Billio, M.; Casarin, R.; Costola, M.; Pasqualini, A. An entropy-based early warning indicator for systematic risk. *J. Int. Financ. Mark. I.* **2016**, *45*, 42–59. [CrossRef]
54. Gradojevic, N.; Caric, M. Predicting systematic risk with entropic indicators. *J. Forecast.* **2017**, *36*, 16–25. [CrossRef]

MDPI
St. Alban-Anlage 66
4052 Basel
Switzerland
Tel. +41 61 683 77 34
Fax +41 61 302 89 18
www.mdpi.com

Entropy Editorial Office
E-mail: entropy@mdpi.com
www.mdpi.com/journal/entropy

www.ingramcontent.com/pod-product-compliance
Lightning Source LLC
LaVergne TN
LVHW070509100526
838202LV00014B/1819